T0213569

Lecture Notes in Computer Science 10548

Commenced Publication in 1973
Founding and Former Series Editors:
Gerhard Goos, Juris Hartmanis, and Jan van Leeuwen

More information about this series at http://www.springer.com/series/7408

Shuvendu Lahiri · Giles Reger (Eds.)

Runtime Verification

17th International Conference, RV 2017
Seattle, WA, USA, September 13–16, 2017
Proceedings

 Springer

Editors
Shuvendu Lahiri
Microsoft Research
Redmond, WA
USA

Giles Reger
The University of Manchester
Manchester
UK

ISSN 0302-9743   ISSN 1611-3349 (electronic)
Lecture Notes in Computer Science
ISBN 978-3-319-67530-5   ISBN 978-3-319-67531-2 (eBook)
DOI 10.1007/978-3-319-67531-2

Library of Congress Control Number: 2017952862

LNCS Sublibrary: SL2 – Programming and Software Engineering

Printed on acid-free paper

This Springer imprint is published by Springer Nature
The registered company is Springer International Publishing AG
The registered company address is: Gewerbestrasse 11, 6330 Cham, Switzerland

Preface

This volume contains the proceedings of the 17th International Conference on Runtime Verification (RV 2017), which was held on September 13–16, 2017 at the Sheraton Hotel, Seattle, USA.

The RV series consists of annual meetings that gather together scientists from both academia and industry interested in investigating novel lightweight formal methods to monitor, analyze, and guide the runtime behavior of software and hardware systems. Runtime verification techniques are crucial for system correctness, reliability, and robustness; they provide an additional level of rigor and effectiveness compared with conventional testing, and are generally more practical than exhaustive formal verification. Runtime verification can be used prior to deployment, for testing, verification, and debugging purposes, and after deployment for ensuring reliability, safety, and security and for providing fault containment and recovery as well as online system repair.

RV started in 2001 as an annual workshop and turned into a conference in 2010. The workshops were organized as satellite events to an established forum, including CAV and ETAPS. The proceedings of RV from 2001 to 2005 were published in the Electronic Notes in Theoretical Computer Science. Since 2006, the RV proceedings have been published in Springer's Lecture Notes in Computer Science. The previous five RV conferences took place in Istanbul, Turkey (2012); Rennes, France (2013); Toronto, Canada (2014); Vienna, Austria (2015); and Madrid, Spain (2016).

RV 2017 received 58 submissions, 47 of which were regular papers, 8 short papers, and 3 regular tool papers. Almost all papers were reviewed by four reviewers. The Program Committee accepted 18 regular papers, 5 short papers, and 4 regular tool papers, where 4 regular papers were accepted as short or tool papers. The evaluation and selection process involved thorough discussions among the members of the Program Committee and external reviewers through the EasyChair conference manager, before reaching a consensus on the final decisions.

To complement the contributed papers, we included in the program three invited speakers covering both industry and academia:

- Rodrigo Fonseca, an associate professor in Brown University's Computer Science Department, gave a talk about the design and applications for a tracing plane for distributed systems;
- Vladimir Levin and Jakob Lichtenberg from Microsoft's driver quality team gave a talk about the Windows Driver Verification Platform;
- Andreas Zeller, a full professor for software engineering at Saarland University, gave a talk about learning input languages for runtime verification.

The conference included three tutorials that took place on the first day. The following tutorials were selected to cover a breadth of topics relevant to RV:

- Adrian Francalanza presented a tutorial on "Foundations for Runtime Monitoring";
- Ankush Desai and Shaz Qadeer presented a tutorial on "P : Modular and Safe Asynchronous Programming";
- Madhusudan Parthasarathy presented a tutorial on "Machine-Learning State Properties".

RV 2017 was also colocated with RV-CuBES, an international workshop on competitions, usability, benchmarks, evaluation, and standardization for runtime verification tools. This workshop was integrated into the RV program as dedicated poster and discussion sessions. RV-CuBES has separate proceedings consisting of tool overview and position papers.

We would like to thank the authors of all submitted papers, the members of the Program Committee, and the external reviewers for their exhaustive task of reviewing and evaluating all submitted papers. We highly appreciate the EasyChair system for the management of submissions. Finally, we would like to extend our special thanks to the general chair, Klaus Havelund, for his leading role in the organization of RV 2017.

September 2017   Shuvendu Lahiri
                                                            Giles Reger

Organization

Program Committee

Wolfgang Ahrendt	Chalmers — University of Gothenburg, Sweden
Cyrille Valentin Artho	KTH Royal Institute of Technology, Sweden
Howard Barringer	University of Manchester, UK
Ezio Bartocci	Vienna University of Technology, Austria
Andreas Bauer	KUKA Systems, Germany
Saddek Bensalem	University of Grenoble Alpes/VERIMAG, France
Eric Bodden	Paderborn University and Fraunhofer IEM, Germany
Borzoo Bonakdarpour	McMaster University, Canada
Christian Colombo	University of Malta, Malta
Ylies Falcone	University Grenoble Alpes/Inria, France
Grigory Fedyukovich	University of Washington, USA
Lu Feng	University of Virginia, USA
Patrice Godefroid	Microsoft Research, USA
Jean Goubault-Larrecq	CNRS/ENS de Cachan, France
Alex Groce	Northern Arizona University, USA
Radu Grosu	Vienna University of Technology, Austria
Sylvain Hallé	Université du Québec à Chicoutimi, Canada
Marieke Huisman	University of Twente, Netherlands
Franjo Ivancic	Google, USA
Bengt Jonsson	Uppsala University, Sweden
Felix Klaedtke	NEC Europe Ltd., Germany
Rahul Kumar	Microsoft, USA
Shuvendu Lahiri	Microsoft Research, USA
Kim Larsen	Aalborg University, Denmark
Insup Lee	University of Pennsylvania, USA
Axel Legay	IRISA/Inria Rennes, France
Martin Leucker	University of Lübeck, Germany
Ben Livshits	Imperial College, UK
David Lo	Singapore Management University, Singapore
Francesco Logozzo	Facebook, USA
P. Madhusudan	University of Illinois at Urbana-Champaign, USA
Leonardo Mariani	University of Milano Bicocca, Italy
Madanlal Musuvathi	Microsoft Research, USA
Ayoub Nouri	University of Grenoble Alpes, France
Gordon Pace	University of Malta, Malta
Doron Peled	Bar Ilan University, Israel
Veselin Raychev	ETH Zurich, Switzerland
Giles Reger	University of Manchester, UK

Grigore Rosu	University of Illinois at Urbana-Champaign, USA
Cesar Sanchez	IMDEA Software Institute, Spain
Gerardo Schneider	Chalmers — University of Gothenburg, Sweden
Rahul Sharma	Microsoft Research, India
Julien Signoles	CEA LIST, France
Scott Smolka	Stony Brook University, USA
Oleg Sokolsky	University of Pennsylvania, USA
Bernhard Steffen	University of Dortmund, Germany
Scott Stoller	Stony Brook University, USA
Volker Stolz	Western Norway University of Applied Sciences, Norway
Frits Vaandrager	Radboud University, Netherlands
Neil Walkinshaw	University of Leicester, UK
Chao Wang	University of Southern California, USA
Eugen Zalinescu	Technical University of Munich, Germany

Additional Reviewers

Alt, Leonardo	Kaufman, Samuel	Poulsen, Danny Bøgsted
Arzt, Steven	Khoury, Raphael	Pun, Ka I
Assaf, Mounir	Komuravelli, Anvesh	Quilbeuf, Jean
Bastani, Osbert	Kuester, Jan-Christoph	Rutle, Adrian
Betti, Quentin	Kusano, Markus	Scheffel, Torben
Bhatia, Sahil	Le, Tien-Duy B.	Schmitz, Malte
Biondi, Fabrizio	Le, Xuan-Bach D.	Selyunin, Konstantin
Chakraborty, Ayon	Lorber, Florian	Serebryany, Konstantin
Chen, Xiaohong	Lukina, Anna	Siddique, Umair
Chimento, Jesus Mauricio	Ma, Lei	Sung, Chungha
Decker, Normann	Mangal, Ravi	Thoma, Daniel
Defrancisco, Richard	Mudduluru, Rashmi	Thorn, Johannes
Demri, Stéphane	Muniz, Marco	Thung, Ferdian
Enescu, Mike	Nguyen, Hung	Traonouez, Louis-Marie
Frohme, Markus	Pardo, Raúl	Vu, Anh-Duy
Ghalebi K., Elahe	Park, Sangdon	Wang, Rui
Guo, Shengjian	Patra, Jibesh	Yang, Junxing
Hirsch, Christian	Phan, Dung	Zhang, Naling
Jakse, Raphaël	Picazo-Sanchez, Pablo	Zhang, Teng
Karpenkov, Egor	Pinisetty, Srinivas	

Machine-Learning State Properties (Tutorial)

Madhusudan Parthasarathy

University of Illinois at Urbana-Champaign, USA

Abstract. Several applications of using machine learning in the realm of software engineering have emerged in recent years. One set of such applications revolve learning properties of program states using a sample of concrete states. There are many ways to obtain concrete states a program can exhibit through runtime information gathered on test runs, through symbolic execution, or through verification engines. Given such a source of discovery of program states, a machine learning algorithm that learns an appropriate generalization of the discovered states can help us synthesize pre-conditions, contracts, and invariants.

This tutorial will be on methods from machine-learning that can be used to learn such state predicates. In particular, we will discuss the various combinations of learning across the following dimensions:

- Classical learning algorithms for various subclasses of Boolean formulae.
- Modifications of algorithms to make them robust for applications in precondition generation, invariants, and inductive invariants.
- Pairing learning algorithms with techniques of state discovery, including dynamic runs, symbolic execution, and verification engines.

Invited Presentations

Learning Input Languages for Runtime Verification

Andreas Zeller

Saarland University, Germany

Abstract. Let us use dynamic tainting to follow the paths of input characters through a program. We will then see that some input fragments end in some variables, and others in others. This allows us to decompose the input into individual parts, one per variable, and consequently, to infer the entire structure of the input as a context-free grammar. In the context of runtime verification, such inferred input grammars have a number of uses. First, they can be used as test drivers, allowing to cover millions of executions in minutes. Second, they can serve to derive dynamic invariants, such as pre- or postconditions. Third, grammars, as well as invariants, can be easily verified dynamically, checking whether inputs and invariants conform to the learned languages. The AUTOGRAM approach will be demonstrated using examples of real programs and (if time permits) even live coding on stage.

The Design and Applications for a Tracing Plane for Distributed Systems

Rodrigo Fonseca

Brown University, USA

Abstract. Many tasks for understanding and managing the execution of systems such as debugging, snapshotting, monitoring, accounting, and providing performance guarantees, are much harder in distributed settings. Correspondingly, many techniques such as distributed timestamps, end-to-end tracing, and taint tracking have been successfully used to help with these tasks. Their deployment, however, is usually fraught with difficulties, including intrusive instrumentation and lack of pervasiveness. In this talk I describe some of the recent successes weve had with these mechanisms, including Pivot Tracing (SOSP 2015) and Retro (NSDI 2015), and will outline a vision for the Tracing Plane, a layered architecture that distills primitives that are common to all these techniques most importantly the causal propagation of generic metadata making traceability a first-class concept in distributed systems. The Tracing Plane simplifies the instrumentation of current and new systems, and lowers the barrier for the adoption of existing and novel introspection and management techniques.

Windows Driver Verification Platform

Vladimir Levin and Jakob Lichtenberg

Microsoft Windows and Devices Group, Redmond, USA
{vladlev, jakobl}@microsoft.com

Abstract. The Windows Driver Verification Platform (DVP) provides compile time and runtime technologies for verifying that device drivers work correctly: Static Driver Verifier (SDV) is a compile time verification tool available for 3rd party developers as part of the Windows Driver Development kit. Runtime Driver Verifier (DV) is integrated directly into the Windows OS and shipped inbox. Both technologies are used by 3rd party driver developers as well as internally at Microsoft and in the entire range of Window devices from IoT devices and all the way up to Microsoft Azure deployments.

Whereas verification paradigms, engines, and abilities are different between SDV and DV, these technologies share a common concept of interface rules between the OS kernel and drivers (kernel extensions, in general). The interface is materialized by a set of APIs supplied by the kernel and sets of callbacks supplied by drivers. In a narrow sense, each of the two technologies is aimed at verifying that drivers follow the interface rules.

The talk will cover the current state of the platform, shared features of the two technologies and their differences. We will also discuss our pipeline for technology transfer from Microsoft Research to Windows.

Contents

Tool Papers

Short Papers

Tutorials

P: Modular and Safe Asynchronous Programming

Ankush Desai[1]([⊠]) and Shaz Qadeer[2]

[1] University of California, Berkeley, USA
ankushd@berkeley.edu
[2] Microsoft Research, Redmond, USA

Abstract. We describe the design and implementation of P, an asynchronous event-driven programming language. P allows the programmer to specify the system as a collection of interacting state machines, which communicate with each other using events. P unifies modeling and programming into one activity for the programmer. Not only can a P program be compiled into executable code, but it can also be validated using systematic testing. P was first used to implement and validate the USB device driver stack that ships with Microsoft Windows 8 and Windows Phone. P is now also being used for the design and implementation of robotics and distributed systems inside Microsoft and in academia.

1 Introduction

An important programming challenge in modern applications is asynchrony, which happens when the requestor of an operation continues without blocking on the completion of the operation in order to keep the application responsive and performant. Asynchrony is difficult to get right because it inevitably leads to concurrency with its notorious pitfalls of race conditions and Heisenbugs. To address the challenges of asynchronous computation, we have developed P [1] (https://github.com/p-org/P), a (domain-specific) programming language for modeling and specifying protocols in asynchronous event-driven applications.

The P programmer writes the protocol and its specification at a high-level. P provides first-class support for modeling concurrency, specifying safety and liveness properties, and checking that the program satisfies its specification [2]. In these capabilities, it is similar to TLA+ [3] and SPIN [4]. Unlike TLA+ and SPIN, a P program can also be compiled into executable C code. This capability bridges the gap between high-level model and low-level implementation and eliminates a huge hurdle to the acceptance of formal modeling and specification among programmers. The programming model in P is based on concurrently-executing state machines communicating via events, each event accompanied by a typed payload value. A memory management system based on linear typing and unique pointers provides safe memory management and data-race free concurrent execution. In this respect, P is similar to modern systems programming languages such as Rust.

© Springer International Publishing AG 2017
S. Lahiri and G. Reger (Eds.): RV 2017, LNCS 10548, pp. 3–7, 2017.
DOI: 10.1007/978-3-319-67531-2_1

P got its start in Microsoft software development when it was used to ship the USB 3.0 drivers in Windows 8.1 and Windows Phone. P enabled the detection and debugging of hundreds of race conditions and Heisenbugs early on in the design of the drivers. Since then, P has been used to ship many more drivers in subsequent versions of Windows. Early positive experience with P in the Windows kernel led to the development of P# [5], a framework that provides state machines and systematic testing via an extension to C#. In contrast to P, the approach in P# is minimal syntactic extension and maximal use of libraries to deliver modeling, specification and testing capabilities.

P is transforming the development of cloud infrastructure in Azure. Azure, similar to other cloud providers, faces the challenge of Heisenbugs caused by unexpected race conditions and software or hardware faults. These bugs result in disruption of live services a huge problem for both customers and providers of cloud services. P and P# are being used to find and debug Heisenbugs in already-deployed services and to design and validate new services before deployment. P allows engineers to precisely model asynchronous interfaces among components in a large Azure service. It also allows engineers to discover and debug problems on their desktops that would otherwise take months and sometimes even years to manifest after the service is deployed.

More recently, P is being used for safe programming of autonomous robotics software stack [6]. Systematic testing of robotics software systems fails to reason about complex robot dynamics and other unknown-uncertainties in the environment. We extended P with runtime verification capabilities to ensure safety of the robot when assumptions made during testing do not hold at runtime [7].

2   Overview: P Programming Framework

P is a domain-specific language for implementing safe asynchronous event-driven systems. Figure 1 provides a pictorial overview of the P tool chain. There are

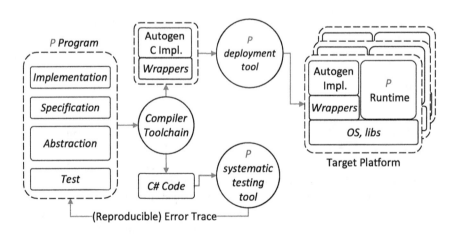

Fig. 1. Overview of P

three main building blocks of the P framework—a *programming language* for implementing and specifying an asynchronous event-driven system, a *compositional testing* tool for efficiently exploring the nondeterminism in a P program, and a *runtime library* for efficiently executing the program.

P *program:* A P program consists of four main components, *implementation*, *specification*, *abstraction* and the *test-driver*. The *implementation* block contains the protocols implementing the application. The computational model underlying a P program is state machines communicating via messages. Each state machine has an input queue, event handlers, and machine-local store for a collection of variables. The state machines run concurrently with each other, each executing an event handling loop that dequeues a message from the input queue, examines the local store, and can execute a sequence of operations. Each operation either updates the local store, sends messages to other machines, or creates new machines. In P, a send operation is non-blocking; the message is simply enqueued into the input queue of the target machine.

The *specification* block captures the correctness properties of the implementation. The specifications of the system are implemented in the form of *monitors*. Each monitor is a state machine that maintains necessary state for asserting a temporal safety or liveness requirement. The implementation is instrumented to send relevant events to each monitor enabling it to check if the system satisfies the specification.

Testing a large distributed system is not scalable as the number of possible executions is extremely large. Instead, P allows the programmer to test each component in the system separately, by replacing any protocols in its environment with the appropriate abstractions. The abstractions of each component used for compositional reasoning constitute the *abstraction* block in a P program.

The *test-driver* block is key to scalable systematic testing of a P program. Each protocol has a separate test-driver to capture the set of executions that must be explored during systematic testing of that protocol. The driver uses P features to compactly specify a large set of executions to be tested. These executions are then automatically generated by the systematic testing tool in P.

Systematic testing: Our tool for systematic testing of P programs is implemented in two parts. The P compiler generates a translation of the program into a C# program. Next, the systematic testing tool takes as input the C# code and systematically enumerates executions resulting from scheduling and explicit nondeterministic choices. Together, these two steps create a single-process interpreter and explorer for the nondeterministic semantics of a P program. A programmer typically spends the initial part of protocol development in the iterative edit-compile-test-debug loop enabled by our systematic testing tool (see the feedback loop in Fig. 1). The feedback from the tool is an error trace that picks a particular sequence of nondeterministic choices leading to the error. Since all nondeterministic choices are explicitly indicated by the tool, the process of debugging becomes considerably simpler that the current practice of correlating logs created at different machines in a live execution.

Execution: The P compiler also generates C code that is compiled by a standard C compiler and linked against the P runtime to generate the executable that can be deployed on the target platform, collection of machines or robotics system. Runtime ensures that the behavior of a P program matches the semantics validated by the systematic testing.

3   Building Distributed and Robotics Systems Using P

We used P to implement two distributed services as case studies: (i) distributed atomic commit of updates to decentralized, partitioned data using two-phase commit [8], and (ii) distributed data structures such as hashtables and lists. These services use State Machine Replication (SMR) for fault-tolerance. Protocols for SMR, like Multi-Paxos [9] and Chain Replication [10], in turn use other protocols like leader election, failure detectors, and network channels. More details about this case-study can be found at: (https://github.com/p-org/P/wiki) More recently, we have been working towards building a programming framework (Drona) for safe robotics. Drona uses P as its front-end programming language (https://drona-org.github.io/Drona/).

4   Conclusion

P is a programming framework that makes it easier to build, specify, and systematically test asynchronous systems. P is being used to implement and validate practical distributed systems and safety critical robotics systems. P's systematic testing has the power to generate and reproduce within minutes, executions that could take months or even years to manifest in a live systems.

References

1. Desai, A., Gupta, V., Jackson, E., Qadeer, S., Rajamani, S., Zufferey, D.: P: safe asynchronous event-driven programming. In: Programming Language Design and Implementation (PLDI), pp. 321–332 (2013)
2. Desai, A., Qadeer, S., Seshia, S.A.: Systematic testing of asynchronous reactive systems. In: Foundations of Software Engineering (FSE), pp. 73–83 (2015)
3. Lamport, L.: Specifying Systems: The TLA+ Language and Tools for Hardware and Software Engineers. Addison-Wesley Longman Publishing Co., Inc, Boston (2002)
4. Holzmann, G.: Spin Model Checker, The: Primer and Reference Manual, 1st edn. Addison-Wesley Professional, Boston (2003)
5. Deligiannis, P., Donaldson, A.F., Ketema, J., Lal, A., Thomson, P.: Asynchronous programming, analysis and testing with state machines. ACM SIGPLAN Not. **50**, 154–164 (2015). ACM
6. Desai, A., Saha, I., Yang, J., Qadeer, S., Seshia, S.A.: DRONA: a framework for safe distributed mobile robotics. In: Proceedings of the 8th International Conference on Cyber-Physical Systems, ICCPS 2017, New York, NY, USA, pp. 239–248. ACM (2017)

7. Desai, A., Dreossi, T., Seshia, S.: Combining model checking and runtime verification for safe robotics. In: International Conference on Runtime Verification (RV) (2017)
8. Gray, J., Lamport, L.: Consensus on transaction commit. ACM Trans. Database Syst. **31**, 133–160 (2006)
9. Lamport, L.: Paxos made simple. ACM SIGACT News **32** (2001)
10. van Renesse, R., Schneider, F.B.: Chain replication for supporting high throughput and availability. In: Proceedings of the 6th Conference on Symposium on Opearting Systems Design & Implementation, OSDI 2004, vol. 6, p. 7. USENIX Association, San Francisco (2004). http://dl.acm.org/citation.cfm?id=1251254.1251261

A Foundation for Runtime Monitoring

Adrian Francalanza[1]([⊠]), Luca Aceto[2], Antonis Achilleos[2],
Duncan Paul Attard[1,2], Ian Cassar[1,2], Dario Della Monica[3,4],
and Anna Ingólfsdóttir[2]

[1] Department of Computer Science, University of Malta, Msida, Malta
adrian.francalanza@um.edu.mt
[2] School of Computer Science, Reykjavík University, Reykjavik, Iceland
[3] Departamento de Sistemas Informáticos y Computación,
Universidad Complutense de Madrid, Madrid, Spain
[4] Dipartimento di Ingegneria Elettrica e Tecnologie dell'Informazione,
Università "Federico II" di Napoli, Naples, Italy

Abstract. Runtime Verification is a lightweight technique that complements other verification methods in an effort to ensure software correctness. The technique poses novel questions to software engineers: it is not easy to identify which specifications are amenable to runtime monitoring, nor is it clear which monitors effect the required runtime analysis correctly. This exposition targets a foundational understanding of these questions. Particularly, it considers an expressive specification logic (a syntactic variant of the modal μ-calculus) that is agnostic of the verification method used, together with an elemental framework providing an operational semantics for the runtime analysis performed by monitors. The correspondence between the property satisfactions in the logic on the one hand, and the verdicts reached by the monitors performing the analysis on the other, is a central theme of the study. Such a correspondence underpins the concept of monitorability, used to identify the subsets of the logic that can be adequately monitored for by RV. Another theme of the study is that of understanding what should be expected of a monitor in order for the verification process to be correct. We show how the monitor framework considered can constitute a basis whereby various notions of monitor correctness may be defined and investigated.

1 Introduction

Runtime Verification (RV) [35] is a lightweight verification technique that checks whether the System Under Scrutiny (SUS) satisfies a correctness property by analysing its *current execution*. It has its origins in model checking, as a more scalable (yet still formal) approach to program verification where state explosion problems (which are inherent to model checking) are mitigated [34,35]. RV is

---

This work was supported by the project "TheoFoMon: Theoretical Foundations for Monitorability" (nr.163406-051) of the Icelandic Research Fund and the Marie Curie INDAM-COFUND-2012 Outgoing Fellowship.

S. Lahiri and G. Reger (Eds.): RV 2017, LNCS 10548, pp. 8–29, 2017.
DOI: 10.1007/978-3-319-67531-2_2

often used to *complement* other verification techniques such as theorem proving, model checking and testing, in a multi-pronged approach towards ensuring system correctness [3–5, 21]. The technique has fostered a number of verification tools such as [6, 10, 12, 16, 18–21, 27, 30, 37–39], to name but a few. It has also been used for a variety of applications, ranging from checking the executions of the NASA Mars Rover software [12] and other autonomous research vehicles [28], to more mundane tasks such as checking for rule violations in financial systems [8], video games [40] and electronic examinations [29].

At its core, RV generally assumes a *logic* describing the correctness specifications that are expected to be satisfied by the SUS. From these specifications, programs called *monitors* are generated and *instrumented* to run with the SUS, so as to analyse its current execution (expressed as a trace of events) and infer any system violations or satisfactions w.r.t. these specifications (see Fig. 1). Violation and satisfaction *verdicts* are typically considered to be definite, *i.e.*, cannot be retracted upon observing further system events. Monitors are themselves computational entities that incur runtime costs, and considerable amounts of effort in RV is devoted to the engineering necessary to keep runtime overheads at feasible levels. Yet, a RV set-up such as the one depicted in Fig. 1 raises additional questions that warrant equal consideration.

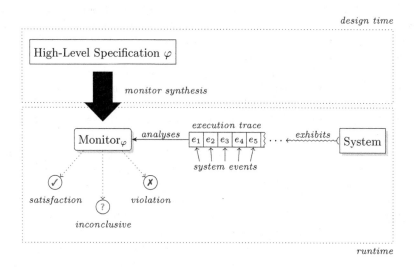

Fig. 1. Runtime monitor synthesis and operational set-up.

We Need to Talk About Monitors. The *expressiveness* of the verification technique w.r.t. the correctness properties that can be described by the logic—an attribute often termed as *monitorability*—should be a central question in RV. In fact, specification logics that are not necessarily wedded to the RV technique may express properties that *cannot* be monitored for at runtime. Particularly, certain aspects of a chosen specification logic can potentially reduce the analytical capabilities of the monitors, such as the ability to express properties describing *multiple or infinite executions* of a system. In such cases, the (finite) trace exhibited by the running system (see Fig. 1) may *not* contain sufficient execution information so as to enable the monitor to determine whether a property under analysis is violated or satisfied by the SUS. Therefore, being able to identify which properties are monitorable is essential for devising an effective strategy in a multi-pronged verification approach that tailors the verification method used to each correctness specification.

Another fundamental question raised by RV concerns monitor *correctness*. Generally, monitors are considered to be part of the *trusted computing base*, and are thus expected to exhibit correct behaviour. When this is not the case, erroneous monitors could invalidate any runtime analysis performed, irrespective of the low overheads a monitor may brandish. On top of that, what is actually expected of these monitors is seldom defined in precise terms, making it hard to ascertain monitor correctness. For instance, in a typical RV set-up such as that of Fig. 1, one would expect detection soundness, whereby *any* rejections (resp. acceptances) flagged by the monitor imply that the system indeed violates (resp. satisfies) the property being monitored. Other settings may also stipulate detection *completeness*, by which *all* property violations (resp. satisfactions) are flagged accordingly by the monitor observing the SUS. One may also require attributes that are independent of the specification logic chosen, such as passivity (*i.e.*, the absence of monitor interference with execution of the SUS), and determinism (*i.e.*, whether the monitor consistently yields the same verification outcome for the same observations).

This paper sheds light on one possible approach for addressing these questions. In particular, it showcases the work embarked upon in *Theoretical Foundations for Monitorability* (TheoFoMon), a three-year project funded by the Icelandic Research Fund with the aim of investigating the expressiveness and correctness issues outlined above. To maintain a general approach, the aforementioned questions are studied in the context of the Hennessy-Milner Logic with recursion (μHML) [33], a reformulation of the expressive and well-studied modal μ-calculus [32]—the logic is agnostic of the verification technique used, and can embed widely used temporal logics such as CTL* [9,17]. Labelled Transition Systems (LTSs) [2], formalisms that have been used to describe a vast range of computational phenomena, are employed to abstractly model the behaviour of systems and monitors in terms of graphs. This generality serves two goals. On the one hand, the LTS operational formalism abstracts away instance details of specific RV settings, facilitating the distillation of the core concepts at play. On the other hand, the considerable expressiveness of the logic immediately extends any findings and observations to other logics that can be embedded within it.

Paper Overview. The preliminaries in Sect. 2 present the basics for modelling systems and provide an introduction to our touchstone logic. Section 3 presents our monitor and instrumentation models. Section 4 links the properties specified by the logic and the verdicts reached by monitors, whereas Sect. 5 discusses notions of monitor correctness. Section 6 surveys extensions on the monitorability and correctness results presented, and Sect. 7 concludes.

2 Preliminaries: Groundhog Day

We provide a brief outline of the main technical machinery used by our exposition, namely, the system model and the specification logic. Interested readers are encouraged to consult [2, 33] for more details.

The Model. LTSs are directed graphs with labelled edges modelling the possible behaviours that can be exhibited by an executing system. Formally, a LTS consists of the triple $\langle \text{Sys}, (\text{Act} \cup \{\tau\}), \longrightarrow \rangle$ comprised of:

- a set of system states $p, q, r \in \text{Sys}$ (every system state may also be used to denote a system that starts executing from that state),
- a set of visible actions $\alpha \in \text{Act}$ and a distinguished silent action τ, where $\tau \notin \text{Act}$ and μ ranges over $(\text{Act} \cup \{\tau\})$, and finally,
- a ternary transition relation between states labelled by actions; we write $p \xrightarrow{\mu} q$ in lieu of $\langle p, \mu, q \rangle \in \longrightarrow$.

The notation $p \xrightarrow{\mu}$ is written when $p \xrightarrow{\mu} q$ for *no* system state q. Additionally, $p \Longrightarrow q$ denotes a sequence of silent actions $p(\xrightarrow{\tau})^* q$ from state p to q, whereas $p \xRightarrow{\alpha} q$, is written in place of $p \Longrightarrow \cdot \xrightarrow{\alpha} \cdot \Longrightarrow q$, to represent a visible action α that may be padded by preceding and succeeding silent actions. We occasionally use the notation $\mathbf{0}$ to refer to a system (state) that is deadlocked and exhibits *no* actions (not even silent ones). We let traces, $t, u \in \text{Act}^*$, range over sequences of *visible* actions and write sequences of transitions $p \xRightarrow{\alpha_1} \ldots \xRightarrow{\alpha_n} p_n$ as $p \xRightarrow{t} p_n$, where $t = \alpha_1, \ldots, \alpha_n$. As usual, ϵ denotes the empty trace.

Example 1. The directed graph in Fig. 2 depicts a LTS describing the implementation of three servers whose events are represented by the set of visible actions $\text{Act} = \{\texttt{req}, \texttt{ack}, \texttt{lim}\}$. State p shows the simplest possible implementation of a server that receives (\texttt{req}) and acknowledges (\texttt{ack}) client requests repeatedly. State q denotes an extension on this implementation that may reach a termination limit (transition \texttt{lim}) after a number or serviced requests (*i.e.,* \texttt{req} followed by \texttt{ack}). Finally state r represents an unpredictable server implementation that occasionally acknowledges a preceding client request twice. ∎

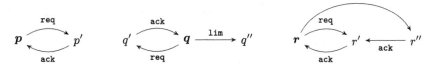

Fig. 2. The LTS depicting the behaviour of three server implementations p, q and r.

Syntax

$$\varphi, \phi \in \mu\text{HML} ::= \quad \textbf{ff} \quad \text{(falsity)} \qquad\qquad | \quad \textbf{tt} \quad \text{(truth)}$$
$$| \quad \varphi \wedge \phi \quad \text{(conjunction)} \qquad | \quad \varphi \vee \phi \quad \text{(disjunction)}$$
$$| \quad [\alpha]\varphi \quad \text{(necessity)} \qquad | \quad \langle\alpha\rangle\varphi \quad \text{(possibility)}$$
$$| \quad \textbf{max}\,X.\varphi \quad \text{(max. fixpoint)} \quad | \quad \textbf{min}\,X.\varphi \quad \text{(min. fixpoint)}$$
$$| \quad X \quad \text{(recursive variable)}$$

Semantics

$$[\![\textbf{ff}, \rho]\!] \stackrel{\text{def}}{=} \emptyset \qquad\qquad\qquad\qquad [\![\textbf{tt}, \rho]\!] \stackrel{\text{def}}{=} \text{Sys}$$

$$[\![\varphi \wedge \phi, \rho]\!] \stackrel{\text{def}}{=} [\![\varphi, \rho]\!] \cap [\![\phi, \rho]\!] \qquad [\![\varphi \vee \phi, \rho]\!] \stackrel{\text{def}}{=} [\![\varphi, \rho]\!] \cup [\![\phi, \rho]\!]$$

$$[\![[\alpha]\varphi, \rho]\!] \stackrel{\text{def}}{=} \left\{ p \mid \forall p'.\ p \stackrel{\alpha}{\Longrightarrow} p' \text{ implies } p' \in [\![\varphi, \rho]\!] \right\}$$

$$[\![\langle\alpha\rangle\varphi, \rho]\!] \stackrel{\text{def}}{=} \left\{ p \mid \exists p'.\ p \stackrel{\alpha}{\Longrightarrow} p' \text{ and } p' \in [\![\varphi, \rho]\!] \right\}$$

$$[\![\textbf{max}\,X.\varphi, \rho]\!] \stackrel{\text{def}}{=} \bigcup \{ S \mid S \subseteq [\![\varphi, \rho[X \mapsto S]]\!] \}$$

$$[\![\textbf{min}\,X.\varphi, \rho]\!] \stackrel{\text{def}}{=} \bigcap \{ S \mid [\![\varphi, \rho[X \mapsto S]]\!] \subseteq S \}$$

$$[\![X, \rho]\!] \stackrel{\text{def}}{=} \rho(X)$$

Fig. 3. The syntax and semantics of μHML.

The Logic. μHML [2,33] is a branching-time logic that can be used to specify correctness properties over systems modelled in terms of LTSs. Its syntax, given in Fig. 3, assumes a countable set of logical variables $X, Y \in \text{LVar}$, thereby allowing formulae to recursively express largest and least fixpoints using $\textbf{max}\,X.\varphi$ and $\textbf{min}\,X.\varphi$ resp.; these constructs bind free instances of the variable X in φ and induce the usual notions of free and closed formulae—we work up to alpha-conversion of bound variables. In addition to the standard constructs for truth, falsity, conjunction and disjunction, the μHML syntax includes the necessity and possibility modalities, one of main distinctive features of the logic.

The semantics of μHML is defined in terms of the function mapping formulae φ to the set of LTS states $S \subseteq \text{Sys}$ satisfying them. Figure 3 describes the semantics for open and closed formulae, and uses a map $\rho \in \text{LVar} \rightharpoonup 2^{\text{Sys}}$ from variables to sets of system states to enable an inductive definition on the structure of the formula φ. The formula $\textbf{tt}$ is satisfied by all processes, while $\textbf{ff}$ is satisfied by none; conjunctions and disjunctions bear the standard set-theoretic meaning of intersection and union. Necessity formulae $[\alpha]\varphi$ state that *for all* system executions producing event α (possibly none), the subsequent system state must then satisfy φ (*i.e.*, $\forall p'$, $p \stackrel{\alpha}{\Longrightarrow} p'$ implies $p' \in [\![\varphi, \rho]\!]$ must hold). Possibility formulae $\langle\alpha\rangle\varphi$ require the existence of *at least one* system execution with event α whereby the subsequent state then satisfies φ (*i.e.*, $\exists p'$, $p \stackrel{\alpha}{\Longrightarrow} p'$ and $p' \in [\![\varphi, \rho]\!]$ must hold). The recursive formulae $\textbf{max}\,X.\varphi$ and $\textbf{min}\,X.\varphi$ are resp. satisfied by the largest and least set of system states satisfying φ. The semantics of recursive variables X w.r.t. an environment instance ρ is given by the mapping of X in ρ, *i.e.*, the set of processes associated with X. *Closed* formulae (*i.e.*, formulae containing no free variables) are interpreted *independently* of the environment ρ, and the shorthand $[\![\varphi]\!]$ is used to denote $[\![\varphi, \rho]\!]$, *i.e.*, the set of system states in SYS that satisfy φ. In view of this, we say that a system (state) p satisfies some closed formula φ whenever $p \in [\![\varphi]\!]$, and conversely, that it violates φ whenever $p \notin [\![\varphi]\!]$. We highlight two basic formulae that are used pervasively in μHML: $\langle \alpha \rangle \mathbf{tt}$ describes systems that *can* produce action α, while $[\alpha]\mathbf{ff}$ describes systems that *cannot* produce action α. Note also that $[\alpha]\mathbf{tt}$ is semantically equivalent to $\mathbf{tt}$ whereas $\langle \alpha \rangle \mathbf{ff}$ equates to $\mathbf{ff}$.

Example 2. Recall the server implementations p, q and r depicted in Fig. 2.

$$\varphi_1 = \langle \text{req} \rangle \langle \text{ack} \rangle \langle \text{req} \rangle \mathbf{tt} \qquad \varphi_2 = [\text{lim}][\text{req}]\mathbf{ff}$$
$$\varphi_3 = [\text{req}][\text{ack}]\langle \text{req} \rangle \mathbf{tt} \qquad \varphi_4 = [\text{req}][\text{ack}]\langle \text{req} \rangle \mathbf{tt} \wedge \langle \text{lim} \rangle \mathbf{tt}$$

$$\varphi_5 = \mathbf{max}\, X.\big([\text{req}]([\text{ack}]X \wedge [\text{ack}][\text{ack}]\mathbf{ff})\big)$$
$$\varphi_6 = \mathbf{min}\, X.\big(\langle \text{req} \rangle \langle \text{ack} \rangle X \vee \langle \text{lim} \rangle \mathbf{tt}\big)$$

Formula φ_1 describes systems that *can* produce a req after *some* serviced request (*i.e.*, a req followed by a ack); all server implementations p, q and r satisfy this property. Formula φ_2 states that *whenever* a system produces the event lim, it *cannot* produce any req actions. Again all three implementations satisfy this property where, in particular, p and r satisfy this trivially since both never produce a lim event. Formula φ_3 strengthens property φ_1 by requiring that a system *can* produce a req after *any* serviced request. While p and q satisfy this requirement, implementation r violates this property at any time it (non-deterministically) transitions to state r''. Formula φ_4 strengthens this property further, by requiring the implementation to be capable of producing the lim event; only q satisfies this property.

Formula φ_5 specifies a (recursive) safety property that prohibits a system from producing duplicate acknowledgements in answer to client requests after *any number* of serviced requests. System r violates φ_5 via any trace in the regular language $(\text{req.ack})^+.\text{ack}$. Finally, φ_6 describes systems that *can* reach a service limit after a number (possibly zero) of serviced requests. System q satisfies φ_6 immediately, as opposed to p and r, which never reach such a state after *any* number of serviced requests. We note that if the minimal fixpoint recursion operator in φ_6 is substituted with a maximal fixpoint, *i.e.*, $\mathbf{max}\, X.(\langle \text{req} \rangle \langle \text{ack} \rangle X \vee \langle \text{lim} \rangle \mathbf{tt})$, implementations p and r would also satisfy it via the *infinite* sequence of events req.ack.req.ack... ∎

3 Dial M for Monitor

In [25, 26], monitors are also perceived as LTSs, expressed through the syntax of Fig. 5. It consists of three *verdict* constructs, **yes**, **no** and **end**, resp. denoting acceptance, rejection and termination (*i.e.*, an inconclusive outcome). The syntax

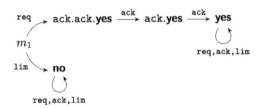

Fig. 4. The LTS representation for monitor $m_1 = (\mathbf{req.ack.ack.yes} + \mathbf{lim.no})$.

also includes action α prefixing, mutually-exclusive (external) choice and recursion, denoted by $\mathbf{rec}\,x.m$, acting as a binder for the recursion variables x in m. All recursive monitors are assumed to be guarded, meaning that all occurrences of bound variables occur under the context of an action prefix. In the sequel, we assume *closed* monitor terms, where all variable occurrences are bound.

Every monitor term may be given a LTS semantics via the transition rules shown in Fig. 5. The rules are fairly standard: for example, $m_1 + m_2 \xrightarrow{\mu} m_3$ (for some m_3) if either $m_1 \xrightarrow{\mu} m_3$ or $m_2 \xrightarrow{\mu} m_3$ (by rules SELL or SELR). The only transition rule worth drawing attention to, VER, specifies that verdicts v may transition with *any* $\alpha \in$ ACT to return to the same state, modelling the assumed requirement from Fig. 1 that verdicts are *irrevocable*.

Example 3. Monitor $m_1 = (\mathbf{req.ack.ack.yes} + \mathbf{lim.no})$ can be represented diagrammatically via the LTS depicted in Fig. 5. This LTS is derived using the monitor dynamics from Fig. 5, by applying the rules that match the edge label

Syntax

$$m, n \in \text{MON} ::= v \qquad | \; \alpha.m \qquad | \; m+n \qquad | \; \mathbf{rec}\,x.m \qquad | \; x$$
$$v, u \in \text{VERD} ::= \mathbf{end} \qquad | \; \mathbf{no} \qquad | \; \mathbf{yes}$$

Dynamics

$$\text{ACT} \frac{}{\alpha.m \xrightarrow{\alpha} m} \qquad\qquad \text{REC} \frac{}{\mathbf{rec}\,x.m \xrightarrow{\tau} m[\mathbf{rec}\,x.m/x]}$$

$$\text{SELL} \frac{m \xrightarrow{\mu} m'}{m+n \xrightarrow{\mu} m'} \qquad \text{SELR} \frac{n \xrightarrow{\mu} n'}{m+n \xrightarrow{\mu} n'} \qquad \text{VER} \frac{}{v \xrightarrow{\alpha} v}$$

Instrumentation

$$\text{MON} \frac{p \xrightarrow{\alpha} p' \quad m \xrightarrow{\alpha} m'}{m \lhd p \xrightarrow{\alpha} m' \lhd p'} \qquad \text{TER} \frac{p \xrightarrow{\alpha} p' \quad m \xcancel{\xrightarrow{\alpha}} \quad m \xcancel{\xrightarrow{\tau}}}{m \lhd p \xrightarrow{\alpha} \mathbf{end} \lhd p'}$$

$$\text{AsS} \frac{p \xrightarrow{\tau} p'}{m \lhd p \xrightarrow{\tau} m \lhd p'} \qquad \text{AsM} \frac{m \xrightarrow{\tau} m'}{m \lhd p \xrightarrow{\tau} m' \lhd p}$$

Fig. 5. Monitors and instrumentation.

and the *structure* of the term under consideration. Every term that results from each rule application essentially represents a LTS *state*. For example, the edge labelled lim from node m_1 to node **no** in Fig. 4 follows from the transition

$$\text{req.ack.ack.yes} + \text{lim.no} \xrightarrow{\;\text{lim}\;} \textbf{no}$$

derived by applying rule SELR and rule ACT. From the LTS in Fig. 4, we can see that monitor m_1 reaches an acceptance verdict whenever it analyses the sequence of events req.ack.ack, and a rejection verdict when the single event lim is analysed. ∎

In [26], a system p can be *instrumented* with a monitor m (referred to hereafter as a *monitored system* and denoted as $m \lhd s$) by composing their respective LTSs. The semantics of $m \lhd s$ is defined by the instrumentation rules in Fig. 5. We highlight the generality of the instrumentation relation $\lhd$. It is parametric w.r.t. the system and monitor abstract LTSs and is largely independent of their specific syntax: it only requires the monitor LTS to contain an inconclusive (persistent) verdict state, **end**. Instrumentation is *asymmetric*, and the monitored system transitions with an observable event only when the system is able to exhibit said event. The suggestive symbol $\lhd$ alludes to this unidirectional composition, indicating that trace events flow from the system into the monitor. The monitor is in this sense *passive* as it does not interact with the system, but transitions in tandem with it according to the rules in Fig. 5. When the system exhibits an observable event that can be analysed by the monitor, the two synchronise and transition in lockstep according to their respective LTSs via the rule MON. When the monitor *cannot* analyse the aforementioned event,[5] and is it *not* able to transition internally to a state that permits it to do so (*i.e.*, it is already stable, $m \not\rightarrow$), the system is not blocked by the instrumentation. Instead, it is allowed to transition, whereas the monitor is aborted to the inconclusive verdict **end**, as per rule TER. The system-monitor synchronisation is limited to visible actions, and both system and monitor can transition independently w.r.t. their own internal τ-action (rules AsS and AsM).

Example 4. Fig. 6 depicts the LTS of the monitored system $m_1 \lhd r$ that results from the composition of system r from Fig. 2 with monitor m_1 from Fig. 4. Any verdict that m_1 arrives at is subject to the execution path that r decides to follow at runtime. In Fig. 6, an acceptance can never be reached since r does not produce event lim. Furthermore, when event req is exhibited by r, the monitored system may non-deterministically transition to either $\text{ack.ack.yes} \lhd r'$ or $\text{ack.ack.yes} \lhd r''$ (cases A and B in Fig. 6)—this impinges on whether m_1 reaches an acceptance verdict or not.

For case A, state r' generates an ack event followed by req; the monitor at this stage, ack.yes, is not expecting a req event, but ack instead. It therefore aborts monitoring, reaching the inconclusive verdict **end** using the instrumentation rule TER (Fig. 5). If instead, the monitored system $m_1 \lhd r$ transitions to

---

[5] This may be due to event knowledge gaps from the instrumentation-side or knowledge disagreements between the monitors and the instrumentation [11].

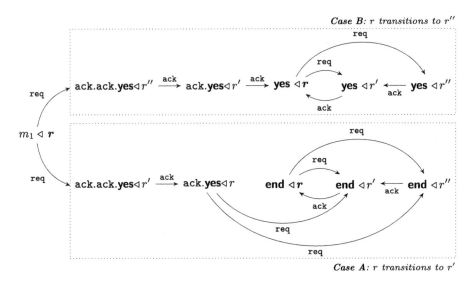

Fig. 6. The LTS depicting the behaviour of the monitored system $m \vartriangleleft r$.

ack.ack.**yes** $\vartriangleleft r''$ (case B), it then reaches an acceptance verdict after analysing two consecutive ack events. In either outcome, the monitor verdict is preserved once it is reached via rule VER.   ∎

4   Sense and Monitorability

To understand monitorability in our setting, we need to relate acceptances (**yes**) and rejections (**no**) reached by a monitor m when monitoring a system p with satisfactions ($p \in \llbracket \varphi \rrbracket$) and violations ($p \notin \llbracket \varphi \rrbracket$) for that system w.r.t. some *closed* μHML formula φ. This will, in turn, allow us to determine when a monitor m *represents* (in some precise sense) a property φ.

Example 5. Consider the simple monitor $m_2 = $ lim.**no** which *rejects all* the systems that produce the event lim. Since any such system p would necessarily violate the property $\varphi_7 = [\text{lim}]\mathbf{ff}$, *i.e.*, $p \notin \llbracket [\text{lim}]\mathbf{ff} \rrbracket$, there exists a tight correspondence between any system rejected by m_2 and the systems violating φ_7. By contrast, the more elaborate monitor $m_3 = \mathbf{rec}\, x.(\text{req.ack}.x + \text{lim}.\mathbf{yes})$ reaches the *acceptance* verdict for systems that exhibit a trace consisting of a sequence of serviced requests (req.ack)* followed by the event lim. It turns out that this monitor can *only* reach an acceptance for systems that satisfy the property $\varphi_6 = \mathbf{min}\, X.(\langle \text{req} \rangle \langle \text{ack} \rangle X \vee \langle \text{lim} \rangle \mathbf{tt})$ from Example 2. Stated otherwise, there is a correspondence between the systems satisfying φ_6, *i.e.*, $p \in \llbracket \varphi_6 \rrbracket$, and those accepted by monitor m_3.   ∎

However such correspondences are not so clear for certain monitors.

Example 6. Monitor m_1 from Example 3 reaches an acceptance verdict when composed with a system $p_\perp$ that exhibits the trace `req.ack.ack`, and a rejection verdict for the *same* system $p_\perp$ when it exhibits the trace `lim` (*i.e.*, $m_1 \lhd p_\perp \xrightarrow{\text{req.ack.ack}}$ **yes** $\lhd \mathbf{0}$ and $m_1 \lhd p_\perp \xrightarrow{\text{lim}}$ **no** $\lhd \mathbf{0}$). If we associate m_1 with a correctness property such as $\varphi_8 = \langle\text{req}\rangle\langle\text{ack}\rangle\langle\text{ack}\rangle\mathbf{tt} \wedge [\text{lim}]\mathbf{ff}$ and attempt to link acceptances to satisfactions and rejections to violations (as in Example 5) we end up with a logical contradiction, namely that $p_\perp \in [\![\varphi_8]\!]$ and $p_\perp \notin [\![\varphi_8]\!]$. ∎

A correspondence between monitor judgements and μHML properties that relies on the following predicates is established in [26]:

$$\mathsf{acc}(p, m) \stackrel{\text{def}}{=} \exists t, p' \text{ such that } m \lhd p \xrightarrow{t} \textbf{yes} \lhd p' \quad \text{(acceptance)}$$
$$\mathsf{rej}(p, m) \stackrel{\text{def}}{=} \exists t, p' \text{ such that } m \lhd p \xrightarrow{t} \textbf{no} \lhd p' \quad \text{(rejection)}$$

Definition 1 (Sound Monitoring). *A monitor m monitors soundly for the property represented by the formula φ, denoted as $\mathsf{smon}(m, \varphi)$, whenever for every system $p \in \textsc{Sys}$ the following conditions hold: (i) $\mathsf{acc}(p, m)$ implies $p \in [\![\varphi]\!]$, (ii) $\mathsf{rej}(p, m)$ implies $p \notin [\![\varphi]\!]$.* ∎

Definition 1 universally quantifies over all system states p satisfying a formula φ that is soundly monitored by a monitor m (this may, in general, be an infinite set). It also rules out contradicting monitor verdicts. For whenever the predicate $\mathsf{smon}(m, \varphi)$ holds for some monitor m and formula φ, and there exists some system p where $\mathsf{acc}(p, m)$, it must be the case that $p \in [\![\varphi]\!]$ by Definition 1. Thus, from the logical satisfaction definition we have $\neg(p \notin [\![\varphi]\!])$, and by the contrapositive of Definition 1, we must also have $\neg\mathsf{rej}(p, m)$. A symmetric argument also applies for any system p where $\mathsf{rej}(p, m)$, from which $\neg\mathsf{acc}(p, m)$ follows. Sound monitoring is arguably the least requirement for relating a monitor with a logical property. Further to this, the obvious additional stipulation would be to ask for the dual of Definition 1, namely *complete monitoring* for m and φ. Intuitively, this would state that for all p, $p \in [\![\varphi]\!]$ implies $\mathsf{acc}(p, m)$, and also that $p \notin [\![\varphi]\!]$ implies $\mathsf{rej}(p, m)$. However, such a demand turns out to be too stringent for a large part of the logic presented in Fig. 3.

Example 7. Consider the core basic formula $\langle\alpha\rangle\mathbf{tt}$, describing processes that can perform action α. One could demonstrate that the simple monitor $\alpha.\textbf{yes}$ satisfies the condition that, for all systems p, $p \in [\![\varphi]\!]$ implies $\mathsf{acc}(p, m)$. However, for this formula, *no* sound monitor exists satisfying the condition that whenever $p \notin [\![\varphi]\!]$ then $\mathsf{rej}(p, m)$. For assume that one such (sound) monitor m exists satisfying this condition. Since $\mathbf{0} \notin [\![\langle\alpha\rangle\mathbf{tt}]\!]$, then $\mathsf{rej}(\mathbf{0}, m)$ follows by our assumption. This means that this particular monitor can reach a rejection *without* needing to observe any actions (*i.e.*, since $\mathbf{0}$ does not produce any actions, we have $m \Longrightarrow$ **no**). Such a statement would, in turn, imply that $\mathsf{rej}(\alpha.\mathbf{0}, m)$ also holds (because m is able to reach a rejection verdict for *any* system) although, clearly, $\alpha.\mathbf{0} \in [\![\langle\alpha\rangle\mathbf{tt}]\!]$. This makes m unsound, contradicting our initial assumption that m was sound. ∎

A dual argument to that of Example 7 can be carried out for another core basic formula in μHML, namely $[\alpha]\mathbf{ff}$, describing the property of not being able to produce action α. Although there are sound monitors m satisfying the condition that for all systems p, if $p \notin [\![[\alpha]\mathbf{ff}]\!]$ then $\mathsf{rej}(p,m)$, there are *none* that also satisfy the condition that for any system p, if $p \in [\![[\alpha]\mathbf{ff}]\!]$ then $\mathsf{acc}(p,m)$.

The counterarguments posed for the core formulae $\langle\alpha\rangle\mathbf{tt}$ and $[\alpha]\mathbf{ff}$ are enough evidence to convince us that requiring complete monitoring would exclude a large number of useful formulae in μHML. In fact, the complete monitoring requirement would severely limit correspondence to formulae that are semantically equivalent to $\mathbf{tt}$ and $\mathbf{ff}$ only—admittedly, this would not be very useful. In view of this, we define a weaker form of completeness where we require completeness w.r.t. either logical satisfactions or violations, but not both.

Definition 2 (Partially-Complete Monitoring). *A monitor m can monitor for a property φ in a satifaction-complete, $\mathsf{scmon}(m,\varphi)$, or a violation-complete, $\mathsf{vcmon}(m,\varphi)$, manner. These are defined as follows:*

$$\mathsf{scmon}(m,\varphi) \overset{\text{def}}{=} \forall p.\, p \in [\![\varphi]\!] \ implies \ \mathsf{acc}(p,m) \qquad (satisfaction\text{-}complete)$$

$$\mathsf{vcmon}(m,\varphi) \overset{\text{def}}{=} \forall p.\, p \notin [\![\varphi]\!] \ implies \ \mathsf{rej}(p,m) \qquad (violation\text{-}complete)$$

A monitor m monitors for formula φ in a partially-complete manner, denoted as $\mathsf{cmon}(m,\varphi)$, when either $\mathsf{scmon}(m,\varphi)$ or $\mathsf{vcmon}(m,\varphi)$ holds. ∎

By defining the partially-complete monitoring predicate $\mathsf{cmon}(m,\varphi)$ of Definition 2 and the sound monitoring predicate of Definition 1, we are now in a position to formalise our touchstone notion for monitor-formula correspondence.

Definition 3 (Monitor-Formula Correspondence). *A monitor m is said to monitor for a formula φ, denoted as $\mathsf{mon}(m,\varphi)$, if it can do it soundly, and in a partially-complete manner:*

$$\mathsf{mon}(m,\varphi) \overset{\text{def}}{=} \mathsf{smon}(m,\varphi) \ and \ \mathsf{cmon}(m,\varphi)$$ ∎

Example 8. Consider the monitor $\alpha.\mathbf{yes}$ and the basic formula $\langle\alpha\rangle\mathbf{tt}$. One can verify that $\alpha.\mathbf{yes}$ monitors for $\langle\alpha\rangle\mathbf{tt}$, *i.e.*, $\mathsf{mon}(\alpha.\mathbf{yes}, \langle\alpha\rangle\mathbf{tt})$. Intuitively, this is because *every* system that $\alpha.\mathbf{yes}$ accepts must generate the trace α, which is precisely the evidence required to show that the system satisfies $\langle\alpha\rangle\mathbf{tt}$. From this information, we can deduce that both requirements of Definition 3, *i.e.*, $\mathsf{smon}(\alpha.\mathbf{yes}, \langle\alpha\rangle\mathbf{tt})$ and $\mathsf{cmon}(\alpha.\mathbf{yes}, \langle\alpha\rangle\mathbf{tt})$, hold.

Consider now the same monitor compared to the formula $\langle\alpha\rangle\langle\beta\rangle\mathbf{tt}$. According to Definition 3, $\alpha.\mathbf{yes}$ does *not* monitor for $\langle\alpha\rangle\langle\beta\rangle\mathbf{tt}$. We can show this via the counterexample system $\alpha.\mathbf{0}$: it is not hard to see that the assertion $\mathsf{acc}(\alpha.\mathbf{0}, \alpha.\mathbf{yes})$ holds, *but* the system being monitored for does not satisfy the formula, *i.e.*, $\alpha.\mathbf{0} \notin [\![\langle\alpha\rangle\langle\beta\rangle\mathbf{tt}]\!]$. This makes the monitor $\alpha.\mathbf{yes}$ unsound, *i.e.*, $\neg\mathsf{smon}(\alpha.\mathbf{yes}, \langle\alpha\rangle\langle\beta\rangle\mathbf{tt})$ from Definition 1.

By Definition 3, the monitor $\alpha.\textbf{no} + \beta.\textbf{no}$ monitors for $[\alpha]\textbf{ff} \wedge [\beta]\textbf{ff}$ by rejecting *all* the systems that violate the property. This is the case because a system violates $[\alpha]\textbf{ff} \wedge [\beta]\textbf{ff}$ if and only if it exhibits either trace α *or* trace β. Such systems are precisely those that are rejected by the monitor $\alpha.\textbf{no} + \beta.\textbf{no}$. ∎

Definition 3 describes the relationship between monitors and logical formulae from the monitor's perspective. Dually, *monitorability* is an attribute of a logical formula, describing its ability to be adequately analysed at runtime by a monitor. The concept of monitorability can also be lifted to sets of formulae (*i.e.,* a sublogic). In this sense, the definition of monitorability is dependent on the monitoring set-up assumed (*i.e.,* the semantics of Fig. 5) and the conditions that constitute an adequate runtime analysis. In what follows, we discuss the monitorability of our logic μHML assuming Definition 3 as our base notion for adequate monitoring.

Definition 4 (Monitorability). *A formula $\varphi \in \mu$HML is monitorable iff there exists a monitor m such that* $\textsf{mon}(m, \varphi)$. *A set of formulae $\mathcal{L} \subseteq \mu$HML is monitorable iff every formula in the set, $\varphi \in \mathcal{L}$, is monitorable.* ∎

Showing that a set of formulae is monitorable is, in general, non-trivial since proving Definition 4 entails two universal quantifications: one for all the formulae in the formula set, and another one for all the systems of the LTS over which the semantics of the formulae is defined. In both cases, the respective sets may be infinite. We immediately note that not all logical formulae in μHML are monitorable. The following example substantiates this claim.

Example 9. Through the witness monitor $\alpha.\textbf{no} + \beta.\textbf{no}$ discussed in Example 8, we can show that formula $[\alpha]\textbf{ff} \wedge [\beta]\textbf{ff}$ is monitorable with a violation-complete monitor. By contrast, the variant formula $[\alpha]\textbf{ff} \vee [\beta]\textbf{ff}$ (swapping the conjunction with a disjunction operator) is *not*. This can be shown by arguing towards a contradiction. Assume that there exists some monitor m such that $\textsf{mon}(m, [\alpha]\textbf{ff} \vee [\beta]\textbf{ff})$. From Definition 3 we know that $\textsf{smon}(m, [\alpha]\textbf{ff} \vee [\beta]\textbf{ff})$ and $\textsf{cmon}(m, [\alpha]\textbf{ff} \vee [\beta]\textbf{ff})$ hold, and by Definition 2, there are two subcases to consider for $\textsf{cmon}(m, [\alpha]\textbf{ff} \vee [\beta]\textbf{ff})$:

- If m is satisfaction-complete, $\textsf{scmon}(m, [\alpha]\textbf{ff} \vee [\beta]\textbf{ff})$, then $\textsf{acc}(\beta.\textbf{0}, m)$ for the specific system $\beta.\textbf{0}$ since $\beta.\textbf{0} \in [\![\, [\alpha]\textbf{ff} \,]\!]$. By the semantics of the logic in Fig. 3 we have $\beta.\textbf{0} \in [\![\, [\alpha]\textbf{ff} \vee [\beta]\textbf{ff} \,]\!]$. From the acceptance $\textsf{acc}(\beta.\textbf{0}, m)$, we know that m must either be able to reach a satisfaction, either autonomously, $m \Longrightarrow \textbf{yes}$, or after observing action β, $m \overset{\beta}{\Longrightarrow} \textbf{yes}$. For both cases we can argue that m also accepts the system $\alpha.\textbf{0} + \beta.\textbf{0}$, since there exists a trace that leads the monitored system $m \lhd \alpha.\textbf{0} + \beta.\textbf{0}$ to an acceptance verdict. This is unsound (Definition 1) since $\alpha.\textbf{0} + \beta.\textbf{0} \notin [\![\, [\alpha]\textbf{ff} \vee [\beta]\textbf{ff} \,]\!]$, contradicting $\textsf{smon}(m, [\alpha]\textbf{ff} \vee [\beta]\textbf{ff})$.
- If m is violation-complete, $\textsf{vcmon}(m, [\alpha]\textbf{ff} \vee [\beta]\textbf{ff})$, then, for the specific system $\alpha.\textbf{0} + \beta.\textbf{0}$, we must have $\textsf{rej}(\alpha.\textbf{0} + \beta.\textbf{0}, m)$ since, by the logic semantics, we know $\alpha.\textbf{0} + \beta.\textbf{0} \notin [\![\, [\alpha]\textbf{ff} \vee [\beta]\textbf{ff} \,]\!]$. Now, from the structure of $\alpha.\textbf{0} + \beta.\textbf{0}$, we can deduce that m can reach verdict **no** along one of the traces ϵ, α or β:

- If it is the empty trace ϵ, then m must also reject the system $\mathbf{0}$. However $\mathbf{0} \in [\![\,[\alpha]\mathbf{ff} \vee [\beta]\mathbf{ff}\,]\!]$ since $\mathbf{0}$ cannot produce any action; this makes the monitor unsound, contradicting $\mathsf{smon}(m, [\alpha]\mathbf{ff} \vee [\beta]\mathbf{ff})$.
- If the trace is α, m must also reject the system $\alpha.\mathbf{0}$ along the same trace α. This also makes the monitor unsound: from $\alpha.\mathbf{0} \in [\![\,[\beta]\mathbf{ff}\,]\!]$ and the semantics of Fig. 3 we deduce $\alpha.\mathbf{0} \in [\![\,[\alpha]\mathbf{ff} \vee [\beta]\mathbf{ff}\,]\!]$. The case for β is analogous. ∎

Definition 5 (Monitorable Logic). *Let* mHML = cHML $\cup$ sHML, *where*

$$\pi, \varpi \in \text{cHML} ::= \mathbf{tt} \quad | \mathbf{ff} \quad | \pi \vee \varpi \quad | \langle \alpha \rangle \pi \quad | \min X.\pi \quad | X$$
$$\theta, \vartheta \in \text{sHML} ::= \mathbf{tt} \quad | \mathbf{ff} \quad | \theta \wedge \vartheta \quad | [\alpha]\theta \quad | \max X.\theta \quad | X \quad ∎$$

In [25,26], the syntactic subset mHML of Definition 5 is shown to be monitorable. At an intuitive level, mHML consists of the co-safe and safe syntactic subsets of μHML, resp. labelled as cHML and sHML. The logical subset cHML describes properties whose satisfying systems can provide a witness trace that enables the monitor to conclusively determine that they are included in the property. Dually, sHML captures properties whose systems are *unable to provide* a single witness trace that permits the monitor to conclude that they violate the property. Note that, for both cHML and sHML, any extension of a witness trace used to reach a verdict is a witness trace itself.

Example 10. Recall formulae φ_1, φ_2, φ_5 and φ_6 from Example 2. We can establish that these are indeed monitorable in the sense of Definition 4 by performing a simple syntactic check against the grammar in Definition 5. This avoids complicated semantic reasoning that is usually harder to automate, such as that shown in Examples 8 and 9. ∎

The work in [25,26] goes even further, and shows that the syntactic subset identified in Definition 5 is maximally expressive w.r.t. the monitorability of Definition 4. This means that all the properties that are monitorable can be expressed in terms of the syntactic fragment described in Definition 5. We are unaware of any other maximality results for monitorability in the field of RV.

Example 11. The formula $\langle \alpha \rangle \mathbf{tt} \wedge \langle \alpha \rangle \mathbf{tt}$ is not part of the monitorable syntactic fragment of Definition 5, as the cHML syntax prohibits possibility modalities (*i.e.*, $\langle \alpha \rangle$) from being combined using conjunctions. However, it turns out that the property denoted by the formula $\langle \alpha \rangle \mathbf{tt} \wedge \langle \alpha \rangle \mathbf{tt}$ is indeed monitorable because it can be monitored for by the monitor $\alpha.\mathbf{yes}$ (see Definition 3). In fact, $\langle \alpha \rangle \mathbf{tt} \wedge \langle \alpha \rangle \mathbf{tt}$ is semantically equivalent to the formula $\langle \alpha \rangle \mathbf{tt}$ which is, in turn, included in the syntactic fragment of Definition 5. More generally, the apparently restrictive mHML fragment of Definition 5 still allows us to describe *all* the monitorable properties expressible in μHML. ∎

5   The Rocky Error Picture Show

A tenet of the basic RV set-up depicted in Fig. 1 is that the monitor used in the configuration is itself correct. Yet, it is perilous to assume that monitors are immune to errors, for erroneous monitors pose a number of risks. To begin with, they could invalidate the runtime analysis performed, resulting in wasted computational overhead (irrespective of how low this might be). Even worse, erroneous monitors may jeopardise the execution of the SUS itself, and a system that originally satisfies a correctness specification ends up violating the same specification after it is instrumented with a monitor. Even though these risks could prove to be as detrimental as that of having high monitoring overheads, few monitors come equipped with correctness assurances. In many cases, is it even unclear what these assurances should be, giving rise to discrepancies between the expected monitor behaviour and the actual monitor implementation.

A formal development such as the monitorability formulation in Sect. 4 may help towards mitigating this. For instance, a synthesis function for the sublogic in Definition 5 was given as a by-product of the monitorability proofs in [25,26]; this synthesis function was shown to generate monitors that satisfy the correspondence requirements of Definition 3. However, these assurances (which mainly focus on the expressiveness of monitors) may not suffice for certain applications. To illustrate, the monitor $\alpha.\textbf{yes} + \alpha.\textbf{end}$ adequately monitors for the formula $\langle\alpha\rangle\textbf{tt}$ according to Definition 3. Yet, it is not hard to see that this does not always yield an acceptance verdict when the SUS produces the witness trace α. In this respect, the monitor $\alpha.\textbf{yes}$ mentioned earlier in Example 8 may be seen as a better, or even, a more correct implementation than $\alpha.\textbf{yes} + \alpha.\textbf{end}$ that monitors for $\langle\alpha\rangle\textbf{tt}$.

The work in [23] studies a possible basis for comparing monitors, that is independent of the specification language used. It develops a number of preorders of the form $m_1 \sqsubseteq m_2$. Intuitively, these denote the fact that, when instrumented with any *arbitrary* system p, if the monitored system $m_1 \triangleleft p$ exhibits certain characteristics, then $m_2 \triangleleft p$ exhibits them as well. For different monitoring characteristics, one obtains different preorders. Such preorders may be used in a variety of ways. They may be employed as notions of refinement, where m_1 represents a monitor specification whose behaviour is preserved by the concrete implementation m_2. Preorders may also be used to determine when one monitor implementation can be safely substituted with another, without affecting the existing characteristics of a monitoring set-up. Importantly, however, they provide a foundation for understanding monitor errors whenever the relation $m_1 \sqsubseteq m_2$ does not hold.

We review the salient aspects of this work in the context of our foundational theory for monitors. To simplify the material that follows, we restrict ourselves to monitors that only reach rejections. This allows us to side-step issues related to soundness (discussed earlier in Sect. 4) and focus on orthogonal behavioural aspects. Note that our preference for rejections over acceptances is arbitrary. We begin by capturing the (complete) execution of a monitored system, which may be described in our setting via the notion of a *computation*, defined below. In

Definition 6 the trailing τ-transitions permit the monitor to stabilise and reach a verdict after a number of internal computational steps.

Definition 6. *The transition sequence with trace t, $m \lhd p \stackrel{t}{\Longrightarrow} m_0 \lhd p_0 \stackrel{\tau}{\longrightarrow} m_1 \lhd p_1 \stackrel{\tau}{\longrightarrow} m_2 \lhd p_2 \stackrel{\tau}{\longrightarrow} \ldots$, is called a t-computation if it is maximal (i.e., either it is infinite or it is finite and cannot be extended further using τ-transitions). A t-computation is called* rejected *(or a rejected computation along t) iff there exists some $n \in \mathbb{N}$ in the transition sequence where $m_n = $* **no**. ∎

Following Definition 3, a criterion for comparing monitors considers the *possible verdicts* that may be reached after observing a *specific execution trace* produced by the SUS. In this sense, a monitor is *as good as* another monitor if it can match all of the rejected computations of the other monitor.

Definition 7. *A monitor m potentially-rejects system p along trace t, denoted as $\mathsf{pr}(m, p, t)$, iff there exists a rejecting t-computation from $m \lhd p$. Monitor m_2 is as good as m_1 w.r.t. potential rejections, denoted as $m_1 \sqsubseteq_{pr} m_2$, iff*

$$for \ all \ systems \ p, \ and \ all \ traces \ t, \ \mathsf{pr}(m_1, p, t) \ implies \ \mathsf{pr}(m_2, p, t).$$

The preorder induces the expected kernel equivalence $m_1 \cong_{pr} m_2 \stackrel{def}{=} (m_1 \sqsubseteq_{pr} m_2$ and $m_2 \sqsubseteq_{pr} m_1)$. We write $m_1 \sqsubset_{pr} m_2$ in lieu of $(m_1 \sqsubseteq_{pr} m_2$ and $m_2 \not\sqsubseteq_{pr} m_1)$. ∎

Example 12. Consider the following monitor descriptions:

$$m_1 = \alpha.\beta.\mathsf{no} \qquad m_2 = \alpha.\mathsf{no} \qquad m_3 = \alpha.\mathsf{no} + \beta.\mathsf{no} \qquad m_4 = \alpha.\mathsf{no} + \beta.\mathsf{no} + \beta.\mathsf{end}$$

We have $m_1 \sqsubset_{pr} m_2$ since, for any p, any rejected t-computation of m_1 (which must have prefix $\alpha\beta$) is also rejected by m_2, but the inverse is not: for some $p \stackrel{\alpha}{\longrightarrow} p'$ we have $\mathsf{pr}(m_2, p, \alpha)$ but *not* $\mathsf{pr}(m_1, p, \alpha)$. For similar reasons, we have

$$m_2 \sqsubset_{pr} m_3 \cong_{pr} m_4$$

Observe that m_3 and m_4 are considered to be potential-rejection equivalent. ∎

Potential rejections may be too weak for certain mission critical applications. For instance, although m_4 can reject traces that start with β, it does not mean that it will, because it may (non-deterministically) follow the branch $\beta.\mathsf{end}$ that does not lead to a rejection. An alternative criterion would thus be to compare monitors w.r.t. their *deterministic* rejections.

Definition 8. *A monitor m deterministically-rejects system p along trace t, denoted as $\mathsf{dr}(m, p, t)$, iff all t-computations from $m \lhd p$ are rejecting. Monitor m_2 is as good as m_1 w.r.t. deterministic rejections, denoted as $m_1 \sqsubseteq_{dr} m_2$, iff*

$$for \ all \ systems \ p, \ and \ all \ traces \ t, \ \mathsf{dr}(m_1, p, t) \ implies \ \mathsf{dr}(m_2, p, t).$$

The respective kernel equivalence, $m_1 \cong_{dr} m_2$, and irreflexive preorder, $m_1 \sqsubset_{dr} m_2$, induced by deterministic rejections are as expected. ∎

Example 13. We have the following following relationships w.r.t. deterministic rejections for the monitors m_1 to m_4 from Example 12:

$$m_1 \sqsubseteq_{\mathsf{dr}} m_2 \cong_{\mathsf{dr}} m_4 \sqsubseteq_{\mathsf{dr}} m_3$$

We note that, whereas in Example 12, m_4 was considered to be strictly better than m_2 w.r.t. potential rejections, it is considered equivalent w.r.t. deterministic rejections, since the rejections of m_4 for traces commencing with a β action are not deterministic and thus ignored.   ∎

It is worth mentioning that defining the preorders of Definitions 7 and 8 in terms of instrumented system executions (instead of just considering the respective monitor traces in isolation) reveals subtleties that would otherwise be missed. These would nevertheless manifest themselves at runtime.

Example 14. Consider the construct $\tau.m$, describing a monitor that performs an internal computation τ before behaving like m. Using the syntax of Figure 5, this may be encoded as **rec** $x.m$, where x is not a free variable in the continuation m (see rule REC). We have the following relations between a monitor that immediately rejects (**no**), and another that performs some internal computation before yielding reject ($\tau.$**no**):

$$\mathbf{no} \cong_{\mathsf{pr}} \tau.\mathbf{no} \qquad\qquad \text{but} \qquad\qquad \tau.\mathbf{no} \sqsubseteq_{\mathsf{dr}} \mathbf{no}$$

It is not hard to see why the monitor **no** is a top element for both preorders $\sqsubseteq_{\mathsf{pr}}$ and $\sqsubseteq_{\mathsf{dr}}$, since it immediately rejects all traces for any given system p (*i.e.,* for any m, we have $m \sqsubseteq_{\mathsf{pr}} \mathbf{no}$ and $m \sqsubseteq_{\mathsf{dr}} \mathbf{no}$). The monitor $\tau.\mathbf{no}$ exhibits the exact behaviour w.r.t. potential rejections and is thus a top element for $\sqsubseteq_{\mathsf{pr}}$ as well. Interestingly, $\tau.\mathbf{no}$ is *not* a top element for $\sqsubseteq_{\mathsf{dr}}$ however. Consider, as a counter example, the system p that goes into an infinite (internal) loop $p \xrightarrow{\tau} p \xrightarrow{\tau} \ldots$. When instrumented with the monitor $\tau.\mathbf{no}$, the monitored system can exhibit the ϵ-computation $\tau.\mathbf{no} \lhd p \xrightarrow{\tau} \tau.\mathbf{no} \lhd p \xrightarrow{\tau} \tau.\mathbf{no} \lhd p \xrightarrow{\tau} \ldots$ effectively starving the monitor $\tau.\mathbf{no}$, and preventing it from ever reaching its rejection verdict, **no**. Thus, we do not have $\mathsf{dr}(\tau.\mathbf{no}, p, \epsilon)$ and, as a result, the inequality $\mathbf{no} \sqsubseteq_{\mathsf{dr}} \tau.\mathbf{no}$ does *not* hold.   ∎

Formulating Definitions 7 and 8 in terms of instrumented system executions also facilitates the classification of anomalous monitor behaviour.

Example 15. Consider the unresponsive monitor m_ω, that goes into an infinite loop without exhibiting any other behaviour (*i.e.,* $m_\omega \xrightarrow{\tau} m_\omega \xrightarrow{\tau} \ldots$). Whereas for the potentially-rejecting preorder, this monitor is clearly a bottom element (*i.e.,* for any m we have $m_\omega \sqsubseteq_{\mathsf{pr}} m$) it is, perhaps surprisingly, *not* a bottom element for the deterministic-rejection preorder. In fact, according to Definition 8, we obtain seemingly peculiar orderings such as the one below (using monitor m_2 defined earlier in Example 12):

$$m_2 \sqsubseteq_{\mathsf{dr}} m_\omega \sqsubseteq_{\mathsf{dr}} \mathbf{no}$$

Note that, according to the instrumentation semantics of Fig. 5, m_ω prevents any system that is composed with it from generating observable events: for arbitrary p, whenever $p \xrightarrow{\alpha} p'$ given some α, rule MON cannot be applied (since $m_\omega \not\xrightarrow{\alpha}$) and neither can rule TER (since $m_\omega \xrightarrow{\tau}$). This means that $\mathsf{dr}(m_\omega, p, t)$ holds for any system p and trace t that is not empty (*i.e.*, $t \neq \epsilon$). This condition holds trivially because no such trace exists, thus explaining why $m_2 \sqsubseteq_{\mathsf{dr}} m_\omega$. The only case where $\mathsf{dr}(m_\omega, p, t)$ does *not* hold is precisely when $t = \epsilon$, leaving us with $m_\omega \sqsubseteq_{\mathsf{dr}} \mathbf{no}$. ∎

Using the two preorders $\sqsubseteq_{\mathsf{pr}}$ and $\sqsubseteq_{\mathsf{dr}}$, we can define a third (more refined) preorder that is an intersection of the two presented thus far, taking into consideration both of their respective criteria when comparing monitors.

Definition 9. *A monitor m_2 is as good as a monitor m_1 w.r.t. rejections, denoted as $m_1 \sqsubseteq_{\mathit{rej}} m_2$, iff $m_1 \sqsubseteq_{\mathsf{pr}} m_2$ and $m_1 \sqsubseteq_{\mathsf{dr}} m_2$.* ∎

Whenever we have $m_1 \sqsubseteq_{\mathsf{rej}} m_2$, we can substitute m_1 with m_2 safe in the knowledge that, all potential and deterministic rejections made by m_1 are preserved by m_2 irrespective of the system these are composed with. Alternatively, should we consider *missed* rejections as our notion of error, then whenever $m_1 \not\sqsubseteq_{\mathsf{rej}} m_2$ we know that when instrumented with a common system, m_2 may *not* exhibit all the rejections that m_1 produces.

Example 16. We obtain the following strict ordering w.r.t. Definition 9:

$$m_1 \sqsubset_{\mathit{rej}} m_2 \sqsubset_{\mathit{rej}} m_4 \sqsubset_{\mathit{rej}} m_3$$
∎

In [23], additional monitor preorders are considered based on other correctness criteria. For instance, monitors are compared w.r.t. to their capability of interfering with the execution of a system, as outlined briefly in Example 15. Apart from devising correctness preorders, the aforementioned work also develops sound compositional techniques that can check for preorder inequalities *without* relying on universal quantifications on systems. Although this is essential for any automated checking of said preorder inequalities, such compositional techniques are outside the scope of this presentation. Interested readers should nevertheless consult [23] for more details.

6   Monitorability and Correctness Now Redux

The concepts outlined in Sects. 4 and 5 served as a basis for various other work related to RV, monitors and monitorability. We here discuss a subset of this work.

Tools. In [6], the monitorability results presented in Sect. 4 (and their respective proofs reported in [26]) were used for the construction of a monitoring tool called detectEr. In this tool, monitorable correctness properties for reactive Erlang programs can be specified using the monitorable syntactic subset of

Definition 5. From these logical specifications, detectEr automatically synthesises monitors that are then instrumented to execute alongside an Erlang SUS, reporting satisfaction or violation verdicts depending on the behaviour exhibited. The need for a more comprehensive instrumentation mechanism for the target language (Erlang), resulted in the development of an aspect-oriented utility called eAOP [15]. This tool is incorporated into the detectEr toolchain, and its development and features (*e.g.* its pointcut definitions) are largely guided by the RV requirements for detectEr. Nevertheless, eAOP can also be used as a standalone utility for other purposes such as Erlang code refactoring.

Monitorability. The work of [7] considers a slightly different monitoring setup to that presented in Fig. 1. Interestingly, it shows how the maximality results for monitorability of Sect. 4 can be extended when working with the new setup. This work views the SUS as a collection of components (instead of treating it as one monolithic block) whereby certian trace events can be attributed to specific components, as shown in Fig. 7. The monitor is equipped with this static information about the SUS to permit it to extend its analytical capabilities. In the case of [7], certain components are known to be execution-independent to one another, meaning that from a particular trace interleaving observed in the current execution trace, the monitor could infer additional (plausible) traces that can also be used for verification purposes.

For instance, in Example 9 we earlier argued why the property $[\alpha]\mathbf{ff} \vee [\beta]\mathbf{ff}$ in the basic setup of Fig. 1 is *not* monitorable. The formula states that a SUS satisfies the property if it either cannot perform α or it cannot perform β. A trace can however only provide us with enough evidence to deduce that only one of the execution subbranches is violated, not both. Yet, if we know that actions α and β can be produced exclusively by independently-executing components C_1 and C_2 resp., from a witness trace of the form $\alpha\beta\ldots$, a monitor in the setup of Fig. 7 could infer that the trace $\beta\alpha\ldots$ can also be generated by the system (for a different execution interleaving of components C_1 and C_2). This allows the

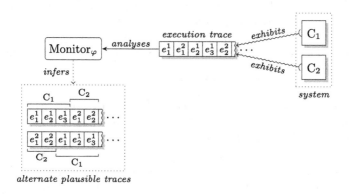

Fig. 7. Monitoring components C_1 and C_2 and inferring their other plausible traces.

monitor to analyse *two* execution traces instead of one: the witness and inferred traces can then be used together to obtain enough evidence to be able to deduce a violation of the property $[\alpha]\mathbf{ff} \vee [\beta]\mathbf{ff}$, making it monitorable.

In other work [22], the authors show how the monitorable subset of Definition 5 can be used to devise a strategy that apportions the verification process between the pre-deployment (via standard techniques such as Model Checking) and post-deployment (using RV) phases of software development. To illustrate, consider the property $\langle\alpha\rangle([\beta]\mathbf{ff}\vee\langle\alpha\rangle\mathbf{tt})$ which clearly does not belong to the monitorable subset of Definition 5. Reformulating it into its semantic equivalent, $\langle\alpha\rangle[\beta]\mathbf{ff} \vee \langle\alpha\rangle\langle\alpha\rangle\mathbf{tt}$, allows us to isolate the runtime-monitorable subformula $\langle\alpha\rangle\langle\alpha\rangle\mathbf{tt}$. One could then check for subformula $\langle\alpha\rangle[\beta]\mathbf{ff}$ prior to deployment, and in cases where this is not satisfied, monitor for the $\langle\alpha\rangle\langle\alpha\rangle\mathbf{tt}$ at runtime.

Monitor Correctness. In [1], the authors consider the use of standard determinisation techniques borrowed from automata theory to determinise monitors and their respective verdicts. The approach would enable a tool to take (non-deterministic) monitor descriptions such as $\alpha.\beta.\mathbf{yes} + \alpha.\gamma.\mathbf{yes}$ (*e.g.* produced by the detectEr tool of [6] when synthesising monitors from the monitorable formula $\langle\alpha\rangle\langle\beta\rangle\mathbf{tt} \vee \langle\alpha\rangle\langle\gamma\rangle\mathbf{tt}$) and obtain the monitor $\alpha.(\beta.\mathbf{yes} + \gamma.\mathbf{yes})$ instead. The key contribution of this work is the establishment of complexity upper bounds (more or less known) and, more interestingly, complexity lower bounds whereby converting a non-deterministic monitor of n states to a deterministic one requires a space complexity of *at least* $2^{2^{\Omega\sqrt{n \log n}}}$.

A fully deterministic monitor behaviour (where every event analysed leads exclusively to one possible monitor state) is too rigid in practice to describe the behaviour of certain monitor implementations. A case in point is monitoring that is conducted via a number of concurrent submonitors [27] that may be subject to different thread interleaving every time they are executed. The monitor framework discussed in Sect. 5 served as a basis for the formulation of a definition for consistently-detecting monitors [24] that allows degrees of non-deterministic behaviour as long as these are *not externally observable* via inconsistent detections. The work in [24] borrows from the compositionality techniques studied in [23] to define an alternative coinductive definition for consistent monitor behaviour based on the notion of *controllability* [31]. It also develops symbolic techniques that facilitate the construction of analysis tools for determining monitor controllability.

Language Design. The work presented in [14] uses the safety fragment sHML from Definition 5 as a basis for defining a scripting language for describing adaptation procedures in a monitor-oriented programming paradigm. It specifically targets systems that are constructed in a layered fashion, with the outer layers adding degrees of functionality in response to the behaviour observed from the inner layers. In this setup, the monitors produced are not passive in the sense that they merely analyse behaviour, but *actively* engage with the observed system via adaptations so as to change its behaviour and mitigate system faults.

Despite of their benefits, runtime adaptations induced by monitors may introduce certain errors themselves. For this reason, in [13] the authors also define language-based methods in the form of a type system to assist monitor construction and to statically detect erroneous adaptations declared in the monitor scripts at design time.

7 Conclusion

In this paper we surveyed a body of work that strives to establish a formal foundation for the RV technique. It focusses on addressing two main questions, namely monitorability for system specifications and monitor correctness. Although the account concentrated mainly on unifying the work presented in [23,25,26], it also showed how this preliminary work has served as a basis for subsequent developments on the subject, such as [1,7,13,14,24]. We are currently working on extending these results even further, by investigating monitorability for diverse monitoring set-ups along the lines of [7], and by considering monitors with augmented capabilities such as those that perform property enforcement [36].

References

1. Aceto, L., Achilleos, A., Francalanza, A., Ingólfsdóttir, A., Kjartansson, S.Ö.: On the complexity of determinizing monitors. In: Carayol, A., Nicaud, C. (eds.) CIAA 2017. LNCS, vol. 10329, pp. 1–13. Springer, Cham (2017). doi:10.1007/978-3-319-60134-2_1
2. Aceto, L., Ingólfsdóttir, A., Larsen, K.G., Srba, J.: Reactive Systems: Modelling, Specification and Verification. Cambridge University Press, Cambridge (2007)
3. Ahrendt, W., Chimento, J.M., Pace, G.J., Schneider, G.: A specification language for static and runtime verification of data and control properties. In: Bjørner, N., de Boer, F. (eds.) FM 2015. LNCS, vol. 9109, pp. 108–125. Springer, Cham (2015). doi:10.1007/978-3-319-19249-9_8
4. Aktug, I., Naliuka, K.: ConSpec - a formal language for policy specification. Sci. Comput. Program. 74(1–2), 2–12 (2008)
5. Artho, C., Barringer, H., Goldberg, A., Havelund, K., Khurshid, S., Lowry, M.R., Pasareanu, C.S., Rosu, G., Sen, K., Visser, W., Washington, R.: Combining test case generation and runtime verification. Theor. Comput. Sci. 336(2–3), 209–234 (2005)
6. Attard, D.P., Francalanza, A.: A monitoring tool for a branching-time logic. In: Falcone, Y., Sánchez, C. (eds.) RV 2016. LNCS, vol. 10012, pp. 473–481. Springer, Cham (2016). doi:10.1007/978-3-319-46982-9_31
7. Attard, D.P., Francalanza, A.: Trace partitioning and local monitoring for asynchronous components. In: SEFM, LNCS (2017, to appear)
8. Azzopardi, S., Colombo, C., Pace, G.J., Vella, B.: Compliance checking in the open payments ecosystem. In: De Nicola, R., Kühn, E. (eds.) SEFM 2016. LNCS, vol. 9763, pp. 337–343. Springer, Cham (2016). doi:10.1007/978-3-319-41591-8_23
9. Baier, C., Katoen, J.P.: Principles of Model Checking. MIT Press, New York (2008)

10. Barringer, H., Goldberg, A., Havelund, K., Sen, K.: Rule-based runtime verification. In: Steffen, B., Levi, G. (eds.) VMCAI 2004. LNCS, vol. 2937, pp. 44–57. Springer, Heidelberg (2004). doi:10.1007/978-3-540-24622-0_5
11. Basin, D., Klaedtke, F., Marinovic, S., Zălinescu, E.: Monitoring compliance policies over incomplete and disagreeing logs. In: Qadeer, S., Tasiran, S. (eds.) RV 2012. LNCS, vol. 7687, pp. 151–167. Springer, Heidelberg (2013). doi:10.1007/978-3-642-35632-2_17
12. Brat, G.P., Drusinsky, D., Giannakopoulou, D., Goldberg, A., Havelund, K., Lowry, M.R., Pasareanu, C.S., Venet, A., Visser, W., Washington, R.: Experimental evaluation of verification and validation tools on martian rover software. Formal Methods Syst. Des. **25**(2–3), 167–198 (2004)
13. Cassar, I., Francalanza, A.: Runtime adaptation for actor systems. In: Bartocci, E., Majumdar, R. (eds.) RV 2015. LNCS, vol. 9333, pp. 38–54. Springer, Cham (2015). doi:10.1007/978-3-319-23820-3_3
14. Cassar, I., Francalanza, A.: On implementing a monitor-oriented programming framework for actor systems. In: Ábrahám, E., Huisman, M. (eds.) IFM 2016. LNCS, vol. 9681, pp. 176–192. Springer, Cham (2016). doi:10.1007/978-3-319-33693-0_12
15. Cassar, I., Francalanza, A., Aceto, L., Ingólfsdóttir, A.: eAOP - an aspect oriented programming framework for erlang. In: Erlang Workshop (2017, to appear)
16. Chen, F., Rosu, G.: MOP: an efficient and generic runtime verification framework. In: OOPSLA, pp. 569–588 (2007)
17. Clarke, E.M., Grumberg, O., Peled, D.A.: Model Checking. MIT Press, Cambridge (1999)
18. Colombo, C., Francalanza, A., Mizzi, R., Pace, G.J.: polyLARVA: runtime verification with configurable resource-aware monitoring boundaries. In: Eleftherakis, G., Hinchey, M., Holcombe, M. (eds.) SEFM 2012. LNCS, vol. 7504, pp. 218–232. Springer, Heidelberg (2012). doi:10.1007/978-3-642-33826-7_15
19. D'Angelo, B., Sankaranarayanan, S., Sánchez, C., Robinson, W., Finkbeiner, B., Sipma, H.B., Mehrotra, S., Manna, Z.: LOLA: runtime monitoring of synchronous systems. In: TIME, pp. 166–174 (2005)
20. Debois, S., Hildebrandt, T., Slaats, T.: Safety, liveness and run-time refinement for modular process-aware information systems with dynamic sub processes. In: Bjørner, N., de Boer, F. (eds.) FM 2015. LNCS, vol. 9109, pp. 143–160. Springer, Cham (2015). doi:10.1007/978-3-319-19249-9_10
21. Decker, N., Leucker, M., Thoma, D.: jUnit[RV]–adding runtime verification to jUnit. In: Brat, G., Rungta, N., Venet, A. (eds.) NFM 2013. LNCS, vol. 7871, pp. 459–464. Springer, Heidelberg (2013). doi:10.1007/978-3-642-38088-4_34
22. Monica, D.D., Francalanza, A.: Towards a hybrid approach to software verification. In: NWPT, number SCS16001 in RUTR, pp. 51–54 (2015)
23. Francalanza, A.: A theory of monitors. In: Jacobs, B., Löding, C. (eds.) FoSSaCS 2016. LNCS, vol. 9634, pp. 145–161. Springer, Heidelberg (2016). doi:10.1007/978-3-662-49630-5_9
24. Francalanza, A.: Consistently-detecting monitors. In: CONCUR. Dagstuhl Publishing (LIPICS) (2017)
25. Francalanza, A., Aceto, L., Ingolfsdottir, A.: On verifying hennessy-milner logic with recursion at runtime. In: Bartocci, E., Majumdar, R. (eds.) RV 2015. LNCS, vol. 9333, pp. 71–86. Springer, Cham (2015). doi:10.1007/978-3-319-23820-3_5
26. Francalanza, A., Aceto, L., Ingolfsdottir, A.: Monitorability for the hennessy-milner logic with recursion. Formal Methods Syst. Des., 1–30 (2017)

27. Francalanza, A., Seychell, A.: Synthesising correct concurrent runtime monitors. Formal Methods Syst. Des. **46**(3), 226–261 (2015)
28. Kane, A., Chowdhury, O., Datta, A., Koopman, P.: A case study on runtime monitoring of an autonomous research vehicle (ARV) system. In: Bartocci, E., Majumdar, R. (eds.) RV 2015. LNCS, vol. 9333, pp. 102–117. Springer, Cham (2015). doi:10.1007/978-3-319-23820-3_7
29. Kassem, A., Falcone, Y., Lafourcade, P.: Monitoring electronic exams. In: Bartocci, E., Majumdar, R. (eds.) RV 2015. LNCS, vol. 9333, pp. 118–135. Springer, Cham (2015). doi:10.1007/978-3-319-23820-3_8
30. Kim, M., Viswanathan, M., Kannan, S., Lee, I., Sokolsky, O.: Java-MaC: a runtime assurance approach for Java programs. Formal Methods Syst. Des. **24**(2), 129–155 (2004)
31. Klamka, J.: system characteristics: stability, controllability, observability. In: Control System, Robotics and Automation, EOLLS, vol. 7 (2009)
32. Kozen, D.: Results on the propositional μ-calculus. Theor. Comput. Sci. **27**, 333–354 (1983)
33. Larsen, K.G.: Proof systems for satisfiability in hennessy-milner logic with recursion. Theor. Comput. Sci. **72**(2&3), 265–288 (1990)
34. Lerda, F., Visser, W.: Addressing dynamic issues of program model checking. In: Dwyer, M. (ed.) SPIN 2001. LNCS, vol. 2057, pp. 80–102. Springer, Heidelberg (2001). doi:10.1007/3-540-45139-0_6
35. Leucker, M., Schallhart, C.: A brief account of runtime verification. J. Log. Algebr. Program. **78**(5), 293–303 (2009)
36. Ligatti, J., Bauer, L., Walker, D.: Edit automata: enforcement mechanisms for run-time security policies. Int. J. Inf. Secur. **4**(1–2), 2–16 (2005)
37. Meredith, P.O., Jin, D., Griffith, D., Chen, F., Rosu, G.: An overview of the MOP runtime verification framework. STTT **14**(3), 249–289 (2012)
38. Neykova, R., Yoshida, N.: Let it recover: multiparty protocol-induced recovery. In: CC, pp. 98–108 (2017)
39. Reger, G., Cruz, H.C., Rydeheard, D.: MarQ: monitoring at runtime with QEA. In: Baier, C., Tinelli, C. (eds.) TACAS 2015. LNCS, vol. 9035, pp. 596–610. Springer, Heidelberg (2015). doi:10.1007/978-3-662-46681-0_55
40. Varvaressos, S., Vaillancourt, D., Gaboury, S., Blondin Massé, A., Hallé, S.: Runtime monitoring of temporal logic properties in a platform game. In: Legay, A., Bensalem, S. (eds.) RV 2013. LNCS, vol. 8174, pp. 346–351. Springer, Heidelberg (2013). doi:10.1007/978-3-642-40787-1_23

Regular Papers

Stream Runtime Monitoring on UAS

Florian-Michael Adolf[2], Peter Faymonville[1]([✉]), Bernd Finkbeiner[1],
Sebastian Schirmer[2], and Christoph Torens[2]

[1] Reactive Systems Group, Saarland University,
Saarbrücken, Germany
faymonville@react.uni-saarland.de
[2] Institute of Flight Systems, DLR (German Aerospace Center),
Braunschweig, Germany

Abstract. Unmanned Aircraft Systems (UAS) with autonomous de-
cision-making capabilities are of increasing interest for a wide area of
applications such as logistics and disaster recovery. In order to ensure the
correct behavior of the system and to recognize hazardous situations or
system faults, we applied stream runtime monitoring techniques within
the DLR ARTIS (Autonomous Research Testbed for Intelligent System)
family of unmanned aircraft. We present our experience from specification elicitation, instrumentation, offline log-file analysis, and online
monitoring on the flight computer on a test rig. The debugging and
health management support through stream runtime monitoring techniques have proven highly beneficial for system design and development.
At the same time, the project has identified usability improvements to
the specification language, and has influenced the design of the language.

1 Introduction

Aerospace is an internationally harmonized, heavily regulated safety-critical
domain. Aircraft development is guided by an uncompromising demand for
safety, and the integration of unmanned aircraft systems (UAS) into populated
airspace is raising a lot of concerns. As the name suggests, there is no human
pilot on board an unmanned aircraft. The pilot is replaced by a number of highly
automated systems, which also ensure proper synchronization with a base station on the ground. The correctness and stability of these systems is critical for
the safety of the aircraft and its operating environment. As a result, substantial efforts in verification and validation activities are required to comply with
standards and the high demand for functional correctness and safety.

Runtime verification has the potential to play a major role in the
development, testing, and operational control of unmanned aircraft. During

---

Partially supported by the European Research Council (ERC) Grant OSARES (No.
683300) and by the German Research Foundation (DFG) as part of the Collaborative
Research Center "Methods and Tools for Understanding and Controlling Privacy"
(SFB 1223).

S. Lahiri and G. Reger (Eds.): RV 2017, LNCS 10548, pp. 33–49, 2017.
DOI: 10.1007/978-3-319-67531-2_3

development, debugging is the key activity. Traditionally, log-files are inspected manually to find unexpected system behaviors. However, the manual analysis quickly becomes infeasible if multiple interacting subsystems need to be considered or if complex computations have to be carried out to correlate the data. Runtime verification can automate this task and thus make debugging dramatically more efficient. During testing, runtime verification can be used to monitor functional correctness of the system behavior. Runtime verification can be integrated into software- and hardware-in-the-loop simulations as well as into full-scale flight tests. In contrast to simple unit testing, a property that is formalized into a runtime monitor can thus not only be tested in a test fixture, but reused in all test phases. During operation, runtime verification can be used to monitor the system health and the validity of environment assumptions. The reason that system failures happen during a flight is often not because of implementation errors, but because unforeseen events occur and the requirement assumptions are no longer valid. Integrating runtime monitoring into operational control makes it possible to enforce safety limitations, such as constraints on the altitude, speed, geographic location and other operational aspects that increase the risk emerging from the unmanned aircraft. If all else fails, the runtime monitor can also initiate contingency procedures and failsafes.

In this paper, we report on a case study, carried out over approximately one year in a collaboration between Saarland University and the German Aerospace Center (DLR). The goal has been to integrate runtime monitoring into the ARTIS (Autonomous Research Testbed for Intelligent Systems) platform. ARTIS consists of a versatile software framework for the development and testing of intelligent functions, as well as a fleet of unmanned aircraft, which include several classes and sizes of aircraft with different technical equipment and resulting autonomous capabilities [1, 20].

Integrating runtime monitoring into a complex flight operation framework like ARTIS is a profound challenge. An immediate observation is that the data to be monitored is complex, and typically requires nontrivial processing, which necessitates a highly expressive specification language. At the same time, there is no separation on the hardware level between the flight control operations and the monitoring engine. Performance guarantees for the monitoring code, in particular with respect to memory usage, are therefore critically important. Finally, we observed that there is a highly beneficial feedback loop between the results of the monitoring and the continued design of the aircraft. The specifications used for monitoring are increasingly used as a documentation of the expected environment conditions and the legal system behavior. Clear, modular specifications that can easily be reused and adapted are therefore a key requirement.

Our runtime verification approach is based on the Lola specification language and monitoring engine [2, 7]. Lola specifications translate input streams, which contain sensor information and other real-time data, into output streams, which contain the processed sensor information and statistical aggregates over time. While Lola is a very expressive specification language, it also comes with strong performance guarantees: the efficiently monitorable fragment, which essentially consists of the full language except that unbounded lookahead into the future is not allowed, can be monitored with constant memory. In principle, Lola is thus clearly in a good position for the task at hand. If Lola would be sufficiently expressive for the monitoring of unmanned aircraft, and whether Lola specifications would be sufficiently modular and understandable for the interaction with the developers, seemed far from obvious at the outset of our study.

The results reported in this paper are very positive. While Lola in its as-is state was in fact not sufficiently expressive, the integration of the missing features, essentially floating point arithmetic and trigonometric functions, turned out to be straightforward. Lola's organizational principle, where more complex output streams are computed in terms of simpler output streams, was adapted easily by developers, who appreciated the similarity to synchronous programming. Small and, in retrospect, almost obvious additions to the language, such as a switch statement for the description of state machines, made the specification of the properties of interest significantly more natural and elegant.

The shortage of published case studies is an often lamented problem for research in runtime verification. We hope that our formalization of common properties of interest in the monitoring of unmanned aircraft can serve as a reference for formalizations in other runtime verification frameworks. The major lesson learned in our work is that while the development of such specifications is extremely difficult and expensive, the benefits in terms of a more effective debugging and testing process, and a mathematically rigorous documentation of the expected system behavior are immense. Conversely, from the perspective of the developer of a runtime verification tool, the insights gained into the practical relevance of various language features are similarly invaluable.

2   Related Work

In the area of unmanned aerial systems, earlier work on applying runtime verification has been performed by Schumann, Rozier et al. at NASA [8,15,17]. The key differences to our approach are our use of a stream-based specification language with direct support for statistics, and that our framework uses a software-based instrumentation approach, which gives access to the internal state of system components. For non-assured control systems, a runtime supervision approach has been described in [9]. A specific approach with a separate, verified hardware system to enforce geo-fencing has been described in [4]. Specification languages for runtime monitoring with similar expressivity include for example eSQL as implemented in the BeepBeep system [10] and the Copilot language in [12], which has been applied to monitor airspeed sensor data agreement.

3   Stream Runtime Monitoring

Lola is a stream-based specification language for monitoring, first presented for monitoring synchronous circuits in [2], but more recently also used in the context of network monitoring [7]. Lola is a declarative specification mechanism based on stream equations and allows the specification of correctness properties as well as statistical properties of the system under observation.

A Lola specification consists of a set of stream equations, which define a set of *input* streams, i.e. the signals of the system to the monitor, and a set of *output* streams, whose values are defined by stream expressions and have access to past, present, and future values of the input streams and other output streams. All streams have a synchronous clock and evolve in a uniform way.

Since the language includes streams with numeric types and the stream expressions allow arithmetic expressions, it is easy to specify incrementally computable statistics. Algorithms for both offline and online monitoring of Lola specifications exist. In online monitoring, future values in stream expressions are evaluated by delaying the evaluation of their output streams.

Consider the following example specification.

```
input   bool valid
input   double height
output double m_height
        := if valid { max(m_height[-1,0.0],height) }
           else  { m_height[-1,0.0] }
```

Here, given the input streams *valid* and *height*, the maximum valid height *m_height* is computed by taking the maximum over the previous *m_height* and the current *height* in case the height is *valid*, otherwise the previous value of *m_height* is used. In Lola, the offset operator $s[x, y]$ handles the access to previous ($x < 0$), present ($x = 0$), or future ($x > 0$) stream values of the stream s. The default value y is used in case an offset x tries to access a stream position past the end or before the beginning of a stream.

In this section, we present syntactic Lola extensions, which were introduced to adapt the language to the domain-specific needs of monitoring unmanned aerial vehicles. For formal definitions of the syntax and semantics of the base language syntax and semantics, we refer to [2] due to space reasons and will restrict ourselves to the extensions.

Extensions to Lola. A Lola Specification is a system of equations of stream expressions over typed stream variables of the following form:

$$\textbf{input } T_1 \; t_1$$

$$\ldots$$

$$\textbf{input } T_m \; t_m$$
$$\textbf{output } T_{m+1} \; s_1 := e_1(t_1, \ldots, t_m, s_1, \ldots s_n)$$

$$\ldots$$

$$\textbf{output } T_{m+n} \; s_n := e_n(t_1, \ldots, t_m, s_1, \ldots s_n)$$

The *independent* stream variables $t_1, \ldots, t_m$ with types $T_1, \ldots, T_m$ refer to input streams, and the *dependent* stream variables $s_1, \ldots, s_n$ with types $T_{m+1}, \ldots, T_{m+n}$ refer to output streams. The *stream expressions* $e_1, \ldots, e_n$ have access to both input streams and output streams. To construct a stream expression e, Lola allows constants, functions, conditionals, and offset expressions to access the values of other streams. Additionally, Lola specifications allow the definition of *triggers*, which are conditional expressions over the stream variables. They generate notifications whenever they are evaluated to *true*.

For a given valuation of input streams $\tau = \langle \tau_1, \ldots, \tau_m \rangle$ of length $N + 1$, the evaluation over the trace is defined as a stream of $N + 1$ tuples $\sigma = \langle \sigma_1, \ldots, \sigma_n \rangle$ for each dependent stream variable s_i, such that for all $1 \leq i \leq n$ and $0 \leq j \leq N$, if the equation $\sigma_i(j) = val(e_i)(j)$ holds, then we call σ an *evaluation model* of the Lola specification for τ. The definition of $val(e_i)(j)$ is given in [2] as a set of partial evaluation rules, which tries to resolve the stream expressions as much as possible for each incoming event.

For the two extensions described here, we extend the definition of the stream expressions $e(t_1, \ldots, t_m, s_1, \ldots s_n)$ and the function val as follows:

- Let a be keyword of type T (e.g. position, int_min, int_max representing the maximal representable numbers), then $e = a$ is an atomic stream expression of type T. This adds direct access to system dependent maximal values for int_min, int_max, double_min, double_max, which is useful for default values. Additionally, we add direct access to the current stream position via $val(\text{position})(j) = j$.
- Let e' be a stream expression of type T, d a constant of type T, and i a positive int, then $e = e' \# [i, d]$ is a stream expression of type T. The value of this absolute offset is defined as,

$$val(e \# [p, d])(j) = \begin{cases} val(e)(p) & \text{if } 0 \leq p \leq N \\ val(d)(j) & \text{otherwise} \end{cases}$$

The *absolute offset operator* $\#$ refers to a position in the trace not relative to the current position, but instead absolute to the start of the trace.

Common abbreviations:

- `const T s := a` $\widehat{=}$ `output T s := a`
- `ite(`e_1`,`e_2`,`e_3`)` $\widehat{=}$ `if `e_1{e_a}`else{`e_b`}`
- `if `e_1{e_a}` elif `e_2{e_b}` else{`e_c`}` $\widehat{=}$ `if `e_1{e_a}` else{if `e_2{e_b}` else{`e_c`}}`
- `if `$e_a = c_1${e_1}` elif `$e_a = c_2${e_2}`...elif `$e_a = c_n${e_n}` else{`e_d`}` $\widehat{=}$
  `switch `e_a{ `case `c_1{e_1}` case `c_2{e_2}` ... case `c_n{e_n}` default{`e_d`}}`

We have also added an extended switch operator, where the switch conditions have to be monotonically ordered. The semantics for this extended switch condition allows us to short-circuit the evaluation of large case switches. There, the evaluation of *lower* cases is omitted which helps e.g. for properties on different flight phases with a large case split (take off, flight, landing, ...) often encountered in the encoding of state machines.

Usability Extensions. We differentiate between two kinds of user feedback. On the one hand, we have online feedback, where notifications are displayed during the execution of the monitoring tool, on the other hand offline feedback, which creates another log-file for further post-analysis. This log-file can then in return be processed individually by the monitoring tool again, and is useful to first extract sections of interest and then process them later in detail.

Online Feedback - Syntax: `obs_kind condition message`
where `condition` is a boolean expression, and `message` is an arbitrary string. The semantics for the different `obs_kind` is defined as follows:

- `trigger`: Prints the `message` whenever the `condition` holds.
- `trigger_once`: Prints the `message` only the first time the `condition` holds.
- `trigger_change`: Prints the `message` whenever the `condition` value changes.
- `snapshot`: Prints the monitor state, i.e. the current stream values.

Offline Feedback - Syntax: `tag as` $y_1, \ldots, y_n$ `if` *cond* `with` $x_1, \ldots, x_n$ `at` l where $x_1, \ldots, x_n$ are stream variables, $y_1, \ldots, y_n$ are pairwise distinct stream names for the new log-file, and *cond* is a boolean expression. The semantics are as following: Whenever *cond* holds, the value of x_i is written to the respective y_i column in the new log-file at location l. These operations are especially interesting in offline post-flight analysis where they can ease the reasoning by generating enhanced log-files or by filtering the bulk of data to relevant fragments.

A special variant of this *tagging* operator is *filtering*, defined syntactically as:
`filter` $s_1, ..., s_n$ `if` *cond*   `at` l :=
`tag as` $s_1, ..., s_n$ `if` *cond* `with` $s_1, ..., s_n$ `at` l
This operator copies all input streams to a new log-file, but filters on *cond*.

The syntax of Lola permits not well-defined specifications, i.e. where no unique evaluation model exists. Since the requirement of a unique evaluation model is a semantic criterion and expensive to check, we check a stronger syntactic criterion, namely *well-formedness*, which implies well-definedness. The well-formedness check can be performed on the *dependency graph* for a Lola specification, where the vertices of the multi-graph are stream names, and edges represent accesses to other streams. Weights on the edges are defined by the offset values of the accesses to other streams. As stated in [2], if the dependency graph of a specification does not contain a zero-weight cycle, then the specification is well-formed. If the dependency graph additionally has no positive-weight cycles, then the specification falls into the *efficiently monitorable* fragment. Intuitively, this means it does not contain unbounded lookahead to future values of streams.

Implementation. For the study, Lola has been implemented in C. Since most of the specifications discovered during this case study fall into the efficiently monitorable fragment, we focused on tuning the performance for this fragment. In [2], the evaluation algorithm maintains two equation stores. Resolved equations are stored in R and unresolved equations are stored in U. Unresolved equations are simplified due to partial evaluation, rewrite, and substitution rules and, if resolved, added to R. Evaluated stream expressions are removed from R whenever their largest offset has passed. Our implementation uses an array for R and an inverted index for U, for convenience we call the array for R *past array* and the inverted index for U *future index*. By analyzing the dependency graph, we are able to calculate the size of the past index and can therefore pre-allocate a memory region *once* on initialization. The future index stores as keys the awaiting stream values and maps them to the respective waiting streams. Here, we use the dependency graph to determine a fixed stream evaluation order to minimize the accesses to yet unresolved stream values. Both data structures offer a fast access to values, the past index due to smart array indexing based on a flattening of the syntax tree of the stream expressions and the future index due to a simple lookup call for streams waiting on the resolution of a value.

4   ARTIS Research Platform

The DLR is researching UAS, especially regarding aspects of system autonomy and safety, utilizing its ARTIS platform. The software framework enables development and test of intelligent functions that can be integrated and used with a whole fleet of UAS, comprised of several classes of aircraft with different technical equipment and autonomous capabilities. The latest addition to the DLR fleet is superARTIS, with a maximum take-off weight of 85 kg, Fig. 1. A number of highly automated subsystems enables unmanned operations and provides required onboard functionality. As strict regulations apply, significant efforts in verification and validation activities are required to comply with standards to ensure functional correctness and safety. For the platform, there has been previous work on software verification as well as certification aspects for UAS [18–21].

Recently published supplements [14] to existing development standards for safety critical software [13] introduced a regulatory framework to apply formal

Fig. 1. One example UAS of the DLR Unmanned Aircraft Fleet: SuperARTIS, a dual rotor configuration vehicle, shown with complete flight computers and sensor setup.

Fig. 2. A simulation of autonomous exploration of an unknown area with onboard perception: path flown (red), virtual distance sensor (green), obstacles mapped (grayscale). (Color figure online)

methods for the verification of aircraft. However, due to a lack of expertise, there are some barriers for introduction of formal methods in industry [3]. Within our cooperation, starting with the use of runtime monitoring, the goal is to gradually introduce formal methods into the ARTIS development. The use of runtime monitoring can support several aspects of research, development, verification, the operation, and even the autonomy of an unmanned aircraft.

ARTIS is based on a *guidance, navigation, control (GNC)* architecture as illustrated in Fig. 3, to be able to define high-level tasks and missions while also maintaining low-level control of the aircraft.

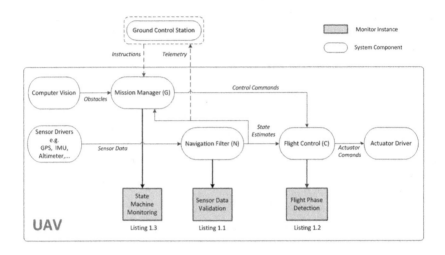

Fig. 3. ARTIS system overview.

The *flight control* realizes the control layer, that uses a model of the flight behavior to command the actuators so that the aircraft achieves desired position, height, speed, and orientation. This system has to cope with external disturbances and keep the aircraft precisely on a given trajectory. The *navigation filter* is responsible for sensor input, such as GPS, inertial measurement, magnetic measurement. The main task of the navigation filter module is the fusion of this heterogeneous information into consistent position information. The top-level component of the guidance layer is the *mission manager*, which does mission planning and execution, breaking high-level objectives such as the exploration and mapping of an unknown area into actionable tasks by generation of suitable waypoints and the path planning to find an optimal route, Fig. 2.

The three-tier architecture has the advantage of different abstraction layers that can be interfaced directly such that each layer represents a level of system autonomy. The ARTIS unmanned aircraft have been evaluated in flight tests with respect to closed-loop motion planning in obstacle rich environments.

In flight, all modules are continuously generating an extensive amount of data, which is logged into files together with sensor data. This logging capability is important for the post flight traceability. Log analysis can however quickly become infeasible due to interacting subsystems and possibly emergent aspects of the system. Data from log-files has to be processed for analysis and may need to be correlated with a context from a different module. Runtime monitoring can support these aspects, by automating the analysis of log-files for specific properties. An important feature is to filter only relevant log data, according to specific properties of the observation and tag it with a keyword for further analysis. These properties can be introduced before conducting an experiment or simulation, or after the fact, since all relevant data is being saved to a log-file.

The software framework consists of a large code base with many modules and interfaces, which is under constant development. Interface changes triggered by a change in a single module are a significant problem during development, since other modules rely on implicit interface assumptions. Those assumptions together with a specification of a module can be monitored to detect inconsistencies early. They include internal properties of a subsystem, interface assumptions of a module, but also environmental assumptions of the overall aircraft.

The explicit specification of assumptions is useful for system documentation, testing and verification, but also for the operation of the aircraft itself. In contrast to simple unit testing, a property that is formalized into a runtime monitor can not only be tested in a test fixture, but scale to the test phase. Runtime monitoring can be integrated into software- and hardware-in-the-loop simulations as well as full-scale flight tests, allowing the direct analysis for complex properties. Since a formal specification mechanism is used, this also allows some reuse in other formal verification methodologies, e.g. for LTL model checking.

System failures often occur not due to implementation errors, but because of the inherent difficulty of specifying all relevant system requirements correctly, completely, and free of contradictions. In nominal operation, the system behaves correctly, but as unforeseen events occur and environment assumptions are no longer valid, the system fails. Integrating runtime monitoring into normal system operation allows to continuously monitor for environmental assumptions and abnormal system behavior and allows to initiate contingency and failsafe procedures in case of unforeseen events. In particular, EASA [5,6] and JARUS [11] are working on concepts for the integration of unmanned aircraft into airspace that rely on the definition of specific operational limitations. Here, the certification is no longer only dependent on the aircraft, but on the combination of it with the specific operation. Limitations, such as constraining the altitude, the speed, the geographic location, etc. of the operation can have a significant impact on the actual safety risk that emerges from the unmanned aircraft. Runtime verification can support the safety of the aircraft by monitoring these limitations.

5   Representative Specifications

In this section, we will give some insights into representative classes of specifications, which have been used for stream runtime monitoring within the DLR ARTIS UAS fleet. These range from low-level sensor data validation and ensuring that the product of the sensor fusion is within the assumptions of the later stages of the control loop, to computing flight phase statistics, and validating the state machine of the mission planning and execution framework. The specifications have been obtained by interviewing the responsible engineers for each component and collaborative specification writing. They have been validated by offline analysis of known test runs. The full set of specifications developed in the study can be found in [16]. Note that due to the time-triggered nature of the system design, all incoming signals to the monitor are timestamped and arrive with a frequency of 50 Hz. For the following specifications, the integration of the respective monitor instance is depicted in Fig. 3.

5.1   Sensor Data Validation

In Listing 1.1, we validate the output of the navigation part of the sensor fusion. Given the sensor data, e.g. GPS position and the inertial measurement, the navigation filter outputs vehicle state estimates, depicted in Fig. 3. Based on this specification, the monitor checks the frequency of incoming signals and detects GPS signal jumps. The detection of frequency deviations can point to problems in the signal-processing chain, e.g. delayed, missing, or corrupted sensor values

```
 1   input   double lat, lon, ug, vg, wg, time_s, time_micros
 2   output double time := time_s + time_micros / 1000000.0
 3   output double flight_time := time - time#[0,0.0]
 4   output double frequency := switch position{
 5                                  case 0  { 1.0 / ( time[1,0.0] - time ) }
 6                                  default { 1.0 / ( time - time[-1,0.0] ) } } }
 7   output double freq_sum := freq_sum[-1,0.0] + frequency
 8   output double freq_avg := freq_sum / double(position+1)
 9   output double freq_max := max( frequency, freq_max[-1,double_min] )
10   output double freq_min := min( frequency, freq_min[-1,double_max] )
11
12   output double velocity := sqrt( ug^2.0 + vg^2.0 + wg^2.0 )
13   const  double R          := 6373000.0
14   const  double pi         := 3.1415926535
15
16   output double lon1_rad := lon[-1,0.0] * pi / 180.0
17   output double lon2_rad := lon * pi / 180.0
18   output double lat1_rad := lat[-1,0.0] * pi / 180.0
19   output double lat2_rad := lat * pi / 180.0
20
21   output double dlon     := lon2_rad - lon1_rad
22   output double dlat     := lat2_rad - lat1_rad
23   output double a := (sin(dlat/2.0))^2.0 +
24                          cos(lat1_rad) *
25                          cos(lat2_rad) *
26                          (sin(dlon/2.0))^2.0
27   output double c := 2.0 * atan2( sqrt(a), sqrt(1.0-a) )
28   output double gps_distance := R * c
29
30   output double passed_time    := time - time[-1,0.0]
31   output double distance_max   := velocity * passed_time
32   output double dif_distance    := gps_distance - distance_max
33   const  double delta_distance := 1.0
34   output bool   detected_jump   := switch position {
35                                        case 0 { false }
36                                        default { dif_distance > delta_distance } }
37   snapshot detected_jump with "Invalid GPS signal received!"
```

Listing 1.1: The specification used for Sensor Data Validation

(Line 4 to 10). Since the vehicle state estimation is used for control decisions, errors would propagate through the whole system. From Line 21 to 37, the GPS signal jumps are computed by the Haversine formula. It compares the traveled distance, first by integrating over the velocity values received by the IMU unit, and second by computing the distance as measured by the GPS coordinates. All calculations are performed in Lola and compared against a threshold. Since the formula expects the latitude and longitude in radians and we receive them in decimal degree, we convert them first (Line 16 to 19).

5.2   Flight Phase Detection

The mission manager describes high-level behaviors, e.g. the hover or the fly-to behavior. The hover behavior implies that the aircraft remains at a fixed location

```
1    input   double  time_s, time_micros, vel_x, vel_y, vel_z,
2                    fuel, power, vel_r_x, vel_r_y, vel_r_z
3    output double time := time_s + time_micros / 1000000.0
4    output double flight_time := time - time#[0,0.0]
5    output double frequency := switch position{
6                            case 0  { 1.0 / ( time[1,0.0] - time ) }
7                            default { 1.0 / ( time - time[-1,0.0] ) } }
8    output double freq_sum := freq_sum[-1,0.0] + frequency
9    output double freq_avg := freq_sum / double(position+1)
10   output double freq_max := max( frequency, freq_max[-1,double_min] )
11   output double freq_min := min( frequency, freq_min[-1,double_max] )
12
13   const  double  vel_bound      := 1.0
14   output double velocity      := sqrt( vel_x^2.0 + vel_y^2.0 + vel_z^2.0 )
15   output double velocity_max  := if reset_max[-1,false] { velocity }
16                                  else { max( velocity, velocity_max[-1,0.0]) }
17   output double velocity_min  := if reset_max[-1,false] { velocity }
18                                  else { min( velocity, velocity_min[-1,0.0]) }
19   output double dif_max       := difference(velocity_max, velocity_min)
20   output bool   reset_max     := dif_max > vel_bound
21   output double reset_time    := if reset_max | position = 0 { time }
22                                  else  { reset_time[-1,0.0] }
23   output int unchanged        := if reset_max[-1,false] { 0 }
24                                  else { unchanged[-1,0] + 1 }
25   snapshot unchanged = 150 with "Phase detected!"
26
27   output double  vel_dev := difference(vel_r_x,vel_x) + difference(vel_r_y,vel_y)
28                          + difference(vel_r_z,vel_z)
29   output double  dev_sum  := vel_dev + dev_sum[-1,0]
30   output double  vel_av   := dev_sum / double((position+1)*3)
31   output int worst_dev_pos := if worst_dev[-1,double_min] < vel_dev { position }
32                               else { worst_dev_pos[-1,0] }
33   output double worst_dev  := if worst_dev[-1,double_min] < vel_dev { vel_dev }
34                               else { worst_dev[-1,0.0] }
35
36   output double fuel_p  := ( ( fuel#[0,0.0] - fuel ) / (fuel#[0,0.0]+0.01) )
37   output double power_p := ( (power#[0,0.0] - power) / (power#[0,0.0]+0.01) )
38   trigger_once fuel_p  < 0.50  with "Fuel below half capacity"
39   trigger_once fuel_p  < 0.25  with "Fuel below quarter capacity"
40   trigger_once fuel_p  < 0.10  with "Urgent: Refill Fuel!"
41   trigger_once power_p < 0.50  with "Power below half capacity"
42   trigger_once power_p < 0.25  with "Power below quarter capacity"
43   trigger_once power_p < 0.10  with "Urgent: Recharge Power!"
```

Listing 1.2: The specification used for Flight Phase Detection whereas the fly-to behavior describes the movement from a source to a destination location. These high-level behaviors are then automatically synthesized into low-level control commands which are send to the flight control. Given the state estimation, the flight control then smoothes the control commands into applicable actuator commands, (vel_r_x, vel_r_y, vel_r_z), depicted in Fig. 3. Hence, the actuator commands implement the desired high-level behavior. Since the actuator movements are limited and therefore smoothed by the flight control, there is a gap between the control commands and the actuator commands.

In Listing 1.2, monitoring is used to recognize flight phases where the velocity of the aircraft stays below a small bound for longer than three seconds (Line 13 to 25). In post-flight analysis, the recognized phases can be compared to the high-level commands to validate the suitability of the property for the respective behavior. Furthermore, from Line 3 to 11, the frequency is examined and, from Line 27 to 34, the deviations between the reference velocity, given by the flight controller, and the actual velocity (vel_x, vel_y, vel_z) are detected. Bound checks on fuel and power detect further boundary conditions and produce notifications for the difference urgency levels.

5.3   Mission Planning and Execution

The mission planning and execution component within the ARTIS control software is responsible for executing uploaded flight missions onboard the aircraft.

```
1    input double time_s, time_micros
2    input int stateID_SC, OnGround
3    const int Start                  := 0
4    const int MissionControllerOff   := 1
5                                        ...
6    const int HammerHeadTurn         := 16
7
8    output double time := time_s + time_micros / 1000000.0
9    output double flight_time := time - time#[0,0.0]
10
11   output bool change_state := switch position {
12                       case 0 { false }
13                       default { stateID_SC != stateID_SC[-1,-1] } }
14   trigger change_state
15
16   output string state_enum := switch stateID_SC {
17                       case 0 { "Start" }
18                       case 1 { "MissionControllerOff" }
19                           ...
20                       case 16{ "HammerHeadTurn" }
21                       default{ "Invalid" }  }
22   output string state_trace :=
23       switch position {  case 0  { state_enum }  default {
24       if change_state { concat(concat(state_trace[-1,""]," -> "),state_enum) }
25       else { state_trace[-1,""] } } }
26
27   output double entrance_time  := if change_state { time }
28                       else { entrance_time[-1,0.0] }
29   const double landing_timebnd := 20.0
30   output double landing_info   := if stateID_SC = Landing { 0.0 }
31                       else { time - entrance_time[-1,0.0] }
32   output bool landing_error    := stateID_SC = Landing & OnGround != 1  &
33                       landing_info > landing_timebound
```

Listing 1.3: The specification used for Mission Planning and Execution

The received mission from the ground control station is planned based on the current state estimate of the vehicle and the sensed obstacles, depicted in Fig. 3. The mission manager and its internal planner essentially consists of a large state machine which controls the parameters of the current flight state. In the corresponding specification seen in Listing 1.3, the state machine is encoded into the specification, and the state trace is recovered from the inputs and converted to a readable form. Starting in Line 27 of the specifications, we record entrance and exit times of certain flight states, and check a landing time bound to ensure a bounded liveness property. With this specification, we are able to detect invalid transition and ensure a landing time bound. In an extended version, we further specified properties for each location. Specifically, we aggregated statistics on the fuel consumption, the average velocity, and the maximal, average, and total time spend in the respective location.

6   Monitoring Experiments

6.1   Offline Experiments

The experiments indicate how Lola performs with the given set of specifications in an offline monitoring context. This mode was especially useful during specification development, because a large number of flight log-files was readily available and could be used to debug the developed specifications.

As offline parameters, Lola receives one or more specifications and the log data file. As an optional parameter, a location for the monitor output can be set. The offline experiments were conducted on a dual-core machine with an 2.6 GHz Intel Core i5 processor with 8 GB RAM. The input streams files were stored on an internal SSD. Runtime results are shown in Fig. 4. Memory consumption was below 1.5 MB. The simulated flight times range up to 15 min.

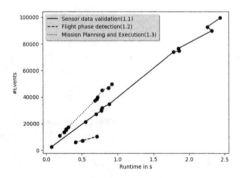

Fig. 4. The results of the offline experiments for the specifications presented in Sect. 5.

The experimental results show that our implementation could process the existing log-files in this application context within seconds. Using an additional helper tool, which automatically runs offline monitoring on a set of given log-files, and further specifications, we were able to identify system boundaries and thresholds without further effort.

6.2   Online Experiments

The Lola online interface is written in C++. Due the absence of both a software bus and a hardware bus, the monitor interface is coupled to the existing logging interface. Therefore, we can use the created log-files to evaluate the monitor impact on the system by comparing the logged frequencies.

The Hardware-in-the-loop (HiL) experiments were run on a flight computer with an Intel Pentium with a 1.8 GHz and 1 GB RAM, running a Unix-based RTOS. As inter-thread communication, we use shared memory for both the stream value delivery and the monitor output. A simulated world environment and a flight mission were set, the worlds and the missions are depicted in Fig. 6. In the experiments, we monitored the system with a superset of the specifications described in Sect. 5. We evaluated the impact of online monitoring as following. For each mission, all experiments flew the same planned route without noticeable deviations, analyzed per manual inspection of an online visualization of the flight as seen in Fig. 6. To measure the system performance impact, we compare the average frequency determined by the timestamps in the monitor, if available for the component, otherwise with the frequency computed afterwards by offline monitoring on the logs of the experiment with the average frequency of a non-monitored execution (Fig. 7).

The results for hardware-in-the-loop testing are given in Fig. 7. The experimental results show that the timing behavior, i.e. the frequencies, are minimally affected. Thus, the current implementation is sufficiently fast for online monitoring in this experimental setting. The monitoring approach can run aside the logging. By setting the evalstep parameter to 100 to simulate a data burst for a monitor evaluation step, the sensitive time-triggered system is slightly affected.

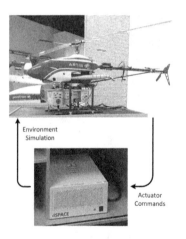

Fig. 5. Test rig for hardware-in-the-loop (HITL) experiments.

Fig. 6. Tracked flight-paths of two scenarios. On top, we see a hover simulation and at the bottom a fly-to simulation.

monitor (evalstep)	online - AvgFreq			offline - AvgFreq			
	nav (Hz)	ctrl (Hz)	mgr (Hz)	gps-p (Hz)	gps-v (Hz)	imu (Hz)	mgn (Hz)
No Monitor	*50.0*	*50.0*	*50.0*	20.0	20.0	100.0	10.0
nav_monitor (1)	**50.0**	*50.0*	*50.0*	20.0	20.0	100.0	10.0
nav_monitor (1)	**50.0**	-	*50.0*	20.0	20.0	100.0	10.0
ctrl_monitor (1)	-	**50.0**	-	″	″	″	″
nav_monitor (1)	**50.0**	-	-	20.0	20.0	100.0	10.0
ctrl_monitor (1)	-	**50.0**	-	″	″	″	″
mgr_monitor (1)	-	-	**50.0**	″	″	″	″
nav_monitor (100)	**50.1**	-	-	20.0	20.0	100.1	10.0
ctrl_monitor (100)	-	**50.3**	-	″	″	″	″
mgr_monitor (100)	-	-	**50.2**	″	″	″	″

Fig. 7. Monitor performance results. The first line denotes the reference values without monitors, and more monitors are added in the further lines. The evalstep parameter represents the amount of buffering of input values before evaluation is triggered. Bold values denote frequencies measured online with Lola, the other frequency values have been determined after the test by offline analysis.

7   Conclusion

We have presented our experience from a successful case study for stream-based runtime monitoring with Lola in a safety-critical application environment. The DLR ARTIS family of unmanned aerial vehicles provides a unique research testbed to explore the applicability of runtime monitoring in this application.

Our experiences show that the integration of runtime monitoring into an existing system has benefits for both the system and its development process. While the primary goal is to ensure the correct behavior of the system, monitor the health of the system components, and possibly trigger fail-safe strategies, there are a number of secondary effects on the system development process, which may aid the adoption of runtime verification techniques. Those benefits include time savings during system debugging, a common and faster way to perform log-file analysis, and a better documentation of interface assumptions of components. The re-use of the same specifications in all contexts increases their appeal. The specification development has already influenced the language and system implementation of our stream-based specification language. The presented extensions improve the readability of specifications, and the insight that efficiently monitorable specifications suffice for online monitoring guides optimization efforts in the implementation. The equation-based, declarative specification style of Lola with a rich type and function supports its use in a real engineering project.

As the adaptation of autonomy into the system designs of regulated industries increases, we expect runtime monitoring to play an important role in the certification process of the future. Runtime verification techniques allow the deployment of trusted, verified components into systems in unreliable environments and may be used to trigger pre-planned contingency measures to robustly control hazardous situations. To perform these important tasks, the monitor needs to comprehensively supervise the internal state of the system components to increase the self-awareness into the system health and to trigger a timely reaction.

References

1. Adolf, F., Thielecke, F.: A sequence control system for onboard mission management of an unmanned helicopter. In: AIAA Infotech@Aerospace Conference (2007)
2. D'Angelo, B., Sankaranarayanan, S., Sánchez, C., Robinson, W., Finkbeiner, B., Sipma, H.B., Mehrotra, S., Manna, Z.: Lola: runtime monitoring of synchronous systems. In: 12th International Symposium on Temporal Representation and Reasoning (TIME 2005), pp. 166–174. IEEE Computer Society Press, June 2005
3. Davis, J.A., Clark, M., Cofer, D., Fifarek, A., Hinchman, J., Hoffman, J., Hulbert, B., Miller, S.P., Wagner, L.: Study on the barriers to the industrial adoption of formal methods. In: Pecheur, C., Dierkes, M. (eds.) FMICS 2013. LNCS, vol. 8187, pp. 63–77. Springer, Heidelberg (2013). doi:10.1007/978-3-642-41010-9_5
4. Dill, E.T., Young, S.D., Hayhurst, K.J.: SAFEGUARD: an assured safety net technology for UAS. In: 2016 IEEE/AIAA 35th Digital Avionics Systems Conference (DASC). IEEE, September 2016. https://doi.org/10.1109/dasc.2016.7778009
5. European Aviation Safety Agency (EASA): Advance Notice of Proposed Amendment 2015-10, Introduction of a regulatory framework for the operation of drones (2015)
6. European Aviation Safety Agency (EASA): Concept of Operations for Drones, A risk based approach to regulation of unmanned aircraft (2015)
7. Faymonville, P., Finkbeiner, B., Schirmer, S., Torfah, H.: A stream-based specification language for network monitoring. In: Falcone, Y., Sánchez, C. (eds.) RV 2016. LNCS, vol. 10012, pp. 152–168. Springer, Cham (2016). doi:10.1007/978-3-319-46982-9_10
8. Geist, J., Rozier, K.Y., Schumann, J.: Runtime observer pairs and Bayesian network reasoners on-board FPGAs: flight-certifiable system health management for embedded systems. In: Bonakdarpour, B., Smolka, S.A. (eds.) RV 2014. LNCS, vol. 8734, pp. 215–230. Springer, Cham (2014). doi:10.1007/978-3-319-11164-3_18
9. Gross, K.H., Clark, M.A., Hoffman, J.A., Swenson, E.D., Fifarek, A.W.: Run-time assurance and formal methods analysis nonlinear system applied to nonlinear system control. J. Aerosp. Inf. Syst. **14**(4), 232–246 (2017). https://doi.org/10.2514/1.i010471
10. Hallé, S., Gaboury, S., Khoury, R.: A glue language for event stream processing. In: BigData, pp. 2384–2391. IEEE (2016)
11. Joint Authorities for Rulemaking of Unmanned Systems (JARUS): JARUS Guidelines on Specific Operations Risk Assessment (SORA) (2016)
12. Pike, L., Niller, S., Wegmann, N.: Runtime verification for ultra-critical systems. In: Khurshid, S., Sen, K. (eds.) RV 2011. LNCS, vol. 7186, pp. 310–324. Springer, Heidelberg (2012). doi:10.1007/978-3-642-29860-8_23
13. Radio Technical Commission for Aeronautics (RTCA): DO-178C/ED-12C Software Considerations in Airborne Systems and Equipment Certification (2011)
14. Radio Technical Commission for Aeronautics (RTCA): DO-333/ED-216 Formal Methods Supplement to DO-178C and DO-278A (2011)

15. Reinbacher, T., Rozier, K.Y., Schumann, J.: Temporal-logic based runtime observer pairs for system health management of real-time systems. In: Ábrahám, E., Havelund, K. (eds.) TACAS 2014. LNCS, vol. 8413, pp. 357–372. Springer, Heidelberg (2014). doi:10.1007/978-3-642-54862-8_24

16. Schirmer, S.: Runtime Monitoring with Lola. Master's Thesis, Saarland University (2016)

17. Schumann, J., Moosbrugger, P., Rozier, K.Y.: R2U2: monitoring and diagnosis of security threats for unmanned aerial systems. In: Bartocci, E., Majumdar, R. (eds.) RV 2015. LNCS, vol. 9333, pp. 233–249. Springer, Cham (2015). doi:10.1007/978-3-319-23820-3_15

18. Torens, C., Adolf, F.: Software verification considerations for the ARTIS unmanned rotorcraft. In: 51st AIAA Aerospace Sciences Meeting Including the New Horizons Forum and Aerospace Exposition, American Institute of Aeronautics and Astronautics, January 2013. http://dx.doi.org/10.2514/6.2013-593

19. Torens, C., Adolf, F.: Using formal requirements and model-checking for verification and validation of an unmanned rotorcraft. In: American Institute of Aeronautics and Astronautics, AIAA Infotech @ Aerospace, AIAA SciTech, 05–09 January 2015. http://dx.doi.org/10.2514/6.2015-1645

20. Torens, C., Adolf, F.M., Goormann, L.: Certification and software verification considerations for autonomous unmanned aircraft. J. Aerosp. Inf. Syst. **11**(10), 649–664 (2014)

21. Torens, C., Adolf, F.M.: Automated verification and validation of an onboard mission planning and execution system for uavs. In: AIAA Infotech@Aerospace (I@A) Conference, Boston, MA, 19–22 August 2013. http://dx.doi.org/10.2514/6.2013-4564

Probabilistic Black-Box Reachability Checking

Bernhard K. Aichernig and Martin Tappler[(✉)]

Institute of Software Technology, Graz University of Technology, Graz, Austria
{aichernig,martin.tappler}@ist.tugraz.at

Abstract. Model checking has a long-standing tradition in software verification. Given a system design it checks whether desired properties are satisfied. Unlike testing, it cannot be applied in a black-box setting. To overcome this limitation Peled et al. introduced black-box checking, a combination of testing, model inference and model checking. The technique requires systems to be fully deterministic. For stochastic systems, statistical techniques are available. However, they cannot be applied to systems with non-deterministic choices. We present a black-box checking technique for stochastic systems that allows both, non-deterministic and probabilistic behaviour. It involves model inference, testing and probabilistic model-checking. Here, we consider reachability checking, i.e., we infer near-optimal input-selection strategies for bounded reachability.

Keywords: Model inference · Statistical model-checking · Reachability analysis · Black-box checking · Testing · Verification

1 Introduction

Model checking has a long-standing tradition in software verification. Given a system design, model-checking techniques determine whether requirements stated as formal properties are satisfied. These techniques, however, fall short if no design is available. Black-box checking, introduced by Peled et al. [27], tackles this issue by establishing methods to check properties of black-box systems. The strategies for black-box checking include a learning-based technique which infers models in the form of deterministic finite automata (DFA) on-the-fly. Inferred models are model checked which may reveal a fault in the system or show that learning was incomplete. Since active automata learning involves repeated (conformance) testing, black-box checking is a combination of model checking and testing. Therefore, we refer to analysed systems as systems under test (SUTs). Note that we use the terms model inference and learning interchangeably.

Inspired by black-box checking, we propose an approach to analyse reactive systems exhibiting stochastic behaviour in a black-box setting. We also follow a learning-based approach involving repeated testing and probabilistic model-checking. Instead of targeting general properties formulated in probabilistic temporal logics, we check reachability as a first step. Since we follow a simulation-based approach, we check bounded reachability. Rather than inferring DFA, we assume that systems can be modelled by Markov decision processes (MDPs).

© Springer International Publishing AG 2017
S. Lahiri and G. Reger (Eds.): RV 2017, LNCS 10548, pp. 50–67, 2017.
DOI: 10.1007/978-3-319-67531-2_4

Hence, we consider systems controllable by inputs, chosen by an environment or a tester. As such, these systems involve non-determinism resulting from the choice of inputs and stochastic behaviour reflected in state transitions and outputs. Given such a system, our goal is to find a input-selection strategy, i.e. a resolution of non-determinism, which maximises the probability of reaching a certain property. A possible application scenario is stress testing of systems with stochastic failures. We could infer a testing strategy that provokes failures.

The approach is depicted in Fig. 1. In a first step, we sample system traces randomly. From these traces we infer an MDP via the method described by Mao et al. [22,23], a variant of ALER-GIA [5]. Once we inferred a hypothesis model $\mathcal{M}_{h1}$, we use the PRISM model checker [16] for a reachability analysis to find the maximal probability of reaching a state satisfying a property ψ. PRISM computes a probability p and a strategy s_1 (also called adversary or scheduler) to reach ψ with p. Since ALERGIA infers models from system traces, the quality of the model $\mathcal{M}_{h1}$ depends on these traces. If ψ is not adequately covered, s_1 inferred from $\mathcal{M}_{h1}$ may perform poorly and rarely reach ψ. To account for that, we follow an incremental process. After initial random sampling, we itera-tively infer models $\mathcal{M}_{hi}$ from which we infer sched-

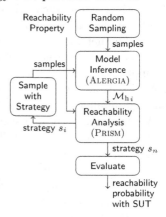

Fig. 1. Overview of the approach.

ulers s_i. To sample new traces for $\mathcal{M}_{hi+1}$ we select inputs randomly and based on s_i. The latter ensures that paths relevant to ψ will be explored more thoroughly. This process is repeated for a fixed number of rounds n. We generally ignore probabilities computed by PRISM because they are based on inferred models which may be inaccurate. Instead, we evaluate the inferred strategy via directed testing of the SUT. Since the behaviour under a strategy is purely probabilistic, this is a form of Monte Carlo simulation. The evaluation provides an estimation of the probability of reaching ψ with the actual SUT under strategy s_n. As a result, the estimation is a lower bound for the optimal probability.

The rest of this paper is structured as follows. In Sect. 2, we will discuss related work. Section 3 introduces preliminaries used in Sect. 4 which discusses the proposed approach. We present evaluation results in Sect. 5. Finally, we provide an outlook on future work and conclude in Sect. 6.

2   Related Work

As discussed before, black-box checking [27] is closely related. In contrast to our technique, it considers non-stochastic systems, but more general properties. Various follow-up work demonstrates the potential of learning-based verification. Extensions, e.g., take existing models into account [15], focus on the composition of black-box and white-box components [11], or check security properties [30].

Mao et al. [21–23] also inferred probabilistic models with the purpose of model checking. In fact, we apply the model-inference technique for MDPs described by them. Wang et al. [35] apply a variant of ALERGIA as well and take properties into account during model inference with the goal of probabilistic model-checking. They apply automated property-specific abstraction/refinement to decrease the model-checking runtime. Nouri et al. [25] also combine stochastic learning and abstraction with respect to some property. Their goal is to improve the runtime of statistical model-checking (SMC). Notably, their approach could also be applied for black-box systems, but does not consider controllability via inputs. Further work on SMC of black-box systems can be found in [29,36].

Although we did not adapt ALERGIA, a passive model-inference technique, we apply it in an active setting. Chen and Nielsen [7] describe active learning of MDPs. However, they do not aim at model checking, but try to reduce the required number of samples by directing sampling towards uncertainties.

We try to find optimal schedulers for MDPs. This problem has to be solved in other simulation-based verification approaches as well, like in SMC. A lightweight approach for finding schedulers in SMC is described in [8,20]. By representing schedulers efficiently, they are able to consider history-dependent schedulers and through "smart sampling" they accomplish finding near-optimal schedulers with low simulation budget. Brázdil et al. [4] presented an approach to unbounded reachability analysis via SMC. The technique is based on delayed Q-learning, a form of reinforcement learning, requiring only limited knowledge of the system (but more than our technique). Another approach using reinforcement learning for strategy inference for reachability objectives has been presented by David et al. [9]. They minimise expected cost while respecting worst-case time bounds.

3   Preliminaries

We introduce background material following [14,23], but consider only finite traces/paths and *bounded* reachability, as we use a simulation-based approach. The restriction to bounded properties is also commonly found in SMC [18], which is also simulation-based and from which we apply concepts. Moreover, SMC of unbounded properties is especially challenging in a black-box setting [19].

Basics. Let Σ^{in} and Σ^{out} be sets of input and output symbols. An input/output string s is an alternating sequence of inputs and outputs, starting with an output, i.e. $s \in \Sigma^{\text{out}} \times (\Sigma^{\text{in}} \times \Sigma^{\text{out}})^*$. We denote by $|s|$ the number of input symbols in s and refer to it also as string/trace length. Given a set S, we denote by $Dist(S)$ the set of probability distributions over S, i.e. for all μ in $Dist(S)$ we have $\mu : S \to [0,1]$ such that $\sum_{s \in S} \mu(s) = 1$. We denote the indicator function by $\mathbf{1}_A$ which returns 1 for $e \in A$ and 0 otherwise.

In Sect. 4, we apply two pseudo-random functions *coinFlip* and *randSel*. These require an initialisation operation which takes a *seed*-value for a pseudo-random number generator and which returns implementations of both functions. The function *coinFlip* implements a biased coin flip and is defined for $p \in [0,1]$ by

$\mathbb{P}(coinFlip(p) = \top) = p$ and $\mathbb{P}(coinFlip(p) = \bot) = 1 - p$. The function $randSel$ takes a set as input and returns a single element of the set, whereby the element is chosen according to a uniform distribution, i.e. $\forall e \in S : \mathbb{P}(randSel(S) = e) = \frac{1}{|S|}$.

Markov Decision Processes. MDPs allow modelling reactive systems with probabilistic responses. An MDP starts in an initial state. During execution, the environment may choose and execute inputs non-deterministically upon which the system reacts according to its current state and its probabilistic transition function. For that, the system changes its state and produces an output.

Definition 1 (Markov decision process (MDP)). *A Markov decision process (MDP) is a tuple $\mathcal{M} = \langle Q, \Sigma^{in}, \Sigma^{out}, q_0, \delta, L \rangle$ where*

- *Q is a finite set of states,*
- *Σ^{in} and Σ^{out} are finite sets of input and output symbols respectively,*
- *$q_0 \in Q$ is the initial state,*
- *$\delta : Q \times \Sigma^{in} \rightarrow Dist(Q)$ is the probabilistic transition function, and*
- *$L : Q \rightarrow \Sigma^{out}$ is the labelling function.*

The transition function δ must be defined for all $q \in Q$ and $i \in \Sigma^{in}$. We consider only deterministic MDPs, i.e. $\forall q \in Q, \forall i : \delta(q, i)(q') > 0 \wedge \delta(q, i)(q'') > 0$ implies $q' = q''$ or $L(q') \neq L(q'')$. Non-determinism thus results only from the non-deterministic choice of inputs by the environment.

We generally set $\Sigma^{out} = \mathcal{P}(AP)$ where AP is a set of relevant propositions and $L(q)$ gives the propositions that hold in state q. A finite path p through an MDP is an alternating sequence of states and inputs, i.e. $p = q_0 i_1 q_1 \cdots i_{n-1} q_{n-1} i_n q_n \in Q \times (\Sigma^{in} \times Q)^*$. The set of all paths of an MDP $\mathcal{M}$ is denoted by $Path_\mathcal{M}$. A path p corresponds to a trace $L(p) = t$, i.e. an input/output string, with $t = o_0 i_1 o_1 \cdots i_{n-1} o_{n-1} i_n o_n$ and $L(q_i) = o_i$. To reason about probabilities of traces and sets of traces, we need a way to resolve non-determinism. To accomplish this, we introduce schedulers which are often also referred to as adversaries or strategies [23]. Schedulers basically choose the next input action (probabilistically) given a history of visited states, i.e. a path.

Definition 2 (Scheduler). *Given an MDP $\mathcal{M} = \langle Q, \Sigma^{in}, \Sigma^{out}, q_0, \delta, L \rangle$, a scheduler for $\mathcal{M}$ is a function $s : Path_\mathcal{M} \rightarrow Dist(\Sigma^{in})$.*

To define a probability distribution over finite paths, we need another component, a probability distribution $p_l \in Dist(\mathbb{N}_0)$ over the length of paths. Given an MDP $\mathcal{M} = \langle Q, \Sigma^{in}, \Sigma^{out}, q_0, \delta, L \rangle$, a length probability p_l and a scheduler s induce a probability distribution $\mathbb{P}^l_{\mathcal{M},s}$ on the set of paths $Path_\mathcal{M}$, defined by:

$$\mathbb{P}^l_{\mathcal{M},s}(q_0 i_1 q_1 \cdots i_n q_n) = p_l(n) \prod_{j=1}^{n} s(q_0 \cdots i_{j-1} q_{j-1})(i_j) \cdot \delta(q_{j-1}, i_j)(q_j) \qquad (1)$$

Probability distributions over finite paths may instead of p_l, e.g., include state-dependent termination probabilities [21]. We take a path-based view because we actively sample from MDPs. As paths correspond to traces, $\mathbb{P}^l_{\mathcal{M},s}$ defines a distribution over traces as well and we control trace length via p_l.

Since we target reachability, we do not need general schedulers, but may restrict ourselves to *memoryless deterministic* schedulers [17]. A scheduler is memoryless if its choice of inputs depends only on the last state, i.e. it is a function from Q to $Dist(\Sigma^{in})$. It is deterministic if for all $p \in Path_\mathcal{M}$, there is exactly one $i \in \Sigma^{in}$ such that $s(p)(i) = 1$. Otherwise, it is called randomised. Example 1 describes an MDP and a scheduler for a faulty coffee machine.

Note that bounded reachability actually requires finite-memory schedulers. However, bounded reachability can be encoded as unbounded reachability by transforming the MDP model [4], at the expense of increased state space.

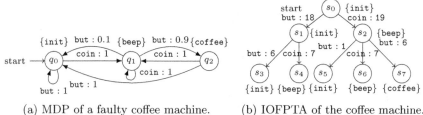

(a) MDP of a faulty coffee machine.   (b) IOFPTA of the coffee machine.

Fig. 2. Coffee machine example.

Example 1. Figure 2a shows an MDP modelling a faulty coffee machine. Edge labels denote input symbols and corresponding transition probabilities, whereas output labels are placed above states. After insertion of a coin and pressing a button, the coffee machine is supposed to provide coffee. However, with a probability of 0.1 it may reset itself instead. A deterministic memoryless scheduler s may provide inputs coin and but in alternation, i.e. $s(q_0) = 1_{\{coin\}}$, $s(q_1) = 1_{\{but\}}$, and $s(q_2) = 1_{\{coin\}}$. By setting $p_l = 1_{\{2\}}$, all strings must have length 2, such that, e.g., $\mathbb{P}^l_{\mathcal{M},s}(p) = 0.9$ for $p = q_0 \cdot coin \cdot q_1 \cdot but \cdot q_2$.

Model Inference. We infer MDPs via an adaptation of ALERGIA [5,22,23]. The technique takes input-output strings as input and constructs an input output frequency prefix tree acceptor (IOFPTA) representing the strings. An IOFPTA is a tree with edges labelled by inputs and nodes labelled by outputs. Additionally, edges are annotated with frequencies denoting how often a corresponding string was present in the sample. An IOFPTA with normalised frequencies represents a tree-shaped MDP whereby tree nodes correspond to MDP states. In a second step, the IOFPTA is transformed through state-merging. For that, the states are partitioned into three sets: *red* states which have been checked, *blue* states which are neighbours of red states, and uncoloured states. Pairs of blue and red states are checked for compatibility and merged if compatible. Otherwise, the blue one is coloured red. This is repeated until all states are coloured. After normalisation of transition probabilities, this adaptation of ALERGIA returns an MDP.

Basically, two states are compatible if they have the same label, and if their successors are sufficiently similar and recursively compatible. A parameter $\epsilon_{\text{ALERGIA}} \in (0, 1]$ controls the significance level of an applied statistical test. We represent calls to ALERGIA by $\text{ALERGIA}(\mathcal{S}, \epsilon_{\text{ALERGIA}}) = \mathcal{M}$ where $\mathcal{S}$ is a set of input-output strings and $\mathcal{M}$ is a resulting MDP.

Figure 2b shows an IOFPTA for the coffee machine from Example 1, but sampled with a (uniformly) randomised scheduler and a different p_l. Edge labels denote inputs and associated frequencies, while outputs are placed next to nodes. At first, q_1 might be merged with q_0 as their successors are similar. Redirecting the but edge from q_1 to q_0 would create the self loop in the initial state.

Statistical Model-Checking. We consider step-bounded reachability. The syntax of formulas ϕ is given by: $\phi = F^{<k}\psi$ with $\psi = \neg\psi|\psi \wedge \psi|\psi \vee \psi|AP$, AP denoting an atomic proposition, and $k \in \mathbb{N}$.

The formula $\phi = F^{<k}\psi$ denotes that ψ should be satisfied in a state reached in less than k steps. We define the satisfaction of $\phi = F^{<k}\psi$ via: a trace $t = o_0 i_1 o_1 \cdots i_{n-1} o_{n-1} i_n o_n$ satisfies ϕ denoted by $t \models \phi$ if there is an $i < k$ such that $o_i \models \psi$. To be able to evaluate whether a trace t satisfies a formula $\phi = F^{<k}\psi$ it must be long enough, i.e. it must contain at least $k - 1$ steps. Therefore, we set the length probability p_l accordingly, i.e. $p_l(j) = 0$ for $j < k - 1$.

The composition of a scheduler s and an MDP $\mathcal{M}$ behaves entirely probabilistically. In fact, it induces a discrete time Markov chain (DTMC) [14]. Hence, we can apply techniques from SMC without considering non-determinism. Furthermore, we can define the probability of satisfying a property ϕ by $\mathbb{P}_{\mathcal{M},s}(\phi) = \mathbb{P}^l_{\mathcal{M},s}(\{p \in Path_\mathcal{M}|L(p) \models \phi\})$ for an appropriate p_l. Note that the value $\mathbb{P}_{\mathcal{M},s}(\phi)$ does not depend on the actual p_l as long as p_l ensures that traces are long enough to allow reasoning about satisfaction of ϕ.

We estimate this probability via SMC [18]. For that, we associate Bernoulli random variables B_i with success probability p with simulations of the SUT. A realisation b_i is 1 if the corresponding sampled trace satisfies ϕ and 0 otherwise. To estimate $p = \mathbb{P}_{\mathcal{M},s}(\phi)$ we apply Monte Carlo simulation. Given n individual simulations, the estimate $\hat{p}$ is the observed relative success frequency, i.e. $\hat{p} = \sum_{i=1}^n \frac{b_i}{n}$. In order to bound the error of the estimation with a certain degree of confidence, we compute the number of required simulations based on a Chernoff bound [18,26]. This bound guarantees that if p is the true probability, then the distance between $\hat{p}$ and p is greater than or equal to some ϵ with a probability of at most δ, i.e. $\mathbb{P}(|\hat{p} - p| \geq \epsilon) \leq \delta$. The required number of simulations n and the parameters ϵ and δ are related by $\delta = 2e^{-2n\epsilon^2}$ [26], i.e. we compute n by

$$n = \left\lceil \frac{\ln(2) - \ln(\delta)}{2\epsilon^2} \right\rceil. \tag{2}$$

4   Probabilistic Black-Box Reachability Checking

We begin with an overview of the approach, discussing each of the steps briefly. Subsequently, we provide in-depth descriptions. For the remainder of this paper, we assume that we interact with an MDP $\mathcal{M} = \langle Q, \Sigma^{in}, \Sigma^{out}, q_0, \delta, L \rangle$ representing the SUT of which we only know Σ^{in}. Basically, we try to find an optimal scheduler for satisfying a given reachability property $\phi = F^{<k}\psi$ with the SUT $\mathcal{M}$. For this purpose, we iteratively sample system traces, learn models from the traces and infer schedulers from the learned models. The inferred schedulers also serve to refine the sampling strategy. This process is also shown in Fig. 1.

Create Initial Samples. The step collects a set of system traces through interaction with $\mathcal{M}$ by uniformly choosing and executing inputs from Σ^{in}.

For *maxRounds* rounds **do**:

  Infer Model. Given the system traces sampled so far, we use ALERGIA to infer an MDP $\mathcal{M}_{hi} = \langle Q_h, \Sigma^{in}, \Sigma^{out}_h, q_{0h}, \delta_h, L_h \rangle$, where h stands for hypothesis and $i \in [1 .. maxRounds]$ denotes the current round.

  Reachability Analysis. Reachability analysis on $\mathcal{M}_{hi}$ with PRISM [16]: i.e. we try to find the maximum probability $P_{\mathcal{M}_{hi}, s_i}(\phi)$ of satisfying ϕ as well as the corresponding scheduler s_i.

  Sample with Scheduler. We extend the set of traces by property-directed sampling unless we are in the last round. For that we choose some inputs according to scheduler s_i and some randomly. With increasing i, we decrease the portion of random choices.

Evaluate. After stopping the iteration, we evaluate the last scheduler we have found. For this evaluation, we sample system traces again, but avoid choosing inputs randomly. The relative frequency of satisfying ϕ now gives us an estimate for the success probability of executing $\mathcal{M}$, the black-box SUT, controlled by scheduler $s_{maxRounds}$. A Chernoff bound [18,26], which is commonly used in SMC, specifies the required number of samples.

Create Initial Samples. In the first step, we sample system traces by choosing input actions randomly according to a uniform distribution. Hence, we sample with a scheduler s_{unif} defined as follows: $\forall q \in Q, s_{unif} : q \mapsto \mu_{unif}(\Sigma^{in})$ where $\forall i \in \Sigma^{in} : \mu_{unif} : i \mapsto \frac{1}{|\Sigma^{in}|}$. Sampling is further controlled by the length probability p_l and by the batch size, i.e. the number of traces n_{batch} collected at once. These parameters also affect subsequent sampling. Additionally, we set a *seed*-value for the initialisation of pseudo-random functions.

As discussed in Sect. 3, we set $p_l(j) = 0$ for $j < k - 1$ if k is the step bound of the property we test for. This would not be necessary for learning but we generally apply this constraint. The length of suffixes, i.e. the trace extensions beyond k, follows a geometric distribution parameterised by $p_{quit} \in [0, 1]$. Before each step, we stop with probability p_{quit}. Hence, the number of input steps $|t|$ in a trace t is distributed according to $p_l(|t|) = (1 - p_{quit})^{|t|-k+1} p_{quit}$ for $|t| \geq k - 1$ and $p_l(|t|) = 0$ otherwise. Both p_{quit} and n_{batch} must be supplied by the user. In the following, $\mathcal{S}_i$ denotes the set of traces created by the ith sampling step, and $\mathcal{S}_{all}$ refers to the set of all traces. Hence, $\mathcal{S}_{all}$ is initially set to $\mathcal{S}_1$, containing n_{batch} traces distributed according to $\mathbb{P}^l_{\mathcal{M}, s_{unif}}$, collected by random testing.

Infer Model. In this step, we use a variant of ALERGIA [22,23] to infer an MDP $\mathcal{M}_{\mathrm{h}i} = \langle Q_{\mathrm{h}}, \Sigma^{\mathrm{in}}, \Sigma^{\mathrm{out}}_{\mathrm{h}}, q_{0\mathrm{h}}, \delta_{\mathrm{h}}, L_{\mathrm{h}} \rangle$, from $\mathcal{S}_i$, i.e. an approximate system model. Strictly speaking, we infer an MDP with a partial transition function, which we make input-complete with a function *complete*. The transition function of an inferred MDP may be undefined for some state-input pair if there is no corresponding execution in $\mathcal{S}_i$. For this reason, we add transitions to a special state labelled with *dontKnow* for undefined state-input pairs. Once we enter that state, we cannot leave it. Formally, we have $\mathcal{M}'_{\mathrm{h}} = \langle Q'_{\mathrm{h}}, \Sigma^{\mathrm{in}}, \Sigma^{\mathrm{out}\prime}_{\mathrm{h}}, q_{0\mathrm{h}}', \delta'_{\mathrm{h}}, L'_{\mathrm{h}} \rangle =$ ALERGIA$(\mathcal{S}_i, \epsilon_{\mathrm{ALERGIA}})$, and $\mathcal{M}_{\mathrm{h}i} = complete(\mathcal{M}'_{\mathrm{h}})$ where $Q_{\mathrm{h}} = Q'_{\mathrm{h}} \cup \{q_{\mathrm{undef}}\}$, $\Sigma^{\mathrm{out}}_{\mathrm{h}} = \Sigma^{\mathrm{out}\prime}_{\mathrm{h}} \cup \{dontKnow\}$, with $dontKnow \notin \Sigma^{\mathrm{out}\prime}_{\mathrm{h}}$, $q_{0\mathrm{h}}' = q_{0\mathrm{h}}$, $\delta_{\mathrm{h}} = \delta'_{\mathrm{h}} \cup \{(q_{\mathrm{undef}}, i) \mapsto \mathbf{1}_{\{q_{\mathrm{undef}}\}} | i \in \Sigma^{\mathrm{in}}\} \cup \{(q, i) \mapsto \mathbf{1}_{\{q_{\mathrm{undef}}\}} | q \in Q'_{\mathrm{h}}, i \in \Sigma^{\mathrm{in}}, \nexists d : (q, i) \mapsto d \in \delta'_{\mathrm{h}}\}$ and $L_{\mathrm{h}} = L'_{\mathrm{h}} \cup \{q_{\mathrm{undef}} \mapsto dontKnow\}$. Following the terminology of active automata learning [2], we refer to $\mathcal{M}_{\mathrm{h}i}$ as the current hypothesis.

Reachability Analysis. Given the current hypothesis inferred in the last step, we use the PRISM model checker [16] to derive a scheduler for satisfying the property ϕ. To accomplish this, we perform the following steps:

1. Translate $\mathcal{M}_{\mathrm{h}i}$ into the PRISM modelling language, whereby we encode
   1.1. states using integers
   1.2. inputs using commands labelled with actions, and
   1.3. outputs using labels.
2. Since PRISM only supports scheduler generation for unbounded reachability properties, we preprocess the translated $\mathcal{M}_{\mathrm{h}i}$ further [4] and encode ϕ as unbounded property:
   2.1. We add a step-counter variable *steps* ranging between 0 and k, corresponding to the trace length.
   2.2. The variable is incremented with every execution of an input.
   2.3. We change ϕ to $\phi' = F(\psi \wedge steps < k)$, i.e. we move the bound from the temporal operator to the property that should be reached.
3. Finally, we use the *sparse engine* of PRISM to compute the maximum probability $\max_s \mathbb{P}_{\mathcal{M}_{\mathrm{h}i},s}(\phi')$ for satisfying ϕ' and export the corresponding scheduler $s_{\mathrm{h}i}$, i.e. we verify the property `Pmax=?[F(psi & steps < k)]`.

PRISM exports memoryless deterministic schedulers for such properties. These schedulers, however, do not define input choices for all states, but only for states reachable by the composition of scheduler and corresponding model. We use $s_{\mathrm{h}i}(q) = \bot$ to denote that $s_{\mathrm{h}i}$ does not define a choice for $q \in Q_{\mathrm{h}}$.

Sample with Scheduler. Property-directed sampling with inferred schedulers aims at exploring parts of the system more thoroughly that have been identified as being relevant to the property. To avoid getting trapped in local minima, we also try explore new paths by choosing actions randomly with a certain probability $p_{\mathrm{rand}i}$, where i corresponds to the current round. This probability is decreased in each round to explore more broadly in the beginning and focus on relevant parts in later rounds. Therefor, the user has to set two parameters: $p_{\mathrm{start}} \in [0, 1]$

Algorithm 1. Property-Directed Sampling

Input: p_{rand_i}, $\mathcal{M}_{\mathrm{h}_i}$, s_{h_i}, n_{batch}, $\phi = F^{<k}\psi$, $\mathcal{S}_{\mathrm{all}}$, c_{change}
Output: $p_{\mathrm{rand}_{i+1}}$, $\mathcal{S}_{i+1}$, $\mathcal{S}_{\mathrm{all}}$
1: $\mathcal{S}_{i+1} \leftarrow \{\}$
2: **while** $|\mathcal{S}_{i+1}| < n_{\mathrm{batch}}$ **do**
3:    $\mathcal{S}_{i+1} \leftarrow \mathcal{S}_{i+1} \cup \{\mathrm{SAMPLE}(p_{\mathrm{rand}_i}, \mathcal{M}_{\mathrm{h}_i}, s_{\mathrm{h}_i}, k)\}$
4: $p_{\mathrm{rand}_{i+1}} \leftarrow p_{\mathrm{rand}_i} \cdot c_{\mathrm{change}}$
5: $\mathcal{S}_{\mathrm{all}} \leftarrow \mathcal{S}_{\mathrm{all}} \cup \mathcal{S}_{i+1}$
6: **function** SAMPLE($p_{\mathrm{rand}_i}, \mathcal{M}_{\mathrm{h}}, s_{\mathrm{h}}, k$)
7:    $trace \leftarrow reset()$
8:    $q_{\mathrm{curr}} \leftarrow q_{0\mathrm{h}}$
9:    **while** $|trace| - 1 < k \vee \neg coinFlip(p_{\mathrm{quit}})$ **do**
10:       **if** $coinFlip(p_{\mathrm{rand}_i}) \vee q_{\mathrm{curr}} = \bot \vee s_{\mathrm{h}}(q_{\mathrm{curr}}) = \bot$ **then**
11:          $input \leftarrow randSel(\Sigma^{\mathrm{in}})$
12:       **else**
13:          $input \leftarrow s_{\mathrm{h}}(q_{\mathrm{curr}})$
14:       $outSut \leftarrow exec(input)$
15:       $trace \leftarrow trace \cdot (input \cdot outSut)$
16:       $distQ_{\mathrm{curr}} = \delta_{\mathrm{h}}(q_{\mathrm{curr}}, input)$
17:       $q_{\mathrm{curr}} \leftarrow \begin{cases} q \in Q_{\mathrm{h}} & \text{such that } L_{\mathrm{h}}(q) = outSut \wedge distQ_{\mathrm{curr}}(q) > 0 \\ \bot & \text{if there is no such } q \end{cases}$
18:    **return** $trace$

---

for the initial probability and $c_{\mathrm{change}} \in [0, 1]$ specifying an exponential decrease, i.e. $p_{\mathrm{rand}_1} = p_{\mathrm{start}}$ and $p_{\mathrm{rand}_{i+1}} = c_{\mathrm{change}} \cdot p_{\mathrm{rand}_i}$.

Basically, we execute both SUT and $\mathcal{M}_{\mathrm{h}_i}$ in parallel. The former ensures that we sample traces of the actual system while the latter is necessary because the inferred scheduler s_{h_i} is defined for $\mathcal{M}_{\mathrm{h}_i}$. Stated differently, we need to simulate the path taken by the SUT on the current hypothesis $\mathcal{M}_{\mathrm{h}_i}$ as well. Doing that enables to select actions with s_{h_i}. However, as $\mathcal{M}_{\mathrm{h}_i}$ is an approximation, two scenarios may occur in which we cannot use s_{h_i}:

– The SUT may show outputs not foreseen by $\mathcal{M}_{\mathrm{h}_i}$, i.e. not only probabilities differ. In such cases, we cannot determine the correct state transition in $\mathcal{M}_{\mathrm{h}_i}$.
– By performing random inputs we may follow a path, that is not optimal with respect to $\mathcal{M}_{\mathrm{h}_i}$ and ϕ. Thus, we may enter a state where s_{h_i} is undefined.

In both kinds of scenarios we default to choosing inputs randomly. The sampling is detailed in Algorithm 1. In the taxonomy of Utting et al. [33], it can be categorised as model-checking-based online testing with a combination of requirements coverage and random input-selection as criterion. In addition to artefacts generated by other steps, sampling requires two auxiliary operations: *reset*, which resets the SUT to the initial state and returns the unique initial output symbol, and *exec* which executes a single input changing the state of the SUT and returning the corresponding output. Both operations are realised by a test adapter. Note that Lines 10 to 17 implement a randomised scheduler derived from s_{h_i}. We will refer to this scheduler as *randomised*(s_{h_i}).

Evaluate. As a result of the reachability analysis, PRISM calculates a probability of reaching ϕ. This probability, however, is derived from a learned model which is possibly inaccurate. Therefore, it may greatly differ from the actual probability of reachability with the SUT. To account for that, we evaluate the scheduler $s_h = s_{h\,maxRounds}$ inferred in the last round. We accomplish this by sampling a set of traces $\mathcal{S}_{eval}$, while generally selecting inputs with s_h, i.e. we execute Algorithm 1 with $p_{rand\,i} = 0$. Thereby, we implicitly sample traces from the DTMC induced by the composition of $\mathcal{M}$ and $randomised(s_h)$. Since this DTMC behaves entirely probabilistic, we can apply SMC. Hence, we estimate $\mathbb{P}_{\mathcal{M},randomised(s_h)}(\phi)$ by $\hat{p}_{\mathcal{M},s_h} = \frac{|\{s \in \mathcal{S}_{eval} | s \models \phi\}|}{|\mathcal{S}_{eval}|}$. To achieve a given error bound with a given confidence, we compute the required number of samples $|\mathcal{S}_{eval}| = n_{batch}$ based on a Chernoff bound [26], i.e. we apply (2). The estimation provides an approximate lower bound of the maximal reachability probability with the SUT.

Convergence and Application. Intuitively, more samples cover the system more thoroughly and therefore, inferred models should be closer to the true model. Correspondingly, inferred schedulers should be closer to the optimal scheduler with increasing number of rounds. Hence, from an intuitive viewpoint n_{batch} and *maxRounds* should be chosen as large as possible. Generally, Mao et al. [23] showed convergence in the large sample limit for ALERGIA. In our case, this entails that the inferred schedulers should converge to the optimal scheduler. However, to transfer these results we would have to restrict the choice of $\epsilon_{ALERGIA}$ and study the influence of our property-directed sampling approach on convergence.

We have observed in experiments that probability estimations converge to the optimal value with increasing number of rounds. Therefore, we are currently working on techniques for detecting convergence. Basically, we statistically test for equivalence between probability estimations derived from samples collected in subsequent rounds. This may allow early stopping and save simulation costs, but may also impair results. As this requires further investigation, we fix the number of rounds *maxRounds* in Sect. 5. Apart from convergence, it may not always be necessary to find a (near-) optimal scheduler. A requirement may state that the probability of reaching an erroneous state must be smaller than some p. Once we found and evaluated a scheduler s_h such that the estimation $\hat{p}_{\mathcal{M},s_h} \geq p$, we basically show with some confidence that the requirement is violated.

We will now briefly discuss the choice of parameters taking our findings into account. The product $n_s = n_{batch} \cdot maxRounds$ defines the overall number of samples for inference, thus it could be chosen as large as the testing/simulation budget permits. Increasing *maxRounds* while fixing n_s increases the time required for model inference and model checking. Intuitively, it improves accuracy as well, as sampling is more frequently adjusted towards the considered property. For the systems we considered, values in the range between 50 and 150 led to reasonable accuracy while incurring acceptable runtime overhead. The value of p_{start} should generally be larger than 0.5, while c_{change} should be close to 1. This ensures broad exploration in the beginning and more directed exploration afterwards. Finally, the choice of p_{quit} depends on the simulation budget and may require domain knowledge. If we, e.g., expect a long initialisation phase, p_{quit} should be low to ensure long tests.

5   Experiments

We evaluated our approach on three case studies from the area of automata learning. For the first case study, we created our own model of the slot machine discussed described by Mao et al. [23] in the context of learning MDPs. The other two case studies consider models of network protocols enhanced with stochastic failures. For that, we transformed deterministic Mealy-machine models inferred via active automata learning as follows:

- Translate Mealy machine into Moore machine: this effectively creates an MDP $\mathcal{M} = \langle Q, \Sigma^{\text{in}}, \Sigma^{\text{out}}, q_0, \delta, L \rangle$ with a non-probabilistic δ.
- Extend Σ^{out} with a new symbol $crash$ and add q_{cr} to Q with $L(q_{\text{cr}}) = crash$.
- For a user-defined probability p_{cr} and for all o in a user-defined set $Crashing$:
  - Find all $q, q' \in Q$, $i \in \Sigma^{\text{in}}$ such that $\delta(q, i)(q') = 1$ and $L(q') = o$
  - Set $\delta(q, i)(q') = 1 - p_{\text{cr}}$ and $\delta(q, i)(q_{\text{cr}}) = p_{\text{cr}}$
  - For all $i \in \Sigma^{\text{in}}$ set $\delta(q_{\text{cr}}, i)(q_{\text{cr}}) = p_{\text{cr}}$ and $\delta(q_{\text{cr}}, i)(q_0) = 1 - p_{\text{cr}}$

Basically, this simulates stochastic failures of outputs belonging to a set $Crashing$. Instead of producing the correct outputs, we output $crash$ and reach a $crash$ state with a certain probability. With the same probability we stay in this state and otherwise we reset the system to q_0 after the crash.

We have complete information of all three case studies. This allows us to compare our results to optimal values. Nevertheless, for evaluation we treat the systems as black boxes. The state spaces of the models without step-counter variables for bounded reachability are of sizes 471, 63, and 157 respectively.

Measurement Setup and Criteria. For a black-box MDP $\mathcal{M}$ and a reachability property ϕ, we compare three approaches to find schedulers s for $\mathbb{P}_{\mathcal{M},s}(\phi)$:

Incremental Scheduler Inference. We apply the incremental approach discussed in Sect. 4. Inferred schedulers are denoted by s_{inc}.

Monolithic Scheduler Inference. To check if the incremental refinement of inferred models pays off, we use the same approach but set $maxRounds = 1$. In other words, we sample traces by solely choosing inputs randomly. Based on this, we perform a single round, inferring a model and a scheduler which we evaluate. To balance the simulation budget, we collect $maxRounds \cdot n_{\text{batch}}$ traces, where $maxRounds$ and n_{batch} are the parameter settings for inferring s_{inc}. We denote monolithically inferred schedulers by s_{mono}.

Uniform Scheduler Inference. As a baseline for comparison we compare to the randomised scheduler s_{unif} which chooses inputs according to a uniform distribution. This resembles random testing without additional knowledge.

Furthermore, let $s_{\text{opt}} = \text{argmax}_s \mathbb{P}_{\mathcal{M},s}(\phi)$ be the optimal scheduler.

As the most important measure of quality, we compare estimates of $\mathbb{P}_{\mathcal{M},s}(\phi)$ to the maximal probability $\mathbb{P}_{\mathcal{M},s_{\text{opt}}}(\phi)$. We consider a scheduler s to be *near optimal*, if the estimate $\hat{p}_{\mathcal{M},s}$ of $\mathbb{P}_{\mathcal{M},s}(\phi)$ derived via SMC is approximately equal to $\mathbb{P}_{\mathcal{M},s_{\text{opt}}}(\phi)$, i.e. $|\hat{p}_{\mathcal{M},s} - \mathbb{P}_{\mathcal{M},s_{\text{opt}}}(\phi)| \leq \epsilon$, for an $\epsilon > 0$. In the following, we use the same ϵ for deciding near optimality as for applying the Chernoff bound (2).

Generally, we try to balance the number of test steps for all approaches, but will discuss computation cost briefly. Finally, we discuss estimations based on model checking inferred models $\mathcal{M}_h$ if possible, i.e. $\max_s \mathbb{P}_{\mathcal{M}_h,s}(\phi)$ calculated by PRISM [16]. These estimations have also been discussed by Mao et al. [23]. They noted that estimations may differ significantly from optimal values in some cases, but generally represent good approximations.

Implementation and Settings. We base the evaluation on our Java implementation of the described technique which can be found at [28]. All experiments were performed with a Lenovo Thinkpad T450 with 16 GB RAM and an Intel Core i7-5600U CPU operating at 2.6 GHz and running Xubuntu Linux 14.04. The systems were modelled with PRISM [16]. PRISM served three purposes:

- We exported the state, transition, and label information from models. This information was used for simulation in a black-box fashion.
- The maximal probabilities were computed via PRISM.
- PRISM's scheduler generation was used for scheduler inference.

Simulation as well as certain aspects discussed in Sect. 4 are controlled by probabilistic choices. To ensure reproducibility we used fixed seeds for pseudo-random number generators controlling the choices. All experiments were run with 20 different seeds. The discussion considers statistics derived from 20 such runs. For the evaluation of schedulers, we applied a Chernoff bound with $\epsilon = 0.01$ and $\delta = 0.01$. Following [23], we used a data-dependent significance level for the compatibility check of ALERGIA, we concretely set $\epsilon_{\text{ALERGIA}} = 100/N$, where N is the combined length of all strings used for inference. As suggested in Sect. 4, we aim at ensuring broad exploration in the beginning and property-directed exploration in later rounds. Therefore, we set $p_{\text{start}} = 0.75$ and $c_{\text{change}} = 0.95$.

Slot Machine. The slot machine was analysed in the context of MDP inference before [23]. Basically, it has three reels which are initially blank and which either show *apple* or *bar* after spinning (one input per reel). With increasing number of spins the probability of bar decreases. A player is given a number of spins m, after which one of three prizes is awarded depending on the reel configuration. A fourth input leads with equal probability either to two extra spins (with a maximum of m), or to stopping the game prematurely including issuance of prizes. For the evaluation, we reimplemented the model, therefore probabilities and state space differ from [23]. As property, we investigated reaching the output *Pr10* if $m = 5$, representing a prize that is awarded after stopping the game if all reels show bar. For that, we set $p_{\text{quit}} = 0.05$, $maxRounds = 100$, and $n_{\text{batch}} = 500$.

In Fig. 3a (Fig. 3b), we show box plots of the probability estimations for reaching *Pr10* in less than 8 (14) steps. The black boxes correspond to the incremental approach, the blue to the monolithic approach, and the dashed line marks the optimal probability. Note that estimations may be slightly larger than the optimal value in rare cases because they are based on simulations. The applied Chernoff bound gives a confidence value for staying within error bound

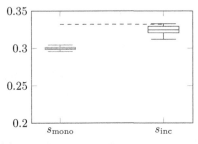
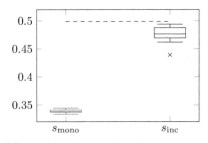

(a) Reaching *Pr10* in less than 8 steps.   (b) Reaching *Pr10* in less than 14 steps.

Fig. 3. Simulation-based probability estimations of reaching *Pr10*.

ϵ in case we actually found an optimal scheduler. Estimations with the baseline s_{unif} are fairly constant, approximately 0.012 for 8 and 0.019 for 14 steps. As estimations with s_{mono} and s_{inc} are significantly higher, this shows that our approach positively influences the probability of reaching a desired event. We further see that the incremental approach performs better than the monolithic, whereby the gap increases with step size. Unlike the monolithic approach, the incremental approach finds near-optimal schedulers in both cases. However, the relative number of near-optimal schedulers decreases with increasing step bound.

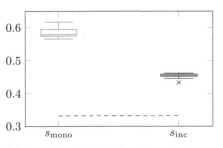
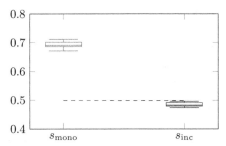

(a) Reaching *Pr10* in less than 8 steps.   (b) Reaching *Pr10* in less than 14 steps.

Fig. 4. Model-checking-based probability estimations of reaching *Pr10*.

Alternatively to simulation-based estimation, estimations may be based on model checking an inferred model [23]. For that, a model $\mathcal{M}_{\text{h}}$ is inferred, either incrementally or in a single step, and then a probabilistic model-checker calculates $\max_s P_{\mathcal{M}_{\text{h}},s}(\phi)$. While this reduces the simulation cost, the inferred probability may differ significantly from $\max_s P_{\mathcal{M},s}(\phi)$, with $\mathcal{M}$ being the black-box system. Figures 4a and 4b show model-checking-based estimations of reaching *Pr10* in less than 8 and 14 steps respectively. Here, s_{mono} denotes that the models $\mathcal{M}_{\text{h}}$ were inferred in one step, while s_{inc} denotes incremental mode-inference. The figures demonstrate that these estimations differ greatly from estimations taking the actual system into account. The monolithic approach overestimates in both cases. The incremental approach leads to more accurate but still too large estimates in Fig. 4a. Hence, the simulation-based estimations are more reliable.

MQTT with Stochastic Failures. This case study is based on a Mealy-machine model of an MQTT [3] broker. More concretely, we translated a model of the EMQ [12] broker interacting with two clients into a Moore machine and added stochastic failures. We discussed the active learning of the model in [31]. Failures were added to connection acknowledgements and subscription acknowledgements for the second client, whereby we set $p_{cr} = 0.1$. For the evaluation we infer schedulers s maximising $\mathbb{P}_{\mathcal{M},s}(F^{<k} crash)$ for $k \in \{5, 8, 11, 14, 17\}$. For the sampling we set $p_{quit} = 0.025$. While this leads to samples longer than necessary for evaluation, e.g., for $k = 5$ the expected length is 43, this increases the chance of seeing $crash$ in a sample which is reflected in inferred models. The simulation budget is limited by $maxRounds = 60$, and $n_{batch} = 100$.

Figure 5 shows box plots for the different approaches, where red boxes correspond to s_{unif}, blue ones to s_{mono} and black ones to s_{inc}. The dashed line is the optimal probability achieved with s_{opt}. The box plots demonstrate that larger probabilities are achievable with model-inference-based approaches than with random testing.

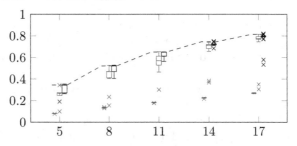

Fig. 5. MQTT: box plots of probability estimations of different inference approaches.

It also shows that the incremental approach achieves near-optimal results more reliably. While both inference-based approaches find at least one near-optimal scheduler out of 20, the probabilities achieved by incremental inference are generally higher. We also see that for large k and especially for s_{inc}, most estimations are in a very small range near to the optimal values. Some outliers approximate the optimal probability quite well, while a few are also significantly lower. Therefore, it makes sense to infer multiple schedulers and discard those performing poorly.

TCP with Stochastic Failures. This case study builds upon a Mealy-machine model of Ubuntu's TCP server learned by Fiterău-Broştean et al. [13,32]. In previous work [1], we have shown that conformance testing of this system is challenging. Here we consider a version with random crashes with $p_{cr} = 0.05$, as discussed in the beginning of this section. We mutated transitions to states outputting an

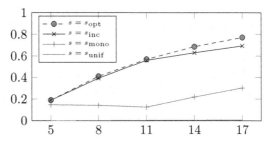

Fig. 6. TCP: average probability estimations of different inference approaches.

acknowledgement which increments both sequence and acknowledgement numbers. For the evaluation, we infer schedulers for $\mathbb{P}_{\mathcal{M},s}(F^{<k}crash)$ with $k \in \{5, 8, 11, 14, 17\}$ and we set $maxRounds = 120$, and $n_{\text{batch}} = 250$.

Figure 6 shows average probability estimations of different schedulers. It demonstrates that random testing is insufficient in this case to reliably reach crashes of the system. Uniform input selection is successful in only 0.7% of the traces for $k = 17$. It further shows that the incremental approach pays off, i.e. it generates near-optimal schedulers, even for this apparently challenging system. Larger bounds, however, cause difficulties in this case study as well. Further analysis shows that the mean values are affected by some outliers. The third quartiles of the probability estimations for the incremental approach are near optimal for all k. As before, this suggests that it would make sense to infer schedulers with different seeds and select the best one. Still, the large difference between the mean values of the estimations $\hat{p}_{\mathcal{M},s_{\text{mono}}}$ and $\hat{p}_{\mathcal{M},s_{\text{inc}}}$ shows that the incremental is more reliable than the monolithic approach.

Runtime. While we simulated previously learned models for the evaluation, the simulation cost would dominate the runtime of the process in general testing scenarios. For instance for the TCP case study, the model-inference and model-checking steps required by incremental inference take on average 13 min if $k = 17$. The monolithic approach performs these steps only once and therefore needs only 13 s on average for such computations. Both approaches, however, require about $1.7 \cdot 10^6$ simulation steps. Assuming each step to take about 10 ms on a real system, the simulation duration would amount to about 4.7 h, thus the incremental runtime overhead is low in comparison. Similar observations can be made for other case studies.

6   Conclusion

We presented an approach to infer near-optimal schedulers for reachability objectives of MDPs. To our knowledge, it is the first such approach to be applicable in a purely black-box setting, where only the input interface is known. This is accomplished by incrementally refining the knowledge about the system, via model inference and based on that property-directed exploration of the system. Section 5 presents promising results, showing that near-optimality can be achieved.

Therefore, we plan to investigate this approach further and extend it. As a first step, we will carry out more case studies. In particular, we are interested in applications for compositional verification. We are also studying the applicability in different testing scenarios. In a testing context, e.g., Nachmanson et al. [24] discussed strategies for bounded reachability games, but with a given model.

Furthermore, non-functional properties like execution time could be considered. For that, we need to devise a model-inference technique which considers both non-deterministic choice of inputs and (continuous) time. Current approaches for probabilistic timed systems do not account for non-determinism of this form [23,34]. If we had such a technique we could, e.g., use PRISM with the digital clocks engine [16] or UPPAAL Stratego [9,10] to infer schedulers. Another possible extension would be to consider more general properties than reachability. This would require replacing PRISM's scheduler generation in our approach. In conclusion, we believe that our results are encouraging and that there are many promising directions for future research.

Acknowledgment. This work was supported by the TU Graz LEAD project "Dependable Internet of Things in Adverse Environments". The authors would like to thank the LEAD project members Roderick Bloem, Masoud Ebrahimi, Franz Pernkopf, Franz Röck, and Tobias Schrank for fruitful discussions.

References

1. Aichernig, B.K., Tappler, M.: Learning from faults: mutation testing in active automata learning. In: Barrett, C., Davies, M., Kahsai, T. (eds.) NFM 2017. LNCS, vol. 10227, pp. 19–34. Springer, Cham (2017). doi:10.1007/978-3-319-57288-8_2
2. Angluin, D.: Learning regular sets from queries and counterexamples. Inf. Comput. **75**(2), 87–106 (1987). doi:10.1016/0890-5401(87)90052-6
3. Banks, A., Gupta, R. (eds.): MQTT Version 3.1.1. OASIS Standard, October 2014. http://docs.oasis-open.org/mqtt/mqtt/v3.1.1/os/mqtt-v3.1.1-os.html, latest version. http://docs.oasis-open.org/mqtt/mqtt/v3.1.1/os/mqtt-v3.1.1-os.html
4. Brázdil, T., Chatterjee, K., Chmelik, M., Forejt, V., Kretínský, J., Kwiatkowska, M.Z., Parker, D., Ujma, M.: Verification of Markov decision processes using learning algorithms. In: Cassez and Raskin [6], pp. 98–114. http://dx.doi.org/10.1007/978-3-319-11936-6_8
5. Carrasco, R.C., Oncina, J.: Learning stochastic regular grammars by means of a state merging method. In: Carrasco, R.C., Oncina, J. (eds.) ICGI 1994. LNCS, vol. 862, pp. 139–152. Springer, Heidelberg (1994). doi:10.1007/3-540-58473-0_144
6. Cassez, F., Raskin, J.-F. (eds.): ATVA 2014. LNCS, vol. 8837. Springer, Cham (2014)
7. Chen, Y., Nielsen, T.D.: Active learning of Markov decision processes for system verification. In: 11th International Conference on Machine Learning and Applications, ICMLA, Boca Raton, FL, USA, December 12–15, 2012, vol. 2, pp. 289–294. IEEE (2012). http://dx.doi.org/10.1109/ICMLA.2012.158
8. D'Argenio, P., Legay, A., Sedwards, S., Traonouez, L.: Smart sampling for lightweight verification of Markov decision processes. STTT **17**(4), 469–484 (2015). doi:10.1007/s10009-015-0383-0
9. David, A., Jensen, P.G., Larsen, K.G., Legay, A., Lime, D., Sørensen, M.G., Taankvist, J.H.: On time with minimal expected cost!. In: Cassez and Raskin [6], pp. 129–145. http://dx.doi.org/10.1007/978-3-319-11936-6_10
10. David, A., Jensen, P.G., Larsen, K.G., Mikučionis, M., Taankvist, J.H.: UPPAAL STRATEGO . In: Baier, C., Tinelli, C. (eds.) TACAS 2015. LNCS, vol. 9035, pp. 206–211. Springer, Heidelberg (2015). doi:10.1007/978-3-662-46681-0_16
11. Elkind, E., Genest, B., Peled, D., Qu, H.: Grey-box checking. In: Najm, E., Pradat-Peyre, J.-F., Donzeau-Gouge, V.V. (eds.) FORTE 2006. LNCS, vol. 4229, pp. 420–435. Springer, Heidelberg (2006). doi:10.1007/11888116_30
12. EMQ. http://emqtt.io/. Accessed 07 May 2017

13. Fiterău-Broştean, P., Janssen, R., Vaandrager, F.: Combining model learning and model checking to analyze TCP implementations. In: Chaudhuri, S., Farzan, A. (eds.) CAV 2016. LNCS, vol. 9780, pp. 454–471. Springer, Cham (2016). doi:10.1007/978-3-319-41540-6_25
14. Forejt, V., Kwiatkowska, M., Norman, G., Parker, D.: Automated verification techniques for probabilistic systems. In: Bernardo, M., Issarny, V. (eds.) SFM 2011. LNCS, vol. 6659, pp. 53–113. Springer, Heidelberg (2011). doi:10.1007/978-3-642-21455-4_3
15. Groce, A., Peled, D., Yannakakis, M.: Adaptive model checking. In: Katoen, J.-P., Stevens, P. (eds.) TACAS 2002. LNCS, vol. 2280, pp. 357–370. Springer, Heidelberg (2002). doi:10.1007/3-540-46002-0_25
16. Kwiatkowska, M., Norman, G., Parker, D.: PRISM 4.0: verification of probabilistic real-time systems. In: Gopalakrishnan, G., Qadeer, S. (eds.) CAV 2011. LNCS, vol. 6806, pp. 585–591. Springer, Heidelberg (2011). doi:10.1007/978-3-642-22110-1_47
17. Kwiatkowska, M., Parker, D.: Automated verification and strategy synthesis for probabilistic systems. In: Hung, D., Ogawa, M. (eds.) ATVA 2013. LNCS, vol. 8172, pp. 5–22. Springer, Cham (2013). doi:10.1007/978-3-319-02444-8_2
18. Larsen, K.G., Legay, A.: Statistical model checking: past, present, and future. In: Margaria, T., Steffen, B. (eds.) ISoLA 2016. LNCS, vol. 9952, pp. 3–15. Springer, Cham (2016). doi:10.1007/978-3-319-47166-2_1
19. Legay, A., Delahaye, B., Bensalem, S.: Statistical model checking: an overview. In: Barringer, H., Falcone, Y., Finkbeiner, B., Havelund, K., Lee, I., Pace, G., Roşu, G., Sokolsky, O., Tillmann, N. (eds.) RV 2010. LNCS, vol. 6418, pp. 122–135. Springer, Heidelberg (2010). doi:10.1007/978-3-642-16612-9_11
20. Legay, A., Sedwards, S., Traonouez, L.-M.: Scalable verification of Markov decision processes. In: Canal, C., Idani, A. (eds.) SEFM 2014. LNCS, vol. 8938, pp. 350–362. Springer, Cham (2015). doi:10.1007/978-3-319-15201-1_23
21. Mao, H., Chen, Y., Jaeger, M., Nielsen, T.D., Larsen, K.G., Nielsen, B.: Learning probabilistic automata for model checking. In: Eighth International Conference on Quantitative Evaluation of Systems, QEST 2011, Aachen, Germany, 5–8, pp. 111–120. IEEE Computer Society (2011). http://dx.doi.org/10.1109/QEST.2011.21
22. Mao, H., Chen, Y., Jaeger, M., Nielsen, T.D., Larsen, K.G., Nielsen, B.: Learning Markov decision processes for model checking. In: Fahrenberg, U., Legay, A., Thrane, C.R. (eds.) Proceedings Quantities in Formal Methods, QFM 2012, Paris, France, 28. EPTCS, vol. 103, pp. 49–63 (2012). http://dx.doi.org/10.4204/EPTCS.103.6
23. Mao, H., Chen, Y., Jaeger, M., Nielsen, T.D., Larsen, K.G., Nielsen, B.: Learning deterministic probabilistic automata from a model checking perspective. Mach. Learn. 105(2), 255–299 (2016). doi:10.1007/s10994-016-5565-9
24. Nachmanson, L., Veanes, M., Schulte, W., Tillmann, N., Grieskamp, W.: Optimal strategies for testing nondeterministic systems. In: Avrunin, G.S., Rothermel, G. (eds.) Proceedings of the ACM/SIGSOFT International Symposium on Software Testing and Analysis, ISSTA 2004, Boston, Massachusetts, USA, July 11–14, 2004, pp. 55–64. ACM (2004). http://doi.acm.org/10.1145/1007512.1007520
25. Nouri, A., Raman, B., Bozga, M., Legay, A., Bensalem, S.: Faster statistical model checking by means of abstraction and learning. In: Bonakdarpour, B., Smolka, S.A. (eds.) RV 2014. LNCS, vol. 8734, pp. 340–355. Springer, Cham (2014). doi:10.1007/978-3-319-11164-3_28
26. Okamoto, M.: Some inequalities relating to the partial sum of binomial probabilities. Ann. Inst. Stat. Math. 10(1), 29–35 (1959). doi:10.1007/BF02883985

27. Peled, D., Vardi, M.Y., Yannakakis, M.: Black box checking. In: Wu, J., Chanson, S.T., Gao, Q. (eds.) Formal Methods for Protocol Engineering and Distributed Systems. IAICT, vol. 28, pp. 225–240. Springer, Boston, MA (1999). doi:10.1007/978-0-387-35578-8_13

28. prob-black-reach - Java implementation of probabilistic black-box reachability checking. https://github.com/mtappler/prob-black-reach. Accessed 07 May 2017

29. Sen, K., Viswanathan, M., Agha, G.: Statistical model checking of black-box probabilistic systems. In: Alur, R., Peled, D.A. (eds.) CAV 2004. LNCS, vol. 3114, pp. 202–215. Springer, Heidelberg (2004). doi:10.1007/978-3-540-27813-9_16

30. Shu, G., Lee, D.: Testing security properties of protocol implementations - a machine learning based approach. In: 27th IEEE International Conference on Distributed Computing Systems (ICDCS 2007), June 25–29, 2007, Toronto, Ontario, Canada, p. 25. IEEE Computer Society (2007). http://dx.doi.org/10.1109/ICDCS.2007.147

31. Tappler, M., Aichernig, B.K., Bloem, R.: Model-based testing IoT communication via active automata learning. In: ICST 2017, pp. 276–287. IEEE Computer Society (2017)

32. TCP models. https://gitlab.science.ru.nl/pfiteraubrostean/tcp-learner/tree/cav-aec/models. Accessed 07 May 2017

33. Utting, M., Pretschner, A., Legeard, B.: A taxonomy of model-based testing approaches. Softw. Test., Verif. Reliab. 22(5), 297–312 (2012). doi:10.1002/stvr.456

34. Verwer, S., Weerdt, M., Witteveen, C.: A likelihood-ratio test for identifying probabilistic deterministic real-time automata from positive data. In: Sempere, J.M., García, P. (eds.) ICGI 2010. LNCS (LNAI), vol. 6339, pp. 203–216. Springer, Heidelberg (2010). doi:10.1007/978-3-642-15488-1_17

35. Wang, J., Sun, J., Qin, S.: Verifying complex systems probabilistically through learning, abstraction and refinement. CoRR abs/1610.06371 (2016). http://arxiv.org/abs/1610.06371

36. Younes, H.L.S.: Probabilistic verification for "Black-Box" systems. In: Etessami, K., Rajamani, S.K. (eds.) CAV 2005. LNCS, vol. 3576, pp. 253–265. Springer, Heidelberg (2005). doi:10.1007/11513988_25

Combining Symbolic Runtime Enforcers for Cyber-Physical Systems

Björn Andersson$^{(\boxtimes)}$, Sagar Chaki, and Dionisio de Niz

Carnegie Mellon University, Pittsburgh, USA
{baandersson,chaki,dionisio}@sei.cmu.edu

Abstract. The problem of composing multiple, possibly conflicting, runtime enforcers for a cyber-physical system (CPS) is considered. A formal definition of utility-agnostic and utility-maximizing CPS enforcers is presented, followed by an algorithm to combine multiple enforcers, and resolve their conflicts based on a design-time prioritization. To implement this combination in an efficient manner, enforcers are encoded symbolically using SMT formulas, and the combination is reduced to a set of SMT satisfiability and optimization operations. Further performance gains are achieved by using the SMT solvers incrementally. The approach is validated via experiments in an indoor area with Parrot minidrones. The incremental enforcer combination is shown to achieve an order of magnitude speedup, and no deadline misses.

1 Introduction

Cyber-Physical Systems (CPS) are "engineered systems that are built from, and depend upon, the seamless integration of computational algorithms and physical components" [1]. They play numeroussafety-critical roles in our day-to-day lives, e.g., in the form of cars, airplanes, nuclear power plants, and medical devices. Verifying safe behavior of CPS is thus an important challenge. At the same time, modern CPS are incorporating advanced AI techniques, such as machine learning, to deliver more features and capabilities. Examples include driverless cars, intelligent patient monitors, and smart home appliances. On the one hand, the added intelligence allows the CPS to operate more effectively and with less human supervision. On the other hand, it also makes "static verification" of the CPS inadequate since the system evolves during operation, and the complete set of its behaviors cannot be modeled precisely prior to deployment.

Some form of "runtime verification" is therefore indispensable for achieving high assurance about the safe behavior of CPS. In this paper, we explore the concept of runtime assurance [15] (RA). Broadly, RA involves adding a runtime monitor (which we call the enforcer) that observes the behavior of the CPS, and intervenes to prevent specific CPS behaviors that could lead to catastrophic results. In particular, if we think of a CPS as a control system, then the enforcer observes, and modifies as needed, actuation signals emitted by the CPS software that determine the CPS's interaction with its physical environment.

© Springer International Publishing AG 2017
S. Lahiri and G. Reger (Eds.): RV 2017, LNCS 10548, pp. 68–84, 2017.
DOI: 10.1007/978-3-319-67531-2_5

In this paper, we address the challenge of soundly composing multiple enforcers that operate on the same set of actuators of a CPS. This is important since a complex CPS has multiple safety-critical requirements involving the same set of actuators that are not guaranteed to be consistent under all situations. Consider two quadcopters (QCs) flying in an open area. Each QC has two enforcers: E_1 attempts to keep the QC within a specific GPS boundary (geo-fencing) and E_2 attempts to keep the QCs at a minimum distance from each other (collision avoidance). Then, in the situation where one QC is backed up against the geo-fence boundary by the other, the two-enforcers produce conflicting actuations – E_1 wants to move the QC away from the boundary (thus closer to the other QC), while E_2 wants to do the opposite. To address this challenge, we make the following contributions.

First, we formalize the logical behavior of enforcers. Intuitively, an enforcer is an algorithm that executes periodically and computes an appropriate actuation based on the observed system state and the command proposed by the application software. Next, we present an algorithm, called select, that combines multiple enforcers ordered by priority. Specifically, select computes an actuation that satisfies a subset of enforcers — determined by the priorities of enforcers. We also present a variant of select, called select* that is utility-maximizing, i.e., computes a legal actuation with maximal utility.

Next, we show how enforcers can be encoded logically using Satisfiability Modulo Theories (SMT) formulas, and how to implement select and select* using optimizing SMT solvers. Our symbolic encoding allows enforcers to be expressed succinctly, and enforcer compositions turn naturally into common logical operations. Thus, we bring into RA the benefits of symbolic reasoning, which have been leveraged in other verification domains over the past decades. CPS enforcers have to be very efficient in order to run with short periods (dictated by the application) and yet be guaranteed that each enforcer finishes execution before the enforcer is requested to execute again. To this end, we present *online* implementations of select and select*, denoted by select† and select*†, that use the SMT solver incrementally, "pushing" and "popping" formulas into dynamically created "contexts," as needed. We present pseudo-code for all variants of select and argue about their correctness.

We used our approach to implement the geo-fencing (a.k.a. tether) and separation enforcers targeting Parrot minidrones. We validated empirically that both enforcers work as expected, individually and in composition, in an indoor area. We also measured the performance of various threads under different variants of the select algorithm. These measurements indicate that our symbolic enforcers are quite efficient, with execution times in the range of tens of milliseconds. Furthermore, our online implementation of enforcers yields an order of magnitude speedup in execution time; thanks to this speedup, in our experiments, we observe zero deadline misses over tens of thousands of invocations.

The rest of the paper is organized as follows. Section 2 surveys related work. Section 3 presents the formal definition of CPS enforcers and their composition. Section 4 presents the symbolic encoding and implementation of enforcers using SMT formulas and optimizing SMT solvers. Section 5 presents our experiments and results, and Sect. 6 concludes.

2   Related Work

A brief overview of runtime enforcement techniques is available in [9,12]. Seto et al. [20] proposed the "Simplex" architecture for resilient control systems, where a monitor switches a system from a complex and more capable, but untrusted, controller C_{comp} to a simple but trusted controller C_{simp}, whenever the system is in danger of becoming unstable. The main focus of this work is on deciding the switching boundary based on control theory. Bak et al. [2] have developed a version of Simplex that combines offline analysis with hybrid reachability at runtime to further push the envelope of recoverability. We focus on efficient implementations of the switching logic, and combining multiple enforcers.

The idea of runtime monitoring has also been used in the context of formal verification [10,11]. The key idea is to check for violations of a target safety property at runtime. This is more tractable than complete static verification since we are only analyzing the states that are reached during execution. Our approach is aimed at implementing runtime monitors using SMT solvers, and resolving conflicting actuation decisions.

In the domain of security, Schneider proposed "security automata" [19] as a formalism to express properties whose violations can be detected at runtime. Originally, security automata were passive, i.e., they only monitored the system for safety violations. Restricted versions of this has been considered: Viswanathan [21, Sect. 4.3] studied the case that the enforcer must be decidable and Fong [8] studied the case where memory is limited. More recently, Ligatti et al. [13] have generalized this idea to "edit automata" that can not only monitor system inputs and outputs, but also modify them as needed. Similarly, Pinisetty et al. [17] monitor and allow changing input and outputs for synchronous systems. This is similar in spirit to our enforcers. However, our enforcers also have real-time constraints (i.e., deadlines) since they are targeted toward CPS. Moreover, we focus on combining multiple enforcers, and efficient and incremental SMT-based implementations.

Falcone et al. [7] explore runtime verification of reactive systems where properties include finite and infinite sequences (i.e., Safety-Progress), and are expressed via (untimed) Streett automata. In contrast, we consider safety properties and consider enforcement in the context of the use of a real-time scheduler. The literature has also considered monitoring of multiple properties. Pinissety and Tripakis [18] use one monitor for each property, and enforce them either sequentially or in parallel. Instead, we construct a single monitor for multiple properties. Previous work [5,22] has also considered synthesizing monitors from a set of properties, assuming they are consistent. We focus on resolving such inconsistencies based on prioritization.

The role of timing in run-time verification deserves mentioning. Timing matters in the sense that the evaluation of the property that is monitored may be a function of the time of events. This is studied in [3,16]. Another aspect of timing, however, is that regardless of whether evaluation of the property that is monitored depends on the timing of event, we would like to run the program that performs the enforcer at the right time; this is the aspect of timing that we have studied in this paper (using a real-time scheduler).

In the domain of real-time scheduling, enforcers have also been used widely, particularly to enforce CPU usage budgets by threads. For example, the ZSRM [6] mixed-criticality scheduler allocates CPU cycles to threads in a way that respects their priorities (during nominal execution) and criticalities (during overload execution). To this end, it uses timers to intercept thread execution and take appropriate preemptive and budget enforcement steps. While we use ZSRM to ensure schedulability of enforcers, our main focus is on symbolic implementation and combination of logical enforcers.

Pike et al. [15] describe COPILOT, a runtime assurance approach for embedded systems. They focus on a single enforcer, which transforms a stream of application commands to commands that will ensure system safety. The enforcer is specified in a high-level domain specific language, from which efficient (but non-symbolic) implementations are automatically generated. A cyclic executive is used for scheduling both the enforcer and applications. We are inspired by this work, and take the same approach when defining the semantics of a single enforcers. However, our main contribution is on efficient symbolic implementations of enforcers using SMT solvers, and combination of multiple enforcers.

3 Enforcers

Let V_S be the set of state variables. Without loss of generality, we assume for each variable, its domain is D. A state $s : V_S \mapsto D$ is an assignment of values to state variables. Let $\mathbf{S}$ be the set of all states. Let V_Σ be the set of action variables. An action $\alpha : V_\Sigma \mapsto D$ is an assignment of values to action variables. Let Σ be the set of actuations, or actions. We consider a system comprising (i) a target system, (ii) a set of enforcers, and (iii) a set of applications. The enforcers and the applications are software. The target system is typically a physical system (but our paper allows the target system to be another software system as well) and the state s describes the state of the target system. Note that an application may have state itself and this is not described by s. Similarly, we envision the enforcer as a *controller* that executes periodically to sense the system's state, compute an appropriate action, and apply it. A user of an enforcer is an application.

The evolution of the system is modeled by the transition relation R, parameterized by the amount of time that elapses during the transition, and the actuation applied at the start of the transition. Formally $R_P(\alpha) \subseteq \mathbf{S} \times \mathbf{S}$ is the relation such that if the action α is applied to the system at time t when it is in state s and subsequently the system is in state s' at time is $t + P$, then $(s, s') \in R_P(\alpha)$. We write $R_P(\alpha, s)$ to mean the set of states related to state s by $R_P(\alpha)$, i.e., $R_P(\alpha, s) = \{s' \mid (s, s') \in R_P(\alpha)\}$.

We are interested in enforcing safety properties. Intuitively, a safety property ϕ states that something bad never happens. It is defined as a set of "safe" states. In particular, we are interested in keeping the system within a set of states that are both safe and enforceable.

Formally, given a safety property ϕ, the set of all ϕ-enforceable states is denoted by C_ϕ and defined as the largest set of states satisfying the following two conditions: $C_\phi \subseteq \phi$ and $\forall s \in C_\phi . \exists \alpha \in \Sigma . R_P(\alpha, s) \subseteq C_\phi$.

We denote by $SafeAct : C_\phi \mapsto 2^\Sigma$ the mapping from ϕ-enforceable states to actuations that will ensure that the system remains enforceable, i.e.,

$$SafeAct(s) = \{\alpha \mid R_P(\alpha, s) \subseteq C_\phi\}$$

Note that by the definition of C_ϕ we know that: $\forall s \in C_\phi . SafeAct(s) \neq \emptyset$. Different actions in $SafeAct(s)$ may have different utilities, i.e., even though all of them would continue to keep the system in a ϕ-enforceable state, there may be additional reasons to prefer some of them over others. Our enforcers, which we define formally next, therefore support the notion of actuation utility.

Definition 1 (Enforcer). *An enforcer for safety property ϕ is a 4-tuple (P, C_ϕ, μ, U) where: (i) P is its period; (ii) C_ϕ is the set of all ϕ-enforceable states; (iii) $\mu : C_\phi \mapsto 2^\Sigma$ is a mapping from enforceable states to actuations such that: $\forall s \in C_\phi . \mu(s) \subseteq SafeAct(s)$; and (iv) $U : C_\phi \times \Sigma \hookrightarrow \mathbb{R}$ maps each ϕ-enforceable state and a corresponding actuation to its utility.*

Note that U is a partial function, and specifically, $Dom(U) = \{(s, \alpha) \mid (s \in C_\phi) \wedge (\alpha \in \mu(s))\}$. Also, the time period P is important since: (i) it specifies how frequently the enforcer must be executed; and (ii) it affects the precise value of C_ϕ. The smaller the value of P, the larger C_ϕ can be. In essence, P is needed because the physical dynamics of the platform and timeliness of enforcement action are crucially important for ensuring safety of a CPS.

Utility-Agnostic Enforcer Operation. Given a non-empty set X, let pick(X) denote an arbitrary element of X. The enforcer $E = (P, C_\phi, \mu, U)$ is executed periodically every P units of time. In each execution, it takes as input the current system state s and user actuation α, and produces an output actuation $\tilde{\alpha}$ defined as follows:

$$\tilde{\alpha} = \begin{cases} \alpha & \text{if } \alpha \in \mu(s) \\ \text{pick}(\mu(s)) & \text{otherwise} \end{cases} \tag{1}$$

Note that if α is an enforcing action at state s, then the enforcer outputs α. Otherwise, it picks and outputs an arbitrary enforcing action α' at state s.

The construction of μ is the crucial step in defining the enforcer. We assume that it is done offline. It could be done via simulations, or analytically (if we have good models), or via some combination of the two.

Utility-Maximizing Enforcer Operation. In general, the enforcer does not have to output the user's command α even if α is enforcing. This is because, in a specific state, different enforcing actions have different utilities and the enforcer may choose the command that maximizes utility. Then the output of the utility maximizing enforcer is defined as follows:

$$\tilde{\alpha} = \begin{cases} \alpha & \text{if } \alpha \in \mu(s) \wedge U(s, \alpha) = \max_{\alpha' \in \mu(s)} U(s, \alpha') \\ \arg\max_{\alpha' \in \mu(s)} U(s, \alpha') & \text{otherwise} \end{cases} \tag{2}$$

Note that (1) is a special case of (2) when U is defined as follows:

$$U(s, \alpha) = \begin{cases} 1 \ if \ \alpha \in \mu(s) \\ 0 \ otherwise \end{cases} \tag{3}$$

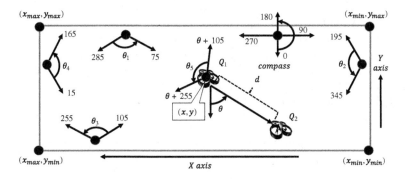

Fig. 1. An example with two enforcers.

3.1 Example

Consider two quadcopters, Q_1 and Q_2, moving in a two-dimensional rectangular zone Z, shown in Fig. 1. The boundaries of Z are aligned to the X and Y axes, and the points (x, y) within Z are defined by $x_{min} \leq x \leq x_{max}$ and $y_{min} \leq y \leq y_{max}$. Directions are measured in degrees, using the reference shown on the right of Fig. 1. Quadcopter Q_1 has two enforcers, defined as follows: (i) *Virtual Tether*: enforcer E_1 keeps Q_1 physically within the zone Z (safety property ϕ_1); (ii) *Separation*: enforcer E_2 keeps Q_1 at a minimum distance of D from Q_2 (safety property ϕ_2). The state variables are $V_S = \{x, y, \theta, d\}$ where (x, y) is the location of Q_1, and θ and d are the direction and distance from Q_1 to Q_2, respectively. An action α attempts to move Q_1 in a specific direction θ_α. Thus, $V_\Sigma = \{\theta_\alpha\}$. The specific range of values of θ_α that can be applied by each enforcer depends on the state of Q_1.

Operations on Angles. In the following, all operations on angles are performed modulo 360, and all angle values are in the range $[0, 360)$. In particular, given two angles θ and θ', we define $\theta \ominus \theta'$ to be the minimum of the two angles between θ and θ' (one measured clockwise, and the other anti-clockwise). For example, we evaluate $350 \ominus 5$ as follows. The clockwise angle between 350 and 5 is 15; the counter-clockwise angle between 350 and 5 is 345; thus $350 \ominus 5 = 15$. We write θ^{opp} to denote the angle opposite to θ, i.e., $\theta^{opp} = (\theta + 180) \mod 360$. For example, $90^{opp} = 270$ and $300^{opp} = 120$.

Tether Enforcer Operation. If Q_1 is too close to the y_{max} boundary of Z, then E_1 applies an enforcement action with $\theta_\alpha \in \tilde{\theta}_1$, where $\tilde{\theta}_1 = [285, 360) \cup [0, 75)$, as shown at the top of Fig. 1. Similarly, if Q_1 is too close to the x_{min} boundary of Z, then E_1 applies an enforcement action with $\theta_\alpha \in \tilde{\theta}_2$ where $\tilde{\theta}_2 = [195, 345]$, as shown at the right of Fig. 1. The other two possible enforcements by E_1, involving enforcement action ranges $\tilde{\theta}_3 = [105, 255]$ and $\tilde{\theta}_4 = [15, 165]$, are also shown in Fig. 1. Let δ_{P1} be the maximum distance that Q_1 can travel along any one dimension in time P, and let δ_{B1} (the braking distance) be the maximum distance that Q_1 can travel in a direction opposing an enforcement action (e.g., toward y_{max} when $\theta_\alpha \in \tilde{\theta}_1$ is applied). Furthermore, we assume that the period P is sufficiently large that once the enforcement action is applied, the QC returns to a state in C_{ϕ_1} within P time units. Let $\delta_{PB1} \equiv \delta_{P1} + \delta_{B1}$. This means that an appropriate enforcement action must be applied as soon as the distance between Q_1 and a boundary of Z falls below δ_{PB1}. Clearly, we are interested in situations when Q_1 is too close to the four boundaries of Z. For this reason, we define b_1, b_2, b_3, and b_4 as

$$b_1 \equiv y_{max} - y \le \delta_{PB1} \qquad\qquad b_2 \equiv x - x_{min} \le \delta_{PB1}$$
$$b_3 \equiv y - y_{min} \le \delta_{PB1} \qquad\qquad b_4 \equiv x_{max} - x \le \delta_{PB1}$$

We specify μ_1 as: $\forall i \in [1, 4] \cdot b_i \implies \mu_1(x, y, \theta, d) \in \tilde{\theta}_i$. In addition, the ϕ_1-enforceable set of states are those corresponding to locations in Z such that there is enough space to prevent a violation, i.e.,

$$C_{\phi_1} = \{(x, y, \theta, d) \mid (x + \delta_{B1}, y + \delta_{B1}) \in Z \wedge (x - \delta_{B1}, y - \delta_{B1}) \in Z\}$$

The utility of an enforcement action is directly related to the degree to which it opposes the movement toward nearby boundaries. It is the sum of four utilities, one for each boundary. Formally,

$$U_1(x, y, \theta, d, \theta_\alpha) = U^1 + U^2 + U^3 + U^4 \text{ such that}$$
$$U^i = 75 - (\theta^i_{mid} \ominus \theta_\alpha) \text{ if } b_i \text{ and } 0 \text{ otherwise, where}$$
$$\theta^1_{mid} = 0 \quad \theta^2_{mid} = 270 \quad \theta^3_{mid} = 180 \quad \theta^4_{mid} = 90$$

Separation Enforcer Operation. When Q_1 is too close to Q_2, E_2 applies an enforcement action to move it away. Recall that θ denotes the direction from Q_1 to Q_2. The enforcement is to move Q_1 in a direction θ_α that is opposite to θ. Specifically, we want $(\theta^{opp} \ominus \theta_\alpha) \le 75$. In Fig. 1, the range of possible values of θ_α is denoted by $\tilde{\theta}_5$. Let δ_{P2} be the largest possible reduction in the value of d within time P, and δ_{B2} be the largest possible reduction in the value of d once the separation enforcement is applied. Let $\delta_{PB2} \equiv \delta_{P2} + \delta_{B2}$. Define condition b_{sep} as $b_{sep} \equiv d \le \delta_{PB2} + D$. We specify μ_2 as: $b_{sep} \implies \mu_2(x, y, \theta, d) \in \tilde{\theta}_5$. In addition, the ϕ_2-enforceable set of states with correct separation, i.e.,

$$C_{\phi_2} = \{(x, y, \theta, d) \mid d + \delta_{B2} \ge D\}$$

The utility of an enforcement action is directly related to the degree to which it is opposite to θ, specifically:

$$U_2(x, y, \theta, d, \theta_\alpha) = 75 - (\theta^{opp} \ominus \theta_\alpha) \text{ if } b_{sep} \text{ and } 0 \text{ otherwise}$$

3.2   Combining Multiple Enforcers

Consider n enforcers $E_1, \ldots, E_n$ such that $E_i = (P, C_{\phi_i}, \mu_i, U_i)$. Without loss of generality, assume that the enforcers are ordered by decreasing priority. When applied in state s, the combined utility-agnostic enforcer returns the action $\texttt{select}(s, \langle E_1, \ldots, E_n \rangle, \alpha)$, which is defined recursively as shown in Fig. 2. Note that since $\texttt{select}(s, \langle E_1, \ldots, E_n \rangle, \alpha)$ is always in $\mu_1(s)$, the system always maintains property ϕ_1. Also note that the second and third cases in the definition of $\texttt{select}(s, \langle E_1, \ldots, E_n \rangle, \alpha)$ cannot be swapped without violating the condition that property ϕ_n must be maintained if at all possible. We assume that utilities are additive. Thus, when combining two enforcers, we assume that the overall utility achieved is the "sum" of the utilities of all the enforcers that are "activated". The utility-maximizing enforcer combination returns the action $\texttt{select}^*(s, \langle E_1, \ldots, E_n \rangle, \alpha)$, which is defined recursively as shown in Fig. 3.

$$\texttt{select}(s, \langle E_1 \rangle, \alpha) = \begin{cases} \alpha & \textit{if } \alpha \in \mu_1(s) \\ \texttt{pick}(\mu_1(s)) & \textit{otherwise} \end{cases}$$

$$\texttt{select}(s, \langle E_1, \ldots, E_n \rangle, \alpha) =$$

$$\begin{cases} \alpha & \textit{if } s \in \bigcap_{i=2,\ldots,n} C_{\phi_i} \wedge \alpha \in \bigcap_{i=1,\ldots,n} \mu_i(s) \\ \texttt{pick}(\bigcap_{i=1,\ldots,n} \mu_i(s)) & \textit{if } s \in \bigcap_{i=2,\ldots,n} C_{\phi_i} \wedge \bigcap_{i=1,\ldots,n} \mu_i(s) \neq \emptyset \\ \texttt{select}(s, \langle E_1, \ldots, E_{n-1} \rangle, \alpha) & \textit{otherwise} \end{cases}$$

Fig. 2. Function $\texttt{select}$ for utility-agnostic enforcer combination.

$$\texttt{select}^*(s, \langle E_1 \rangle, \alpha) = \begin{cases} \alpha & \textit{if } \alpha \in \mu_1(s) \wedge U_1(s, \alpha) = \max_{\alpha' \in \mu_1(s)} U_1(s, \alpha') \\ \arg\max_{\alpha' \in \mu_1(s)} U_1(s, \alpha') & \textit{otherwise} \end{cases}$$

$$\texttt{select}^*(s, \langle E_1, \ldots, E_n \rangle, \alpha) =$$

$$\begin{cases} \alpha & \textit{if } s \in \bigcap_{i=2,\ldots,n} C_{\phi_i} \wedge \alpha \in \bigcap_{i=1,\ldots,n} \mu_i(s) \wedge \\ & \sum_{i=1,\ldots,n} U_i(s, \alpha) = \max_{\alpha' \in \bigcap_{i=1,\ldots,n} \mu_i(s)} \left(\sum_{i=1,\ldots,n} U_i(s, \alpha') \right) \\ \arg\max_{\alpha' \in \bigcap_{i=1,\ldots,n} \mu_i(s)} \left(\sum_{i=1,\ldots,n} U_i(s, \alpha') \right) & \textit{if } s \in \bigcap_{i=2,\ldots,n} C_{\phi_i} \wedge \bigcap_{i=1,\ldots,n} \mu_i(s) \neq \emptyset \\ \texttt{select}^*(s, \langle E_1, \ldots, E_{n-1} \rangle, \alpha) & \textit{otherwise} \end{cases}$$

Fig. 3. Function $\texttt{select}^*$ for utility-maximizing enforcer combination.

4   Enforcer Implementation

In this section, we focus on implementing enforcers in an efficient manner. Recall, from Definition 1, that an enforcer is a 4-tuple (P, C_ϕ, μ, U). The most critical parts to implement here are C_ϕ, μ and U. In particular, following Fig. 3, such an implementation must support the operations shown in the left column of Table 1. In this paper, we propose to represent both C_ϕ and μ symbolically, as logical formulas, and implement the above operations using an SMT solver. We now present this in more detail.

Table 1. Enforcer operations and their symbolic implementations.

Enforcer operation	Symbolic implementation
$s \in \bigcap_{i=2,\ldots,n} C_{\phi_i}$	$\text{sat}(V_S = s \land \bigwedge_{i=2,\ldots,n} C_{\phi_i})$
$\alpha \in \bigcap_{i=1,\ldots,n} \mu_i(s)$	$\text{sat}(V_S = s \land V_\Sigma = \alpha \land \bigwedge_{i=1,\ldots,n} \mu_i)$
$\bigcap_{i=1,\ldots,n} \mu_i(s) = \emptyset$	$\neg\text{sat}(V_S = s \land \bigwedge_{i=1,\ldots,n} \mu_i)$
$\text{pick}(\bigcap_{i=1,\ldots,n} \mu_i(s))$	$\text{soln}(V_S = s \land \bigwedge_{i=1,\ldots,n} \mu_i, V_\Sigma)$
$\sum_{i=1,\ldots,n} U_i(s,\alpha) = \max_{\alpha' \in \bigcap_{i=1,\ldots,n} \mu_i(s)} \left(\sum_{i=1,\ldots,n} U_i(s,\alpha') \right)$	$\neg\text{sat}(\Omega(s,\alpha,n))$ where $\Omega(s,\alpha,n) =$ $\begin{pmatrix} V_S = s \land V_\Sigma = \alpha \land k = \sum_{i=1,\ldots,n} U_i \land \\ V_S' = s \land \bigwedge_{i=1,\ldots,n} \mu_i' \land k' = \sum_{i=1,\ldots,n} U_i' \land \\ k < k' \end{pmatrix}$
$\underset{\alpha' \in \bigcap_{i=1,\ldots,n} \mu_i(s)}{\arg\max} \left(\sum_{i=1,\ldots,n} U_i(s,\alpha') \right)$	$\text{opt}(V_S = s \land \bigwedge_{i=1,\ldots,n} \mu_i, \sum_{i=1,\ldots,n} U_i, V_\Sigma)$

Recall that a state is an assignment to state variables V_S, and an action is an assignment to action variables V_Σ. Thus, a logical formula F over V_S, denoted $F(V_S)$, represents a set of states S in the sense that a state s belongs to S iff the assignment to V_S corresponding to s makes $F(V_S)$ true. In the same way, a formula $F(V_\Sigma)$ represents a set of actions, and a formula $F(V_S, V_\Sigma)$ represents a relation over S and Σ. In addition, a state s is representable as a logical formula over V_S, and an action α is representable as a logical formula over V_Σ.

We therefore represent C_ϕ as a logical formula over V_S, μ as a logical formula over $V_S \cup V_\Sigma$, and U as a function over $V_S \cup V_\Sigma$. Also, let $V_S = s$ denote the formula that assigns state variables to the specific state s, and $V_\Sigma = \alpha$ denote the formula that assigns action variables to the specific action α. We introduce fresh "primed" copies of variables in V_S and V_Σ, and denote them by V_S' and V_Σ', respectively. We write μ' and U_i' to mean $\mu(V_S', V_\Sigma')$ and $U_i(V_S', V_\Sigma')$, respectively. Then, the right column of Table 1 shows the implementations of the necessary enforcer operations using the following logical primitives:

- $\text{sat}(F)$ returns TRUE iff F is satisfiable, and FALSE otherwise;
- $\text{soln}(F, V)$ returns a satisfying solution of F but restricts the assignment to variables in V, i.e., it returns a satisfying solution of $\exists(V_S \cup V_\Sigma \setminus V) \cdot F$. If F is not satisfiable, then $\text{soln}(F, V)$ returns a special value $\bot$.
- $\text{opt}(F, \Psi, V)$ returns a satisfying solution of F that maximizes the objective function Ψ but restricts the assignment to variables in V. If F is not satisfiable, then $\text{opt}(F, \Psi, V)$ returns a special value $\bot$.

We assume that all logical formulas are over an underlying theory T for which $\text{sat}(F)$ is decidable, and $\text{soln}(F, V)$ and $\text{opt}(F, \Psi, V)$ are effectively computable. For our experiments, we use linear arithmetic over rationals, for which these two conditions hold. Specifically, we use the z3[14] SMT solver to implement $\text{sat}(F)$ and $\text{soln}(F, V)$, and νz [4] solver to implement $\text{opt}(F, \Psi, V)$.

```
1 proc select(s, α, n) {
2    if (n = 1) {
3       if (sat(V_S = s ∧ V_Σ = α ∧ μ_1))
4          return α;
5       return soln(V_S = s ∧ μ_1, V_Σ);
6    }
7    b := sat(V_S = s ∧ C^n);
8    if (¬b) return select(s, α, n − 1);
9    if (sat(V_S = s ∧ V_Σ = α ∧ μ^n))
10      return α;
11   α' := soln(V_S = s ∧ μ^n, V_Σ);
12   if (α' ≠ ⊥) return α';
13   return select(s, α, n − 1);
14 }
```

(a)

```
1 proc select*(s, α, n) {
2    if (n = 1) {
3       if (sat(V_S = s ∧ V_Σ = α ∧ μ_1)∧
4          ¬sat(Ω(s, α, 1))) return α;
5       return opt(V_S = s ∧ μ_1, U_1, V_Σ);
6    }
7    b := sat(V_S = s ∧ C^n);
8    if (¬b) return select*(s, α, n − 1);
9    if (sat(V_S = s ∧ V_Σ = α ∧ μ^n) ∧
10      ¬sat(Ω(s, α, n))) return α;
11   α' := opt(V_S = s ∧ μ^n, ∑_{i=1,...,n} U_i, V_Σ);
12   if (α' ≠ ⊥) return α';
13   return select*(s, α, n − 1);
14 }
```

(b)

Fig. 4. (a) Pseudo-code for utility-agnostic enforcer composition; $C^n \equiv \bigwedge_{i=2,...,n} C_{\phi_i}$; $\mu^n \equiv \bigwedge_{i=1,...,n} \mu_i$; (b) Pseudo-code for utility-maximizing enforcer composition; the formula $\Omega(s, \alpha, n)$ is defined in Table 1.

Example. Recall our example with two enforcers from Sect. 3.1. Enforcer E_1 is specified symbolically as follows:

$$\mu_1 \equiv (b_1 \implies (285 \leq \theta_\alpha < 360) \vee (0 \leq \theta_\alpha \leq 75)) \wedge (b_2 \implies (195 \leq \theta_\alpha \leq 345))$$
$$\wedge (b_3 \implies (105 \leq \theta_\alpha \leq 255)) \wedge (b_4 \implies (15 \leq \theta_\alpha \leq 165))$$
$$C_{\phi_1} \equiv (x_{min} + \delta_{B1} \leq x \leq x_{max} - \delta_{B1}) \wedge (y_{min} + \delta_{B1} \leq y \leq y_{max} - \delta_{B1})$$
$$U_1 \equiv U^1 + U^2 + U^3 + U^4 \text{ (Sect. 3.1)}$$

Similarly, enforcer E_2 is specified symbolically as follows:

$$\mu_2 \equiv d \leq \delta_{PB2} + D \implies (\theta^{opp} \ominus \theta_\alpha) \leq 75$$
$$C_{\phi_2} \equiv d + \delta_{B2} \geq D \qquad U_2 \equiv 75 - (\theta^{opp} \ominus \theta_\alpha)$$

Pseudo-Code. Figure 4(a) shows the pseudo-code for the utility-agnostic enforcer composition. The code follows from the definition of function select in Fig. 2 and the definition of symbolic operations in Table 1. However, we have refactored various program statements to avoid calling $\mathrm{sat}(V_S = s \wedge C^n)$ – an expensive operation – multiple times. Also, we eliminated the call to $\mathrm{sat}(V_S = s \wedge \mu^n)$ since the result can also be obtained via the call to $\mathrm{soln}(V_S = s \wedge \mu^n, V_S)$, which is needed in any case.

Similarly, Fig. 4(b) shows the pseudo-code for the utility-maximizing enforcer composition. It follows from the definition of function select* in Fig. 3 and the definition of symbolic operations in Table 1. Again, we have refactored the program to avoid calling $\mathrm{sat}(V_S = s \wedge C^n)$ multiple times. Also, we eliminated the call to $\mathrm{sat}(V_S = s \wedge \mu^n)$ since the result can also be obtained via the (necessary) call to $\mathrm{opt}(V_S = s \wedge \mu^n, \sum_{i=1,\ldots,n} U_i, V_\Sigma)$.

4.1 Optimized and Online Versions

We propose three additional optimizations to the pseudo-code shown in Fig. 4. OPT1 replaces the recursion with iteration. This optimization is possible since both select() and select* are tail-recursive functions. It eliminates stack operations and limits the possibility of stack overflows. OPT2 precomputes commonly used formulas C^i and μ^i for $1 \leq i \leq n$, and uses them as needed, instead of creating and destroying them repeatedly. Finally, OPT3 uses the SMT solver in an online manner. Specifically, the online SMT solver maintains a stack of asserted formulas (a.k.a. the context), and updates it via operations push(F) and pop(F) as follows: (i) push(F) pushed formula F to the context; and (ii) pop() pops a formula from the context. Moreover, new operations $\mathrm{sat}^\dagger$, $\mathrm{soln}^\dagger$, and $\mathrm{opt}^\dagger$ are defined as follows (here θ denotes the conjunctions of all the formulas in the current context):

$$\mathrm{sat}^\dagger() \equiv \mathrm{sat}(\theta) \qquad \mathrm{soln}^\dagger(V) \equiv \mathrm{soln}(\theta, V) \qquad \mathrm{opt}^\dagger(\Psi, V) \equiv \mathrm{opt}(\theta, \Psi, V)$$

Both Z3 and νz support such online operation. In OPT3, the commonly used C^i's and μ^i's are always kept in contexts. Other formulas are pushed prior to an operation, and popped afterwards, as needed. We use the following shorthand:

$$b := \mathrm{sat}^\dagger(\Gamma) \equiv \mathrm{push}(\Gamma); b := \mathrm{sat}^\dagger(); \mathrm{pop}()$$
$$\alpha := \mathrm{sat}^\dagger(\Gamma, V) \equiv \mathrm{push}(\Gamma); \alpha := \mathrm{soln}^\dagger(V); \mathrm{pop}()$$
$$\alpha := \mathrm{opt}^\dagger(\Gamma, \Psi, V) \equiv \mathrm{push}(\Gamma); \alpha := \mathrm{opt}^\dagger(\Psi, V); \mathrm{pop}()$$

Optimizations OPT2 and OPT3 both trade-off memory in favor of time. Our experiments indicate that this is a good trade-off, yielding significant performance gain at the cost of a small memory footprint increase, due to the modest complexity of SMT formulas involved. Indeed, we expect this to be the general case since enforcer logics are expected to be much simpler than the target systems.

Figure 5 shows optimized versions of select() and select*() – denoted select†() and select*† respectively – with all three optimizations applied.

```
                                      1 proc init*() {
                                      2   for i = 1 to n, for j = 1 to i:
1 proc init() {                       3     push_{i,1}(μ_j); push_{i,2}(C_{φ_j}); push_{i,3}(μ'_j);
2   for i = 1 to n, for j = 1 to i:   4   for i = 1 to n: push_{i,3}(K^i)
3     push_{i,1}(μ_j); push_{i,2}(C_{φ_j}); 5 }
4 }                                    6 proc select*†(s, α, n) {
5 proc select†(s, α, n) {             7   for i = n to 1 {
6   for i = n to 1 {                  8     if (i = 1) {
7     if (i = 1) {                     9       b := sat†_{i,1}(V_S = s ∧ V_Σ = α);
8       b := sat†_{i,1}(V_S = s ∧ V_Σ = α); 10      b' := sat†_{i,3}(V_S = s ∧ V_Σ = α ∧ V'_S = s');
9       if (b) return α;              11       if (b ∧ ¬b') return α;
10      α' := soln†_{i,1}(V_S = s, V_Σ); 12      α' := opt†_{i,1}(V_S = s, U_1, V_Σ);
11      return α';                    13       return α';
12    }                               14     }
13    b := sat_{i,2}(V_S = s);        15     b := sat_{i,2}(V_S = s);
14    if (¬b) continue;              16     if (¬b) continue;
15    b := sat†_{i,1}(V_S = s ∧ V_Σ = α); 17     b := sat†_{i,1}(V_S = s ∧ V_Σ = α);
16    if (b) return α;               18     b' := sat†_{i,3}(V_S = s ∧ V_Σ = α ∧ V'_S = s');
17    α' := soln†_{i,1}(V_S = s, V_Σ); 19     if (b ∧ ¬b') return α;
18    if (α' ≠ ⊥) return α';         20     α' := opt†_{i,1}(V_S = s, Σ_{i=1,...,n} U_i, V_Σ);
19  }                                 21     if (α' ≠ ⊥) return α';
20 }                                  22   }
                                      23 }
           (a)                                        (b)
```

Fig. 5. (a) Pseudo-code for optimized utility-agnostic enforcer composition; (b) Pseudo-code for fully optimized utility-maximizing enforcer composition; $K^i \equiv (\sum_{j=1,...,i} U_j) < (\sum_{j=1,...,i} U'_j)$.

For $\text{select}^\dagger()$, we use $2 \times n$ contexts. Contexts $(1,1), \ldots, (n,1)$ are used for operations involving μ_i's, while contexts $(1,2), \ldots, (n,2)$ are used for operations involving C_{ϕ_i}'s. All contexts are initialized once via $\text{init}()$ at startup. We use subscripts for $\text{push}()$, $\text{pop}()$, $\text{sat}^\dagger()$, $\text{soln}^\dagger()$, and $\text{opt}^\dagger()$ to indicate the context involved. For example, $\text{push}_{i,j}(F)$ indicates a push of formula F to the (i,j)-th context. For $\text{select}^{*\dagger}()$, we use $3 \times n$ contexts, initialized via $\text{init}^*()$.

4.2   Correctness of Optimizations

Correctness of $\text{select}^\dagger$. We argue about the correctness of procedure $\text{select}^\dagger$ by showing its correspondence to procedure select. Assume that the contexts have been initialized via init. Then the lines of $\text{select}^\dagger$ correspond to those of select as follows: (i) lines 7–12 correspond to lines 2–6 of select; (ii) lines 13–14 correspond to lines 7–8 of select; (iii) lines 15–16 correspond to lines 9–10 of select; and (iv) lines 17–18 correspond to lines 11–12 of select. Note that the loop invariant maintained by $\text{select}^\dagger$ is that context $(i,1)$ contains the formulas $\{\mu_j \mid 1 \le j \le i\}$, and context $(i,2)$ contains the formulas $\{C_{\phi_j} \mid 1 \le j \le i\}$. To maintain this invariant, formulas pushed in each iteration are always popped before the next iteration, or before $\text{select}^\dagger$ returns.

Correctness of select*†. We argue about the correctness of procedure select*† by showing its correspondence to procedure select*. Assume that the contexts have been initialized via init*. The lines of select*† correspond to those of select* as follows: (i) lines 8–14 correspond to lines 2–6 of select*; (ii) lines 15–16 correspond to lines 7–8 of select*; (iii) lines 17–19 correspond to lines 9–10 of select*; and (iv) lines 20–21 correspond to lines 11–12 of select*. The loop invariant maintained by select*† is that context $(i, 1)$ contains the formulas $\{\mu_j \mid 1 \leq j \leq i\}$, context $(i, 2)$ contains the formulas $\{C_{\phi_j} \mid 1 \leq j \leq i\}$, and context $(i, 3)$ contains the formulas $\{\mu'_j \mid 1 \leq j \leq i\}$. To maintain this invariant, formulas pushed in each iteration are always popped before the next iteration, or before select*† returns.

5   Experimental Evaluation

To evaluate the proposed techniques, we created an indoor arena consisting of: (i) a laptop running Ubuntu 16.04; (ii) an Optitrack localization system with 8 cameras; (iii) two Parrot Travis mini-QCs; and (iv) two XBox gamepads. Optitrack sets up a coordinate system with six dimensions – X, Y, Z, roll, pitch and yaw – and multicasts the locations of the QCs in real-time at 120 Hz over a wired LAN. The enforcer for each QC runs periodically on the laptop. It receives the locations from Optitrack via the LAN, and the user's command to the QC via the gamepad. Next, it uses the select algorithm, or one of its presented variants, to compute an appropriate actuation command and sends it to the Parrot QC via Bluetooth. We used existing open-source software for Bluetooth communication with the QCs, and with interface with the gamepads.

Thread Structure. Even though our running example is two-dimensional, for our experiments we implemented a three-dimensional enforcer. Specifically, the movement of a QC is specified via a pair of angles (α, α_1), where α is the same as in our example, and α_1 is an angle in the range $[-90, 90]$ w.r.t. to the horizontal plane. The enforcers are updated accordingly. The enforcement software running on the laptop for each QC consisted of the following periodic threads with fixed priorities: (i) T_{CL} receives and responds to commands from Optitrack; (ii) T_{FL} receives and records localization data from Optitrack; (iii) T_{EL} executes the select algorithm and computes the actuation; (iv) T_{RS} sends the command to the QC over Bluetooth; and (v) T_{Log} logs messages to a file. Table 2 shows the periods and priorities of all threads. The bottom 16 rows correspond to the T_{EL} thread executing different variants of select. Priorities were assigned rate-monotonically, i.e., shorter periods imply higher priorities. We made the periods as large as possible without sacrificing experiment quality. For example, further increasing the periods of T_{FL} and T_{EL} compromises unacceptably localization accuracy and enforcer responsiveness, respectively. Similarly, a higher period of T_{RS} causes the QCs to become unstable due to controller limitations.

Thread Scheduling. During experiments, all threads were bound to core 0, assigned their respective priorities, and the SCHED_FIFO scheduling policy. In this way, we achieve a single-core processing environment, and a pre-emptive fixed priority scheduler. Since we do not have precise worst-case execution time estimates for the threads, we do not analyze the system for schedulability. Instead, if a job misses its deadline (which always equals the task's period) the next job is delayed so that it starts at the next multiple of the task's period. For example, suppose a job of T_{RS} starts at time 10, and finishes at time 60. Since it misses its deadline (at time 50), the next job of T_{RS} starts at time 90. Clearly, we want to minimize deadline misses. While transient deadline misses are acceptable, a long series of deadline misses can cause the CPS to behave in an unsafe manner. In particular, a deadline miss by the enforcer thread reduces the effectiveness of the RA mechanism. We now present results demonstrating the effectiveness of the different enforcers presented earlier.

Enforcer Effectiveness. We implemented the tether and separation enforcers (E_1 and E_2) and evaluated them individually and in composition. Visually, both enforcers caused the QCs to behave as expected. When we flew a QC with only E_1, the enforcer prevented the QC from exiting the tether region even when the operator attempted to make it do so. When we flew both QCs together with E_2 running on each, the enforcers prevented the two QCs from crashing into each other even when the operators tried to make them crash. Next we flew QC_1 with both E_1 and E_2, given E_1 higher priority. We manually moved QC_2 closer to QC_1. We observed that this caused QC_1 to move further away till it reached the tether boundary. At this point, since E_1 has higher priority, QC_1 did not move away even if QC_2 was brought even closer to it. We ran a similar experiment by reversing the priorities of E_1 and E_2. This time, as expected, QC_1 continued to move away from QC_2 even if this caused QC_1 to violate the tether boundary.

Enforcer Efficiency. Each periodic execution of a thread is called a *job*. The *response time* of a job is the difference between its arrival and completion times. The *execution time* of a job is the amount of CPU time during which it actually executes (i.e., is not preempted by a higher priority thread). For each thread, we measured the response time and execution time of each job, and then computed their minimum, maximum, mean and standard deviation. Table 2 shows the results for the various threads in our system. As can be seen, our symbolic approach leads to quite efficient enforcers with execution times in the order of tens of milliseconds. In general, utility-maximizing enforcers are slightly less efficient (and have more deadline misses) than their utility-agnostic counterparts. This is expected since maximizing utilities requires solving an optimization problem. Finally, select† and select*† deliver around $10\times$ speedups in average execution times consistently, and sometimes almost $20\times$, e.g., $\langle E_2 \rangle^\dagger$ vs. $\langle E_2 \rangle$. Consequently, select† and select*† never miss deadlines while select and select* have frequent deadline misses. Overall, select*† is the best choice since it delivers optimal actuations in a timely manner. Finally, note that the execution times of enforcers have large standard deviations, indicating that overload conditions occur regularly. However, as can be seen by the modest number of deadline misses, ZSRM is able to handle overloads gracefully.

Table 2. Response time and execution time measurements of various threads; Per= period in ms; Prio = priority; Flt-Time = total flight time (sec); DL-Miss = # of jobs that missed deadlines (i.e., response time > period); RespTime = response time (max/avg/stdev) in ms; ExecTime = execution time (max/avg/stdev) in ms; the superscript of $\langle \cdot \rangle$ denotes the variant of `select` used, e.g., $\langle E_1, E_2 \rangle^{*\dagger}$ means that `select`*† was used with the enforcer ordering $\langle E_1, E_2 \rangle$. Note that Flt-Time < Per × #Jobs since it does not include experiment times (at start and end) when the QCs are not airborne.

Thread	Per	Prio	Flt-Time	#Jobs	DL-Miss	RespTime	ExecTime
T_{FL}	5	9	2358.22	530841	0	1.099/0.151/0.039	1.099/0.150/0.039
T_{CL}	50	2	2358.22	53059	26	250.994/0.146/4.281	0.101/0.014/0.008
T_{RS}	40	7	2358.22	64996	19	238.114/0.118/2.842	0.776/0.030/0.015
T_{Log}	1000	1	2358.22	2656	0	31.849/1.198/3.598	0.895/0.330/0.114
$\langle E_1 \rangle$	20	8	145.98	7743	572	83.626/5.579/7.709	39.164/5.415/7.453
$\langle E_1 \rangle^\dagger$	20	8	147.99	8397	0	7.196/0.323/0.439	3.553/0.322/0.434
$\langle E_1 \rangle^*$	20	8	197.11	8295	2564	33.910/9.798/10.237	32.722/9.558/9.984
$\langle E_1 \rangle^{*\dagger}$	20	8	353.03	19684	0	7.539/1.015/1.435	7.310/1.012/1.427
$\langle E_2 \rangle$	20	8	219.07	11338	660	45.079/5.752/7.515	42.942/5.611/7.329
$\langle E_2 \rangle^\dagger$	20	8	146.55	8368	0	2.732/0.361/0.480	2.732/0.361/0.480
$\langle E_2 \rangle^*$	20	8	188.14	8099	2327	36.035/9.940/10.264	34.776/9.705/10.018
$\langle E_2 \rangle^{*\dagger}$	20	8	234.75	13258	0	11.623/0.999/1.856	11.242/0.986/1.817
$\langle E_1, E_2 \rangle$	20	8	100.77	3479	2118	46.066/15.415/11.633	44.547/15.088/11.384
$\langle E_1, E_2 \rangle^\dagger$	20	8	101.23	5605	0	3.834/0.637/0.787	3.834/0.637/0.788
$\langle E_1, E_2 \rangle^*$	20	8	130.74	4396	2657	48.932/16.053/12.269	47.564/15.731/12.017
$\langle E_1, E_2 \rangle^{*\dagger}$	20	8	89.79	5009	0	13.640/1.815/2.579	13.157/1.796/2.537
$\langle E_2, E_1 \rangle$	20	8	55.61	2447	920	57.623/10.631/11.434	56.112/10.416/11.192
$\langle E_2, E_1 \rangle^\dagger$	20	8	81.71	4629	0	3.898/0.561/0.762	3.899/0.561/0.762
$\langle E_2, E_1 \rangle^*$	20	8	69.50	2795	1152	45.360/13.066/13.464	44.214/12.801/13.176
$\langle E_2, E_1 \rangle^{*\dagger}$	20	8	96.15	5315	0	16.940/2.656/3.770	16.371/2.586/3.647

6   Conclusion

We addressed the problem of combining multiple runtime enforcers for a CPS that may produce conflicting actuation commands. We proposed an algorithm that resolves such conflicts at runtime by considering a design-time prioritization of the enforcers. Specifically, our algorithm produces an action that satisfies the maximum number of high-priority enforcers, ignoring the low-priority ones as needed. Our approach also supports a notion of utility-maximization that enables us to implement enforcers that yield the best possible actuation under any given situation. To enable efficient implementations, needed to meet tight schedulability and periodicity constraints, we encode the enforcers symbolically as SMT formulas, and compute their combination via incremental SMT solver operations. Experiments on a CPS testbed involving geo-fencing and collision avoidance among flying minidrones demonstrates the effectiveness of our approach. We see at least two important areas of future work: (i) supporting "skipping" of enforcement actions necessary due to extreme overload conditions; and (ii) supporting multiple enforcer threads operating in the same system.

Acknowledgment. Copyright 2017 Carnegie Mellon University[1].

References

1. NSF Definition of Cyber-Physical Systems. https://www.nsf.gov/funding/pgm_summ.jsp?pims_id=503286
2. Bak, S., Johnson, T., Caccamo, M., Sha, L.: Real-time reachability for verified simplex design. In: Proceedings of the 35th Real-Time Systems Symposium, RTSS 2014 (2014)
3. Basin, D., Jugé, V., Klaedtke, F., Zălinescu, E.: Enforceable security policies revisited. ACM Trans. Inf. Syst. Secur. (TISSEC) (2013)
4. Bjørner, N., Phan, A.-D., Fleckenstein, L.: νZ - An optimizing SMT solver. In: Baier, C., Tinelli, C. (eds.) TACAS 2015. LNCS, vol. 9035, pp. 194–199. Springer, Heidelberg (2015). doi:10.1007/978-3-662-46681-0_14
5. Bloem, R., Könighofer, B., Könighofer, R., Wang, C.: Shield synthesis: runtime enforcement for reactive systems. In: Baier, C., Tinelli, C. (eds.) TACAS 2015. LNCS, vol. 9035, pp. 533–548. Springer, Heidelberg (2015). doi:10.1007/978-3-662-46681-0_51
6. deNiz, D., Lakshmanan, K., Rajkumar, R.: On the scheduling of mixed-criticality real-time task sets. In: Proceedings of the 30th Real-Time Systems Symposium, RTSS 2009 (2009)
7. Falcone, Y., Mounier, L., Fernandez, J.C., Ricier, J.L.: Runtime enforcement monitors: composition, synthesis, and enforcement abilities. Form. Methods Syst. Des. (FMSD) **38**, 223–262 (2011)
8. Fong, P.: Access control by tracking shallow execution history. In: IEEE Security and Privacy (2004)
9. Havelund, K., Goldberg, A.: Verify your runs. In: Meyer, B., Woodcock, J. (eds.) VSTTE 2005. LNCS, vol. 4171, pp. 374–383. Springer, Heidelberg (2008). doi:10.1007/978-3-540-69149-5_40
10. Havelund, K., Rosu, G.: Monitoring programs using rewriting. In: Proceedings of the 16th International Conference on Automated Software Engineering, ASE 2001 (2001)

---

[1] All Rights Reserved. This material is based upon work funded and supported by the Department of Defense under Contract No. FA8702-15-D-0002 with Carnegie Mellon University for the operation of the Software Engineering Institute, a federally funded research and development center. NO WARRANTY. THIS CARNEGIE MELLON UNIVERSITY AND SOFTWARE ENGINEERING INSTITUTE MATERIAL IS FURNISHED ON AN "AS-IS" BASIS. CARNEGIE MELLON UNIVERSITY MAKES NO WARRANTIES OF ANY KIND, EITHER EXPRESSED OR IMPLIED, AS TO ANY MATTER INCLUDING, BUT NOT LIMITED TO, WARRANTY OF FITNESS FOR PURPOSE OR MERCHANTABILITY, EXCLUSIVITY, OR RESULTS OBTAINED FROM USE OF THE MATERIAL. CARNEGIE MELLON UNIVERSITY DOES NOT MAKE ANY WARRANTY OF ANY KIND WITH RESPECT TO FREEDOM FROM PATENT, TRADEMARK, OR COPYRIGHT INFRINGEMENT. [DISTRIBUTION STATEMENT A] This material has been approved for public release and unlimited distribution. Please see Copyright notice for non-US Government use and distribution. DM17-0207.

11. Kim, M., Viswanathan, M., Ben-Abdallah, H., Kannan, S., Lee, I., Sokolsky, O.: Formally specified monitoring of temporal properties. In: Proceedings of the 11th Euromicro Conference on Real-Time Systems, ECRTS 1999 (1999)
12. Leucker, M., Schallhart, C.: A brief account of runtime verification. In: JLAP (2008)
13. Ligatti, J., Bauer, L., Walker, D.: Edit automata: enforcement mechanisms for run-time security policies. Int. J. Inf. Secur. (IJIS) **4**, 2–16 (2005)
14. de Moura, L., Bjørner, N.: Z3: an efficient SMT solver. In: Ramakrishnan, C.R., Rehof, J. (eds.) TACAS 2008. LNCS, vol. 4963, pp. 337–340. Springer, Heidelberg (2008). doi:10.1007/978-3-540-78800-3_24
15. Pike, L., Wegmann, N., Niller, S., Goodloe, A.: Copilot: monitoring embedded systems. Innov. Syst. Softw. Eng. (ISSE) **9**, 235–255 (2013)
16. Pinisetty, S., Falcone, Y., Jéron, T., Marchand, H., Rollet, A., Timo, O.: Runtime enforcement of timed properties. In: Proceedings of the 2nd International Conference on Runtime Verification, RV 2012 (2012)
17. Pinisetty, S., Roop, P., Smyth, S., Tripakis, S., Hanxleden, R.: Runtime enforcement of reactive systems using synchronous enforcers. coRR abs/1612.05030 (2016)
18. Pinisetty, S., Tripakis, S.: Compositional runtime enforcement. In: Rayadurgam, S., Tkachuk, O. (eds.) NFM 2016. LNCS, vol. 9690, pp. 82–99. Springer, Cham (2016). doi:10.1007/978-3-319-40648-0_7
19. Schneider, F.: Enforceable security policies. ACM Trans. Inf. Syst. Secur. (TISSEC) **3**, 30–50 (2000)
20. Seto, D., Krogh, B., Sha, L., Chutinan, A.: The simplex architecture for safe online control system upgrades. In: Proceedings of the American Control Conference (1998)
21. Viswanatha, M.: Foundations for the run-time analysis of software systems. Ph.D. thesis, University of Pennsylvania (2000)
22. Wu, M., Zeng, H., Wang, C.: Synthesizing runtime enforcer of safety properties under burst error. In: Rayadurgam, S., Tkachuk, O. (eds.) NFM 2016. LNCS, vol. 9690, pp. 65–81. Springer, Cham (2016). doi:10.1007/978-3-319-40648-0_6

Almost Event-Rate Independent Monitoring of Metric Dynamic Logic

David Basin, Srđan Krstić[(⊠)], and Dmitriy Traytel[(⊠)]

Institute of Information Security, Department of Computer Science,
ETH Zürich, Zurich, Switzerland
srdan.krstic@inf.ethz.ch, traytel@inf.ethz.ch

Abstract. Linear temporal logic (LTL) and its quantitative extension metric temporal logic (MTL) are standard languages for specifying system behaviors. Regular expressions are an even more expressive formalism in the non-metric setting and several extensions of LTL, including the recently proposed linear dynamic logic (LDL), offer regular-expression-like constructs. We extend LDL with past operators and quantitative features. The resulting *metric dynamic logic* (MDL) offers the quantitative temporal conveniences of MTL while increasing its expressiveness. We develop and evaluate an online monitoring algorithm for MDL whose space-consumption is *almost event-rate independent*—a notion that characterizes monitors that scale to high-velocity event streams.

1 Introduction

Runtime monitoring is a well-established paradigm for verifying system properties by comparing system events against a specification formalizing which event sequences are allowed. Numerous monitoring algorithms have been developed for both the *online* setting, where events are monitored in real-time, as they occur, and for the *offline* setting, where the monitor analyzes events stored in logs. In this paper we address the *online monitoring problem*: Given a stream of events and a property formalized in a formal specification language, identify all the points in the stream that violate the property.

A standard specification language is linear temporal logic (LTL) with past and future temporal operators, which express qualitative temporal constraints like "*A* must follow (or be preceded by) *B*." Metric temporal logic (MTL) extends LTL to formulate quantitative temporal constraints like "*A* must be followed by *B* within an hour." There are numerous semantics for MTL and we work here with a discrete, point-based time model (Sect. 2). This model faithfully captures the imprecision of physical clocks and is algorithmically easier to handle than the dense, interval-based model [8].

We recently developed a monitor for MTL based on dynamic programming that scales to high-volume and high-velocity event streams [5]. The central notion in this work is *almost event-rate independence* (Sect. 2): the monitor's space consumption may only depend logarithmically on the number of events per time-unit. This requirement is stronger than the traditionally used trace-length independence, as it accounts for a high velocity of events. Future temporal constraints make it hard for a monitor to be event-rate independent. This is because the monitor may be unable to output verdicts

© Springer International Publishing AG 2017
S. Lahiri and G. Reger (Eds.): RV 2017, LNCS 10548, pp. 85–102, 2017.
DOI: 10.1007/978-3-319-67531-2_6

for events, since the verdicts may depend on future events and the number of such events can exceed the event rate. To overcome this problem, our monitor outputs *equivalence verdicts* in addition to the standard Boolean verdicts. With an equivalence verdict, the monitor indicates that it does not know the exact verdict for an event, but it knows that the verdict will be equivalent to the verdict of another (also presently unknown) event.

LTL falls short of expressing all regular languages. For example, one cannot express that some event occurs at every other position in a stream. This limitation is often a problem in practice [29] and carries over to the point-based semantics of MTL [9]. A realistic example that cannot be expressed in MTL is that, within the next day, an action is approved and executed and the approval event happens before the execution event.

To overcome this limitation, researchers have developed numerous, more expressive extensions of LTL and MTL by adding regular-expression-like constructs to the language [30]. This resulted in specification languages such as the industrially standardized property specification language [29] (PSL), regular linear temporal logic [22,23] (RLTL), and more recently linear dynamic logic [14] (LDL). We survey these and other languages in Sect. 6. All of them lack some of the features that make MTL an attractive choice: either its support for past operators or its quantitative features.

Our contributions in this paper are as follows. First, we propose metric dynamic logic (MDL), an extension of LDL with past operators and quantitative features (Sect. 3). Second, we develop, implement, and optimize an almost event-rate independent monitoring algorithm for MDL that substantially extends our earlier algorithm for MTL and Antimirov's results on partial derivatives of regular expressions [3] (Sect. 4). Finally, we empirically evaluate our algorithm and show that it outperforms state-of-the-art monitoring tools for MTL and timed regular expressions (Sect. 5).

2   Metric Temporal Logic and Event-Rate Independence

We present our discrete, point-based time model [8] below, briefly introduce metric temporal logic (MTL) [21], and the notion of event-rate independence for monitors [5].

Let Σ be a set of atomic propositions. An *event* is a pair (τ, π), where $\tau \in \mathbb{N}$ is a *time-stamp* and $\pi \subseteq \Sigma$ is a set of propositions that are true at that event. An *event stream* is an infinite sequence of events $\rho = \langle (\tau_0, \pi_0), (\tau_1, \pi_1), (\tau_2, \pi_2), \ldots \rangle$ with monotonically increasing time-stamps: $\tau_i \le \tau_{i+1}$ for all $i \in \mathbb{N}$. We write Δ_i for the non-negative time-stamp difference $\tau_{i+1} - \tau_i$. We call the indices in ρ *time-points*, i.e., event (τ_i, π_i) occurs at time-point i. Moreover, we require that time progresses: for all time-stamps τ there exists a time-point i with $\tau_i > \tau$. The *event rate* $\mathrm{er}_\rho(\tau)$ of a stream ρ at time-stamp τ is the number of time-points with that time-stamp, i.e., $\mathrm{er}_\rho(\tau) = |\{i \mid \tau_i = \tau\}|$.

Metric temporal logic (MTL) [21] is a commonly used language to formulate properties of event streams. Its syntax is given by the grammar

$$\varphi = p \mid \neg \varphi \mid \varphi \vee \varphi \mid \bigcirc_I \varphi \mid \bullet_I \varphi \mid \varphi \, \mathcal{S}_I \, \varphi \mid \varphi \, \mathcal{U}_I \, \varphi,$$

where $p \in \Sigma$ and $I \in \mathbb{I}$. Here, $\mathbb{I}$ denotes the set of non-empty intervals over $\mathbb{N}$. We write $[a, b]$ for the interval $\{x \in \mathbb{N} \mid a \le x \le b\}$, where $a \in \mathbb{N}$, $b \in \mathbb{N} \cup \{\infty\}$, and $a \le b$. For an interval I and $n \in \mathbb{N}$, we define $I - n$ to be the interval $\{x - n \mid x \in I\} \cap \mathbb{N}$ and I^- to be the set of intervals $\{I - n \mid n \in \mathbb{N}\}$, which is always finite. Along with the standard Boolean operators, MTL includes the past temporal operators $\bullet_I$ (*previous*) and $\mathcal{S}_I$ (*since*) and the future temporal operators $\bigcirc_I$ (*next*) and $\mathcal{U}_I$ (*until*), which may be nested freely. A formula is interpreted with respect to a fixed event stream ρ at a time-point i. As this is standard, we only show the $\mathcal{U}_I$ case (omitting the fixed event stream ρ):

$$i \models \varphi \, \mathcal{U}_I \, \psi \text{ iff } j \models \psi \text{ for some } j \geq i \text{ with } \tau_j - \tau_i \in I \text{ and } k \models \varphi \text{ for all } i \leq k < j.$$

A (*traditional online*) *monitor* for MTL takes as input an MTL formula φ and events from ρ, one at a time, and outputs a stream of *Boolean verdicts* $\langle 0 \models \varphi, 1 \models \varphi, 2 \models \varphi, \ldots \rangle$. Note that for future formulas (i.e., those containing $\mathcal{U}_I$ or $\bigcirc_I$), the monitor cannot in general output the verdict at time-point i before it has seen some of the events at future time-points $j > i$. Taking this to the extreme, for the formula $p \, \mathcal{U}_{[0,\infty]} \, q$ with atomic propositions p and q and the event stream ρ with $\tau_i = i$ and $\pi_i = \{p\}$ for all i, the monitor can never output a verdict at time-point 0 because it always sees only a finite prefix of the stream. Moreover, even with bounded future intervals, the number of events that a monitor might need to wait for is unbounded, since non-increasing time-stamps are allowed in our model. It follows that the memory consumption of any monitor depends on the event rate as it must allocate at least one bit for each time-point at which it has not yet produced an output.

In earlier work [5], we developed an MTL monitor that is robust against increasing event rates. Our *almost event-rate independent* monitor differs from traditional monitors in its output: additionally to outputting Boolean verdicts, it may output *equivalence verdicts* between time-points $i \equiv j$. Such an equivalence means that the Boolean verdicts at both i and j are presently unknown (since they depend on future events). However, independent of the future events, they are guaranteed to be equal. Moreover, the monitor may output verdicts out of order with respect to time-points. For the above example, for $p \, \mathcal{U}_{[0,\infty]} \, q$ the monitor would forever output equivalence verdicts $\langle 0 \equiv 1, 0 \equiv 2, \ldots \rangle$. These changes in how the monitor outputs verdicts are crucial and result in monitor's space requirement being *almost* event-rate independent. Namely, while reading a sequence of time-points with identical time-stamps, the monitor keeps the current value of the time-stamp, as well as the offset between the current and the first time-point with the same time-stamp. The monitor therefore requires space only logarithmic in the event-rate, i.e. the number of bits needed to encode the above-mentioned offset.

3 Metric Dynamic Logic

In this section, we introduce metric dynamic logic (MDL). This logic extends LDL [14] with past temporal operators and time intervals associated with temporal formulas. MDL's syntax is defined by the following grammar, where $p \in \Sigma$ denotes an atomic proposition, and $I \in \mathbb{I}$ denotes a non-empty interval.

$$\psi = p \mid \neg\psi \mid \psi \vee \psi \mid \langle r \rangle_I \, \psi \mid \psi_I \langle r \rangle \qquad r = \star \mid \psi? \mid r + r \mid r \cdot r \mid r^*$$

Aside from Boolean operators, MDL contains dynamic modalities like the metric future diamond operator $\langle r \rangle_I \, \varphi$ which expresses that formula φ is true at some future time-point with a time difference bounded by the interval I and that the regular expression r matches the portion of the event stream from the current point up to that future time-point. The past diamond operator $\varphi_I\langle r\rangle$ expresses the same property about a past time-point. Regular expressions in MDL match portions of the event stream, i.e., words over 2^Σ. The expression $\star$ matches any character and $\varphi?$ matches the empty word starting at time-point i if the formula φ holds at i. Moreover, $+, \cdot$, and $*$ are the standard alternation, concatenation, and (Kleene) star operators. The semantics of formulas and regular expressions is defined by mutual induction. A formula is interpreted over a fixed event stream $\rho = \langle(\tau_i, \pi_i)\rangle_{i\in\mathbb{N}}$ and a position $i \in \mathbb{N}$. The semantics of a regular expression r is given by a relation $\mathcal{R}(r) \subseteq \mathbb{N} \times \mathbb{N}$ that contains pairs of time-points (i, j) with $i \leq j$ such that the sequence $\pi_i, \ldots, \pi_j$ (or $\pi_j, \ldots, \pi_i$ for past) from the fixed ρ matches r.

$$i \models p \text{ iff } p \in \pi_i$$
$$i \models \neg\varphi \text{ iff } i \not\models \varphi$$
$$i \models \varphi_1 \vee \varphi_2 \text{ iff } i \models \varphi_1 \text{ or } i \models \varphi_2$$
$$i \models \langle r\rangle_I \varphi \text{ iff } j \models \varphi \text{ for some } j \geq i$$
$$\text{with } \tau_j - \tau_i \in I \text{ and } (i, j) \in \mathcal{R}(r)$$
$$i \models \varphi_I\langle r\rangle \text{ iff } j \models \varphi \text{ for some } j \leq i$$
$$\text{with } \tau_i - \tau_j \in I \text{ and } (j, i) \in \mathcal{R}(r)$$

$$\mathcal{R}(\star) = \{(i, i+1) \mid i \in \mathbb{N}\}$$
$$\mathcal{R}(\varphi?) = \{(i, i) \mid i \models \varphi\}$$
$$\mathcal{R}(r+s) = \mathcal{R}(r) \cup \mathcal{R}(s)$$
$$\mathcal{R}(r \cdot s) = \{(i, k) \mid \exists j. (i, j) \in \mathcal{R}(r)$$
$$\text{and } (j, k) \in \mathcal{R}(s)\}$$
$$\mathcal{R}(r^*) = \{(i, i) \mid i \in \mathbb{N}\} \cup$$
$$\{(i_0, i_k) \mid \exists i_1, \ldots, i_{k-1}. (i_j, i_{j+1}) \in \mathcal{R}(r)$$
$$\text{for all } 0 \leq j < k\}$$

We employ the usual syntactic sugar for additional Boolean constants and operators: $true = p \vee \neg p$, $false = \neg true$, and $\varphi \wedge \psi = \neg(\neg\varphi \vee \neg\psi)$. The ability to arbitrarily nest the negation operator allows us to define the metric future and past box operators $[r]_I \varphi$ and $\varphi_I[r]$ as $\neg(\langle r\rangle_I \neg\varphi)$ and $\neg(\neg\varphi_I\langle r\rangle)$, respectively. We use the abbreviations $\langle\varphi\rangle_I \psi$ and $\psi_I\langle\varphi\rangle$ for $\langle\varphi? \cdot \star\rangle_I \psi$ and $\psi_I\langle\star \cdot \varphi?\rangle$. We perform the same implicit *cast* of a formula φ to the regular expression $\varphi? \cdot \star$ in the context of a future regular expression (or $\star \cdot \varphi?$ in the context of a past regular expression) for any formula that occurs as an argument to one of the $+, \cdot$, and $*$ constructors. For example, $\langle\varphi^*\rangle_I \psi$ abbreviates $\langle(\varphi? \cdot \star)^*\rangle_I \psi$.

For an MDL formula φ, let $\mathsf{SF}(\varphi)$ denote the set of its subformulas defined as usual. Note that $\varphi \in \mathsf{SF}(\varphi)$. We extend this set to the set of *interval-skewed subformulas* $\mathsf{ISF}(\varphi) = \mathsf{SF}(\varphi) \cup \{\psi_J\langle r\rangle \mid \psi_I\langle r\rangle \in \mathsf{SF}(\varphi), J \in I^-\} \cup \{\langle r\rangle_J \psi \mid \langle r\rangle_I \psi \in \mathsf{SF}(\varphi), J \in I^-\}$, which contains all temporal formulas with the same structure as existing temporal subformulas of φ, except with intervals shifted by constants.

Theorem 1. *For every MTL formula there exists an equivalent MDL formula.*

Proof. We prove this constructively by defining a syntactic translation ξ:

$$\xi(p) = p; \quad \xi(\varphi \vee \psi) = \xi(\varphi) \vee \xi(\psi); \quad \xi(\neg\varphi) = \neg\xi(\varphi); \quad \xi(\bigcirc_I \varphi) = \langle\star\rangle_I \xi(\varphi);$$
$$\xi(\varphi \mathcal{U}_I \psi) = \langle\xi(\varphi)^*\rangle_I \xi(\psi); \quad \xi(\bullet_I \varphi) = \xi(\varphi)_I\langle\star\rangle; \quad \xi(\varphi \mathcal{S}_I \psi) = \xi(\psi)_I\langle\xi(\varphi)^*\rangle.$$

Given an MTL formula φ and a fixed stream ρ, one can prove that $\forall i. \, i \models \xi(\varphi)$ $\Leftrightarrow i \models \varphi$ by induction on the structure of φ. (Note that we overload the notation for satisfiability $\models$ for both logics.) We show the proof only for $\mathcal{U}_I$. The other cases follow similarly.

$$i \models \xi(\varphi \, \mathcal{U}_I \, \psi) \stackrel{\text{def. } \xi}{\Leftrightarrow} i \models \langle \xi(\varphi)^* \rangle_I \, \xi(\psi) \stackrel{\text{cast}}{\Leftrightarrow} i \models \langle (\xi(\varphi)? \cdot \star)^* \rangle_I \, \xi(\psi)$$

$$\stackrel{\text{def. } \models}{\Leftrightarrow} j \models \xi(\psi) \text{ for some } j \geq i \text{ with } \tau_j - \tau_i \in I \text{ and } (i, j) \in \mathcal{R}((\xi(\varphi)? \cdot \star)^*)$$

$$\stackrel{\text{IH } \psi}{\Leftrightarrow} j \models \psi \text{ for some } j \geq i \text{ with } \tau_j - \tau_i \in I \text{ and } (i, j) \in \mathcal{R}((\xi(\varphi)? \cdot \star)^*)$$

$$\stackrel{\text{def. } \mathcal{R}}{\Leftrightarrow} j \models \psi \text{ for some } j \geq i \text{ with } \tau_j - \tau_i \in I \text{ and } k \models \xi(\varphi) \text{ for all } i \leq k < j$$

$$\stackrel{\text{IH } \varphi}{\Leftrightarrow} j \models \psi \text{ for some } j \geq i \text{ with } \tau_j - \tau_i \in I \text{ and } k \models \varphi \text{ for all } i \leq k < j$$

$$\stackrel{\text{def. } \models}{\Leftrightarrow} i \models \varphi \, \mathcal{U}_I \, \psi$$

$\square$

Since MDL extends LDL, it can express any ω-regular language [14]. For instance, the property "the event a occurs at every even position" can be expressed as $[(true \cdot true)^*] \, a$. This property cannot be expressed by any LTL or MTL formula. Similarly, the property "both b and c occur within the next two time-units and b occurs before c" cannot be expressed in MTL with point-based semantics [9]. It can, however, be expressed in MDL with the formula $\langle true^* \cdot b \cdot true^* \rangle_{[0,2]} \, c$.

4 The Monitoring Algorithm

Our almost event-rate independent monitor for MTL [5] uses dynamic programming in a way that extends the classic monitor for past-only LTL by Havelund and Roşu [18]. For MDL we follow the same approach. We recapitulate the algorithm in the simpler setting of MTL (Subsect. 4.1) and afterwards we use incremental reasoning about dynamic modalities (Subsect. 4.2) to extend the algorithm to MDL (Subsect. 4.3). Finally, we present several important performance optimizations (Subsect. 4.4).

4.1 An Almost Event-Rate Independent Monitor for MTL

At its core, the MTL monitor relies on an alternative recursive definition of the satisfiability of temporal formulas. For example, for a fixed stream ρ, $\mathcal{U}_I$'s definition reads:

$$i \models \varphi \, \mathcal{U}_I \, \psi \text{ iff } a = 0 \text{ and } i \models \psi, \text{ or } \Delta_i \leq b, i \models \varphi, \text{ and } i + 1 \models \varphi \, \mathcal{U}_{I - \Delta_i} \, \psi, \quad (1)$$

where $I = [a, b]$. The key observation is that the satisfiability of $\varphi \, \mathcal{U}_I \, \psi$ at time-point i is fully determined by the satisfiability of φ and ψ at the current time-point i and the satisfiability of the interval-skewed formula $\varphi \, \mathcal{U}_{I - \Delta_i} \, \psi$ at the next time-point $i + 1$, along with some interval boundary checks. For $\mathcal{S}_I$, a symmetric characterization refers to an interval-skewed formula at the previous time-point $i - 1$.

Figure 1 (left) illustrates these dependencies as arrows for verdicts at time point i for the formula $(p \, \mathcal{S}_{[0,5]} \, \varphi) \, \mathcal{U}_{[2,4]} \, \psi$ and its subformula $p \, \mathcal{S}_{[0,5]} \, \varphi$. Note that the future

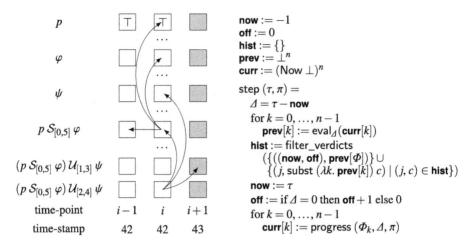

Fig. 1. Example excerpt of the MTL monitor's state (left) and pseudocode (right)

dependencies can, in general, only be resolved after having seen the event at time-point $i + 1$. Our monitor treats such future dependencies symbolically as Boolean variables. To monitor the formula Φ, the algorithm stores a Boolean expression for each interval-skewed subformula $\varphi \in \mathsf{ISF}(\Phi)$ in an array **curr**, ordered such that, for any formula φ at index k, each of its proper subformulas occurs at a lower index $l < k$. We write Φ_k for the formula occurring at index k and sometimes use formulas synonymously as indices, e.g., by writing **curr**$[\varphi]$ for the **curr**'s entry at position k, given that $\varphi = \Phi_k$. We use Boolean expressions in negation normal form, defined inductively as:

$$bexp = \bot \mid \top \mid \mathsf{Var}\ \mathbb{N} \mid \neg\mathsf{Var}\ \mathbb{N} \mid bexp \wedge bexp \mid bexp \vee bexp.$$

Negation $\neg$ is applied to arbitrary Boolean expressions by pushing it down to the leaves.

With each arriving event, the array **curr** is updated following Eq. 1 (and analogous equations). The variables in expressions at time-point i represent pointers into the monitor's array **curr** *after* processing the event at time-point $i + 1$. Instead of using pointers to the past time-point $i - 1$, the monitor directly uses the expressions from the array at time-point $i - 1$ to build from them new expressions at time-point i.

For future formulas, there is an additional complication: before the monitor has seen the time-stamp at position $i + 1$, it cannot know which of the interval-skewed future formulas to refer to. Therefore, we work with so called *future expressions* defined as $fexp = \mathsf{Now}\ bexp \mid \mathsf{Later}\ (\mathbb{N} \rightarrow bexp)$, where the parameter of Later is the time-stamp difference between the time-points $i + 1$ and i. The functions $\wedge_{fexp}$, $\vee_{fexp}$, $\neg_{fexp}$ lift Boolean operators to future expressions while propagating Boolean values eagerly, for example, by simplifying $\mathsf{Now}\ \top \vee_{fexp} x$ to $\mathsf{Now}\ \top$ and $\mathsf{Now}\ \bot \vee_{fexp} x$ to x. Given a time-stamp difference Δ, a future expression evaluates to a Boolean expression: $\mathsf{eval}_\Delta(\mathsf{Now}\ c) = c$ and $\mathsf{eval}_\Delta(\mathsf{Later}\ f) = f(\Delta)$.

We are now set to describe our almost event-rate independent monitor. Figure 1 (right) depicts its (OCaml-like) pseudocode. The monitor's state consists of five variables initialized as shown, where n is the number of interval-skewed subformulas of Φ.

To denote their mutability, we write them in boldface. The variable **now** is the current time-stamp and together with it the natural number **off** identifies the current time-point. Note that we represent time-points as pairs (τ, k), where the second component is an offset into a block of time-points labeled with time-stamp τ. The history **hist** is a set of pairs of Boolean expressions and time-points (again stored as time-stamp-offset pairs). It contains all time-points at which no verdict was output so far, since the verdict depends on future events. The variable **curr** is the array of length n of future expressions for all interval-skewed subformulas at the current time-point. The variable **prev** is another array of length n of Boolean expressions that belong to the previous time-point. The monitor updates its state using the step function for each incoming event (τ, π).

The step function first computes the time-stamp difference Δ between τ and the previous time-stamp stored in **now**. It uses Δ to translate future expressions from **curr** to Boolean expressions and store them in **prev**, thereby discarding any old expression stored in **prev**. Next the history **hist** is updated. This step is the key to obtaining almost event-rate independence. The variables of all Boolean expressions stored in the history refer to the latest seen time-point. To maintain this invariant, we first update all expressions in the history by substituting their variables (pointing to what used to be in **curr** before the call of step) with the actual Boolean expressions contained in **curr** (that is now stored in **prev**). The substitution is performed by the higher-order function subst, whose definition is omitted. Moreover, the expression **prev**$[\Phi]$ is added as a new element to the history. Then, the function filter_verdicts (whose formal definition is omitted, too) performs two verdict output steps. First, it iterates over the history and removes (and outputs as Boolean verdicts) all Boolean expressions equivalent to $\top$ or $\bot$. Second, it finds all pairwise equivalent pairs of expressions from the history and for each such pair it removes the expression with the larger time-point from the history and outputs an equivalence verdict. By guaranteeing that only semantically different Boolean expressions in at most n variables are contained in the history, the monitor is almost event-rate independent, as only offset's size depends on the event rate. Note that if the second step were omitted, we would obtain a standard monitor that is event-rate dependent. Finally, after a trivial update of **now** and **off**, the progress function fills the **curr** array with new future expressions. We only show its definition for $\mathcal{U}_I$, following Eq. 1.

$$\text{progress} \, (\varphi \, \mathcal{U}_{[a,b]} \, \psi, \Delta, \pi) = (\text{Now} \, (a = 0) \wedge_{fexp} \textbf{curr}[\psi]) \vee_{fexp}$$
$$\text{Later} \, (\lambda \Delta'. \, \Delta' \leq b \wedge \text{eval}_{\Delta'}(\textbf{curr}[\varphi]) \wedge \text{Var} \, (\varphi \, \mathcal{U}_{[a,b] - \Delta'} \, \psi))$$

For other formulas, the update works similarly, for example, by inspecting the π argument for atomic propositions. Note that the parameter Δ is not used for $\mathcal{U}_I$, as it is the time-stamp difference between the current and previous time-point. In contrast, Δ' from the Later argument is the appropriate time-stamp difference for $\mathcal{U}_I$. It will be instantiated to a concrete value after the next event (including its time-stamp) is received. To refer to the satisfiability of $\varphi \, \mathcal{U}_{[a,b] - \Delta'} \, \psi$ at position $i + 1$ as stipulated by Eq. 1, we use the Var constructor applied to (the index of) $\varphi \, \mathcal{U}_{[a,b] - \Delta'} \, \psi$.

In the presented algorithm, only the progress function and the computation of interval-skewed subformulas are specific to MTL. In the following subsections we will replace these ingredients to obtain a monitor for MDL.

4.2 Derivatives of Dynamic Modalities

To build on ideas from the above algorithm for MDL, we need an alternative recursive definition of the past and future modalities that refer only to the $(i-1)$st and $(i+1)$st time-point. For a fixed stream ρ, the following characterization holds.

$$i \models \langle r \rangle_I \, \varphi \text{ iff } a = 0, \varepsilon_i(r), \text{ and } i \models \varphi, \text{ or } \Delta_i \leq b \text{ and } i+1 \models \langle \delta_i(r) \rangle_{I-\Delta_i} \, \varphi \tag{2}$$

$$i \models \varphi_I \langle r \rangle \text{ iff } a = 0, \varepsilon_i(r), \text{ and } i \models \varphi, \text{ or } \Delta_{i-1} \leq b \text{ and } i-1 \models \varphi_{I-\Delta_{i-1}} \langle \eth_i(r) \rangle \tag{3}$$

Here, $I = [a, b]$, $\varepsilon_i(r)$ is the Boolean denoting whether $(i, i) \in \mathcal{R}(r)$ (i.e., r matches the empty word), and $\delta_i(r)$ is the Brzozowski derivative [10] of the regular expression r (and $\eth_i(r)$ its symmetric counterpart). For plain regular expressions, the Brzozowski derivative $\delta_c(r)$ computes a regular expression whose language is the left quotient $\{w \mid cw \in L(r)\}$ of the input expression's language $L(r)$ by a given letter c. One may view the derivative as a deterministic automaton whose states are labeled by regular expressions, whereby reading c in a state r takes the automaton to $\delta_c(r)$. For MDL formulas, the time-point i takes the place of the given letter c and "reading c" means querying a subformula's satisfaction at time-point i. The inductive definitions of ε, δ, and $\eth$ follow. They all are implicitly parameterized by the fixed ρ.

$$
\begin{aligned}
\varepsilon_i(\star) &= \bot & \delta_i(\star) &= \top? & \eth_i(\star) &= \top? \\
\varepsilon_i(\varphi?) &= i \models \varphi & \delta_i(\varphi?) &= \bot? & \eth_i(\varphi?) &= \bot? \\
\varepsilon_i(r+s) &= \varepsilon_i(r) \vee \varepsilon_i(s) & \delta_i(r+s) &= \delta_i(r) + \delta_i(s) & \eth_i(r+s) &= \eth_i(r) + \eth_i(s) \\
\varepsilon_i(r \cdot s) &= \varepsilon_i(r) \wedge \varepsilon_i(s) & \delta_i(r \cdot s) &= \delta_i(r) \cdot s + & \eth_i(r \cdot s) &= r \cdot \eth_i(s) + \\
& & &\quad \varepsilon_i(r)? \cdot \delta_i(s) & &\quad \varepsilon_i(s)? \cdot \eth_i(r) \\
\varepsilon_i(r^*) &= \top & \delta_i(r^*) &= \delta_i(r) \cdot r^* & \eth_i(r^*) &= r^* \cdot \eth_i(r)
\end{aligned}
$$

The definition of δ is faithful to Brzozowski's original definition. Note that $\mathcal{R}(\top?) = \{(i, i) \mid i \in \mathbb{N}\}$, $\mathcal{R}(\bot?) = \{\}$, and $\varepsilon_i(r)? \cdot \delta_i(s)$ is equivalent to if $\varepsilon_i(r)$ then $\delta_i(s)$ else $\bot?$, which is more commonly used to define Brzozowski derivatives. The equations for the right derivative $\eth$ are symmetric for the concatenation and star cases. Thereby, $\eth$ matches the regular expression from right to left. It is easy to verify that the Eqs. 2 and 3 hold for those definitions by structural induction on the regular expression r.

How can we integrate Eqs. 2 and 3 into our monitor? Since the equations refer to the satisfiability of formulas $\langle \delta_i(r) \rangle_{I-\Delta_i} \, \varphi$ and $\varphi_{I-\Delta_{i-1}} \langle \eth_i(r) \rangle$, those formulas must occur in our interval-skewed subformulas array. In other words, we must monitor $\langle \delta_i(r) \rangle_I \, \varphi$ simultaneously to $\langle r \rangle_I \, \varphi$ (and all their interval-skewed variants). But by the same reasoning, $\langle \delta_j(\delta_i(r)) \rangle_I \, \varphi$ must be monitored, too. Hence, we must monitor all formulas that can be reached by repeatedly computing the derivative of the original subexpressions. Fortunately, Brzozowski has proved that the set of expressions reachable by repeatedly taking derivatives is finite, provided that one rewrites expressions to a normal form with respect to associativity, commutativity, and idempotence (ACI) of the $+$ constructor. Unfortunately, the number of all such Brzozowski derivatives is exponential in the size of the initial expression r. This is hardly surprising, since regular expressions are exponentially more concise than deterministic automata and the set of all Brzozowski derivatives represents exactly the set of states of a deterministic automaton.

With the size of the array exponential in the size of the input formula, we would still obtain an almost event-rate independent monitor, but not one that is very time-efficient. We can do better by resorting to nondeterministic automata, which are as concise as regular expressions. The equivalent of the Brzozowski derivative for nondeterministic automata are Antimirov's partial derivatives of regular expressions [3]. Instead of computing only one successor expressions, a partial derivative computes a set of expressions, analogous to the transition function of a nondeterministic automaton. The partial derivative ∂ and its symmetric counterpart G are defined inductively as follows.

$$
\begin{aligned}
\partial_i(\star) &= \{\top?\} & \mathsf{G}_i(\star) &= \{\top?\} \\
\partial_i(\varphi?) &= \{\} & \mathsf{G}_i(\varphi?) &= \{\} \\
\partial_i(r+s) &= \partial_i(r) \cup \partial_i(s) & \mathsf{G}_i(r+s) &= \mathsf{G}_i(r) \cup \mathsf{G}_i(s) \\
\partial_i(r \cdot s) &= \partial_i(r) \odot s \cup \varepsilon_i(r)? \odot \partial_i(s) & \mathsf{G}_i(r \cdot s) &= r \odot \mathsf{G}_i(s) \cup \varepsilon_i(s)? \odot \mathsf{G}_i(r) \\
\partial_i(r^*) &= \partial_i(r) \odot r^* & \mathsf{G}_i(r^*) &= r^* \odot \mathsf{G}_i(r)
\end{aligned}
$$

Here, $\odot$ lifts $\cdot$ to sets of expressions. Overloading notation we have $r \odot X = \{r \cdot s \mid s \in X\}$ and $X \odot r = \{s \cdot r \mid s \in X\}$.

Partial derivatives enjoy nice properties: the sum of all expressions in $\partial_i(r)$ is equivalent to $\delta_i(r)$. Moreover, the number of different expressions reachable from r by repeated application of the partial derivative is bounded by $n+1$, where n is r's size [3]. In other words, partial derivatives convert a regular expression of size n into a nondeterministic automaton of size $n+1$. The states of this automaton are labeled by the $n+1$ reachable expressions, and these are exactly the ones our monitor will need to keep track of to follow the following partial derivative variant of Eqs. 2 and 3.

$$i \models \langle r \rangle_I \varphi \text{ iff } a = 0, \varepsilon_i(r), \text{ and } i \models \varphi, \text{ or } \Delta_i \leq b \text{ and } \bigvee_{s \in \partial_i(r)} i+1 \models \langle s \rangle_{I-\Delta_i} \varphi \quad (4)$$

$$i \models \varphi_I \langle r \rangle \text{ iff } a = 0, \varepsilon_i(r), \text{ and } i \models \varphi, \text{ or } \Delta_i \leq b \text{ and } \bigvee_{s \in \mathsf{G}_i(r)} i-1 \models \varphi_{I-\Delta_i} \langle s \rangle \quad (5)$$

Those equations follow by structural induction on r, using the distributivity of the diamond operators over $+$, i.e., $i \models \langle r+s \rangle_I \varphi \Leftrightarrow i \models \langle r \rangle_I \varphi \vee \langle s \rangle_I \varphi$.

We must know which regular expressions to keep track of before actually running the monitor. We can overapproximate this set by replacing $\varepsilon_i(\varphi?)$ with $\top$ instead of $i \models \varphi$. Then both ε and ∂ become independent of the fixed ρ and i. The number of expressions in the approximation is still bounded by the size of the original expression (+1).

4.3 An Almost Event-Rate Independent Monitor for MDL

The recursive equations are a useful blueprint. However, we cannot use the ε and partial derivative operations directly, since they rely on the satisfiability of subformulas that are arguments of _?. But the monitor might not know at time-point i whether some subformula φ is satisfied, since φ could refer to the future. However, the monitor does know the symbolic future expression **curr**$[\varphi]$ denoting φ's satisfiability at i. This knowledge allows us to compute the ε symbolically as a future expression:

$$\varepsilon(\star) = \mathsf{Now} \perp \qquad\qquad \varepsilon(r+s) = \varepsilon(r) \vee_{fexp} \varepsilon(s)$$
$$\varepsilon(\varphi?) = \mathbf{curr}[\varphi] \qquad\qquad \varepsilon(r \cdot s) = \varepsilon(r) \wedge_{fexp} \varepsilon(s) \qquad\qquad \varepsilon(r^*) = \mathsf{Now} \top$$

Unlike previous definitions of ε, this definition does not depend on any fixed stream ρ.

For the symbolic version of partial derivatives, an additional complication arises. The above definition of ∂ computes a set of expressions and relies on the Boolean verdicts of certain subformulas. When we work with future expressions, we do not know for sure whether to include the partial derivatives of s when computing the partial derivatives $r \cdot s$, since $\varepsilon(r)$ is not a Boolean value but a future expression. Therefore, the derivative's result must be something like a decision tree with sets of regular expressions as leaves. Equations 4 and 5 illustrate, however, that in fact we are not interested in expressions as such, but rather in expressions wrapped into some fixed past or future diamond operators and ultimately the satisfiability of the resulting formulas. Satisfiability queries are much easier to represent using our machinery (as future expressions) than decision tree with sets of regular expressions as leaves. Using continuation-passing-style programming, we obtain the symbolic partial derivative ∂ (and the symmetric $\wp$) that computes a future expression corresponding to $\bigvee_{s \in \partial_i(r)} i+1 \models \langle s \rangle_{I-\Delta_i} \varphi$. The function ∂ takes two arguments: a regular expression r and a continuation function κ that is supposed to wrap a regular expressions in a past or future diamond operator and create a variable pointing to the corresponding formula in the $(i+1)$st time-point.

$$\partial(\star, \kappa) = \kappa(\top?) \qquad\qquad\qquad \wp(\star, \kappa) = \kappa(\top?)$$
$$\partial(\varphi?, \kappa) = \mathsf{Now} \perp \qquad\qquad\quad \wp(\varphi?, \kappa) = \mathsf{Now} \perp$$
$$\partial(r+s, \kappa) = \partial(r, \kappa) \vee_{fexp} \partial(s, \kappa) \qquad \wp(r+s, \kappa) = \wp(r, \kappa) \vee_{fexp} \wp(s, \kappa)$$
$$\partial(r \cdot s, \kappa) = \partial(r, \lambda t.\, \kappa\,(t \cdot s)) \vee_{fexp} \qquad \wp(r \cdot s, \kappa) = \wp(s, \lambda t.\, \kappa\,(r \cdot t)) \vee_{fexp}$$
$$(\varepsilon(r) \wedge_{fexp} \partial(s, \kappa)) \qquad\qquad (\varepsilon(s) \wedge_{fexp} \wp(r, \kappa))$$
$$\partial(r^*, \kappa) = \partial(r, \lambda t.\, \kappa\,(t \cdot r^*)) \qquad\quad \wp(r^*, \kappa) = \wp(r, \lambda t.\, \kappa\,(r^* \cdot t))$$

Observe how the continuation is altered in the concatenation and star cases. The standard partial derivative first calculates recursively the set $\partial_i(r)$ before concatenating s to each expression in $\partial_i(r)$. Here, we extend the continuation κ to perform the concatenation via $\lambda t.\, \kappa\,(t \cdot s)$ at the leaves of the recursion tree.

Finally, we define the progress function for MDL. The function takes as input a subformula φ, the time-stamp difference Δ between the current and the previous time-point, and the set of currently true atomic predicates π. Moreover, it assumes, that the array **prev** contains the Boolean expressions denoting the satisfiability at the previous time-point for all interval-skewed variants of φ and that the array **curr** contains the future expression denoting the satisfiability at the current time-point for all subformulas of φ. It computes a future expression denoting the satisfiability of φ at the current time-point.

$$\text{progress } (\varphi, \Delta, \pi) = \text{case } \varphi \text{ of}$$

$\quad | \; p \qquad\qquad \Rightarrow \mathsf{Now} \; (p \in \pi)$

$\quad | \; \neg\psi \qquad\quad\; \Rightarrow \neg_{fexp} \, \mathbf{curr}[\psi]$

$\quad | \; \psi_1 \vee \psi_2 \quad\; \Rightarrow \mathbf{curr}[\psi_1] \vee_{fexp} \mathbf{curr}[\psi_2]$

$\quad | \; \langle r \rangle_{[a,b]} \, \psi \Rightarrow (\mathsf{Now} \; (a = 0) \wedge_{fexp} \varepsilon(r) \wedge_{fexp} \mathbf{curr}[\psi]) \vee_{fexp}$

$\qquad\qquad\qquad \mathsf{Later} \; (\lambda\Delta'. \, \Delta' \leq b \wedge \mathsf{eval}_{\Delta'}(\partial \; (r, \lambda s. \, \mathsf{Now} \; (\mathsf{Var} \; (\langle s \rangle_{[a,b]-\Delta'} \, \psi)))))$

$\quad | \; \psi_{[a,b]} \langle r \rangle \Rightarrow (\mathsf{Now} \; (a = 0) \wedge_{fexp} \varepsilon(r) \wedge_{fexp} \mathbf{curr}[\psi]) \vee_{fexp}$

$\qquad\qquad\qquad (\mathsf{Now} \; (\Delta \leq b) \wedge_{fexp} \, \mathsf{\lozenge} \; (r, \lambda s. \, \mathsf{subst} \; (\lambda k. \, \mathbf{curr}[k]) \, \mathbf{prev}[\psi_{[a,b]-\Delta} \langle s \rangle]))$

Only the cases for the diamond operators are interesting. They implement Eqs. 4 and 5. The first disjunct is the same for both the future and past, since it covers the case when the regular expression matches the empty word. For the future diamond, the second disjunct is a Later future expression, since it does not know the time-stamp difference between the current and the next time-point. The argument to Later is the conjunction of the Boolean from the interval boundary test with the symbolic partial derivative ∂ (evaluated to a Boolean expression using the abstracted time-difference Δ'). The continuation κ wraps a given regular expression into a future diamond formula and creates a variable denoting the satisfiability of the resulting formula at the next time-point. For the past diamond, the second disjunct is a conjunction of the interval boundary test and the right derivative $\mathsf{\lozenge}$. The continuation function for the latter wraps a given regular expression into a past diamond formula and retrieves the Boolean expression denoting the formula's satisfaction at the previous time-point from **prev**. The variables in this expression point to the current time-point. The function subst updates those variables to the next time-point by accessing **curr**.

Using this progress function in the algorithm shown in Subsect. 4.1 results in our almost event-rate independent monitor for MDL.

Theorem 2. *Our monitor is sound: for an MDL formula Φ and any prefix of the event-stream ρ, whenever it outputs a Boolean verdict b at time-point i, then $i \models \varphi \Leftrightarrow b$ and whenever it outputs an equivalence verdict between time-points i and j, then $i \models \varphi \Leftrightarrow j \models \varphi$. Moreover, the monitor outputs each verdict as soon as it has seen enough events to compute the verdict and its space consumption is almost event-rate independent.*

Proof. For lack of space, we refer to the similar proof in our previous work for the MTL monitor [5, Sect. 5.3]. Since we have only modified the progress function, the only part that must be adjusted is the calculation given there in the proof of Lemma 2.   □

To process an event, our monitor solves several NP-complete problem instances. However, the Boolean equivalences arising in practice are simple and tractable (Sect. 5).

4.4   Optimizations

AERIAL [1] is a concise OCaml implementation of our monitoring algorithms for MTL and MDL. In previous work [5], we reported on a PolyML implementation of the homonymous MTL monitor. The OCaml successor employs several optimizations, used in both logics, that substantially improve its performance for MTL.

Following Havelund and Roşu [18], our arrays store only expressions for temporal subformulas. The expressions for the Boolean connectives are computed on the fly accessing the **curr** array for temporal subformulas and are not stored.

A central operation in our monitor is the access to the **curr** and **prev** arrays based on a subformula's index. This raises the question of how to efficiently retrieve a subformula's index. Searching the array of subformulas is of course not an efficient option (although our previous PolyML implementation did just that). A standard more efficient solution would be to use a hash table, but some preliminary experiments showed that computing hashes of formulas very quickly becomes a bottleneck, too. Instead, AERIAL stores the indices for all subformulas directly in the formulas as annotations on the constructors. In the progress function, we then still need to compute the index of a formula based on the indices of its subformulas and the interval. However, the stored index allows us to avoid computing the indices of the subformulas recursively. For MTL it is easy to compute the exact position of a temporal formula $\varphi \, \mathcal{U}_I \, \psi$ based on this information by using a canonical order on subformulas as in $[\ldots, \varphi, \ldots, \psi, \ldots, \varphi \, \mathcal{U}_{I-2} \, \psi, \varphi \, \mathcal{U}_{I-1} \, \psi, \varphi \, \mathcal{U}_I \, \psi]$: the index of $\varphi \, \mathcal{U}_I \, \psi$ is just the index of ψ increased by b, where $I = [a, b]$. For MDL this is still problematic, since the derivatives are hard to align in a predictable way. We resort to memoizing the derivative functions ∂ and $\mathfrak{b}$ to compute a symbolic expression not only in the verdicts at the $(i+1)$st time-point but also in the verdicts at the ith time-point. Thereby, the search for indices happens only once during the initialization of the monitor and not in the progress function. The progress function merely needs to substitute the symbolic variables pointing to the ith time-point with the current values of **curr**.

Another crucial question is how to represent Boolean expressions. AERIAL offers the choice between two representations: the one reported in the paper and one based on binary decision diagrams (BDDs). For the former, it is important to keep the expressions small. To achieve this, we normalize expressions with respect to the associativity, commutativity, and idempotence of $\wedge$ and $\vee$, as well as Boolean tautologies such as $\top \wedge c = c$. Boolean expressions offer a low-cost substitution operation, but are expensive to check for equivalence. In fact, the equivalence check translates expressions into BDDs. The BDD version always works with the BDD representation thereby avoiding the costly translation. In contrast, the substitution operation becomes more expensive. In our experiments, the Boolean expression version outperformed the BDD version.

5   Evaluation

In our evaluation, we distinguish between two variants of our tool: AERIAL MDL and AERIAL MTL and we compare them with MONPOLY [6,7], a state-of-the-art monitor for *metric first-order temporal logic* (*MFOTL*) and MONTRE [27,28], a state-of-the-art matcher for *timed regular expressions* (*TRE*). We aim to answer the following questions:

Q1: *How does* AERIAL MDL *scale with respect to the event rate?*
Q2: *How does* AERIAL MDL *scale with respect to the size of the monitored formula?*
Q3: *Does* AERIAL MDL *perform better then state-of-the-art tools?*

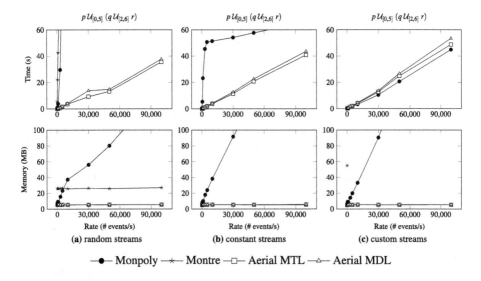

Fig. 2. Time (top) and memory (bottom) usage with respect to the event rate

We ran all our experiments on a 2.6 GHz quad-core Intel Core i7 processor with 16 GB RAM. We measure the tools' total execution time and maximal memory usage via the Unix time command. We use GNU Parallel [24] both to generate the streams and run the four tools. Our evaluation can be divided into two parts: analyzing the tools' scalability with respect to (1) the event rate and (2) the size of the monitored formula. In the first part, we monitor a fixed set of formulas ($\Diamond_{[0,5]} p$, $p\,\mathcal{U}_{[0,5]}\,q$, $p\,\mathcal{U}_{[0,5]}\,(q\,\mathcal{S}_{[2,6]}\,r)$, and $p\,\mathcal{U}_{[0,5]}\,(q\,\mathcal{U}_{[2,6]}\,r)$) over streams with an increasing event rate. In the second part, we monitor formulas of increasing size over a set of streams with a fixed event rate.

The finite prefixes of the synthetic streams used in the experiments span 100 time units, with the event rate (the number of time-points labeled with the same time-stamp) ranging from 100 to 100,000 on average ($\pm 10\%$) per stream. The streams contain three events, $\Sigma = \{p, q, r\}$, and their distribution depends on three different generation strategies: *random*, *constant*, and *custom*. The random generation strategy uses the uniform probability distribution for each event. Under the constant strategy, each stream has identical events at every time-point. Since $|\Sigma| = 3$, there are exactly eight distinct constant streams, including the stream with all empty time-points, and the stream with all events at all time-point. Constant streams are useful to test edge cases in the monitors' implementations and often trigger worst-case monitor execution time and memory usage. Finally, the custom generation strategy uses event probability distributions tailored to the particular formulas. For example, for the formula $\Diamond_{[0,5]} p$, the probability of p occurring is very small, which makes the tools wait longer before producing a verdict.

For each generation strategy and event rate, we generated eight different streams. We also converted each of these streams to the format supported by MONTRE. Since MONTRE supports only strictly monotonic time-stamps, our conversion simulated large event rates by increasing the time granularity of the MONTRE streams. Namely, time-points that share the same time-stamp in the original stream are converted into a sequence of time-points with time-stamps that strictly increase by one time unit. The granularity of the time unit in the converted stream is proportional to the event rate.

We have developed a random MTL and MDL formula generator parameterized by the formula's size using QCheck [2], a QuickCheck implementation for OCaml. For our evaluation, we measure the formula size simply as the number of subformulas and we separately check the scalability of the monitors with respect to different interval sizes in the formulas. Note that the tools can only be compared on commonly supported logical fragments. Propositional MTL with both future and past is the common fragment supported by AERIAL MDL, AERIAL MTL, and MONPOLY, while future MDL formulas in positive normal form belong to the common fragment of AERIAL MDL and MONTRE. To supply the correct input to each tool, the formula generator implements a translation from MTL to fragments of MDL, MFOTL, and a translation from MDL to TRE. The translation to TRE also scales the intervals appropriately to match the different time granularity of MONTRE-compliant streams. In contrast to monitors that report violations, MONTRE outputs all parts of the stream that match a TRE pattern. Hence, to properly compare the tools, we negate the formulas inputed to the other monitors. We generated ten arbitrary formulas for each formula size ranging from 5 to 100.

We set a timeout for each monitoring run to be 100 s, coinciding with the streams' time span. Moreover, we enforce the following disqualification scheme: If a tool times out for all the traces with the same event rate (or for all formulas with the same size) it will not be invoked for traces with larger event rates (or, respectively, for formulas with larger size). When computing the average values, a timeout counts as 100 s (although the actual run may take longer) and skews the curves to converge to the 100 s margin. Therefore, in our plots we only show average values below 50 s. The memory used before a timeout contributes to the average memory usage.

Figure 2 shows the results of the first part of the evaluation classified according to the stream generation strategy. We show the plots for formula $p\,\mathcal{U}_{[0,5]}\,(q\,\mathcal{U}_{[2,6]}\,r)$, which had least favorable outcome for AERIAL MDL. Each data point in the plots represents a value averaged over eight different streams with a fixed event rate. To answer Q1, we note that the space consumption of both versions of AERIAL is constant. As expected, the increasing memory consumption of other tools significant increases the overall processing time. MONTRE was almost immediately disqualified in the case of constant and custom streams. To answer Q2, we note that, even for the largest formula, AERIAL MDL requires only 12 MB of space compared to MONPOLY, which uses almost 2 GB (see Fig. 3a). These experiments were performed on random traces and random formulas and each data point is an average value over eight random traces and ten random formulas with the same size. During the experiment indicated in Fig. 3b, MONTRE timed out 392 times which is over 50% of all its invocations. Figure 3c shows that all the tools are mostly unaffected by the size of the time interval N in the formula $p\,\mathcal{U}_{[0,N]}\,(q\,\mathcal{S}_{[N/2,N]}\,r)$. Finally, we observe that in all tests AERIAL MDL performs only marginally worse than AERIAL MTL, while supporting a strictly more expressive logic.

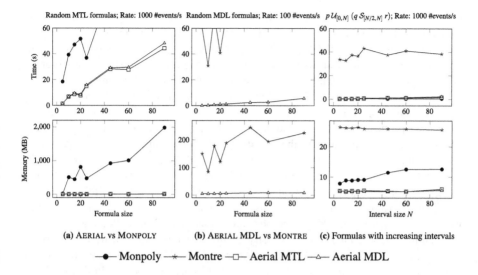

Fig. 3. Time (top) and memory (bottom) usage with respect to the formula size

6 Related Work

We survey temporal logics similar to MDL and we describe and compare monitoring algorithms for those logics most closely related to ours.

MTL is a well known temporal logic for specifying real-time properties. Thati and Roşu [25] provide an event-rate independent, dynamic programming monitoring algorithm for MTL based on derivatives of MTL formulas. However, their algorithm implements a non-standard semantics of MTL, truncated to finite traces. When handling future temporal operators, the algorithm outputs verdicts without looking at future events, which can potentially alter the verdicts. Computing verdicts this way defeats the purpose of (top-level) future operators: An *until* that is not satisfied at the current time-point, but only at the next one, is reported as a violation. Basin et al. [7,8] introduce techniques to handle MTL and metric first-order temporal logic with bounded future operators, adhering to the standard non-truncated semantics for future formulas. Their monitor uses a queue to postpone the evaluation of a future formula to a time-point at which all needed information is present. Their algorithm stores in the worst case all time-points while it waits and its space complexity is therefore linear in the event rate. Our previous work [5] is, up to now, the only almost event-rate independent monitoring algorithm for MTL with the standard semantics for future operators.

Dynamic LTL [19] (DLTL) is one of the earliest attempts to extend LTL's until operator to express all ω-regular languages. Leucker and Sánchez [22] propose regular LTL (RLTL) that further improves on DLTL by allowing regular expressions to be nested arbitrarily as LTL subformulas. RLTL's power operator is also more suitable for extensions that can handle past. Sánchez and Leucker [23] extend RLTL with past operators and show that it can be translated into a 2-way alternating parity automaton with size linear in the size of the RLTL formula. But 2-way automata are not ideally suited for the online monitoring of high-velocity event streams, and removing bidirectionality incurs an exponential blowup [20]. Dax et al. [11] propose a similar extension of the property specification language [29] (PSL) with additional past operators, called regular temporal logic (RTL). They translate RTL formulas into nondeterministic Büchi automata with the worst-case size doubly exponential in the size of the RTL formula.

More recently, De Giacomo and Vardi [14] revisited this problem for the finite-trace semantics and introduced linear dynamic logic (LDL$_f$). It was inspired by the well-known propositional dynamic logic (PDL) [17], but its semantics closely resemble LTL. The authors do not discuss the past diamond operator and do not provide a monitoring algorithm. However, they do provide a general translation from LDL formulas to alternating finite state automata that employs partial derivatives in a similar fashion as our monitoring algorithm. De Giacomo et al. [12, 13] provide a direct translation from LDL$_f$ formulas to nondeterministic automata that are more suitable for monitoring. Faymonville et al. [15, 16] propose an extension of LDL called parametric linear dynamic logic (PLDL) that can specify quantitative temporal constraints. However, PLDL does not support past operators and its point-based time model does not include time-stamps, but rather time is implicitly encoded in the time-points. In this work, we chose to extend LDL with metric features (as opposed to PSL, RTL, or RLTL) due to its convenient and elegant mutual nesting of logical formulas and regular expressions.

Asarin et al. [4] introduce *timed regular expressions* (TRE) and prove their equivalence to timed automata. Additionally, some of the authors propose offline [27] and online [28] pattern matching algorithms for TRE, implemented as an open source tool called MONTRE [26]. Although TRE was originally defined over both discrete point-based and dense interval-based time models, MONTRE assumes the latter model.

7 Conclusion

We have introduced metric dynamic logic (MDL), a new logic that combines the expressive power of regular expressions with the ability to reference the past and the future in both a quantitative and qualitative way, as in metric temporal logic. Moreover, we have extended our previous almost event-rate independent monitoring algorithm for MTL to support MDL. Our evaluation shows that our implementation of this monitor, AERIAL, outperforms other state-of-the-art monitoring tools.

As future work, we would like to extend the presented ideas to the first-order setting, where events may carry data and formulas may quantify over the data's domain.

Acknowledgment. Felix Klaedtke pointed us to a motivating example of a property not expressible in MTL. Bhargav Bhatt, Domenico Bianculli, and three anonymous reviewers provided helpful feedback on earlier drafts of this paper. Srđan Krstić is supported by the Swiss National Science Foundation grant Big Data Monitoring (167162). The authors are listed alphabetically.

References

1. Aerial: An almost event-rate independent monitor for metric temporal logic (2017). https://bitbucket.org/traytel/aerial
2. QCheck: QuickCheck inspired property-based testing for OCaml (2017). https://github.com/c-cube/qcheck
3. Antimirov, V.: Partial derivatives of regular expressions and finite automaton constructions. Theor. Comput. Sci. **155**(2), 291–319 (1996)
4. Asarin, E., Caspi, P., Maler, O.: Timed regular expressions. J. ACM **49**(2), 172–206 (2002)
5. Basin, D.A., Bhatt, B.N., Traytel, D.: Almost event-rate independent monitoring of metric temporal logic. In: Legay, A., Margaria, T. (eds.) TACAS 2017. LNCS, vol. 10206, pp. 94–112. Springer, Heidelberg (2017). doi:10.1007/978-3-662-54580-5_6
6. Basin, D.A., Klaedtke, F., Müller, S., Pfitzmann, B.: Runtime monitoring of metric first-order temporal properties. In: Hariharan, R., Mukund, M., Vinay, V. (eds.) FSTTCS 2008. LIPIcs, vol. 2, pp. 49–60. Schloss Dagstuhl - Leibniz-Zentrum fuer Informatik (2008)
7. Basin, D.A., Klaedtke, F., Müller, S., Zălinescu, E.: Monitoring metric first-order temporal properties. J. ACM **62**(2), 1–45 (2015)
8. Basin, D.A., Klaedtke, F., Zălinescu, E.: Algorithms for monitoring real-time properties. In: Khurshid, S., Sen, K. (eds.) RV 2011. LNCS, vol. 7186, pp. 260–275. Springer, Heidelberg (2012). doi:10.1007/978-3-642-29860-8_20
9. Bouyer, P., Chevalier, F., Markey, N.: On the expressiveness of TPTL and MTL. Inf. Comput. **208**(2), 97–116 (2010)
10. Brzozowski, J.A.: Derivatives of regular expressions. J. ACM **11**(4), 481–494 (1964)
11. Dax, C., Klaedtke, F., Lange, M.: On regular temporal logics with past. Acta Inf. **47**(4), 251–277 (2010)
12. De Giacomo, G., De Masellis, R., Grasso, M., Maggi, F.M., Montali, M.: LTLf and LDLf monitoring: A technical report. CoRR abs/1405.0054 (2014)
13. De Giacomo, G., De Masellis, R., Grasso, M., Maggi, F.M., Montali, M.: Monitoring business metaconstraints based on LTL and LDL for finite traces. In: Sadiq, S., Soffer, P., Völzer, H. (eds.) BPM 2014. LNCS, vol. 8659, pp. 1–17. Springer, Cham (2014). doi:10.1007/978-3-319-10172-9_1
14. De Giacomo, G., Vardi, M.Y.: Linear temporal logic and linear dynamic logic on finite traces. In: Rossi, F. (ed.) IJCAI-13, pp. 854–860. AAAI Press (2013)
15. Faymonville, P., Zimmermann, M.: Parametric linear dynamic logic. In: Peron, A., Piazza, C. (eds.) Proceedings 5th GandALF 2014, EPTCS, vol. 161, pp. 60–73 (2014)
16. Faymonville, P., Zimmermann, M.: Parametric linear dynamic logic. Inf. Comput. **253**, 237–256 (2017)
17. Fischer, M.J., Ladner, R.E.: Propositional dynamic logic of regular programs. J. Comput. Syst. Sci. **18**(2), 194–211 (1979)
18. Havelund, K., Roşu, G.: Synthesizing monitors for safety properties. In: Katoen, J.-P., Stevens, P. (eds.) TACAS 2002. LNCS, vol. 2280, pp. 342–356. Springer, Heidelberg (2002). doi:10.1007/3-540-46002-0_24
19. Henriksen, J.G., Thiagarajan, P.: Dynamic linear time temporal logic. Ann. Pure Appl. Logic **96**(1), 187–207 (1999)
20. Kapoutsis, C.: Removing bidirectionality from nondeterministic finite automata. In: Jędrzejowicz, J., Szepietowski, A. (eds.) MFCS 2005. LNCS, vol. 3618, pp. 544–555. Springer, Heidelberg (2005). doi:10.1007/11549345_47
21. Koymans, R.: Specifying real-time properties with metric temporal logic. Real-Time Syst. **2**(4), 255–299 (1990)

22. Leucker, M., Sánchez, C.: Regular linear temporal logic. In: Jones, C.B., Liu, Z., Woodcock, J. (eds.) ICTAC 2007. LNCS, vol. 4711, pp. 291–305. Springer, Heidelberg (2007). doi:10. 1007/978-3-540-75292-9_20

23. Sánchez, C., Leucker, M.: Regular linear temporal logic with past. In: Barthe, G., Hermenegildo, M. (eds.) VMCAI 2010. LNCS, vol. 5944, pp. 295–311. Springer, Heidelberg (2010). doi:10.1007/978-3-642-11319-2_22

24. Tange, O.: GNU parallel - the command-line power tool.;login: USENIX Mag. **36**(1), 42–47 (2011). http://www.gnu.org/s/parallel

25. Thati, P., Roşu, G.: Monitoring algorithms for metric temporal logic specifications. Electr. Notes Theor. Comput. Sci. **113**, 145–162 (2005)

26. Ulus, D.: Montre: A tool for monitoring timed regular expressions. arXiv preprint (2016). arXiv:1605.05963

27. Ulus, D., Ferrère, T., Asarin, E., Maler, O.: Timed pattern matching. In: Legay, A., Bozga, M. (eds.) FORMATS 2014. LNCS, vol. 8711, pp. 222–236. Springer, Cham (2014). doi:10. 1007/978-3-319-10512-3_16

28. Ulus, D., Ferrère, T., Asarin, E., Maler, O.: Online timed pattern matching using derivatives. In: Chechik, M., Raskin, J.-F. (eds.) TACAS 2016. LNCS, vol. 9636, pp. 736–751. Springer, Heidelberg (2016). doi:10.1007/978-3-662-49674-9_47

29. Vardi, M.Y.: From Church and Prior to PSL. In: Grumberg, O., Veith, H. (eds.) 25 Years of Model Checking. LNCS, vol. 5000, pp. 150–171. Springer, Heidelberg (2008). doi:10. 1007/978-3-540-69850-0_10

30. Wolper, P.: Temporal logic can be more expressive. Inform. Control **56**(1/2), 72–99 (1983)

Annotation Guided Collection of Context-Sensitive Parallel Execution Profiles

Zachary Benavides[1]([⊠]), Rajiv Gupta[1], and Xiangyu Zhang[2]

[1] University of California, Riverside, USA
zbena001@ucr.edu
[2] Purdue University, West Lafayette, USA

Abstract. Studying the relative behavior of an application's threads is critical to identifying performance bottlenecks and understanding their root causes. We present *context-sensitive parallel* (CSP) execution profiles, that capture the relative behavior of threads in terms of the *user selected code regions* they execute. CSPs can be analyzed to compute execution times spent by the application in interesting *behavior states*. To capture *execution context*, code regions of interest can be given static and dynamic names using a versatile set of annotations. The CSP divides the execution time of a multithreaded application into a sequence of time intervals called *frames*, during which no thread transitions between code regions. By appropriate selection and naming of code regions, the user can obtain a CSP that captures all occurrences of arbitrary behavior states. We provide the user with a powerful *query language* to facilitate the analysis of CSPs. Our implementation for collection of CSPs of C++ programs has *low overhead* and *high accuracy*. Collection of CSPs of full executions of 12 Parsec programs incurred overhead of at most 7% in execution time. The accuracy of CSPs was validated in the context of common performance problems such as load imbalance in pipeline stages and the presence of straggler threads.

Keywords: Parallel behaviors · Contention · Load imbalance · Stragglers · Overhead

1 Introduction

Understanding the runtime behavior of parallel programs is hard. Thus, tools have been developed to understand parallel program behavior for performance debugging [5,6,21]. Existing works are aimed at specific metrics to identify performance bugs, e.g., normalized execution time [3], critical paths [11], slack [13] etc. However, it is desirable to develop a single *versatile* framework that allows the user to capture a wide range of program behaviors using a variety of metrics to understand their causes. In addition, the framework should be *accurate* and *lightweight*. The instrumentation must be lightweight to minimize its intrusive effects that can alter the program's runtime behavior. Sampling can be used to

This work is supported by NSF grants CCF-1318103 and CCF-1524852 to UCR.

© Springer International Publishing AG 2017
S. Lahiri and G. Reger (Eds.): RV 2017, LNCS 10548, pp. 103–120, 2017.
DOI: 10.1007/978-3-319-67531-2_7

reduce runtime overhead [2,9,18]; however, it sacrifices the precision with which the runtime behavior is captured.

We present a framework for the collection and representation of runtime profiles of parallel executions that is versatile, accurate, and lightweight. Its key components are as follows:

1. Code Region Annotations. Our framework provides annotations using which code regions of interest are marked and named by the user. The names of regions can have static and/or dynamic components that allow region executions to be captured in a *context-sensitive* fashion. Annotations make our system versatile – user can select code regions of different types (e.g., code blocks, loops, functions, etc.), categorize their executions according to context (e.g., call and return sites, locks held) to match the needs for detecting interesting program behaviors (e.g., lock contention, straggler threads, bottleneck pipeline stages). The annotations guide the introduction of lightweight instrumentation using which *thread local timestamped event traces* are collected independently. Instrumentation overhead is kept low via use of unsynchronized local clocks (e.g., the Intel Timestamp Counter) and by only instrumenting the regions of interest. The error introduced by lack of synchronization has a negligible impact on the results of our analyses.

2. Context Sensitive Parallel Profile: Capture and Representation. Following execution, the collected thread local event traces are converted into a novel representation called *Context Sensitive Parallel* (CSP) profiles. A CSP divides the execution time of a multithreaded application into time intervals or a *sequence of frames* such that during each frame the code regions being executed in parallel by application threads remain unchanged. This representation is compact and yet precise. Interesting program *behavior states* involving multiple threads (e.g., contention, straggler threads, load imbalance) can be easily characterized in terms of frames they generate and thus can be captured by CSPs.

3. Querying CSPs. Since the CSP contains the activities of individual threads and their relative timing of execution, a wide range of queries of frequencies and runtime durations of parallel behaviors can be evaluated from them. We have developed and implemented a powerful query language using which it is easy to construct queries that detect the time spent by a parallel application in interesting behavior states. Thus, queries can be constructed not only to identify performance bottlenecks, but also to understand their root causes.

Our evaluation shows that the overhead of our system is low and case studies show that CSPs help in understanding the causes of performance bottlenecks.

2   CSP Execution Profiles

.8The steps of our approach are shown in Fig. 1. Based upon a hypothesis for the cause of poor performance, the user introduces annotations into source code identifying code regions of interest. The

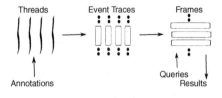

Fig. 1. Overview

annotations lead to instrumentation of the program that when executed produces timestamped traces for individual threads – thread local collection of event traces via lightweight instrumentation leads to *minimal perturbation* of program behavior and *low overhead*. The event traces are analyzed offline to generate a sequence of frames which describe what activities were performed by threads in parallel. Finally, the user constructs queries that reveal how often and how long threads run in behavior states of interest, which reveals the absence or presence of hypothesized performance problem.

2.1   Code Region Annotations

Here we present the annotation framework available to the user. A set of easy to use annotations are supported that allow the user to mark code regions. The annotations provide the user with a great deal of flexibility via two features: alternate ways of *naming* the region; and allowing *conditional* collection of region information.

Purpose	Annotation
ENTRY	#Region [NAME] [CONDITION]
EXIT	#~Region [NAME] [CONDITION]
NAME	(RID CNST : [CVAR])
CONDITION	if (EXP)
RELATED	#SubRegion [NAME] [CONDITION] ⋯
NESTED	⋯ #~SubRegion [NAME] [CONDITION]
CONTEXT	#Context STMT ;

Fig. 2. Summary of supported annotations.

Figure 2 provides a list of supported annotations which consist of the following components:

– Marking region entry and exit. The annotations #Region and #~Region mark the entry and exit of the region respectively. The corresponding SubRegion annotations are used to express related nested regions as will be described later.
– Naming regions. As the user may mark multiple regions of interest, names are assigned to them to distinguish their executions. The user provides a *static name* in form a constant (CNST). In addition, the user may also provide a *dynamic name* component in form an expression (EXP). This dynamic name is useful when the user wishes to distinguish executions of a given region into a finite number of categories according to their *execution context* (e.g., functions called, locks held, paths followed etc.). The context itself is captured in a variable by the #Context annotation (for instance, with STMT being CVAR = EXP;).
– Conditional regions. A user may be interested in only some of the executions of a marked region which can be selected at runtime based upon an associated condition (see CONDITION) defined in terms of the program's runtime state. The #SubRegion and #~SubRegion annotations can be used to couple nested conditional regions, such that instances of the inner region are not captured unless instances of the outer region are captured as well.

Next we illustrate the use of above features through examples. A region can be a single-entry-single-exit or a single-entry-multiple-exit code region.

Static-name-only *regions.* Let us consider the use of static names. It is often useful to analyze the relative execution times of a pair of regions. For example, in Fig. 3, region 1 captures the time spent waiting on a condition relative to the time spent in the surrounding for loop (region 0). In Fig. 4, the time spent waiting on a lock (region 1) is captured relative to the time spent in the surrounding function (region 0). Consider another example of *barrier synchronization* where it is useful to identify the presence of a *straggler thread* causing excessive waiting. Let us see how via appropriate region selection we can detect and find the cause of this behavior. By using the annotations shown on in Fig. 5, we can determine the wait time for each thread at the barrier (region 1) as well as the total time spent in the loop (region 0). If it is found that all threads except one thread wait for a significant duration at the barrier, then that one thread is the straggler. By comparing the execution time of the loop (region 0) with the time spent at the barrier (region 1) we can see if barrier causes significant performance degradation. Having detected the presence of a straggler, we can see if the same thread

```
#Region (RID  0:)
while ( ... )  {
    ...
    #Region (RID  1:)
    cond . wait ( );
    #~Region
    ...
}
#~ Region
```

Fig. 3. Wait time

```
void  f ()  {
    #Region (RID  0:)
    ...
    #Region (RID  1:)
    mutex . lock ( );
    #~Region
    ...
    shared++;
    ...
    mutex . unlock ( );
    ...
    #~Region
}
```

Fig. 4. Lock contention

```
#Region (RID  0:)
for  ( ... )  {
    //Loop  body
    ...
    #Region (RID  1:)
    barrier_wait ( );
    #~Region
}
#~ Region
```

Fig. 5. Identifying straggler thread

```
for  ( ... )  {
    #Region (RID  0:)
    //Loop  body
    ...
    #~Region
    #Region (RID  1:)
    barrier_wait ( );
    #~Region
}
```

Fig. 6. Straggler thread

```
class  Lock  {
    void  acquire ()  {
        #Region (RID  0: this )
        ...
        #~Region
    }
}
```

Fig. 7. Adding dynamic names for different locks using **this** pointer.

```
for  ( ... )  {
    #Region (RID  0:)
    // Loop  body
    ...
    if  ()  {
        #Context  fname  = 1
        f ()  }  else  {
        #Context  fname  = 2
        g ()  }
    #~Region (RID  : fname )
    #Region (RID  1:)
    barrier_wait ( );
    #~Region
}
```

Fig. 8. Dynamic names as execution context.

acts as a straggler or whether the straggler's identity varies. In the latter case, this behavior may be the result of variability in the amount of work performed by the loop body. This can be verified by using the modified annotation shown in Fig. 6 where region 0 captures the time spent on the work performed during each loop iteration. If during an iteration, the thread identified as the straggler is also the one that spends the most time in region 0, then we know the cause is the code in region 0.

In the above examples because we only considered single-entry single-exit regions, we were able to assign static names upon entry. However, for single-entry multiple-exit code regions where we want to treat each exit as forming a different region, we must name the region on exit since the region id is known at the exit point. For example, consider a function with multiple return points. We can use region ids 0, 1, 2 etc. to distinguish different return points.

Context-sensitive dynamic-name *regions*. The user may want to collect additional execution `context` information to better understand the causes of observed timing behavior. In such situations, in addition to using a static name, a *dynamic name* is also assigned. Let us consider the example of some code that acquires of a lock. The user may be interested in capturing the time spent in `acquire()` of various locks by each thread. As shown in Fig. 7, this can be achieved by assigning a static name 0 to mark the code region and assigning a dynamic name using the *lock address* as the execution context. Thus, the time spent by a thread in acquiring locks can be divided among the different locks it acquires. Here the context (i.e., `&thislock`) was already available at the start of region 0 and thus it was directly referenced while creating the dynamic name. In general to ensure that the execution context is available at region entry or exit point, it may be necessary to first collect it explicitly at an appropriate execution point. In such a case we use `#Context` annotations for collection.

Consider the loop shown in Fig. 8 which is an expanded version of the loop on the right in Figs. 5 and 6. Further assume that we want to capture the function called (f() or g()) during the execution of each loop iteration because the user suspects that one of these functions is responsible for creating the straggler effect. As shown in the Fig. 8, this can be achieved by specifying a static name in the annotation that marks the entry of the region as before and, in addition, using the context variable `fname` as the dynamic name in the annotation that marks the exit of the region. The context is captured at the call sites of the functions via the two `#Context` annotations. As a result each execution of the loop body is assigned the name `0:1` or `0:2` depending upon where function f() or g() are called. Let us assume that we observe that a given thread acts as straggler when it calls f() but not g(), then we would know that we must optimize the code in f() to eliminate the straggler effect. Thus, dynamic names help the user to narrow and relate the cause of observed behavior to smaller code segments within marked regions.

Conditional regions. To handle situations in which we may not be interested in capturing all executions of an annotated region we support *conditional regions.* By specifying a condition as part of the annotation we can selectively capture executions of a region. This is yet another way of capturing context sensitive information. However, it is different from capturing context using names. This is because, con-

```
while  (...) {
  #Region(RID  0:)  for  Thread(TID = 1)
    ...
  #Context  sample = 0
  while  (...) {
    #Context  sample++
    #SubRegion(RID  1:)  if (sample % 5==0)
      if () {
        #Context  fname = 1
        f() }
      else {
        #Context  fname = 2
        g() }
    #~SubRegion(RID  :fname) }
  #~Region }
```

Fig. 9. Conditional profiling of regions.

ditional regions collect only relevant information corresponding to interesting contexts. Figure 9 illustrates the use of annotations for specifying conditional regions. The region corresponding to the outer loop indicates that the execution of this region is only captured if the region is being executed by the thread with id 1. The second region in the inner loop uses the condition to sample the execution of its loop iterations – every fifth loop iteration is sampled. Further note that the inner region uses the `SubRegion` annotation. This couples its sampling to the outer region, i.e. it is only sampled when the outer region is being captured. Also note that here the context annotations are being used to create the variable `sample` needed to implement sampling.

Dealing with unannotated exits. Note that in the examples so far, all exits from regions were marked by the user. However, it is possible that the user may forget to mark an exit. We deal with this problem by checking the integrity of generated traces.

Automating Instrumentation. For many types of analyses, automating the instrumentation phase is feasible using a tool like Clang to get access to the AST of the program. For instance, calls to barriers could be found automatically, and the barrier waits along with their associated loop bodies could have calls to the instrumentation library inserted directly around them.

2.2   CSP Representation

First we describe the thread local event trace that is generated when an annotated program is executed. Since event traces are thread local, they do not introduce any form of inter-thread synchronization, and thus minimally perturb program behavior. Moreover, the overhead of trace collection is low because it uses lightweight instrumentation. Second we present a novel CSP representation consisting of a series of frames that is derived offline. The local event trace of a thread tells us when the thread is executing a region of interest and when it is not. The frame sequence divides the application execution time into intervals where each frame captures the parallel behavior in terms of regions being executed by the threads in the interval.

The **Thread Local Event Trace** represents the execution history of a single thread as a series of events and the times at which they took place. The event trace of thread t that begins execution at time s_t, ends execution at time e_t, and along the way encounters region entry and exit events $e_1 \cdots e_n$ at times $x_1 \cdots x_n$ is denoted as follows:

$$[t@s_t \triangleright e_1@x_1 \triangleright e_2@x_2 \triangleright e_3@x_3 \triangleright \cdots \triangleright e_n@x_n \triangleright]@e_t$$

The types of events captured by the event trace are:

- Thread creation and termination. A thread trace begins and ends with the events [tid and] marking the creation of thread identified by tid and its termination respectively.
- Region entry and exit. Intervening events are either region entry or region exit that are of the form: Named only on entry → (rid ....); Named only on exit → (.... rid); or Named on entry and exit → (rid .... rid).

As an example, consider the event traces of threads T_1 and T_2 in Fig. 10 where, during the execution shown, T_2 executes nested regions R_1 and R_2 and later R_3 while thread T_2 executes regions R_1 and R_3. The execution of a thread that does not execute a region of interest is named ϕ.

We implement the instrumentation by transforming the region annotations into instrumentation library function calls. Each function call generates an event object, which contains a fresh timestamp, the region id if one was provided, and a tag to indicate whether this event was an entry or an exit. We also have a grammar that is used to test the integrity of the generated event trace and ensure that the user has not overlooked annotating any region exits. Due to space limitations we have omitted implementation details.

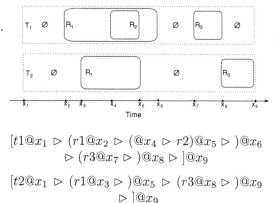

$$[t1@x_1 \triangleright (r1@x_2 \triangleright (@x_4 \triangleright r2)@x_5 \triangleright)@x_6$$
$$\triangleright (r3@x_7 \triangleright)@x_8 \triangleright]@x_9$$

$$[t2@x_1 \triangleright (r1@x_3 \triangleright)@x_5 \triangleright (r3@x_8 \triangleright)@x_9$$
$$\triangleright]@x_9$$

Fig. 10. Per thread event traces.

A **CSP** is represented in the form of a sequence of frames where each frame corresponds to the longest time interval over which the region being executed by each thread remains constant. Note that the region could be a region of interest or ϕ. A frame is represented as follows where the time interval that it represents begins at s (inclusive) and ends at e (exclusive) and each $S(tid_i)$ represents the state of thread tid_i in terms of the region(s) that it is executing.

$$[s, e) \rightarrow \{S(tid_1), S(tid_2), \ldots S(tid_n)\}$$

If thread tid is in an unnested region, then $S(tid)$ is given by:

$$S(tid) = \begin{cases} \phi & \text{if thread } tid \text{ is in an unmarked region} \\ rid & \text{if thread } tid \text{ is in a marked region } rid \end{cases}$$

On the other hand if tid is nested in n regions, then $S(tid)$ has following form:

$$S(tid) = rid_1 \rhd rid_2 \cdots \rhd rid_n$$

where rid_1 is outermost region and rid_n is the innermost.

Figure 11 shows the sequence of frames corresponding the event traces of Fig. 10. As we can see, each frame indicates the regions being executed by the two threads. When an event causes the region of some thread to change, a new frame begins. We have crossed out two frames as in these frames none of the threads is executing an annotated region. Moreover, these frames can be inferred from other frames.

$$
\begin{aligned}
[x_1, x_2) &\rightarrow \{S(T_1) = \phi, & S(T_2) = \phi\} \\
[x_2, x_3) &\rightarrow \{S(T_1) = R_1, & S(T_2) = \phi\} \\
[x_3, x_4) &\rightarrow \{S(T_1) = R_1, & S(T_2) = R_1\} \\
[x_4, x_5) &\rightarrow \{S(T_1) = R_1 \rhd R_2, S(T_2) = R_1\} \\
[x_5, x_6) &\rightarrow \{S(T_1) = R_1, & S(T_2) = \phi\} \\
[x_6, x_7) &\rightarrow \{S(T_1) = \phi, & S(T_2) = \phi\} \\
[x_7, x_8) &\rightarrow \{S(T_1) = R_3, & S(T_2) = \phi\} \\
[x_8, x_9) &\rightarrow \{S(T_1) = \phi, & S(T_2) = R_3\}
\end{aligned}
$$

Fig. 11. CSP - Frame sequence.

To construct the frame sequence, events are processed in the order of their occurrence one at a time – the ordering of events is made possible by the timestamps. With each event the current frame is updated to reflect the effect it has on the state of the relevant thread, producing the next frame in the sequence. By streaming events from log files and constructing frames one at a time, we construct and iterate over the frame sequence in constant space, enabling efficient trace analysis, even when traces are too large to fit in memory.

Behavior States. Since CSPs give the global picture of the execution, it is easy to characterize interesting behavior states in terms of the frames. For example, given the annotations in Fig. 6, we would detect a straggler thread by searching for frames of the following form where region R_1 (RID 0) represents the loop body preceding the barrier and region R_2 (RID 1) represents the barrier itself:

$$[x_1, x_2) \rightarrow \{S(T_1) = \cdots = S(T_{n-1}) = R_2, S(T_n) = R_1\}$$

Note that threads $T_1 \cdots T_{n-1}$ are waiting at the barrier while thread T_n is executing the code preceding the barrier. The duration for which threads $T_1 \cdots T_{n-1}$ wait at the barrier for thread T_n is simply given by $x_2 - x_1$. In the next section we will present additional examples that show how our query language allows user to easily analyze program behavior.

Accuracy of frames constructed. We generate timestamps using **RDTSCP** instruction available on modern x86 based architectures [1]. This instruction reads the value of the timestamp counter register, which holds the number of cycles that have elapsed since the processor was last restarted. It ensures that all instructions that come before it have been executed before it reads the timestamp counter, and the values that are read are guaranteed to be monotonically increasing. **RDTSCP** instruction has two benefits. First, since it is a single instruction, it is much faster than a typical standard library time gathering function. Second, it measures time in terms of *cycles*. There is one issue however – since each core of the processor has a separate timestamp counter, and these timestamp counters are *not synchronized*, there can be inaccuracy in the measured frame durations. If this inaccuracy is too large, it can lead to observing a different event order, which will result in frames showing up that did not actually occur. We show that this inaccuracy is too small to have any meaningful impact on information collected and inferences made.

Using the approach proposed in [22], we measured the drift Δ between the timestamp counters of a pair of cores on the same socket and on different sockets of the machine used. Δ, computed as a range, was found to be $[0, 24]$ and $[0, 44]$ cycles respectively for intra-socket and inter-socket cases. Consider a frame that starts at time S on one core and finishes at time F on another core. Since the times F and S are determined by **RDTSCP** using different counters, the absolute error in the measured frame duration is $\Delta/(F - S)$. For this error to be less than 0.1% of the frame duration, and assuming worst case Δ of 44 cycles, the frame duration should be $> 44{,}000$ cycles. That is, all frames with measured duration of $\leq 44{,}000$ cycles can have $> 0.1\%$ error.

Program	%Time
blacksholes	0.0000459
bodytrack	1.5
canneal	0.331
dedup	14.9
facesim	0.849
ferret	0.125
fluidanimate	0.0782
raytrace	0.0295
streamcluster	1.64
swaptions	0.00000353
vips	0.556
x264	0.676

Fig. 12. %age execution time due to frames with duration $< 44{,}000$ cycles.

In Fig. 12, for Parsec programs instrumented to detect waiting times at barriers and conditional variables, %Time is the percentage of execution time spent in frames smaller than 44,000 cycles. We see, excluding **dedup** where a large number of active threads in pipeline stages transition between regions, these frames represent less than 2% of the total execution time, i.e. frames representing over 98% of the execution have error $< 0.1\%$ of their durations.

2.3   Querying CSPs for Performance Tuning

Once the CSP consisting of a sequence of frames has been generated, the user can construct a query to extract the subset of *pruned frames* representing interesting program behaviors. Each *pruned frame*

$$[\, Measures \mid Attributes \,]\, FrQuery\, [\, Interval\,]$$

$Measures \rightarrow Duration \mid MaxPar \mid Area$
$Attributes \rightarrow WhichThreads \mid WhatRegions$
$FrQuery \rightarrow \overline{[\,\neg\,]}\, Quantifier\, ID\, Constraints\, :\, Predicate$
$Quantifier \rightarrow \forall \mid \exists \mid \exists_{Nat}$
$Var \rightarrow ID \mid Nat \qquad Nat \rightarrow 0|1|2|...$
$Constraints \rightarrow (\, = \mid \neq\,)\, Var\, [\,(\wedge \mid \vee)\, ID\, Constraints\,]$
$Predicates \rightarrow \overline{[\,\neg\,]}\, (Thread, Region)\, [\,(\wedge \mid \vee)\, Predicates\,]$
$Thread \rightarrow Var \qquad Region \rightarrow Var$

Fig. 13. Query language.

contains the maximal part of the frame, called the *sub-frame*, that satisfies the query. Our query language is presented in Fig. 13. A *FrQuery*, evaluated over the entire execution or period of execution specified by the *Interval*, is constructed to specify properties of interest and its evaluation yields a subset of pruned frames for which various *Measures* and *Attributes* are computed as follows:

– **Measures** are a means of computing summary information for a set of frames. We support three forms of measures. The first measure, *Duration*, returns the sum of the durations of the subset of frames, i.e. it corresponds to the total elapsed time. The second measure, *MaxPar*, returns the maximum number of threads that were active among the given subset of frames. A thread is considered *active* if it is in some region of interest, i.e. it is not in the ϕ state. Therefore this measure corresponds to the degree of parallelism. The last measure is *Area*, which represents the total work done by a subset of frames. *Area* is computed by summing the areas of each of the individual frames, where the area of an individual frame is its *Duration* times its *MaxPar*.

– **Attributes** return the set of threads (*WhichThreads*) or regions involved (*WhatRegions*) in a subset of frames.

– A **FrQuery** is constructed to express the forms of frames that satisfy properties of interest in a time interval that may be specified. When no interval is specified, the entire execution is analyzed. A *FrQuery*, when evaluated, returns a subset of pruned frames from the profile that satisfy the query. The returned frames are pruned so that they contain the maximal sub-frame that makes the query true. For instance, consider a query that returns the set of frames in which there is at least one thread inside region 0. Each of those frames is pruned to contain *only* those threads which are actually in region 0.

The basic construct in a query is a *Predicate* that asserts that some thread is inside some region. Using logical operators $(\wedge \mid \vee)$ we can construct arbitrarily large predicates over multiple threads and regions. Examples of such queries are shown in Fig. 14 – see the first two queries.

We permit quantification over both *Threads* and *Regions*. We provide three quantifiers: $\forall$, $\exists$, and $\exists_{Nat}$, which we use as an exact existential quantifier. The quantifier $\exists_k$ states that there exist exactly k of some object (either *Threads* or *Regions*) satisfying some property. The names bound by quantifiers can have equality constraints imposed upon them as well.

Query	Returns frames such that –
$(0,0)$	– thread *0* is in region *0*
$(0,0) \wedge (1,1)$	– thread *0 & 1* are in region *0 & 1*
$\forall t : (t,0)$	– *all* threads are in region 0
$\exists t : (t,0)$	– *some* thread is in region 0
$\exists_1 t : (t,0)$	– there is *exactly one* thread in region *0*
$\forall r : \exists t : (t,r)$	– there is *some* thread in *every* region
$\forall t : \exists_1 r : (t,r)$	– *each* thread is in *outermost* region

Fig. 14. Some queries and their meaning.

The quantifiers range over the active threads and regions of each frame. The third through fifth queries in Fig. 14 are examples of using the three quantifiers.

Finally, the last two complex queries in the figure employ two quantifiers, one over the threads and the other over the regions. Note that constraints on quantified variables must involve the variable captured by the quantifier. In this section all the discussion assumes is based on static region names. However, in general, dynamic names can be used to further subdivide multiple executions of a static region into distinct groups corresponding to their dynamic names.

Case Studies. Next we illustrate the usage of queries to identify opportunities for program restructuring to improve performance. We improve performance of two Parsec suite programs `blacksholes` and `cannel` by 36% and 17% respectively. In these case studies we use the largest available native inputs.

– **blackscholes** assigns prices to each of a set of input options. The pricing of individual options is independent, so the benchmark is parallelized by dividing the set of options evenly among the available threads, and simply having each of those threads price its own subset of options. There is no synchronization among the threads that calculate the prices.

We began our analysis by marking the start function for each thread and calculating their total execution times using the query $Duration(t, m)$, individually for every t and m. We found that the main thread executed for approximately twice as long as each of the pricing threads. When we examined this thread further, we saw that there were three stages to the main thread: (1) read input data, (2) launch threads to price the data and wait for them to terminate, and (3) write the prices to disk. We then measured the time spent performing task 2 using the query: $Duration(\exists t : (t, \texttt{bs\_thread})$. The result of this query was about 48% of the overall execution time. This suggests that hiding the latency of stages 1 and 3 could result in significant performance improvement.

We modified the program by adding two more threads: one which produces values by reading them from disk, and one which consumes values by writing them to disk. Between these threads are the application threads, which transform options into prices. Application threads receive options from the producer, and give prices to the consumer. Lock-free queues are used as buffers between each of these stages. Implementing this change led to 36% reduction in execution time.

– **canneal** We begin this case study with the same analysis as for blackscholes, which reveals the same I/O structure. In this case however, we cannot apply the same optimization, since the input is used to construct a single shared data structure as opposed to a stream of items to be processed. We notice that the threads spawned by main all run the same function, namely `annealer_thread::Run`, and so we turn our attention there.

This function contains the main loop of the simulated annealing algorithm. There is a barrier at the end of each iteration which serves to keep the annealing temperature synchronized between the threads. By evaluating the query $Duration(\exists t : (t, Barrier))$ we see that the time each thread spends waiting on this barrier is between 11% and 15% of the overall execution time. By removing this barrier, we improved the average runtime of the program by 17%, while increasing the average routing cost of the solution by only .003%, which is a negligible change for a randomized algorithm like simulated annealing.

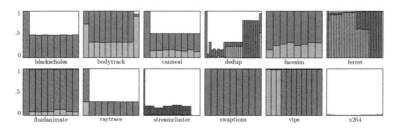

Fig. 15. Execution time for each thread divided into wait time (gold) and total time (blue), normalized wrt the main thread. (Color figure online)

3   Evaluation: Overhead and Accuracy

3.1   Overhead of Collecting CSPs

To measure the time and space overhead of CSPs, we performed a realistic analysis of twelve out of the thirteen benchmarks from the Parsec benchmark suite (all of the benchmarks which included pthreads parallelizations.) We created a histogram of all threads showing the their total time broken down into waiting time and running time. For code regions we chose waits on condition variables and barriers, as well as the entry function for each thread. For each thread t, we determined the total time by evaluating the query $Duration(t, entry_t)$, where $entry_t$ is the entry function for thread t. We determined the waiting time by evaluating the query $Duration(t, w)$, where w is the static region ID corresponding to the barrier and condition waits. This analysis is typical of a first step one might take in analyzing the runtime behavior of a parallel program, since it gives a rough idea of which threads are doing the most work and how efficiently that work is parallelized. Our experiments were conducted on a Dell Poweredge T410, having two 2.27 GHz quad core Intel Xeon E5607 processors (no hyperthreading) for a total of 8 physical cores with 32GB of RAM. For all benchmarks, native inputs (the largest available) were used, and a thread count of 8 was used in the launch options.

Benchmark	Min(+prof)	Max(+prof)	Avg(+prof)
blackscholes	60.50(-0.69)	62.61(+0.61)	61.13(-0.22)
bodytrack	73.27(+0.21)	76.57(-1.91)	74.07(-0.11)
canneal	94.11(+2.78)	100.67(+4.05)	97.93(+2.33)
dedup	12.22(+0.87)	13.37(+0.05)	12.78(+0.45)
facesim	189.91(+2.74)	199.28(+2.93)	193.30(+1.77)
ferret	76.54(-0.18)	77.14(+0.06)	76.86(+0.03)
fluidanimate	95.42(+11.26)	123.17(+4.74)	110.61(+1.95)
raytrace	103.91(-0.15)	107.77(-1.00)	105.80(-0.51)
streamcluster	107.88(+2.21)	111.08(+0.41)	109.48(+1.38)
swaptions	50.86(-0.09)	51.21(-0.04)	51.02(-0.09)
vips	23.07(+0.06)	26.41(-1.12)	24.26(-0.47)
x264	22.27(+0.91)	29.35(+2.82)	24.19(+3.14)

Fig. 16. Time overhead in seconds. Numbers in parentheses is overhead of profiling.

In Fig. 15 the blue regions correspond to total time, and gold regions correspond to waiting time. All measurements are normalized with respect to the total execution time of the main thread. About half of the benchmarks show very little gold, suggesting they are efficiently parallelized and require little or no waiting. The others have waiting times from 15% to 40%, suggesting that they are harder to efficiently parallelize. Of particular interest are streamcluster and x264, which employ dynamic parallelization, launching 49 and 1024 threads respectively. Neither exhibit large waiting times.

Figure 16 shows the time overhead. In five out of the twelve cases, the time overhead was within the variance of the unmodified runtime. In six of the remaining seven cases, the time overhead was less than 5%. The x264 benchmark has high overhead due to large number of threads launched. Since our instrumentation gathers thread local buffers that must be written to disk upon thread termination, a parallelization that launches a large number of threads with relatively little work causes a large serial overhead when those buffers are saved to disk. Even in this case, the runtime overhead is modest.

Benchmark	Min(+prof)	Max(+prof)	Avg(+prof)
blackscholes	627048(-12)	627088(+1872)	627069(+414)
bodytrack	33872(+13764)	33948(+16072)	33912(+15516)
canneal	962436(+3560)	968508(-296)	964042(+2902)
dedup	1642340(+93244)	1760540(+2210)	1717930(+32310)
facesim	324576(+29124)	329840(+34948)	326874(+30664)
ferret	117992(+4920)	130232(-2836)	121317(+4443)
fluidanimate	693100(+3256)	693304(+5324)	693192(+4482)
raytrace	1161224(252)	1162460(-270)	1161950(-160)
streamcluster	113504(+24984)	117896(+23992)	114980(+24977)
swaptions	6220(-20)	8220(-44)	7715(-953)
vips	61432(+7276)	65808(+7564)	63171(+7609)
x264	299528(+6604)	303408(+10912)	302154(+8320)

Fig. 17. Peak memory overhead in Kilobytes.

Figure 17 shows the space overhead. In nine out of twelve benchmarks, the space overhead is less than 10%. Two of the remaining three have overhead less than 25%. The highest overhead was exhibited by the bodytrack benchmark at 45.75%. These overheads are acceptable as experiments were conducted by holding all generated events in memory and only writing them out to disk at thread termination.

Benchmark	Min(+prof)	Max(+prof)	Avg(+prof)
blackscholes	627048(-12)	627088(+1872)	627069(+414)
bodytrack	33872(+13764)	33948(+16072)	33912(+15516)
canneal	962436(+3560)	968508(-296)	964042(+2902)
dedup	1642340(+93244)	1760540(+2210)	1717930(+32310)
facesim	324576(+29124)	329840(+34948)	326874(+30664)
ferret	117992(+4920)	130232(-2836)	121317(+4443)
fluidanimate	693100(+3256)	693304(+5324)	693192(+4482)
raytrace	1161224(252)	1162460(-270)	1161950(-160)
streamcluster	113504(+24984)	117896(+23992)	114980(+24977)
swaptions	6220(-20)	8220(-44)	7715(-953)
vips	61432(+7276)	65808(+7564)	63171(+7609)
x264	299528(+6604)	303408(+10912)	302154(+8320)

Fig. 18. Log file sizes in Kilobytes.

If peak memory consumption becomes a problem, then we can periodically flush the thread local buffers to disk.

Finally, Fig. 18 shows the size of the log files generated. Only one benchmark (facesim) had log files with an average size in excess of one MB. These small log files, as well as the very small execution time overhead and modest memory overhead are strong evidence of the efficiency of CSPs for the analysis of real world, long running multi-threaded programs.

3.2   Accuracy of Captured Behaviors

To test the accuracy of our profiler, we studied three microbenchmarks with predictable behavior. The control over their operating parameters allows us to effectively study CSP's accuracy.

(a) Accuracy of Pipeline Behavior. Software pipelining is commonly used for parallelization. In a typical implementation of a software pipeline, each pipeline stage is represented by a thread pool and a function which implements the work of that stage. Data is passed from one stage to the next, and threads in a pool cooperate to transform that data in some way and pass it along to the next stage. Synchronization between stages occurs during this hand off of data. Since each stage is data-dependent on the one before it, the overall performance of the pipeline is limited by the slowest stage. Analyzing these types of applications using traditional tools can be challenging since most of those see threads as individual actors instead of cooperating entities. CSP queries make this type of aggregation very convenient, as shown below.

We characterize the performance of a software pipeline by measuring the amount of time that each stage is caused to wait due to every other stage. For a pipeline with n stages, this can be summarized in what we call a *waiting matrix*:

$$W_{m,n} = \begin{pmatrix} w_{1,1} & w_{1,2} & \cdots & w_{1,n} \\ w_{2,1} & w_{2,2} & \cdots & w_{2,n} \\ \vdots & \vdots & \ddots & \vdots \\ w_{m,1} & w_{m,2} & \cdots & w_{m,n} \end{pmatrix}$$

in which the entry $w_{i,j}$ denotes the amount of time stage i spent waiting for stage j. These quantities can be calculated in a straightforward manner using CSPs. Let $threads(k)$ be the threads that implement stage k of the pipeline (i.e., $threads(1)$ are the threads belonging to the pool of the first stage). Furthermore, let B be the pipeline stage barrier for stage i, and let P be the work region for stage j. The query which calculates this quantity has two parts. The first part specifies that stage i has completed. Another way to say this is that all of the threads which belong to stage i are waiting at the pipeline barrier. This query can be written as:

$$Duration(\forall t \in threads(i) : (t, B))$$

The second part specifies that pipeline stage j has not completed. Another way of saying this is that there is at least one thread from stage j which is still executing that stage region. This query can be written as:

$$Duration(\exists t \in threads(j) : (t, P))$$

The final query is just a conjunction of these two queries, or:

$$Duration(\forall t \in threads(i) : (t, B) \land \forall t' \in threads(j) : (t', P))$$

In this microbenchmark, we set up a pipeline with 3 stages. Each stage does some amount of work, which is split among a set of threads. The amount of work, the number of threads per stage, and the distribution of the work among the threads of the pipeline stage is configurable via command line arguments. We simulate the passing of data between the stages of the pipeline by having each of the stages synchronize with each other. That is, a stage cannot proceed to the next iteration until all other stages have completed.

In experiments related to this microbenchmark, we use our profiler to create a waiting matrix as defined above, with the entries normalized with respect to the stage length execution time. We allocate three threads to the first stage, three threads to the second stage, and two threads to the third stage.

– **Balanced Stages.** For our first experiment, we gave each thread in each stage equal amount of work (2^{30} increments). For any waiting matrix, we expect the diagonal entries to be exactly zero since it is not possible for a pipeline stage to be waiting for itself. For the other entries of this matrix, we expect the values to be close to zero, since the work is balanced across stages. The waiting matrix (W), and the expected waiting matrix ($\mathcal{W}$) for this experiment are shown below. We observe the measured values are close to expected values.

$$\mathcal{W} = \begin{pmatrix} 0 & 0 & 0 \\ 0 & 0 & 0 \\ 0 & 0 & 0 \end{pmatrix} \quad W = \begin{pmatrix} 0 & 0 & 6.41 \times 10^{-2} \\ 8.96 \times 10^{-3} & 0 & 7.3 \times 10^{-2} \\ 0 & 0 & 0 \end{pmatrix}$$

– **Single Stage Imbalance.** For our second experiment, we removed the workload for the threads in the third stage of the pipeline. Since the threads in this stage now have no work, we expect the third row of the resulting matrix to have values very close to one. The resulting waiting matrix is given below. Once again we can see the measured values are very close to expected values.

$$\mathcal{W} = \begin{pmatrix} 0 & 0 & 0 \\ 0 & 0 & 0 \\ 1 & 1 & 0 \end{pmatrix} \quad W = \begin{pmatrix} 0 & 8.57 \times 10^{-4} & 0 \\ 0 & 0 & 0 \\ 9.99 \times 10^{-1} & 1 & 0 \end{pmatrix}$$

– **Double Stage Imbalance.** For our final experiment, we removed the workload for the threads in the second stage as well. We now expect to see very high values for $W_{2,1}$ and $W_{3,1}$, but very low values for the other entries in these rows. As in previous cases, the resulting waiting matrix is shown below and conforms closely with our expectations.

$$\mathcal{W} = \begin{pmatrix} 0 & 0 & 0 \\ 1 & 0 & 0 \\ 1 & 0 & 0 \end{pmatrix} \quad W = \begin{pmatrix} 0 & 0 & 0 \\ 9.98 \times 10^{-1} & 0 & 0 \\ 9.99 \times 10^{-1} & 0 & 0 \end{pmatrix}$$

(b) Accuracy of Straggler Degrees. Next we show how we can use the frame query language to detect and identify *straggler threads*. Let L and B denote the regions corresponding to some loop and a barrier at the end of each iteration of that loop respectively. The presence of a straggler is indicated by frames where one thread is in region L while all other threads are in region B. The performance impact of the straggler can be characterized by computing the ratio of

StagglerDuration and *LoopDuration* which represent the time all other threads spend waiting at the barrier for the straggler thread and the total time spent on executing the entire loop respectively. We denote this as *StragglerDegree* whose value falls between 0 and 1 with closer to one being worse:

$$\text{LoopDuration} = Duration(\exists t : (t, L))$$
$$\text{StragglerDuration} = Duration(\exists_1 t : (t, L) \wedge \forall t' \neq t : (t', B))$$
$$\text{StragglerDegree} = \frac{\text{StragglerDuration}}{\text{LoopDuration}}$$

There can be multiple causes for the presence of a straggler. (1) A thread may be assigned relatively too much work. (2) The code representing the work preceding the barrier can exhibit a great deal of variability in its execution time and thus different threads manifest as stragglers during different executions of the barrier. To determine the actual scenario we can identify the *StragglerDegree* for each thread t using concretization below:

$$\text{StragglerDuration}_t = Duration((t, L) \wedge \forall t' \neq t : (t', B))$$
$$\text{StragglerDegree}_t = \frac{\text{StragglerDuration}_t}{\text{LoopDuration}}$$

The straggler microbenchmark is structured around a single function which executes a loop for a predetermined number of iterations. The body of this loop contains a call to a function which simulates work by incrementing a local variable w times. Each iteration of the loop is guarded at the beginning and the end by a barrier. This ensures that no thread is executing the work region if there is some other thread in a different iteration of the loop. This function is executed concurrently by 8 threads. In each experiment we mark the work function and loop barriers as code regions, spawn 8 threads, and perform the straggler analysis as above.

– **Even Work Distribution.** In this experiment, each thread is given the same amount of work so we expect every thread to finish its iteration at approximately the same time. This leads to an expected straggler degree of close to zero for every thread. The results in Fig. 19 are close to this expectation.

Tid	StragglerDegree
1	0.000172
2	0.000191
3	0.000139
4	0.000151
5	0.000164
6	0.000162
7	0.000179
8	0.000168

Fig. 19. Even Dist.

Tid	StragglerDegree
1	0.497517
2	0.000000
3	0.000000
4	0.000000
5	0.000000
6	0.000000
7	0.000000
8	0.000000

Fig. 20. Uneven Dist.

– **Uneven Work Distribution.** In this experiment, we assigned twice as much work to the first thread as to the remaining seven threads. We expect the last seven threads to finish their work by the time the first thread is halfway through its work. The straggler degree for the first thread should be close to 0.5 and the straggler degree for the last seven threads close to zero (see Fig. 20).

4   Conclusion

We presented a framework to capture the runtime profile of a parallel application, to represent it in a readily analyzable representation, and to query the profiles enabling them to be automatically analyzed for the presence of performance bottlenecks. Our experience shows that CSPs capture runtime behavior with high precision and low overhead. The flexibility of our framework allows implementation of existing techniques that are: based upon different normalized execution time measures [3,8,10,15]; rely on critical path analyses to find bottlenecks [3,4,11,12,14,16,17,20]; and are aimed at detecting lock contention [6,19,21]. While some tools rely upon hardware performance counters to reduce overhead [2,9,18], we do so by limiting logging of events as in [7].

References

1. Intel 64 and ia-32 architectures software developer's manual, volume 2: Instruction set reference, a-z (2015). http://www.intel.com/content/dam/www/public/us/en/documents/manuals/64-ia-32-architectures-software-developer-instruction-set-reference-manual-325383.pdf. Accessed 22 July 2016
2. Adhianto, L., Banerjee, S., Fagan, M., Krentel, M., Marin, G., Mellor-Crummey, J., Tallent, N.R.: Hpctoolkit: tools for performance analysis of optimized parallel programs. Concurrency Comput. Pract. Experience 22(6), 685–701 (2010)
3. Anderson, T.E., Lazowska, E.D.: Quartz: a tool for tuning parallel program performance. In: Proceedings of the ACM SIGMETRICS Conference on Measurement and Modeling of Computer Systems. Citeseer (1990)
4. Böhme, D., Wolf, F., de Supinski, B.R., Schulz, M., Geimer, M.: Scalable critical-path based performance analysis. In: 2012 IEEE 26th International Parallel & Distributed Processing Symposium (IPDPS), pp. 1330–1340. IEEE (2012)
5. Curtsinger, C., Berger, E.D.: Coz: finding code that counts with causal profiling. In: Proceedings of the 25th Symposium on Operating Systems Principles, pp. 184–197. ACM (2015)
6. David, F., Thomas, G., Lawall, J., Muller, G.: Continuously measuring critical section pressure with the free-lunch profiler. In: OOPSLA 2014. ACM (2014)
7. Ding, R., Zhou, H., Lou, J.G., Zhang, H., Lin, Q., Fu, Q., Zhang, D., Xie, T.: Log2: a cost-aware logging mechanism for performance diagnosis. In: 2015 USENIX Annual Technical Conference (USENIX ATC 15), pp. 139–150 (2015)
8. Du Bois, K., Sartor, J.B., Eyerman, S., Eeckhout, L.: Bottle graphs: visualizing scalability bottlenecks in multi-threaded applications. In: Proceedings of the 2013 ACM SIGPLAN International Conference on Object Oriented Programming Systems Languages & Applications, OOPSLA 2013, NY, USA, pp. 355–372 (2013). doi:10.1145/2509136.2509529
9. Geimer, M., Wolf, F., Wylie, B.J., Ábrahám, E., Becker, D., Mohr, B.: The scalasca performance toolset architecture. Concurrency Comput. Pract. Experience 22(6), 702–719 (2010)
10. Graham, S.L., Kessler, P.B., Mckusick, M.K.: Gprof: a call graph execution profiler. In: Proceedings of the 1982 SIGPLAN Symposium on Compiler Construction, SIGPLAN 1982, NY, USA, pp. 120–126 (1982). doi:10.1145/800230.806987

11. Hollingsworth, J.K.: An online computation of critical path profiling. In: Proceedings of the SIGMETRICS Symposium on Parallel and Distributed Tools, pp. 11–20. ACM (1996)

12. Hollingsworth, J.K., Miller, B.P.: Parallel program performance metrics: a comprison and validation. In: Proceedings of the 1992 ACM/IEEE Conference on Supercomputing, pp. 4–13. IEEE Computer Society Press (1992)

13. Hollingsworth, J.K., Miller, B.P.: Slack: a new performance metric for parallel programs (1994)

14. Jeon, D., Garcia, S., Louie, C., Taylor, M.B.: Kismet: Parallel speedup estimates for serial programs. In: Proceedings of the 2011 ACM International Conference on Object Oriented Programming Systems Languages and Applications, OOPSLA 2011, NY, USA, pp. 519–536 (2011). doi:10.1145/2048066.2048108

15. Kambadur, M., Tang, K., Kim, M.A.: ParaShares: finding the important basic blocks in multithreaded programs. In: Silva, F., Dutra, I., Santos Costa, V. (eds.) Euro-Par 2014. LNCS, vol. 8632, pp. 75–86. Springer, Cham (2014). doi:10.1007/978-3-319-09873-9_7

16. Miller, B.P., Clark, M., Hollingsworth, J., Kierstead, S., Lim, S.S., Torzewski, T.: IPS-2: The second generation of a parallel program measurement system. IEEE Trans. Parallel Distrib. Syst. 1(2), 206–217 (1990)

17. Oyama, Y., Taura, K., Yonezawa, A.: Online computation of critical paths for multithreaded languages. In: Rolim, J. (ed.) IPDPS 2000. LNCS, vol. 1800, pp. 301–313. Springer, Heidelberg (2000). doi:10.1007/3-540-45591-4_40

18. Shende, S., Malony, A.D., Cuny, J., Beckman, P., Karmesin, S., Lindlan, K.: Portable profiling and tracing for parallel, scientific applications using c++. In: Proceedings of the SIGMETRICS Symposium on Parallel and Distributed Tools, pp. 134–145. ACM (1998)

19. Tallent, N.R., Mellor-Crummey, J.M., Porterfield, A.: Analyzing lock contention in multithreaded applications. In: 2010 ACM SIGPLAN Symposium on Principles and Practice of Parallel Programming, PPoPP 2010 (2010)

20. Yang, C.Q., Miller, B.P.: Critical path analysis for the execution of parallel and distributed programs. In: 8th International Conference on Distributed Computing Systems, pp. 366–373. IEEE (1988)

21. Yu, X., Han, S., Zhang, D., Xie, T.: Comprehending performance from real-world execution traces: a device-driver case. In: ASPLOS. Citeseer (2014)

22. Yuan, X., Wu, C., Wang, Z., Li, J., Yew, P.C., Huang, J., Feng, X., Lan, Y., Chen, Y., Guan, Y.: ReCBuLC: reproducing concurrency bugs using local clocks. In: Proceedings of the 37th International Conference on Software Engineering-Volume 1, pp. 824–834. IEEE Press (2015)

Signal Clustering Using Temporal Logics

Giuseppe Bombara$^{(\boxtimes)}$ and Calin Belta

Boston University, Boston, USA
gbombara@bu.edu

Abstract. This paper introduces a new method for clustering signals using their temporal logic properties. Specifically, we propose a hierarchical clustering algorithm for efficiently processing a set of input signals. The input data is unlabeled, that is, no further information about properties of the signals are available to the learning algorithm other than the signals themselves. The algorithm produces a hierarchical structure where the internal nodes test some temporal properties of the data, and each terminal node contains a cluster (i.e., a group of similar signals). Each cluster can be mapped to a Signal Temporal Logic (STL) formula that describes its signals. The obtained formulae can be used directly for monitoring purposes but also, more generally, to acquire knowledge about the system under analysis. We present two case studies to illustrate the characteristics of our proposed algorithm. The first case study is related to a maritime surveillance problem, and the second is a fault classification problem in an automatic transmission system.

Keywords: Signal Temporal Logic · Specification mining · Clustering · Knowledge discovery · Formal methods · Unsupervised learning · Logic inference

1 Introduction

In recent years, there has been a great interest in applying machine learning based techniques to the formal methods field. In particular, some efforts have been made on inferring formal descriptions of the behaviors of a system from its execution traces [3,4,6,7,13,15–17]. The system behaviors can be described using an appropriate temporal logic, such as Signal Temporal Logic (STL) [19].

This approach, named *Temporal Logic Inference* (TLI) in [17], while retaining many qualities of traditional classifiers, presents several additional advantages. In particular, classical machine learning methods are often overly specific to the task. That is, they focus solely on solving the problem at hand and offer no other understanding about the system where they have been applied. On the contrary, temporal logic formulae have a precise meaning and allow for a rich specification of the behaviors of a system that is *interpretable* by human experts. In this research field, the initial work focused on finding the optimal parameters for a formula when the formula structure has been fixed [3,15,16]. Later, some attempts were made to tackle the *supervised two-class classification*

© Springer International Publishing AG 2017
S. Lahiri and G. Reger (Eds.): RV 2017, LNCS 10548, pp. 121–137, 2017.
DOI: 10.1007/978-3-319-67531-2_8

problem [4,6,7,13,17], where the goal is to build a discriminative formula given a set of *labeled* traces (normal and anomalous).

In this paper, we turn our attention to the *unsupervised clustering problem*. In this scenario, it is assumed that only a set of *unlabeled* signals is available, that is, it is not known a priori if a signal exhibits a specific behavior or satisfies some property, and the end goal is to group *similar* signals together, in a so-called *cluster*, and to describe each cluster with a formula. We propose a hierarchical clustering approach for partitioning the input signals. Our algorithm produces a tree, where each internal node contains a formula that tests some temporal logic property of the data. The terminal nodes, or leaves, are connected with the actual clusters and each leaf can be mapped to an STL formula that *describes* the respective cluster.

The hierarchical approach provides several advantages. First, the number of signals to be processed at once decreases at each level of the hierarchy, and, more importantly, the number of clusters does *not* need to be known beforehand. We present a method for exploring the relationship between the number of clusters and the diversity in the data explained by the induced tree. We argue that this information provides useful insights on the trade-off between the complexity of the formulae inferred and the clustering effectiveness. Moreover, we will show that our unsupervised algorithm achieves classification performances on-par with the supervised algorithm in [6] and better than [17] in a case study. The formulae learned by our algorithm can be used as monitors directly during the deployment phase of a system. However, the implications of this research are even broader. The obtained formulae are in fact very useful for *acquiring knowledge* about the system under analysis. That is, they provide the designers a formal description of the possible behaviors of the system.

The paper is organized as follows. In Sect. 2, we briefly survey some previous research contributions regarding the learning of temporal logic formulae from data. In Sect. 3, we define the syntax and semantics of Signal Temporal Logic (STL), describe its parameterized variant PSTL, and review some common distance measures used to asses the similarity between signals. The unsupervised clustering problem of signals with STL formulae is discussed in Sect. 4 along with a motivating maritime surveillance case study. In Sect. 5, we describe in detail our hierarchical algorithm. We present an automotive case study in Sect. 6 and analyze the results obtained with our method in Sect. 7, along with some comparisons with related work. We conclude in Sect. 8 with a brief review of the work done and an outlook on future research directions.

2   Related Work

Attempts have been made in the recent years to learn temporal logic formulae from data. In this field, the initial work has focused on finding the optimal parameters for a formula when a formula template is given [3,15,16]. This problem is called *parameter mining*, and the parameters for the formula are selected so that the resulting formula barely satisfies the input signals [15,16], or strongly satisfies them [3] (in the sense of the robustness degree). These approaches essentially differ in the way the underlying optimization problem is formulated and solved.

Later, work was performed within the so-called *supervised two-class classification problem* [4,6,7,13,17]. In this setting, the goal is to build a temporal logic formula, *both* the formula structure and its parameters, that can distinguish signals belonging to one of two possible classes. The dataset is given as a finite set of pairs of signals and labels, where each label indicates whether the respective signal exhibits some desired system behavior or not. The approaches to solve this problem generally follow an iterative two-step procedure. In particular, [17] construct the formula structure by exploring a fragment of STL that admits a partial ordering, whereas the parameter optimization is performed using an SVM-like objective function. In [4,7], the formula structure is additively constructed by means of heuristics [7] or a genetic algorithm [4], while the parameter space is explored through a Statistical Model Checking approach on the likelihood ratio of two generative probabilistic models, which were previously fit to the available data. Finally, a decision-tree based approach to solve the two-class problem has been proposed in [6]. In this approach, a special binary tree is first constructed. Afterward, this tree is mapped to an STL formula that is used for classification.

3   Preliminaries

A temporal logic is a system of rules and symbols used for reasoning about propositions in terms of the flow of time. Linear Temporal Logic (LTL) and Computation Tree Logic (CTL) are the most commonly used temporal logics [8]. Signal Temporal Logic (STL) has emerged recently as a generalization of LTL, where time is continuous and the predicates can be defined over real values [19]. STL has found important applications in formal verification of hybrid systems where it is used to state and monitor requirements. In this section, we briefly review the syntax and the semantics of this logic.

Let $\mathbb{R}$ be the set of real numbers. For $t \in \mathbb{R}$, we denote the interval $[t, \infty)$ by $\mathbb{R}_{\geq t}$. We use $\mathcal{S} = \{s : \mathbb{R}_{\geq 0} \to \mathbb{R}^n\}$ with $n \in \mathbb{N}$ to denote the set of all continuous parameterized curves in the n-dimensional Euclidean space $\mathbb{R}^n$. In this paper, an element of $\mathcal{S}$ is called a *signal* and its parameter is interpreted as *time*. Given a signal s, the components of s are denoted by s_i, $i \in \{1, \ldots, n\}$. The set $\mathcal{F}$ contains the projection operators from a signal s to one of its components s_i, that is $\mathcal{F} = \{f_i : \mathbb{R}^n \to \mathbb{R}, f_i(s) = s_i, i = \{1, \ldots, n\}\}$.[1] The *suffix* at time $t \geq 0$ of a signal is denoted by $s[t] \in \mathcal{S}$, and it represents the signal s shifted forward in time by t time units, i.e., $s[t](\tau) = s(\tau + t)$ for all $\tau \in \mathbb{R}_{\geq 0}$.

The syntax of *Signal Temporal Logic* (STL) is defined as follows [19]:

$$\phi ::= \top \mid f(x) \sim \mu \mid \neg\phi \mid \phi_1 \wedge \phi_2 \mid \phi_1 \mathbf{U}_{[a,b)} \phi_2$$

where $\top$ is the Boolean *true* constant ($\bot$ for *false*); $f(x) \sim \mu$ is a predicate over $\mathbb{R}^n$ defined by a function $f \in \mathcal{F}$, a real number $\mu \in \mathbb{R}$, and an order relation

---

[1] A more general definition of the set $\mathcal{F}$ is used in [19].

$\sim\in \{\leq, >\}$; $\neg$ and $\wedge$ are the Boolean operators negation and conjunction; and $\mathbf{U}_{[a,b)}$ is the bounded temporal operator *until*.

The semantics of STL is defined over signals in $\mathcal{S}$ as [19]:

$$
\begin{aligned}
s[t] &\models \top & &\Leftrightarrow \top \\
s[t] &\models f(x) \sim \mu & &\Leftrightarrow f(s(t)) \sim \mu \\
s[t] &\models \neg\phi & &\Leftrightarrow \neg(s[t] \models \phi) \\
s[t] &\models (\phi_1 \wedge \phi_2) & &\Leftrightarrow (s[t] \models \phi_1) \wedge (s[t] \models \phi_2) \\
s[t] &\models (\phi_1 \mathbf{U}_{[a,b)} \phi_2) & &\Leftrightarrow \exists t_u \in [t+a, t+b) \text{ s.t. } \big(s[t_u] \models \phi_2\big) \\
& & &\wedge \big(\forall t_1 \in [t, t_u) \; s[t_1] \models \phi_1\big)
\end{aligned}
$$

A signal $s \in \mathcal{S}$ is said to satisfy an STL formula ϕ if and only if $s[0] \models \phi$. Other Boolean operations, such as disjunction, implication, and equivalence, are defined in the usual way. The temporal operators *eventually* and *globally* are defined respectively as

$$
\mathbf{F}_{[a,b)}\phi \equiv \top\mathbf{U}_{[a,b)}\phi, \qquad \mathbf{G}_{[a,b)}\phi \equiv \neg\mathbf{F}_{[a,b)}\neg\phi
$$

In addition to the Boolean semantics defined above, some *quantitative semantics* have been proposed for STL [9,11]. These semantics are formalized through the introduction of a real valued function called *robustness*, which quantifies the *degree* of satisfaction of a signal with respect to a formula.

Parametric Signal Temporal Logic (PSTL) was introduced in [2] as an extension of STL where formulae are parameterized. A PSTL formula is similar to an STL formula, however all the time bounds in the time intervals associated with temporal operators and all the constants in the inequality predicates are replaced by free parameters. These two types of parameters are called *time* and *space* parameters, respectively. If ψ is a PSTL formula, then every parameter assignment $\theta \in \Theta$ (where Θ is the parameter space of ψ) induces a corresponding STL formula $\phi = \psi(\theta)$, where all the space and time parameters of ψ have been fixed according to θ. This assignment is also referred to as valuation θ of ψ. For example, given $\psi = \mathbf{F}_{[a,b)}(f_1(x) > \pi)$ and $\theta = [1.1, 2.3, 3.7]$, we obtain the STL formula $\psi(\theta) = \mathbf{F}_{[1.1, 2.3)}(f_1(x) > 3.7)$.

Even though STL is defined using a dense-time semantics and natively supports predicates over reals, its monitoring algorithms work in practice with *sampled* signals and assume that the signals are piece-wise constant (or piece-wise linearly interpolated) [9]. The sampling rate does not have to be constant.

To measure the similarity between two signals, a *distance* function is generally used. Let $\bar{s}^1$ and $\bar{s}^2$ be two n-dimensional series of samples corresponding to the signals s^1 and s^2 in $\mathcal{S}$, respectively. The most straightforward distance function is the familiar Euclidean distance, extended to the case of multi-dimensional time-series. It is defined as:[2]

---

[2] If the original sampling times of s^1 and s^2 are not the same, the signals can be re-interpolated to obtain values for matching sampling times.

$$d^2(s^1, s^2) = \sum_{i=1}^{n} \sum_{t=t_0}^{t_f} \left(\bar{s}_i^1(t) - \bar{s}_i^2(t) \right)^2$$

where t_0 and t_f are the first and last sampling time, respectively.

In the last decade, Dynamic Time Warping (DTW) has emerged as another popular distance measure for time series in various machine learning problems [20]. The core idea is to align two series by warping the time axis iteratively until an optimal alignment is found. There exist two possible extensions of DTW to the multi-dimensional signal case: (1) independent warping of each dimension (DTW_I), or (2) coordinated/dependent warping along all signal dimensions (DTW_D). Refer to [22] for a formal definition. While Euclidean distance is very sensitive to distortions in the time axis, DTW provides flexibility to match signals that are similar but locally out of phase [20]. Usually, a restriction on the amount of allowed warping is imposed as percentage of the signal length and is called the *warping factor*. The choice of the *right* distance function should reflect the kind of similarity measure the user is interested in and it is often application dependent.

4   Motivating Example and Problem Description

The motivating example and first case study is a maritime surveillance problem. It is assumed that the routes of the ships can be tracked in an area of interest. This surveillance problem, along with the related synthetic dataset, was initially proposed in [17], based on the scenarios described in [18]. Some example trajectories are show in Fig. 1a. In the first scenario, a vessel approaching from open sea heads directly towards the harbor. This behavior is considered normal. In the second scenario, a ship veers to the island first and then heads to the harbor. This behavior is compatible with human trafficking. In the third scenario, a boat tries to approach other vessels in the passage between the peninsula and the island and then veers back to the open sea. This scenario is compatible with terrorist activity. The signals in this dataset are represented as 2D trajectories with planar coordinates $[x(t), y(t)]$ and were generated using a Dubins' model with additive Gaussian noise [17]. The dataset is made of 2000 total trajectories, with 61 sample points per trace. There are 1000 normal trajectories, 500 human trafficking trajectories, and 500 terrorist activity trajectories.

In [6,17], a *supervised* learning problem based on this surveillance dataset was considered. Each training trajectory could be either normal, human trafficking, or terrorist activity, and its type was *known* beforehand. This information, along with the signals themselves, was exploited by the learning algorithm to construct a formula that distinguishes normal and anomalous behaviors.

The major shortcoming of supervised methods is their need of *labeled* examples during training. In the vast majority of real applications, only unlabeled data is available. For supervised algorithms to work, the raw trajectories have to be manually analyzed by a human expert (e.g. the port authority), who partitions and labels the data recorded. This generally is a time-consuming and error-prone

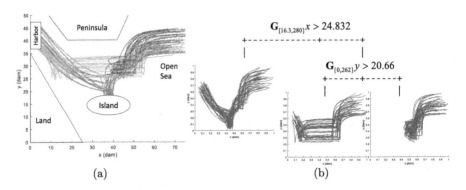

(a)   (b)

Fig. 1. (a) Maritime surveillance dataset. The vessels behaving normally are shown in green. The magenta and blue trajectories represent two types of anomalous routes: human trafficking and terrorist activity, respectively. (b) Tree induced for the maritime case study. The second cluster contains the normal trajectories. (Color figure online)

process. We wanted to develop an unsupervised algorithm that works directly on raw recorded trajectories to discover and represent the possible behaviors of the ships in the area. The algorithm should be able to partition the trajectories into separate groups and devise formulae to describe and discriminate them.

More formally, given a set of unlabeled signals, i.e., where the class (or type) of each signal is *not* known, the algorithm should: (1) partition the input data into separate groups, where each group contains only *similar* signals, and (2) associate each group of signals with an STL formula. In machine learning, the problem of grouping together similar objects is know as *clustering*. In our specific application, the objects are signals, and our objective is not just to partition similar signals into clusters but also to *describe* each cluster, that is, each type of behavior of the system, with an STL formula.

5   Hierarchical Clustering with STL

In literature, many algorithms have been proposed to solve clustering problems, such as K-means or DBSCAN [5]. Each approach has advantages and disadvantages, often depending on the particular application at hand. For our specific problem, we chose to design a divisive hierarchical clustering algorithm, which does not require the user to pre-assign the number of clusters beforehand (like K-means) and does not impose a probabilistic model on the data (like Gaussian Mixture Models). In general, these methods produce a hierarchy of clusters where the initial node contains the complete dataset and subgroups with more *similar* objects are present as one moves down the hierarchy. Our aim is to construct the hierarchy with a special structure so that every node can also be associated with a corresponding STL formula that represents it. To this end, we will expand the connection between STL formulae and trees as introduced in [6].

Given a set of unlabeled signals, our algorithm constructs a binary tree, where each internal node contains a simple formula that tests some temporal logic property of the signals. This formula is chosen from a set of formulae, called *primitives*, so that the signals in the resulting children nodes are more *homogeneous*, that is, they contain signals overall more *similar* to each other than their parent. The terminal nodes, or leaves, of the tree are connected with the final clusters, and each leaf is mapped to an STL formula that *describes* its respective cluster. Figure 1b shows a tree induced by our algorithm for the maritime surveillance case study. Two internal nodes partition the signals in three clusters.

This section is organized as follows. In Sect. 5.1, we first describe how binary trees can be connected with a fragment of STL by means of PSTL primitives in the nodes. In Sect. 5.2, we define some suitable *homogeneity measures* used during the optimization process to select the best primitive at each node. Finally, in Sect. 5.3 we describe our hierarchical clustering algorithm, and we conclude in Sect. 5.4 with some comments on the evaluation of its results and address the problem of choosing the appropriate number of clusters.

5.1 STL Formulae and Decision Trees

In a tree, we define: the root as the initial node; the depth of a node as the length of the path from the root to that node; the parent of a node as the neighbor whose depth is one less; the children of a node as the neighbors whose depths are one more. A node with no children is called a leaf, and all other nodes are called non-terminal nodes. We focus on *binary* trees, where every non-terminal node has exactly two children and every leaf contains a cluster.

In [6], it was proposed to split the signals reaching a node using a simple formula, chosen from a finite set of PSTL template formulae, called *primitives*. Trivially, the signals satisfying the node's primitive are routed to the left child while the signals violating the node's primitive are routed to the right child. A tree-structured sequence of questions such as this is referred to as *decision tree*. In this work, we use the following set of primitives.

Definition 1 (PSTL Primitives). *Let S be the set of signals with values in $\mathbb{R}^n$, we define*

$$\mathcal{P} = \left\{ \mathbf{F}_{[\tau_1,\tau_2]}(f_i(x) \sim \mu) \ or \ \mathbf{G}_{[\tau_1,\tau_2]}(f_i(x) \sim \mu) \mid i \in \{1,\dots,n\}, \ \sim \in \{\leq,>\}\right\}$$

The parameters for the PSTL formulae in $\mathcal{P}$ are $(\mu, \tau_1, \tau_2]$ and the space of parameters is $\Theta = \{(a,b,c) \mid a \in \mathbb{R}, \ b < c, \ b,c \in \mathbb{R}_{\geq 0}\}$.

The primitive $\mathbf{F}_{[\tau_1,\tau_2]}(f_i(x) \sim \mu)$ is used to express that the predicate $f_i(x) \sim \mu$ must be true for at least one time instance in the interval $[\tau_1, \tau_2]$, while the primitive $\mathbf{G}_{[\tau_1,\tau_2]}(f_i(x) \sim \mu)$ expresses that $f_i(x) \sim \mu$ must be true for all time in the interval.

Every leaf of a tree with this structure can be mapped to an equivalent STL formula that describes the signals falling in that leaf. Starting from a leaf of interest and backtracking to the root of the tree, the STL formula can be recursively obtained by (1) conjunction with the parent node's primitive if the current node is its left child; or (2) conjunction with the negation of the parent node's primitive if the current node is its right child. For example, in the naval surveillance case study, the formula corresponding to the cluster that contains the normal trajectories is (Fig. 1b)

$$\phi_{norm} = \mathbf{F}_{[16.3,280]}(x \leq 24.832) \wedge \mathbf{G}_{[0,262]}(y > 20.66) \tag{1}$$

Notice also the insight we can gain from the plain English translation of this formula: "The normal ship x coordinate is eventually below 24.83 in the time interval $[16.3, 280]$", i.e., it eventually approaches the port, and "the normal ship y coordinate is always above 20.66", i.e., it never approaches the island.

Remark 1. It is important to stress that the set of primitives $\mathcal{P}$ in Eq. 1 is not the only possible set. A user may define other primitives, for instance generic primitives using nested temporal operators (such as $\mathbf{G}_{[\tau_1,\tau_2]}\mathbf{F}_{[0,\tau_3]}(f_i(x) \sim \mu)$), or specific ones, guided by the particular nature of the learning problem at hand. For space restrictions, we do not investigate other primitives in this paper. However, the proposed algorithm works without modifications using other sets of primitives. The fragment of STL that is mapped with decision trees corresponds to the Boolean closure of the valuations from $\mathcal{P}$ [6].

5.2 Homogeneity Measures

The previous section describes how an STL formula can be associated to each leaf of a tree that contains primitives of $\mathcal{P}$ in its nodes. It is also necessary to define a criterion with which to select the primitive that best splits the data at each node. Our goal is to divide the signals so that the resulting two groups are more *homogeneous*. This means that each child produced contains signals more *similar* with each other and more different from the signals in the other child. To formalize this concept, we need to define (1) a measure of homogeneity for a set of signals and (2) a measure of the increase in homogeneity obtained by splitting the signals using a certain formula.

Definition 2 (Inertia-based Homogeneity Measure I). *Let S be a finite set of signals in $\mathcal{S}$, we define*

$$I(S) = \frac{1}{2}\frac{1}{|S|^2}\sum_{i=1}^{|S|}\sum_{j=1}^{|S|}d^2(s^i, s^j)$$

where $d(\cdot, \cdot)$ is a suitable distance function between two signals, such as the Euclidean Distance or Dynamic Time Warping (See Sect. 3).

$I(S)$ is the average squared distance of the signals in set S and, intuitively, a set is homogeneous when this quantity is low, i.e., the signals are close to each other.

Remark 2. As the name suggests, the Inertia-based homogeneity measure in Definition 2 recalls the *moment of inertia* concept in physics. When the distance function $d(\cdot, \cdot)$ is Euclidean, this measure is also related to the *variance* concept [1,21]. For brevity, we only present one homogeneity measure. However, others are possible, for instance by exploiting the various *linkage criteria* (i.e., single-linkage, complete-linkage, etc.) from the agglomerative clustering literature [1,5].

Definition 3 (Homogeneity Gain HG**).** *Let S be a finite set of signals and ϕ an STL formula, the Homogeneity Gain is defined as*

$$HG(S, \phi) = I(S) - \left[\frac{|S_\top|}{|S|} \cdot I(S_\top) + \frac{|S_\perp|}{|S|} \cdot I(S_\perp) \right] \tag{2}$$

where $S_\top = \{s^i \in S \mid s^i \models \phi\}$ and $S_\perp = \{s^i \in S \mid s^i \not\models \phi\}$ are the subsets of signals from S satisfying and not satisfying the formula ϕ, respectively.

Intuitively, a positive value of $HG(S, \phi)$ means that by splitting the set S with the formula ϕ, we obtain two sets $S_\top$ and $S_\perp$ with a *reduced overall diversity* or, equivalently, we *gained homogeneity*. The homogeneity gain in Definition 3 is connected to the so-called *Ward's criterion* in the clustering literature [1,21].

The defined homogeneity gain guides the primitive selection and parameter optimization process. In particular, given a set of primitives $\mathcal{P}$ and a set of signals S, we select the primitive $\psi^* \in \mathcal{P}$, and its optimal parameters $\theta^* \in \Theta$, so that the resulting STL formula $\psi^*(\theta^*)$ maximizes the homogeneity gain:

$$\psi^*, \theta^* = \arg\max_{\psi \in \mathcal{P}, \theta \in \Theta} HG(S, \psi(\theta)) \tag{3}$$

This problem is decomposed into $|\mathcal{P}|$ optimization problems over a small number of real-valued parameters ($|\Theta|$), which can be solved using any global non-linear optimization algorithm.

Remark 3. To solve the parameter optimization problem in Eq. (3) we used Simulated Annealing with satisfactory results. However, we feel there is room for improvement. In the future, we plan to investigate alternative optimization routines, such as Differential Evolution, and try to exploit the *monotonic* property of some PSTL formulae to speed up the optimization process [2,16].

5.3   Clustering Algorithm

In Algorithm 1 we show our parameterized clustering procedure with a high-level object oriented notation. The meta-parameters of Algorithm 1 are: (1) a set of PSTL primitives $\mathcal{P}$; (2) a set of stopping criteria *stop*; and (3) three measure functions $d()$, $I()$, $HG()$ (distance, homogeneity, and homogeneity gain, respectively) described in the previous sections. The algorithm is *iterative* and takes as input argument a set of unlabeled training signals S_{tr}. At the beginning, an empty tree is created. This tree has a single leaf, which is also the root, that

---

Algorithm 1. Hierarchical Clustering Algorithm - HClustSTL()

Parameter: $\mathcal{P}$ – set of PSTL primitives
Parameter: $stop$ – set of stopping criteria
Parameter: d, I, HG – distance, homogeneity, and homogeneity gain measures
Input: S_{tr} – set of training signals
Output: T – a Tree

1 $T \leftarrow$ createEmptyTree(S_{tr})
2 **while** $stop()==false$ **do**
3     $L \leftarrow T$.selectDivLeaf()
4     $\psi^*, \theta^* \leftarrow \arg\max_{\psi \in \mathcal{P}, \theta \in \Theta} HG(L.S, \psi(\theta))$
5   T.nonTerminal(L, $\psi^*(\theta^*)$)
6     $S_\top^*, S_\bot^* \leftarrow$ partition($L.S, \psi^*(\theta^*)$)
7   T.createLeftLeaf(L, $S_\top^*$)
8   T.createRightLeaf(L, $S_\bot^*$)

9 **return** T

---

contains all the input signals (line 1). At each iteration, the least homogeneous leaf is selected for further processing (line 3). This is the leaf L that contains the most diverse signals $L.S$ according to the homogeneity measure $I()$. The algorithm proceeds to find the optimal STL formula, among all the valuations of PSTL formulae from the set of primitives $\mathcal{P}$, to split the signals in L (line 4). The goal here is to get more homogeneous children, and the optimality is assessed using the homogeneity gain measure $HG()$ according to Eqs. (2)–(3). Next, the leaf L is converted to a non-terminal node, and it is associated with the formula $\psi^*(\theta^*)$ (line 5). The induced partition of the signals $S_\top^*, S_\bot^*$ is computed (line 6), and for each outcome of the split, a corresponding child leaf is created (lines 7–8). The stopping conditions are checked at every iteration (line 2), and the constructed tree T is returned when they are met. Several stopping criteria can be set for Algorithm 1. The most common strategy is to stop if the tree has reached a certain prespecified depth. Another strategy is to stop when the leaves' diversity is below a certain threshold. As we will discuss in the next section, it is generally good practice to use permissive stopping conditions and then assess the quality of the induced hierarchy using other tools.

Remark 4. We implemented and tested Algorithm 1 using MATLAB. The only computationally expensive step of the algorithm is the optimization in line 4. This problem becomes easier as the depth of the tree increases because fewer signals need to be processed. Aside from the optimization routine itself (see Remark 3), the computation of the objective function $HG(S, \psi(\theta))$ implicitly requires the construction of the partition $S_\top, S_\bot$ induced by $\psi(\theta)$ and the computation of the distances among the signals in S. To speed up the execution, we precompute and store a *distance matrix* that contains the distances, taken pairwise, of the signals in the dataset S_{tr}. Moreover, since the distance computations involve multi-dimensional signals, normalizing the dataset before the execution of the algorithm has proven to be useful.

5.4   Clustering Evaluation

Evaluating the quality of clustering results is a difficult task [1]. If independent labeled data is available, it is possible to assess how similar the returned clusters are to the predetermined classes, treating the latter as a *gold standard* during the evaluation. Several performance metrics used for classification tasks can be adapted for this purpose, such as the misclassification rate (MCR). However, there is no unanimous agreement that this is an adequate way of assessing the performance of a clustering algorithm [12]. Specifically, manually assigned labels only represent *one* possible partitioning of the dataset, which does not imply that there are no other, equal or more meaningful, partitions. Moreover, in general, labeled data is not available at all, and clustering algorithms should be interpreted more as *exploratory* and *knowledge discovery* tools [1,21] that assist the human user who is the ultimate (and subjective) judge. In this context, clustering is a trial and error process and may involve several attempts. Our algorithm, with explicit support for meta-parameters, e.g., different distance measures, is well suited for this task.

An important related issue is deciding the number of clusters. One of the major advantages of hierarchical clustering algorithms is that the number of clusters does not have to be *prefixed* before the execution of the algorithm. Given a constructed hierarchy of clusters, some methods have been proposed in literature to help the user decide the appropriate number of clusters without requiring explicit data labeling [1]. We used the so-called *elbow* method. The core idea is to explore the relationship between the number of clusters and the remaining diversity in the clusters. The latter is quantified with the *percentage of unexplained diversity* defined as the ratio between the weighted sum of inhomogeneity in the clusters and the initial inhomogeneity of the whole dataset. The percentage of unexplained diversity is plotted against the number of clusters. Generally, the first splits of the tree explain a lot of diversity in the data, but at some point the marginal decrease will drop, giving an angle in the graph (hence the elbow name). This information can be exploited to stop the algorithm, if a satisfactory solution has been found, or to prune the tree in order to remove unnecessary clusters. Moreover, since there is a direct connection in our method between depth of induced tree, number of clusters, and length of the formulae representing the clusters, this analysis provides insights on the trade-off between formulae complexity and clustering effectiveness.

For the maritime surveillance case study, we obtained excellent results with the classical Euclidean norm. Algorithm 1 was set to run until a tree of depth 4 was constructed. The elbow analysis in Fig. 2 shows that the last major drop in unexplained diversity happens when there are three leaves, and this corresponds to the tree shown in Fig. 1b. In this case, each cluster can be mapped with one of the original scenarios of the dataset.

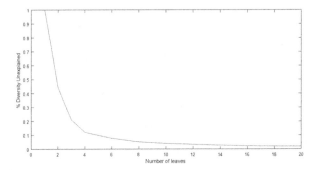

Fig. 2. Maritime surveillance case study - elbow analysis

6   Automotive Case Study

The second case study is a fault classification problem in an automatic transmission system. We constructed this dataset for the purposes of this investigation by modifying a built-in Simulink model [23]. We selected this model because it includes all the complexities of real world industrial models, such as continuous and discrete blocks, look-up tables, and Stateflow charts. Moreover, this model was proposed as a benchmark for the Hybrid Systems community in [14] and variations of the base scheme have been used as case studies in some recent formal methods papers [10,16,24].

In this section, we briefly describe the base model and our modifications. Consider the closed-loop vehicle model with four speeds and an automatic transmission controller of [23]. The transmission subsystem allows the internal combustion engine to run at appropriate rotational speeds in order to provide a range of speeds and torques necessary for the vehicle to move and maneuver effectively. The goal of the controller is to automatically change gear, freeing the driver from having to shift gears manually. The system has two inputs: the throttle opening and the brake. The throttle can take any value between 0 (fully closed) and 100 (fully open). The brake can also take values between 0 and 100, and it is used to model the variable load on the engine, such as the vehicle going uphill or downhill. The system has two continuous and one discrete state variables. The continuous state variables are the engine speed (in rpm) and the vehicle speed (in mph). The discrete state variable is the gear, which takes an integer value between 1 and 4. The engine speed and the vehicle speed are also used as outputs of the system.

For the simulation, we consider the vehicle starting from rest and subsequently performing a surpass maneuver. Specifically, the vehicle starts with zero speed, engine at 1000 RPM, and with throttle at 50%. The surpass maneuver begins at a random time, between 15 and 25 s, when the driver steps the throttle to 90%. The overall simulation time is 50 s. Noise has also been injected in the system. In particular, independent Gaussian random noise was added to the engine speed, the transmission speed, and the vehicle's speed sensor.

In this case study, three types of faults have been simulated. The first type of fault models a malfunction in the vehicle's speed sensor. The fault can manifest at anytime during the execution and the readings of the sensor are substituted with a random (erratic) value between 0 and 100 mph. The second and third types of faults are obtained by tampering with the gear shifting logic, which is implemented with a Stateflow chart in the Simulink model. In the second type of fault, the Stateflow chart is modified so that the vehicle is unable to engage the fourth gear. For the third type of fault, the Stateflow chart is modified so that the automatic transmission switches directly from second gear to fourth gear, and vice versa, by skipping the third gear altogether.

We performed 1500 total simulations with different settings. In detail, we obtained: 750 traces where the system was working normally; 250 traces with a fault in the vehicle's speed sensor (Type 1 fault); 250 traces with an *unable to engage the fourth gear* fault (Type 2 fault); 250 traces with a *skip the third gear* fault (Type 3 fault). For every trace, we collected the system's output values, that is, the speed of the engine (variable x_1) and the speed of the vehicle (variable x_2). Some sample traces are shown in Fig. 3a.

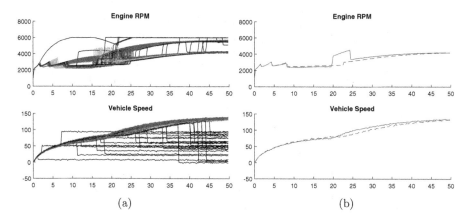

Fig. 3. Automatic transmission - (a) Example trajectories: Normal in blue, anomalous in black (Type 1-`sensor fault`), red (Type 2-`no 4th`), and green (Type 3-`skip 3rd`). (b) Two qualitatively different normal scenarios: (1) shift sequence 4th-3rd-4th with a solid line, and (2) stay in 4th gear with a dashed line. (Color figure online)

7   Results

For the automotive case study, we executed Algorithm 1 with the aim of reconstructing the different types of faults and the normal conditions present in the dataset. We obtained the best results using the *dependent* multi-dimensional dynamic time-warping distance (DTW_D) with 0.2 warping factor. This is due to the fact that the components of each signal come from the same system and share the same clock. Moreover, the signals in the dataset can be shifted and distorted in time due to the varying input throttle and the noise injected. Algorithm 1 was set to run until a tree of depth 4 was constructed. The elbow analysis in this case shows that there is not much gain after six clusters have been created (Fig. 4b). This corresponds to the tree shown in Fig. 4a.

Type 1 and Type 2 faults are mapped with a cluster each. Type 3 faults are mapped with two clusters, and there are also two separate clusters containing normal signals. This happens because, when the surpassing maneuver starts, two scenarios are possible. In the first scenario, the transmission downshifts from the fourth gear to the third gear and the engine jumps from about 2500 RPM to about 4000 RPM. The engine torque is thus increased and so is the mechanical advantage of the transmission. With continued heavy throttle, the vehicle accelerates and eventually shifts back to the forth gear (Fig. 3b - solid line). In the second scenario, the automatic transmission deems the gear change not necessary, according to the shift schedule, and the vehicle stays in the forth gear for the whole time (Fig. 3b - dashed line). Using a simple disjunction, we can obtain a single formula that overall describes the normal conditions (it encompasses the signals contained in both clusters):

$$\phi_{norm} = \begin{aligned} &\mathbf{G}_{[33.1,45.9]}x_1 \leq 4609.8 \wedge ((\mathbf{G}_{[31.6,45.3]}x_2 > 110.02 \wedge \mathbf{F}_{[20.8,46]}x_1 > 4266.1) \\ &\vee (\mathbf{F}_{[31.6,45.3]}x_2 \leq 110.02 \wedge (\mathbf{F}_{[46.3,46.7]}x_2 > 111.18 \wedge \mathbf{G}_{[4.41,5.88]}x_1 > 2517.2))) \end{aligned}$$

Since labeled data is available for this case study, we tested the classification performance of this formula using an independent test set and achieved a misclassification rate of 0.031.

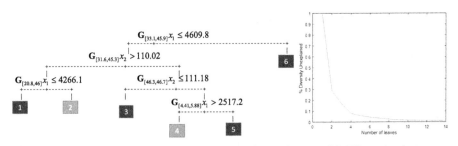

(a) Cluster Tree - Leaves 2 and 4 contain normal signals   (b) Elbow Analysis

Fig. 4. Automatic transmission results

We return to the maritime surveillance case study for some final remarks. This case study was also investigated in [17], with their SVM-based approach, and in [6], using a decision-tree based algorithm. Both these works tackle the *supervised two-class classification* problem. Even though the problem settings are quite different, we can still try to make some comparisons since our algorithm was able to recover the same class structure of the original dataset (as shown in

Fig. 1). In terms of classification performance, the formula in Eq. (1) achieves a misclassification rate of 0.0079 on an independent test set. This outperforms the results obtained in [17], improving the misclassification rate by a factor of 20, and is on par with the results of the supervised algorithm in [6]. This result is quite impressive considering that our algorithm does *not* use labeled examples and yet it is able to achieve similar accuracy. For the naval case study, the execution time of Algorithm 1 was 283 s, which is still far better than [17] but roughly three times slower with respect to [6].[3] The difference with [6] is due to two main factors: (1) the computation of distances, which are not needed in supervised algorithms, and (2) the greater depth at which the tree is initially induced, since labels are not available to guide the algorithm termination. Moreover, it must be noted that the exploratory nature of clustering generally requires more than one execution.

8   Conclusion

We introduced a novel method for learning signal classifiers in the form of STL formulae from raw data. Specifically, we tackled the clustering problem. In this challenging scenario, no labels are available for the signals, and the end goal is to cluster similar signals together and represent each cluster with an STL formula.

We exploited the connection between binary trees and STL formulae introduced in [6] and constructed an hierarchical clustering algorithm that partitions signals using PSTL primitives to test simple temporal logic properties of the data. The best primitives, along with their parameters, are chosen by optimizing some appropriately defined *homogeneity* measures, which capture how well a formula splits the signals according to their similarity. Finally, each leaf of the tree is associated with a cluster and can be mapped to an STL formula that describes it. *Both* the formula structure and its parameters are derived from the input data.

This work is in line with the recent interest in learning temporal specification from data and is motivated by the need to construct formulae that provide good clustering performance while being interpretable. This allows the designers to acquire some knowledge over the derived clusters and the specific application domain. Moreover, the inferred formulae can be used in other contexts, such as system monitoring. The proposed algorithm has been tested on two case studies in the maritime surveillance and automotive fields. We showed that the algorithm is able to capture relevant characteristics of the signals in both cases and achieves solid classification accuracy.

In the future, we plan to investigate other homogeneity measures, especially some measures derived from information theory, and then perform a comparative study of the behavior of the proposed algorithm for each measure. Future work also includes improving the local optimization procedure, which will speed up the overall performance of the algorithm.

---

[3] We ran our experiments on a Windows PC with an Intel 5920K CPU.

Acknowledgments. This work was partially supported by DENSO CORPORATION and by the Office of Naval Research under grant N00014-14-1-0554. The authors would like to acknowledge Hirotoshi Yasuoka (DENSO CORPORATION) and Rachael Ivison (Boston University) for providing valuable feedback during this research. We also thank the anonymous reviewers for their comments.

References

1. Aggarwal, C.C., Reddy, C.K.: Data Clustering: Algorithms and Applications Chapman & Hall/CRC, 1st edn. CRC Press, Boca Raton (2013)
2. Asarin, E., Donzé, A., Maler, O., Nickovic, D.: Parametric Identification of Temporal Properties. In: Khurshid, S., Sen, K. (eds.) RV 2011. LNCS, vol. 7186, pp. 147–160. Springer, Heidelberg (2012). doi:10.1007/978-3-642-29860-8_12
3. Bartocci, E., Bortolussi, L., Nenzi, L., Sanguinetti, G.: System design of stochastic models using robustness of temporal properties. Theoret. Comput. Sci. **587**, 3–25 (2015)   ·
4. Bartocci, E., Bortolussi, L., Sanguinetti, G.: Data-driven statistical learning of temporal logic properties. In: Legay, A., Bozga, M. (eds.) FORMATS 2014. LNCS, vol. 8711, pp. 23–37. Springer, Cham (2014). doi:10.1007/978-3-319-10512-3_3
5. Bishop, C.M.: Pattern Recognition and Machine Learning. Information Science and Statistics. Springer, New York (2006)
6. Bombara, G., Vasile, C.I., Penedo, F., Yasuoka, H., Belta, C.: A decision tree approach to data classification using signal temporal logic. In: Proceedings of the 19th International Conference on Hybrid Systems: Computation and Control, HSCC 2016, pp. 1–10. ACM, New York (2016)
7. Bufo, S., Bartocci, E., Sanguinetti, G., Borelli, M., Lucangelo, U., Bortolussi, L.: Temporal logic based monitoring of assisted ventilation in intensive care patients. In: Margaria, T., Steffen, B. (eds.) ISoLA 2014. LNCS, vol. 8803, pp. 391–403. Springer, Heidelberg (2014). doi:10.1007/978-3-662-45231-8_30
8. Clarke, E.M., Grumberg, O., Peled, D.: Model Checking. MIT Press, Cambridge (1999)
9. Donzé, A., Maler, O.: Robust satisfaction of temporal logic over real-valued signals. In: Chatterjee, K., Henzinger, T.A. (eds.) FORMATS 2010. LNCS, vol. 6246, pp. 92–106. Springer, Heidelberg (2010). doi:10.1007/978-3-642-15297-9_9
10. Fainekos, G., Sankaranarayanan, S., Ueda, K., Yazarel, H.: Verification of automotive control applications using S-TaLiRo. In: American Control Conference (ACC), vol. 2012, pp. 3567–3572, June 2012
11. Fainekos, G.E., Pappas, G.J.: Robustness of temporal logic specifications for continuous-time signals. Theoret. Comput. Sci. **410**(42), 4262–4291 (2009)
12. Färber, I., Günnemann, S., Kriegel, H.P., Kröger, P., Müller, E., Schubert, E., Seidl, T., Zimek, A.: On using class-labels in evaluation of clusterings. In: MultiClust: 1st International Workshop on Discovering, Summarizing and Using Multiple Clusterings Held in Conjunction with KDD 2010 (2010)
13. Grosu, R., Smolka, S.A., Corradini, F., Wasilewska, A., Entcheva, E., Bartocci, E.: Learning and detecting emergent behavior in networks of cardiac myocytes. Commun. ACM **52**(3), 97–105 (2009)
14. Hoxha, B., Abbas, H., Fainekos, G.: Benchmarks for temporal logic requirements for automotive systems. In: Proceedings of Applied Verification for Continuous and Hybrid Systems (2014)

15. Hoxha, B., Dokhanchi, A., Fainekos, G.: Mining parametric temporal logic properties in model-based design for cyber-physical systems. Int. J. Softw. Tools Technol. Transfer, 1–15 (2017)
16. Jin, X., Donzé, A., Deshmukh, J., Seshia, S.A.: Mining requirements from closed-loop control models. IEEE Trans. Comput. Aided Des. Integr. Circuits Syst. **PP**(99), 1 (2015)
17. Kong, Z., Jones, A., Medina Ayala, A., Aydin Gol, E., Belta, C.: Temporal logic inference for classification and prediction from data. In: Proceedings of the 17th International Conference on Hybrid Systems: Computation and Control, HSCC 2014, pp. 273–282. ACM, New York (2014)
18. Kowalska, K., Peel, L.: Maritime anomaly detection using Gaussian Process active learning. In: 2012 15th International Conference on Information Fusion (FUSION), pp. 1164–1171, July 2012
19. Maler, O., Nickovic, D.: Monitoring temporal properties of continuous signals. In: Lakhnech, Y., Yovine, S. (eds.) FORMATS/FTRTFT -2004. LNCS, vol. 3253, pp. 152–166. Springer, Heidelberg (2004). doi:10.1007/978-3-540-30206-3_12
20. Ratanamahatana, C.A., Keogh, E.: Everything you know about dynamic time warping is wrong. In: Third Workshop on Mining Temporal and Sequential Data. Citeseer (2004)
21. Ripley, B.D.: Pattern Recognition and Neural Networks. Cambridge University Press, Cambridge (1996)
22. Shokoohi-Yekta, M., Wang, J., Keogh, E.: On the non-trivial generalization of dynamic time warping to the multi-dimensional case. In: Proceedings of the 2015 SIAM International Conference on Data Mining, Proceedings, Society for Industrial and Applied Mathematics, pp. 289–297, June 2015
23. The MathWorks Inc: MATLAB and Simulink R2017a. Natick, Massachusetts (2017)
24. Zhao, Q., Krogh, B.H., Hubbard, P.: Generating test inputs for embedded control systems. IEEE Control Syst. **23**(4), 49–57 (2003)

Space Efficient Breadth-First and Level Traversals of Consistent Global States of Parallel Programs

Himanshu Chauhan$^{(\boxtimes)}$ and Vijay K. Garg

University of Texas at Austin, Austin, USA
himanshu@utexas.edu, garg@ece.utexas.edu

Abstract. Enumerating *consistent* global states of a computation is a fundamental problem in parallel computing with applications to debugging, testing and runtime verification of parallel programs. Breadth-first search (BFS) enumeration is especially useful for these applications as it finds an erroneous consistent global state with the least number of events possible. The total number of executed events in a global state is called its *rank*. BFS also allows enumeration of all global states of a given rank or within a range of ranks. If a computation on n processes has m events per process on average, then the traditional BFS (Cooper-Marzullo and its variants) requires $\mathcal{O}(\frac{m^{n-1}}{n})$ space in the worst case, whereas our algorithm performs the BFS requires $\mathcal{O}(m^2 n^2)$ space. Thus, we reduce the space complexity for BFS enumeration of consistent global states exponentially, and give the first polynomial space algorithm for this task. In our experimental evaluation of seven benchmarks, traditional BFS fails in many cases by exhausting the 2 GB heap space allowed to the JVM. In contrast, our implementation uses less than 60 MB memory and is also faster in many cases.

1 Introduction

Parallel programs are not only difficult to design and implement, but once implemented are also difficult to debug and verify. The technique of predicate detection [12,17] is helpful in verification of these implementations as it allows inference based analysis to check many possible system states based on one execution trace. The technique involves execution of the program, and modeling of its trace as a partial order. Then all possible states of the model that are consistent with the partial order are visited and evaluated for violation of any constraints/invariants. A large body of work uses this approach to verify distributed applications, as well as to detect data-races and other concurrency related bugs in shared memory parallel programs [11,14,19,23]. Finding consistent global states of an execution also has critical applications in snapshotting of modern distributed file systems [1,27].

A fundamental requirement for this approach is the traversal of all possible consistent global states, or *consistent cuts*, of a parallel execution. Let us call the execution of a parallel program a *computation*. The set of all consistent cuts

© Springer International Publishing AG 2017
S. Lahiri and G. Reger (Eds.): RV 2017, LNCS 10548, pp. 138–154, 2017.
DOI: 10.1007/978-3-319-67531-2_9

of a computation can be represented as a directed acyclic graph in which each vertex represents a consistent cut, and the edges mark the transition from one global state to another by executing one operation. Moreover, this graph has a special structure: it is a distributive lattice [24]. Multiple algorithms have been proposed to traverse the lattice of consistent cuts of a parallel execution. Cooper and Marzullo's algorithm [12] starts from the source — a consistent cut in which no operation has been executed by any process — and performs a breadth-first-search (BFS) visiting the lattice level by level. Alagar and Venkatesan's algorithm [2] performs a depth-first-search (DFS) traversal of the lattice, and Ganter's algorithm [15] enumerates global states in lexical order.

The BFS traversal of the lattice is particularly useful in solving two key problems. First, suppose a programmer is debugging a parallel program to find a concurrency related bug. The global state in which this bug occurs is a counter-example to the programmer's understanding of a correct execution, and we want to halt the execution of the program on reaching the first state where the bug occurs. Naturally, finding a small counter example is quite useful in such cases. The second problem is to check all consistent cuts of given rank(s). For example, a programmer may observe that her program crashes only after k events have been executed, or while debugging an implementation of Paxos [22] algorithm, she might only be interested in analyzing the system when all processes have sent their *promises* to the leader. Among the existing traversal algorithms, the BFS algorithm provides a straightforward solution to these two problems. It is guaranteed to traverse the lattice of consistent cuts in a level by level manner where each level corresponds to the total number of events executed in the computation. This traversal, however, requires space proportional to the size of the biggest level of the lattice which, in general, is *exponential* in the size of the computation. In this paper, we present a new algorithm to perform BFS traversal of the lattice in space that is polynomial in the size of the computation. In short, the contribution of this paper are:

- For a computation on n processes such that each process has m events on average, our algorithm requires $\mathcal{O}(m^2 n^2)$ space in the worst case, whereas the traditional BFS algorithm requires $\mathcal{O}(\frac{m^{n-1}}{n})$ space (exponential in n).
- Our evaluation on seven benchmark computations shows the traditional BFS runs out of the maximum allowed 2 GB memory for three of them, whereas our implementation can traverse the lattices by using less than 60 MB memory for each benchmark.

The exponential reduction in space may come at the cost of a longer runtime to perform the BFS traversal. In the worst case, our algorithm may take $\mathcal{O}(m^2 n^2)$ time per consistent cut. However, our experimental evaluation shows our runtimes are within the same order of magnitude to those of the traditional BFS.

2   Background

We model a computation $P = (E, \rightarrow)$ on n processes $\{P_1, P_2, \ldots, P_n\}$ as a partial order on the set of events, E. The events are ordered by Lamport's *happened-*

before ($\rightarrow$) relation [21]. This partially ordered set (poset) of events is partitioned into chains:

Definition 1 (Chain Partition). *A chain partition of a poset places every element of the poset on a chain that is totally ordered. Formally, if α is a chain partition of poset $P = (E, \rightarrow)$ then α maps every event to a natural number such that*

$$\forall x, y \in E : \alpha(x) = \alpha(y) \Rightarrow (x \rightarrow y) \vee (y \rightarrow x).$$

Generally, a computation on n processes is partitioned into n chains such that the events executed by process P_i ($1 \le i \le n$) are placed on i^{th} chain.

Mattern [24] and Fidge [13] proposed *vector clocks*, an approach for time-stamping events in a computation such that the happened-before relation can be tracked. For a program on n processes, each event's vector clock is a n-length vector of integers. Note that vector clocks are dependent on chain partition of the poset that models the computation. For an event e, we denote $e.V$ as its vector clock. Throughout this paper, we use the following representation for interpreting chain partitions and vector clocks: if there are n chains in the chain partition of the computation, then the lowest chain (process) is always numbered 1, and the highest chain being numbered n. A vector clock on n chains is represented as a n-length vector: $[c_n, c_{n-1}, ..., c_i, ..., c_2, c_1]$ such that c_i denotes the number of events executed on process P_i. Hence, if event e was executed on process P_i, then $e.V[i]$ is e's index (starting from 1) on P_i. Also, for any event f in the computation: $e \rightarrow f \Leftrightarrow \forall j : e.V[j] \le f.V[j] \wedge \exists k : e.V[k] < f.V[k]$. A pair of events, e and f, is concurrent iff $e \not\rightarrow f \wedge f \not\rightarrow e$. We denote this relation by $e||f$. Figure 1a shows a sample computation with six events and their corresponding vector clocks. Event b is the second event on process P_1, and its vector clock is $[0, 2]$. Event g is the third event on P_2, but it is preceded by f, which in turn is causally dependent on b on P_1, and thus the vector clock of g is $[3, 2]$.

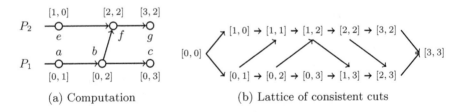

(a) Computation (b) Lattice of consistent cuts

Fig. 1. A computation with vector clocks of events, and its consistent cuts

Definition 2 (Consistent Cut). *Given a computation $(E, \rightarrow)$, a subset of events $C \subseteq E$ forms a consistent cut if C contains an event e only if it contains all events that happened-before e. Formally, $(e \in C) \wedge (f \rightarrow e) \implies (f \in C)$.*

A consistent cut captures the notion of a possible global state of the system at some point during its execution [6]. Consider the computation shown in Fig. 1a. The subset of events $\{a, b, e\}$ is a consistent cut, whereas $\{a, e, f\}$ is not; because $b \rightarrow f$ (b happened-before f) but b is not included in the subset.

Vector Clock Notation of Cuts: So far we have described how vector clocks can be used to time-stamp events in the computation. We also use them to represent cuts of the computation. If the computation is partitioned into n chains, then for any cut G, its vector clock is a n-length vector such that $G[i]$ denotes the number of events from P_i included in G. Note that in our vector clock representation the events from P_i are at the ith index from the right.

For example, consider the state of the computation in Fig. 1a when P_1 has executed events a and b, and P_2 has only executed event e. The consistent cut for this state, $\{a, b, e\}$, is represented by $[1, 2]$. Note that cut $[2, 1]$ is not consistent, as it indicates execution of f on P_2 without b being executed on P_1. The computation in Fig. 1a has twelve consistent cuts; and the lattice of these consistent cuts (in their vector clock representation) is shown in Fig. 1b.

Rank of a Cut: Given a cut G, we define $rank(G) = \sum G[i]$. The rank of a cut corresponds to the total number of events, across all processes, that have been executed to reach the cut.

In Fig. 1b, there is one source cut ($[0, 0]$) with rank 0, then there are two cuts each of ranks 1 to 5, and finally there is one cut ($[3, 3]$) has rank 6.

2.1 Breadth-First Traversal of Lattice of Consistent Cuts

Consider a parallel computation $P = (E, \rightarrow)$. The lattice of consistent cuts, $\mathcal{C}(E)$, of P is a DAG whose vertices are the consistent cuts of $(E, \rightarrow)$, and there is a directed edge from vertex u to vertex v if state represented by v can be reached by executing one event on u; hence we also have $rank(v) = rank(u) + 1$. The source of $\mathcal{C}(E)$ is the empty set: a consistent cut in which no events have been executed on any process. The sink of this DAG is E: the consistent cut in which all the events of the computation have been executed. Breadth-first search (BFS) of this lattice starts from the source vertex and visits all the cuts of rank 1; it then visits all the cuts of rank 2 and continues in this manner till reaching the last consistent cut of rank $|E|$. For example, in Fig. 1b the BFS algorithm will traverse cuts in the following order: $[0, 0], [0, 1], [1, 0], [0, 2], [1, 1], [0, 3], [1, 2], [1, 3], [2, 2], [2, 3], [3, 2], [3, 3]$.

The standard BFS on a graph needs to store the vertices at distance d from the source to be able to visit the vertices at distance $d + 1$ (from the source). Hence, in performing a BFS on $\mathcal{C}(E)$ we are required to store the cuts of rank r in order to visit the cuts of rank $r + 1$. Observe that in a parallel computation there may be exponentially many cuts of rank r. Thus, traversing the lattice $\mathcal{C}(E)$ requires space which is exponential in the size of input. The optimized vector clock based BFS traversal takes $\mathcal{O}(n^2)$ time per cut [16], where n is the number of processes in the computation.

2.2   Related Work

Cooper and Marzullo [12] gave the first algorithm for global states enumeration which is based on breadth first search (BFS). Let $i(P)$ denote the total number of consistent cuts of a poset P. Cooper-Marzullo algorithm requires $\mathcal{O}(n^2 \cdot i(P))$ time, and exponential space in the size of the input computation. The exponential space requirement is due to the standard BFS approach in which consistent cuts of rank r must be stored to traverse the cuts of rank $r + 1$.

There is also a body of work on enumeration of consistent cuts in order different than BFS. Alagar and Venkatesan [3] presented a depth first algorithm using the notion of global interval which reduces the space complexity to $\mathcal{O}(|E|)$. Steiner [29] gave an algorithm that uses $\mathcal{O}(|E| \cdot i(P))$ time, and Squire [28] further improved the computation time to $\mathcal{O}(log|E| \cdot i(P))$. Pruesse and Ruskey [26] gave the first algorithm that generates global states in a combinatorial Gray code manner. The algorithm uses $\mathcal{O}(|E| \cdot i(P))$ time and can be reduced to $\mathcal{O}(\Delta(P) \cdot i(P))$ time, where $\Delta(P)$ is the in-degree of an event; however, the space grows exponentially in $|E|$. Later, Jegou et al. [20] and Habib et al. [18] improved the space complexity to $\mathcal{O}(n \cdot |E|)$.

Ganter [15] presented an algorithm, which uses the notion of lexical order, and Garg [16] gave the implementation using vector clocks. The lexical algorithm requires $\mathcal{O}(n^2 \cdot i(P))$ time but the algorithm itself is *stateless* and hence requires no additional space besides the poset. Paramount [8] gave a parallel algorithm to traverse this lattice in lexical order, and QuickLex [7] provides an improved implementation for lexical traversal that takes $\mathcal{O}(n \cdot \Delta(P) \cdot i(P))$ time, and $\mathcal{O}(n^2)$ space overall.

3   Uniflow Chain Partition

A uniflow partition of a computation's poset $P = (E, \rightarrow)$ is its partition into n_u chains $\{P_i \mid 1 \leq i \leq n_u\}$ such that no element (event of E) in a higher numbered chain is smaller than any element in lower numbered chain; that is if any event e is placed on a chain i then all causal dependencies of e must be placed on chains numbered lower than i. For poset $P = (E, \rightarrow)$, chain partition μ is uniflow if

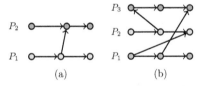

Fig. 2. Posets in uniflow partitions

$$\forall x, y \in P : \mu(x) < \mu(y) \Rightarrow \neg(y \not\rightarrow x) \qquad (1)$$

Visually, in a uniflow chain partition all the edges, capturing happened-before relation, between separate chains always point upwards because their dependencies — elements of poset that are smaller — are always placed on lower chains. Figure 2 shows two posets with uniflow partition. Whereas Fig. 3 shows two posets with partitions that do not satisfy the uniflow property. The poset in

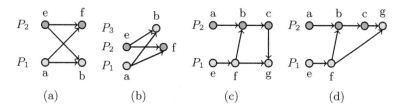

Fig. 3. Posets in (a) and (c) are not in uniflow partition: but (b) and (d) respectively are their uniflow partitions

Fig. 3(a) can be transformed into a uniflow partition of three chains as shown in Fig. 3(b). Similarly, Fig. 3(c) can be transformed into a uniflow partition of two chains shown in Fig. 3(d). Observe that:

Lemma 1. *Every poset has at least one uniflow chain partition.*

Proof. Any total order derived from the poset is a uniflow chain partition in which each element is a chain by itself. In this trivial uniflow chain partition the number of chains is equal to the number of elements in the poset.

The structure of uniflow chain partitions can be used for efficiently obtaining consistent cuts of larger ranks.

Lemma 2 (Uniflow Cuts Lemma). *Let P be a poset with a uniflow chain partition $\{P_i \mid 1 \leq i \leq n_u\}$, and G be a consistent cut of P. Then any $H_k \subseteq P$ for $1 \leq k \leq n_u$ is also a consistent cut of P if it satisfies:*

$$\forall i : k < i \leq n_u : H_k[i] = G[i], \text{ and}$$
$$\forall i : 1 \leq i \leq k : H_k[i] = |P_i|.$$

Proof. Using Eq. 1, we exploit the structure of uniflow chain partitions: the causal dependencies of any element e lie only on chains that are lower than e's chain. As G is consistent, and H_k contains the same elements as G for the top $n_u - k$ chains, all the causal dependencies that need to be satisfied to make H_k have to be on chain k or lower. Hence, including all the elements from all of the lower chains will naturally satisfy all the causal dependencies, and make H_k consistent.

For example, in Fig. 2(b), consider the cut $G = [1, 2, 1]$ that is a consistent cut of the poset. Then, picking $k = 1$, and using Lemma 2 gives us the cut $[1, 2, 3]$ which is consistent; similarly choosing $k = 2$ gives us $[1, 3, 3]$ that is also consistent. Note that the claim may not hold if the chain partition does not have uniflow property. For example, in Fig. 3(c), $G = [2, 2]$ is a consistent cut. The chain partition, however, is not uniflow and thus applying the Lemma with $k = 1$ gives us $[2, 3]$ which is not a consistent cut as it includes the third event on P_1, but not its causal dependency — the third event on P_2.

3.1 Finding a Uniflow Partition

The problem of finding a uniflow chain partition is a direct extension of finding the *jump number* of a poset [5,10,30]. Multiple algorithms have been proposed to find the jump number of a poset; which in turn arrange the poset in a uniflow chain partition. Finding an optimal (smallest number of chains) uniflow chain partition of a poset is a hard problem [5,10]. Bianco et al. [5] present a heuristic algorithm to find a uniflow partition, and show in their experimental evaluation that in most of the cases the resulting partitions are relatively close to optimal. We use a vector clock based online algorithm to find a uniflow partition for a computation. We present this algorithm in the extended version of the paper [9]. Note that we need to re-generate vector clocks of the events for the uniflow partition. This is a simple task using existing vector clock implementation techniques, and we omit these details.

4 Polynomial Space Breadth-First Traversal of Lattice

BFS traversal of the lattice of consistent cuts of any poset can be performed in space that is polynomial in the size of the poset. We do so by first obtaining the poset's uniflow chain partition, and then using this partition for traversal of cuts in increasing order of ranks. We start from the empty cut, and then traverse all consistent cuts of rank 1, then all consistent cuts of rank 2 and so on. For rank r, $1 \leq r \leq |E|$, we traverse the consistent cuts in the following lexical order:

Definition 3 (Lexical Order on Consistent Cuts). *Given any chain partition of poset P that partitions it into n chains, we define a total order called* lexical order *on all consistent cuts of P as follows. Let G and H be any two consistent cuts of P. Then, $G <_l H \equiv \exists k : (G[k] < H[k]) \wedge (\forall i : n \geq i > k : G[i] = H[i])$.*

Recall from our vector clock notation (Sect. 2) that the right most entry in the vector clock is for the least significant (lowest) chain. Consider the poset with a non-uniflow chain partition in Fig. 4(a). The vector clocks of its events are shown against the four events. The lexical order on the consistent cuts of this chain partition is: $[0,0] <_l [0,1] <_l [1,0] <_l [1,1] <_l [1,2] <_l [2,1] <_l [2,2]$. For the same poset, Fig. 4(b) shows the equivalent uniflow partition, and the corresponding vector clocks. The lexi-

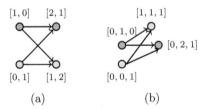

Fig. 4. Vector clocks of a computation in its original form, and in its uniflow partition

cal order on the consistent cuts for this uniflow chain partition is: $[0,0,0] <_l [0,0,1] <_l [0,1,0] <_l [0,1,1] <_l [0,2,1] <_l [1,1,1] <_l [1,2,1]$. Note that the number of consistent cuts remains same for both of these chain partitions, and there is a one-to-one mapping between the consistent cuts in the two partitions. Hence, if the computation's uniflow partition is different from its original chain

Algorithm 1. TRAVERSEBFSUNIFLOW(P)

Input: A poset $P = (E, \rightarrow)$ that has been partitioned into a uniflow chain partition of n_u chains, and the vector clock of the events have been regenerated for this partition.

1: $G = $ new int$[n_u]$ // initial consistent cut
2: enumerate(G) // evaluate the predicate on empty cut G.
3: **for** $(r = 1; r \leq |E|; r + +)$ **do**
4:    //make G lexically smallest cut of given rank
5:    $G = $ GETMINCUT(G, r)
6:    **while** $G \neq $ null **do**
7:       enumerate(G) // evaluate the predicate on G.
8:       //find the next bigger lexical cut of same rank
9:       $G = $ GETSUCCESSOR(G, r)

---

partition, we re-map the consistent cuts in uniflow partition to cuts in original partition.

Algorithm 1 shows the steps of our BFS traversal using a computation in a uniflow chain partition. From Lemma 1, we know that every poset has a uniflow chain partition. Recall that the vector clocks of the events depend on the chain partition of the poset. Thus, in generating this input we need two pre-processing steps: (a) finding a uniflow partition, and (b) regenerating vector clocks for this partition. For example, given a computation on two processes shown in Fig. 4(a), we will first convert it to the computation shown in Fig. 4(b). These steps are performed only once for a computation, and are relatively inexpensive in comparison to the traversal of lattice.

For each rank r, $1 \leq r \leq |E|$, Algorithm 1 first finds the lexically smallest consistent cut at of rank r. This is done by the GETMINCUT (shown in Algorithm 2) routine that returns the lexically smallest consistent cut of P bigger than G of rank r. For example, in Fig. 5, GETMINCUT($[0, 0, 0], 4$) returns $[0, 1, 3]$. Given a consistent cut G of rank r, we repeatedly find the next lexically bigger consistent cut of rank r using the routine GETSUCCESSOR given in Algorithm 3. For example, in Fig. 5, GETSUCCESSOR($[0, 0, 3], 3$) returns the next lexically smallest consistent cut $[0, 1, 2]$.

The GETMINCUT routine on poset P assumes that the rank of G is at most r and that G is a consistent cut of the P. It first computes d as the difference between r and the rank of G. We need to add d elements to G to find the smallest consistent cut of rank r. We exploit the Uniflow Cut Lemma (Lemma 2) by adding as many elements from the lowest chain as possible. If all the elements from the lowest chain are already in G, then we continue with the second lowest chain, and so on. For example in Fig. 5, consider finding smallest consistent cut of rank 5 starting from $G = [0, 0, 2]$. In this case, we add all three elements from P_1 to reach $[0, 0, 3]$, and then add first two elements from P_2 to get the answer as $[0, 2, 3]$.

The GETSUCCESSOR routine (Algorithm 3) finds the lexical successor of G at rank r. The approach for finding a lexical successor is similar to counting numbers in a decimal system: if we are looking for successor of 2199, then we cannot increment the two 9s (as we are only allowed digits 0–9), and hence the first possible increment is for entry 1. We increment it to 2, but we must now reset the entries at lesser significant digits. Hence, we reset the two 9s to 0s, and get the successor as 2200.

Algorithm 2. GetMinCut(G, r)

Input: G: a consistent cut of poset P from Algorithm 1

Output: Smallest consistent cut of rank r that is lexically greater than or equal to G.

1: $d = r - rank(G)$ // difference in ranks
2: **for** ($j = 1; j \leq n_u; j = j + 1$) **do**
3:   **if** $d \leq |P_j| - G[j]$ **then**
4:     $G[j] = G[j] + d$
5:     **return** G
6:   **else** // take all the elements from chain j
7:     $G[j] = G[j] + |P_j|$
8:     $d = d - |P_j|$

Algorithm 3. GetSuccessor(G, r)

Input: G: a consistent cut of rank r

Output: K: lexical successor of G of rank r

1: $K = G$ // Create a copy of G in K
2: **for** ($i = 2; i \leq n_u; i++$) **do** // lower chains to higher
3:   **if** next element on P_i exists **then**
4:     $K[i] = K[i] + 1$ // increment cut
5:     **for** ($j = i - 1; j > 0; j--$) **do**
6:       $K[j] = 0$ // reset lower chains
7:     //fix dependencies on lower chains
8:     **for** ($j = i + 1; j \leq n_u; j++$) **do**
9:       **for** ($k = i - 1; k > 0; k--$) **do**
10:        $vc =$ vector clock of event
11:          number $G[j]$ on P_j
12:        $K[k] = $ MAX($vc[k], K[k]$)
13:   **if** $rank(K) \leq r$ **then**
14:     **return** GetMinCut(K, r)
15: **return** null // no candidate cut

P_3 $[1,2,0]$ $[2,2,0]$ $[3,2,2]$

P_2 $[0,1,0]$ $[0,2,0]$ $[0,3,1]$

P_1 $[0,0,1]$ $[0,0,2]$ $[0,0,3]$

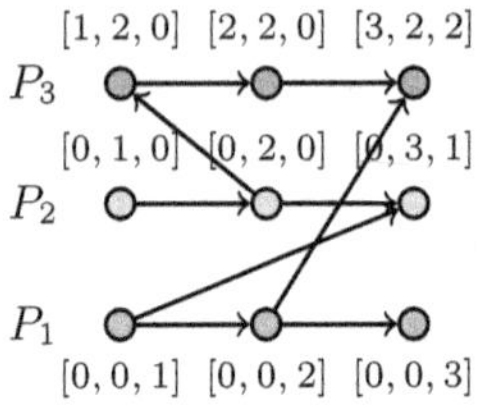

Fig. 5. Illustration: GetSuccessor

In our GetSuccessor routine, we start at the second lowest chain in a uniflow poset, and if possible increment the cut by one event on this chain. We then reset the entries on lower chains, and then make the cut consistent by satisfying all the causal dependencies. If the rank of the resulting cut is less than or equal to r, then calling the GetMinCut routine gives us the lexical successor of G at rank r. Line 1 copies cut G in K. The for loop covering lines 2–13 searches for an appropriate element not in G such that adding this element makes the resulting consistent cut lexically greater than G. We start the search from chain 2, instead of chain 1, because for a non-empty cut G adding any event from the lowest chain to G will only increase G's rank as there are no lower chains to reset. Line 3 checks if there is any possible element to add in P_i. If yes, then lines 4–6 increment K at chain i, and then set all its values for lower chains to 0. To ensure that K is a consistent cut, for every element in K, we add its causal dependencies to K in lines 7–11. Line 12 checks whether the resulting consistent cut is of rank $\leq r$. If $rank(K)$ is at most r, then we have found a suitable cut that can be used to find the next lexically bigger consistent cut and we call GETMINCUT routine to find it. If we have tried all values of i and did not find a suitable cut, then G is the largest consistent cut of rank r and we return null.

In Fig. 5, consider the call of GETSUCCESSOR $([1, 2, 3], 6)$. As there is no next element in P_1, we consider the next element in P_2. After line 5, the value of K is $[1, 3, 0]$, which is not consistent. Lines 7–10 make K a consistent cut, now $K = [1, 3, 1]$. Since $rank(K)$ is 5, we call GETMINCUT at line 13 to find the smallest consistent cut of rank 6 that is lexically bigger than $[1, 3, 1]$. This consistent cut is $[1, 3, 2]$.

The proof of correctness is given in the extended version of the paper [9].

4.1   Optimization for Time Complexity

We can find the lexical successor of any consistent cut in $\mathcal{O}(n_u^2)$ time, instead of $\mathcal{O}(n_u^3)$ time taken in GETSUCCESSOR, by using additional $\mathcal{O}(n_u^2)$ space.

Observe that GETSUC-CESSOR routine iterates over $n_u - 1$ chains in the outer loop at line 2, and the two inner loops at lines 8 and 9 perform $\mathcal{O}(n_u^2)$ work in the worst case. When we cannot find a suitable cut of rank less than or equal to r (check performed at line 12), we move to a higher chain (with the outer loop at line 2). Thus, we repeat a large fraction of the

---

Algorithm 4. COMPUTEPROJECTIONS(G)

Input: G: a consistent cut of rank r
1: **for** $(i = n_u; i \geq 1; i--)$ **do** // go top to bottom
2:    $val = G[i]$ // event number in G on chain i
3:    $vc =$ vector clock of event num val on chain i
4:    **if** $i == n_u$ **then** // on highest chain
5:       $proj[i] = vc$
6:    **else** // process relevant entries in vector
7:       **for** $(j = i; j > 0; j--)$ **do**
8:          //projection on chain i:
9:          $proj[i][j] =$MAX$(vc[j], proj[i + 1][j])$

$\mathcal{O}(n_u^2)$ work in the two inner loops at lines 8 and 9 for this higher chain. We can avoid this repetition by storing the combined causal dependencies from higher chains on each lower chain.

Let us illustrate this with an example. Consider the uniflow computation shown in Fig. 6. Suppose we want the lexical successor of $G = [1, 3, 2]$. Then, for each chain, starting from the top we compute the projection of events included in G on lower chains. For example, $G[3] = 1$, and thus on the top-most chain, the projection is only the vector clock of

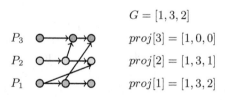

$G = [1, 3, 2]$

$proj[3] = [1, 0, 0]$

$proj[2] = [1, 3, 1]$

$proj[1] = [1, 3, 2]$

Fig. 6. Projections of a cut on chains

the first event on P_3, which is $[1, 0, 0]$. Thus $proj[3] = [1, 0, 0]$. On P_2, the projection must include the combined vector clocks of $G[3]$ and $G[2]$ — the events from top two chains. As $G[2] = 3$, we use the vector clock of third event on P_2, which is $[0, 3, 1]$ as that event is causally dependent on first event on P_1. Combining the two vectors gives us the projection on P_2 as $proj[2] = [1, 3, 1]$.

Algorithm 4 shows the steps involved in computing the projections of a cut on each chain. We create an auxiliary matrix, $proj$, of size $n_u \times n_u$, to store these projections. In GetSuccessor routine, once we have computed a new successor by using some event on chain i, we need to update the stored projections on chains lower than i; and not all n_u chains. This is because the projections for unchanged entries in G above chain i will not change on chain i, or any chain above it. Hence, we only update the relevant rows and columns — rows and columns with number i or lower — in $proj$; i.e. only the upper triangular part of the matrix $proj$. We keep track of the chain that gave us the successor cut, and pass it as an additional argument to Algorithm 4. We read and update $n_u^2/2$ entries in the matrix, and not all n_u^2 of them.

Hence, the optimized implementation of finding the lexical successor of G requires two changes. First, every call of GetSuccessor (G, r) starts with first computing the projections of G using Algorithm 4. Second, we replace the two inner for loops at lines 8 and 9 in GetSuccessor by one $\mathcal{O}(n_u)$ loop to compute the max of the two vector clocks: vector clock of $K[i]$, and $proj[i]$. See the extended version of the paper for details [9].

4.2   Re-mapping Consistent Cuts to Original Chain Partition

The number of consistent cuts of a computation is independent of the chain partition used. Their vector clock representation, however, varies with chain partitions as the vector clocks of events in the computation depend on the chain partition used to compute them. There is a one-to-one mapping between a consistent cut in the original chain partition of the computation on n chains (processes), and its uniflow chain partition on n_u chains. We now show how to map a consistent cut in a uniflow chain partition to its equivalent cut in the original chain partition of the computation. Let $P = (E, \rightarrow)$ be a computation on n processes, and let n_u be the number of chains in its uniflow chain partition. If G_u is a consistent cut in the uniflow chain partition, then its equivalent consistent cut G for the original chain partition (of n chains) can be found in $\mathcal{O}(n_u + n^2)$ time.

We do so by mapping two additional entries with the new vector clock of each event for uniflow chain partition: the chain number c, and event number e from the original chain partition over n chains. For example, in Fig. 4(b), for uniflow vector clock $[1, 1, 1]$, its chain number in original poset is 1, and its event number on that chain is 2. When generating the uniflow vector clocks, we populate these entries in a map. Given a uniflow vector clock uvc, the call to OriginalChain(uvc) returns c, and OriginalEvent(uvc) returns e. To compute G from G_u, we use these two values from the corresponding event for each entry in G_u. We start with I as an all-zero vector of length n. Now, we iterate over G_u, and we update I by setting $I[c] = max(I[c], e)$. As vector G_u has length n_u, this step takes $\mathcal{O}(n_u)$ time. We now initiate G as an all-zero vector clock of length n, and for each entry $I[k]$, $1 \leq k \leq n$, we get the vector clock, vce, of event $I[k]$ on chain k in the original computation. We then set G

to the component-wise maximum of G and vce. As there are n entries in I, and for each non-zero entry we perform $\mathcal{O}(n)$ work in updating G (in lines 11–14 in Algorithm 5) the total work in this step is $\mathcal{O}(n^2)$.

Algorithm 5. REMAP(G_u, n_u, n)

Input: G_u: a consistent cut in uniflow chain partition on n_u chains
Output: G: equivalent consistent cut in original chain partition on n chains
1:   $G = $ new int$[n]$ // allocate memory for G
2:   $I = $ new int$[n_u]$ // reduction vector
3:   **for** $(i = n_u; i \geq 1; i - -)$ **do**   // go over all the uniflow chains
4:       $uvc = $ event number $G_u[i]$'s vector-clock on uniflow chain i
5:       //chain of this event in original poset
6:       $c = $ ORIGINALCHAIN(uvc)
7:       //uvc's event number on chain c in original poset
8:       $e = $ ORIGINALEVENT(uvc)
9:       **if** $I[c] < e$ **then**   // update indicator with e
10:         $I[c] = e$
11:   **for** $(j = n; i \geq 1; i - -)$ **do**   // go over chains in original poset
12:       $vce = $ event number $I[j]$'s vector-clock on chain j in original poset
13:       **for** $(k = n; k \geq 1; k - -)$ **do**   // update G entries
14:         $G[k] = $ MAX$(G[k], vce[k])$
15: **return** G

4.3   Traversing Consistent Cuts of a Given Rank

A key benefit of our algorithm is that it can traverse all the consistent cuts of a given rank, or within a range of ranks, without traversing the cuts of lower ranks. In contrast, the traditional BFS traversal must traverse, and store, consistent cuts of rank $R-1$ to traverse cuts of rank R, which in turn requires it to traverse cuts of rank $R - 2$ and so on.

To traverse all the cuts of rank R, we only need to change the loop bounds at line 3 in Algorithm 1 to for $(r = R; r \leq R; r + +)$. Thus, starting with an empty cut we can find the lexically smallest consistent cut of rank r in $\mathcal{O}(n_u)$ time with the GETMINCUT routine. Then we repeatedly find its lexical successor of the same rank, until we have traversed the lexically biggest cut of rank R. Similarly, consistent cuts between the ranks of R_1 and R_2 can be traversed by changing the loop at line 3 in Algorithm 1 to: for $(r = R_1; r \leq R_2; r + +)$.

Lemma 3. *Let L_k denote the number of consistent cuts of rank k for a computation $(E, \rightarrow)$. Then, traversing consistent cuts of rank r takes $\mathcal{O}(n_u^2 L_r)$ time with Algorithm 1. For the same traversal, the traditional BFS algorithm requires $\mathcal{O}(n^2 \sum_{k=1}^{r} L_k)$ time, and Lex algorithm takes $\mathcal{O}(n^2 \sum_{k=1}^{|E|} L_k)$ time.*

5   Time and Space Complexity

Algorithm 1 requires a computation in its uniflow chain partition. Multiple polynomial time algorithms exist to find a non-trivial uniflow chain partition of a poset, and we give a vector clock based online algorithm to find one that takes $\mathcal{O}(n)$ time per event. We analyze the worst case time and space complexities of our algorithms.

Given any computation on n processes and E events, we can find its trivial uniflow chain partition in $\mathcal{O}(n|E|log|E|)$ time by lexically ordering the vector clocks of all the events. Suppose the number of chains in the uniflow partition is n_u, then the step of computing new vector clocks takes $\mathcal{O}(n_u|E|\cdot\Delta)$ time where Δ is the maximum in-degree of any event in the computation; note that $\Delta \leq n$. The GETMINCUT sub-routine has only one for loop that iterates over the chains of the uniflow partition. Hence, it takes $\mathcal{O}(n_u)$ time in the worst case. The optimized version of finding the successor, sub-routine GETSUCCESSOROPTIMIZED, takes $\mathcal{O}(n_u^2)$ time in the worst case due to the two nested for loops at lines 3, and 10. Hence, for any rank, our algorithm requires $\mathcal{O}(n_u^2)$ time per consistent cut in the uniflow partition. Re-mapping this cut to the original computation takes $\mathcal{O}(n_u + n^2)$ time. Thus, we take $\mathcal{O}(n_u^2 + n^2)$ time per consistent cut.

Theorem 1. *Given a computation $P = (E, \rightarrow)$ on n processes, Algorithm 1 performs breadth-first traversal of its lattice of consistent cuts using $\mathcal{O}((n_u + n)|E|)$ space which is polynomial in the size of the computation.*

Proof. Storing the original computation requires $\mathcal{O}(n|E|)$ space — each event's vector clock having at most n integers. Vector clocks for the uniflow chain partition with n_u chains takes $\mathcal{O}(n_u)$ space per event. Thus, we require $\mathcal{O}(n_u)|E|$ additional space overall to store the computation in its uniflow form. Traversing the lattice as per Algorithm 1 only requires $\mathcal{O}(n_u^2)$ space as at most two vectors of length n_u are stored/created during this traversal, and we use the auxiliary matrix of $n_u \times n_u$ size in the optimized implementation of GETSUCCESSOR. From Lemma 1 we know that $n_u \leq |E|$. Thus, the worst case space complexity is $\mathcal{O}(|E|^2 + n|E|)$ which is polynomial in the size of the input.

6   Experimental Evaluation

We conduct an experimental evaluation to compare the space and time required by BFS, Lex, and our uniflow based traversal algorithm to traverse consistent cuts of specific ranks, as well as all consistent cuts up to a given rank. We do not evaluate DFS implementation as previous studies have shown that Lex implementation outperforms DFS based traversals in both time and space [7,8,16]. Lexical enumeration is significantly better for enumerating all possible consistent cuts of a computation [7,8]. However, it is not well suited for only traversing cuts of specified ranks, or finding the smallest counter example. For these tasks, BFS· traversal remains the algorithm of choice. We optimize the traditional BFS implementation as per [16] to enumerate every global state exactly once. We use seven benchmark computations from recent literature on traversal of consistent cuts [7,8]. The details of these benchmarks are shown in first four columns of Table 1. Benchmarks *d-100, d-300* and *d-500* are randomly generated posets for modeling distributed computations. The benchmarks *bank*, and *hedc* are computations obtained from real-world concurrent programs that are used by [11,14,31] for evaluating their predicate detection algorithms. The benchmark *bank* contains a typical error pattern in concurrent programs, and *hedc* is a web-crawler. Benchmarks *w-4* and *w-8* have 480 events distributed over 4 and 8 processes respectively, and help to highlight the influence of degree of parallelism on the performance of enumeration algorithms. We conduct two sets of experiments: (a) complete traversal of lattice of consistent cuts (of the computation) in BFS manner, and (b) traversal of cuts of specific ranks. We conduct all the experiments on a Linux machine with an Intel Core i7 3.4 GHz CPU, with L1, L2 and L3 caches of size 32 KB, 256 KB, and 8192 KB respectively. We compile and run the programs on Oracle Java 1.7, and limit the maximum heap size for Java virtual machine (JVM) to 2 GB. For each run of our traversal algorithm, we use the online partition algorithm (see Appendix B in [9]) to find the uniflow chain partition of the poset. The runtimes and space reported for our uniflow traversal implementation include the time and space needed for finding and storing the uniflow chain partition of the poset.

Table 1. Benchmark details, heap-space consumed (in MB) and runtimes (in seconds) for two BFS implementations to traverse the full lattice of consistent cuts. $T_{part}=$ time (seconds) to find uniflow partition; $\times$ = out-of-memory error

Name	n	$|E|$	Approx. # of cuts	n_u	T_{part}	Traditional BFS		Uniflow BFS	
						Space	Time	Space	Time
d-100	10	100	1.2×10^6	26	0.030	108	0.48	31	0.37
d-300	10	300	4.3×10^7	68	0.031	842	16.84	33	46.20
d-500	10	500	4.9×10^9	112	0.033	893	108.07	34	607.55
bank	8	96	8.2×10^8	8	0.023	$\times$	$\times$	59	73.2
hedc	12	216	4.5×10^9	26	0.028	$\times$	$\times$	56	1129
w-4	4	480	9.3×10^6	121	0.036	258	0.99	25	8.59
w-8	8	480	7.3×10^9	63	0.032	$\times$	$\times$	40	1445.57

Table 1 compares the size of JVM heap and runtimes for traditional BFS and our uniflow based BFS traversal of lattice of consistent cuts of the benchmarks. The traditional BFS implementations runs out of memory on *hedc, bank*, and *w-8*. Our implementation requires significantly less memory, and even though it is slower, it enables us to do BFS traversal on large computations — something that is impossible with traditional BFS due to its memory requirement.

Table 2 highlights the strength of our algorithm in traversing consistent cuts of specific ranks. We compare our implementation with traditional BFS as well

Table 2. Runtimes (in seconds) for tbfs: Traditional BFS, lex: Lexical, and uni: Uniflow BFS implementations to traverse cuts of given ranks

Name	$r = \frac{|E|}{4}$			$r = \frac{|E|}{2}$			$r = \frac{3|E|}{4}$			$r \leq 32$		
	tbfs	lex	uni	tbfs	lex	uni	tbfs	lex	uni	tbfs	lex	uni
d-100	0.12	0.10	0.04	0.22	0.11	0.05	0.20	0.89	0.04	0.19	0.93	0.12
d-300	0.39	1.23	0.05	2.70	1.15	0.07	6.33	1.25	0.13	0.20	1.22	0.14
d-500	2.29	5.73	0.11	7.83	6.52	0.33	67.59	6.86	1.48	0.19	4.93	0.19
bank	3.36	16.80	0.27	×	16.34	3.07	×	17.02	0.32	45.43	16.87	5.70
hedc	4.72	16.50	0.40	×	152.76	15.70	×	153.54	0.51	0.23	128.60	0.12
w-4	0.09	0.18	0.07	0.53	0.18	0.10	0.93	0.19	0.09	0.01	0.13	0.05
w-8	26.39	143.08	0.72	×	171.23	120.27	×	169.21	3.09	0.02	196.21	0.05

as the implementation of Lexical traversal. For traversing consistent cuts of three specified ranks (equal to quarter, half, and three-quarter of number of events) our algorithm is consistently and significantly faster than both traditional BFS, as well as Lex algorithm. Thus, it can be extremely helpful in quickly analyzing traces when the programmer has knowledge of the conditions when an error/bug occurs. In addition, there are many cases when we are not interested in checking all consistent cuts of a computation. It has been argued that most concurrency related bugs can be found relatively early in execution traces [4, 25]. We also perform well in visiting all consistent cuts of rank less than or equal to 32. Hence, our implementation is faster on most benchmarks for smaller ranks, and requires much less memory (memory consumption details for this experiment are given in the extended version of the paper at [9]). These results emphasize that our algorithm is useful for practical debugging tasks while consuming less resources.

7   Future Work and Conclusion

Algorithm 1 can perform the BFS traversal without regenerating the vector clocks for uniflow chain partitions. This is particularly beneficial for the computations in which $|E| \gg n$, and hence the $\mathcal{O}(|E|^2)$ space needed to regenerate the vector clocks is expensive. Observe that any chain partition, including a uniflow chain partition, of a computation is only an arrangement of its graph. Hence, we can implement Algorithm 1 without regenerating new vector clocks, and by only finding the positions of the events in the uniflow chain partition. To do so, we assign a unique id to each event, and then place this event id on its corresponding uniflow chain. We also store a mapping of original vector clocks against the event ids. The space requirement for our algorithm will reduce to $\mathcal{O}(n_u \cdot n)$ as we do not regenerate vector clock, and computation of projections can be performed using $n_u \times n$ space instead of $n_u \times n_u$ space. As a future work, we plan to implement and evaluate this strategy.

As Algorithm 1 traverses cuts of rank $r + 1$ independently of those of rank r, we can parallelize rank traversals using a parallel-for loop at line 3 of Algorithm 1. We intend to implement this parallel approach and compare its performance against parallel traversal algorithms such as Paramount [8].

For verification and analysis of parallel programs, breadth-first-search based traversal of global states is a crucial routine. We have reduced the space complexity of this routine from exponential to quadratic in the size of input computation. This reduction in space complexity allows us to analyze computation with high degree of parallelism with relatively small memory footprint — a task that is practically impossible with traditional BFS implementations.

References

1. Alagappan, R., Ganesan, A., Patel, Y., Pillai, T.S., Arpaci-Dusseau, A.C., Arpaci-Dusseau, R.H.: Correlated crash vulnerabilities. In: 12th USENIX Symposium on Operating Systems Design and Implementation (OSDI 16), GA, pp. 151–167. USENIX Association (2016)

2. Alagar, S., Venkatesan, S.: Hierarchy in testing distributed programs. In: Fritzson, P.A. (ed.) AADEBUG 1993. LNCS, vol. 749, pp. 101–116. Springer, Heidelberg (1993). doi:10.1007/BFb0019404

3. Alagar, S., Venkatesan, S.: Techniques to tackle state explosion in global predicate detection. IEEE Trans. Softw. Eng. **27**, 412–417 (2001)

4. Ball, T., Burckhardt, S., Coons, K.E., Musuvathi, M., Qadeer, S.: Preemption sealing for efficient concurrency testing. In: Esparza, J., Majumdar, R. (eds.) TACAS 2010. LNCS, vol. 6015, pp. 420–434. Springer, Heidelberg (2010). doi:10.1007/978-3-642-12002-2_35

5. Bianco, L., Dell Olmo, P., Giordani, S.: An optimal algorithm to find the jump number of partially ordered sets. Comput. Optim. Appl. **8**(2), 197–210 (1997)

6. Chandy, K.M., Lamport, L.: Distributed snapshots: determining global states of distributed systems. ACM Trans. Comput. Syst. **3**(1), 63–75 (1985)

7. Chang, Y., Garg, V.K.: Quicklex: a fast algorithm for consistent global states enumeration of distributed computations. In: 19th International Conference on Principles of Distributed Systems, OPODIS 2015, December 14–17, 2015, Rennes, France, pp. 25:1–25:17 (2015)

8. Chang, Y.-J., Garg, V.K.: A parallel algorithm for global states enumeration in concurrent systems. In: ACM SIGPLAN Notices, vol. 50, pp. 140–149. ACM (2015)

9. Chauhan, H., Garg, V.K.: Space efficient breadth-first and level traversals of consistent global states of parallel programs (extended version). https://arxiv.org/abs/1707.07788

10. Chein, M., Habib, M.: The jump number of dags and posets: an introduction. Ann. Discrete Math. **9**, 189–194 (1980)

11. Chen, F., Serbanuta, T.F., Roşu, G.: jPredictor: a predictive runtime analysis tool for java. In: Proceedings of the International Conference on Software Engineering, pp. 221–230 (2008)

12. Cooper, R., Marzullo, K.: Consistent detection of global predicates. In: Proceedings of the Workshop on Parallel and Distributed Debugging, Santa Cruz, CA, pp. 163–173, May 1991

13. Fidge, C.J.: Timestamps in message-passing systems that preserve the partial-ordering. In: Raymond, K. (ed.) Proceedings of the 11th Australian Computer Science Conference (ACSC), pp. 56–66, February 1988
14. Flanagan, C., Freund, S.N.: FastTrack: efficient and precise dynamic race detection. In: Proceedings of the Conference on Programming Language Design and Implementation, pp. 121–133 (2009)
15. Ganter, B.: Two basic algorithms in concept analysis. In: Kwuida, L., Sertkaya, B. (eds.) ICFCA 2010. LNCS, vol. 5986, pp. 312–340. Springer, Heidelberg (2010). doi:10.1007/978-3-642-11928-6_22
16. Garg, V.K.: Enumerating global states of a distributed computation. In: Proceedings of the International Conference on Parallel and Distributed Computing Systems, pp. 134–139 (2003)
17. Garg, V.K., Waldecker, B.: Detection of weak unstable predicates in distributed programs. IEEE Trans. Parallel Distrib. Syst. 5(3), 299–307 (1994)
18. Habib, M., Medina, R., Nourine, L., Steiner, G.: Efficient algorithms on distributive lattices. Discrete Appl. Math. 110(2–3), 169–187 (2001)
19. Huang, J., Zhang, C.: Persuasive prediction of concurrency access anomalies. In: Proceedings of the International Symposium on Software Testing and Analysis, pp. 144–154 (2011)
20. Jegou, R., Medina, R., Nourine, L.: Linear space algorithm for on-line detection of global predicates. In: Proceedings of the International Workshop on Structures in Concurrency Theory, pp. 175–189 (1995)
21. Lamport, L.: Time, clocks, and the ordering of events in a distributed system. Commun. ACM (CACM) 21(7), 558–565 (1978)
22. Lamport, L., et al.: Paxos made simple. ACM Sigact News 32(4), 18–25 (2001)
23. Lu, S., Tucek, J., Qin, F., Zhou, Y.: AVIO: detecting atomicity violations via access interleaving invariants. In: Proceedings of the International Conference on Architectural Support for Programming Languages and Operating Systems, pp. 37–48 (2006)
24. Mattern, F.: Virtual time and global states of distributed systems. In: Parallel and Distributed Algorithms: Proceedings of the Workshop on Distributed Algorithms (WDAG), pp. 215–226 (1989)
25. Musuvathi, M., Qadeer, S.: Iterative context bounding for systematic testing of multithreaded programs. In Proceedings of Conference on Programming Language Design and Implementation, pp. 446–455 (2007)
26. Pruesse, G., Ruskey, F.: Gray codes from antimatroids. Order 10, 239–252 (1993)
27. Song, W., Gkountouvas, T., Birman, K., Chen, Q., Xiao, Z.: The freeze-frame file system. In: ACM Symposium on Cloud Computing (SOCC) (2016)
28. Squire, M.B.: Enumerating the ideals of a poset. In: Ph.D. Dissertation, Department of Computer Science, North Carolina State University (1995)
29. Steiner, G.: An algorithm to generate the ideals of a partial order. Oper. Res. Lett. 5(6), 317–320 (1986)
30. Sysło, M.M.: Minimizing the jump number for partially ordered sets: a graph-theoretic approach. Order 1(1), 7–19 (1984)
31. von Praun, C., Gross, T.R.: Object race detection. In: Proceedings of the Conference on Object-Oriented Programming, Systems, Languages, and Applications, pp. 70–82 (2001)

Witnessing Network Transformations

Chaoqiang Deng[1] and Kedar S. Namjoshi[2]([envelope])

[1] New York University, New York, USA
deng@cs.nyu.edu
[2] Bell Laboratories, Nokia, Murray Hill, USA
kedar.namjoshi@nokia-bell-labs.com

Abstract. Software-defined networking (SDN) is transforming the way networks are managed, as fixed distributed protocols give way to flexible route calculation software. The shift brings to the forefront the issue of software errors, which may produce wrong routes, and cause significant network disruption. We propose a run-time certification mechanism that rejects any wrongly calculated route before it is installed in the network. Certification is done through a strategy called *witnessing*, where a witness (i.e., a justification) is generated by the software for each routing decision. The witness provided for a route change is validated against the original user request, using a formal network model, before the change is installed on the real network. Witnessing shifts trust away from the complex system software to a relatively simple witness checker. We define a formal language to specify connection-based user requests ("intents"), witnesses for each type of intent, and the checking algorithm. We also formulate a notion of refinement between networks, and show that it preserves the realizability of intents across abstraction levels.

1 Introduction

Computer networks have long been managed with standardized, distributed protocols. The advent of software-defined networking (SDN) (cf. [9]) is radically transforming this view to one where flexible, programmable routing engines operate on a formal network model. This makes it possible to apply sophisticated route selection algorithms and to experiment with variations.

Such flexibility, however, comes with potential dangers. Increasing algorithmic sophistication increases the likelihood of errors in their implementation. A miscalculated route may fail to meet the original request or, worse still, disrupt traffic on existing routes by over-committing available bandwidth. In this work, we design a run-time certification mechanism to detect wrongly calculated routes and prevent them from being installed on the real network. The central concept is to require all route selection programs to produce a formal justification – which we call a "witness" – for each routing decision. A valid witness guarantees that the associated routing changes do not adversely affect active routes.

We show how to instantiate this design for an emerging class of *network operating systems* (NOS's) – examples include ONOS [1] and OpenDaylight [2]

© Springer International Publishing AG 2017
S. Lahiri and G. Reger (Eds.): RV 2017, LNCS 10548, pp. 155–171, 2017.
DOI: 10.1007/978-3-319-67531-2_10

– which use SDN principles to unify the management and operation of a collection of networks built with different technologies (e.g., IP, optical, and wireless), each with its own protocols and management software. To facilitate this goal, all networks, regardless of the underlying technology, are represented uniformly as graphs with capacitated connections between nodes. In response to a connectivity request, a global route is calculated by the NOS on the graph model; individual route segments are later configured locally in technology-specific ways. Existing NOS's do not guard against errors in global route calculation, nor do they have a principled mechanism for defining connectivity patterns. Our work makes a number of contributions beyond efficient certification.

- We define a formal language of connectivity patterns on graphs, called *intents*. This includes common patterns such as paths, chains, and trees, with constraints on bandwidth and delay, and allowance for backup paths
- We propose an augmented architecture of a *certifying* NOS. Route selection programs are required to generate a witness (a set of paths) as justification for each routing decision
- We show that witness checking has worst-case linear complexity in the size of the witnesses and in the number of intents. An incremental checking algorithm further reduces the complexity in the common case. Experimental results on a family of synthetic networks support the theoretical analysis
- We define a formal notion of refinement between networks which preserves the realizability of intents: i.e., any intent satisfied on the abstract network can be realized in the concrete network. This allows route selection algorithms to operate on smaller abstract networks, reducing complexity.

The architecture of a certifying network operating system ensures that new route selection algorithms can be implemented and tested quickly, with the "safety-net" guarantee that certification makes it impossible to install erroneous routes that may disrupt network operation. The refinement notions ensure that solutions computed on an abstract network remain realizable at more concrete levels, which makes it possible to chain route selection algorithms operating at different levels of granularity. Taken together, these mechanisms significantly increase the robustness and the safety of a network operating system.

1.1   Overview

A network operating system computes and installs routes on the fly in response to a stream of incoming user requests. The ideal is a formally verified OS, whose output is guaranteed to be correct. Constructing a formally verified network operating system is, however, an enormously difficult undertaking. We propose an alternative solution based on the run-time certification of the results computed by the operating system.

A schematic view of a network operating system (NOS, for short) is shown in Fig. 1(a). The operating system reacts to explicit external requests for routes (referred to as "intents"), and implicitly to changes in the underlying network,

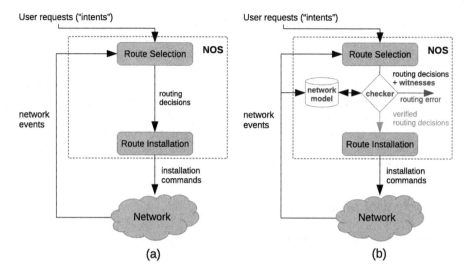

Fig. 1. Network operating system structure: (a) current, (b) with formal certification. (Color figure online)

such as failure or degradation of nodes or links (referred to as "events"). In response, the system uses route selection algorithms to make decisions to set up new routes and, possibly, to move old routes, aiming to preserve all active intents. Those decisions are then configured and installed on the real network. A network operating system is, in essence, a network transformer; it maps a network with allocated routes and a request to a network with modified routes. The standard architecture in Fig. 1(a) leaves no room for error: one must trust the correctness of the route selection algorithms and their implementations. A mistake in either may result in a routing decision that disrupts network traffic.

Our proposal is shown in Fig. 1(b). Two key aspects are the use of formal network models and the generation and checking of witnesses (i.e., justifications) for each intent. The new architecture requires the route selection algorithm to provide a witness, a collection of paths in the network, for every decision. The checker has to perform two tasks: (1) ensure that the route decision (which could be presented in a different format, e.g., as a sequence of commands) is consistent with the supplied witness paths; and (2) check that the supplied paths prove that the network meets the new intent *and* continues to meet all earlier intents. Only if these checks succeed are the changes instantiated on the real network.

The certification step shifts trust away from the complex operating software to a relatively simple checker. There is no need to verify the implementation of the routing algorithm: if a mistake results in a wrong route or an incorrect witness, the error is detected by the checker. The route installation process (lower blue rectangle in the NOS figure) relies on standardized mechanisms such as NETCONF [3] and is a trusted component.

In this paper, we address task (2), defining a formal language of intents, their witnesses, and an algorithm for witness checking. We do not address task (1), as it is specific to the format used by the NOS to represent its routing decision. A general strategy for task (1) is to simulate the route-change commands on the network model and verify that network links are reconfigured exactly as stated in the witness paths.

Real networks have an immense amount of detail, not all of which is relevant for route selection. In the second part of this paper, we formulate a network abstraction notion, and show that it preserves realizability: i.e., every intent realizable on the abstract model is also realizable on the concrete network.

Detailed proofs and additional explanations are provided in the extended version of this paper [7].

2   Networks and Intents

We define the formal network model, the intent language, and intent satisfaction.

2.1   Network Model

A *network* is a hierarchical system of graphs. It is defined by a vector of graphs, say $(G_0, G_1, \ldots, G_n)$, for $n \geq 0$. A graph G_i is either a primitive graph with a single node, or a non-primitive graph where each node is a reference to a copy of a graph G_j, where $j < i$, giving the entire network a hierarchical structure. The graph G_n is the root of the hierarchy.

A network *attribute* is a quantity such as bandwidth, bit-error rate (BER), cost, or delay, which takes values from the appropriate domain. An *attribute vector* is a map from the set of attributes to their domains. E.g., "(bandwidth=1.0, BER=1.0E-5, cost=20, delay=2.5)" is an example vector. For concreteness, we focus on two important attributes: bandwidth and delay, so the vector is written as (bandwidth, delay). Attribute vectors are ordered by a partial relation, $\succeq$ (read as "better than"), defined appropriately. For bandwidth and delay, the relation $(b, d) \succeq (b', d')$ is defined as $(b \geq b') \wedge (d \leq d')$. I.e., (b, d) is better than (b', d') if b represents more bandwidth than b', and d represents a smaller delay than d'. The inverse relation, $\preceq$, is read as "worse than".

A *primitive* graph has only one node whose ports are all *external*. It represents an atomic building block of the network. There can be zero or more internal *links* between each pair of ports. Each link is associated with a *capability*, which is an attribute vector. The implicit understanding is that all links in a primitive graph represent *independent* connections. The capability of the i'th link from port p to port q of node n (if defined) is denoted $\mathsf{cap}(n, p, q, i)$.

Examples of primitive graphs are channels and mux/demux elements. A *channel* has one input port and one output port. A multiplexer (*mux*) has one output port, say q, and multiple input ports; a link is defined only for pairs (x, q), where $x \neq q$. A demultiplexer has one input port, say p, and multiple output ports; a link is defined only for pairs (p, x), where $p \neq x$.

A non-primitive graph, G_i, has internal structure that is given by a pair (N, C), where N is a set of *nodes*, and C is a set of *connections*. Every node has an associated set of *ports*. A connection is a pair of the form $((n,p),(n',p'))$, indicating that port p of node n is to be identified with port p' of node n'. The *external* ports of a graph are those ports that are not part of any connection. Every node of G_i contains a reference to a graph G_j, where $j < i$, along with an isomorphism between the ports of the node and the external ports of G_j. Nodes may have *region* labels, used to state routing constraints that require paths to stay within a certain geographic or network region.

A flat (i.e., non-hierarchical) network can be obtained by starting from G_n and recursively expanding each node into a copy of the graph to which it refers, if that graph is non-primitive. The satisfaction of intents is defined over the flattened graph, which may be exponentially larger than the network description. For convenience, by the links of a node we mean the links of its primitive graph.

Paths. The tuple $(p_i', n_i, l_i, w_i, p_{i+1})$ represents the l_i'th link between input port p_i' and output port p_{i+1} on node n_i, with an associated attribute weight vector w_i. A *path* from port p of node n to port q of node m, represented as $(p_0', n_0, l_0, w_0, p_1), (p_1', n_1, l_1, w_1, p_2), \ldots, (p_k', n_k, l_k, w_k, p_{k+1})$, is a sequence of such links, with $k \geq 0$, $(p_0', n_0) = (p, n)$, and $(n_k, p_{k+1}) = (m, q)$. A path should meet the following conditions.

(a) p_i' and p_{i+1} are ports of n_i for all i, and l_i is a valid link between those ports
(b) w_i represents an allocation that is worse than the capability of its link, i.e., $w_i \preceq \mathsf{cap}(n_i, p_i', p_{i+1}, l_i)$ for all i (I.e., w_i allocates less bandwidth and assumes a higher delay than the actual capability of the link), and
(c) For all i such that $i < k$, the pair $((n_i, p_{i+1}), (n_{i+1}, p_{i+1}'))$ is a connection.

The *allocated weight* of a path π is an attribute vector (b, d) such that b is the least bandwidth entry and d is the sum of all the delay entries in the set of weights $\{w_i\}$. The *capability* of π is the attribute vector (b', d') such that b' is the least bandwidth entry and d' is the sum of all the delay entries in the set of capabilities $\{\mathsf{cap}(n_i, p_i', p_{i+1}, l_i)\}$. Requirement (b) ensures that the capability of a path is better than its allocated weight.

2.2   Network Intents: Syntax

An *intent* is a connectivity pattern between a set of ports. The pattern includes constraints on minimum bandwidth, or maximum delay. A *region* constraint is defined by a requirement to either *avoid* or to stay *within* the region. We define three common types of intents, and show later how these can be considered as examples of a quite general class of polynomially-checkable intents.

(Basic Segment). A *basic segment* specifies a connection between port p of node n and port q of node m, with constraints on attributes and regions.

(Protected Segment). A *protected segment* specifies a connection between port p of node n and port q of node m that has a degree of failure protection. The protection is defined as a set of basic segments between (n, p) and (m, q). For simplicity, in this paper we suppose that there are only two such segments, one referred to as the primary, and the other as the backup. This is commonly referred to as $1 + 1$ protection. Each basic segment has its own constraints on attributes and regions.

(Chain). A *chain* is specified as a sequence of segments where the end point of each segment in the chain is connected to the start point of its successor segment (if any). Each segment is specified independently, i.e., some may be protected, while others are basic. A chain may also have end-to-end attribute constraints (i.e., between its endpoints), and globally applicable region constraints. Chains are used to represent paths that must pass through a series of so-called middle-boxes in the network where packet processing occurs.

2.3   Network Intents: Semantics

Consider path $\pi = (p'_0, n_0, l_0, w_0, p_1), (p'_1, n_1, l_1, w_1, p_2), \ldots, (p'_k, n_k, l_k, w_k, p_{k+1})$. It satisfies a minimum bandwidth B if the bandwidth entry in each of the weights $\{w_i\}$ is at least B. It satisfies a maximum delay D if the sum of all the delay entries in the set of weights $\{w_i\}$ is at most D. It satisfies an avoids(R) constraint, for region R, if none of the nodes on the path is labeled with R, and a within(R) constraint if all of the nodes on the path are labeled with R. We can now define what it means for an intent to be satisfied.

(Basic Segment). A basic segment between port p of node n and port q of node m is satisfied if there exists a path π from (n, p) to (m, q) such that π satisfies all the attribute and region constraints for the segment.

(Protected Segment). A protected segment between (n, p) and (m, q) with two basic segments x_0, x_1 is satisfied if there are two paths, π_0, π_1 from (n, p) to (m, q) such that for each i, path π_i satisfies the requirements of the segment x_i and, moreover, π_0 and π_1 have no node-port combination in common except the two end points. i.e., the paths are node and port disjoint. Operationally, this implies that a single node or port failure cannot affect both paths, unless it is at the originating or terminating end.

(Chain). A chain from (n, p) to (m, q) is satisfied if there exist path(s) associated with each segment of the chain such that (i) the constraints for each segment are satisfied by its associated path(s), (ii) the end point (i.e., (node, port)) of the path witnessing a segment has a connection to the start point of the path witnessing the next segment, and (iii) the end-to-end constraints and global region constraints for the chain are satisfied on all end-to-end paths that can be constructed from the per-segment paths.

2.4   Witnesses and Satisfaction

For each satisfied intent, there is a network path (or paths) that explain *why* the intent is satisfied. That set of paths is called the *witness* for that intent. Figure 2 illustrates the three types of intents, corresponding witnesses, and how to check that a witness meets its intent. For instance, the witness for the protected segment is a pair of paths connecting Los Angeles to New York: green for

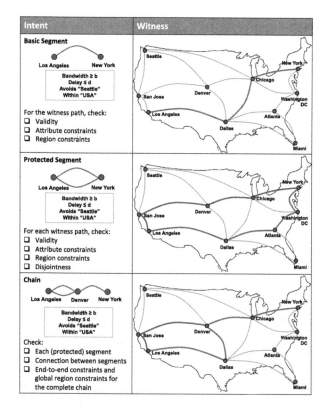

Fig. 2. Example: three types of intents and corresponding witnesses. (Color figure online)

the primary and red for the backup segment. To determine if this witness is correct, one checks that the witness paths are valid in the network, the constraints on attribute and regions are be satisfied, and that the paths are disjoint.

Joint Satisfaction. A collection of intents is *jointly satisfied* if there are witnesses for each intent such that the witness paths *together* do not over-subscribe the bandwidth on any common link. Given a set of intents, if all the intents can be jointly satisfied, then each individual intent can be satisfied. However, the converse is *not* necessarily true. A trivial counter-example is a graph with a single channel of bandwidth 2. It is possible to individually satisfy intents with min. bandwidth 1 and with bandwidth 1.5, but joint satisfaction is impossible.

The inability to decompose the satisfaction of intents is one reason why route selection algorithms have high complexity. In a graph where all links have bandwidth 1, two basic segments between the same endpoints with bandwidth at least 1 require disjoint paths, which is an NP-complete problem on directed graphs. Another source of complexity is that intents must be satisfied in an *online* fashion, which may lead to sub-optimal decisions. E.g., consider two points connected by disjoint paths π and π', with resp. bandwidths 1 and 2. A request for bandwidth 1 can be satisfied by either path; say it is assigned to π'. A following request for bandwidth 2 cannot then be satisfied, unless the first is re-assigned to π.

Witness Generation. For these reasons, the actual route selection algorithm may be quite complex. However, its natural output is the set of paths that form the witness. With standard algorithmic schemes, no additional work is needed. Such algorithms allocate new routes on a residual capacity network, where the capacity of a link is the amount that remains after satisfying previous intents. If a new request is met on the residual network, its witness does not interfere with those for previous intents, so the algorithm merely reports previously stored witnesses. However, the algorithm may need to backtrack to recover from suboptimal decisions. In that case, the set of witnesses it needs to report are for the intents that are re-assigned paths. In either case, witness generation does not require additional work. As the validation procedure checks joint satisfaction, witness paths for *all* intents are provided with each routing decision.

3   Witness Checking

The algorithm to check whether a witness matches a basic intent type on a flat network model is shown in Fig. 3. The algorithm follows quite directly from the definitions, as formalized in Sect. 2, and is easy to implement. For each intent type, the algorithm checks that the witness paths provided are (a) valid paths in the network, and (b) satisfy the attribute and region constraints specified for the intent. The capacity of the network is reduced by the bandwidth consumed by the witness paths; the algorithm outputs a network with the remaining capacity. The algorithm operates in linear time in the size of witness. (The disjointness check in Case 2 can be done in linear time on average using hashing.)

The algorithm works on a fully flattened network, which is obtained by flattening the hierarchical network before a NOS is deployed to receive intents. An optimization is to retain the hierarchical form, and flatten only those sections of the network which are traversed by the witness paths. It is an open question whether the check can be performed in polynomial time without flattening, we conjecture that this may not be possible. As the check removes bandwidth from the components through which a witness path passes, copies of the same component may, over time, diverge in the set of feasible paths. This is not the case for pure reachability queries, which can be checked without flattening [4].

General Forms of Intents. The intent types discussed so far fit the following general form, which is inspired by Fagin's beautiful characterization of NP in terms of existential second order formulae on graphs [8]. An intent specifies a sub-graph over a set of points, H, such that there exist sub-graphs $X_0, \ldots, X_n$ for which $\varphi(H, X_0, \ldots, X_n)$ holds, where φ is a polynomial-time checkable property. As an illustration, for a protected segment, the two endpoints (defining H)

Function wcheck(i : *intent*, w : *witness*, M : *flat network*) : *flat network*

    Check that each witness path in w is a valid path in network M

    if i *is a basic segment* **then**

        Check that the path defined by w satisfies the attribute and region constraints in i as defined in Section 2

        Let M' be obtained from M by reducing the bandwidth on each link by the amount reserved for that link on w

        return M'

    else if i *is a protected segment of intents* i_0, i_1 *with witnesses* w_0, w_1 **then**

        Check that the paths w_0, w_1 are node and port disjoint

        $M_0 := $ wcheck(i_0, w_0, M)

        $M_1 := $ wcheck(i_1, w_1, M_0)

        return M_1

    else i is a chain of intents $i_0, \ldots, i_n$ with witnesses $w_0, \ldots, w_n$, end-to-end constraints delay D and bandwidth B, and global region constraints

        $D_n := D$

        for k *from* n *down to* 0 **do**

            if $k > 0$ **then**

                Check that start point of w_k is connected to end point of w_{k-1}

            end

            Let i'_k be i_k with additional constraints of min. bandwidth B, max. delay D_k and global region constraints.

            $M := $ wcheck(i'_k, w_k, M)

            $D_{k-1} := D_k - $ maxdelay(w_k)

        end

        return M

    end

Fig. 3. Witness checking algorithm

are connected by path-shaped sub-graphs X_0 and X_1, with φ asserting that the paths are disjoint and satisfy the attribute and region constraints. The witness for an intent in general form is the instantiation given to $X_0, \ldots, X_n$, while witness checking is the evaluation of φ on this instantiation. A number of practically useful connectivity patterns can be specified in this manner. Examples include broadcast and multicast trees, possibly with disjoint backup paths; virtual networks that interconnect several ports; and grid topologies.

3.1   Incremental Checking

Starting from the un-allocated network model, the algorithm above is used to check each witness in succession. This takes time linear in the number of active intents. We describe an efficient incremental algorithm, which checks only those intents whose witnesses have changed.

The key underlying observation is that the order in which a set of witnesses are checked does not matter. Consider witnesses w and w' provided for intents a and a', respectively. Starting from a network M, if the check succeeds in the order $w; w'$, it must also succeed in the order $w'; w$. This is because the check can be split into a step which determines the connectivity of witness paths, ignoring capacity; and another that reduces network capacity along the witness paths, while ensuring that the residual capacity on each link is non-negative. If no link has negative capacity when witness paths are allocated in the order $w; w'$, that is also true for the reverse order $w'; w$.

The algorithm stores the residual capacity network, M, and the list of active intent-witness pairs, W, with the invariant that M represents the residual capacity after processing W on the un-allocated network N. Route selection produces a list of intent-witness pairs, W', listing only the intents that have new witnesses. The incremental algorithm proceeds as follows.

1. For each (i, w') in W', if there is an entry for intent i, say (i, w), in W, undo the capacity reduction effect of checking w by adding back the capacity used by links w to M. Remove the (i, w) entry from W
2. Add into M the effects of any network change that *reduces* the capacity of a link l; if the new capacity of l is negative, *stop with error*
3. Add into M the effects of any network change that adds new links or *increases* link capacity. We suppose that such links are disjoint from those whose capacity has been reduced
4. Check the intent-witness entries in W' on M with the wcheck algorithm, updating the residual capacity in M
5. Append W' to W to obtain the new active list

Incremental algorithms usually trade off increased state (e.g., storage for partial results) for speed. It is interesting that this algorithm uses no additional space. We show the following correctness theorem.

Theorem 1. *The incremental and basic algorithms produce the same result.*

4   Experiments

This section presents an experimental evaluation of our witness checking implementation. We do not have access to real network designs, so the experiments are on a synthetic network, a parameterized grid of size n, shown in Fig. 6, where each link has bandwidth and delay 1. The parameterization makes it simple to scale up network size to assess its influence on witness checking.

For the experiments, a grid network is set up for a particular value of n. Then endpoints and intents connecting them are generated at random. The type of intent (basic or protected) is also chosen at random. Corresponding witnesses paths are calculated via depth first search (DFS) while keeping track of residual capacity. The search is prioritized to prefer links closer to the destination node. The DFS algorithm approximates the work of actual route selection algorithms used in networks. It suffices for our purpose, which is to measure the performance of witness checking, not the quality of the chosen routes.

The implementation is in Java, it includes network creation, intents generation, witness calculation and checking. The checker is about 300 lines of Java code. All of the experiments are performed on a MacBook Pro machine with a 2.4 GHz Intel Core i7, and 8GB 1600 MHz DDR3, running on Mac OS X 10.10.5.

In the experiment, we simulate networks of size from 10 to 1000; accordingly, the number of nodes varies from one hundred to one million. In each network, 500 intents are randomly generated, and corresponding witnesses are calculated and checked by our algorithm in Fig. 3. The results are shown in Fig. 4. The x-axis shows the network size n (there are n^2 network nodes). The left-hand y-axis shows the average time cost of checking a witness for a single intent, and the right-hand y-axis shows the average size of a witness. It is clear that the average time cost of checking is negligible (e.g. for a large network of one million nodes, checking a witness takes only about 1 ms, in the meanwhile, according to our experiment log which is not presented here, witness generation by DFS takes about 20 ms). The graph shows also that the cost of checking is proportional to the witness size, both of which scale as $O(n)$, on average. A second experiment fixes the network size to 1000 but varies the number of intent requests. The results support the theoretical analysis, showing that the cost of the incremental algorithm is essentially constant, while that of the basic algorithm increases linearly with the number of requests.

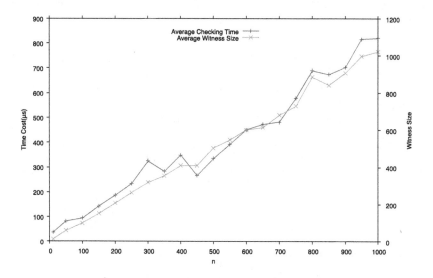

Fig. 4. Time cost of witness checking on networks of n^2 nodes.

5   Network Abstraction

The witness checking algorithm introduced in previous sections works on the complete network. It is, however, often the case that only a small part of a network needs to be examined to select routes. E.g., for an intent requesting a connection between two cities in the east coast, say New York City and Washington DC, it would be superfluous to examine networks in the west coast, as well as tedious to use detailed information about networks inside a single city. Thus, we propose to operate algorithms on abstracted networks. It is vital, however, that the routes discovered at an abstract level are realizable as routes at the concrete level; otherwise, there is no benefit to perform the abstraction.

In this section we introduce *network abstraction*. The general idea is to get an abstract network by collapsing a specified sub-network of a concrete real network into a single node. We define a notion of refinement from the concrete to the abstract level, and show that this preserves the realizability of routes.

5.1   Abstraction and Refinement with Single Nodes

We consider the case where a graph G is abstracted to a new primitive graph H whose external ports are isomorphic to the external ports of G. The key question is to define a relation between paths and capabilities in G with those in H, so that routes in H can be realized as routes in G. As H is primitive, routes in H are links between ports; routes in G are paths through the graph G.

Refinement. A *refinement* map R from H to G is a function such that the following properties hold:

(a) Each link (n, p, q, i) in H (i.e., the i'th link between port p and q of node n) is mapped by R to a path π between ports p and q in G, where the capability of π in G is better than the capability of link (n, p, q, i) in H, and
(b) The set of paths $\{R(n, p, q, i) \mid (n, p, q, i) \text{ is a link in } H\}$ are node and port disjoint in G, and
(c) Node n and all nodes of G have the same abstract region labels.

The refinement map constrains the capabilities, not the weights of the corresponding paths. Hence, it is possible that a different algorithm can be applied to G to arrange the weights.

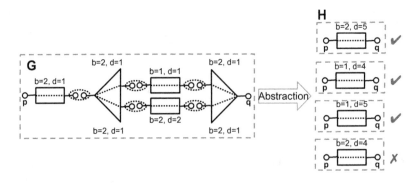

Fig. 5. Collapsing a sub-network into a single node via refinement.

Example. A simple example of refinement is shown in Fig. 5. For the sake of clarity, we do not use the formal notion of graph references, but rather show the details directly. Ports are shown as circles, a long rectangle is a channel, and a triangle is a mux/demux. A dashed line between two ports is a link, and a dashed ellipse with two ports inside shows that those ports are part of a connection. (E.g. in G, the right port of left channel is connected to the left port of demux.) The capability of the single link for each pair of ports is shown near the host node. (E.g. in G, "$b = 2, d = 1$" above the left triangle means that, for the upper link inside the demux, the bandwidth is 2 and delay is 1.) Between ports p and q in G, there are two non-disjoint paths: one path goes through the upper channel in the middle, and has capability "$b = 1, d = 4$"; the other path goes through the lower channel in the middle, and has capability "$b = 2, d = 5$". We show four possible abstractions; the upper three are correct (i.e. there is a refinement connecting H to G). The first two represent the capabilities of the paths in G described above; the third is a manufactured capability representing the worst of the two paths. The bottom abstraction is incorrect, however, as there is no path in G from p to q with capability better than "$b = 2, d = 4$".

5.2 Abstraction and Refinement for Networks

We say that network A is an *abstraction* of network $C = (G_0, G_1, \ldots, G_n)$ if there is a chosen subset GS of $\{G_0, G_1, \ldots, G_n\}$, and A is gained from C by replacing each graph G_i in GS with a primitive graph H_i such that there is a refinement R_i from primitive graph H_i to graph G_i. The *size of abstraction* is defined as the cardinality of GS.

Example. Figure 7 illustrates the process of network abstraction. The concrete network C has two graphs (G_0, G_1), where G_1 contains two connected nodes referring to G_0. There is a refinement relation from the primitive graph H_0 to G_0, thus by replacing G_0 with H_0 we obtain an abstract network (H_0, G_1') where $G_1' = G_1[G_0 := H_0]$ (the brackets indicate substitution of references to G_0 by references to H_0). The size of this abstraction is 1. Furthermore, another abstraction of size 1 can be performed on (H_0, G_1') by replacing it with the primitive graph H_1, since there is an abstraction refinement from H_1 to G_1'. Now an ultimately abstract network (H_0, H_1) is obtained, and no more abstraction can be applied. Furthermore, H_0 can be removed since it is not referred by any network. It is not difficult to find that for any set of intents that can be jointly satisfied in the abstract network (H_1), it can be jointly satisfied in the original network (G_0, G_1) too.

Theorem 2. *Let network A be an abstraction of network C. Every set I of intents that can be jointly satisfied in A can also be jointly satisfied in C.*

Proof Sketch: Suppose the size of abstraction from C to A is k. We generate a series of networks $N_1 = A, N_2, N_3, \ldots, N_k = C$ such that N_{i+1} is a refinement of N_{i+1} with an abstraction of size 1. We show that any set of intents that can

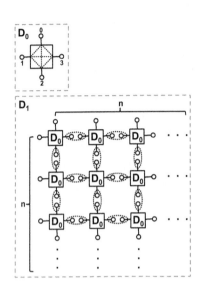

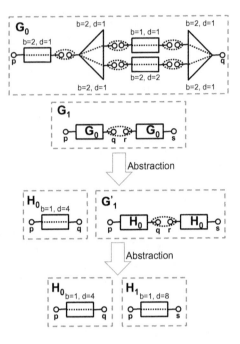

Fig. 6. Virtual network of size n.   **Fig. 7.** Network abstraction

be jointly satisfied in N_i, can also be jointly satisfied in N_{i+1}. By induction, it follows that any set I of intents that is jointly satisfied in A is also jointly satisfied in C. **EndProof.**

As illustrated in Fig. 7, realizability is preserved across multiple abstract levels, i.e. if network A abstracts B and B abstracts C, then any set of intents that can be jointly satisfied in A can also jointly satisfied in C.

6   Related Work and Conclusions

The certification strategy is inspired by research on methods to verify compiler transformations. Run-time compiler verification, generally referred to as Translation Validation, uses heuristics to determine whether the resulting program refines the behavior of the original (cf. [20,22,27]). Our recent proposal [19], building on the idea of proof certificates [21,23], suggests having the compiler itself generate candidate refinements; valid refinements are called witnesses. We adopt this general scheme and terminology.

There are, however, fundamental differences between Translation Validation and network validation. For compiler optimizations, correctness is established by showing that the optimized program refines the behavior of the original. A routing decision, however, may change routes arbitrarily so long as the intent is met; thus, correctness does not correspond to a natural refinement on networks. Instead, the criterion adopted here is that the transformed network should satisfy all active intents with the particular route witnesses supplied by the network transformation algorithm. This differs from the model-checking question "Does the transformed network satisfy all intents?", which implicitly checks for the existence of satisfying routes.

Emerging network operating systems based on SDN principles (cf. [24]), such as ONOS [1] and OpenDaylight [2], make it easy to replace route selection methods. These NOS's do not, however, guard against potential network disruption caused by miscalculated routes. The lack of error-checking is a significant omission, which this work aims to fill.

There is a growing body of work on formalization of various aspects of SDN at the IP level: reasoning frameworks such as NetKAT [5], verified compilers [12] for OpenFlow [18] and model checkers for network invariants (cf. [6,14,17]). Run-time checking has been investigated at the IP level: the Veriflow [15] system checks routing table modifications against fixed network properties such as the absence of a forwarding loop. Reachability properties can be checked off-line by the system in [16]. As discussed in the introduction, our work applies to NOS's that work at a different (higher) level of abstraction, managing combinations of networks with diverse technologies. Thus, the existing techniques do not apply.

The network model in this paper is inspired by NetML [10,25], which was designed to describe connectivity in multi-layered networks. Our model expands on NetML to include link attributes such as bandwidth and delay. In turn, this requires new forms of abstraction to preserve the realizability of intents. Work on abstraction in the IP model includes [26], which describes an IP network as a virtual "big switch" (cf. [13]); routes programmed at the virtual level are then refined into routes on a physical topology. This refinement notion preserves reachability but may not preserve path disjointness.

Network management is clearly moving towards increasing levels of abstraction and programmability. With increasing sophistication, however, comes the danger that software errors may result in significant disruption in large area networks. This work has presented a run-time certification method which acts as a safety net, preventing incorrect routing decisions from affecting network operations. The checking process is efficient, and naturally handles a variety of user-defined specifications and dynamic network changes. A promising direction is to explore witnessing for IP networks, particularly where model checking is difficult (e.g., checking reachability in the presence of packet filters is NP-hard [17]).

Acknowledgements. We wish to thank colleagues at Bell Labs for many helpful comments. Kedar Namjoshi was supported, in part, by NSF grant CCF-1563393 during the preparation of this paper.

References

1. ONOS: Open Network Operating System. http://onosproject.org/
2. Open Daylight. https://www.opendaylight.org/
3. RFC 6241 - Network Configuration Protocol (NETCONF). https://tools.ietf.org/html/rfc6241

4. Alur, R., Yannakakis, M.: Model checking of hierarchical state machines. ACM Trans. Program. Lang. Syst. **23**(3), 273–303 (2001). doi:10.1145/503502.503503

5. Anderson, C.J., Foster, N., Guha, A., Jeannin, J., Kozen, D., Schlesinger, C., Walker, D.: NetKAT: semantic foundations for networks. In: Jagannathan, S., Sewell, P. (eds.) The 41st Annual ACM SIGPLAN-SIGACT Symposium on Principles of Programming Languages, POPL 2014, San Diego, CA, USA, January 20–21, 2014, pp. 113–126. ACM (2014). doi:10.1145/2535838.2535862

6. Canini, M., Venzano, D., Peresíni, P., Kostic, D., Rexford, J.: A NICE way to test openflow applications. In: Gribble and Katabi [11], pp. 127–140. https://www.usenix.org/conference/nsdi12/technical-sessions/presentation/canini

7. Deng, C., Namjoshi, K.S.: Witnessing network transformations (2017). Extended version of this paper, at http://cs.nyu.edu/~deng/

8. Fagin, R.: Generalized first-order spectra and polynomial-time recognizable sets. In: Karp, R. (ed.) Complexity of Computation, SIAM-AMS Proc., pp. 27–41 (1974)

9. Feamster, N., Rexford, J., Zegura, E.W.: The road to SDN: an intellectual history of programmable networks. Comput. Commun. Rev. **44**(2), 87–98 (2014). doi:10.1145/2602204.2602219

10. Fortune, S.: Equivalence and generalization in a layered network model. J. Comput. Syst. Sci. **81**(8), 1698–1714 (2015). doi:10.1016/j.jcss.2015.06.004

11. Gribble, S.D., Katabi, D. (eds.) Proceedings of the 9th USENIX Symposium on Networked Systems Design and Implementation, NSDI 2012, San Jose, CA, USA, April 25–27, 2012. USENIX Association (2012). https://www.usenix.org/publications/proceedings/?f[0]=im_group_audience%3A279

12. Guha, A., Reitblatt, M., Foster, N.: Machine-verified network controllers. In: Boehm, H., Flanagan, C. (eds.) ACM SIGPLAN Conference on Programming Language Design and Implementation, PLDI 2013, Seattle, WA, USA, June 16–19, 2013, pp. 483–494. ACM (2013). doi:10.1145/2462156.2462178

13. Kang, N., Liu, Z., Rexford, J., Walker, D.: Optimizing the "one big switch" abstraction in software-defined networks. In: Almeroth, K.C., Mathy, L., Papagiannaki, K., Misra, V. (eds.) Conference on emerging Networking Experiments and Technologies, CoNEXT 2013, Santa Barbara, CA, USA, December 9–12, 2013, pp. 13–24. ACM (2013). doi:10.1145/2535372.2535373

14. Kazemian, P., Varghese, G., McKeown, N.: Header space analysis: static checking for networks. In: Gribble and Katabi[11], pp. 113–126. https://www.usenix.org/conference/nsdi12/technical-sessions/presentation/kazemian

15. Khurshid, A., Zou, X., Zhou, W., Caesar, M., Godfrey, P.B.: Veriflow: Verifying network-wide invariants in real time. In: Feamster, N., Mogul, J.C. (eds.) Proceedings of the 10th USENIX Symposium on Networked Systems Design and Implementation, NSDI 2013, Lombard, IL, USA, April 2–5, 2013, pp. 15–27. USENIX Association (2013). https://www.usenix.org/conference/nsdi13/technical-sessions/presentation/khurshid

16. Lopes, N.P., Bjørner, N., Godefroid, P., Jayaraman, K., Varghese, G.: Checking beliefs in dynamic networks. In: 12th USENIX Symposium on Networked Systems Design and Implementation, NSDI 15, Oakland, CA, USA, May 4–6, 2015, pp. 499–512. USENIX Association (2015). https://www.usenix.org/conference/nsdi15/technical-sessions/presentation/lopes

17. Mai, H., Khurshid, A., Agarwal, R., Caesar, M., Godfrey, B., King, S.T.: Debugging the data plane with Anteater. In: Keshav, S., Liebeherr, J., Byers, J.W., Mogul, J.C. (eds.) Proceedings of the ACM SIGCOMM 2011 Conference on Applications, Technologies, Architectures, and Protocols for Computer Communications, Toronto, ON, Canada, August 15–19, 2011, pp. 290–301. ACM (2011). doi:10.1145/2018436.2018470

18. McKeown, N., Anderson, T., Balakrishnan, H., Parulkar, G.M., Peterson, L.L., Rexford, J., Shenker, S., Turner, J.S.: Openflow: enabling innovation in campus networks. Comput. Commun. Rev. **38**(2), 69–74 (2008). doi:10.1145/1355734.1355746

19. Namjoshi, K.S., Zuck, L.D.: Witnessing program transformations. In: Logozzo, F., Fähndrich, M. (eds.) SAS 2013. LNCS, vol. 7935, pp. 304–323. Springer, Heidelberg (2013). doi:10.1007/978-3-642-38856-9_17

20. Necula, G.: Translation validation of an optimizing compiler. In: Proceedings of the ACM SIGPLAN Conference on Principles of Programming Languages Design and Implementation (PLDI) 2000, pp. 83–95 (2000)

21. Necula, G., Lee, P.: Safe kernel extensions without run-time checking. In: OSDI (1996)

22. Pnueli, A., Shtrichman, O., Siegel, M.: The code validation tool (CVT) - automatic verification of a compilation process. Softw. Tools Technol. Transf. **2**(2), 192–201 (1998)

23. Rinard, M.C., Marinov, D.: Credible compilation with pointers. In: FLoC Workshop on Run-Time Result Verification (1999)

24. Shenker, S., Casado, M., Koponen, T., McKeown, N.: The future of networking and the past of protocols. Open Networking Summit (2011)

25. Simsarian, J.E., Choi, N., Kim, Y.J., Fortune, S., Thottan, M.K.: Netgraph data model applied to multilayer carrier networks. In: OFC (2016). doi:10.1364/OFC.2016.Th4G.2

26. Smolka, S., Eliopoulos, S.A., Foster, N., Guha, A.: A fast compiler for netkat. In: Fisher, K., Reppy, J.H. (eds.) Proceedings of the 20th ACM SIGPLAN International Conference on Functional Programming, ICFP 2015, Vancouver, BC, Canada, September 1–3, 2015, pp. 328–341. ACM (2015). doi:10.1145/2784731.2784761

27. Zuck, L.D., Pnueli, A., Goldberg, B.: VOC: a methodology for the translation validation of optimizing compilers. J. UCS **9**(3), 223–247 (2003)

Combining Model Checking and Runtime Verification for Safe Robotics

Ankush Desai$^{(\boxtimes)}$, Tommaso Dreossi, and Sanjit A. Seshia

University of California at Berkeley, Berkeley, CA, USA
{ankushd,tommasodreossi,sseshia}@berkeley.edu

Abstract. A major challenge towards large scale deployment of autonomous mobile robots is to program them with formal guarantees and high assurance of correct operation. To this end, we present a framework for building safe robots. Our approach for validating the end-to-end correctness of robotics system consists of two parts: (1) a high-level programming language for implementing and systematically testing the reactive robotics software via model checking; (2) a signal temporal logic (STL) based online monitoring system to ensure that the assumptions about the low-level controllers (discrete models) used during model checking hold at runtime. Combining model checking with runtime verification helps us bridge the gap between software verification (discrete) that makes assumptions about the low-level controllers and the physical world, and the actual execution of the software on a real robotic platform in the physical world. To demonstrate the efficacy of our approach, we build a safe adaptive surveillance system and present software-in-the-loop simulations of the application.

1 Introduction

Recent advances in robotics have led to the adoption of autonomous mobile robots across a broad spectrum of applications like surveillance [1], precision agriculture [2], warehouse [3], and delivery systems [4]. As autonomous robots are finding applications in complex real-world systems that have acute *safety* and *reliability* requirements, programmability with high assurance and provable robustness guarantees remains a major barrier to their large-scale adoption.

At the heart of an autonomous robot is the specialized on-board software that ensures safe operation without any human intervention. Controller software stacks usually consist of several interacting modules that can be grouped into two categories: *high-level* modules, taking discrete decisions and planning to ensure that the robot safely achieves complex tasks, and *low-level* modules, usually consisting of closed-loop controllers and actuators that determine the robot's

This work is funded in part by the DARPA BRASS program under agreement number FA8750-16-C-0043, NSF grants CNS-1646208 and CCF-1139138, and by TerraSwarm, one of six centers of STARnet, a Semiconductor Research Corporation program sponsored by MARCO and DARPA.

S. Lahiri and G. Reger (Eds.): RV 2017, LNCS 10548, pp. 172–189, 2017.
DOI: 10.1007/978-3-319-67531-2_11

continuous dynamics. Ensuring safe and reliable operation therefore requires reasoning about both high and low levels of the software stack in the external environment in which the robot is operating.

High-level controllers must be reactive to inputs from the physical world and from other software components. These controllers are therefore generally implemented as concurrent event-driven systems, whose testing and debugging is notoriously difficult due to nondeterministic interactions arising from inputs and scheduling of event handlers. Model checking is therefore a good fit for verifying such software. However, model checking such software monolithically is impossible due to the intractable state space. Moreover, software model checking invariably relies on having reasonable assumptions on interactions with the physical world and on other software components. Not all software components are amenable to model checking. Additionally, the dynamics of the physical world is often highly non-linear, and in some cases, good environment models are not even available. Simulation-based falsification of cyber-physical systems (CPSs), including both software components and physical sub-systems, has recently shown much promise (e.g. [5]); however, such techniques typically require models of the entire closed-loop CPS, which is not always available in robotics systems operating in uncertain and unknown environments. Thus, verifying the combination of the software and the physical environment of robots is virtually impossible today.

To address these problems, we present a framework for designing safe complex real-world robotic applications. In our scheme, trusted software components that must satisfy key properties are written in a high-level programming language called P [6]. We use model checking to verify properties of this discrete, event-driven portion of the robotic software system. Moreover, it uses a brand of execution-driven, explicit-state model checking that has been found effective for large software systems. Since such model checking may not exhaustively enumerate all states of the software, we will use the phrase "systematic testing" interchangeably with "model checking". However, this model checking still requires assumptions on the interfaces of the checked software with the physical world and with other untrusted software components. We capture such assumptions in *signal temporal logic* (STL), a specification language that has proved effective for CPS. We provide a framework for online monitoring of STL properties and a system for feeding back the results of online monitoring to the decision making in the robot's software stack. Thus, we use a combination of software model checking and runtime monitoring of STL to provide a high level of assurance on the operation of robotic systems.

To summarize, there are three key features that enable our methodology:

1. The event-driven programming language P [6] for implementing and model checking high-level robotic logics; P analysis assumes a discrete abstraction of the continuous robot dynamics;
2. A combination of Signal Temporal Logic (STL) [7] and regression methods to infer the parameters under which the assumptions made in (1) are satisfied;

3. An online monitoring based approach to ensure that the specifications defined in (2) are not violated by the robot at runtime.

We implemented the proposed framework in a tool called Drona and we used it to build and analyze a real-world surveillance application, where an autonomous drone safely patrols a workspace. Our evaluation shows that the methods implemented in Drona help find several critical bugs in the drone implementation. Moreover, STL online-monitoring successfully catches instances when the drone violates low-level assumptions during flight.

This paper is structured as follows: we first provide an overview of our proposed methodology using a motivating example (Sect. 2) and define some basic terminology (Sect. 3); we next briefly describe the trusted software stack (Sect. 4); in Sect. 5 we introduce STL and define specifications that, in combination with regression analysis, formalize the assumptions made on low-level dynamics; in Sect. 6 we define online monitors and their usage; Sect. 7 discusses Drona implementation details and shows application of Drona to build a surveillance system; the paper ends in Sect. 8 with related work.

2   Overview

We consider a surveillance system using autonomous aerial drones as a case study to present the challenges in building safe robotics systems and to demonstrate how Drona can be used to address them.

Motivating example: Let us consider an application where a drone must patrol a set of locations in a city. Figure 1a shows a snapshot of the workspace from the Gazebo simulator [8]. Figure 1b presents the obstacle map for the workspace with some surveillance points (blue dots) and a possible path that the autonomous drone can take when performing the surveillance task (black trajectory). Obstacles such as houses and cars are considered to be static.

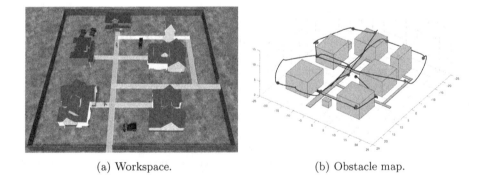

(a) Workspace.   (b) Obstacle map.

Fig. 1. Surveillance system using drones: (a) Workspace created in Gazebo simulator, (b) Obstacle map for the workspace with surveillance points (blue) and an example trajectory of the drone (black). (Color figure online)

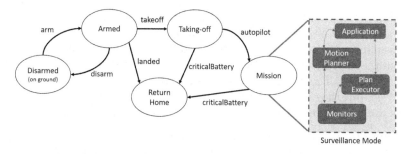

Fig. 2. Operation modes of autonomous drone.

High level controllers of an autonomous drone performing complex tasks, such as surveillance, usually involve several modes that change during the span of a mission. Figure 2 presents an example of a high level controller and shows how different modes are organized and connected by triggering events. A controller execution can look like: the drone starts in `Disarmed` state; on receiving the `arm` command it moves to `Armed` state where rotors are started; on receiving the `takeoff` command followed by the `autopilot` command, the drone moves to the `Mission` mode where it starts performing the surveillance mission. In each mode, different components cooperate with the goal of performing the desired operations. For instance, in the `mission` mode components like application, motion planner, and plan executor together ensure that the robot safely performs the surveillance mission. Irrespective of the mode of operation, the high level controller must handle critical events that can happen at any time. For example, a `criticalBattery` event must be handled correctly by aborting all operations and safely returning to home location.

Implementing a high-level controller that satisfies desired properties is notoriously hard. For example, in surveillance applications, the drone should:

(P1) *Sequencing*: Visit all the surveillance points in priority order;
(P2) *Coverage*: Eventually visit all the surveillance points;
(P3) *Obstacle avoidance*: Never collide with an obstacle;
(P4) *Valid trajectory*: Compute valid trajectories leading to the goal location;
(P5) *Safe trajectories:* Follow the reference trajectory within an error bound.

These properties involve different reasoning domains and robot components. For instance, properties P1–P2 are application specific and comprise discrete events. Contrarily, properties P3–P5 are generic (i.e., they should be satisfied by any safe robotics system) and concern both discrete and continuous domains. Moreover, properties P3–P4 must be ensured by the motion planner (discrete) that generates trajectories, whereas the property P5 is dependent on the low-level controllers (continuous).

These observations motivate the need for decomposing the verification problem into subproblems that can be tackled by using the right technique.

For instance, traditional model checking approaches can address properties P1-P2, they could be used to reason on properties P3-P4 under some abstractions/assumption (e.g., state space discretization or robot dynamics linearization), but they hardly provide guarantees about P5 due to the infinite/continuous domains involved. The simulation and testing-based approaches can handle properties P1-P5 but they suffer a lack of guarantees, in the sense that an exhaustive analysis would require an infeasible infinite number of simulations.

Approach Overview: We now give an overview of the new methodology proposed in this paper based on the software stack of a robotics system built using our framework. The software stack is organized into four main blocks (Fig. 3): (1) the *application block* that implements the application specific logic; (2) the *trusted software stack* that focuses on modules that can be reused across different applications; (3) the *low-level controllers* layer that implements the primitive controllers and state-estimators (possibly provided by third-parties); (4) the *runtime verification* block that implements online monitoring to ensure that robot always performs safe control actions. The edges in Fig. 3 represents interaction between different blocks, for example, the components in the trusted software stack can create monitors that observe the state of the robot by processing the sensor streams and inform components in trusted software stack if the monitored properties are violated.

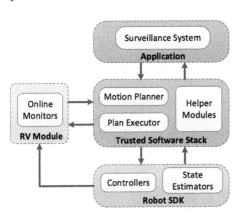

Fig. 3. Robotics software stack

To design and reason about the blocks (1) and (2), we use P [6], an event-driven programming language for implementing and model checking asynchronous reactive systems. A P program comprises *state machines* communicating asynchronously with each other using events accompanied by typed data values. For blocks (3) and (4) we use Signal Temporal Logic (STL) [7], a formalism suitable to describe properties on real-values signals over real-time. STL is used to define properties related to assumptions needed by the blocks (1) and (2) and to monitor their status at runtime while the drone performs a mission.

Our approach can be used to validate properties P1-P4 using the traditional model checking approaches and simultaneously ensures that the system satisfies property P5 using runtime verification based on STL online monitoring.

3   Terminology and Definitions

In this section, we formalize the definitions needed for the rest of the paper.

Workspace: We represent the workspace for a robot $W \subseteq \mathbb{R}^3$ as a 3-D occupancy map, where obstacles are assumed to be convex (Fig. 1b). The set of all locations occupied by obstacles is denoted by Ω. The set of free locations in the workspace is denoted by F, where $F = W \setminus \Omega$.

Tasks: In an autonomous robotics system, tasks can be generated dynamically and assigned to the robot. An atomic task is represented by the goal location $g \in F$ that the robot must visit in order to accomplish the task. A complex task can be represented as a sequence of atomic tasks. For example, moving from one surveillance point to another is an atomic task and periodically visiting all the surveillance points is an example of a complex task.

Trajectory: The motion of a robot operating in W can be expressed by the rule $\mathbf{q}' = f(\mathbf{q}, \mathbf{u})$ where $\mathbf{q} \in F$ is the current robot position, $\mathbf{u} \in \mathbb{R}^m$ is the current input, and $\mathbf{q}' \in F$ is the future robot position under the influence of $\mathbf{u}$. We consider the robot as a black-box as we do not explicitly know f, but we can observe the generated trajectories of a robot. A *trajectory* is a function $\tau : T \to F$ from a linearly-ordered time domain to a location in the workspace.

Let $\mathbf{q}_i, \mathbf{q}_g \in W$ be two locations and $\mathbf{q} \in F$ be the current robot position. Let $d(\mathbf{q}, \mathbf{q}_g)$ be the Euclidean distance between $\mathbf{q}$ and $\mathbf{q}_g$, and $d(\mathbf{q}, (\mathbf{q}_i, \mathbf{q}_g))$ be the distance between $\mathbf{q}$ and the line passing through $\mathbf{q}_i$ and $\mathbf{q}_g$.

ϵ-close: A robot is ϵ-close to a location $\mathbf{q}_g$ represented by $close(\mathbf{q}_g, \epsilon)$ if $close(\mathbf{q}_g, \epsilon) := d(\mathbf{q}, \mathbf{q}_g) < \epsilon$.

ϵ-tube: A robot is within the ϵ-tube surrounding the line passing through points $\mathbf{q}_i$ and $\mathbf{q}_g$, represented by $tube((\mathbf{q}_i, \mathbf{q}_g), \epsilon)$, if the distance between its current position and the line is bounded by ϵ, i.e., $tube((\mathbf{q}_i, \mathbf{q}_g), \epsilon) := d(\mathbf{q}, (\mathbf{q}_i, \mathbf{q}_g)) < \epsilon$.

Motion primitives: Motion primitives are a set of short closed-loop trajectories of a robot under the action of a set of precomputed control laws [9,10]. The set of motion primitives form the basis of the motion of a robot. A robot moves from its current location to a destination location by executing a motion plan which is a sequence of motion primitives. The low-level controllers can be used to move the robot from one location to another by continuously changing either its velocity or thrust. We leverage these controllers to implement a motion primitive, called goto, that moves the robot from its current location to the goal location along the straight line joining the locations.

Given the complex dynamics of a robot, noisy sensors, and environmental disturbances ensuring that the robot precisely follow a fixed trajectory is extremely hard (see Fig. 5). Hence, we assume that on executing goto($\mathbf{q}_g$), the robot takes any trajectory from its current location $\mathbf{q}_i$ to the goal location $\mathbf{q}_g$ such that $tube((\mathbf{q}_i, \mathbf{q}_g), \epsilon)$ holds for the duration of the goto, where ϵ is error bound by which the robot can drift. In Sect. 5, we present formal specification of goto using STL and describe an approach for learning error bound ϵ such that the specification of goto is robust.

4   Trusted Robotics Software Stack

The first part of the proposed framework consists of a generic trusted software stack that implements the common components required for building safe autonomous robots. Our trusted software stack consists of three main components (Fig. 3):

1. *Motion planner*, that computes a safe motion plan from the current position to the goal location of the current task,
2. *Plan executor*, that ensures that the robot correctly executes the generated motion plan;
3. *Helper modules*, consisting of helper state-machines that continuously observe the sensor streams published by the robot sensors and inform the high-level components of important events.

Given a high level task, the motion planning problem is to compute a safe motion-plan such that on executing it the robot follows a safe trajectory to its goal location without colliding with any obstacle.

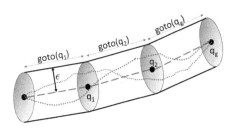

Fig. 4. Motion plan as a sequence of goto (Color figure online)

The adopted motion planning technique is based on the composition of motion primitives [11]. A motion plan is defined as a sequence of motion primitives that move the robot from its current location to the goal location $\mathbf{q}_g$. We use a sampling based approach to compute a motion plan denoted by the sequence $\mu = (\text{goto}(\mathbf{q}_1)\ldots\text{goto}(\mathbf{q}_g))$, such that, on executing μ, the resultant trajectory does not collide with any obstacle and takes the robot to the goal location (see Sect. 7 for implementation details). Our plan executor ensures that the motion primitives are executed in timely fashion so that the robot follows a safe trajectory. Obstacle collision avoidance is guaranteed by the assumption that the paths taken by the robot lie inside a safe tube (see Fig. 4; safe (green) and reference (red) trajectories). The motion planner ensures that the plan tube does not collide with any obstacle. In the following, we will show how such a safe tube can be determined (Sect. 5) and we will provide a method to monitor whether the drone actually flies inside it (Sect. 6).

Verification approach: To model check our trusted software stack, we implemented each high-level component as a collection of P state machines. The P compiler generates code that can be model checked using state-of-the-art search prioritization techniques (for details, see Sect. 7). We use *over-approximating* models for all motion primitives and the robot state during testing, and replace them with their implementations for real execution. In most cases, computing a safe motion plan involves usage of complex constraint solvers [11,12] or graph search (sampling) algorithms [13]. Hence, some part of the motion planner is not implemented in P and is considered as a black-box. When verifying the software stack, creating a sound model of such a motion planner is hard. To resolve this problem, we use execution based model checking [14], a verification technique based on executing the actual program implementation whenever the sound model is not available during the systematic exploration. We extended the model checker such that, whenever the motion planner invokes an external function, it executes its native implementation. This technique is sound because same implementation code is used during model checking and actual execution.

To summarize, we provide a method to implement verified motion planners and plan executors (e.g., that satisfy properties like P3–P4). However, the verified properties hold only under some specific assumptions, for instance, the trajectories taken by the robot are contained by a safe tube (see Fig. 4).

5   Validating Low-Level Controllers

When model-checking the high-level software we assumed a discrete abstraction of the motion primitives used to control robot's motion. For instance, when a goto command is invoked, we assume that the drone reaches the target location in a reasonable amount of time without drifting too much from the nominal line connecting its current position and the target point. In this section, we first specify the motion primitives using parametric Signal Temporal Logic. Next, we use linear regressions to learn the specification parameters for a given robot. Finally, we evaluate these specifications on several observed trajectories.

The formalization and analysis of the assumptions about motion primitives allow us to bridge the gap between their discrete abstractions used during model checking and their low-level implementation.

5.1   Signal Temporal Logic

We begin by introducing Signal Temporal Logic [7] (STL), a formalism particularly suitable for the specification of properties of real-values signals over real-time, such as trajectories generated by robots.

A *signal* is a function $s : D \to S$, with $D \subseteq \mathbb{R}_{\geq 0}$ an interval and either $S \subseteq \mathbb{B}$ or $S \subseteq \mathbb{R}$, where $\mathbb{B} = \{\top, \bot\}$ and $\mathbb{R}$ is the set of reals. Signals defined on $\mathbb{B}$ are called *booleans*, while those on $\mathbb{R}$ are said *real-valued*. A *trace* $w = \{s_1, \ldots, s_n\}$ is a finite set of real-valued signals defined over the same interval D.

Let $\Sigma = \{\sigma_1, \ldots, \sigma_k\}$ be a finite set of predicates $\sigma_i : \mathbb{R}^n \to \mathbb{B}$, with $\sigma_i \equiv p_i(x_1, \ldots, x_n) \lhd 0$, $\lhd \in \{<, \leq\}$, and $p_i : \mathbb{R}^n \to \mathbb{R}$ a function in the variables $x_1, \ldots, x_n$. An STL formula is defined by the following grammar:

$$\varphi := \sigma \mid \neg\varphi \mid \varphi \wedge \varphi \mid \varphi \ \mathsf{U}_I \ \varphi \tag{1}$$

where $\sigma \in \Sigma$ is a predicate and $I \subset \mathbb{R}_{\geq 0}$ is a closed non-singular interval. Other common temporal operators can be defined as syntactic abbreviations in the usual way, like for instance $\varphi_1 \vee \varphi_2 := \neg(\neg\varphi_1 \wedge \neg\varphi_2)$, $\mathsf{F}_I \ \varphi := \top \ \mathsf{U}_I \ \varphi$, or $\mathsf{G}_I \ \varphi := \neg\mathsf{F}_I \ \neg\varphi$. Given a $t \in \mathbb{R}_{\geq 0}$, a shifted interval I is defined as $t + I = \{t + t' \mid t' \in I\}$.

Definition 1 (Robustness semantics). Let w be a trace, $t \in \mathbb{R}_{\geq 0}$, and φ be an STL formula. The *robustness* ρ of φ for a trace w at time t is defined as:

$$
\begin{aligned}
\rho(p(x_1, \ldots, x_n) \lhd 0, w, t) &= p(w(t)) \text{ with } \lhd \in \{<, \leq\} \\
\rho(\neg\varphi, w, t) &= -\rho(\varphi, w, t) \\
\rho(\varphi_1 \wedge \varphi_2, w, t) &= \min(\rho(\varphi_1, w, t), \rho(\varphi_2, w, t)) \\
\rho(\varphi_1 U_I \varphi_2, w, t) &= \sup_{t' \in t+I} \min(\rho(\varphi_2, w, t'), \inf_{t'' [t, t']} \rho(\varphi_1, w, t''))
\end{aligned}
\tag{2}
$$

A trace w satisfies a formula φ (denoted by $w \models \varphi$) if and only if $\rho(\varphi, w, 0) > 0$. The *robustness* signal of a formula φ with respect to w is the signal $\rho(\varphi, w, \cdot)$. Note that a robot trajectory $\tau : T \to F$ falls under the definition of trace (see Sect. 3). With a slight notation overload, we say that a trajectory $\tau : T \to F$ satisfies a formula φ (denoted by $\tau \models \varphi$) if and only if $\rho(\varphi, \tau, 0) > 0$.

Differently from classic qualitative semantics, STL robustness provides quantitative information on the evaluated formula, i.e., it tells how strongly the specification is satisfied or violated by the considered trace. In our context, we can use robustness to understand how close a robot trajectory is to a specification violation. For instance, a small positive robustness value means that a slight change in the robot trajectory might lead to a violation. The ability of reasoning on trajectories combined with the qualitative semantics makes STL the right formalism to capture the assumptions that low-level controllers must satisfy.

5.2   Assumptions as STL Formulas

In this section, we use STL to formally specify the goto motion primitive and the motion plan which is a sequence of motion primitives.

The assumptions made about the goto motion primitive can be specified as:

$$
goto(\mathbf{q}_g, t, \epsilon) := tube((\mathbf{q}_i, \mathbf{q}_g), \epsilon) \, U_{[0,t]} \, close(\mathbf{q}_g, \epsilon)
\tag{3}
$$

This formula holds if the drone stays in the ϵ-tube connecting its original position $\mathbf{q}_i$ and the destination $\mathbf{q}_g$ until it eventually is ϵ-close to the goal point $\mathbf{q}_g$. The time interval $[0, t]$ imposes a time constraint on the execution time of the goto command.

Recollect that the robot moves from its current location to a goal location by executing a motion plan (a sequence of gotos) generated by the planner (Fig. 4). We next specify the set of trajectories that the robot can take when executing a motion plan $\mu = (goto(\mathbf{q}_{g_1}), \ldots, goto(\mathbf{q}_{g_n}))$. Let $\xi = (\mathbf{q}_{g_1}, \ldots, \mathbf{q}_{g_n})$, $t = (t_1, \ldots, t_{n-1})$, and $\epsilon = (\epsilon_1, \ldots, \epsilon_{n-1})$ be sequences of goto locations, the execution times of each goto, and ϵ the parameter corresponding to each goto, respectively. $traj(\xi, t, \epsilon)$ is recursively defined as follow:

$$
traj(\xi, t, \epsilon) := \begin{cases} tube(\mathbf{q}_{g_1}, \mathbf{q}_{g_2}, \epsilon_1) \, U_{[0,t_1]} \, close(\mathbf{q}_{g_2}, \epsilon_1) & \text{if } n = 2 \\ tube(\mathbf{q}_{g_1}, \mathbf{q}_{g_2}, \epsilon_1) \, U_{[0,t_1]} \, (close(\mathbf{q}_{g_2}, \epsilon_1) \wedge traj(\xi', t', \epsilon')) & \text{otherwise} \end{cases}
\tag{4}
$$

where $\xi' = (\mathbf{q}_{g_2}, \ldots, \mathbf{q}_{g_n})$, $t' = (t_2, \ldots, t_{n-1})$, and $\epsilon' = (\epsilon_2, \ldots, \epsilon_{n-1})$.

For the base case, similarly to the *goto* case, the specification asks the robot to lie in the ϵ_1-tube between $\mathbf{q}_{g_1}$ and $\mathbf{q}_{g_2}$ until it is ϵ_1-close to the target position $\mathbf{q}_{g_2}$. In the general case, a series of nested until specifications are imposed in order to force the robot to follow the desired sequences of target locations with their corresponding execution times and ϵ-tubes.

5.3   Parameter Prediction

We next describe how we learn the parameter values (ϵ and t) for the *goto* and *traj* specifications (Eqs. 3 and 4) such that they tightly represent the correct sets of behaviors for a given robot.

One way to instantiate the specification parameters is to manually choose an upper bound value on the basis of knowledge about the system. However, one value of the parameter might not suffice different templates of the same specification. For instance, consider two **goto** executions, one to a close location and the other to a distant target location. The duration of the former is likely to be shorter than the latter. A large parameter value for the time duration t satisfies both cases, but for the first one it leads to a highly conservative specification. Similar argument holds for the value of ϵ, setting it to a large value means that the radius of ϵ-tube is large which makes the motion planner conservative discarding potentially feasible motion plans.

In general, we want a mechanism to dynamically tune the parameters depending on the motion primitive. In our case, e.g., **goto**($\mathbf{q}_g$) executed at location $\mathbf{q}_i$, we want to define two parameter prediction functions $f_t, f_\epsilon : F \times F \to \mathbb{R}_{\geq 0}$ that return the expected duration $t = f_t(\mathbf{q}_i, \mathbf{q}_g)$ and overshoot $\epsilon = f_\epsilon(\mathbf{q}_i, \mathbf{q}_g)$ such that the instantiated STL formula $goto(\mathbf{q}_g, t, \epsilon)$ represents the set of valid trajectory specifically for the start location $\mathbf{q}_i$ and goal location $\mathbf{q}_g$.

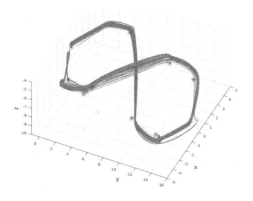

Fig. 5. goto trajectories evaluation using learned STL specification. (Color figure online)

To this end, we adopt regression analysis to estimate ϵ and t as functions of the initial and target locations. We estimate the relationship between the dependent variables ϵ and t and the independent variables $l \in \mathbb{R}_{\geq 0}$ and $\mathbf{v} \in [-1, 1]^3$, where $l = \|\mathbf{q}_g - \mathbf{q}_i\|$ and $\mathbf{v} = (\mathbf{q}_g - \mathbf{q}_i)/l$ are the distance and the normalized direction between $\mathbf{q}_i$ and $\mathbf{q}_g$, respectively. We chose distance and direction as independent variables since we noticed that in our experiments the overshoots (ϵ) and execution times (t) are influenced by the direction and distance of the target position.

A possible approach to defining prediction functions is to use multilinear regression analysis [15] where the functions are of the form $f_t(\mathbf{q}_i, \mathbf{q}_g) = \mathbf{x}^T \beta_t + \varepsilon_t$

and $f_\epsilon(\mathbf{q}_i, \mathbf{q}_g) = \mathbf{x}^T \beta_\epsilon + \varepsilon_\epsilon$ where $\mathbf{x} = (l\ \mathbf{v})$ are the independent variables, $\beta_t, \beta_\epsilon \in \mathbb{R}^4$ are the parameter vectors, and $\varepsilon_t, \varepsilon_\epsilon \in \mathbb{R}$ are the error terms.

Learning parameters: Using multilinear regression, we learned the parameters $\beta_t, \beta_\epsilon, \varepsilon_t, \varepsilon_\epsilon$ analyzing more than 1000 trajectories generated by goto of random lengths. The learned parameters led to the prediction functions:

$$f_t(\mathbf{q}, \mathbf{q}_g) = 30.3438l + 2.3065\mathbf{v}_1 - 0.9014\mathbf{v}_2 - 221.1588\mathbf{v}_3 + 217.6745$$
$$f_\epsilon(\mathbf{q}, \mathbf{q}_g) = 0.1060l - 0.0010\mathbf{v}_1 - 0.0139\mathbf{v}_2 + 0.0806\mathbf{v}_3 + 0.6180$$
(5)

To demonstrate that the parameters learnt using regressions tightly capture the correct set of behaviors, we present another experiment where the learnt parameter prediction functions are used to automatically instantiate the parameters of STL specifications.

Specification instantiation: We analyze the trajectories of the drone repeatedly flying along a tilted eight loop (see Fig. 5). From the given way points (stars), we generate the *traj* STL formula template (Eq. 4) and we instantiate it using the prediction functions previously learned (Eq. 5). We then evaluate the observed trajectory against the specifications. Figure 5 present 50 trajectories. Green trajectories robustly satisfy the specification (i.e., robustness larger than 0.2); orange ones have a weak positive robustness (i.e., between 0.0 and 0.2); red ones violate the specification (i.e., negative robustness). Note how most of the trajectories satisfy the *traj* specification and only two violate it, demonstrating that the learnt parameters are tight.

This example shows how the proposed parameter prediction method is useful to determined tight parameter evaluations and can be used to validate discrete abstractions used during model checking. However, as these specifications are tight but not sound, it is desirable to have runtime verification for catching outliers.

6   Online Monitoring

In this section, we provide a method to monitor at runtime the specifications learned in Sect. 5. An online monitor is useful as it can determine if any of the assumptions (specifications) are violated and notify the operator about the unexpected behavior or trigger some correcting input actions to fix the problem.

Differently from the offline approach used in the previous section, online STL algorithms assume that partial traces are provided to the monitor. Partial trajectories might prevent the monitor from computing definitive robustness values. However, online monitors usually provide estimates (upper and lower bounds) of the robustness by quantifying how close is the monitored trace to the violation/satisfaction. To clarify the notion of robustness estimates, consider the formula $\mathsf{G}_{[0,10]}(x \geq 0)$. This specification can be declared satisfied only after observing x on the whole time interval $[0, 10]$. However, its distance from the violation provides an upper bound of the final robustness. It is important to note that a negative upper bound implies the violation of the specification.

There are several methods to online monitor temporal properties [16–18]. In this work, we adopt the technique presented in [19] where the monitor incrementally computes upper and lower bounds of the robustness by reasoning on the provided partial trace. Intuitively, the online robustness semantics, slightly different from the standard one (Definition 1), provides a best and worst robustness estimates for the partially observed trace.

STL online monitoring: We monitor online the *traj* specification (Eq. 4) on one example trajectory. The drone is asked to pass through the way points (stars) that generate a tilted eight loop (see Fig. 6). The *traj* monitor is instantiated with the parameters learnt in Sect. 5.3.

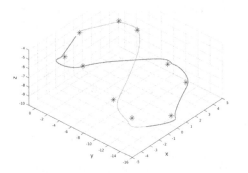

Fig. 6. Online goto monitoring using learned STL specification. (Color figure online)

Figure 6 depicts the upper bound robustness signal colored according to its robustness values. Green segments strongly satisfy the specification (i.e., robustness larger than 0.2) while orange ones have a weak positive robustness (i.e., between 0.0 and 0.2). We can observe how the upper bound robustness signal changes from strongly positive (green) to weak positive (orange) along the trajectory. This provides us the exact point at which the trajectory does not strongly (high robustness) satisfy the property, i.e., the instant in which the assumption is getting close to a violation. In our framework, we use the decreasing robustness during online monitoring as a warning to take preemptive action against potential erroneous behavior.

To summarize, when a motion plan is executed by a robot in order to accomplish a high-level task, the following sequence of steps are performed:

1. A template of an STL formula is generated corresponding to the motion plan (see Sect. 5.2);
2. The parameters of the specification are computed using the functions described in Sect. 5.3;
3. A online monitor is created to monitor the STL specification and take preemptive action based on the robustness value.

7   Implementation and Experimental Evaluation

Our past work on Drona [12] was in the context of distributed mobile robotics. For this work, we reimplemented the framework with runtime verification capabilities and applied to real-world robot systems.

In this section, we first describe the implementation of Drona, followed by the empirical evaluation to demonstrate its efficacy for building real-world safe robotics applications. Videos and further details of the conducted experiments are available at https://drona-org.github.io/Drona/.

7.1   Implementation

Figure 7 provides an overview of the Drona framework. The application and the trusted robotics software stack are implemented using the programming language P that allows programmers to write the implementation and its specification at a high-level as a collection of communicating state-machines. P provides first-class support for modeling concurrency, specifying safety and liveness properties, and checking that the program satisfies its specification [6, 20, 21]. We extend P so that programmer can syntactically specify the workspace configuration like obstacle size and its position. The compiler generates code for both execution-based model-checking and real execution when deployed on a target platform.

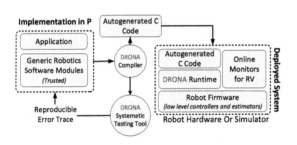

Fig. 7. Overview of Drona tool chain

We modified an open-source implementation of the sampling-based motion planner RRT* [13, 22] to generate plans as compositions of goto motion primitives. When executing a motion plan, the RV module automatically generates an STL specification (as discussed in Sect. 5) and performs online monitoring to catch violations. We use Matlab toolbox Breach [23] to online monitor the STL specifications. For our experiments, we use 3DR Iris [24] drone that comes with the open-source Pixhawk PX4 [25] autopilot. We implemented a collection of motion primitives using the low-level controllers provided by the PX4 firmware that is used to control the drone in autopilot mode.

Some examples of the implemented motion primitives are arm, takeoff, goto. When invoked, motion primitives are converted into series of MAVLINK messages (a protocol for communicating with unmanned vehicles) and sent to drone via User Datagram Protocol (UDP).

7.2   Evaluation

As a case study, we implemented a safe real-world surveillance application.

Safe surveillance: The entire surveillance system, which includes application and the trusted software stack, was implemented in around 3500 lines of P code and was systematically tested using the execution-based model-checker. We found some critical bugs in our high-level software implementation. For example, we did not check that when the battery is low the drone should not take-off.

This bug was uncovered by the model checker within a few minutes but was not found during simulations as the simulator always starts in full battery state.

After model-checking, we also performed stress-testing by running the surveillance application for several hours performing software-in-the-loop simulation. We did not find any new bugs in our implementation, except for some bugs at the interface of the P and external C code. This example demonstrates that model checking performs better than simulation-based testing in providing test-coverage and finding bugs in robotics software.

Obstacle avoidance: We next present simulation results to demonstrate the effectiveness of our STL-based online monitoring approach. We created a surveillance workspace in Gazebo [8] simulator environment (Fig. 1a) that is internally represented by Drona as an obstacle map (Fig. 1b). In our simulations, we execute the PX4 firmware in the loop, meaning that we considered a real low-level controller implementation that can be executed in the real deployment.

We consider an obstacle avoidance scenario, where the drone must never get closer than 0.5 m to any obstacle in the workspace during its 120 s of flight. The corresponding STL formula is:

$$\varphi_{obs} := \bigwedge_{j=1}^{n} \neg \mathbf{F}_{[0,120]}(d(\mathbf{q}, obs_j) < 0.5) \tag{6}$$

where $\mathbf{q} \in F$ is the robot current position, and $d(\mathbf{q}, obj_j)$ represents the distance between robot current position and the j-th obstacle.

We online monitored the requirement φ_{obs} on all the trajectories generated by the drone during the surveillance task. Figure 8 shows two views of a faulty trajectory of the drone with the upper bound of its online robustness. Note how online monitoring detects a specification violation (red trace), meaning that the drone gets too close (<0.5 m) to an obstacle. Also, observe that the robot robustly satisfy the specification in most part of the trajectory, with the exception of few segments where the robustness is between 0 and 0.5 (orange traces).

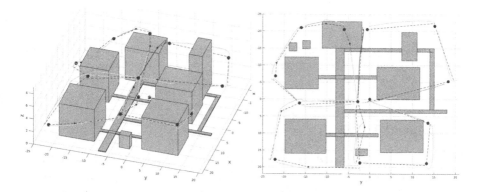

Fig. 8. Online obstacle avoidance monitoring (Eq. 6). Robustness legend: green $[0.5, +\infty)$, orange $(0, 0.5)$, red $[-\infty, 0)$. (Color figure online)

Plan execution: In this case, we monitor the correctness of the trajectories taken by the drone with respect to the reference ones computed by the motion planner. Recollect that given a task, the motion planner returns a sequence of waypoints or locations whose linear interpolation takes the drone from its current position to the goal location. For every such path, we are interested in checking whether the drone reaches all the waypoints while remaining inside a safe ϵ-tube. To this end, we generated the STL specification in Eq. 4 on the fly using the locations returned by the motion plan and instantiated its parameters using the prediction functions learned in Sect. 5.3. Note that Drona builds an STL specification for every generated plan. Once that the specification is generated, the online monitoring module checks it against the actual trajectory.

Figure 9 shows the robustness upper bound for an example trajectory computed online. It is interesting to note how there are two falsifying segments (red), i.e., parts of the trajectory that do not satisfy the generated STL specifications. Note how both these segments refer to parts where the drone strays away from the reference trajectories (dashed). The graph also shows some nonrobust traces (orange) where the drone is quite distant from the reference trajectories but does not violate the generated specification. Finally, note how in most part of the trajectory the robustness is green as it is always close to the reference.

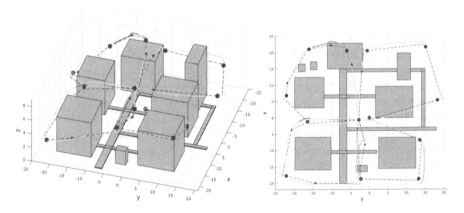

Fig. 9. Online trajectory following (Eq. 4 with predicted parameters of Eq. 5). Robustness legend: green $[0.2, +\infty)$; orange $(0, 0.2)$; red $[-\infty, 0)$. (Color figure online)

8   Related Work

Recently, there is increased interest towards using temporal logic formalism for synthesizing reactive robotics software [26–31]. This approach provides strong guarantees of correctness. However, the problem with automated synthesis techniques is that they scale poorly both with the complexity of the mission and the size of the workspace.

Reachability analysis techniques [32–35] have been used to verify robots modeled as hybrid systems. Differently from our work, reachability methods require an explicit representation of the robot dynamics and often suffer from scalability issues. Simulation-based tools for the falsification [23,36,37] of black-box systems (such as Simulink or Stateflow models) are more scalable than reachability methods but generally, they do not provide any formal guarantees. In this case, the goal of the falsifier is to generate a model simulation that does not satisfy a given specification.

Finally, the idea of synthesizing monitors from specifications [38–40] is well studied in the runtime verification community. Runtime verification has been applied to robotics [41–44] where monitors are used to checking the status of path planner and tasks executions.

The method proposed in this paper combines ideas from these well-known approaches in a practical and scalable way to build real-world robotics applications.

References

1. Marino, A., Parker, L., Antonelli, G., Caccavale, F.: Behavioral control for multi-robot perimeter patrol: a finite state automata approach. In: International Conference on Robotics and Automation, ICRA, pp. 831–836. IEEE (2009)
2. Barrientos, A., Colorado, J., del Cerro, J., Martinez, A., Rossi, C., Sanz, D., Valente, J.: Aerial remote sensing in agriculture: a practical approach to area coverage and path planning for fleets of mini aerial robots. J. Field Robot. **28**(5), 667–689 (2011)
3. Kehoe, B., Patil, S., Abbeel, P., Goldberg, K.: A survey of research on cloud robotics and automation. IEEE Trans. Autom. Sci. Eng. **12**(2), 398–409 (2015)
4. Omachonu, V.K., Einspruch, N.G.: Innovation in healthcare delivery systems: a conceptual framework. Publ. Sect. Innov. J. **15**(1), 1–20 (2010)
5. Yamaguchi, T., Kaga, T., Donzé, A., Seshia, S.A.: Combining requirement mining, software model checking, and simulation-based verification for industrial automotive systems. In: Proceedings of the IEEE International Conference on Formal Methods in Computer-Aided Design (FMCAD), October 2016
6. Desai, A., Gupta, V., Jackson, E., Qadeer, S., Rajamani, S., Zufferey, D.: P: safe asynchronous event-driven programming. In: Programming Language Design and Implementation (PLDI), pp. 321–332 (2013)
7. Maler, O., Nickovic, D.: Monitoring temporal properties of continuous signals. In: Lakhnech, Y., Yovine, S. (eds.) FORMATS/FTRTFT -2004. LNCS, vol. 3253, pp. 152–166. Springer, Heidelberg (2004). doi:10.1007/978-3-540-30206-3_12
8. Koenig, N., Howard, A.: Design and use paradigms for gazebo, an open-source multi-robot simulator. In: Intelligent Robots and Systems, IROS, vol. 3, pp. 2149–2154. IEEE (2004)
9. LaValle, S.M.: Planning Algorithms. Cambridge University Press, Cambridge (2006)
10. Mellinger, D., Kumar, V.: Minimum snap trajectory generation and control for quadrotors. In: International Conference on Robotics and Automation (ICRA), pp. 2520–2525 (2011)

11. Saha, I., Ramaithitima, R., Kumar, V., Pappas, G.J., Seshia, S.A.: Automated composition of motion primitives for multi-robot systems from safe ltl specifications. In: Intelligent Robots and Systems, IROS, pp. 1525–1532. IEEE (2014)
12. Desai, A., Saha, I., Yang, J., Qadeer, S., Seshia, S.A.: Drona: a framework for safe distributed mobile robotics. In: Proceedings of the 8th International Conference on Cyber-Physical Systems, ICCPS 2017, pp. 239–248. ACM, New York (2017)
13. Karaman, S., Frazzoli, E.: Incremental sampling-based algorithms for optimal motion planning. In: Robotics Science and Systems VI, vol. 104 (2010)
14. Godefroid, P.: Model checking for programming languages using verisoft. In: Proceedings of the 24th ACM SIGPLAN-SIGACT Symposium on Principles of Programming Languages, pp. 174–186. ACM (1997)
15. Neter, J., Kutner, M.H., Nachtsheim, C.J., Wasserman, W.: Applied Linear Statistical Models, vol. 4. Irwin, Chicago (1996)
16. Maler, O., Ničković, D.: Monitoring properties of analog and mixed-signal circuits. Int. J. Softw. Tools Technol. Transf. **15**(3), 247–268 (2013)
17. Ho, H.-M., Ouaknine, J., Worrell, J.: Online monitoring of metric temporal logic. In: Bonakdarpour, B., Smolka, S.A. (eds.) RV 2014. LNCS, vol. 8734, pp. 178–192. Springer, Cham (2014). doi:10.1007/978-3-319-11164-3_15
18. Dokhanchi, A., Hoxha, B., Fainekos, G.: On-line monitoring for temporal logic robustness. In: Bonakdarpour, B., Smolka, S.A. (eds.) RV 2014. LNCS, vol. 8734, pp. 231–246. Springer, Cham (2014). doi:10.1007/978-3-319-11164-3_19
19. Deshmukh, J.V., Donzé, A., Ghosh, S., Jin, X., Juniwal, G., Seshia, S.A.: Robust online monitoring of signal temporal logic. In: Bartocci, E., Majumdar, R. (eds.) RV 2015. LNCS, vol. 9333, pp. 55–70. Springer, Cham (2015). doi:10.1007/978-3-319-23820-3_4
20. P Github (2017). https://github.com/p-org/P
21. Desai, A., Qadeer, S., Seshia, S.A.: Systematic testing of asynchronous reactive systems. In: Foundations of Software Engineering (FSE), pp. 73–83 (2015)
22. Şucan, I.A., Moll, M., Kavraki, L.E.: The open motion planning library. IEEE Robot. Autom. Mag. **19**, 72–82 (2012). http://ompl.kavrakilab.org
23. Donzé, A.: Breach, a toolbox for verification and parameter synthesis of hybrid systems. In: Touili, T., Cook, B., Jackson, P. (eds.) CAV 2010. LNCS, vol. 6174, pp. 167–170. Springer, Heidelberg (2010). doi:10.1007/978-3-642-14295-6_17
24. 3D Robotics (2017). https://3dr.com/
25. PX4 Autopilot (2017). https://pixhawk.org/
26. Kupferman, O., Vardi, M.Y.: Model checking of safety properties. Formal Methods Syst. Des. **19**(3), 291–314 (2001)
27. Kress-Gazit, H., Fainekos, G.E., Pappas, G.J.: Temporal-logic-based reactive mission and motion planning. IEEE Trans. Robot. **25**(6), 1370–1381 (2009)
28. Saha, I., Ramaithitima, R., Kumar, V., Pappas, G.J., Seshia, S.A.: Implan: scalable incremental motion planning for multi-robot systems. In: International Conference on Cyber-Physical Systems (ICCPS), pp. 1–10. IEEE (2016)
29. Fainekos, G.E., Kress-Gazit, H., Pappas, G.J.: Temporal logic motion planning for mobile robots. In: International Conference on Robotics and Automation, ICRA, pp. 2020–2025. IEEE (2005)
30. Fainekos, G.E., Girard, A., Kress-Gazit, H., Pappas, G.J.: Temporal logic motion planning for dynamic robots. Automatica **45**(2), 343–352 (2009)
31. Saha, I., Ramaithitima, R., Kumar, V., Pappas, G.J., Seshia, S.A.: Automated composition of motion primitives for multi-robot systems from safe ltl specifications. In: International Conference on Intelligent Robots and Systems (IROS), pp. 1525–1532. IEEE (2014)

32. Frehse, G., et al.: SpaceEx: scalable verification of hybrid systems. In: Gopalakrishnan, G., Qadeer, S. (eds.) CAV 2011. LNCS, vol. 6806, pp. 379–395. Springer, Heidelberg (2011). doi:10.1007/978-3-642-22110-1_30

33. Chen, X., Ábrahám, E., Sankaranarayanan, S.: Flow*: an analyzer for non-linear hybrid systems. In: Sharygina, N., Veith, H. (eds.) CAV 2013. LNCS, vol. 8044, pp. 258–263. Springer, Heidelberg (2013). doi:10.1007/978-3-642-39799-8_18

34. Dreossi, T.: Sapo: reachability computation and parameter synthesis of polynomial dynamical systems. In: Hybrid Systems: Computation and Control, HSCC, HSCC 2017, pp. 29–34 (2017)

35. Duggirala, P.S., Mitra, S., Viswanathan, M., Potok, M.: C2E2: a verification tool for stateflow models. In: Baier, C., Tinelli, C. (eds.) TACAS 2015. LNCS, vol. 9035, pp. 68–82. Springer, Heidelberg (2015). doi:10.1007/978-3-662-46681-0_5

36. Dreossi, T., Dang, T., Donzé, A., Kapinski, J., Jin, X., Deshmukh, J.V.: Efficient guiding strategies for testing of temporal properties of hybrid systems. In: Havelund, K., Holzmann, G., Joshi, R. (eds.) NFM 2015. LNCS, vol. 9058, pp. 127–142. Springer, Cham (2015). doi:10.1007/978-3-319-17524-9_10

37. Annpureddy, Y., Liu, C., Fainekos, G., Sankaranarayanan, S.: S-TaLiRo: a tool for temporal logic falsification for hybrid systems. In: Abdulla, P.A., Leino, K.R.M. (eds.) TACAS 2011. LNCS, vol. 6605, pp. 254–257. Springer, Heidelberg (2011). doi:10.1007/978-3-642-19835-9_21

38. Havelund, K., Roşu, G.: Synthesizing monitors for safety properties. In: Katoen, J.-P., Stevens, P. (eds.) TACAS 2002. LNCS, vol. 2280, pp. 342–356. Springer, Heidelberg (2002). doi:10.1007/3-540-46002-0_24

39. Stoller, S.D., Bartocci, E., Seyster, J., Grosu, R., Havelund, K., Smolka, S.A., Zadok, E.: Runtime verification with state estimation. In: Khurshid, S., Sen, K. (eds.) RV 2011. LNCS, vol. 7186, pp. 193–207. Springer, Heidelberg (2012). doi:10.1007/978-3-642-29860-8_15

40. Bartocci, E., Grosu, R., Karmarkar, A., Smolka, S.A., Stoller, S.D., Zadok, E., Seyster, J.: Adaptive runtime verification. In: Qadeer, S., Tasiran, S. (eds.) RV 2012. LNCS, vol. 7687, pp. 168–182. Springer, Heidelberg (2013). doi:10.1007/978-3-642-35632-2_18

41. Gat, E., Slack, M.G., Miller, D.P., Firby, R.J.: Path planning and execution monitoring for a planetary rover. In: Robotics and Automation, pp. 20–25. IEEE (1990)

42. Pettersson, O.: Execution monitoring in robotics: a survey. Robot. Auton. Syst. 53(2), 73–88 (2005)

43. Lotz, A., Steck, A., Schlegel, C.: Runtime monitoring of robotics software components: increasing robustness of service robotic systems. In: 2011 15th International Conference on Advanced Robotics (ICAR), pp. 285–290. IEEE (2011)

44. Lee, I., Ben-Abdallah, H., Kannan, S., Kim, M., Sokolsky, O., Viswanathan, M.: A monitoring and checking framework for run-time correctness assurance (1998)

Monitoring Hyperproperties

Bernd Finkbeiner, Christopher Hahn[(⊠)], Marvin Stenger,
and Leander Tentrup

Reactive Systems Group, Saarland University, Saarbrücken, Germany
{finkbeiner,hahn,stenger,tentrup}@react.uni-saarland.de

Abstract. We investigate the runtime verification problem of hyper-properties, such as non-interference and observational determinism, given as formulas of the temporal logic HyperLTL. HyperLTL extends linear-time temporal logic (LTL) with trace quantifiers and trace variables. We show that deciding whether a HyperLTL formula is monitorable is PSPACE-complete. For monitorable specifications, we present an efficient monitoring approach. As hyperproperties relate multiple computation traces with each other, it is necessary to store previously seen traces, and to relate new traces to the traces seen so far. If done naively, this causes the monitor to become slower and slower, before it inevitably runs out of memory. In this paper, we present techniques that reduce the set of traces that new traces must be compared against to a minimal subset. Additionally, we exploit properties of specifications such as reflexivity, symmetry, and transitivity, to reduce the number of comparisons. We show that this leads to much more scalable monitoring with, in particular, significantly lower memory consumption.

1 Introduction

Hyperproperties [10] generalize trace properties in that they not only check the correctness of individual traces, but can also relate multiple computation traces to each other. This is needed, for example, to express information flow security policies like the requirement that the system behavior appears to be deterministic, i.e., independent of certain secrets, to an external observer. Monitoring hyperproperties is difficult, because it is no longer possible to analyze traces in isolation: a violation of a hyperproperty in general involves a set of traces, not just a single trace. A naive approach would be to simply store all traces seen so far. This would create two problems: a memory problem, because the needed memory grows with the number of traces observed by the monitor, and a time problem, because one needs to relate every newly observed trace against the growing set of stored traces.

This work was partially supported by the German Research Foundation (DFG) under the project SpAGAT (grant no. FI 936/2-1) in the priority program "Reliably Secure Software Systems – RS3" and as part of the Collaborative Research Center "Methods and Tools for Understanding and Controlling Privacy" (SFB 1223).

© Springer International Publishing AG 2017
S. Lahiri and G. Reger (Eds.): RV 2017, LNCS 10548, pp. 190–207, 2017.
DOI: 10.1007/978-3-319-67531-2_12

There are hyperproperties where this effect cannot be avoided. An example is the hyperproperty with two atomic propositions p and q, where any pair of traces that agree on their p labeling must also agree on their q labeling. Clearly, for every p labeling seen so far, we must also store the corresponding q labeling. In practice, however, it is often possible to greatly simplify the monitoring. Consider, for example, the hyperproperty that states that all traces have the same q labeling (independently of the p labeling). In the temporal logic HyperLTL [9], this property is specified as the formula $\forall \pi. \forall \pi'. \Box (p_\pi \leftrightarrow p_{\pi'})$. The naive approach would store all traces seen so far, and thus require $O(n)$ memory after n traces. A new trace would be compared against every stored trace twice, once as π and once as π', resulting in a $O(2n)$ running time for each new trace. Obviously, however, it is sufficient in this example to store the first trace, and compare all further incoming traces against this reference. The required memory is thus, in fact, constant in the number of traces. A further observation is that the specification is symmetric in π and π'. Hence, a single comparison suffices.

In this paper, we present a monitoring approach for hyperproperties that reduces the set of traces that new traces must be compared against to a minimal subset. Our approach comes with a strong correctness guarantee: our monitor produces the same verdict as a naive monitor that would store all traces and, additionally, we keep a sufficient set of traces to always provide an actually observed witness for the monitoring verdict. Our monitoring thus delivers a result that is equally informative as the naive solution, but is computed faster and with less memory.

We introduce two analysis techniques: *Trace analysis* reduces the stored set of traces to a minimum, thus minimizing the required memory. *Specification analysis* identifies symmetry, transitivity, and reflexivity in the specification, in order to reduce the algorithmic workload that needs to be carried out on the stored traces.

Trace Analysis. As an example for a system where confidentiality and information flow is of outstanding importance for the intended operation, we consider a conference management system. There are a number of confidentiality properties that such a system should satisfy, like *"The final decision of the program committee remains secret until the notification"* and *"All intermediate decisions of the program committee are never revealed to the author"*. We want to focus on important hyperproperties of interest beyond confidentiality, like the property that no paper submission is lost or delayed. Informally, one formulation of this property is *"A paper submission is immediately visible for every program committee member"*. More formally, this property relates pairs of traces, one belonging to an author and one belonging to a program committee member. We assume this separation is indicated by a proposition pc that is either disabled or enabled in the first component of those traces. Further propositions in our example are the proposition s, denoting that a paper has been submitted, and v denoting that the paper is visible.

Given a set of traces T, we can verify that the property holds by checking every pair of traces $(t, t') \in T \times T$ with $pc \notin t[0]$ and $pc \in t'[0]$ that $s \in t[i]$ implies $v \in t'[i+1]$ for every $i \geq 0$. When T satisfies the property, $T \cup \{t^*\}$, where t^* is a new trace, amounts to checking new pairs (t^*, t) and (t, t^*) for $t \in T$. This, however, leads to an increasing size of T and thereby to an increased number of checks: the monitoring problem becomes inevitable costlier over time. To circumvent this, we present a method that keeps the set of traces *minimal* with respect to the underlying property. When monitoring hyperproperties, traces may pose *requirements* on future traces. The core idea of our approach is to characterize traces that pose strictly stronger requirements on future traces than others. In this case, the traces with the weaker requirements can be safely discarded. As an example, consider the following set of traces

$$\boxed{\{s\}}\boxed{\{\}}\boxed{\{\}}\boxed{\{\}}\boxed{\{\}} \quad \textit{an author immediately submits a paper} \tag{1}$$

$$\boxed{\{\}}\boxed{\{s\}}\boxed{\{\}}\boxed{\{\}}\boxed{\{\}} \quad \textit{an author submits a paper after one time unit} \tag{2}$$

$$\boxed{\{\}}\boxed{\{s\}}\boxed{\{s\}}\boxed{\{\}}\boxed{\{\}} \quad \textit{an author submits two papers} \tag{3}$$

A satisfying PC trace would be $\{pc\}\{v\}\{v\}\{v\}\emptyset$ as there are author traces with paper submissions at time step 0, 1, and 2. For checking our property, one can safely discard trace 2 as it poses no more requirements than trace 3. We say that trace 3 dominates trace 2. We show that, given a property in the temporal logic HyperLTL, we can automatically reduce trace sets to be minimal with respect to this dominance. On relevant and more complex information flow properties, this reduces the memory consumption dramatically.

Specification Analysis. For expressing hyperproperties, we use the recently introduced temporal logic HyperLTL [9], which extends linear-time temporal logic (LTL) [22] with explicit trace quantification. We construct a monitor template, containing trace variables, from the HyperLTL formula. We initialize this monitor with explicit traces resulting in a family of monitors checking the relation, defined by the hyperproperty, between the traces. Our specification analysis technique allows us to reduce the number of monitors in order to detect violation or satisfaction of a given HyperLTL formula. We use the decision procedure for the satisfiability problem of HyperLTL [15] to check whether or not a universally quantified HyperLTL formula is symmetric, transitive, or reflexive. If a hyperproperty is *symmetric*, then we can omit every symmetric monitor, thus, performing only half of the language membership tests. A canonical example for a symmetric HyperLTL formula is $ObsDet := \forall \pi. \forall \pi'. (O_\pi = O_{\pi'}) \mathcal{W} (I_\pi \neq I_{\pi'})$, a variant of observational determinism [21,24,30]. Symmetry is particular interesting, since many information flow policies have this property. If a hyperproperty is *transitive*, then we can omit every, except for one, monitor, since we can check every incoming trace against any reference trace. One example for a transitive HyperLTL formula is equality $EQ := \forall \pi. \forall \pi'. \square (a_\pi \leftrightarrow a_{\pi'})$. If a hyperproperty is *reflexive*, then we can omit the monitor where every trace variable is initialized with the same trace. For example, both hyperproperties above are reflexive.

Related Work. The temporal logic HyperLTL was introduced to model check security properties of reactive systems [9,17]. For one of its predecessors, SecLTL [13], there has been a proposal for a white box monitoring approach [14] based on alternating automata. The problem of monitoring HyperLTL has been considered before [1,7]. Agrawal and Bonakdarpour [1] gave a syntactic characterization of monitorable HyperLTL formulas and a monitoring algorithm based on Petri nets. In subsequent work, a constraint based approach has been proposed [7]. Like our monitoring algorithm, they do not have access to the implementation (black box), but in contrast to our work, they do not provide witnessing traces for a monitor verdict. For certain information flow policies, like non-interference and some extensions, dynamic enforcement mechanisms have been proposed. Techniques for the enforcement of information flow policies include tracking dependencies at the hardware level [27], language-based monitors [2,3,5,25,29], and abstraction-based dependency tracking [8,18,19]. Secure multi-execution [12] is a technique that can enforce non-interference by executing a program multiple times in different security levels. To enforce non-interference, the inputs are replaced by default values whenever a program tries to read from a higher security level.

2 Monitorability of HyperLTL

Let AP be a finite set of atomic propositions and let $\Sigma = 2^{\text{AP}}$ be the corresponding finite *alphabet*. A finite (infinite) trace is a finite (infinite) sequence over Σ. We denote the concatenation of a finite trace $u \in \Sigma^*$ and a finite or infinite trace $v \in \Sigma^* \cup \Sigma^\omega$ by uv and write $u \preceq v$ if u is a prefix of v. Further, we lift the prefix operator to sets of traces, i.e., $U \preceq V := \forall u \in U. \exists v \in V. u \preceq v$ for $U \subseteq \Sigma^*$ and $V \subseteq \Sigma^* \cup \Sigma^\omega$. We denote the powerset of a set A by $\mathcal{P}(A)$ and define $\mathcal{P}^*(A)$ to be the set of all finite subsets of A.

HyperLTL. HyperLTL [9] is a temporal logic for specifying hyperproperties. It extends LTL [22] by quantification over trace variables π and a method to link atomic propositions to specific traces. The set of trace variables is $\mathcal{V}$. Formulas in HyperLTL are given by the grammar

$$\varphi ::= \forall \pi. \varphi \mid \exists \pi. \varphi \mid \psi \text{ , and}$$
$$\psi ::= a_\pi \mid \neg \psi \mid \psi \vee \psi \mid \bigcirc \psi \mid \psi \, \mathcal{U} \, \psi \text{ ,}$$

where $a \in \text{AP}$ and $\pi \in \mathcal{V}$. We call a HyperLTL formula an LTL formula if it is quantifier free. The semantics is given by the satisfaction relation $\vDash_P$ over a set of traces $T \subseteq \Sigma^\omega$. We define an assignment $\Pi : \mathcal{V} \to \Sigma^\omega$ that maps trace variables to traces. $\Pi[i, \infty]$ denotes the trace assignment that is equal to $\Pi(\pi)[i, \infty]$ for all π.

$$\Pi \vDash_T a_\pi \qquad \text{if } a \in \Pi(\pi)[0]$$
$$\Pi \vDash_T \neg\varphi \qquad \text{if } \Pi \nvDash_T \varphi$$
$$\Pi \vDash_T \varphi \vee \psi \quad \text{if } \Pi \vDash_T \varphi \text{ or } \Pi \vDash_T \psi$$
$$\Pi \vDash_T \bigcirc\varphi \qquad \text{if } \Pi[1,\infty] \vDash_T \varphi$$
$$\Pi \vDash_T \varphi \,\mathcal{U}\, \psi \quad \text{if } \exists i \geq 0.\, \Pi[i,\infty] \vDash_T \psi \wedge \forall 0 \leq j < i.\, \Pi[j,\infty] \vDash_T \varphi$$
$$\Pi \vDash_T \exists\pi.\,\varphi \quad \text{if there is some } t \in T \text{ such that } \Pi[\pi \mapsto t] \vDash_T \varphi$$

We write $T \vDash \varphi$ for $\{\} \vDash_T \varphi$ where $\{\}$ denotes the empty assignment. The language of a HyperLTL formula φ, denoted by $\mathcal{L}(\varphi)$, is the set $\{T \subseteq \Sigma^\omega \mid T \vDash \varphi\}$. Let φ be a HyperLTL formula with trace variables $\mathcal{V} = \{\pi_1, \ldots, \pi_k\}$ over alphabet Σ. We define $\Sigma_\mathcal{V}$ to be the alphabet where p_π is interpreted as an atomic proposition for every $p \in \text{AP}$ and $\pi \in \mathcal{V}$. We denote by $\vDash_{\text{LTL}}$ the LTL satisfaction relation over $\Sigma_\mathcal{V}$. We define the π-projection, denoted by $\#_\pi(s)$, for a given $s \subseteq \Sigma_\mathcal{V}$ and $\pi \in \mathcal{V}$, as the set of all $p_\pi \in s$.

Lemma 1. *Let ψ be an LTL formula over trace variables $\mathcal{V}$. There is a trace assignment A such that $A \vDash_\emptyset \psi$ if, and only if, ψ is satisfiable under LTL semantics over atomic propositions $\Sigma_\mathcal{V}$. The models can be translated effectively.*

Monitorability. For the remainder of this section, we develop the notion of monitorability for hyperproperties and show that deciding whether a HyperLTL formula is monitorable is PSPACE-complete, i.e., no harder than the corresponding problem for LTL. This result extends earlier characterizations based on restricted syntactic fragments of HyperLTL [1].

For trace languages, monitorability is the property whether language containment can be decided by finite prefixes [23]. Given a trace language $L \subseteq \Sigma^\omega$, the set of *good* and *bad* prefixes is $good(L) := \{u \in \Sigma^* \mid \forall v \in \Sigma^\omega.\, uv \in L\}$ and $bad(L) := \{u \in \Sigma^* \mid \forall v \in \Sigma^\omega.\, uv \notin L\}$, respectively. L is *monitorable* if $\forall u \in \Sigma^*.\, \exists v \in \Sigma^*.\, uv \in good(L) \vee uv \in bad(L)$. The decision problem, i.e., given an LTL formula φ, decide whether φ is monitorable, is PSPACE-complete [4].

A *hyperproperty* H is a set of trace properties, i.e., $H \subseteq \mathcal{P}(\Sigma^\omega)$. Analogous to the previous definition, we define monitorability for hyperproperties. Given $H \subseteq \mathcal{P}(\Sigma^\omega)$. The set of *good* and *bad prefix traces* is $good(H) := \{U \in \mathcal{P}^*(\Sigma^*) \mid \forall V \in \mathcal{P}(\Sigma^\omega).\, U \preceq V \Rightarrow V \in H\}$ and $bad(H) := \{U \in \mathcal{P}^*(\Sigma^*) \mid \forall V \in \mathcal{P}(\Sigma^\omega).\, U \preceq V \Rightarrow V \notin H\}$, respectively. H is *monitorable* if

$$\forall U \in \mathcal{P}^*(\Sigma^*).\, \exists V \in \mathcal{P}^*(\Sigma^*).\, U \preceq V \Rightarrow V \in good(H) \vee V \in bad(H) \ .$$

We present a method to decide whether an alternation-free HyperLTL formula is monitorable.

Lemma 2. *Given a HyperLTL formula $\varphi = \forall\pi_1 \ldots \forall\pi_k.\,\psi$, where ψ is an LTL formula. It holds that $good(\mathcal{L}(\varphi)) = \emptyset$ unless $\psi \equiv true$.*

Theorem 1. *Given a HyperLTL formula $\varphi = \forall\pi_1 \ldots \forall\pi_k.\,\psi$, where $\psi \not\equiv true$ is an LTL formula. φ is monitorable if, and only if, $\forall u \in \Sigma_\mathcal{V}^*.\, \exists v \in \Sigma_\mathcal{V}^*.\, uv \in bad(\mathcal{L}(\psi))$.*

Proof. Assume $\forall u \in \Sigma_{\mathcal{V}}^*. \exists v \in \Sigma_{\mathcal{V}}^*. uv \in bad(\mathcal{L}(\psi))$ holds. Given an arbitrary prefix $U \in \mathcal{P}^*(\Sigma^*)$. Pick an arbitrary mapping from U to $\Sigma_{\mathcal{V}}^*$ and call it u'. By assumption, there is a $v' \in \Sigma_{\mathcal{V}}^*$ such that $u'v' \in bad(\mathcal{L}(\psi))$. We use this v' to extend the corresponding traces in U resulting in $V \in \mathcal{P}^*(\Sigma^*)$. It follows that for all $W \in \mathcal{P}(\Sigma^\omega)$ with $V \preceq W$, $W \nvDash \varphi$, hence, $V \in bad(\mathcal{L}(\varphi))$.

Assume φ is monitorable, thus, $\forall U \in \mathcal{P}^*(\Sigma^*). \exists V \in \mathcal{P}^*(\Sigma^*). U \preceq V \Rightarrow V \in good(\mathcal{L}(\varphi)) \vee V \in bad(\mathcal{L}(\varphi))$. As the set of good prefixes $good(\mathcal{L}(\varphi))$ is empty by Lemma 2 we can simplify the formula to $\forall U \in \mathcal{P}^*(\Sigma^*). \exists V \in \mathcal{P}^*(\Sigma^*). U \preceq V \Rightarrow V \in bad(\mathcal{L}(\varphi))$. Given an arbitrary $u \in \Sigma_{\mathcal{V}}^*$, we translate it into the (canonical) U' and get a V' satisfying the conditions above. Let $v' \in \Sigma_{\mathcal{V}}^*$ be the finite trace constructed from the extensions of u in V' (not canonical, but all are bad prefixes since $V' \in bad(\mathcal{L}(\varphi))$). By assumption, $u'v' \in bad(\mathcal{L}(\psi))$.   □

Corollary 1. *Given a HyperLTL formula $\varphi = \exists \pi_1 \ldots \exists \pi_k.\psi$, where ψ is an LTL formula. φ is monitorable if, and only if, $\forall u \in \Sigma_{\mathcal{V}}^*. \exists v \in \Sigma_{\mathcal{V}}^*. uv \in good(\mathcal{L}(\psi))$.*

Theorem 2. *Given an alternation-free HyperLTL formula φ. Deciding whether φ is monitorable is PSPACE-complete.*

Proof. We consider the case that $\varphi = \forall \pi_1 \ldots \forall \pi_2. \psi$, the case for existentially quantified formulas is dual. We apply the characterization from Theorem 1. First, we have to check validity of ψ which can be done in polynomial space [26]. Next, we have to determine whether $\forall u \in \Sigma_{\mathcal{V}}^*. \exists v \in \Sigma_{\mathcal{V}}^*. uv \in bad(\mathcal{L}(\psi))$. We use a slight modification of the PSPACE algorithm given by Bauer [4]. Hardness follows as the problem is already PSPACE-hard for LTL.   □

3   Monitoring HyperLTL

There are many obstacles to overcome in monitoring hyperproperties (see [6] for an overview of the challenges), such that classic monitoring approaches of trace properties need to be carefully adjusted. In this section, we define a finite trace semantics for HyperLTL and present our automata-based monitoring approach.

Finite Trace Semantics. We define a finite trace semantics for HyperLTL based on the finite trace semantics of LTL [20]. In the following, when using $\mathcal{L}(\varphi)$ we refer to the finite trace semantics of a HyperLTL formula φ. Let t be a finite trace, ϵ denotes the empty trace, and $|t|$ denotes the length of a trace. Since we are in a finite trace setting, $t[i, \ldots]$ denotes the subsequence from position i to position $|t| - 1$. Let $\Pi_{fin} : \mathcal{V} \to \Sigma^*$ be a partial function mapping trace variables to finite traces. We define $\epsilon[0]$ as the empty set. $\Pi_{fin}[i, \ldots]$ denotes the trace assignment that is equal to $\Pi_{fin}(\pi)[i, \ldots]$ for all π. We define a subsequence of t as follows.

$$t[i, j] = \begin{cases} \epsilon & \text{if } i \geq |t| \\ t[i, min(j, |t| - 1)], & \text{otherwise} \end{cases}$$

$$\Pi_{fin} \vDash_T a_\pi \quad \text{if } a \in \Pi_{fin}(\pi)[0]$$
$$\Pi_{fin} \vDash_T \neg\varphi \quad \text{if } \Pi_{fin} \nvDash_T \varphi$$
$$\Pi_{fin} \vDash_T \varphi \vee \psi \quad \text{if } \Pi_{fin} \vDash_T \varphi \text{ or } \Pi_{fin} \vDash_T \psi$$
$$\Pi_{fin} \vDash_T \bigcirc\varphi \quad \text{if } \Pi_{fin}[1,\ldots] \vDash_T \varphi$$
$$\Pi_{fin} \vDash_T \varphi\,\mathcal{U}\,\psi \quad \text{if } \exists i \geq 0.\, \Pi_{fin}[i,\ldots] \vDash_T \psi \wedge \forall 0 \leq j < i.\, \Pi_{fin}[j,\ldots] \vDash_T \varphi$$
$$\Pi_{fin} \vDash_T \exists\pi.\varphi \quad \text{if there is some } t \in T \text{ such that } \Pi_{fin}[\pi \mapsto t] \vDash_T \varphi$$

Monitoring Algorithm. In this subsection, we describe our automata-based monitoring algorithm for HyperLTL. We employ standard techniques for building LTL monitoring automata and use this to instantiate this monitor by the traces as specified by the HyperLTL formula.

Let AP be a set of atomic propositions and $\mathcal{V} = \{\pi_1,\ldots,\pi_n\}$ a set of trace variables. A deterministic monitor template $\mathcal{M} = (\Sigma, Q, \delta, q_0)$ is a four tuple of a finite alphabet $\Sigma = 2^{\mathrm{AP}\times\mathcal{V}}$, a non-empty set of states Q, a partial transition function $\delta : Q \times \Sigma \to Q$, and a designated initial state $q_0 \in Q$. The automata runs in parallel over traces $(2^{\mathrm{AP}})^*$, thus we define a run with respect to a n-ary tuple $N \in ((2^{\mathrm{AP}})^*)^n$ of finite traces. A run of N is a sequence of states $q_0 q_1 \cdots q_m \in Q^*$, where m is the length of the smallest trace in N, starting in the initial state q_0 such that for all i with $0 \leq i < m$ it holds that

$$\delta\left(q_i, \bigcup_{j=1}^{n}\ \bigcup_{a\in N(j)(i)} \{(a, \pi_j)\}\right) = q_{i+1}\ .$$

A tuple N is accepted, if there is a run on $\mathcal{M}$. For LTL, such a deterministic monitor can be constructed in doubly-exponential time in the size of the formula [11,28].

Example 1. We consider again the conference management example from the introduction. We distinguish two types of traces, *author traces* and *program committee member traces*, where the latter starts with proposition pc. Based on this traces, we want to verify that no paper submission is lost, i.e., that every submission (proposition s) is visible (proposition v) to every program committee member in the following step. When comparing two PC traces, we require that they agree on proposition v. The monitor template for the following HyperLTL formalization is depicted in Fig. 1.

$$\forall\pi.\forall\pi'.\ \big((\neg pc_\pi \wedge pc_{\pi'}) \to \bigcirc\square(s_\pi \to \bigcirc v_{\pi'})\big) \wedge \big((pc_\pi \wedge pc_{\pi'}) \to \bigcirc\square(v_\pi \leftrightarrow v'_\pi)\big) \quad (4)$$

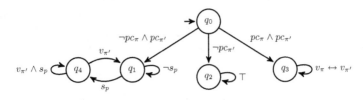

Fig. 1. Visualization of a monitor template corresponding to formula given in Eq. 4. We use a symbolic representation of the transition function δ.

The offline and online algorithms for monitoring HyperLTL formulas are presented in Fig. 2. The *offline* algorithm takes a HyperLTL formula φ and a set of traces T as input. After building the deterministic monitoring automaton $\mathcal{M}_\varphi$, it checks every n-ary tuple $N \in T^n$. If some trace tuple N is not accepted by $\mathcal{M}_\varphi$, then this path assignment violates the formula φ. The *online* algorithm is similar, but proceeds with the pace of the incoming stream, which has an indicator when a new trace starts. We have a variable S that maps tuples of traces to states of the deterministic monitor. Whenever a trace progresses, we update the states in S according to the transition function δ. If on this progress, there is a violation, we return the corresponding tuple of traces as a witness. When a new trace t starts, only new tuples are considered for S, that are tuples $N \in (T \cup \{t\})^n$ containing the new trace t, i.e., $N \notin T^n$.

input : $\forall^n$ HyperLTL formula φ
    set of traces T
output: satisfied or n-ary tuple
    witnessing violation

$\mathcal{M}_\varphi = \texttt{build\_template}(\varphi)$;

for *each tuple $N \in T^n$* **do**
  if $\mathcal{M}_\varphi$ *accepts* N **then**
  | proceed;
  else
  | return N;
  end
end
return satisfied;

Algorithm 1: Offline Algorithm.

input : $\forall^n$ HyperLTL formula φ
output: satisfied or n-ary tuple
    witnessing violation

$\mathcal{M}_\varphi = (\Sigma, Q, \delta, q_0) = \texttt{build\_template}(\varphi)$;
$S : T^n \to Q$;
$T := \emptyset$;
$t := \epsilon$;

while $p \leftarrow$ *new element* **do**
  if p *is new trace* **then**
  | $T \cup \{t\}$;
  | $t := \epsilon$;
  | $S := \{q_0 \mid$ for new n-tuple$\}$;
  else
  | $t := t\, p$;
  | progress every state in S according to δ;
  | **if** *violation* **then**
  | | return witnessing tuple;
  | **end**
  end
end
return satisfied;

Algorithm 2: Online Algorithm.

Fig. 2. Evaluation algorithms for monitoring $\forall^n$ HyperLTL formulas.

In contrast to previous approaches, our algorithm returns a witness for violation. This highly desired property comes with a price. In constructed worst case scenarios, we have to remember every system trace in order to return an explicit witness. However, it turns out that practical hyperproperties satisfy certain properties such that the majority of traces can be pruned during the monitoring process.

4   Minimizing Trace Storage

The main obstacle in monitoring hyperproperties is the potentially unbounded space consumption. In the following, we present two analysis phases of our algorithm. The first phase is a specification analysis, which is a preprocessing step that analyzes the HyperLTL formula under consideration. We use the recently introduced satisfiability solver for hyperproperties EAHyper [16] to detect whether a formula is (1) *symmetric*, i.e., we halve the number of instantiated monitors, (2) *transitive*, i.e., we reduce the number of instantiated monitors to two, or (3) *reflexive*, i.e., we can omit the self comparison of traces. The second analysis phase is applied during runtime. We analyze the incoming trace to detect whether or not this trace poses strictly more requirements on future traces, with respect to a given HyperLTL formula.

4.1   Specification Analysis

Symmetry. Symmetry is particular interesting since many information flow policies satisfy this property. Consider, for example, observational determinism $ObsDet := \forall \pi. \forall \pi'. (O_\pi = O_{\pi'}) \, W \, (I_\pi \neq I_{\pi'})$. We detect symmetry by translating this formula to a formula $ObsDet_{symm}$ that is unsatisfiable if there exists no set of traces for which every trace pair violates the symmetry condition:

$$ObsDet_{symm} := \exists \pi. \exists \pi'. \left((O_\pi = O_{\pi'}) \, W \, (I_\pi \neq I_{\pi'}) \right) \nleftrightarrow \left((O'_\pi = O_\pi) \, W \, (I'_\pi \neq I_\pi) \right)$$

This is a sufficient condition for the invariance of $ObsDet$ under π and π', which we define in the following, and, therefore, $ObsDet$ is symmetric.

Definition 1. *Given a HyperLTL formula $\varphi = \forall \pi_1 \ldots \forall \pi_n. \psi$, where ψ is an LTL formula over trace variables $\{\pi_1, \ldots, \pi_n\}$. We say φ is invariant under trace variable permutation $\sigma : \mathcal{V} \to \mathcal{V}$, if for any set of traces $T \subseteq \Sigma^\omega$ and any assignment $\Pi : \mathcal{V} \to T$, $\Pi \vDash_T \psi \Leftrightarrow (\Pi \circ \sigma) \vDash_T \psi$. We say φ is symmetric, if it is invariant under every trace variable permutation in $\mathcal{V} \to \mathcal{V}$.*

We generalize the previous example to formulas with more than two universal quantifiers. We use the fact, that the symmetric group for a finite set $\mathcal{V}$ of n trace variables is generated by the two permutations $(\pi_1 \; \pi_2)$ and $(\pi_1 \; \pi_2 \; \cdots \; \pi_{n-1} \; \pi_n)$. If the HyperLTL-SAT solver determines that the input formula is invariant under these two permutations, then the formula is invariant under every trace variable permutation and thus symmetric.

Theorem 3. *Given a HyperLTL formula $\varphi = \forall \pi_1 \ldots \forall \pi_n. \psi$, where ψ is an LTL formula over trace variables $\{\pi_1, \ldots, \pi_n\}$. φ is symmetric if and only if $\varphi_{symm} = \exists \pi_1 \ldots \exists \pi_n. (\psi(\pi_1, \pi_2, \ldots, \pi_{n-1}, \pi_n) \nleftrightarrow \psi(\pi_2, \pi_1, \ldots, \pi_{n-1}, \pi_n)) \lor (\psi(\pi_1, \pi_2, \ldots, \pi_{n-1}, \pi_n) \nleftrightarrow \psi(\pi_2, \pi_3, \ldots, \pi_n, \pi_1))$ is unsatisfiable.*

Transitivity. While symmetric HyperLTL formulas allow us to prune half of the monitor instances, transitivity of a HyperLTL formula has an even larger impact on the required memory. Observational Determinism, considered above, is not transitive. However, equality, i.e., $EQ := \forall \pi. \forall \pi'. \Box(a_\pi \leftrightarrow a_{\pi'})$, for example, is transitive and symmetric and allow us to reduce the number of monitor instances to one, since we can check equality against any reference trace.

Definition 2. *Given a HyperLTL formula* $\varphi = \forall \pi_1. \forall \pi_2. \psi$, *where* ψ *is an LTL formula over trace variables* $\{\pi_1, \pi_2\}$. *Let* $T = \{t_1, t_2, t_3\} \in \Sigma^\omega$ *be three-elemented set of traces. We define the assignment* $\Pi_{i,j} : \mathcal{V} \to \Sigma^\omega$ *by* $\Pi_{i,j} := \{\pi_1 \mapsto t_i, \pi_2 \mapsto t_j\}$. *We say* φ *is transitive, if* T *was chosen arbitrary and* $(\Pi_{1,2} \vDash_T \psi) \wedge (\Pi_{2,3} \vDash_T \psi) \Rightarrow \Pi_{1,3} \vDash_T \psi$.

Theorem 4. *Given a HyperLTL formula* $\varphi = \forall \pi_1. \forall \pi_2. \psi$, *where* ψ *is an LTL formula over trace variables* $\{\pi_1, \pi_2\}$. φ *is transitive if and only if* $\varphi_{trans} = \exists \pi_1 \exists \pi_2 \exists \pi_3. (\psi(\pi_1, \pi_2) \wedge \psi(\pi_2, \pi_3)) \nrightarrow \psi(\pi_1, \pi_3)$ *is unsatisfiable.*

Reflexivity. Lastly, we introduce a method to check whether a formula is reflexive, which enables us to omit the composition of a trace with itself in the monitoring algorithm. Both HyperLTL formulas considered in this section, *ObsDet* and *EQ*, are reflexive.

Definition 3. *Given a HyperLTL formula* $\varphi = \forall \pi_1 \dots \forall \pi_n. \psi$, *where* ψ *is an LTL formula over trace variables* $\{\pi_1, \dots, \pi_n\}$. *We say* φ *is reflexive, if for any trace* $t \in \Sigma^\omega$ *and the corresponding assignment* $\Pi : \mathcal{V} \to \{t\}$, $\Pi \vDash_{\{t\}} \psi$.

Theorem 5. *Given a HyperLTL formula* $\varphi = \forall \pi_1 \dots \forall \pi_n. \psi$, *where* ψ *is an LTL formula over trace variables* $\{\pi_1, \dots, \pi_n\}$. φ *is reflexive if and only if* $\varphi_{refl} = \exists \pi. \neg \psi(\pi, \pi, \dots, \pi)$ *is unsatisfiable.*

4.2   Trace Analysis

In the previous subsection, we described a preprocessing step to reduce the number of monitor instantiations. The main idea of the trace analysis, considered in the following, is to check whether a trace contains new requirements on the system under consideration. If this is not the case, then this trace will not be stored by our monitoring algorithm. We denote $\mathcal{M}_\varphi$ as the monitor template of a $\forall^*$ HyperLTL formula φ.

Definition 4. *Given a HyperLTL formula* φ, *a trace set* T *and an arbitrary* $t \in TR$, *we say that* t *is* (T, φ)-*redundant if* T *is a model of* φ *if and only if* $T \cup \{t\}$ *is a model of* φ *as well. Formally denoted as follows.*

$$\forall T' \supseteq T. \ T' \in \mathcal{L}(\varphi) \Leftrightarrow T' \cup \{t\} \in \mathcal{L}(\varphi).$$

Example 2. Consider, again, our example hyperproperty for a conference management system. *"A user submission is immediately visible for every program committee member and every program committee member observes the same."* We formalized this property as a $\forall^2$ HyperLTL formula in Eq. 4. Assume our algorithm observes the following three traces of length five.

$$\boxed{\{\} \;\; \{s\} \;\; \{\} \;\; \{\} \;\; \{\}} \qquad \textit{an author submits a paper} \qquad\qquad\qquad (5)$$

$$\boxed{\{\} \;\; \{\} \;\; \{s\} \;\; \{\} \;\; \{\}} \qquad \textit{an author submits a paper one time unit later} \quad (6)$$

$$\boxed{\{\} \;\; \{\} \;\; \{s\} \;\; \{s\} \;\; \{\}} \qquad \textit{an author submits two papers} \qquad\qquad\qquad (7)$$

Trace 6 contains, with respect to φ above, no more information than trace 7. We say that trace 7 dominates trace 6 and, hence, trace 6 may be pruned from the set of traces that the algorithm has to store. If we consider a PC member trace, we encounter the following situation.

$$\boxed{\{\} \;\; \{s\} \;\; \{\} \;\; \{\} \;\; \{\}} \qquad \textit{an author submits a paper} \qquad\qquad\qquad (8)$$

$$\boxed{\{\} \;\; \{\} \;\; \{s\} \;\; \{s\} \;\; \{\}} \qquad \textit{an author submits two papers} \qquad\qquad\qquad (9)$$

$$\boxed{\{\} \;\; \{pc\} \;\; \{v\} \;\; \{v\} \;\; \{v\}} \qquad \textit{a PC member observes three submissions} \qquad (10)$$

Our algorithm will detect no violation, since the program committee member sees all three papers. Intuitively, one might expect that no more traces can be pruned from this trace set. However, in fact, trace 10 dominates trace 8 and trace 9, since the information that three papers have been submitted is preserved in trace 10. Hence, it suffices to remember the last trace to detect, for example, the following violations.

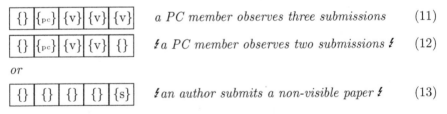

$$\boxed{\{\} \;\; \{pc\} \;\; \{v\} \;\; \{v\} \;\; \{v\}} \qquad \textit{a PC member observes three submissions} \qquad (11)$$

$$\boxed{\{\} \;\; \{pc\} \;\; \{v\} \;\; \{v\} \;\; \{\}} \qquad \lightning\textit{a PC member observes two submissions}\lightning \quad (12)$$

or

$$\boxed{\{\} \;\; \{\} \;\; \{\} \;\; \{\} \;\; \{s\}} \qquad \lightning\textit{an author submits a non-visible paper}\lightning \quad (13)$$

Note that none of the previous user traces, i.e., trace 5 to trace 9, are needed to detect a violation.

Definition 5. *Given $t, t' \in TR$, we say t dominates t' if t' is $(\{t\}, \varphi)$-redundant.*

The observations from Example 2 can be generalized to a language inclusion check (cf. Theorem 6), to determine whether a trace dominates another trace. For proving this, we first prove the following two lemmas. For the sake of simplicity, we consider $\forall^2$ HyperLTL formulas. The proofs can be generalized. We denote $\mathcal{M}_\varphi[t/\pi]$ as the monitor where trace variable π of the template Monitor $\mathcal{M}_\varphi$ is initialized with explicit trace t.

Lemma 3. *Let φ be a $\forall^2$ HyperLTL formula over trace variables $\{\pi_1, \pi_2\}$. Given an arbitrary trace set T and an arbitrary trace t, $T \cup \{t\}$ is a model of φ if and only if T is still accepted by the following two monitors: (1) only π_1 is initialized with t (2) only π_2 is initialized with t. Formally, the following equivalence holds.*

$$\forall T \subseteq TR, \forall t \in TR. T \cup \{t\} \in \mathcal{L}(\varphi) \Leftrightarrow T \subseteq \mathcal{L}(\mathcal{M}_\varphi[t/\pi_1]) \wedge T \subseteq \mathcal{L}(\mathcal{M}_\varphi[t/\pi_2])$$

Lemma 4. *Given a $\forall^2$ HyperLTL formula φ over trace variables $\mathcal{V} := \{\pi_1, \ldots, \pi_n\}$ and two traces $t, t' \in TR$, the following holds: t dominates t' if and only if*

$$\mathcal{L}(\mathcal{M}_\varphi[t/\pi_1]) \subseteq \mathcal{L}(\mathcal{M}_\varphi[t'/\pi_1]) \wedge \mathcal{L}(\mathcal{M}_\varphi[t/\pi_2]) \subseteq \mathcal{L}(\mathcal{M}_\varphi[t'/\pi_2])$$

Proof. Assume for the sake of contradiction that (a) t dominates t' and w.l.o.g. (b) $\mathcal{L}(\mathcal{M}_\varphi[t/\pi_1]) \nsubseteq \mathcal{L}(\mathcal{M}_\varphi[t'/\pi_1])$. Thus, by definition of subset, there exists a trace $\tilde{t}$ with $\tilde{t} \in \mathcal{L}(\mathcal{M}_\varphi[t/\pi_1])$ and $\tilde{t} \notin \mathcal{L}(\mathcal{M}_\varphi[t'/\pi_1])$. Hence, $\Pi = \{\pi_1 \mapsto t, \pi_2 \mapsto \tilde{t}\}$ is a valid trace assignment, whereas $\Pi' = \{\pi_1 \mapsto t', \pi_2 \mapsto \tilde{t}\}$ is not. On the other hand, from (a) the following holds by Definition 5: $\forall T'$ with $\{t\} \subseteq T'$ it holds that $T' \in \mathcal{L}(\varphi) \Leftrightarrow T' \cup \{t'\} \in \mathcal{L}(\varphi)$. We choose T' as $\{t, \tilde{t}\}$, which is a contradiction to the equivalence since we know from (a) that Π is a valid trace assignment, but Π' is not a valid trace assignment.

For the other direction, assume that $\mathcal{L}(\mathcal{M}_\varphi[t/\pi_1]) \subseteq \mathcal{L}(\mathcal{M}_\varphi[t'/\pi_1])$ and $\mathcal{L}(\mathcal{M}_\varphi[t/\pi_2]) \subseteq \mathcal{L}(\mathcal{M}_\varphi[t'/\pi_2])$. Let T' be arbitrary such that $\{t\} \subseteq T'$. We distinguish two cases:

- Case $T' \in \mathcal{L}(\varphi)$, then (a) $T' \subseteq \mathcal{L}(M_\varphi[t/\pi_1]) \subseteq \mathcal{L}(M_\varphi[t'/\pi_1])$ and (b) $T' \subseteq \mathcal{L}(M_\varphi[t/\pi_2]) \subseteq \mathcal{L}(M_\varphi[t'/\pi_2])$. By Lemma 3 and $T' \in \mathcal{L}(\varphi)$, it follows that $T' \cup \{t'\} \in \mathcal{L}(\varphi)$.
- Case $T' \notin \mathcal{L}(\varphi)$, then $T' \cup \{\hat{t}\} \notin \mathcal{L}(\varphi)$ for an arbitrary trace $\hat{t}$.

A generalization leads to the following theorem, which serves as the foundation of our trace storage minimization algorithm.

Theorem 6. *Given a $\forall^n$ HyperLTL formula φ over trace variables $\mathcal{V} := \{\pi_1, \ldots, \pi_n\}$ and two traces $t, t' \in TR$, the following holds: t dominates t' if and only if*

$$\bigwedge_{\pi \in \mathcal{V}} L(\mathcal{M}_\varphi[t/\pi]) \subseteq L(\mathcal{M}_\varphi[t'/\pi]) \ .$$

Corollary 2. *Given an $\exists^n$ HyperLTL formula φ over trace variables $\mathcal{V} := \{\pi_1, \ldots, \pi_n\}$ and two traces $t, t' \in TR$, the following holds: t dominates t' if and only if $\bigwedge_{\pi \in \mathcal{V}} \mathcal{L}(\mathcal{M}_\varphi[t'/\pi]) \subseteq \mathcal{L}(\mathcal{M}_\varphi[t/\pi])$.*

Theorem 7. *Algorithm 3 preserves the minimal trace set T, i.e., for all $t \in T$ it holds that t is not $(T \setminus \{t\}, \varphi)$-redundant.*

5   Monitoring Alternating HyperLTL Formulas

With the classic definition of monitorability (cf. Sect. 2), hardly any alternating HyperLTL formula is monitorable as their satisfaction cannot be characterized by a finite trace set, even for safety properties. Consider, for example, the formula $\varphi = \forall \pi. \exists \pi'. \Box(a_\pi \to b_{\pi'})$. Assume a finite set of traces T does not violate the formula. Then, one can construct a new trace t where $a \in t[i]$ and $b \notin t[i]$ for some position i, and for all traces $t' \in T$ it holds that $b \notin t'[i]$. Thus, the new trace set violates φ. Likewise, if there is a finite set of traces that violates φ, a sufficiently long trace containing only b's stops the violation.

If we fix a set of traces, we can check the satisfaction of an alternating HyperLTL formula with a modification of the offline monitoring algorithm presented earlier. This way, we can verify alternating hyperproperties after the execution of a system based on recorded traces. In our conference management system example, the property *"There was a submission for every paper that is visible for a program committee member."* is a hyperproperty that utilizes alternation and can be formalized as the $\forall \exists$HyperLTL formula

$$\forall \pi. \exists \pi'. pc_{\pi'} \wedge (\neg pc_\pi \to \bigcirc \Box(s_\pi \to \bigcirc v_{\pi'})) \ . \tag{14}$$

In the following, we present an extension to our offline algorithm for monitoring $\forall \exists$HyperLTL and $\exists \forall$HyperLTL formulas. Further, we show that the trace storage minimization technique is also applicable for alternating HyperLTL formulas, allowing to determine at runtime whether a trace needs to be stored or not.

We considered offline monitoring of universally quantified $\forall^n$HyperLTL in Sect. 3 by checking whether $\mathcal{M}_\varphi$ accepts N for every $N \in T^n$, given a trace set T and a HyperLTL formula φ. In contrast, an offline monitor for a $\forall^n \exists^m$HyperLTL and $\exists^m \forall^n$HyperLTL formula has to perform the checks

$$\bigwedge_{N \in T^n} \bigvee_{M \in T^m} \text{check if } \mathcal{M}_\varphi \text{ accepts } N \times M \ , \text{ and}$$

$$\bigvee_{M \in T^m} \bigwedge_{N \in T^n} \text{check if } \mathcal{M}_\varphi \text{ accepts } M \times N \ , \text{ respectively.}$$

We give a characterization of the trace dominance introduced in the last section for HyperLTL formulas with one alternation. These characterizations can be checked similarly to the algorithm depicted in Fig. 3.

Theorem 8. *Given a HyperLTL formula $\forall \pi. \exists \pi'. \psi$ two traces $t, t' \in TR$, the following holds: t dominates t' if and only if*

$$\mathcal{L}(\mathcal{M}_\varphi[t/\pi]) \subseteq \mathcal{L}(\mathcal{M}_\varphi[t'/\pi]) \text{ and } \mathcal{L}(\mathcal{M}_\varphi[t'/\pi']) \subseteq \mathcal{L}(\mathcal{M}_\varphi[t/\pi']) \ .$$

Corollary 3. *Given a HyperLTL formula $\exists \pi. \forall \pi'. \psi$ two traces $t, t' \in TR$, the following holds: t dominates t' if and only if*

$$\mathcal{L}(\mathcal{M}_\varphi[t'/\pi]) \subseteq \mathcal{L}(\mathcal{M}_\varphi[t/\pi]) \text{ and } \mathcal{L}(\mathcal{M}_\varphi[t/\pi']) \subseteq \mathcal{L}(\mathcal{M}_\varphi[t'/\pi']) \ .$$

input : $\forall^n$ HyperLTL formula φ,
  redundancy free set of traces T
  trace t
output: redundancy free set of traces $T_{min} \subseteq T \cup \{t\}$

$\mathcal{M}_\varphi = $ build_template(φ)

foreach $t' \in T$ **do**
  if $\bigwedge_{\pi \in \mathcal{V}} \mathcal{L}(\mathcal{M}_\varphi[t'/\pi]) \subseteq \mathcal{L}(\mathcal{M}_\varphi[t/\pi])$ **then**
    | return T
  end
end
foreach $t' \in T$ **do**
  if $\bigwedge_{\pi \in \mathcal{V}} \mathcal{L}(\mathcal{M}_\varphi[t/\pi]) \subseteq \mathcal{L}(\mathcal{M}_\varphi[t'/\pi])$ **then**
    | $T := T \setminus \{t'\}$
  end
end
return $T \cup \{t\}$

Fig. 3. Storage minimization algorithm.

Example 3. We show the effect of the dominance characterization on two example formulas. Consider the HyperLTL formula $\forall \pi. \exists \pi'. \Box(a_\pi \rightarrow b_{\pi'})$ and the traces $\{b\}\emptyset$, $\{b\}\{b\}$, $\{a\}\emptyset$, and $\{a\}\{a\}$. Trace $\{a\}\{a\}$ dominates trace $\{a\}\emptyset$ as instantiating π requires two consecutive b's for π' where $\{a\}\emptyset$ only requires a b at the first position (both traces do not contain b's, so instantiating π' leads to the same language). Similarly, one can verify that $\{b\}\{b\}$ dominates trace $\{b\}\emptyset$.
    Consider alternatively the formula $\exists \pi. \forall \pi'. \Box(a_\pi \rightarrow b_{\pi'})$. In this case, $\{a\}\emptyset$ dominates $\{a\}\{a\}$ and $\{b\}\emptyset$ dominates $\{b\}\{b\}$.

For our conference management example formula given in Eq. 14, a trace $\{pc\}\emptyset\{v\}$ dominates $\{pc\}\emptyset\emptyset$ and $\emptyset\{s\}\emptyset$ dominates $\emptyset\emptyset\emptyset$, but $\emptyset\{s\}\emptyset$ and $\{pc\}\emptyset\{v\}$ are incomparable with respect to the dominance relation.

6   Evaluation

In this section, we report on experimental results of the presented algorithm and the accompanying optimizations. Our results show that those optimizations are orthogonal, i.e., none of the techniques subsumes the other. For the specification analysis, we checked variations of observational determinism, quantitative non-interference [17], equality and our conference management example for symmetry, transitivity, and reflexivity. The results are depicted in Table 1. The specification analysis comes with low costs (every check was done in under a second), but with a high reward in terms of constructed monitor instances (see Fig. 5). For hyperproperties that do not satisfy one of the properties, e.g., our conference management example, our trace analysis will still dramatically reduce the memory consumption.
    For evaluating our trace analysis, we use a scalable, bounded variation of observational determinism: $\forall \pi. \forall \pi'. \Box_{<n}(I_\pi = I_{\pi'}) \rightarrow \Box_{<n+c}(O_\pi = O_{\pi'})$.

Table 1. Specification analysis for universally quantified hyperproperties.

		symm	trans	refl
ObsDet1	$\forall\pi.\forall\pi'.\,\Box(I_\pi = I_{\pi'}) \rightarrow \Box(O_\pi = O_{\pi'})$	✓	✗	✓
ObsDet2	$\forall\pi.\forall\pi'.\,(I_\pi = I_{\pi'}) \rightarrow \Box(O_\pi = O_{\pi'})$	✓	✗	✓
ObsDet3	$\forall\pi.\forall\pi'.(O_\pi = O'_\pi)\,W\,(I_\pi \neq I'_\pi)$	✓	✗	✓
QuantNoninf	$\forall\pi_0\ldots\forall\pi_c.\ \neg((\bigwedge_i I_{\pi_i} = I_{\pi_0}) \wedge \bigwedge_{i \neq j} O_{\pi_i} \neq O_{\pi_j})$	✓	✗	✓
EQ	$\forall\pi.\forall\pi'.\Box(a_\pi \leftrightarrow a_{\pi'})$	✓	✓	✓
ConfMan	$\forall\pi\forall\pi'.\,\big((\neg pc_\pi \wedge pc_{\pi'}) \rightarrow \bigcirc\Box(s_\pi \rightarrow \bigcirc v_{\pi'})\big)$ $\wedge\big((pc_\pi \wedge pc_{\pi'}) \rightarrow \bigcirc\Box(v_\pi \leftrightarrow v'_\pi)\big)$	✗	✗	✗

Figure 4 shows a family of plots for this benchmark class, where c is fixed to three. We randomly generated a set of 10^5 traces. The blue (dashed) line depicts the number of traces that need to be stored, the red (dotted) line the number of traces that violated the property, and the green (solid) line depicts the pruned traces. When *increasing the requirements* on the system, i.e., decreasing n, we prune the majority of incoming traces with our trace analysis techniques.

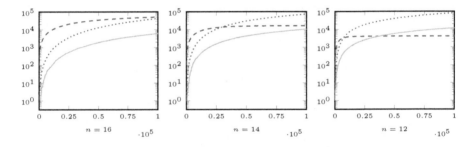

Fig. 4. Absolute numbers of violations in red (dotted), number of instances stored in blue (dashed), number of instances pruned in green (solid) for 10^5 randomly generated traces of length 100000. The y axis is scaled logarithmically. (Color figure online)

In Fig. 5 we compare the running time of the monitoring optimizations presented in this paper to the naive approach. As a specification, we use the observational determinism property with a single input and a single output proposition. We compare the naive monitoring approach to the monitor using specification analysis and trace analysis, as well as a combination thereof. We randomly built traces of length 2000, with one byte of low input, i.e., one atomic proposition is allowed to appear for 8 steps. The remaining atomic propositions are one low output and five high in and outputs. Applying both of our techniques results in a tremendous speed up of the monitoring algorithm.

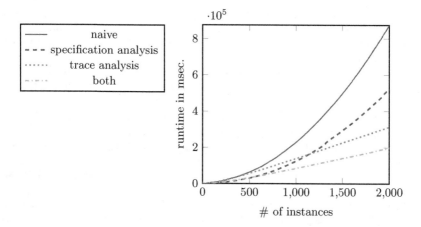

Fig. 5. Runtime comparison of naive monitoring approach with a version using specification analysis, trace analysis, and a combination of both.

7   Conclusion

In this paper, we have presented an automata based monitoring approach for HyperLTL. We showed that deciding whether an alternation-free formula is monitorable is PSPACE-complete. We presented two optimizations tackling different problems in monitoring hyperproperties. Trace analysis minimizes the needed memory, by minimizing the stored set of traces. Specification analysis reduces the algorithmic workload by reducing the number of comparisons between a newly observed trace and the previously stored traces. Combined, we have made significant progress towards the practical monitoring of hyperproperties.

References

1. Agrawal, S., Bonakdarpour, B.: Runtime verification of k-safety hyperproperties in HyperLTL. In: Proceedings of CSF, pp. 239–252. IEEE Computer Society (2016)
2. Askarov, A., Sabelfeld, A.: Tight enforcement of information-release policies for dynamic languages. In: Proceedings of CSF, pp. 43–59. IEEE Computer Society (2009)
3. Austin, T.H., Flanagan, C.: Permissive dynamic information flow analysis. In: Proceedings of PLAS, p. 3. ACM (2010)
4. Bauer, A.: Monitorability of omega-regular languages. CoRR abs/1006.3638 (2010)
5. Bichhawat, A., Rajani, V., Garg, D., Hammer, C.: Information flow control in WebKit's JavaScript bytecode. In: Abadi, M., Kremer, S. (eds.) POST 2014. LNCS, vol. 8414, pp. 159–178. Springer, Heidelberg (2014). doi:10.1007/978-3-642-54792-8_9
6. Bonakdarpour, B., Finkbeiner, B.: Runtime verification for HyperLTL. In: Falcone, Y., Sánchez, C. (eds.) RV 2016. LNCS, vol. 10012, pp. 41–45. Springer, Cham (2016). doi:10.1007/978-3-319-46982-9_4

7. Brett, N., Siddique, U., Bonakdarpour, B.: Rewriting-based runtime verification for alternation-free HyperLTL. In: Legay, A., Margaria, T. (eds.) TACAS 2017. LNCS, vol. 10206, pp. 77–93. Springer, Heidelberg (2017). doi:10.1007/978-3-662-54580-5_5

8. Chudnov, A., Kuan, G., Naumann, D.A.: Information flow monitoring as abstract interpretation for relational logic. In: Proceedings of CSF, pp. 48–62. IEEE Computer Society (2014)

9. Clarkson, M.R., Finkbeiner, B., Koleini, M., Micinski, K.K., Rabe, M.N., Sánchez, C.: Temporal logics for hyperproperties. In: Abadi, M., Kremer, S. (eds.) POST 2014. LNCS, vol. 8414, pp. 265–284. Springer, Heidelberg (2014). doi:10.1007/978-3-642-54792-8_15

10. Clarkson, M.R., Schneider, F.B.: Hyperproperties. J. Comput. Secur. 18(6), 1157–1210 (2010)

11. d'Amorim, M., Roşu, G.: Efficient monitoring of ω-languages. In: Etessami, K., Rajamani, S.K. (eds.) CAV 2005. LNCS, vol. 3576, pp. 364–378. Springer, Heidelberg (2005). doi:10.1007/11513988_36

12. Devriese, D., Piessens, F.: Noninterference through secure multi-execution. In: Proceedings of SP, pp. 109–124. IEEE Computer Society (2010)

13. Dimitrova, R., Finkbeiner, B., Kovács, M., Rabe, M.N., Seidl, H.: Model checking information flow in reactive systems. In: Kuncak, V., Rybalchenko, A. (eds.) VMCAI 2012. LNCS, vol. 7148, pp. 169–185. Springer, Heidelberg (2012). doi:10.1007/978-3-642-27940-9_12

14. Dimitrova, R., Finkbeiner, B., Rabe, M.N.: Monitoring temporal information flow. In: Margaria, T., Steffen, B. (eds.) ISoLA 2012. LNCS, vol. 7609, pp. 342–357. Springer, Heidelberg (2012). doi:10.1007/978-3-642-34026-0_26

15. Finkbeiner, B., Hahn, C.: Deciding hyperproperties. In: Proceedings of CONCUR, LIPIcs, vol. 59, pp. 13:1–13:14. Schloss Dagstuhl - Leibniz-Zentrum fuer Informatik (2016)

16. Finkbeiner, B., Hahn, C., Stenger, M.: EAHyper: satisfiability, implication, and equivalence checking of hyperproperties. In: Majumdar, R., Kunčak, V. (eds.) CAV 2017. LNCS, vol. 10427. Springer, Cham (2017). doi:10.1007/978-3-319-63390-9_29

17. Finkbeiner, B., Rabe, M.N., Sánchez, C.: Algorithms for model checking HyperLTL and HyperCTL*. In: Kroening, D., Păsăreanu, C.S. (eds.) CAV 2015. LNCS, vol. 9206, pp. 30–48. Springer, Cham (2015). doi:10.1007/978-3-319-21690-4_3

18. Le Guernic, G., Banerjee, A., Jensen, T., Schmidt, D.A.: Automata-based confidentiality monitoring. In: Okada, M., Satoh, I. (eds.) ASIAN 2006. LNCS, vol. 4435, pp. 75–89. Springer, Heidelberg (2007). doi:10.1007/978-3-540-77505-8_7

19. Kovács, M., Seidl, H.: Runtime enforcement of information flow security in tree manipulating processes. In: Barthe, G., Livshits, B., Scandariato, R. (eds.) ESSoS 2012. LNCS, vol. 7159, pp. 46–59. Springer, Heidelberg (2012). doi:10.1007/978-3-642-28166-2_6

20. Manna, Z., Pnueli, A.: Temporal Verification of Reactive Systems - Safety. Springer, New York (1995)

21. McLean, J.: Proving noninterference and functional correctness using traces. J. Comput. Secur. 1(1), 37–58 (1992)

22. Pnueli, A.: The temporal logic of programs. In: Proceedings of FOCS, pp. 46–57. IEEE Computer Society (1977)

23. Pnueli, A., Zaks, A.: PSL model checking and run-time verification via testers. In: Misra, J., Nipkow, T., Sekerinski, E. (eds.) FM 2006. LNCS, vol. 4085, pp. 573–586. Springer, Heidelberg (2006). doi:10.1007/11813040_38

24. Roscoe, A.W.: CSP and determinism in security modelling. In: Proceedings of SP, pp. 114–127. IEEE Computer Society (1995)
25. Sabelfeld, A., Myers, A.C.: Language-based information-flow security. IEEE J. Sel. Areas Commun. **21**(1), 5–19 (2003)
26. Sistla, A.P., Clarke, E.M.: The complexity of propositional linear temporal logics. In: Proceedings of STOC, pp. 159–168. ACM (1982)
27. Suh, G.E., Lee, J.W., Zhang, D., Devadas, S.: Secure program execution via dynamic information flow tracking. In: Proceedings of ASPLOS, pp. 85–96. ACM (2004)
28. Tabakov, D., Rozier, K.Y., Vardi, M.Y.: Optimized temporal monitors for systemc. Formal Methods Syst. Des. **41**(3), 236–268 (2012)
29. Vanhoef, M., Groef, W.D., Devriese, D., Piessens, F., Rezk, T.: Stateful declassification policies for event-driven programs. In: Proceedings of CSF, pp. 293–307. IEEE Computer Society (2014)
30. Zdancewic, S., Myers, A.C.: Observational determinism for concurrent program security. In: Proceedings of CSF, p. 29. IEEE Computer Society (2003)

TeLEx: Passive STL Learning Using Only Positive Examples

Susmit Jha[1]([⊠]), Ashish Tiwari[1], Sanjit A. Seshia[2], Tuhin Sahai[3],
and Natarajan Shankar[1]

[1] CSL, SRI International, Menlo Park, USA
{jha,tiwari,shankar}@csl.sri.com
[2] EECS, UC Berkeley, Berkeley, USA
sseshia@eecs.berkeley.edu
[3] United Technologies Research Center, East Hartford, USA
tuhin.sahai@utrc.utc.com

Abstract. We propose a novel passive learning approach, TeLEx, to infer signal temporal logic formulas that characterize the behavior of a dynamical system using only observed signal traces of the system. The approach requires two inputs: a set of observed traces and a template Signal Temporal Logic (STL) formula. The unknown parameters in the template can include time-bounds of the temporal operators, as well as the thresholds in the inequality predicates. TeLEx finds the value of the unknown parameters such that the synthesized STL property is satisfied by all the provided traces and it is *tight*. This requirement of *tightness* is essential to generating interesting properties when only positive examples are provided and there is no option to actively query the dynamical system to discover the boundaries of legal behavior. We propose a novel quantitative semantics for satisfaction of STL properties which enables TeLEx to learn tight STL properties without multidimensional optimization. The proposed new metric is also smooth. This is critical to enable use of gradient-based numerical optimization engines and it produces a 30×–100× speed-up with respect to the state-of-art gradient-free optimization. The approach is implemented in a publicly available tool.

1 Introduction

Signal Temporal Logic (STL) [26] is a discrete linear time temporal logic used to reason about the future evolution of a continuous time behaviour. Generally, this formalism is useful in describing the behaviours of trajectories of differential equations or hybrid models. Several approaches [14,20,21,25,30,31] have been recently proposed to automatically design systems and controllers to satisfy given temporal logic specifications. But practical systems are still often created as an assembly of components - some of which are manually designed. Further, many practical systems also include the physical plant, and the overall property of such systems are not known a-priori. Consequently, specification mining has emerged as an effective approach to create abstractions of monitored behavior to better understand complex systems, particularly in autonomy and robotics.

© Springer International Publishing AG 2017
S. Lahiri and G. Reger (Eds.): RV 2017, LNCS 10548, pp. 208–224, 2017.
DOI: 10.1007/978-3-319-67531-2_13

Existing approaches to learning STL properties fall into two categories. The approaches in the first category are classifier-learning techniques which rely on the presence of both positive and negative examples to learn STL formula as a classifier. The approaches in the second category are active-learning approaches that require the capability to experiment with the system to actively try falsifying candidate STL properties in order to obtain counterexamples. In this paper, we address the problem of learning STL properties where negative examples are not provided and it is not possible to actively experiment with the system in a safe manner. For example, learning properties of a vehicle-deployed autonomous driving system must rely on only positive examples. We neither have easy access to negative example trajectories that the system will never execute nor do have an easy way to design safe experiments for falsifying properties.

We propose a novel technique, TeLEx that addresses this challenge of data-driven learning of STL formulae from just positive example trajectories. An initial learning bias is provided to TeLEx as a template formula. TeLEx is restricted to learning parameters of the provided template STL formula and not its structure. TeLEx does not have access to either negative examples or the model of the system for falsification. Thus, the boundaries of legal behaviour are not directly available. It has to be inferred just from positive examples. The challenge is to avoid over-generalization in absence of negative examples or counterexamples obtained from active falsification. TeLEx addresses this research gap of mining temporal specifications of systems where active experimentation is not possible and failing traces (negative examples) are not available.

TeLEx uses a novel quantitative metric that measures the tightness of satisfiability of STL formulas over the traces. This metric uses smooth functions to represent predicates and temporal operators. This keeps the metric differentiable, which would not be possible by just taking the absolute value of standard robustness-metric or directly using the qualitative metric. While sigmoid and exponential-like functions are often used in fields such as deep-learning which rely on numerical-optimization, TeLEx is the first to use these to *smoothly* represent tight-satisfiability of STL formulas. The smoothness of the proposed metric allows the effective use of gradient-based numerical optimization techniques. TeLEx can be used with a number of different numerical optimization back-ends to synthesize parameters that minimize the new metric over positive examples, and thus, learn a tight STL formula consistent with all the traces.

2   Preliminaries

We present some preliminary concepts and definitions used in our work.

Definition 1. *An interval I is a convex subset of $\mathbb{R}$. A singular interval $[a, a]$ contains exactly one point and $\emptyset$ denotes empty interval. Let $I = [a, b]$, $I_1 = [a_1, b_1]$, and $I_2 = [a_2, b_2]$ be three closed intervals. Then,*
1. $-I = [-b, -a]$ 2. $c+I = [c+a, c+b]$ 3. $I_1 \oplus I_2 = [a_1+a_2, b_1+b_2]$ 4. $\min(I_1, I_2) = [\min(a_1, a_2), \min(b_1, b_2)]$ 5. $I_1 \cap I_2 = [\max(a_1, a_2), \min(b_1, b_2)]$ *if* $\max(a_1, a_2) \leq \min(b_1, b_2)$ *and* $\emptyset$ *o.w.*

These definitions for various operations are naturally extended to closed, open-closed, and closed-open intervals.

Definition 2. *A time domain ST is a finite or infinite set of time instants such that $ST \subseteq \mathbb{R}^{\geq 0}$ with $0 \in ST$. A signal or signal-trace τ is a function from ST to a domain $\mathcal{X} \subseteq \mathbb{R}$. We assume the domain of all signals to be $\mathbb{R}$ to simplify notation. We also refer to signal-trace as simply trace or trajectory.*

Monitors used in cyberphysical systems, as well as simulation frameworks, typically provide signal values at discrete time instants due to discrete sampling, or due to limitations of numerical integration techniques. The actual signal can be reconstructed from discrete-time samples using some form of interpolation. In this paper, we assume constant interpolation to reconstruct the signal $\tau(t)$, that is, given a sequence of time-value pairs $(t_0, x_0), \ldots, (t_n, x_n)$, for all $t \in [t_0, t_n)$, we define $\tau(t) = x_i$ if $t \in [t_i, t_{i+1})$, and $\tau(t_n) = x_n$. The signal temporal logic (STL) formula are used to describe properties of signals. The syntax of STL is given as follows:

Definition 3. *A formula $\phi \in \mathcal{F}$ of bounded-time STL is defined as follows:*

$$\phi := \bot \mid \top \mid \mu \mid \neg\phi \mid \phi \vee \phi \mid \phi \wedge \phi \mid \phi\mathbf{U}_{[t_1,t_2]}\phi \mid \mathbf{F}_{[t_1,t_2]}\phi \mid \mathbf{G}_{[t_1,t_2]}\phi$$

where $0 \leq t_1 < t_2 < \infty$ and the atomic predicates $\mu : \mathbb{R}^n \rightarrow \{\top, \bot\}$ are inequalities on a set X of n signals, that is, $\mu(X)$ is of the form $g(X) \geq \alpha$, where $\alpha \in \mathbb{R}$ and $g : \mathbb{R}^n \rightarrow \mathbb{R}$ is a continuous function.

The eventually $\mathbf{F}$ and globally $\mathbf{G}$ operators are shorthands for $\top\mathbf{U}_{[t_1,t_2]}\phi$ and $\neg(\top\mathbf{U}_{[t_1,t_2]}\neg\phi)$ respectively. We keep them, nonetheless, to aid clarity when presenting the different ways of assigning semantics to these operators. We refer to [10, 26], and the survey in [27], for detailed discussion on STL. We briefly summarize its qualitative semantics in Definition 4. Let $\mathcal{T}$ denote the set of all signal-traces.

Definition 4. *The qualitative semantics of STL formulas is given by the function $\psi : \mathcal{F} \times \mathcal{T} \times ST \rightarrow \texttt{Bool}$ that maps an STL formula ϕ, a given signal-trace $\tau \in \mathcal{T}$, and a time $t \in ST$ to a Boolean value (True $\top$, or False $\bot$) such that*

- $\psi(\top, \tau, t) = \top$
- $\psi(\mu, \tau, t) = \mu(\tau(t))$
- $\psi(\neg\phi, \tau, t) = \neg\psi(\phi, \tau, t)$
- $\psi(\phi_1 \vee \phi_2, \tau, t) = \psi(\phi_1, \tau, t) \vee \psi(\phi_2, \tau, t))$
- $\psi(\phi_1 \wedge \phi_2, \tau, t) = \psi(\phi_1, \tau, t) \wedge \psi(\phi_2, \tau, t))$
- $\psi(\mathbf{F}_{[t_1,t_2]}\phi, \tau, t) = \exists t' \in [t + t_1, t + t_2] \ \psi(\phi, \tau, t')$
- $\psi(\mathbf{G}_{[t_1,t_2]}\phi, \tau, t) = \forall t' \in [t + t_1, t + t_2] \ \psi(\phi, \tau, t')$
- $\psi(\phi_1\mathbf{U}_{[t_1,t_2]}\phi_2, \tau, t) = \exists t' \in [t + t_1, t + t_2](\psi(\phi_2, \tau, t') \wedge \forall t'' \in [t, t') \ \psi(\phi_1, \tau, t''))$

Motivated by the need to define how robustly a trace satisfies a formula, formulas in STL were given a quantitative semantics, where formulas are interpreted over numbers such that positive numbers indicate that the formula is True, and negative numbers indicate falsehood. We summarize the quantitative semantics (robustness metric) from [11, 13] below.

Definition 5. *The robustness metric ρ maps an STL formula $\phi \in \mathcal{F}$, a signal trace $\tau \in \mathcal{T}$, and a time $t \in ST$ to a real value, that is, $\rho : \mathcal{F} \times \mathcal{T} \times ST \to \mathbb{R} \cup \{\infty, -\infty\}$ such that:*

- $\rho(\top, \tau, t) = +\infty$
- $\rho(\mu, \tau, t) = g(\tau(t)) - \alpha$ *where* $\mu(X)$ *is* $g(X) \geq \alpha$
- $\rho(\neg \phi, \tau, t) = -\rho(\phi, \tau, t)$
- $\rho(\phi_1 \vee \phi_2, \tau, t) = \max(\rho(\phi_1, \tau, t), \rho(\phi_2, \tau, t))$
- $\rho(\mathbf{F}_{[t_1, t_2]} \phi, \tau, t) = \sup\limits_{t' \in [t+t_1, t+t_2]} \rho(\phi, \tau, t')$
- $\rho(\mathbf{G}_{[t_1, t_2]} \phi, \tau, t) = \inf\limits_{t' \in [t+t_1, t+t_2]} \rho(\phi, \tau, t')$
- $\rho(\phi_1 \mathbf{U}_{[t_1, t_2]} \phi_2, \tau, t) = \sup\limits_{t' \in [t+t_1, t+t_2]} (\min(\rho(\phi_2, \tau, t'), \inf\limits_{t'' \in [t, t']} \rho(\phi_1, \tau, t'')))$

A STL formula ϕ is satisfied by a trace τ at time t, that is, $\psi(\phi, \tau, t) = \top$ if and only if $\rho(\phi, \tau, t) \geq 0$. Intuitively, ρ quantifies the *degree of satisfiability*. This has motivated its use in learning STL formulae for specification mining [7,11,18,23], diagnosis [24], falsification [1,2,6], and system synthesis [4,9,31].

3   Related Work

In this section, we summarize related work on learning STL formulae and contrast them to the approach presented in this paper. We categorize related work into three groups: learning STL formula, quantitative metrics for temporal logic and learning concepts from positive examples.

Learning STL formula: Existing techniques for learning STL formulae can be broadly classified into active and passive methods. Active STL learning methods rely on availability of a simulation model on which candidate temporal properties can be falsified [1,3,6,33]. This generates counterexamples. Since these models are often complex executable models, black-box optimization techniques such as simulated annealing are used in falsification of candidate temporal logic properties. If the falsification succeeds, the incorrect parameter values are eliminated and the obtained negative example is used in the next iteration of inferring new candidate parameters values of the temporal logic property. We address a different problem of learning signal temporal logic formula when the simulation model is not available. Further, instead of using gradient-free optimization methods such as simulated annealing, Monte Carlo and ant colony optimization to falsify models, we use more scalable gradient-based numerical optimization methods to infer tightest STL property consistent with a given set of traces. Gradient-based methods for falsification [2] have also been proposed recently to exploit the differentiable nature of simulation models but our approach does not have access to a simulation model. Instead, we define a *smooth* tightness metric for satisfiability of STL properties, and use gradient-based methods to search over the parameter space of STL formulae.

Passive data driven approaches for learning STL formula from positive and negative example traces have also been proposed in literature. Learning STL formula is reduced to a two class supervised classification problem [7, 15, 24] that is solved using a mixture of discrete and continuous optimization using decisions trees and simulated annealing. A model based approach that relies on statistical induction of models before learning STL formulae is presented in [7]. In contrast, TeLEx addresses the problem of passive learning of STL formulae in presence of only positive examples.

Metrics for STL Satisfiability: Signal temporal logic was introduced [11, 26] within the context of monitoring temporal properties of signals. It is possible to quantify the degree of satisfiability of an STL property on a signal trace, thus going beyond the Boolean interpretation. Robustness metric was proposed [11, 13] to provide such a quantitative metric, as described in Sect. 2. Intuitively, this metric captures the closest distance between the signal trace and the boundary of set of signals satisfying the STL property. This is the worst-case measure of degree of satisfiability. More recently, an *average robustness metric* has also been proposed [25] in the context of task and motion planning application where the min (inf) operator in the metric definition for globally properties is replaced by an averaging operator. This allows more efficient encoding to linear programs for certain planning problems. These metrics are monotonic, that is, the measure is higher for formulas that are more robustly satisfiable.

If we use robustness metric to learn STL properties from a set of positive example traces, then we would learn very weak properties. This is because a weaker STL property would have a higher robustness value for any given set of positive example signal traces. For example, even if $G(x > 0)$ holds for a given set of traces, the formula $G(x > -100)$ holds more robustly, and would be preferred if we optimized for the standard robustness metric. Hence, in this paper, we define a new metric that captures *tight satisfiability* of an STL property over positive example traces.

A possible approach for finding a tight formula would be to seek a formula that minimizes the absolute-value of the robustness-metric. However, this is not ideal because the absolute-value function is non-differentiable at the optimum and hence, optimizing such a metric would be very challenging. Our proposed novel metric uses smooth functions, such as sigmoid and exponentials, to model tight-satisfiability while still retaining differentiability to aid optimization.

Learning from Positive Examples: Learning from positive examples has been investigated extensively in machine learning. Gold et al. [16] showed that even learning regular languages from a class with at least one infinite language is not possible with only positive examples in a deterministic setting. Horining [17] considered the case of stochastic context-free grammars and assumed that the positive examples were generated by sampling from the unknown grammar according to the probabilities assigned to the productions. He proved that such positive examples could be used to converge to the correct grammar in the limit with probability one. Angluin [5] generalized these results to identifying any unknown formal language in the limit with probability one as long as positive examples are drawn according to an associated probability distribution. Apart from the literature on language learning, Muggleton [28] showed that logic programs are learnable with arbitrarily low expected error just from positive examples within a Bayesian framework. Valiant [32] showed monomials and k-CNF formulas are Probably Approximately Correct (PAC) learnable using only positive examples. While learning from positive examples and its limitations have been studied for other concept classes [22], our approach is the first to consider learning STL properties from positive examples.

4   Learning STL from Positive Examples

Before we present the proposed approach for learning STL properties from just positive examples, we present a simple motivating example.

Illustrative Example: Let us consider an autonomous vehicle system where the steering angle ang and speed spd are being observed. Each element of the observed trace is a tuple of the form $(\texttt{timestamp}, \texttt{ang}, \texttt{spd})$. We would like to learn an STL property with the template: $\phi = |\texttt{ang}| \geq 0.2 \Rightarrow F_{[0,6]}\texttt{spd} \leq \alpha$, which intuitively means that we would like to learn the minimum speed α reached within $6\,\mathrm{s}$ of initiating a turn. Let us consider a timestamped signal trace: $\tau = (0, 0.1, 15), (2, 0.2, 14), (4, 0.3, 12), (6, 0.35, 10), (8, 0.4, 8), \ldots$. For this trace, we notice that $(|\texttt{ang}| \geq 0.2 \Rightarrow F_{[0,6]}\texttt{spd} \leq 8)$ would tightly fit the data. But if we used the robustness metric for optimization, increasing the value of α would be preferred since it increases the robustness value. The robustness metric value for the instantiated template ϕ and the trajectory τ is $\rho(\phi, \tau, 0) = 0$ when $\alpha = 8$, $\rho(\phi, \tau, 0) = 2$ when $\alpha = 10$, $\rho(\phi, \tau, 0) = 992$ when $\alpha = 1000$, and so on. A weak property like $|\texttt{ang}| \geq 0.2 \Rightarrow F_{[0,6]}\texttt{spd} \leq 1000$ has higher robustness score than the tight property $|\texttt{ang}| \geq 0.2 \Rightarrow F_{[0,6]}\texttt{spd} \leq 8$ but clearly, the latter is a more fitting description of the observed behavior.

Problem Definition: We next present some definitions essential to formulating the problem of learning STL properties from positive examples.

Definition 6. *A template STL formula $\phi(p_1, p_2, \ldots, p_k)$ with k unknown parameters is a negation-free bounded-time signal temporal logic formula with the syntax in Definition 3 where some of the time bounds of temporal operators and thresholds of atomic predicates are not constants but instead, free parameters. The parameters are optionally associated with interval constraints providing lower and upper bounds; that is, $l_i \leq p_i \leq u_i$ for $1 \leq i \leq k$ where l_i, u_i are constant bounds.*

Note that we assume templates are negation free. If there are no **U** operator in a formula ϕ, then the negation in $\neg\phi$ can be pushed inside a formula until we are only left with negated atomic predictes. Negated predicates can themselves be rewritten in negation-free form.

We say that an STL formula $\phi(v_1, v_2, \ldots, v_k)$ completes the STL template if the values $v_i \in \mathbb{R}$ for parameters p_i satisfy all the bound constraints on p_i.

Definition 7. *Given a temporal logic property $\phi(v_1, v_2, \ldots, v_k)$ that completes a template $\phi(p_1, p_2, \ldots, p_k)$, we define the ϵ-neighborhood of $\phi(v_1, v_2, \ldots, v_k)$ as $\mathcal{N}_\epsilon(\phi(v_1, v_2, \ldots, v_k)) = \{\phi(v_1', v_2', \ldots, v_k') \text{ s.t. } |v_i - v_i'| \leq \epsilon \text{ for } 1 \leq i \leq k\}$.*

We now formally define the problem of learning signal temporal logic formula. The second condition in Definition 8 ensures ϵ-tightness while the first condition ensures that the STL formula is consistent with positive examples.

Definition 8. *Given a set of traces $\mathcal{T}$ and template STL $\phi(p_1, p_2, \ldots, p_k)$, the problem of learning ϵ-tight STL formula is to learn the values of the parameters, $p_i = v_i^*$, such that*

- *the STL formula $\phi(v_1^*, v_2^*, \ldots, v_k^*)$ holds over all traces in $\mathcal{T}$, that is, $\forall \tau \in \mathcal{T} : \tau \models \phi(v_1^*, v_2^*, \ldots, v_k^*)$ and*
- *there exists some $\phi(v_1, v_2, \ldots, v_k) \in \mathcal{N}_\epsilon(\phi(v_1^*, v_2^*, \ldots, v_k^*))$ that does not hold over at least one trace in $\mathcal{T}$; that is, $\exists \tau \in \mathcal{T} : \tau \not\models \phi(v_1, v_2, \ldots, v_k)$*

We have used the notation $\tau \models \phi$ here to denote $\psi(\phi, \tau, 0) = \top$, where ψ is the qualitative semantics presented in Definition 4. We can solve the problem of learning ϵ-tight STL formulas by formulating the following constrained multi-objective optimization problem where minimization is done with respect to free parameters $p_1, \ldots, p_k$.

$$\texttt{minimize } \{|\epsilon_1|, |\epsilon_2|, \ldots, |\epsilon_k|\} \text{ s.t.}$$
$$\epsilon_1 = p_1 - p_1', \epsilon_2 = p_2 - p_2', \ldots, \epsilon_k = p_k - p_k'$$
$$\forall \tau \in \mathcal{T} \ \tau \models \phi(p_1, p_2, \ldots, p_k), \ \exists \tau' \in \mathcal{T} \ \tau' \not\models \phi(p_1', p_2', \ldots, p_k')$$

We can check if the solution of the above problem solves our ϵ-tight learning problem by checking if $\max\{|\epsilon_1|, \ldots, |\epsilon_k|\}$ is less than the desired ϵ (or, we could alternatively change the above optimization problem to a min-max problem). However, the above optimization problem is difficult to solve in practice for two reason - first, it requires multi-objective optimization where the number of objectives, k, grows with the number of parameters in the signal temporal logic formula. Further, the constraints require checking satisfiability of the bounded-time STL formula over finite traces which is itself an NP hard problem.

The robustness metric for quantitative satisfiability of STL formula allows us to replace satisfiability checking with nonlinear constraints in the above optimization problem.

$$\texttt{minimize } \{|\epsilon_1|, |\epsilon_2|, \ldots, |\epsilon_k|\} \text{ s.t.}$$
$$\epsilon_1 = p_1 - p_1', \epsilon_2 = p_2 - p_2', \ldots, \epsilon_k = p_k - p_k'$$
$$\forall \tau \in \mathcal{T} \ \rho(\phi(p_1, p_2, \ldots, p_k), \tau, 0) \geq 0, \ \exists \tau' \in \mathcal{T} \ \rho(\phi(p_1', p_2', \ldots, p_k'), \tau', 0) < 0$$

Next, we notice that the robustness metric is continuous in the parameters p_i corresponding to inequality thresholds and time-bounds and hence, one could expect that we will obtain a reasonable solution for the above problem by solving the following simpler scalar optimization problem:

$$\texttt{minimize}_{p_1, p_2, \ldots, p_k} \ \min_{\tau \in \mathcal{T}} |\rho(\phi(p_1, p_2, \ldots, p_k), \tau, 0)|$$

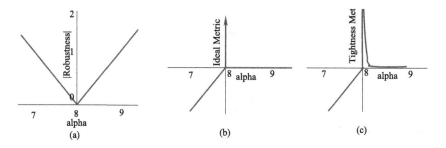

Fig. 1. (a) The absolute value of robustness metric reaches 0 at $\alpha = 8$. It is close to 0 even at 7.99 even though the temporal property corresponding to $\alpha = 7.99$ is violated by the trace. (b) The ideal metric should be negative when $\alpha < 8$ and jump to ∞ when $\alpha = 8$ and drop down to 0 when $\alpha > 8$. (c) A metric which is negative for $\alpha < 8$, reaches its maxima between 8 and $8 + \epsilon$ and then drops to 0.

There are two problems with this approach of solving the tight-STL learning problem using the above optimization problem. This optimization problem uses the absolute value of the robustness metric. This metric is generally not differentiable at $\rho(\phi(p_1, p_2, \ldots, p_k)) = 0$. Further, if we get an ϵ-approximate solution for the above optimization problem, it no longer guarantees that all traces will satisfy the instantiated template ϕ. This is because the absolute value can be a small positive number even when the actual value is a small negative number. In Fig. 1, we use the example at the beginning of the section to illustrate the problem. Figure 1(b) illustrates an ideal metric, because it achieves its maximum at the boundary of satisfiability and unsatisfiability. Maximizing this metric would yield tight STL property but optimizing such a discontinuous function is difficult. Figure 1(c) illustrates a more practical incarnation of the ideal metric, which is not discontinuous but still useful to learn ϵ tight STL property. Our main contribution is designing such a metric.

We begin by first defining a tightness metric for predicates. We would like the metric to achieve its maximum value at the boundary in order to discover tight STL properties. For a predicate $\mu(,) := g() \geq \alpha$, recall that the robustness metric is $\rho(\mu, \tau, t) = g(\tau(t)) - \alpha = r$. We would like to define a tightness metric $\theta(\mu, \tau, t)$ such that it is similar to Fig. 1(c), and hence we define it to be

$$\frac{1}{r + e^{-\beta r}} - e^{-r}$$

where $\beta \geq 1$ is an adjustable parameter. This function is plotted in Fig. 2 and it approaches the ideal function in Fig. 1(b) as β increases albeit at the cost of numerical stability during optimization. This function is smooth (its deriv-

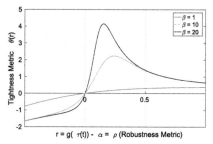

Fig. 2. Tightness metric θ for predicate

ative is defined and also continuous), and hence, is amenable to gradient-based numerical optimization techniques. Finding an ϵ-tight value of α reduces to maximizing θ with appropriate choice of β - lower values of ϵ require higher values of β.

Apart from the predicates, the other difficult cases for defining the tightness metric (θ) happen to be the temporal operators. The requirement here is that the metric θ should be defined such that it prefers longer time intervals for globally operator and shorter for eventually operator as illustrated in Fig. 3.

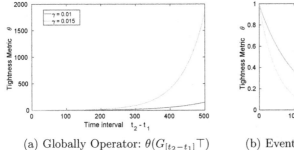
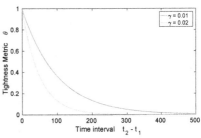

(a) Globally Operator: $\theta(G_{[t_2-t_1]}\top)$ (b) Eventually Operator: $\theta(F_{[t_2-t_1]}\top)$

Fig. 3. Tightness metric θ

We next formally define the tight quantitative semantics over negation-free STL properties and show how it can be used to formulate the problem of learning consistent and tight STL property as a numerical optimization problem over a single (scalar) cost metric. If the original formula has negation, it is pushed inwards through Boolean combinations, F and G temporal operations, and the inequality in predicate is flipped. Negation can also be pushed inwards through discrete bounded time U operator via case-splitting. Further, since we deal with continuous signals, we consider only non-strict inequalities as predicates and relax strict inequalities if needed.

Definition 9. *The tightness metric* $\theta : \mathcal{F} \times \mathcal{T} \times ST \mapsto \mathbb{R} \cup \{-\infty, \infty\}$ *maps an STL formula* $\phi \in \mathcal{F}$, *a trace* $\tau \in \mathcal{T}$, *and a sampled time instance* $t \in ST$ *to a real value s.t.:*

- $\theta(\top, \tau, t) = \infty, \quad \theta(\bot, \tau, t) = -\infty$
- $\theta(\mu, \tau, t) = \mathrm{P}(g(\tau(t)) - \alpha)$ *where* $\mu() := (g() \geq \alpha)$
- $\theta(\phi_1 \wedge \phi_2, \tau, t) = \min(\theta(\phi_1, \tau, t), \theta(\phi_2, \tau, t))$
- $\theta(\phi_1 \vee \phi_2, \tau, t) = \max(\theta(\phi_1, \tau, t), \theta(\phi_2, \tau, t))$
- $\theta(\mathbf{F}_{[t_1,t_2]}\phi, \tau, t) = \mathrm{C}(\gamma, t_1, t_2) \displaystyle\sup_{t' \in [t+t_1, t+t_2]} \theta(\phi, \tau, t')$
- $\theta(\mathbf{G}_{[t_1,t_2]}\phi, \tau, t) = \mathrm{E}(\gamma; t_1, t_2) \displaystyle\inf_{t' \in [t+t_1, t+t_2)} \theta(\phi, \tau, t')$
- $\theta(\phi_1 \mathbf{U}_{[t_1,t_2]}\phi_2, \tau, t)$
  $\mathrm{E}(\gamma, t_1, t_2) \displaystyle\sup_{t' \in [t+t_1, t+t_2]} (\min(\theta(\phi_2, \tau, t'), \inf_{t'' \in [t, t')} \theta(\phi_1, \tau, t'')))$ $=$

where the peak function $P(r) = \frac{1}{r+e^{-\beta r}} - e^{-r}$, *the contraction function* $C(\gamma, t_1, t_2) = \frac{2}{1+e^{\gamma(t_2-t_1+1)}}$, *the expansion function* $E(\gamma, t_1, t_2) = \frac{2}{1+e^{-\gamma(t_2-t_1+1)}}$, $\beta \geq 1$ *is a coefficient chosen to determine sharpness of peak and* $\gamma \geq 0$ *is a coefficient chosen to trade-off tightness in time vs tightness over predicates for a given time-scale and spread of continuous variables. We choose to use the expansion function* E *in the definition of tightness of* U-*formulae. We could replace* E *by* C *if shorter time-intervals are preferred in the* U-*operator.*

If both the time-interval and predicate threshold is unknown for a temporal operator, then there is a choice in either tightening time-intervals and discovering predicates that hold over these or to find tighter predicates over longer (in case of eventually) and shorter (in case of globally) operators. Increasing γ would result in tighter time-intervals. Increasing β would result in tighter predicates. In the following theorem, we summarize the relation between the tightness metric and satisfaction of STL formula.

Theorem 1. *The tightness metric for a given STL formula* ϕ, *namely* $\theta(\phi, \tau, t)$ *is nonnegative if and only if* τ *satisfies* ϕ *at time* t.

Proof. We first show that $\theta(\phi, \tau, t) \geq 0$ if and only if $\rho(\phi, \tau, t) \geq 0$ using structural induction. We have only two nontrivial cases:

- Atomic Predicates: We know that $\frac{1}{r+e^{-\beta r}} - e^{-r} \geq 0$ where $\beta \geq 1$ if and only if $r \geq 0$. Hence, $\theta(\mu, \tau, t) = \frac{1}{r+e^{-\beta r}} - e^{-r} \geq 0$ if and only if $r = g(\tau(t)) - \alpha = \rho(\mu, \tau, t) \geq 0$
- Temporal Operators: $C(\gamma, t_1, t_2) = \frac{2}{1+e^{\gamma(t_2-t_1+1)}} \geq 0$ for all $t_2 > t_1$ and $E(\gamma, t_1, t_2) = \frac{2}{1+e^{-\gamma(t_2-t_1+1)}} \geq 0$ for all $t_2 > t_1$. Hence, θ has the same sign as ρ, that is, $\theta(\phi, \tau, t) \geq 0$ if and only if $\rho(\phi, \tau, t) \geq 0$.

Thus, $\theta(\phi, \tau, t) \geq 0$ if and only if $\rho(\phi, \tau, t) \geq 0$ and we know that $\rho(\phi, \tau, t) \geq 0$ if and only if τ satisfies ϕ at time t. □

The theorem above shows that a STL formula ϕ that has positive tightness metric (over all the traces τ in some set $\mathcal{T}$) will also evaluate to True in all these traces. But we want a formula that is not only consistent with the traces, but also tight on the traces. The following lemma says that optimizing for the tightness metric results in tight formulas.

Lemma 1. *Given a trace* τ *and a template STL formula* $\phi(p_1, p_2, \ldots, p_k)$ *with* k *unknown parameters (Definition 6), let*

$$(v_1^*, v_2^*, \ldots, v_k^*) = \arg \max_{p_1, p_2, \ldots, p_k} \theta(\phi(p_1, p_2, \ldots, p_k), \tau, 0)$$

be a solution $\boldsymbol{v}^* = (v_1^*, \ldots, v_k^*)$ *such that* $\theta(\phi(\boldsymbol{v}^*), \tau, 0)$ *is a finite nonnegative value. Then* $\boldsymbol{v}^*$ *is a solution for the* ϵ-*tight STL learning problem on the singleton set* $\{\tau\}$ *of traces for any value of* ϵ *such that* $\epsilon > \eta$, *where* η *is no more than the robustness* $\rho(\phi(\boldsymbol{v}^*), \tau, 0)$ *of the discovered instantiated formula. The value* η *can be made arbitrarily small with appropriate choice of* β, γ.

Proof (Sketch). We again argue by structural induction over the template ϕ. Since ϕ is negation-free, we have three cases. (Case 1) If the top symbol of ϕ is a temporal operator with a time bound $[t_1, t_2]$ such that either t_1 or t_2 is a parameter, then our definition of θ guarantees that the interval $[t_1^*, t_2^*]$ (in the instantiated solution) is maximally elongated or contracted, and hence $\phi(\boldsymbol{v}^*)$ can be falsified by an ϵ perturbation to the interval, for any $\epsilon > 0$. (Case 2) If ϕ is an atomic predicate, then the robustness measure ρ clearly defines the minimum perturbation required to falsify it. (Case 3) If the top symbol of ϕ is $\vee$ or $\wedge$, we can reason inductively one or both of the subformulas.

For the second part, note that we can decrease η by choosing a large β and $\gamma > 0$. (Case 1) The value of r at which the function $\frac{1}{r+e^{-\beta r}} - e^{-r}$ peaks monotonically decreases with β and hence, more tight predicates (smaller r) can be learnt by increasing β. Hence, η decreases by increasing β. (Case 2) From the definition of C, we observe that the function $\frac{2}{1+e^{\gamma(\Delta t+1)}}$ decreases monotonically with γ and the function $\frac{2}{1+e^{-\gamma(\Delta t+1)}}$ increases monotonically with γ. Thus, if $\gamma > 0$, these functions cause us to learn the largest or smallest possible time interval, and hence changing the learnt intervals even slightly falsifies the formula. Hence, if $\gamma > 0$, then $\eta = 0$ for formulas that have a parametric temporal operator at the top. $\qquad \square$

We can lift Lemma 1 to a set of traces, but we lose the ability to arbitrarily decrease η.

Theorem 2. *Given a set of traces $\mathcal{T}$ and a template STL formula $\phi(p_1, p_2, \ldots, p_k)$, let*

$$(v_1^*, v_2^*, \ldots, v_k^*) = \arg \max_{p_1, p_2, \ldots, p_k} \left[\min_{\tau \in \mathcal{T}} \theta(\phi(p_1, p_2, \ldots, p_k), \tau, 0) \right]$$

define the solution $\boldsymbol{v}^* = (v_1^*, \ldots, v_k^*)$ such that $\min_{\tau \in \mathcal{T}} \theta(\phi(\boldsymbol{v}^*), \tau, 0)$ is nonnegative. Then the learnt formula $\phi(\boldsymbol{v}^*)$ solves the ϵ-tight STL learning problem for a value of ϵ such that $\epsilon > \eta$, where $\eta = \min_{\tau \in \mathcal{T}} \rho(\phi(v_1^*, \ldots, v_k^*), \tau, 0)$ is the standard robustness measure of the discovered instantiated formula. The value η gets no larger by increasing β and γ.

We use an off-the-shelf solver - quasi-Newton algorithm [12,34] to solve the above optimization problem. It uses gradient during optimization where the search direction in each iteration i is computed as $d_i = -H_i g_i$. H_i is the inverse of the Hessian matrix and g_i is the current derivative. The Hessian is a matrix of second-order partial derivatives of the cost function and describes its local curvature. Due to the smoothness of the defined tightness metric θ, gradient-based optimization techniques are very effective in solving the STL learning problem since both the gradient and the Hessian can be conveniently computed. We also used the gradient-free optimization to experimentally validate the advantage of smoothness of tightness metric. The optimization engine behind gradient-free optimization is differential evolution [29].

5   Experimental Evaluation

The presented approach is implemented in a publicly available tool: TeLEx[1].
We evaluated the effectiveness of TeLEx on a number of synthetic and real case-
studies. All experiments were conducted on a quad core Intel Core i5-2450M
CPU @ 2.50 GHz with 3 MB cache per core and 4 GB RAM.

1. Temporal Bounds on Signal $x(t) = t \sin(t^2)$

This case-study was designed to evaluate the scalability of TeLEx as well as
the tightness of learnt STL formulae using a synthetic trajectory for which we
already know the correct answer. We also compare gradient-based TeLEx with
gradient-free optimization to demonstrate the utility of smoothness of proposed
tightness metric. We consider the signal $x(t) = t \sin(t^2)$. We consider 12 STL
templates of the form:

$$template(k) \equiv \bigwedge_{i=0}^{k} (G_{[i,i+1]}(x \leq p_{2i} \wedge x \geq p_{2i+1}))$$

where $k = 0, 1, \ldots, 11$. Thus, the number of parameters in these templates grow
from 2 to 24. We repeated learning experiments 10 times in each case since
numerical optimization routines are not deterministic.

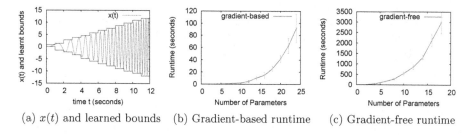

(a) $x(t)$ and learned bounds   (b) Gradient-based runtime   (c) Gradient-free runtime

Fig. 4. Tightness and scalability of TeLEx using gradient based optimization

Figure 4(a) shows the signal trace from time $t = 0$ to $t = 12$ along with the
bounds discovered by TeLEx while synthesizing the STL property using template
$template(12)$ (the largest template) and gradient-based optimization. The tightness of bounds demonstrates that the learnt STL properties are tight (and have
very low variance) even with 24 parameters. The robustness values for learnt STL
properties were always very small (between 0.02 and 0.12). We observed that
gradient-free differential evolution also discovered tight properties in all cases
(robustness value between (0.06 and 0.35) in which it terminated. Figure 4(b)
and (c) show the runtime of gradient-based and gradient-free optimization techniques respectively. Gradient-free methods did not terminate in an hour for more

---

[1] https://github.com/susmitjha/TeLEX.

than 18 parameters. We plot the mean runtime (along with standard deviation) from 10 runs with respect to the number of parameters being learnt for each of the 12 templates. The variability in runtime (standard deviation plotted as error bars) increases with the number of parameters. We observe a speed-up of 30X-100X using gradient-based approach due to the smoothness of tightness metric (scales of y-axis in Fig. 4(b) and (c) are different).

2. Two Agent Surveillance

We consider a two agent surveillance system in which both agents monitor a 10×10 grid as illustrated in Fig. 5. Intruders can pop up at any of the 8 locations marked by circles. But at any point, there are at most two intruders.

The two agents are initially at $0, 0$ and $10, 10$ respectively. The agents follow a simple protocol. At each time-instant, the agents calculate the distance from their current location to the intruders (if any), then they select the intruder closest to them as their target for inspection and move towards it. The target of an agent might change while moving (when second intruder pops up and it is closer to the agent moving towards first). After an intruder location is inspected, it is considered neutralized and the agent stays there until new target emerges. The simulator for this

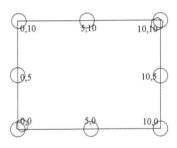

Fig. 5. Two agent surveillance

simple surveillance protocol is available at the tool website[2]. We simulated this for 1000 time-steps and then used TeLEx to learn STL corresponding to the following two properties.

- The maximum time between intruder popping up and being neutralized is 39.001 time-steps.
- The distance between the two agents is at least 4.998. This non-collision between agents is an emergent property due to "move-to-closest" policy of agents and the fact that there are at most two intruders at any given time.

3. Udacity Autonomous-Car Driving Public Data-set

In this case-study, we use the data made available publicly by Udacity as a part of its second challenge for autonomous driving[3]. The data corresponds to an instrumented car (2016 Lincoln MKZ) driving along El Camino Real (a major road in San Francisco Bay Area) starting from the Udacity office in Mountain View and moving north towards San Francisco. We use HMB_1 data-set which is a 221 s snippet with a total of over 13205 samples. It has a mixture of turns and straight driving. The data-set includes steering angle, applied torque, speed, throttle, brake, GPS and image. For our purpose, we focus on non-image data.

---

[2] https://github.com/susmitjha/TeLEX/blob/master/tests/twoagent.py.
[3] https://github.com/udacity/self-driving-car/tree/master/challenges/challenge-2.

The goal of this data-set is to provide real-world training sample for autonomous driving. Figure 6 shows how the angle and speed vary in the Udacity data-set.

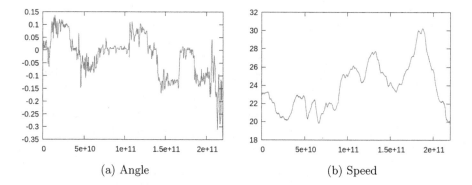

(a) Angle   (b) Speed

Fig. 6. Angle and speed for a subset of Udacity data

We use the tight STL learning approach presented in this paper to learn temporal properties relating angle, torque and speed. Such learned temporal properties could have several utilities. It could be used to examine whether a driving pattern (autonomous or manual) is too conservative or too risky. It could be used to extract sensible logical relations that must hold between different control inputs (say, speed and angle) from good manual driving data, and then enforce these temporal properties on autonomous driving systems. It could also be used to compare different autonomous driving solutions. We are interested in the following set of properties and we present the result of extracting these using **TeLEx**. We would like the robustness metric to be as close to 0 as possible and in all experiments below, we found it to be below 0.005.

1. The speed of the car must be below some upper bound $a \in [15, 25]$ if the angle is larger than 0.2 or below -0.2. Intuitively, this property captures required slowing down of the car when making a significant turn.

   Template STL: $G[0, 2.2e11](((angle \geq 0.2)|(angle \leq -0.2)) \Rightarrow (speed \leq a?15; 25))$
   Synthesized STL: $G[0.0, 2.2e11](((angle \geq 0.2)|(angle \leq -0.2)) \Rightarrow (speed \leq 22.01))$
   Performance: Tightness Metric = 0.067, Robustness Metric = 0.004
   Runtime: 8.64 s

2. Similar to the property above, the speed of the car must be low while applying a large torque (say, more than 1.6). Usually, torque is applied to turn along with brake when driving safely to avoid slipping.

   Template STL: $G[0, 2.2e11](((torque \geq 1.6)|(torque \leq -1.6)) \Rightarrow (speed \leq a?15; 25))$
   Synthesized STL: $G[0.0, 2.2e11](((torque \geq 1.6)|(torque \leq -1.6)) \Rightarrow (speed \leq 23.64))$
   Performance: Tightness Metric = 0.221, Robustness Metric = 0.005
   Runtime: 10.12 s

3. Another property of interest is to ensure that when the turn angle is high (say, above 0.06), the magnitude of negative torque applied is below a threshold. This avoids unsafe driving behavior of making late sharp compensation torques to avoid wide turns.

Template STL: $G[0, 2.2e11]((angle \geq 0.06) \Rightarrow (torque \geq b? - 2; -0.5))$
Synthesized STL: $G[0.0, 2.2e11]((angle \geq 0.06) \Rightarrow (torque \geq -1.06))$
Performance: Tightness Metric = 0.113, Robustness Metric = 0.003
Runtime: 7.30 s

4. Similarly, when the turn angle is low (say, below -0.06), the magnitude of positive torque applied is below a threshold to avoid late sharp compensating torques.

Template STL: $G[0, 2.2e11]((angle \leq -0.06) \Rightarrow (torque \leq b?0.5; 2))$
Synthesized STL: $G[0.0, 2.2e11]((angle \leq -0.06) \Rightarrow (torque \leq 1.25))$
Performance: Tightness Metric = 0.472, Robustness Metric = 0.002
Runtime: 5.00 s

5. The torque also must not be so low that the turns are very slow and so, we require that application of negative torque should decrease the angle below a threshold within some fixed time.

Template STL: $G[0, 2.2e11]((torque \leq 0.0) \Rightarrow F[0.0, 1.2e8](angle \leq a? - 1; 1))$
Synthesized STL: $G[0.0, 2.2e11]((torque \leq 0.0) \Rightarrow F[0.0, 1.2e8](angle \leq 0.01))$
Performance: Tightness Metric = 0.727, Robustness Metric = 0.002
Runtime: 46.59 s

6   Conclusion

In this paper, we presented a novel approach to learn tight STL formula using only positive examples. Our approach is based on a new tightness metric that uses smooth functions. The problem of learning tight STL properties admits a number of pareto-optimal solutions. We would like to add the capability of specifying preference in which parameters are tightened. Further, computation of the metrics on traces over optimization can be easily parallelized. Another dimension is to study other metrics proposed in literature to quantify conformance and extend tightness over these metrics [8, 19]. In conclusion, TeLEx automates the learning of high-level STL properties from observed time-traces given user-guidance in form of templates. It relies on a novel tightness metric defined in this paper which is smooth and amenable to gradient-based numerical optimization techniques.

Acknowledgement. This work is supported in part by DARPA under contract FA8750-16-C-0043 and NSF grant CNS-1423298.

References

1. Abbas, H., Hoxha, B., Fainekos, G., Ueda, K.: Robustness-guided temporal logic testing and verification for stochastic cyber-physical systems. In: 2014 IEEE 4th Annual International Conference on Cyber Technology in Automation, Control, and Intelligent Systems (CYBER), pp. 1–6. IEEE (2014)
2. Abbas, H., Winn, A., Fainekos, G., Julius, A.A.: Functional gradient descent method for metric temporal logic specifications. In: 2014 American Control Conference (ACC), pp. 2312–2317. IEEE (2014)
3. Akazaki, T.: Falsification of conditional safety properties for cyber-physical systems with Gaussian process regression. In: Falcone, Y., Sánchez, C. (eds.) RV 2016. LNCS, vol. 10012, pp. 439–446. Springer, Cham (2016). doi:10.1007/978-3-319-46982-9_27
4. Aksaray, D., Jones, A., Kong, Z., Schwager, M., Belta, C.: Q-learning for robust satisfaction of signal temporal logic specifications. In: 2016 IEEE 55th Conference on Decision and Control (CDC), pp. 6565–6570. IEEE (2016)
5. Angluin, D.: Identifying languages from stochastic examples. Technical report, YALEU/DCS/RR-614, Yale University, Department of Computer Science (1988)
6. Annpureddy, Y., Liu, C., Fainekos, G., Sankaranarayanan, S.: S-TaLiRo: a tool for temporal logic falsification for hybrid systems. In: Abdulla, P.A., Leino, K.R.M. (eds.) TACAS 2011. LNCS, vol. 6605, pp. 254–257. Springer, Heidelberg (2011). doi:10.1007/978-3-642-19835-9_21
7. Bartocci, E., Bortolussi, L., Sanguinetti, G.: Data-Driven Statistical Learning of Temporal Logic Properties. In: Legay, A., Bozga, M. (eds.) FORMATS 2014. LNCS, vol. 8711, pp. 23–37. Springer, Cham (2014). doi:10.1007/978-3-319-10512-3_3
8. Deshmukh, J.V., Majumdar, R., Prabhu, V.S.: Quantifying conformance using the Skorokhod metric. In: Kroening, D., Păsăreanu, C.S. (eds.) CAV 2015. LNCS, vol. 9207, pp. 234–250. Springer, Cham (2015). doi:10.1007/978-3-319-21668-3_14
9. Donzé, A.: Breach, a toolbox for verification and parameter synthesis of hybrid systems. In: Touili, T., Cook, B., Jackson, P. (eds.) CAV 2010. LNCS, vol. 6174, pp. 167–170. Springer, Heidelberg (2010). doi:10.1007/978-3-642-14295-6_17
10. Donzé, A.: On signal temporal logic. In: Legay, A., Bensalem, S. (eds.) RV 2013. LNCS, vol. 8174, pp. 382–383. Springer, Heidelberg (2013). doi:10.1007/978-3-642-40787-1_27
11. Donzé, A., Maler, O.: Robust satisfaction of temporal logic over real-valued signals. In: Chatterjee, K., Henzinger, T.A. (eds.) FORMATS 2010. LNCS, vol. 6246, pp. 92–106. Springer, Heidelberg (2010). doi:10.1007/978-3-642-15297-9_9
12. Facchinei, F., Lucidi, S., Palagi, L.: A truncated newton algorithm for large scale box constrained optimization. SIAM J. Optim. 12(4), 1100–1125 (2002)
13. Fainekos, G.E., Pappas, G.J.: Robustness of temporal logic specifications. In: Havelund, K., Núñez, M., Roşu, G., Wolff, B. (eds.) FATES/RV -2006. LNCS, vol. 4262, pp. 178–192. Springer, Heidelberg (2006). doi:10.1007/11940197_12
14. Fu, J., Topcu, U.: Synthesis of joint control and active sensing strategies under temporal logic constraints. IEEE Trans. Autom. Control 61(11), 3464–3476 (2016). doi:10.1109/TAC.2016.2518639
15. Giuseppe, B., Cristian Ioan, V., Francisco, P.A., Hirotoshi, Y., Calin, B.: A decision tree approach to data classification using signal temporal logic. In: Hybrid Systems: Computation and Control (HSCC), Vienna, Austria, pp. 1–10, April 2016
16. Gold, E.M.: Language identification in the limit. Inf. Control 10(5), 447–474 (1967)

17. Horning, J.J.: A study of grammatical inference. Technical report, DTIC Document (1969)
18. Hoxha, B., Dokhanchi, A., Fainekos, G.: Mining parametric temporal logic properties in model based design for cyber-physical systems. arXiv preprint arXiv:1512.07956 (2015)
19. Jakšić, S., Bartocci, E., Grosu, R., Ničković, D.: Quantitative monitoring of STL with edit distance. In: Falcone, Y., Sánchez, C. (eds.) RV 2016. LNCS, vol. 10012, pp. 201–218. Springer, Cham (2016). doi:10.1007/978-3-319-46982-9_13
20. Jha, S., Raman, V.: Automated synthesis of safe autonomous vehicle control under perception uncertainty. In: Rayadurgam, S., Tkachuk, O. (eds.) NFM 2016. LNCS, vol. 9690, pp. 117–132. Springer, Cham (2016). doi:10.1007/978-3-319-40648-0_10
21. Jha, S., Raman, V.: On optimal control of stochastic linear hybrid systems. In: Fränzle, M., Markey, N. (eds.) FORMATS 2016. LNCS, vol. 9884, pp. 69–84. Springer, Cham (2016). doi:10.1007/978-3-319-44878-7_5
22. Jha, S., Seshia, S.A.: A theory of formal synthesis via inductive learning. Acta Inform. (2017). doi:10.1007/s00236-017-0294-5
23. Jin, X., Donzé, A., Deshmukh, J.V., Seshia, S.A.: Mining requirements from closed-loop control models. IEEE Trans. Comput. Aided Des. Integr. Circuits Syst. 34(11), 1704–1717 (2015)
24. Kong, Z., Jones, A., Medina Ayala, A., Aydin Gol, E., Belta, C.: Temporal logic inference for classification and prediction from data. In: Proceedings of the 17th International Conference on Hybrid Systems: Computation and Control, pp. 273–282. ACM (2014)
25. Lindemann, L., Dimarogonas, D.V.: Robust control for signal temporal logic specifications using average space robustness. arXiv preprint arXiv:1607.07019 (2016)
26. Maler, O., Nickovic, D.: Monitoring temporal properties of continuous signals. In: Lakhnech, Y., Yovine, S. (eds.) FORMATS/FTRTFT -2004. LNCS, vol. 3253, pp. 152–166. Springer, Heidelberg (2004). doi:10.1007/978-3-540-30206-3_12
27. Maler, O., Nickovic, D., Pnueli, A.: Checking temporal properties of discrete, timed and continuous behaviors. In: Avron, A., Dershowitz, N., Rabinovich, A. (eds.) Pillars of Computer Science. LNCS, vol. 4800, pp. 475–505. Springer, Heidelberg (2008). doi:10.1007/978-3-540-78127-1_26
28. Muggleton, S.: Learning from positive data. In: Muggleton, S. (ed.) ILP 1996. LNCS, vol. 1314, pp. 358–376. Springer, Heidelberg (1997). doi:10.1007/3-540-63494-0_65
29. Price, K., Storn, R.M., Lampinen, J.A.: Differential Evolution: A Practical Approach to Global Optimization. Springer Science & Business Media, New York (2006)
30. Raman, V., Donzé, A., Maasoumy, M., Murray, R.M., Sangiovanni-Vincentelli, A.L., Seshia, S.A.: Model predictive control with signal temporal logic specifications. In: CDC, pp. 81–87, December 2014
31. Sadraddini, S., Belta, C.: Robust temporal logic model predictive control. In: 2015 53rd Annual Allerton Conference on Communication, Control, and Computing (Allerton), pp. 772–779. IEEE (2015)
32. Valiant, L.G.: A theory of the learnable. Commun. ACM 27(11), 1134–1142 (1984)
33. Yang, H., Hoxha, B., Fainekos, G.: Querying parametric temporal logic properties on embedded systems. In: Nielsen, B., Weise, C. (eds.) ICTSS 2012. LNCS, vol. 7641, pp. 136–151. Springer, Heidelberg (2012). doi:10.1007/978-3-642-34691-0_11
34. Zhu, C., Byrd, R.H., Lu, P., Nocedal, J.: Algorithm 778: fortran subroutines for large-scale bound-constrained optimization. ACM Trans. Math. Softw. (TOMS) 23(4), 550–560 (1997)

From Model Checking to Runtime Verification and Back

Katarína Kejstová, Petr Ročkai[(✉)], and Jiří Barnat

Faculty of Informatics, Masaryk University, Brno, Czech Republic
{xkejstov,xrockai,barnat}@fi.muni.cz

Abstract. We describe a novel approach for adapting an existing software model checker to perform precise runtime verification. The software under test is allowed to communicate with the wider environment (including the file system and network). The modifications to the model checker are small and self-contained, making this a viable strategy for re-using existing model checking tools in a new context.

Additionally, from the data that is gathered during a single execution in the runtime verification mode, we automatically re-construct a description of the execution environment which can then be used in the standard, full-blown model checker. This additional verification step can further improve coverage, especially in the case of parallel programs, without introducing substantial overhead into the process of runtime verification.

1 Introduction

While model checking is a powerful technique for software verification, it also has certain limitations and deficiencies. Many of those limitations are related to the fact that a model checker must, by design, fully isolate the program from any outside effects. Therefore, for verification purposes, the program under test is placed into an artificial environment, which gives non-deterministic (but fully reproducible) responses to the program. The existence of this model environment immediately requires trade-offs to be made. If the environment model is too coarse, errors may be missed, or spurious errors may be introduced. Creating a detailed model is, however, more costly, and the result is not guaranteed to exactly match the behaviour of the actual environment either. Moreover, a detailed model may be too rigid: programs are often executed in conditions that have not been fully anticipated, and a certain amount of coarseness in the model of the environment can highlight such unwarranted assumptions.

Many of those challenges are, however, not unique to model checking. In the context of automated testing, the test environment plays a prominent role, and a large body of work deals with related problems. Unfortunately, adapting the methods used in automated testing to the context of model checking is far

---

This work has been partially supported by the Czech Science Foundation grant No. 15-08772S and by Red Hat, Inc.

S. Lahiri and G. Reger (Eds.): RV 2017, LNCS 10548, pp. 225–240, 2017.
DOI: 10.1007/978-3-319-67531-2_14

from straightforward. Making existing test-based setups easier to use with model checking tools is a core contribution of this paper.

Both manual and automated testing are established, core techniques which play an important role in virtually every software development project. In a certain sense, then, testing provides an excellent opportunity to integrate rigorous tools into the software development process. A number of verification tools specifically tailored for this mode of operation have seen great success in the software development community, for instance the memcheck tool from the valgrind suite. We show that it is possible to tap into this potential also with a traditionally-designed software model checker: we hope that this will help put powerful verification technology into the hands of software developers in a natural and seamless fashion. The second important contribution of this paper, then, is an approach to build a runtime verification tool out of an existing software model checker.

Our main motivating application is extending our existing software model checker, DIVINE [1], with a runtime verification mode. In its latest version, DIVINE has been split into a number of well-defined, reusable components [11] and this presented an opportunity to explore the contexts in which the new components could be used. Based on this motivation, our primary goal is to bring traditional (software) model checking and runtime verification closer together. As outlined above, there are two sides to this coin. One is to make model checking fit better into existing software development practice, the second is to derive powerful runtime verification tools from existing model checkers. To ensure that the proposed approach is viable in practice, we have built a prototype implementation, which allowed us to execute simple C and C++ programs in the resulting runtime verifier.

The rest of the paper is organised as follows: Sect. 2 describes prior art and related work, while Sect. 3 lays out our assumptions about the model checker and its host environment. Section 4 describes adapting a model checker to also work as a runtime verifier and Sect. 5 focuses on how to make use of data gathered by the runtime verifier in the context of model checking. Section 6 describes our prototype implementation based on DIVINE (including evaluation) and finally, Sect. 7 summarises and concludes the paper.

2   Related Work

There are two basic approaches to runtime verification [3]: online (real time) monitoring, where the program is annotated and, during execution, reports its actions to a monitor. In an offline mode, the trace is simply collected for later analysis. Clearly, an online-capable tool can also work in offline mode, but the reverse is not always true. An extension of the online approach allows the program to be monitored also in production, and property violations can invoke a recovery procedure in the program [7]. Our work, in principle, leads to an online verifier, albeit with comparatively high execution overhead, which makes it, in most cases, unsuitable for executing code in production environments. Depending on the model checker used, it can, however, report violations to the program and invoke recovery procedures and may therefore be employed this way in certain special cases.

Since our approach leads to a runtime verification tool, this can be compared to other such existing tools. With the exception of `valgrind` [8], most tools in this category focus on Java programs. For instance, Java PathExplorer [4] executes annotated Java byte code, along with a monitor which can check various properties, including past-time LTL. Other Java-based tools include Java-MOP [5] with focus on continuous monitoring and error recovery and Java-MaC [6] with focus on high-level, formal property specification.

Our *replay mode* (described in Sect. 5) is also related to the approach described in [2], where data collected at runtime is used to guide the model checker, with the aim of reducing the size of the state space. In our case, the primary motivation is to use the model checker for verifying more complex properties (including LTL) and to improve coverage of runtime verification.

3   Preliminaries

There are a few assumptions that we need to make about the mode of operation of the model checker. First, the model checker must be able to restrict the exploration to a single execution of the program, and it must support explicitly-valued operations. The simplest case is when the model checker in question is based on an explicit-state approach (we will deal with symbolic and/or abstract values in Sect. 3.1). If all values are represented explicitly in the model checker, exploration of a single execution is, in a sense, equivalent to simply running the program under test. Of course, since this is a model checker, the execution is subject to strict error checking.

3.1   Abstract and Symbolic Values

The limitation to exploring only a single execution is, basically, a limitation on *control flow*, not on the representation of variables. The root cause for the requirement of exploring only one control flow path is that we need to insert actions into the process of model checking that will have consequences in the outside world, consequences which cannot be undone or replayed. Therefore, it is not viable to restore prior states and explore different paths through the control flow graph, which is what normally happens in a model checker. It is, however, permissible to represent data in an abstract or symbolic form, which essentially means the resulting runtime verifier will also act as a symbolic executor. In this case, an additional requirement is that the values that reach the outside world are all concrete (the abstract representation used in the model checker would not be understood by the host operating system or the wider environment). Luckily, most tools with support for symbolic values already possess this capability, since it is useful in a number of other contexts.

3.2   Environments in Model Checking

A model checker needs a complete description of a system, that is, including any environment effects. This environment typically takes the form of code in the same language as the program itself, in our case C or C++. For small programs or program fragments, it is often sufficient to write a custom environment from scratch. This is analogous to how unit tests are written: effects from outside of the program are captured by the programmer and included as part of the test.

When dealing with larger programs or subsystems, however, the environment becomes a lot more complicated. When the program refers to an undefined function, the model checker will often provide a fallback implementation that gives completely undetermined results. This fallback, typically, does not produce any side effects. Such fallback functions constitute a form of synthetic model environment. However, this can be overly coarse: such model environment will admit many behaviours that are not actually possible in the real one, and vice versa, lasting side effects of a program action (for instance a change in file content) may not be captured at all. Those infidelities can introduce both false positives and false negatives. For this reason, it is often important to provide a more realistic environment.

A typical model checker (as opposed to a runtime verifier) cannot make use of a real operating system nor of testing-tailored, controlled environment built out of standard components (physical or virtual machines, commodity operating systems, network equipment and so on). A possible compromise is to implement an operating system which is designed to run inside a model checker, as a stand-in for the real OS. This operating system can then be re-used many times when constructing environments for model checking purposes. Moreover, this operating system is, to a certain degree, independent of the particular model checker in use. Like with standard operating systems, a substantial part of the code base can be re-used when porting the OS (that is, the host model checker is akin to a processor architecture or a hardware platform in standard operating systems).

Many programs of interest are designed to run on POSIX-like operating systems, and therefore, POSIX interfaces, along with the interfaces mandated by ISO C and C++ are a good candidate for implementation. This has the additional benefit that large parts of all these specifications are implemented in open source C and/or C++ code, and again, large parts of this code are easily ported to new kernels. Together, this means that a prefabricated environment with POSIX-like semantics is both useful for verifying many programs and relatively simple to create.

In the context of a model checker, the kernel of the operating system can be linked directly to the program, as if it were a library. In this approach, the model checker in question does not need any special support for loading kernel-like objects or even for privilege separation.

3.3   System Calls

In this section, we will consider how traditional operating systems, particularly in the POSIX family, define and implement system calls. A traditional operating system consists of many different parts, but in our context, the most important are the kernel and the user-space libraries which implement the operating system API (the most important of these libraries is, on a typical Unix system, `libc`). From the point of view of a user program, the `libc` API *is* the interface of the operating system. However, many functions which are mandated as part of this interface cannot be entirely implemented in the user space: they work with resources that the user-space code is unable to directly access. Examples of such functions would be `read` or `write`: consider a `read` from a file on a local file system. If the implementation was done in the user space, it would need direct access to the hardware, for instance the PCI bus, in order to talk to the hard drive which contains the requisite blocks of data which represent the file system. This is, quite clearly, undesirable, since granting such access to the user program would make access control and resource multiplexing impossible.

For these reasons, it is standard practice to implement parts of this functionality in separate, system-level code with a restricted interface, which makes access control and resource sharing possible. In operating system designs with monolithic kernels, this restricted interface consists of what is commonly known as system calls.[1] A system call is, then, a mechanism which allows the user-space code to request that the system-level software (the kernel) executes certain actions on behalf of the program (subject to appropriate permission and consistency checks). The actual implementation of syscall invocation is platform-specific, but it always involves a switch from user (non-privileged) mode into kernel mode (privileged mode, *supervisor* mode or *ring 0* on x86-style processors).

On POSIX-like systems, `libc` commonly provides a generic `syscall` function (it first appeared in 3BSD). This function allows the application to issue syscalls based on their number, passing arguments via an ellipsis (i.e. by taking advantage of variadic arguments in the C calling convention). In particular, this means that given a description of a system call (its number and the number and types of its arguments), it is possible to automatically construct an appropriate invocation of the `syscall` function.

3.4   Overview of Proposed Extensions

Under the proposed extensions, we have a model checker which can operate in two modes: *run* and *verify*. In the *run* mode, a single execution of the program is explored, in the standard execution order. We expect that all behaviour checking (enforcement of memory safety, assertion checks, etc.) is still performed in this mode. The *verify* mode, on the other hand, uses the standard model checking algorithm of the given tool.

The system under test (the input to this model checker), then, consists of the user program itself, along with the environment, the latter of which contains a stand-in operating system. The situation is illustrated in Fig. 1. The operating system has 3 different modes:

---

[1] In microkernel and other design schools, syscalls in the traditional sense only exist as an abstraction, and are implemented through some form of inter-process communication.

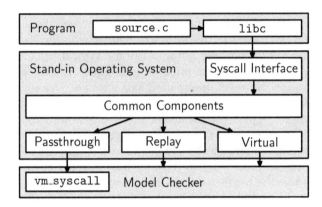

Fig. 1. A scheme of components involved in our proposed approach.

1. a *virtual* mode, in which all interaction with the real world is simply simulated – for example, a virtual file system is maintained in-memory and is therefore part of the state of the system under test; this OS mode can be used with both *run* and *verify* modes of the model checker
2. a *passthrough* mode, which uses the vm_syscall model checker extension to execute system calls in the host operating system and stores a trace of all the syscalls it executed for future reference; this OS mode can only be used in the *run* mode of the model checker
3. a *replay* mode, which reads the system call trace recorded in the *passthrough* mode, but does not interact with the host operating system; this OS mode can be again used in both the *run* and *verify* mode of the model checker

4   Syscall Passthrough

In order to turn a model checker into a runtime verifier, we propose a mechanism which we call *syscall passthrough*, where the virtual, stand-in operating system (see Sect. 3.2) gains the ability to execute syscalls in the host operating system (see also Sect. 3.3). Of course, this is generally *unsafe*, and only makes sense if the model checker can explore a single run of the program and do so *in order*.

Thanks to the architecture of system calls in POSIX-like kernels, we only need a single new primitive function to be implemented in the model checker (we will call this new primitive function vm_syscall from now on; first, we need to avoid confusion with the POSIX function syscall, second, the model checker acts as a virtual machine in this context). The sole purpose of the function is to construct and execute, in the context of the host operating system, an appropriate call to the host syscall function (the interface of which is explained in more detail in Sect. 3.3).

We would certainly like to avoid any system-specific knowledge in the implementation of vm_syscall – instead, any system-specific code should reside in the stand-in OS, which is much easier to modify than the model checker proper. To this end, the arguments to our `vm_syscall` primitive contain metadata describing the arguments `syscall` expects, in addition to the data itself. That is, `vm_syscall` needs to know whether a particular argument is an input or an output argument, its size, and if it is a buffer, the size of that buffer. The exact encoding of these metadata will be described in Sect. 4.1, along with more detailed rationale for this approach.

Finally, most of the implementation work is done in the context of the (stand-in) operating system (this is described in more detail in Sect. 4.2). This is good news, because most of the code in the operating system, including all of the code related to syscall passthrough, is in principle portable between model checkers.

4.1 Model Checker Extension

The model checker, on the other hand, only needs to provide one additional primitive. As already mentioned, we call this primitive `vm_syscall`, and it should be available as a variadic C function to the system under test. This is similar to other built-in functions often provided by model checkers, like `malloc` or a non-deterministic choice operator. While in the program under test, invocations of such built-ins look just like ordinary C function calls, they are handled differently in the model checker and often cause special behaviour that is not otherwise available to a C program.

We would like this extension to be as platform-neutral as possible, while maintaining simplicity. Of course not all platforms provide the `syscall` primitive described in Sect. 3.3, and on these platforms, the extension will be a little more complicated. Namely, when porting to a platform of this type, we need to provide our own implementation of `syscall`, which is easy to do when the system calls are available as C functions, even if tedious. In this case, we can simply assign numbers to system calls and construct a single `switch` statement which, based on a number, calls the appropriate C function.

Therefore, we can rely on the `syscall` system-level primitive without substantial loss of generality or portability. The next question to ask is whether a different extension would serve our purpose better – in particular, there is the obvious choice of exposing each syscall separately as a model checker primitive. There are two arguments against this approach.

First, it is desirable that the syscall-related machinery is all in one place and not duplicated in both the stand-in operating system and in the model checker. However, in the *virtual* and *replay* modes, this machinery must be part of the stand-in operating system, which suggests that this should be also the case in the *passthrough* mode.

Second, the number of system calls is quite large (typically a few hundred functions) and the functions are system-dependent. When the code that is specific to the host operating system resides in the stand-in operating system, it can be ported once and multiple model checkers can benefit. Of course, the stand-in operating system needs to be ported to the model checker in question, but this offers many additional advantages (particularly the virtual mode).

Now if we decide that a single universal primitive becomes part of the model checker, we still need to decide the syntax and the semantics of this extension. Since different system calls take different arguments with varying meaning, the primitive itself will clearly need to be variadic. Since one of the main reasons for choosing a single-primitive interface was platform neutrality, the primitive itself should not possess special knowledge about individual syscalls. First of all, it does not know the bit widths of individual arguments (on most systems, some arguments can be 32 bit – for instance file descriptors – and other 64 bit – object sizes, pointers, etc.). This information is crucial to correctly set up the call to syscall (the variadic arguments must line up). Moreover, some pointer-type arguments represent variable-sized *input* data (the buffer argument to write, for example) and others represent *output* data (the buffer argument to read). In both cases, the size of the memory allocated for the variable-sized argument must be known to vm_syscall, so that this memory can be correctly copied between the model checker and the system under test.

```
vm_syscall( SYS_read,
           _VM_SC_Out | _VM_SC_Int32, &read,
           _VM_SC_In  | _VM_SC_Int32, fd,
           _VM_SC_Out | _VM_SC_Mem, length, buffer,
           _VM_SC_In  | _VM_SC_Int32, length );
```

Fig. 2. An example invocation of vm_syscall performing a read passthrough.

For these reasons, the arguments to vm_syscall also contain metadata: for each real argument that ought to be passed on to syscall, 2 or 3 arguments are passed to vm_syscall. The first one is always type information: whether the following argument is a scalar (32 b or 64 b integer) or a pointer, whether it is an input or an output. If the value is a scalar input, the second argument is the value itself, if it is a scalar output, the following argument is a pointer to an appropriate-sized piece of memory. If the value is a pointer, the size of the pointed-to object comes second and the pointer itself comes third. An example invocation of vm_syscall is shown in Fig. 2. The information passed to vm_syscall this way is sufficient to both construct a valid call to syscall and to copy inputs from the system under test to the host system and pass back the outputs.

4.2   Operating System Extension

The vm_syscall interface described above is a good low-level interface to pass syscalls through to the host operating system, but it is very different from the usual POSIX way to invoke them, and it is not very intuitive or user-friendly either. It is also an unsafe interface, because wrong metadata passed to vm_syscall can crash the model checker, or corrupt its memory.

The proper POSIX interface is to provide a separate C function for each syscall, essentially a thin wrapper that just passes the arguments along. Calling these dedicated wrappers is more convenient, and since they are standard C functions, their use can be type-checked by the compiler. In the *virtual* mode of the operating system, those wrappers cause the execution to divert into the kernel. We can therefore re-use the entire `libc` without modifications, and implement syscall passthrough at the kernel level, where we have more control over the code.

In our OS design, the kernel implements each system call as a single C++ method of a certain class (a *component*). Which exact components are activated is decided at boot time, and it is permissible that a given system call is implemented in multiple components. Since the components are arranged in a stack, the topmost component with an implementation of a given system call "wins". In this system, implementing a passthrough mode is simply a question of implementing a suitable passthrough component and setting it up. When `libc` invokes a system call, the control is redirected into the kernel as usual, and the passthrough component can construct an appropriate invocation of `vm_syscall`.

This construction requires the knowledge of a particular system call. Those are, luckily, more or less standardised by POSIX and the basic set is therefore reasonably portable. Moreover, we already need all of this knowledge in the implementation of the virtual mode, and hence most of the code related to the details of argument passing can be shared. As mentioned earlier, this means that the relevant `libc` code and the syscall mechanism it uses internally is identical in all the different modes of operation. The passthrough mode is, therefore, implemented entirely in the kernel of the stand-in operating system.

4.3   Tracing the Syscalls

The architecture of syscall passthrough makes it easy to capture argument values and results of every invoked syscall, in addition to actually passing it on to the host operating system. Namely, the implementation knows exactly which arguments are inputs and which are outputs and knows the exact size of any buffer or any other argument passed as a pointer (both input and output). This allows the implementation to store all this data in a file (appending new records as they happen). This file can then be directly loaded for use in the *replay mode* of the stand-in operating system.

5   Syscall Replay

In a model checker, all aspects of program execution are fully repeatable. This property is carried over into the *virtual* operating mode (as described in this paper), but not into the *passthrough* mode. System calls in the host operating system are, in general, not repeatable: files appear and disappear and change content, network resources come and go and so on, often independently of the execution of the program of interest.

What the passthrough mode can do, however, is recording the answers from the host operating system (see Sect. 4.3). When we wish to repeat the same execution of the program (recall that everything apart from the values coming from vm_syscall is under the full control of the model checker), we do not need to actually pass on the syscalls to the host operating system: instead, we can read off the outputs from a trace. This is achieved by simply replacing all invocations of vm_syscall by a different mechanism, which we will call replay_syscall. This new function looks at the trace, ensures that the syscall invoked by the program matches the one that comes next in the trace and then simply plays back the effects observable in the program. Since the program is otherwise isolated by the model checker, those effects are limited to the changes the syscall caused in its output parameters and the value of errno. The appropriate return value is likewise obtained from the trace.

5.1 Motivation

There are two important applications of the replay mode. First, if the model checker in question provides interactive tools to work with the state space, we can use those tools to look at real executions of the program, and in particular, we can easily step backwards in time. That is, if we have an interactive simulator (like, for example, presented in [10]), we can derive a reversible debugger essentially for free by recording an execution in the passthrough mode and then exploring the corresponding path through the state space in the *replay* mode.

Second, if the behaviour of the program depends on circumstances other than the effects and return values of system calls, it is often the case that multiple different executions of the program will result in an identical sequence of system calls. As an example, if the program contains multiple threads, one of which issues syscalls and others only participate in computation and synchronisation, the exact thread interleaving will only have a limited effect on the order and arguments of system calls, if any. The model checker is free to explore all such interleavings, as long as they produce the same syscall trace.

That this is a practical ability is easily demonstrated. A common problem is that a given program, when executed in a controlled environment, sometimes executes correctly and other times incorrectly. In this case, by a controlled environment we mean that files and network resources did not change, and that the behaviour of the program does not depend on the value of the real-time clock. Therefore, we can reasonably expect the syscall trace to be identical (at least up to the point where the unexpected behaviour is encountered). If this is the case, the model checker will be able to reliably detect the problem based on a single syscall trace, regardless of whether the problem did or did not appear while running in the passthrough mode.

5.2 Constructing the State Space

As explained above, we can use the replay mode to explore behaviours of the program that result in an identical syscall trace, but are not, computation-wise, identical to the original passthrough execution. In this case, it is important that the model checker explores only executions with this property. A primitive which is commonly available in model checkers and which can serve this purpose is typically known as assume[2]. The effect of this primitive is to instruct the model checker to abandon any executions where the condition of the assume does not hold. Therefore, our replay_syscall, whenever it detects a mismatch between the syscall issued by the program and the one that is next in the trace, it can simply issue assume(false). The execution is abandoned and the model checker is forced to explore only those runs that match the external behaviour of the original.

5.3 Causality-Induced Partial Order

The requirement that the traces exactly match up is often unnecessarily constraining. For instance, it is quite obvious that the order of two read operations (with no intervening write operations) can be flipped without affecting the outcome of either of the two reads. In this sense, such two reads are not actually ordered in the trace. This means that the trace does not need to be ordered linearly – the two reads are, instead, incomparable in the causal ordering. In general, it is impossible to find the exact causal relationships between syscalls, especially from the trace alone – a write to a file may or may not have caused certain bytes to appear on the stdin of the program. We can, however, construct an approximation of the correct partial order, and we can do so safely: the constructed ordering will always respect causality, but it may order certain actions unnecessarily strictly.

We say that two actions a and b (system call invocations) *commute* if the outcome of both is the same, regardless of their relative ordering (both a and b have the same individual effect, whether they are executed as a, b or as b, a). Given a sequence of system calls that respects the causal relationships, swapping two adjacent entries which commute will lead to a new sequence with the same property. We can obtain an approximate partial order by constructing all such sequences and declaring that $a < b$ iff this is the case in all of the generated sequences.

6 Prototype Implementation

We have implemented the approach described in this paper, using the DIVINE 4 software model checker as a base. In particular, we rely on the DiVM component in DIVINE, which is a verification-focused virtual machine based on the LLVM intermediate representation (more details in Sect. 6.1). The architecture of DIVINE 4, as a model checker, is illustrated in Fig. 3. First, we have extended DiVM with the vm_syscall primitive (cf. Section 4). Taking advantage of this extension, we have implemented the requisite support code in DiOS, as described in Sect. 4.2. DiOS is a pre-existing stand-in operating system component which

---

[2] The assume primitive is a counterpart to assert and has a similar interface. It is customary that a single boolean value is given as a parameter to the assume statement (function call), representing the assumed condition.

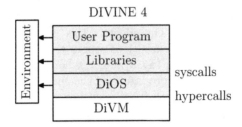

Fig. 3. The architecture of DIVINE 4. The shaded part is, from a model checking point of view, the system under test. However, DiOS and most of the libraries are shipped as part of DIVINE.

originally supported only the *virtual* mode of operation. As part of the work presented in this paper, we implemented both a passthrough and a replay mode in DiOS.

In the rest of this section, we will describe the underpinnings of DIVINE 4 in more detail. The first important observation is that, since DIVINE is based on interpreting LLVM bitcode, it can use a standard compiler front-end to compile C and C++ programs into the bitcode form, which can then be directly verified. We will also discuss the limitations of the current implementation and demonstrate its viability using a few examples.

6.1   LLVM Bitcode

LLVM bitcode (or intermediate representation) [9] is an assembly-like language primarily aimed at optimisation and analysis. The idea is that LLVM-based analysis and optimisation code can be shared by many different compilers: a compiler front end builds simple LLVM IR corresponding to its input and delegates all further optimisation and native code generation to a common back end. This architecture is quite common in other compilers: as an example, GCC contains a number of different front ends that share infrastructure and code generation. The major innovation of LLVM is that the language on which all the common middle and back end code operates is exposed and available to 3rd-party tools. It is also quite well-documented and LLVM provides stand-alone tools to work with both bitcode and textual form of this intermediate representation.

From a language viewpoint, LLVM IR is in partial SSA form (single static assignment) with explicit basic blocks. Each basic block is made up of instructions, the last of which is a *terminator*. The terminator instruction encodes relationships between basic blocks, which form an explicit control flow graph. An example of a terminator instruction would be a conditional or an unconditional branch or a `ret`. Such instructions either transfer control to another basic block of the same function or stop execution of the function altogether.

Besides explicit control flow, LLVM also strives to make much of the data flow explicit, taking advantage of partial SSA for this reason. It is, in general, impossible to convert entire programs to a full SSA form; however, especially within a single function, it is possible to convert a significant portion of code. The SSA-form values are called *registers* in LLVM and only a few instructions can "lift" values from memory into registers and put them back again (most importantly `load` and `store`, respectively, plus a handful of atomic memory access instructions).

6.2   Runtime Verification with LLVM

While LLVM bitcode is primarily designed to be transformed and compiled to native code, it can be, in principle, executed directly. Of course, this is less convenient than working with native code, but since the bitcode is appreciably more abstract than typical processor-level code, it is more amenable to model checking. The situation can be improved by providing tools which can work with hybrid object files, which contain both native code and the corresponding LLVM bitcode. This way, the same binary can be both executed natively and analysed by LLVM-based tools.

6.3   LLVM Extensions for Verification

Unfortunately, LLVM bitcode alone is not sufficiently expressive to describe real programs: most importantly, it is not possible to encode interaction with the operating system into LLVM instructions. When LLVM is used as an intermediate step in a compiler, the lowest level of the user side of the system call mechanism is usually provided as an external, platform-specific function with a standard C calling convention. This function is usually implemented in the platform's assembly language. The system call interface, in turn, serves as a gateway between the program and the operating system, unlocking OS-specific functionality to the program. An important point is that the gateway function itself cannot be implemented in portable LLVM.

To tackle these problems, a small set of primitives was proposed in [11] (henceforth, we will refer to this enriched language as DiVM). With these primitives, it is possible to implement a small, isolated operating system in the DiVM language alone. DIVINE already provides such an operating system, called DiOS – the core OS is about 2500 lines of C++, with additional 5000 lines of code providing *virtual* POSIX-compatible file system and socket interfaces. Our implementation of the ideas outlined in Sect. 4.2 can, therefore, re-use a substantial part of the existing code of DiOS.

6.4   Source Code

The implementation consists of two parts. The model checker extension is about 200 lines of C++, some of which is quite straightforward. The DiOS extension is more complex: the passthrough component is about 1400 lines, while the replay component is less than 600. All the relevant source code, including the entire DIVINE 4 model checker, can be obtained online[3].

---

[3] https://divine.fi.muni.cz/2017/passthrough/.

6.5   Limitations

There are two main limitations in our current implementation. The first is caused by a simplistic implementation of the *run* mode of our model checker (see Sect. 3.4). The main drawback of such a simple implementation is that syscalls that block may cause the entire model checker to deadlock. Specifically, this could happen in cases where one program thread is waiting for an action performed by another program thread. Since there is only a single model checker thread executing everything, if it becomes blocked, no program threads can make any progress. There are two possible counter-measures: one is to convert all system calls to non-blocking when corresponding vm_syscall invocations are constructed, another is to create multiple threads in the model checker, perhaps even a new thread for each system call. Only the latter approach requires additional modifications to the model checker, but both require modifications to the stand-in operating system.

The second limitation stems from the fact that our current libc implementation only covers a subset of POSIX. For instance, the gethostbyname interface (that is, the component of libc known as a resolver) is not available. This omission unfortunately prevents many interesting programs from working at the moment. However, this is not a serious limitation in principle, since the resolver component from an existing libc can be ported. Many of the networking-related interfaces are already present and work (in particular, TCP/IP client functionality has been tested, cf. Section 6.6).

Finally, a combination of both those limitations means that the fork system call, which would create a new process, is not available. In addition to problems with blocking calls, there are a few attributes that are allocated to each process, and those attributes can be observed by certain system calls. For example, one such attribute is the pid (process identifier), obtainable with a getpid system call, another is the working directory of the process, available through getcwd. Again, there are multiple ways to resolve this problem, some of which require modifications in the model checker.

6.6   Evaluation

Mainly due to the limitations outlined in Sect. 6.5, it is not yet possible to use our prototype with many complete, real-world programs. The domain in which DIVINE has been mainly used so far are either small, self-contained programs and unit tests for algorithms and data structures. Both sequential and parallel programs can be verified. The source distribution of DIVINE includes about 600 test cases for the model checker, many of which also use POSIX interfaces, leveraging the existing *virtual* mode of DiOS. As a first part of our evaluation, we took all those test cases and executed them in the new *passthrough* mode, that is, in a mode when DIVINE acts as a runtime verifier. A total of 595 tests passed without any problems, 3 timed out due to use of blocking system calls and 9 timed out due to presence of infinite loops. Of course, since runtime verification is not exhaustive, not all errors present in the 595 tests were uncovered in this mode.

The second part of our evaluation was to write small programs that specifically test the *passthrough* and the *replay* mode:

- `pipe`, which creates a named pipe and two threads, one writer and one reader and checks that data is transmitted through the pipe
- `rw` which simply creates, writes to and reads from files
- `rw-par` in which one thread writes data to a file and another reads and checks that data
- `network`, a very simple HTTP client which opens a TCP/IP connection to a fixed IP address, performs an HTTP request and prints the result

We tested these programs in both the *passthrough* mode and in the *replay* mode. While very simple, they clearly demonstrate that the approach works. The source code of those test programs is also available online[4]. Clearly, our verifier incurs appreciable overhead, since it interprets the program, instead of executing it directly. Quantitative assessment of the runtime and memory overhead is subject to future work (more complex test cases are required).

7 Conclusions and Future Work

We have described an approach which allows us to take advantage of an existing software model checking tool in the context of runtime verification. On one hand, this approach makes model checking more useful by making it usable with real environments while retaining many of its advantages over testing. On the other hand, it makes existing model checking tools useful in cases when runtime verification is the favoured approach. The approach is lightweight, since the modification to the model checker is small and self-contained. The other component required in our approach, the stand-in operating system, is also reasonably portable between model checkers. The overall effort associated with our approach is small, compared to implementing two dedicated tools (a model checker and a runtime verifier).

In the future, we plan to remove the limitations described in Sect. 6.5 and offer a production-ready implementation of both a passthrough and a replay mode in DIVINE 4. Since the results of the preliminary evaluation are highly encouraging, we firmly believe that a runtime verification mode based on the ideas laid out in this paper will be fully integrated into a future release of DIVINE.

References

1. Barnat, J., Brim, L., Havel, V., Havlíček, J., Kriho, J., Lenco, M., Ročkai, P., Still, V., Weiser, J.: DiVinE 3.0 – an explicit-state model checker for multithreaded C & C++ programs. In: Sharygina, N., Veith, H. (eds.) CAV 2013. LNCS, vol. 8044. Springer, Heidelberg (2013). doi:10.1007/978-3-642-39799-8_60

---

[4] https://divine.fi.muni.cz/2017/passthrough/.

2. Havelund, K.: Using runtime analysis to guide model checking of Java programs. In: Havelund, K., Penix, J., Visser, W. (eds.) SPIN 2000. LNCS, vol. 1885, pp. 245–264. Springer, Heidelberg (2000). doi:10.1007/10722468_15

3. Havelund, K., Rosu, G.: Efficient monitoring of safety properties. STTT **6**(2), 158–173 (2004). doi:10.1007/s10009-003-0117-6

4. Havelund, K., Rosu, G.: An overview of the runtime verification tool Java PathExplorer. Formal Methods Syst. Des. **24**(2), 189–215 (2004). doi:10.1023/B:FORM.0000017721.39909.4b

5. Jin, D., O'Neil Meredith, P., Lee, C., Roşu, G.: JavaMOP: efficient parametric runtime monitoring framework. In: International Conference on Software Engineering (ICSE), pp. 1427–1430. IEEE, June 2012. doi:10.1109/ICSE.2012.6227231

6. Kim, M., Viswanathan, M., Kannan, S., Lee, I., Sokolsky, O.: Java-MaC: a run-time assurance approach for java programs. Formal Methods Syst. Des. **24**(2), 129–155 (2004). doi:10.1023/B:FORM.0000017719.43755.7c. ISSN:1572–8102

7. O'Neil Meredith, P., Jin, D., Griffith, D., Chen, F., Roşu, G.: An overview of the MOP runtime verification framework. Int. J. Softw. Tools Technol. Transfer **14**(3), 249–289 (2012). doi:10.1007/s10009-011-0198-6. ISSN:1433–2787

8. Nethercote, N., Seward, J.: Valgrind: a framework for heavyweight dynamic binary instrumentation. In: PLDI (2007)

9. The LLVM Project. LLVM language reference manual (2016). http://llvm.org/docs/LangRef.html

10. Petr Ročkai and JiříBarnat. A simulator for LLVM bitcode. 2017. Preliminary version. https://arxiv.org/abs/1704.05551

11. Ročkai, P., Štill, V., Černà, I., Barnat, J.: DiVM: model checking with LLVM and graph memory (2017). Preliminary version. https://arxiv.org/abs/1703.05341

Verifying Policy Enforcers

Oliviero Riganelli[1]([⊠]), Daniela Micucci[1], Leonardo Mariani[1],
and Yliès Falcone[2]

[1] University of Milano Bicocca, Viale Sarca 336, 20126 Milan, Italy
{riganelli,micucci,mariani}@disco.unimib.it
[2] Univ. Grenoble Alpes, CNRS, Inria, Grenoble INP, LIG,
38000 Grenoble, France
ylies.falcone@univ-grenoble-alpes.fr

Abstract. Policy enforcers are sophisticated runtime components that can prevent failures by enforcing the correct behavior of the software. While a single enforcer can be easily designed focusing only on the behavior of the application that must be monitored, the effect of multiple enforcers that enforce different policies might be hard to predict. So far, mechanisms to resolve interferences between enforcers have been based on priority mechanisms and heuristics. Although these methods provide a mechanism to take decisions when multiple enforcers try to affect the execution at a same time, they do not guarantee the lack of interference on the global behavior of the system.

In this paper we present a verification strategy that can be exploited to discover interferences between sets of enforcers and thus safely identify a-priori the enforcers that can co-exist at run-time. In our evaluation, we experimented our verification method with several policy enforcers for Android and discovered some incompatibilities.

Keywords: Proactive library · Self-healing · Android · Resource usage · API · Policy enforcement · Runtime enforcement

1 Introduction

Software ecosystems provide new challenges to verification and validation techniques. An ecosystem is typically composed of a marketplace, where software applications are published and made available to the public, application developers, who implement and share their applications through the marketplace, and customers, who search, download, and use the applications in the marketplace [22]. Notable examples of marketplaces are Android's Google Play, and Apple's App Store.

Marketplaces represent useful channels that enable direct communication between developers and customers. However, marketplaces also expose customers to several threats. In fact, it is extremely hard to control the quality of every application published on a marketplace, and thus marketplaces end up containing a number of unreliable, unsafe, and unstable applications [5,7,34,36,37].

© Springer International Publishing AG 2017
S. Lahiri and G. Reger (Eds.): RV 2017, LNCS 10548, pp. 241–258, 2017.
DOI: 10.1007/978-3-319-67531-2_15

In addition to enriching marketplaces with advanced mechanisms to check the quality of the published applications [25], customers can exploit richer execution environments to protect themselves from the execution of untrusted software applications. In this context, the *policy enforcement* technology provides mechanisms to automatically detect the violations of correctness policies and enforce the correct behavior at runtime. These solutions have been already experienced in several contexts, including the Android environment [8,12,16,24,32].

While activating a single enforcer that can guarantee that a given policy is satisfied is not problematic, there might be issues when multiple policies should be guaranteed simultaneously. In fact, the policy enforcers might *interfere* one with the other, introducing unexpected behaviors whose effect might be even worse than the result produced by the monitored application without the enforcers.

So far, the problem of interfering enforcers has been addressed using *priority mechanisms* that can disambiguate at runtime which enforcer to execute when multiple enforcers need to react to a same event in different ways [9]. While these mechanisms can be effective in some cases, they suffer from three limitations:

- *Direct Interference:* Priority mechanisms are not adequate when enforcers have to modify a same execution at multiple points to guarantee a sound behavior of the application. For instance, an enforcer may automatically release the microphone acquired by an app when the app is paused, but may also need to acquire and assign the microphone back to the same app when the execution of the app is resumed. If the conflict resolution policy let the enforcer modify the execution only once, for instance because a second higher priority (interfering) enforcer prevents the acquisition of the microphone by the first enforcer, the resulting execution may produce highly undesirable results. For instance, the app may fail once the execution is resumed because the formerly acquired microphone is not available anymore.
- *Indirect Interference:* Enforcers might interfere even if not impacting on exactly the same events. For instance, two enforcers may independently act on two dependent resources (e.g., the Android media recorder and the microphone) producing an interference. In fact, releasing the Android media recorder also releases the microphone which cannot be used anymore unless it is acquired again. Thus an enforcer monitoring the usage of the media recorder while enforcing certain policies may interfere with an enforcer doing the same for the microphone.
- *Late Detection of Interferences:* Even when interferences are on the same events, priority mechanisms are heuristic solutions that operate at runtime to guarantee that at least one policy is correctly enforced. On the contrary, an a-priori analysis of possible interferences allows to detect the interferences in advance. This information is useful both to users, who might be prohibited to activate incompatible sets of enforcers, and to developers, who could redesign the enforcers in such a way that all the policies are correctly enforced.

In this paper, we present an interference detection strategy that overcomes the aforementioned problems for enforcers defined as *edit automata*, which is the most used formalism to define the behavior of enforcers that can manipulate executions [27]. The analysis is designed for enforcers that prevent applications from misusing the resources available in their execution environment. In order to apply the analysis, the *lifecyle* of the applications, which is the same for every application, and the *usage protocol* of the resources, which does not depend on the specific app that uses the resources, must be known.

Note that if a set of enforcers that monitor interactions with some resources does not interfere according to our analysis, they can be activated together regardless of the specific applications that are executed, because the application lifecycle and the usage policies are always the same.

We applied the analysis to 25 enforcers designed to guarantee that Android apps use resources appropriately, and we have been able to verify the compatibility of the enforcers, also discovering some interferences.

The paper is organized as follows. Section 2 provides background definitions. Section 3 introduces a motivating case that is used to illustrate the analysis. Section 4 presents the analysis for interference detection. Section 5 presents our experience with Android. Finally, Sects. 6 and 7 discuss related work and provide final remarks, respectively.

2   Background

This section defines three concepts that are exploited in the paper to define the interference analysis: policies, edit automata, and I/O automata.

2.1   Policy

Let Σ denote a finite set of observable program actions a. An *execution* σ is a finite or infinite non-empty sequence of actions $a_1; a_2; \ldots; a_n$. The notation $\sigma[i]$ denotes the i-th action in the sequence. The notation $\sigma[\ldots i]$ represents the prefix of σ until the i-th actions, and $|\sigma|$ represents the length of the sequence. The symbol ϵ denotes the empty sequence, that is, an execution with no actions.

Σ^* is the set of all finite sequences, while Σ^ω is the of infinite sequences. Finally Σ^∞ is the set of all the sequences (both finite and infinite).

Given a set of executions $\chi \subseteq \Sigma^\infty$, a *policy* is a predicate P on χ. A policy P is satisfied by a set of executions χ if and only if $P(\chi)$ evaluates to *true*.

Policy Example. The Android framework includes the `MediaPlayer` API for the playback of audio/video files and streams. To use the media player in their applications, developers must obtain an instance of a `MediaPlayer` by invoking the class method `create()`. The acquired media player instance can be released by invoking the instance method `release()`.

According to the Android documentation, to make the media player available to other applications and to avoid resource leaks, the usage of the `MediaPlayer` should be governed by the following policy:

Policy 1: *"if you are using a MediaPlayer and your activity receives a call to onStop, you must release the MediaPlayer."* [2]

For the purpose of the analysis presented in this paper, we represent policies as CTL formulas [6]. We use CTL because it is the language supported by UPAAL [10], which is the verification tool that we used in the empirical evaluation. However, our properties express linear-time behaviour, thus they could also be expressed with LTL. For example, *Policy 1* can be defined as

AG(MediaPlayer.create $\Rightarrow$

AXA[¬Activity.onStop W(MediaPlayer.release)])

which states that "once the MediaPlayer is created, the Activity can be stopped only after the MediaPlayer' has been released".

2.2   Edit Automata

Edit automata can be used to describe how policies can be enforced at runtime [26]. An edit automaton is an abstract machine that specifies how an execution is transformed by inserting and suppressing actions. More formally, an edit automaton A_E is a tuple $< \Sigma, Q, q_0, \delta >$ where:

– Σ is a finite or countably infinite set of *actions*;
– Q is a finite or countably infinite set of *states*;
– q_0 is the *initial state*;
– $\delta : Q \times \Sigma \rightarrow Q \times \Sigma^*$ is the *transition function* that maps a state and an action to the new state reached by the automaton and the finite or empty sequence of actions emitted by the automaton that is indicated by the second component in the returned pair. When the emitted action is the same as the accepted action, the automaton does not affect the execution. In the other cases, the actions that are actually executed are influenced by the edit automaton. Action suppression is represented with the empty sequence.

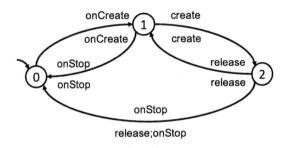

Fig. 1. Edit Automaton EA_{p1} enforcing *Policy 1*

Example of edit automata. Figure 1 shows the EA_{p1} edit automaton, which can enforce policy *Policy 1* at runtime. The symbol above a transition indicates the input symbol accepted by the automaton, while the sequence below a transition indicates the output sequence emitted by the automaton when the input sequence is accepted.

In the initial state (state 0), EA_{p1} accepts a call to the onCreate callback method, which represents the creation of an activity[1]. The creation of an activity causes a transition from state 0 to state 1 in the model. When the activity is destroyed, the onStop callback is emitted and the model moves back to state 0. In these cases, the execution is never modified, that is, the transition always emits the accepted action.

State 1 also accepts a call to the create method, which returns an instance of the MediaPlayer. This case corresponds to the app starting to use the MediaPlayer. It causes a transition to state 2 in the model, while the execution is left unaltered by the edit automaton. State 2 is the state that can detect the violation of the resource usage policy, if any. In fact, if the onStop callback method is detected, the application is paused without releasing the MediaPlayer. The automaton fixes the execution by intercepting the call to onStop and emitting the sequence release;onStop (transition from state 2 to state 0), which forces the release of the MediaPlayer. On the contrary, if release is emitted, *Policy 1* is satisfied and the model does not change the execution.

2.3 I/O Automata

An input/output automaton is a labeled state machine typically used for modelling the behavior of reactive and distributed systems [28]. Formally, an I/O automaton A is a tuple $\langle states, start, sig, trans \rangle$, where:

- *states* is a finite or infinite set of *states*;
- *start* $\subseteq$ *states* is a set of *initial states*;
- *sig* is the set of *actions* of A partitioned into input actions *in*, internal actions *int* and output actions *out*.
- *trans* $\subseteq$ *states* $\times$ *sig* $\times$ *states* is a set of *transitions* such that for every state $s \in$ *states* and every input action $\pi \in$ *in*, there is a transition $(s, \pi, s') \in$ *trans*.

Input and output actions enable the communication between the automaton and the environment: the environment controls input actions, while the automaton controls the output (and internal) actions. For any state s and action π, if I/O automaton A has some transitions of the form (s, π, s'), then π is said to be enabled in s. Since an I/O automaton is unable to block any input, input actions in set *in* should be enabled in every state.

---

[1] Android apps are composed of multiple components called activities.

3   Motivating Example

This section presents a motivating example that is also a case of interference
that we discovered in our evaluation. It consists of two enforcers that work
correctly when used individually, but that interfere when activated simultaneously. The two enforcers implement different usage policies for the Android
MediaPlayer API.

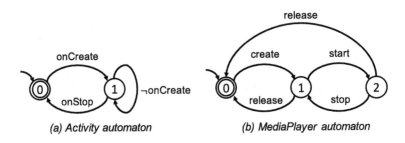

Fig. 2. System automata for the MediaPlayer example.

In order to describe the two enforcers, we also need to specify the behavior
of a generic Android application, in terms of the lifecycle events, and the usage
protocol of the MediaPlayer API. Note that these two elements are invariant
for every application, that is, regardless of the application that is executed at
runtime, the lifecycle events and the usage protocol of a MediaPlayer are always
the same.

To keep the example small and simple, we only represent the actions that are
relevant to the policies that we want to enforce. Figure 2(a) shows the model of
the Android activity lifecycle [4] limited to the creation and the stopping of an
activity. Figure 2(b) shows the usage protocol for the MediaPlayer API derived
from the Android specifications [2].

In this example, we consider the enforcement of two policies extracted from
technical and scientific documentation about the MediaPlayer API. The first
policy is *Policy 1* introduced in Sect. 2, while the second policy about stopping
the execution of the player is the following one:

Policy 2: "*if you started a MediaPlayer and your activity receives a call
to onStop, you must stop the MediaPlayer.*" [37]

The edit automaton EA_{p1} that can enforce *Policy 1* is shown in Fig. 1 and
has been discussed in Sect. 2.

Figure 3 shows EA_{p2}, the edit automaton that can enforce *Policy 2*. As long
as the MediaPlayer is started after the activity has been created and is stopped
before the activity is stopped, the enforcer does not change the execution. However, if the activity is stopped without first stopping the MediaPlayer (transition

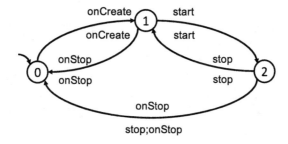

Fig. 3. Edit Automaton EA_{p2} enforcing `Policy 2`

from state 2 to state 0), the enforcer changes the execution inserting the `stop` action, before the execution of `onStop`.

The enforcers in Figs. 1 and 3 can interfere if they are both in their respective states 2 and the Android framework produces the `onStop` callback. In this case, both enforcers capture the `onStop` callback and attempt to change the execution. The interference occurs when the enforcer for *Policy 1* changes the execution before the enforcer for *Policy 2*.

In particular, if the automaton enforcing *Policy 1* outputs the `release` of the `MediaPlayer` instance before the other enforcer outputs the `stop` action, the `MediaPlayer` instance will be released, and the system will reach a deadlock state. In fact, the enforcer for *Policy 2* is no longer able to invoke the `stop` operation of the `MediaPlayer` instance because this call is not accepted by the `MediaPlayer` API protocol as shown in Fig. 2(b). Since the model of the resource forbids to call method *stop* from state 0, the interference results in a deadlock at the level of the models. In practice, the call to *stop* is issued by the enforcer and the execution fails due to an exception produced by the resource.

In the next section, we show how this conflict can be detected in advance and then eliminated by the developers.

4   Interference Analysis

The goal of the interference analysis is to check whether a set of policy enforcers can jointly operate without causing any interference. An *interference* occurs when two or more enforcers are no longer able to enforce the policies that they can enforce individually. More formally, let us assume that Enf_1 and Enf_2 are two enforcers that can operate in environment Env to enforce policies $Policy_1$ and $Policy_2$, respectively. We write $Env||Enf_1 \models Policy_1$ and $Env||Enf_2 \models Policy_2$. The two enforcers Enf_1 and Enf_2 *interfere* if $Env||(Enf_1||Enf_2) \not\models Policy_1$ or $Env||(Enf_1||Enf_2) \not\models Policy_2$ or $Env||(Enf_1||Enf_2)$ includes deadlocks. This is exactly the case of the motivating example where the enforcer for *Policy 1* can release the `MediaPlayer` instance before the enforcer for *Policy 2* stops the player causing a deadlock.

In our setting, the environment consists of an Android app that uses multiple resources. We represent the generic behavior of an app and the resources using

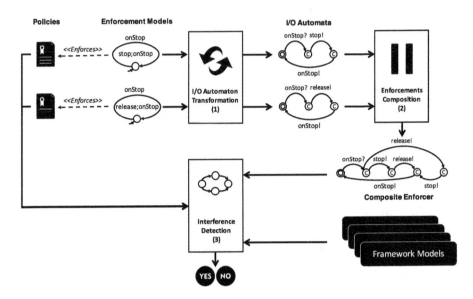

Fig. 4. Interference analysis.

one model for the app and one model for each resource, as done for the example in Fig. 2. We call these models the *framework models*. Note that although we first experienced this solution in the Android environment, it is indeed valid in any environment where applications must obey to a pre-defined lifecycle and resources must be used according to a protocol, as it happens in many frameworks for the development of Web and server-side applications.

Figure 4 shows the overall structure of the interference analysis that starting from a set of *enforcement models*, the corresponding *policies*, and a set of *framework models* verifies whether the enforcers can coexist to enforce the policies without causing interferences. Since the enforcers, the apps, and the resources are communicating components, we run our analysis representing the behavior of each component as an I/O automaton. Since I/O automata provide good expressive power and a flexible framework for modeling the behavior of communicating components, they are also able to precisely capture the behavior of the components involved in real-world enforcement tasks. We thus first map the enforcers, specified as edit automata, into their corresponding I/O automata (see the *I/O automaton transformation* step in Fig. 4). We then compose the enforcers to derive the *composite enforcer*, which is a single model that encapsulates the collective behavior of all the enforcers considered in the analysis (see the *enforcers composition* step in Fig. 4). To check for interferences, the analysis composes the composite enforcer with the framework models and checks for the satisfaction of the policies and for the absence of deadlocks on the resulting model (see the *interference detection* step in Fig. 4).

In the rest of this section, we describe these three steps in details.

4.1 I/O Automaton Transformation

In this step, each model of enforcer encoded as an edit automaton $A_E = \langle \Sigma, Q, q_0, \delta \rangle$ is transformed into the corresponding I/O automaton $A = \langle states, start, sig, trans \rangle$ according to the strategy defined below.

Since each transition in an edit automata can accept an action and produce multiple actions in response, this same behavior requires multiple transitions, and thus multiple states, to be represented in an I/O automaton. To this end, we define $states$ as the union of the $origStates$, which are the same states than the states in the edit automaton, and the $newStates$, which are the additional states introduced in the I/O automaton to produce sequences of actions consistently with the transitions in the edit automaton. Since the need of these intermediate states depends on the length of the sequences that are emitted by each transition of the edit automaton, we directly exploit these sequences in the representation of the states. More formally, $states = origStates \cup newStates$, where:

- $origStates = \{\langle q, \epsilon \rangle \mid q \in Q\}$,
- $newStates = \{\langle q, s \rangle \mid q \in Q, s = a; \sigma[...i], a \in in, \delta(q, a) = \langle q', \sigma \rangle, i < |\sigma|\}$,

To preserve the intuition that these sequences of actions should be emitted quickly in response to an input, we define all the states in $newStates$ as committed states. The initial state is the same as the one of the edit automaton, thus $start = \{\langle q_0, \epsilon \rangle\}$.

The operations that can be performed by the edit automaton are duplicated into input and output operations. Actually, whether an operation is an input or an output depends on whether it is accepted or emitted by a transition in the edit automaton. More formally, $sig = in \cup int \cup out$, where: $in = \{a? \mid a \in \Sigma\}$, $int = \{\}$, $out = \{a! \mid a \in \Sigma\}$.

We distinguish two main cases for the transitions. When the transition in the edit automaton suppresses the action, that is, no action is emitted, there is no need of introducing additional states in the I/O automaton to map the transition. Otherwise, extra states and transitions are needed. Formally, $trans = suppression \cup insertion$, with $suppression = \{\langle\langle q, \epsilon \rangle, a, \langle q', \epsilon \rangle\rangle \mid q, q' \in Q, a \in in, \delta(q, a) = \langle q', \epsilon \rangle\}$. In the case of $insertion$, the transitions in the edit automaton requires multiple transitions in the I/O automaton to be represented correctly. We thus distinguish three kinds of transitions that may occur in $insertion$: the first transition of a sequence, that is a transition that starts from a state in $origStates$ and reaches a state in $newStates$, an intermediate transition of a sequence, that is a transition that starts from a state in $newStates$ and reaches a state in $newStates$, and finally the last transition of a sequence, that is a transition that starts from $newStates$ and reaches a state in $origStates$. More formally, $insertion = startInsertion \cup ongoingInsertion \cup endInsertion$, where:

- $startInsertion = \{\langle\langle q, \epsilon \rangle, a, \langle q, a; \sigma[i] \rangle\rangle \mid q \in Q, a \in in, \delta(q, a) = \langle q', \sigma \rangle\}$
- $ongoingInsertion = \{\langle\langle q, a; \sigma[...i] \rangle, \sigma[i], \langle q, a; \sigma[...i+1] \rangle\rangle \mid q \in Q, a \in in, \delta(q, a) = \langle q', \sigma \rangle, \sigma[i] \in out, 0 < i < |\sigma|\}$
- $endInsertion(A) = \{\langle\langle q, a; \sigma[...|\sigma|] \rangle, \sigma[|\sigma|], \langle q', \epsilon \rangle\rangle \mid q, q' \in Q, a \in in, \delta(q, a) = \langle q', \sigma \rangle, \sigma[|\sigma|] \in out\}$.

Figure 5 shows the output of the I/O automaton transformation step applied to the running example. Figures 5(a) and (b) show the I/O automata derived from the enforcement models for *Policy 1* and *Policy 2*, respectively. The numbered states are in *origStates* and the numbering is consistent with the states in the original edit automaton. States marked with *c* are the committed states in *newStates*.

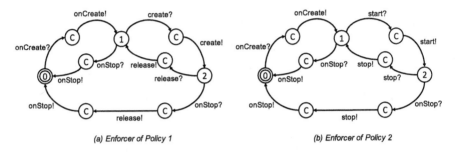

(a) Enforcer of Policy 1   (b) Enforcer of Policy 2

Fig. 5. I/O Automaton Transformation of the Running Example: (a) I/O automaton IOA_{p1} for *Policy 1*, (b) I/O automaton IOA_{p2} for *Policy 2*.

The equivalence between the languages accepted by original edit automaton and the corresponding I/O automaton is pretty straightforward. By construction, every transition t in the edit automaton has a corresponding linear sequence of transitions that starts by accepting an input action and continue producing the output actions consistently with t, and viceversa. These sequences are also linked to *origStates* consistently with the edit automaton and the initial state is also preserved.

The only difference that the I/O automaton introduces with respect to the corresponding edit automaton is in the composition of multiple models. In fact, an output sequence emitted by the edit automaton in response to an event is atomic, while the corresponding sequence emitted through multiple states and transitions in the I/O automaton could be interrupted, although the presence of the committed states guarantee that this may happen only from another committed state. This difference is desirable in our context since the atomicity of the sequence could not be guaranteed in practice and the behavior of the enforcers should be verified without considering this property, as we do by running our analysis on the I/O automaton derived from the edit automaton.

4.2   Enforcers Composition

This step derives a composite enforcer which represents the collective behavior of all the enforcers. Since the behavior of the enforcers must be synchronized, the interference analysis derives the composite automaton using CSP (Communicating Sequential Processes)-like synchronization [21]. Thus the states of the composite automaton are the cartesian product of the states of the composed automata and its behavior is the interleaving of the behaviors of the composed I/O automata.

Considering the I/O automata derived in the motivating example (Fig. 5), the state space of the resulting composite I/O automaton $CA_{p1,p2}$ is represented by pairs $\langle s_1, s_2 \rangle$, where s_1 is a state of I/O automaton IOA_{p1}, and s_2 is a state of I/O automaton IOA_{p2}. Figure 6 shows the portion of the $CA_{p1,p2}$ responsible for the interference. When the onStop? action is executed and $CA_{p1,p2}$ is in state $\langle 2, 2 \rangle$ the model can produce both the sequences stop!;release! and release!stop!. If release!stop! is produced, the policies are not enforced correctly.

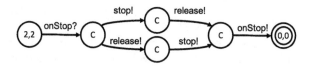

Fig. 6. Excerpt of composite automaton

4.3   Interference Detection

This step verifies that all the policies are correctly enforced by the composite enforcer without introducing any deadlock in the system. To this end, the analysis reconstructs the global behavior of the system by composing the composite enforcer with both the framework models (i.e., the generic model of an app life-cycle and the models of the used resources) and an environment model which is simply used to generate every possible combination of actions that the app and the resources can produce (i.e., this model is used to consider every possible execution scenario in the analysis).

In this case, the composed models are I/O automata that communicate using binary synchronization channels which let pairs of automata synchronize on shared input-output actions (e.g., the output action a! with the input action a?). Since every action emitted by the environment must be first intercepted by the composite enforcer, which reacts by generating the actions for the app and the resources, the analysis automatically renames actions to reflect the way components communicate in practice. In particular, the action produced by the environment and the corresponding actions in the framework models are renamed adding different suffixes (e.g., the onCreate() method is changed into onCreate-env()! when emitted from the environment, and into onCreate-app()? when received by the app). This simple strategy prevents direct communication between the environment and the framework models. The actions in the composite enforcer are renamed to receive actions from the environment and emit actions for the app and the resources. For instance, if a transition of the enforcer receives onCreate()? and the following transition emits onCreate()!, the actions are renamed into onCreate-env()?, to receive the action from the environment, and `onCreate-app()`! to propagate the action to the app. This simple renaming strategy is sufficient to fully model a communication mediated by the enforcers.

To check if the enforcers can interfere, the interference analysis checks all the enforced policies specified as Computation Tree Logic (CTL)-like formulas [13] on the model resulting from the composition of the framework models, the composite enforcer, and the environment model after renaming (of course the name of the actions in the CTL formulas are renamed consistently with the model). An interference is detected if the model checker, in our case UPAAL [10], reports a counterexample that violates any policy, or the system may reach a deadlock state.

In the running example, an interference is detected because the system may reach a deadlock state. Indeed, the resulting automaton cannot proceed with the execution because the `stop` action cannot be executed on the `MediaPlayer` once it has been released. The analysis identifies the problem as a deadlock because the model of the resource does not allow the execution of `stop` after `release`. In practice, the enforcer anyway tries to invoke the `stop` method on the resource and the execution fails due to an exception returned by the resource.

5   Analysis of Resource Usage Policies in Android

To evaluate the effectiveness of the interference analysis, we focus on misuses of the APIs that provide access to critical system resources, such as camera and the media player. Misuses of these APIs are frequent in Android [20,37] and often cause resource leaks which lead to performance degradation and crashes.

To identify the correctness policies that can be enforced on Android apps that interact with system resources, we exploited the recommendations about API usage derived from the Android documentation [1,3] by Wu et al. [37]. We identified ten different resources that must satisfy multiple policies, for a total of twenty-five policies. We encoded each policy as a CTL formula and defined the corresponding enforcer. We finally used the interference analysis presented in this paper to detect interferences between enforcers, that is, enforcers that work well in isolation but fail to enforce the policies when used jointly with other enforcers.

Table 1 shows the obtained results. Column **API** indicates the API that provides access to a specific resource. Below the name of the API we report the name of its package. Column *Resource Usage Policy* lists the set of policies that each API must satisfy. We have written the policies in the form "<acquire method>/<release method>: <callback>" which should be interpreted as: if the app invokes <acquire method>, it should also invoke <release method> when a call to <callback> is received, unless <release method> has been already invoked before. Column *Interference* indicates the result of the interference analysis of the enforcers that enforce the specified policies: *No* indicates that the enforcers combined together are still able to successfully enforce all the policies, while *Yes* indicates that an interference among the enforcers has been detected.

Table 1. Interference analysis of resource usage policies

API	Resource usage policy	Interference
BluetoothAdapter (android.bluetooth)	enable/disable: onDestroy	No
	startDiscovery/cancelDiscovery: onDestroy	
	getProfielProxy/closeProfileProxy: onDestroy	
Camera (android.hardware)	lock/unlock: onPause	**Yes**
	open/release: onPause	
	startFaceDetection/stopFaceDetection: onPause	
	startPreview/stopPreview:onPause	
AudioManager (android.media)	requestAudioFocus/abandonAudioFocus: onPause	No
	startBluetoothSco/stopBluetoothSco: onPause	
	loadSoundEffects/unloadSoundEffects: onPause	
MediaCodec (android.media)	createDecoderByType/release: onPause	**Yes**
	start/stop: onPause	
MediaPlayer (android.media)	<init >/release: onStop	**Yes**
	create/release: onStop	
	start/stop: onStop	
MediaRecorder (android.media)	<init>/release: onStop	**Yes**
	start/stop: onStop	
NfcAdapter (android.nfc)	enableForegroundDispatch/ disableForegroundDispatch: onPause	No
	enableForegroundNdefPush/ disableForegroundNdefPush: onPause	
RemoteCallbackList (android.os)	beginBroadcast/finishBroadcast: onDestroy	No
	register/unregister: onDestroy	
Surface (android.view)	<init>/release: onDestroy	**Yes**
	lockCanvas/unlockCanvasAndPost: onDestroy	
SurfaceHolder (android.view)	addCallback/removeCallback: onDestroy	No
	LockCanvas/unlockCanvasAndPost: onDestroy	

In order to observe the impact that interferences have on the actual execution of an app, we have implemented and deployed the analyzed enforcers on a real device as described in [32]. After activating the interfering enforcers and opening an app that violates the policy, we execute a test case that reproduces the scenario with the misuse and we observed that in all the cases interference caused the crash of the app.

Interestingly, we reported an interference for 5 out of 10 analyzed APIs. This result shows that interference among policy enforcers can be a major obstacle to the successful deployment of the policy enforcers technology. The mechanism presented in this paper can be a useful tool to avoid these situations. It can be used to decide which enforcers to activate and which enforcers to not activate. For instance, it is not possible to activate the four enforcers specified for the `Camera` API, but our analysis reveals that the first and third enforcers of the camera are compatible and thus can be activated together. Moreover, the developers can exploit this result to redesign some of the enforcers.

This result also suggests that sets of enforcers cannot be designed in a completely independent way, but their co-existence must be planned in advance and reflected in their definition. In this paper we do not discuss how to evolve enforces in this direction, we left this research direction for future work.

6   Related Work

Runtime solutions for avoiding and mitigating the impact of failures have been studied in many different contexts, including Web applications [29], mobile applications [15,16,31,32], operative systems [35], and Cloud environments [14].

In the context of the Android environment, runtime enforcement mechanisms have been focused on the enforcement of privacy [16] and resource usage policies [32], obtained respectively by applying mechanisms for detecting and disabling suspicious method calls, and by augmenting classic Android libraries with proactive mechanisms able to automatically suppress and insert API calls. Both approaches are not intrinsically limited to security and resource usage policies, but could be potentially exploited to generally enforce correctness policies.

So far, these approaches focused on the definition of the enforcement mechanisms and paid little attention to the interference between mechanisms, which might be an issue when multiple policies must be enforced. The work presented in this paper is complementary to these approaches because it provides an analysis framework for checking the compatibility between enforcers.

The problem of handling interferences has been considered in the work by Bauer et al. [9]. In their work, Bauer et al. present a framework that can be used by the developers to specify how the enforcement mechanism should behave when multiple enforcers directly interfere, that is, multiple enforcers try to alter an execution as a reaction to a same action. To address these situations, Bauer et al. [9] define several composition operators that can be used to obtain a strategy to solve these situations. General composition operators for enforcers, which might be potentially used to reason on interferences, have been also defined by Falcone et al. [19]. Compared to these strategies, the analysis presented in this paper can address a broader set of situations, not only the direct inference. Moreover, it can also be exploited to know a-priori if a set of enforcers are compatible, instead of lately discovering it at run-time, once their interference or the lack of application of some enforcers may have serious consequences for the health of the system.

A body of work formally studied the classes of properties that can be enforced using different models and languages, with an emphasis on security policies [17,23,26,27,33]. Interestingly these approaches should be complemented with appropriate analysis routines to check that the result of the enforcement is in line with what the enforcers are expected to achieve. The gap between the policies to be enforced and the enforced behaviors has been highlighted by Bielova et al. [11] who show that often there is little guarantee that enforcers fix the bad sequences in the desired way. This result further stresses the need of analysis strategies similar to the one presented in this paper.

7 Conclusions and Future Work

Conclusions. The reliability of software applications can be improved by exploiting advanced execution environments equipped with mechanisms to enforce correctness policies, such as security [16,27] and resource usage policies [16,32]. Although enforcers can be effective when used in isolation, their effect on the application and the execution environment when executed jointly might be hard to predict and potentially harmful. In particular, a set of enforcers may fail to enforce the policies that they are designed to enforce individually.

To address this problem, we presented an analysis framework that can be used to detect interferences among enforcers. The analysis can be exploited by both the developers, to improve the enforcement strategies and implement enforcers that can safely co-exist, and the users, to identify sets of policies that can be enforced without introducing side-effects.

Our initial evaluation with several enforcers designed to guarantee the correct usage of multiple Android resources revealed that enforcers may easily interfere. This result suggests that defining techniques to design interference-free enforcers, as well as defining efficient and effective verification mechanisms, are important challenges for the future.

Future work. In this work we present a possible analysis, but there are several complementary aspects worth to be analyzed. For instance, timing aspects in runtime enforcement [18,30] have not been considered, but timing could be another source of interferences. For instance, the joint activation of two enforcers may successfully cause the enforcement of some security policies, but may cause serious slow downs that dramatically annoy users.

Finally, while in this work we focused on revealing interferences, we plan to investigate mechanisms to semi-automatically or automatically fix interferences.

Acknowledgment. This work has been partially supported by the H2020 Learn project, which has been funded under the ERC Consolidator Grant 2014 program (ERC Grant Agreement n. 646867), the GAUSS national research project, which has been funded by the MIUR under the PRIN 2015 program (Contract 2015KWREMX), and the COST Action ARVI IC1402, supported by COST (European Cooperation in Science and Technology).

References

1. Android: API Guides. https://developer.android.com/guide/index.html. Accessed 6 May 2017
2. Android: MediaPlayer. https://developer.android.com/reference/android/media/MediaPlayer.html. Accessed 6 May 2017
3. Android: Package Index. https://developer.android.com/reference/packages.html. Accessed 6 May 2017
4. Android: The Activity Lifecycle. https://developer.android.com/guide/components/activities/activity-lifecycle.html. Accessed 6 May 2017
5. Azim, M.T., Neamtiu, I., Marvel, L.M.: Towards self-healing smartphone software via automated patching. In: Proceedings of the International Conference on Automated Software Engineering (ASE) (2014)
6. Baier, C., Katoen, J.P., Larsen, K.G.: Principles of Model Checking. MIT Press, Cambridge (2008)
7. Banerjee, A., Chong, L.K., Chattopadhyay, S., Roychoudhury, A.: Detecting energy bugs and hotspots in mobile apps. In: Proceedings of the ACM SIGSOFT International Symposium on Foundations of Software Engineering (FSE) (2014)
8. Bauer, A., Küster, J., Vegliach, G.: Runtime verification meets Android security. In: Proceedings of the International Symposium on Formal Methods (NFM) (2012)
9. Bauer, L., Ligatti, J., Walker, D.: Composing security policies with polymer. In: Proceedings of the ACM SIGPLAN Conference on Programming Language Design and Implementation (PLDI) (2005)
10. Bengtsson, J., Larsen, K., Larsson, F., Pettersson, P., Yi, W.: UPPAAL — a tool suite for automatic verification of real-time systems. In: Alur, R., Henzinger, T.A., Sontag, E.D. (eds.) HS 1995. LNCS, vol. 1066, pp. 232–243. Springer, Heidelberg (1996). doi:10.1007/BFb0020949
11. Bielova, N., Massacci, F.: Do you really mean what you actually enforced? edited automata revisited. Int. J. Inform. Secur. (IJIS) **10**(4), 239–254 (2011)
12. Chircop, L., Colombo, C., Pace, G.J.: Device-centric monitoring for mobile device management. In: Proceedings of the International Workshop on Formal Engineering approaches to Software Components and Architectures (FESCA) (2016)
13. Clarke, E.M., Emerson, E.A., Sistla, A.P.: Automatic verification of finite-state concurrent systems using temporal logic specifications. ACM Trans. Program. Lang. Syst. (TOPLAS) **8**(2), 244–263 (1986)
14. Dai, Y., Xiang, Y., Zhang, G.: Self-healing and hybrid diagnosis in cloud computing. In: Jaatun, M.G., Zhao, G., Rong, C. (eds.) CloudCom 2009. LNCS, vol. 5931, pp. 45–56. Springer, Heidelberg (2009). doi:10.1007/978-3-642-10665-1_5
15. Daian, P., Falcone, Y., Meredith, P., Şerbănuţă, T.F., Shiriashi, S., Iwai, A., Rosu, G.: RV-Android: efficient parametric android runtime verification, a brief tutorial. In: Bartocci, E., Majumdar, R. (eds.) RV 2015. LNCS, vol. 9333, pp. 342–357. Springer, Cham (2015). doi:10.1007/978-3-319-23820-3_24
16. Falcone, Y., Currea, S., Jaber, M.: Runtime verification and enforcement for Android applications with RV-Droid. In: Proceedings of the International Conference on Runtime Verification (RV) (2012)
17. Falcone, Y., Fernandez, J.C., Mounier, L.: What can you verify and enforce at runtime? Int. J. Softw. Tools Technol. Transfer **14**(3), 349–382 (2012)

18. Falcone, Y., Jéron, T., Marchand, H., Pinisetty, S.: Runtime enforcement of regular timed properties by suppressing and delaying events. Syst. Control Lett. **123**, 2–41 (2016)
19. Falcone, Y., Mounier, L., Fernandez, J.C., Richier, J.L.: Runtime enforcement monitors: composition, synthesis, and enforcement abilities. Formal Methods Syst. Des. **38**(3), 223–262 (2011)
20. Guo, C., Zhang, J., Yan, J., Zhang, Z., Zhang, Y.: Characterizing and detecting resource leaks in android applications. In: Proceedings of the International Conference on Automated Software Engineering (ASE) (2013)
21. Hoare, C.A.R.: Communicating sequential processes. In: Hansen, P.B. (ed.) The Origin of Concurrent Programming, pp. 413–443. Springer, New York (1978)
22. Hyrynsalmi, S., Suominen, A., Mäkilä, T., Knuutila, T.: Mobile application ecosystems: an analysis of android ecosystem. In: Encyclopedia of E-Commerce Development, Implementation, and Management, chap. 100, vol. II, pp. 1418–1434. IGI Global (2016)
23. Khoury, R., Tawbi, N.: Which security policies are enforceable by runtime monitors? a survey. Comput. Sci. Rev. **6**(1), 27–45 (2012)
24. Küster, J., Bauer, A.: Monitoring real android malware. In: Proceedings of the International Conference on Runtime Verification (RV) (2015)
25. Li, L., Bissyandé, T.F., Octeau, D., Klein, J.: DroidRA: taming reflection to support whole-program analysis of android apps. In: Proceedings of the International Symposium on Software Testing and Analysis (ISSTA) (2016)
26. Ligatti, J., Bauer, L., Walker, D.: Edit automata: enforcement mechanisms for run-time security policies. Int. J. Inform. Secur. **4**(1), 2–16 (2005)
27. Ligatti, J., Bauer, L., Walker, D.: Run-time enforcement of nonsafety policies. ACM Trans. Inform. Syst. Secur. (TISSEC) **12**(3), 19:1–19:41 (2009)
28. Lynch, N.A., Tuttle, M.R.: An introduction to input/output automata. CWI Q. **2**(3), 219–246 (1988)
29. Magalhães, J.P., Silva, L.M.: SHÕWA: a self-healing framework for web-based applications. ACM Trans. Auton. Adapt. Syst. **10**(1), 4:1–4:28 (2015)
30. Pinisetty, S., Falcone, Y., Jéron, T., Marchand, H., Rollet, A., Nguena-Timo, O.: Runtime enforcement of timed properties revisited. Formal Methods Syst. Des. **45**(3), 381–422 (2014). https://doi.org/10.1007/s10703-014-0215-y
31. Riganelli, O., Micucci, D., Mariani, L.: Healing data loss problems in android apps. In: Proceedings of the International Workshop on Software Faults (IWSF), Co-located with the International Symposium on Software Reliability Engineering (ISSRE) (2016)
32. Riganelli, O., Micucci, D., Mariani, L.: Policy enforcement with proactive libraries. In: Proceedings of the International Symposium on Software Engineering for Adaptive and Self-Managing Systems (SEAMS) (2017)
33. Schneider, F.B.: Enforceable security policies. ACM Trans. Inform. Syst. Secur. (TISSEC) **3**(1), 30–50 (2000)
34. Shan, Z., Azim, T., Neamtiu, I.: Finding resume and restart errors in android applications. In: Proceedings of the ACM SIGPLAN International Conference on Object-Oriented Programming, Systems, Languages, and Applications (OOPSLA) (2016)
35. Sidiroglou, S., Laadan, O., Perez, C., Viennot, N., Nieh, J., Keromytis, A.D.: ASSURE: automatic software self-healing using rescue points. In: Proceedings of the International Conference on Architectural Support for Programming Languages and Operating Systems (ASPLOS) (2009)

36. Wei, L., Liu, Y., Cheung, S.C.: Taming android fragmentation: characterizing and detecting compatibility issues for android apps. In: Proceedings of the IEEE/ACM International Conference on Automated Software Engineering (ASE) (2016)

37. Wu, T., Liu, J., Xu, Z., Guo, C., Zhang, Y., Yan, J., Zhang, J.: Light-weight, inter-procedural and callback-aware resource leak detection for android apps. IEEE Trans. Softw. Eng. (TSE) **42**(11), 1054–1076 (2016)

Hierarchical Non-intrusive In-situ Requirements Monitoring for Embedded Systems

Minjun Seo[✉] and Roman Lysecky[✉]

Department of Electrical and Computer Engineering, University of Arizona,
Tucson, AZ, USA
mjseo@email.arizona.edu, rlysecky@ece.arizona.edu

Abstract. Accounting for all operating conditions of a system at the design stage is typically infeasible for complex systems. In-situ runtime monitoring and verification can enable a system to introspectively ensure the system is operating correctly in the presence of dynamic environment, to rapidly detect failures, and to provide detailed execution traces to find the root cause thereof. In this paper, we seek to address two challenges faced in using in-situ runtime verification for embedded systems, including (1) efficiently defining and automatically constructing a requirements model for embedded system software and (2) minimizing the runtime overhead of observing and verifying the runtime execution adheres to the requirements model. We present a methodology to construct a hierarchical runtime monitoring graph from system requirements specified using multiple UML sequence diagrams, which are already commonly used in software development. We further present the design of on-chip hardware that nonintrusively monitors the system at runtime to ensure the execution matches the requirements model. We evaluate the proposed methodology using a case study of a fail-safe autonomous vehicle subsystem and analyze the relationship between event coverage, detection rate, and hardware requirements.

Keywords: Runtime requirement monitoring · Embedded systems · Nonintrusive system monitoring

1 Introduction

Defining and verifying system requirements are critical challenges in embedded systems. During development, verification often includes both test-based and formal verification methods [27], often comprising as much as 75% of the design effort [10]. Even with this considerable design-time effort, runtime verification is essential for many embedded systems due to both system complexity and the highly dynamic nature of applications and the environments in which they operate. Exhaustively testing for all possible data inputs, application configurations, and environmental conditions is at best infeasible or cost prohibitive and at worst impossible. Thus, for safety-critical and life-critical embedded systems, runtime monitoring and verification methods are needed to continually verify correct system execution at runtime and *in-situ*.

© Springer International Publishing AG 2017
S. Lahiri and G. Reger (Eds.): RV 2017, LNCS 10548, pp. 259–276, 2017.
DOI: 10.1007/978-3-319-67531-2_16

Embedded systems present unique opportunities and challenges in monitoring correctness. In-situ runtime monitoring and verification of embedded systems can enable the system to introspectively ensure the system is operating correctly in the presence of dynamic environment, rapidly detect failures or deviations in the expected system execution, and provide detailed execution traces to find the root cause of those unexpected behaviors. Importantly, runtime verification can ensure embedded systems adhere to system requirements and verified execution requirements in the presence of unknown environmental, physical, and operating conditions. However, due to strict resource constraints, runtime monitoring should be non-intrusive, as intrusive monitoring methods would perturb a system's behavior and result in negative side effects. For example, timing changes from an intrusive monitoring system may change the system execution such that synchronization and scheduling issues are introduced, which in the worst case can lead to system failure. Tight integration of hardware and software means monitoring methods must consider both hardware and software aspects, which increases the monitoring complexity.

In this paper, we seek to address two primary challenges of using runtime verification for embedded systems, including (1) efficiently defining a requirements model for embedded software and (2) minimizing the runtime overhead of monitoring and verifying that the execution adheres to the requirements model. To address these challenges, we present a methodology to extract and synthesize a hierarchical runtime monitoring graph from system requirements specified using UML sequence diagrams. UML sequence diagram have been widely used in software development and can be used to model both synchronous and asynchronous operations as well with interactions between software and hardware components. Additionally, system developers can model different execution scenarios and requirements using multiple sequence diagrams. As such, UML sequence diagrams can be leveraged to extract system requirements without requiring distinct and separate requirements models, which often necessitate error-prone and time consuming manual efforts. We present a formal Hierarchical Runtime Monitoring Graph (HRMG) model that compactly represents system requirements extracted from the sequence diagrams and enables efficient runtime verification using non-intrusive hardware. We present the design of on-chip Non-intrusive In-situ Requirements Monitoring (NIRM) hardware that monitors the system execution to ensure the execution matches the requirements model. In the event of a detected violation, the runtime verification hardware maintains detailed information of the execution that led to the failure, which can be used for root cause analysis.

2   Related Work

2.1   Requirements Models for Runtime Verification

Numerous models exist for specifying requirements for runtime monitoring and verification. Formal models such as timed automata and linear temporal logic use a mathematical framework to completely define requirements for the entire system. Linear temporal logic (LTL) define system states and temporal properties about the systems' states [21], which can be verified at runtime to ensure those properties remain true throughout a system's execution. Real-time extensions of LTL such as metric interval temporal logic (MITL) have been proposed to specify real-time requirements supporting a concept of specific time interval for LTL.

Timed Automata (TA) [1] model is another well-known formal modeling approach for specifying how a system operates and modeling the time constraints for transitioning between system states. TA models are typically used by model checking techniques, primarily at the component level to evaluate properties such as reachability, safety, and liveness properties. However, TA models face challenges in modeling the interactions at the system-level (e.g., hardware integration and interactions).

While both LTL and TA (along with many related formal requirements models) can succinctly specify system requirements and can be used at runtime to verify systems correctness, these modeling techniques are not commonly used by software developers. Integrating the use of LTL or TA in standard software development processes would require developers to maintain multiple system models, which is time consuming and error prone, and would require extensive training [5].

UML sequence diagrams [23] are widely used in software development and can be considered a standard model. Early versions of sequence diagrams had limited support to model execution scenarios, which thus limited their use for runtime verification. However, the UML current standard's sequence diagrams support modeling multiple scenarios using combined fragments and support both synchronous and asynchronous operations. Notably, sequence diagrams are also used to model system level interaction between components, including software and hardware components.

UML sequence diagrams have been used for verification, including several approaches that convert the sequence diagrams to TA models [6, 8]. However, there are several limitations. One approach converts each sequence diagram to a separate TA model [6], which requires later combining those models, leading to the well-known state explosion problem. Another approach supports converting hierarchical UML models to hierarchical timed automata [6], but still requires multiple TA models. Overall, TA models are not ideal for non-intrusive runtime monitoring and verification due to the hardware resources required to support system-level TA models.

2.2 Software-Based Runtime Monitoring and Verification Methods

Software-based runtime monitoring and verification execute additional software to observe system events and ensure the system execution adheres to the requirements model or ensures system properties hold true. However, the instrumentation and analysis of software-based approaches incur significant runtime overheads.

Time triggered runtime verification (TTRV) is an approach that seeks to minimize the software overhead of runtime verification for multicore systems [19]. During the design process, TTRV seeks to find an optimal mapping of software components to processors cores and an optimal configuration of monitoring frequency in order to minimize overhead of the monitoring and verification software. While TTRV reduces the overhead by up to 34.1%, the runtime monitoring and verification software still incurs a 7% performance overhead and a 51% memory overhead.

EgMon reduces the software overhead for runtime verification by focusing on monitoring messages transmitted between components, specifically monitoring messages broadcast over a CAN bus and verifying requirements defined using bounded metric temporal logic [13]. EgMon uses a separate device on the CAN bus through USB connection, which reduces the performance overhead for the system, but does not eliminate it, due to the added delay of the EgMon device.

Chai et al. presented a runtime verification systems that utilizes live sequence charts (LSCs) [5]. LSCs are similar to UML sequence diagrams and enable support modeling multiple system behaviors, conditional execution sequences, and activation timing [4]. This approach concatenates several LSCs to define the possible system states that can be examined, and then transforms the concatenated LSC into linear temporal logic (LTL). Although LSC can be transformed to LTL, the number of events in the resulting LTL can be exponential. Also, LTL model checking is powerful verification method, it is not ideal for hardware-based implementation.

Copilot is a compiler-assisted approach that automatically instruments a software binary with custom verification code compiled from a requirements specification language [20]. While this approach reduces the effort required to verify hard real-time constraints for the system, any changes in requirements mandate re-verifying that the hard real-time constraints are met.

Although these methods try to minimize or control the overhead, software-based approaches still incur significant runtime overheads that can negatively impact the system execution and present challenges for design time verification.

2.3   Hardware-Based Runtime Monitoring and Verification Methods

Alternatively, hardware based runtime monitoring can be utilized to dynamically verify that the system implementation adheres to the required system properties. However, most runtime monitoring methods are not specifically targeted at verifying system requirements at runtime, but are more geared toward testing and debugging.

Trace-based methods for monitoring system events (e.g., CoreSight [17], ChipScope [26], SignalTap [25], RTNI [9]) allow designers to specify a set of signals that can be traced at runtime without affecting the system performance. MAMon is a hardware-based approach for kernel operations within an RTOS, including context switches, system calls, and interrupts [24]. However, those trace methods typically require external hardware or dedicated processors to access the traced signals and only allow a small subset of signals to be traced.

P2 V is a hardware-based verification method that extends the memory access stage of a MIPS processor to implement a monitor unit (MU) [15]. The P2 V approach synthesizes requirements specified using a subset of property specification language (PSL) to a custom dedicated hardware component integrated with the memory access stage. This approach enables non-intrusive verification, but is limited to verifying memory accesses and does not support software updates.

Reinbacher et al. present an approach that automatically synthesizes requirements specified in past-time Metric Temporal Logic (ptMTL) to hardware that verifies those requirements over fixed time intervals [22]. This approach observes communication-based events by monitors either the system bus, network-on-chip, or physical IO, which limits the types of events that can be monitored.

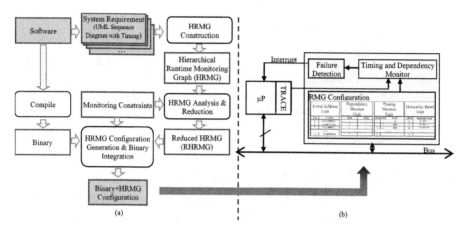

Fig. 1. (a) Design methodology for automated requirements model construction for runtime verification. (b) System integration of non-intrusive runtime monitoring hardware. *System inputs include software and multiple UML sequence diagrams. The output is a software binary integrated with a configuration for the NIRM hardware monitor.*

Backasch et al. utilize a hidden in-circuit emulator (hidICE) to non-intrusively detect events within the main system and report those events to an external emulator using a dedicated port [2]. The runtime verification is then performed using the external emulator, which ensures the main system's execution is unaffected. While non-intrusive, the external emulator requires significant area and energy overheads, and the number of monitored events is limited by the bandwidth of the external interface.

Hofmann et al. presented a hybrid monitoring technique that combines software instrumentation to detect events or specific conditions with hardware that monitors those events [11]. Alternatively, NUVA uses hardware-based instrumentation enabled by custom instructions to detect events and dedicated hardware that verify system require-ments specified using parametric FSMs [18]. While the use of custom instructions reduces the performance overhead compared to software-based instrumentation, a performance overhead of approximately 5% is still incurred.

3 Non-intrusive In-situ Requirement Monitoring (NIRM)

The NIRM methodology for in-situ requirements monitoring and verification consists of: (1) a design time methodology for system requirements specification, analysis, and model construction and (2) in-situ, non-intrusive hardware for monitoring and verifying requirements at runtime within the deployed system. Figure 1(a) presents the NIRM methodology consisting of: (1) initial software development and UML sequence diagram modeling, (2) requirements analysis, (3) automated hierarchical runtime monitoring graph (HRMG) construction, (4) HRMG analysis and reduction (optional), (5) RMG configuration generation and binary integration, and (6) in-situ, non-intrusive monitoring of system execution as represented in Fig. 1(b).

4   Hierarchical Runtime Monitoring Graph

We define a hierarchical runtime monitoring graph (HRMG) that is automatically constructed from sequence diagrams, which capture all requirements that can be monitored. The HRMG defines the set of events (or probes) observed at runtime, the correct execution orders of those events, and timing constraints between events, where applicable. All messages and causality of messages (i.e., sender and receiver) within the sequence diagrams are considered system events.

Definition 1:   An HRMG is a tuple $G = \langle V_G, E_G \rangle$ where:

- V_G is a finite set of vertices, where each vertex represents a system event.
- E_G is a set edges representing dependencies between vertices. Each edge $E \in E_G$, defined as $E = V_G \rightarrow V_G'$, represents a dependency between two events V_G and V_G'. V_G is the *source* event and V_G' is the *sink* event.
- If a time constraint exists between V_G and V_G', an edge E may also specify a worst-case execution *time* (WCET) constraint, defined as $V_G \overset{time}{\rightarrow} V_G'$. Note that the WCET can be obtained using static or probabilistic analysis [28].
- An edge has a *type* $\in \{strong, weak\}$ that specifies if the dependency is mandatory or optional. *strong* (solid arrow) represents a mandatory dependency. *weak* (dashed arrow) represents an optional dependency.
- A hierarchical event $H \in V_G$ is defined by a tuple $H = \langle V_H, E_H, H_I, H_F \rangle$. $H_I \in V_H$ is the initial vertex for H. External edges to H connect only to H_I. $H_F \in V_H$ is the final vertex for H. External edges from H only originate from H_F.
- For a hierarchical event H, all incoming edges to H_I must have the same edge type (i.e., incoming edges must all be strong or weak dependencies).

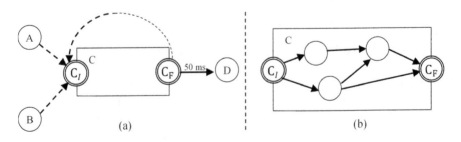

Fig. 2. Example HRMG: (a) top-level HRMG including hierarchical event C, and (b) internal events and dependencies for hierarchical event C.

Figure 2 presents an illustrative example of the HRMG model. Figure 2(a) shows the top-level view of a graph consisting of 5 events, one of which is a hierarchical event, 3 weak dependencies, and 2 strong dependencies. The hierarchical event C graphically depicts the initial (C_I) and final (C_F) events. C_I has three incoming edges from A, B, and C_F, all of which represent weak dependencies. Figure 2(b) shows the events and dependencies within hierarchical event C, which consists of a total of 5 events, including the initial (C_I) and final (C_F) events. The edge $C1 \xrightarrow{1\ ms} C3$ indicates that event C3 should occur no more than 1 ms after C3.

4.1 HRMG Evaluation Metrics

Given system complexity and limitations on area, memory, and energy, the NIRM hardware may be configured with a reduced HRMG (RHRMG). The RHRMG is a subgraph of the HRMG specifying a subset of events to monitor. To evaluate the requirements coverage of the RHRMG, three evaluation metrics are considered: execution path coverage (EPC), timing path coverage (TPC), and average path coverage (APC). The path coverage metrics integrate the percentage of paths and precision with which paths in the HRMG are covered in the RHRMG. A path precision index (PPI) measures how much information is maintained in the RHRMG (i.e., how closely a path in the RHRMG matches the original path in the HRMG). We separately calculate an execution path precision index (EPPI) and a timing path precision index (TPPI).

Execution Path Coverage (EPC). For a path, P_i, in the RHRMG, the EPPI calculates the number of events in the path compared to the number of events in the closest matching path in the original HRMG. EPC calculates the average EPPI for all paths.

$$EPPI(P_i) = \frac{NumEvents(P_i)}{NumEvents(NearestPath(HRMG, P_i))}$$

$$EPC(RHRMG) = \frac{\sum_{P_n \in RHRMG} EPPI(P_n)}{NumPaths(HRMG)} * 100$$

NumEvents() calculates the number of events in a path, and *NumPaths()* calculates the number of paths in a HRMG or RHRMG.

Timed Path Coverage (TPC). TPC is the percentage of timing information within the HRMG that is covered within the RHRMG. The TPPI calculates the number of timed events within a path compared to the original path in the HRMG. The TPC calculates the average TPPI for all timed paths.

$$TPPI(P_i) = \frac{NumTimedEvents(P_i)}{NumTimedEvents(NearestPath(HRMG, P_i))}$$

$$TPC(RHRMG) = \frac{\sum_{P_n \in RHRMG} TPPI(P_n)}{NumTimedPaths(HRMG)} * 100$$

NumTimedEvents() calculates the number of timed events in a path and *NumTimed-Paths()* calculates the number of timed paths in RMG or RRMG.

Average Path Coverage (APC). As an HRMG encapsulates both execution sequence and timing requirements, the average path coverage (APC) is calculated as the average of the EPC and TPC:

$$APC(RHRMG) = \frac{EPC(RHRMG) + TPC(RHRMG)}{2}$$

Because the APC averages coverage of timing and sequence requirements, it is intended to estimate the overall detection rate for timing and dependency failures.

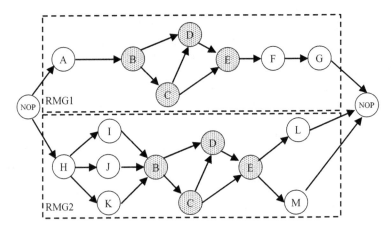

Fig. 3. An example RMG RMG1, RMG2, and the combined graph.

Multi-phase Greedy Iterative Algorithm. A multi-phase greedy iterative algorithm is utilized to select the RHRMG given a constraint on the maximum number of events in the RHRMG. The algorithms' phase starts with the full HRMG, and iteratively removes one event until the number of RHRMG events is less than the constraint. In each iteration, the algorithm removes the event with the smallest requirements coverage loss, as measured by the average path coverage (APC). A second refinement phase iteratively re-evaluates the selection of each event in the RHRMG. For each event, the refinement phase evaluates if replacing the selected event with any of the non-selected events increases the APC. If so, the event is replaced. Using this refinement phase, the APC is increased by up to 3%. Although not detailed here, the greedy approach yields APC within 4% of a simulated annealing-based algorithm.

5   HRMG Construction from Sequence Diagrams

Since UML sequence diagrams are commonly used in software development, automatically converting sequence diagram into a requirement model for runtime verification holds significant promise. A sequence diagram consists of explicit messages that represent the order of executions for a specific execution scenario, from which the systems' events and dependencies between events within the HRMG can be constructed. As each sequence diagram, or sequence diagram fragment, is used to specify a single execution scenario, multiple sequence diagrams must be combined to create the HRMG for the complete system. Additionally, as sequence diagrams may share common sequences of operations, automatically extracting hierarchy to create the HRMG reduces the model complexity. As such, the HRMG construction utilizes three construction techniques: (1) converting a UML sequence diagram to a flat RMG, (2) combining RMGs and adding hierarchy for common execution sequences, and (3) converting a UML sequence diagram's combined fragments to the HRMG.

5.1   Combining RMGs and Defining Hierarchy

As UML sequence diagrams, and in general different execution scenarios, have common sequences of operations, a critical step within the HRMG construction is combining RMG for multiple sequence diagrams and then identifying common sequences which can be represented using hierarchy. To combine multiple RMGs, two NOP (No operation) vertices, a *source* NOP and a *sink* NOP, are added to the RMG model. For each event with an in-degree of 0, an edge from the source NOP to the event is added. For each event with an out-degree of 0, an edge from the event to the sink NOP is added. Figure 3 shows show an RMG that combines two: RMG1 and RMG2.

After combining RMGs, a maximum common subgraph (MCS) algorithm, specifically the Durand-Pasari algorithm [7], is used to identify common operation sequences within the RMG to create hierarchal events. The MCS algorithm finds the largest completely connected subgraph starting with an event and ending with an event, creating a hierarchical event for the subgraph. The MCS is iteratively applied to until no new hierarchical events can be found. When converting subgraphs to hierarchical events, edges to the hierarchical events are converted to weak dependencies as multiple executions may now occur before the hierarchical event, but not all events must occur. After the MCS algorithm finishes, the source and sink NOP vertices are removed from the resulting HRMG. Figure 4 shows the HRMG resulting from executing the MSC algorithm for the RMG in Fig. 3. In the example, the subgraph containing events B, C, D, and E is converted to a hierarchical event. Because multiple events may occur before event B, the edges $A \rightarrow B$, $I \rightarrow B$, $J \rightarrow B$, and $K \rightarrow B$ become weak dependencies.

5.2   UML Sequence Diagram Combined Fragment

UML sequence diagrams support several methods of defining combined fragments, including options, alternatives, and loops. We provide an overview of the process for constructing events and dependencies within the RMG for these combined fragments.

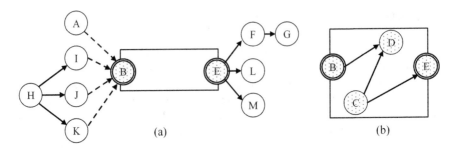

Fig. 4. HRMG resulting from executing the MCS algorithm for the RMG in Fig. 3 showing the (a) top-level HRMG and (b) the internal details of the hierarchical event.

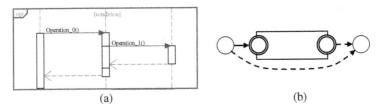

Fig. 5. Conversion of an (a) optional combined fragment to an (b) HRMG.

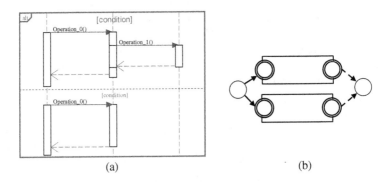

Fig. 6. Conversion of on (a) alternative combined fragment to an (b) HRMG.

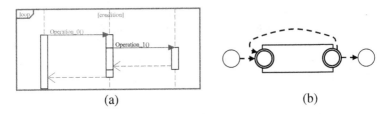

Fig. 7. Conversion of a (a) loop combined fragment to an (b) HRMG.

An optional combined fragment is converted to a hierarchical event with the weak dependencies that indicate the hierarchical event optionally executes. Figure 5 illustrates the conversion of an optional combined fragment to events in the HRMG. An alternative combined fragment represents the mutual exclusive execution of two fragments, such as an if-else construct. Each of the alternative fragments is converted to a hierarchical event with weak dependencies connecting to a common sink event, as illustrated in Fig. 6. A loop combined fragment implicitly specifies that a fragment executes n times, which can be converted to a hierarchical event with a cyclic dependency connected from the event's final vertex to the initial vertex, as shown in Fig. 7.

6 NIRM Hardware

Figure 8 represents a high-level overview of the NIRM hardware. The NIRM hardware in directly integrated on-chip within the system-on-a-chip (SOC) architecture and interfaces with the processor's trace port to non-intrusively monitor the software application to detect system events. Integrating the NIRM on-chip and using the processor trace port has the advantage of not requiring any internal modifications to processor cores and of avoiding the limited bandwidth of external interfaces.

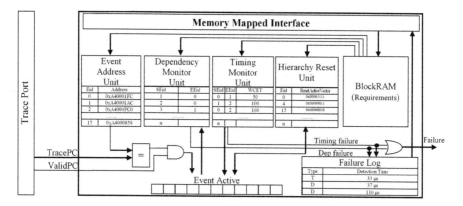

Fig. 8. NIRM hardware architecture.

The NIRM hardware consists of: (a) an event address unit, (b) a dependency monitoring unit, (c) a timing monitor unit, (d) a hierarchy reset unit, (e) a small RAM storing the system requirements, (f) a failure log, and (g) event active register. The NIRM hardware detects events by monitoring two signals from the processor trace port, namely *TracePC* and *ValidPC*. *TracePC* provides the program counter address and *ValidPC* indicates if the program counter address is valid (i.e., the processor is currently executing the instruction located at that address). For each event within the HRMG, the event address unit maps unique event IDs (*Eid*) to each event's PC address. Each event corresponds to a distinct sender or receiver within the UML sequence diagram. Whenever the PC matches the address of a monitored event, the corresponding bit in the *EventActive* register is set. The dependency monitor unit stores the start event ID (*SEid*) and end event ID (*EEid*) for each dependency in the HRMG. The dependency monitoring unit detects requirement violations at runtime by detecting changes in the *EventActive* register that violate the specified dependencies. The timing monitoring unit stores the start event ID (*SEid*), end event ID (*EEid*), and WCET for timing requirements specified in the HRMG. The timing monitoring unit measures the current execution of each monitored event to detect if the execution time exceeds the WCET. The hierarchy reset unit detects the occurrence of a hierarchical event's final, and when detected, the *EventResetVector* is used to reset the affected events within the *EventActive* register. When a dependency or timing violation is detected, the *FailureLog* unit stores details of the violation, and the NIRM hardware asserts a non-maskable interrupt to inform the system of the failure.

During software compilation, a NIRM configuration stub is incorporated. Given an RMG and compiled software binary, the RMG configuration generation will analyze the binary to identify the addresses corresponding to each monitored event, and output a final configuration for the NIRM hardware. The empty configuration within the configuration stub is then updated with the RMG configuration.

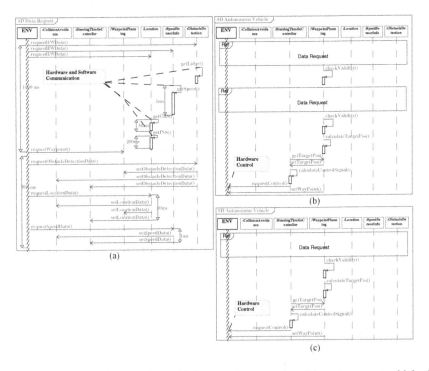

Fig. 9. UML sequence diagrams for multiple execution scenarios of the autonomous vehicle: (a) common sequence diagram for sensor data request operations, (b) sequence diagram for navigation and steering control in which invalid sensor data is received, and (c) sequence diagram for navigation and steering control without sensor errors.

7   Experimental Results

We developed an FPGA-based prototype for an embedded application modeling the high-level operations of an autonomous vehicle's navigation, speed, and steering controls. The system is implemented using a Xilinx Artix-7 FPGA (XC7A200T), which enables the integration of the NIRM hardware with a MicroBlaze processor. The NIRM hardware implemented within the prototype supports an HRMG with up to 128 events, requiring 6271 LUTs, 2101 FFs, and two 36 KB BRAM.

Figure 9 presents the UML sequence diagrams for the autonomous vehicles navigation, speed, and steering control operations. The autonomous vehicle operations consist of two scenarios shown in Fig. 9(b) and (c). Figure 9(b) models the execution scenario in which abnormal sensor data is received, and the system requests new sensor data before making navigation decisions and controlling the vehicle's actuators. Figure 9(c) models the scenario in which the initial sensor data is valid, and the system immediately makes the navigation and control. Figure 9(a) is the UML sequence diagram for the common sequence used to request the required sensor data. The HRMG constructs three RMGs which are then merged and processed into the HRMG shown in Fig. 10, where (a) shows the top-level HRMG and (b) shows the events within the hierarchical event A. In total, the HRMG consists of 34 events with 44 strong dependencies, 2 weak dependencies, and 9 timing requirements.

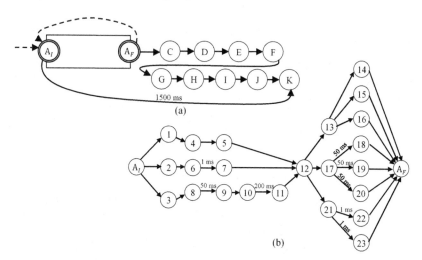

Fig. 10. HRMG for fail-safe autonomous vehicle: (a) top-level and (b) a hierarchical event A.

Figure 11(a) presents the EPC, TPC, and APC for the resulting HRMG as the number of events is decreased from 34 to 14. To evaluate the advantage of the hierarchical model, we further compare the path coverage of the HRMG to a flat RMG (FRMG) model, shown in Fig. 11(b). We observe that for the HRMG the TPC decreases more slowly than EPC. The HRMG achieves a TPC of 100% with just 15 events. However, for an HRMG this small, the APC is only 61% due to a low EPC. In contrast, the FRMG achieves much lower path coverage, with an APC of just 58% for 25 events. Across event constraints, the FRMG achieves an APC 23.6% lower than the HRMG.

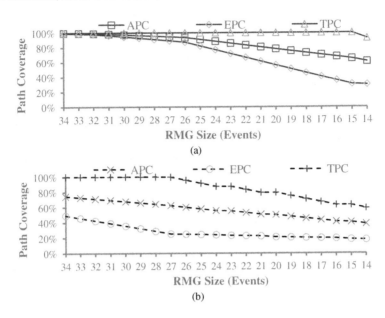

(a)

(b)

Fig. 11. Path coverage metrics for (a) HRMG and (b) FRMG for decreasing number of events.

Table 1 presents an overview of common types of failures that we utilized to evaluate the failure detection of our runtime verification approach. The failures are classified into timing failures, dependency failures, synchronization failures, and sensor failures, based on reported failures for similar systems [3, 12, 14, 16]. For each failure type, we injected a failure within the autonomous vehicle system at randomized locations and executed

Table 1. Summary of failure types and corresponding failure injection method.

Failure	Description	Failure injection method
Timing failure	Task execution takes longer than the WCET for that task, leading to violation(s) of real-time constraints	Insert timing delays ranging from 500 µs to 1 ms within targeted tasks
Dependency failure	Operations with implicit dependencies are executed out of order	Randomize execution order of dependent operations
Synchronization failure	Synchronization failures leading to system deadlocks	Randomize mutex lock/unlock failures, and randomize priority of threads
Sensor failure	Sensor failures resulting in incorrect data and control decisions	Simulate erroneous sensor data and processing of erroneous data as if it were valid

the system 100 times to measure the detection rate using the runtime verification of the NIRM hardware. In total, we conducted 2400 experiments for the different failure scenarios and for different size HRMGs using the prototype system implementation to determine the actual detection rate.

Figure 12 presents the detection rate for the four failures types using HRMGs of various sizes, ranging from the full HRMG with 34 events to an HRMG with only 14 events. The NIRM approach achieves high detection rates for timing, synchronization, and sensor failures, with a 100% detection rate for an HRMG with 26 events. Even with just 14 events, the NIRM approach achieves detection rates of 91%, 100%, and 92%, respectively. In contrast, for dependency failures, a detection rate of 85% is achieved with 18 events, and 56% with 14 events. The detection rate for dependency failures decreases faster as the number of events decreases, which is due to the reduction algorithms' tendency to eliminate events not associated with time constraints.

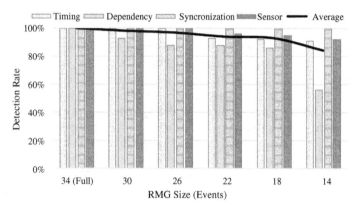

Fig. 12. Detection rate for timing, dependency, synchronization, and sensor failures for decreasing number of events within the HRMG.

Finally, we evaluate the detection latency for the NIRM approach. The detection latency is the time elapsed between when the failure occurred and when the failure was detected. Table 2 presents the minimum, maximum, and average detection latencies for various sized HRMGs for the synchronization failure case. Although the synchronization failure achieves a 100% detection rate for HRMG sizes, the size of the HRMG has a considerable impact on the detection latency. For the full HRMG, the detection latency ranges from 36 µs to 100 ms. With 18 events, the detection latency ranges from 89 µs to 110 ms, with an average increase of 12.3 ms. When the HRMG is reduced to just 14 events, a significant increase in detection latency is observed, requiring a minimum of 20 ms to detect the failures. Table 2 further presents the breakdown in the detection source, listing the percentage of the failures detected by timing violations or dependency violations. As one might expect, the majority of synchronization failures are detected from dependency violations, accounting at least 91% of the detected failures across the different HRMG sizes. We note that in some cases, a failure is simultaneously detected by both a timing and dependency failures.

Table 2. Relationship between RMG size, detection latency, and breakdown of the detection source for the synchronization failures.

HRMG size	Detection latency (μs)			Detection source	
	Min	Max	Avg	Timing	Dependency
34	36.35	100604.15	49966.82	*4%	*100%
30	44.92	100688.44	50892.65	*5%	*100%
26	87.2	100682.71	58018.80	9%	91%
22	51.75	100733.85	59794.78	6%	94%
18	89.47	110052.03	62156.18	4%	96%
14	20256.82	130830.93	101026.27	1%	99%

*Note that a failure may be simultaneously detected by timing and dependency failures.

8   Conclusions and Future Work

We presented non-intrusive requirements monitoring methodology for automatically constructing a hierarchical requirements model from UML sequence diagrams and verifying system correctness at runtime using non-intrusive on-chip in-situ hardware. Experimental results demonstrate the effectiveness of the NIRM approach for detecting several common failure types within embedded systems, achieving a 100% detection rate while monitoring only 40% of the events with the system requirements model. The HRMG model enables better coverage of system requirements and more efficient hardware implementation compared to a flat requirements model using a similar formalism. These results demonstrate the feasibility of the proposed NIRM approach, which holds promise to enable the use of UML sequence diagrams for runtime verification. Future work includes developing tools for optimizing path coverage of an HRMG subject to energy constraints for runtime verification, integration of sequence models for hardware components supporting full system-level integration, and modeling of data-dependent timing and sequence requirements.

References

1. Alur, R.: Timed automata. In: Halbwachs, N., Peled, D. (eds.) CAV 1999. LNCS, vol. 1633, pp. 8–22. Springer, Heidelberg (1999). doi:10.1007/3-540-48683-6_3
2. Backasch, R., et al.: Runtime verification for multicore SoC with high-quality trace data. ACM Trans. Des. Autom. Electron. Syst. **18**(2), 18 (2013)
3. Bonakdarpour, B., Navabpour, S., Fischmeister, S.: Sampling-based runtime verification. In: Butler, M., Schulte, W. (eds.) FM 2011. LNCS, vol. 6664, pp. 88–102. Springer, Heidelberg (2011). doi:10.1007/978-3-642-21437-0_9
4. Brill, M., Damm, W., Klose, J., Westphal, B., Wittke, H.: Live sequence charts. In: Ehrig, H., Damm, W., Desel, J., Große-Rhode, M., Reif, W., Schnieder, E., Westkämper, E. (eds.) Integration of Software Specification Techniques for Applications in Engineering. LNCS, vol. 3147, pp. 374–399. Springer, Heidelberg (2004). doi:10.1007/978-3-540-27863-4_21

5. Chai, M., Schlingloff, B.-H.: Monitoring systems with extended live sequence charts. In: Bonakdarpour, B., Smolka, S.A. (eds.) RV 2014. LNCS, vol. 8734, pp. 48–63. Springer, Cham (2014). doi:10.1007/978-3-319-11164-3_5
6. David, A.: Hierarchical modeling and analysis of timed systems. IT Tech. Rep. Ser. 2003-50 (2003)
7. Durand, P.J., et al.: An efficient algorithm for similarity analysis of molecules. Internet J. Chem. 2(17), 1–16 (1999)
8. Firley, T., Huhn, M., Diethers, K., Gehrke, T., Goltz, U.: Timed sequence diagrams and tool-based analysis — a case study. In: France, R., Rumpe, B. (eds.) UML 1999. LNCS, vol. 1723, pp. 645–660. Springer, Heidelberg (1999). doi:10.1007/3-540-46852-8_45
9. Fryer, R.: FPGA based CPU instrumentation for hard real-time embedded system testing. ACM SIGBED Rev. 2(2), 39–42 (2005)
10. Hailpern, B., Santhanam, P.: Software debugging, testing, and verification. IBM Syst. J. 41(1), 4–12 (2002)
11. Hofmann, R., et al.: Distributed performance monitoring: methods, tools, and applications. IEEE Trans. Parallel Distrib. Syst. 5(6), 585–598 (1994)
12. Jones, M.: What really happened on mars rover pathfinder. Risks Dig. 19(49), 1–2 (1997)
13. Kane, A., Chowdhury, O., Datta, A., Koopman, P.: A case study on runtime monitoring of an Autonomous Research Vehicle (ARV) system. In: Bartocci, E., Majumdar, R. (eds.) RV 2015. LNCS, vol. 9333, pp. 102–117. Springer, Cham (2015). doi: 10.1007/978-3-319-23820-3_7
14. Leveson, N.G., Turner, C.S.: An investigation of the Therac-25 accidents. Computer (Long. Beach. Calif) 26(7), 18–41 (1993)
15. Lu, H.: The design and implementation of P2V, an architecture for zero-overhead online verification of software programs. Science (80), August 2007
16. Macaulay, K.: ATSB preliminary factual report, in-flight upset, Qantas Airbus A330, 154 Km West of Learmonth, WA, 7 October 2008. Australian Transport Safety Bureau Media Release, 14 November 2008 (1992)
17. Mijat, R.: Better trace for better software: introducing the new arm coresight system trace macrocell and trace memory controller. ARM, White Pap. (2010)
18. Nassar, A., et al.: NUVA: architectural support for runtime verification of parametric specifications over multicores. In: 2015 International Conference on Compilers, Architecture and Synthesis for Embedded Systems, CASES 2015, pp. 137–146 (2015)
19. Navabpour, S., Bonakdarpour, B., Fischmeister, S.: Time-triggered runtime verification of component-based multi-core systems. In: Bartocci, E., Majumdar, R. (eds.) RV 2015. LNCS, vol. 9333, pp. 153–168. Springer, Cham (2015). doi:10.1007/978-3-319-23820-3_10
20. Pike, L., Niller, S., Wegmann, N.: Runtime verification for ultra-critical systems. In: Khurshid, S., Sen, K. (eds.) RV 2011. LNCS, vol. 7186, pp. 310–324. Springer, Heidelberg (2012). doi:10.1007/978-3-642-29860-8_23
21. Pnueli, A.: The temporal logic of programs. In: 18th Annual Symposium on Foundations of Computer Science (SFCS 1977), pp. 46–57. IEEE (1977)
22. Reinbacher, T., Függer, M., Brauer, J.: Real-time runtime verification on chip. In: Qadeer, S., Tasiran, S. (eds.) RV 2012. LNCS, vol. 7687, pp. 110–125. Springer, Heidelberg (2013). doi:10.1007/978-3-642-35632-2_13
23. Rumbaugh, J., et al.: The Unified Modeling Language Reference Manual. Addison-Wesley, Boston (2005)
24. El Shobaki, M.: On-chip monitoring of single-and multiprocessor hardware real-time operating systems. In: Proceedings of the 8th International Conference on Real-Time Computing Systems and Applications (RTCSA) (2002)

25. Tool, A.V.: SignalTap II Embedded Logic Analyzer (2006)
26. Tool, X.V.: ChipScope Pro (2006)
27. Whalen, M., Cofer, D., Miller, S., Krogh, B.H., Storm, W.: Integration of formal analysis into a model-based software development process. In: Leue, S., Merino, P. (eds.) FMICS 2007. LNCS, vol. 4916, pp. 68–84. Springer, Heidelberg (2008). doi: 10.1007/978-3-540-79707-4_7
28. Wilhelm, R., et al.: The worst-case execution-time problem-overview of methods and survey of tools. ACM Trans. Embed. Comput. Syst. 7(3), 1–53 (2008)

Monitoring Partially Synchronous Distributed Systems Using SMT Solvers

Vidhya Tekken Valapil[1]([✉]), Sorrachai Yingchareonthawornchai[1],
Sandeep Kulkarni[1], Eric Torng[1], and Murat Demirbas[2]

[1] Michigan State University, East Lansing, MI 48823, USA
{tekkenva,sandeep}@cse.msu.edu, {yingchar,torng}@msu.edu
[2] SUNY Buffalo, University of Buffalo, Buffalo, NY 14260, USA
demirbas@buffalo.edu

Abstract. In this paper, we discuss the feasibility of monitoring partially synchronous distributed systems to detect latent bugs, i.e., errors caused by concurrency and race conditions among concurrent processes. We present a monitoring framework where we model both system constraints and latent bugs as Satisfiability Modulo Theories (SMT) formulas, and we detect the presence of latent bugs using an SMT solver. We demonstrate the feasibility of our framework using both synthetic applications where latent bugs occur at any time with random probability and an application involving exclusive access to a shared resource with a subtle timing bug. We illustrate how the time required for verification is affected by parameters such as communication frequency, latency, and clock skew. Our results show that our framework can be used for real-life applications, and because our framework uses SMT solvers, the range of appropriate applications will increase as these solvers become more efficient over time.

1 Introduction

In this paper, we focus on runtime monitoring of latent concurrency bugs in loosely synchronized, distributed, safety-involved systems with the help of SMT solvers. By distributed, we mean that the processes/components are linked by a network and communicate with each other by passing messages, though our approach could also be used for shared memory processes. By loosely synchronized, we mean that the processes employ some form of clock synchronization such as NTP ensuring that clock drift is bounded by some specified value ϵ. By safety-involved, we mean that failure of the distributed system may put lives or the environment at risk; in the extreme, these systems may be safety-critical where failures would lead to loss of life and/or environmental damage.

Examples of such systems include embedded systems, e.g., different components in a car that communicate with each other, vehicular systems, a set of cars on a highway that need to coordinate with each other to avoid collision and maximize their performance, and distributed sensor networks that are used for intrusion detection.

© Springer International Publishing AG 2017
S. Lahiri and G. Reger (Eds.): RV 2017, LNCS 10548, pp. 277–293, 2017.
DOI: 10.1007/978-3-319-67531-2_17

Since we are dealing with safety-involved and potentially safety-critical systems, we must ensure that the deployed systems function correctly. Unfortunately, due to the inherent uncertainty and complexity of these systems, it is difficult to eliminate all bugs before deployment. Therefore, it is necessary to monitor deployed systems at runtime to ensure that they function correctly and to detect any violations of safety specifications as early as possible.

One of the most challenging correctness issues of complex distributed systems is latent concurrency bugs that are caused by concurrency issues/race conditions. Since we assume that the processes are only loosely synchronized, we cannot totally order all the events in the system; but the events obey some partial order. This means that any observation of the system is some serialization of the partial order of events. We define latent concurrency bugs to be bugs that are only visible in some but not all serializations of the partial order of events in the system. To simplify terminology, we refer to latent concurrency bugs as latent bugs in the rest of the paper.

Latent bugs are important, as they indicate a potential for something to go wrong. If detected early, these bugs may be fixed by using stronger synchronization, introducing delays and so on. Unfortunately, identifying latent bugs is a very challenging problem. Straightforward enumeration of all serializations is not efficient as the number of serializations is likely exponential in the several factors. In fact, in some cases, identifying latent bugs is an NP-hard problem [5].

We propose to address this challenge using SMT solvers. An SMT solver takes a formula and a list of constraints as its input. The solver then identifies whether the formula can be satisfied while simultaneously satisfying all constraints. If satisfiable, it produces a satisfying variable assignment for the formula. Otherwise, it reports that the formula cannot be satisfied. We propose to use SMT solvers as follows. First, we develop a formula to represent that the violation of a safety specification. This formula is developed once for the system. Then during runtime, we propose a lightweight method for the monitor to generate the system events and constraints that define the partial order on the system events that any serialization must follow. The SMT solver then determines if there is a serialization of events that would lead to violation of the safety specification. Our main focus is on developing the lightweight method for generating system events and constraints that define the partial order on system events.

Relying on SMT solvers for runtime monitoring has several advantages. The most important advantage is correctness. Since an SMT solver evaluates all possible combinations of variables before declaring the formula unsatisfiable, it guarantees the correctness of the monitor; i.e., it will not miss an error and it will not identify phantom errors. Also, the field of SMT solvers is an active field where new advances result in more efficient solvers. Thus, over time, runtime monitors based on SMT solvers will be able to monitor more complex systems.

We give two justifications for the use of SMT solvers. First, we show that monitoring a distributed system with perfect accuracy, concurrent execution and efficiency (ACE) is *impossible* unless P = NP; this result is a restatement of a known result in asynchronous systems [5]. The second justification is that the impossibility result is for the worst case. In practice, traces often have some structure [1] that can be exploited by highly optimized SMT solvers. The major question regarding the use of SMT solvers in performing runtime monitoring is whether they are fast enough to allow the monitor to keep up with the system processes. This is a valid question since we are asking them to solve potentially NP-hard satisfiability input instances on the fly. We note that any runtime monitoring solution that guarantees correctness has to solve the same problem, so the difficulty of keeping up is not limited to SMT solvers. With this motivation, we present an algorithm to map runtime execution of distributed programs into instances that can be evaluated using SMT solvers. We use the SMT solver Z3 [9] for this purpose. We also analyze the effectiveness of using Z3 in two applications: first in a synthetic application to evaluate the role of different system parameters (communication frequency, clock skew etc). The second in a shared memory access program that has a subtle bug.

Organization of the paper. The rest of the paper is organized as follows. In Sect. 2, we define the system, monitor model and introduce the monitoring problem. We show how any monitor must choose among accuracy, concurrency, and efficiency in Sect. 3. We illustrate latent bugs in Sect. 4. We describe the necessary instrumentation in Sect. 5 and how to generate the SMT formulas in Sect. 6. We present our experimental results in Sect. 7. Finally, we discuss related work in Sect. 8 and provide concluding remarks in Sect. 9.

2 Preliminaries

2.1 System Model

Our system model is similar to the quasi-synchronous model in [8]. We consider a system that consists of n application processes numbered 1 to n where each process i has its own clock. We assume that the underlying system guarantees that clocks of any two processes differ by at most ϵ, the clock skew, by using a protocol such as NTP. The processes communicate via messages. The minimum and maximum message delays between processes are δ_{min} (could be 0) and δ_{max} (could be ∞), respectively. Each process i is also associated with a single variable v_i. Our techniques can be easily extended to processes having multiple variables. Each process execution is a sequence of events. The two main events are message send or receive events and variable events (the variable changes its value). The local clock when event e occurred at process i is denoted by $pt.i(e)$.

2.2 Monitor Model

In our initial discussion, we assume that monitoring for latent bugs is performed by one or more dedicated monitoring processes that are different from the application processes. (During analysis of experimental results, we also consider an alternate implementation where each process devotes a part of its computational resource to the task of monitoring.) Each application process reports its events to the monitor using messages. We assume that the messages from each application process arrive at the monitor in a FIFO order for that process.

We assume that we can characterize latent bugs with a predicate P that is defined over n variables of the application processes. For example, if we were implementing a token passing structure, v_i might be a Boolean variable that denotes that process i has the token, and an event e would occur when process i takes the token to change v_i from 0 to 1 and when process i releases the token v_i changes from 1 to 0. P would be that there is no time t where $\sum_{i=1}^{n} v_i > 1$, i.e., the token is never possessed by more than one process simultaneously.

The monitor processes the events it receives from the application processes to determine if there is a legal serialization of events such that predicate P is true in that serialization. We evaluate a monitor in terms of precision, recall, and latency. By precision, we mean that if the monitor declares that predicate P as true, then some legal serialization (defined precisely in Sect. 2.3) of events will cause the system to reach a state where P is true. By recall, we mean that if some legal serialization of application events causes the system to reach a state where P is true, then it is detected by the monitor. By latency, we mean the time spent between reaching a state where P is true and the monitor concluding that P is true. We define a monitor to be a Δ-latency monitor if at any time t, the monitor can verify whether P has been satisfied by time $t - \Delta$. Ideally, we would like to have 0-latency monitors, but this is not possible for a variety of reasons including message delay and processing time. Instead, we try to minimize Δ.

2.3 Concurrent Events, Happened Before Relation, Valid Snapshots

We briefly recall notions of concurrent events, happened before relation and consistent snapshots [19]. We define the goal of monitoring as determining if there is some legal serialization of application events that causes the system to reach a state where P is true. By state, we mean an assignment of values for the n process variables. We now define what is a legal serialization of application events and how the monitor might detect when the system could reach a state where P is true. A priori, we assume that all events might be concurrent and thus all serializations are legal. We rule out some events from being concurrent and thus some possible serializations using happened before relation, where event A cannot be concurrent with event B if A happened before B, or vice versa.

Definition 1. *Given two events A and B, we say that event A happened before event B, denoted as $A \xrightarrow{hb} B$ iff one of the following four conditions holds.*

- **Local Events.** *Events A, B are at the same process i and $pt.i(A) < pt.i(B)$.*
- **Communication.** *A is a send event, B is the corresponding receive event.*
- **Clock Synchronization.** *Event A happens on process i and event B happens on process j and $pt.j(B) - pt.i(A) > \epsilon$.*
- **Transitivity.** *There exists an event C such that $A \xrightarrow{hb} C$ and $C \xrightarrow{hb} B$.*

Clearly, if $A \xrightarrow{hb} B$, then in any legal serialization of events, A must appear before B.

Definition 2. *Events* A, B *are possibly concurrent,* $A\|B$, *if* $A \overset{hb}{\not\longrightarrow} B \wedge$ $B \overset{hb}{\not\longrightarrow} A$.

If $A\|B$, then a legal serialization of events might have A appear before B or B appear before A. If all events are pairwise possibly concurrent, the number of legal serializations of x events would be $|x|!$. With the partial order defined by the happened before relation, many of these serializations are eliminated. One of the factors that makes monitoring difficult is if the number of serializations is large. A common approach for searching for a legal serialization of events is to search for what is known as a *consistent snapshot* which we define as follows.

Definition 3. *A snapshot is a set S of n events, one per process. A snapshot S is consistent if for any two events $A, B \in S$, A and B are possibly concurrent.*

In our analysis, we assume that frontier events of the snapshot correspond to local events; if the designer wants frontier events to be send events (respectively, receive events) then we create a new local event just before (respectively, after) the event chosen by the designer.

We need the snapshot to be consistent, and the predicate P to be true in this consistent snapshot. Thus, we define the following term.

Definition 4. *A snapshot S is valid if and only if it is consistent and the predicate being detected is satisfied at the time of this snapshot.*

Restating the monitoring goal, the monitor strives to find a valid snapshot as soon as possible after that snapshot first exists.

2.4 Hybrid Logical Clocks

To help the monitor accurately identify when two events might be concurrent or when one event happened before another, we use hybrid logical clocks (HLC) [14] to timestamp an event e with an HLC value $hlc.e$. The local physical time is not sufficient for this purpose because of clock drift. For example, because of clock drift, the local physical time for a send event e might be larger than the local physical time for the corresponding receive event f even though e clearly happened before f. HLC timestamps provide a simple and efficient way to ensure that if one event e happened before another event f, then $hlc.e < hlc.f$.

We now briefly describe how HLC ensures this. A timestamp $hlc.e$ associated with event e consists of two integers $l.e$ and $c.e$. The value of $l.e$ captures the maximum physical clock value that a process was aware of when event e was created. In many cases, $l.e$ is the same as the physical clock of the process where e was created. However, if this process receives a message with a higher l value than its own clock, $l.e$ reflects that higher value. In $hlc.e$, $c.e$ acts as a counter to capture situations where $l.e$ alone cannot determine the timestamp of the newly generated event. Also, $hlc.e < hlc.f$ if and only if $(l.e < l.f) \vee ((l.e = l.f) \wedge (c.e < c.f))$. (Complete algorithm for HLC can be found in [14].) Since $l.e$ captures the maximum clock that the process was aware of when event e was created, if $|l.e - l.f| < \epsilon$, it is possible that e and f could have happened at the same time. Hence, in the absence of additional information (e.g., a message sent after e and received before f), we can treat that they are possibly concurrent. Our overall discussion does not depend upon the implementation of HLC; it only relies on its property that it provides logical clocks and that $l.e$ is within ϵ of the physical clock and that $e \xrightarrow{hb} f => (l.e < l.f) \vee ((l.e = l.f) \wedge (c.e < c.f))$.

3   Worst-Case Impossibility Result

We identify three desirable properties for any monitor: (1) Accuracy (Precision and Recall), (2) Concurrency (Non-intrusiveness), and (3) Efficiency (Polynomial time execution). An accurate monitor provides perfect precision and recall which means the monitor claims that the predicate is satisfiable iff there exists a valid snapshot. A concurrent or non-intrusive monitor does not interrupt or block the normal execution of the system. For example, the monitor never asks a process to delay sending messages or delay performing its computation. An efficient monitor performs detection in polynomial time. We define an ACE monitor to be a monitor that is accurate, concurrent, and efficient. ACE monitors are desirable when runtime verification of distributed system is necessary. Unfortunately, Garg's result for asynchronous systems [5] also applies to our setting with partially synchronous systems which means that for arbitrary Boolean predicates, ACE monitors are impossible unless P = NP. In our technical report [22], we briefly recap Garg's NP-completeness proof highlighting the modification needed to handle our partially synchronous setting. Although the NP-completeness result implies that there is no general ACE monitor, there is hope for a good monitor in the partially synchronous setting that we study. First, the NP-hardness reduction requires that all processes have variable events within an ϵ window. Second, each application has a specific predicate rather than arbitrary predicates. Many specific predicates such as conjunctive predicates can be handled in polynomial time. Also, even for harder predicates, many specific instances may be solved efficiently, especially with modern SAT/SMT solvers.

4   Latent/Concurrency Bugs

We now illustrate latent bugs using a simple protocol for exclusive access to shared data. To simplify the example, we use only two processes, and the invariant property that we wish to monitor is that at any moment, only one process accesses the shared resource. Exclusive access can be implemented in many ways such as using time division multiplexing, message passing, or their combination.

We first illustrate how the use of time division multiplexing with improper care for clock skew can lead to a latent bug. Suppose we use time division multiplexing where Process 1 is given exclusive access to the shared resource in the interval $[0, 50)$ while Process 2 is given exclusive access to the shared resource in the interval $[50, 100)$. Further suppose that Process 1 uses its exclusive access in the interval $[45, 50)$ while Process 2 uses its exclusive access in the interval $[55, 60)$ as shown in Fig. 1(a). If the clock drift $\epsilon < 5$, then this execution is fine and there is no possibility of simultaneous access of the shared resource. On the other hand, if the clock drift $\epsilon > 5$, then moments $\langle 50, 0 \rangle$ and $\langle 55, 0 \rangle$ are potentially concurrent which means both processes might be simultaneously accessing the shared resource. In this example, for the given clock drift, process P_1 should not access the resource this close to the end of its exclusive access time window to prevent this from occurring.

We next illustrate how messages can potentially ensure proper operation. Suppose instead of using time division multiplexing, the processes use message passing to pass a token. Suppose Process 1 initially possesses the token exclusively in the interval $[45, 50)$, then passes the token to Process 2 in a message that it sends at time 51 which is received at Process 2 at time 54 as shown in Fig. 1(b), and Process 2 exclusively accesses in the interval $[55, 60)$. Because of message m, no matter how large the clock skew ϵ is, moments $\langle 50, 0 \rangle$ and $\langle 55, 0 \rangle$ are not potentially concurrent. Specifically, $\langle 50, 0 \rangle \xrightarrow{hb} \langle 55, 0 \rangle$, and thus there is no concurrent access of shared resource. We will return to this example later to illustrate how we generate the SMT formula necessary for identifying potential errors by performing runtime monitoring using an SMT solver.

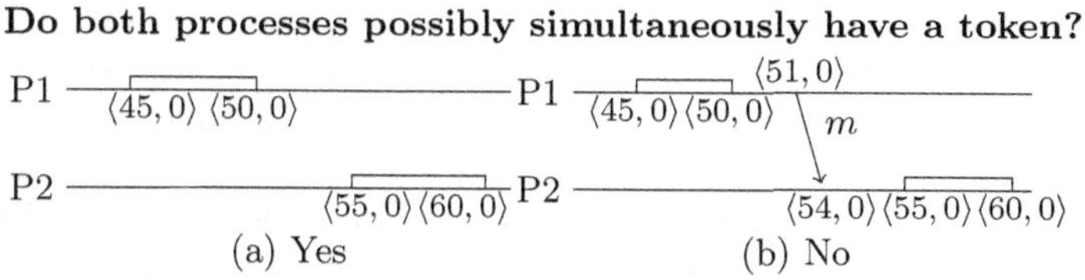

Do both processes possibly simultaneously have a token?

(a) Yes   (b) No

Fig. 1. Example of a token passing system with 2 nodes. In (a), there are four variable events and no messages. Due to clock drift, it is possible that both processes simultaneously share the token if $\epsilon > 5$. Part (b), has the same four variable events plus a message m. Because of the message, the two processes cannot share the token regardless of ϵ.

5   Instrumentation for Runtime Monitoring

In this section, we identify the instrumentation required to support runtime monitoring. We describe how each application process reports changes in variable values and inter-process messages to the monitor process. In practice if messages are being sent over a network, it could be observed by the monitor directly.

5.1   Reporting a Change in Variable Value

Every time when the value of the variable v_i changes, process P_i sends a message with three pieces of information to the monitor: the previous value of v_i, the

HLC timestamp of the previous variable event, and the current HLC timestamp associated with the new variable event. The two timestamps are sent as an interval that includes the left endpoint but excludes the right endpoint.

To make this work, we assume process P_i starts with an HLC value of $\langle 0, 0 \rangle$ and initially $v_i = a_i$. The information for the new variable event will be captured in the next variable event message sent to the monitor. Providing the previous value and HLC timestamp allows the monitor to process messages correctly even if they arrive out of order, though out of order messages may delay detection of predicate satisfaction. To illustrate these variable event messages, consider the run of the program in Fig. 1(a) or (b) where each process's Boolean variable v_i is true when process P_i accesses the shared data and is false otherwise. Process P_1 sends two variable event messages to the monitor. The first message has $v_1 = False$, $[\langle 0, 0 \rangle, \langle 45, 0 \rangle)$ and is sent at $\langle 45, 0 \rangle$. The second message has $v_1 = True$, $[\langle 45, 0 \rangle, \langle 50, 0 \rangle)$ and is sent at $\langle 50, 0 \rangle$. Likewise process P_2 sends two messages to the monitor. The first message has $v_2 = False$, $[\langle 0, 0 \rangle, \langle 55, 0 \rangle)$. The second message has $v_2 = True$, $[\langle 55, 0 \rangle, \langle 60, 0 \rangle)$.

5.2 Reporting Message Events

We report inter-process message events by having the process that receives a message report both the send and receive events to the monitor. Specifically, the process reports four things to the monitor: the sender process ID and the HLC timestamp for the send event (information that is included in the message by the sender process before sending the message), the receiver process ID, and the HLC timestamp for the receive event. For example, in Fig. 1(b), process P_2 sends a message to the monitor with the sender ID P_1, the send event timestamp $\langle 51, 0 \rangle$, the receiver process ID P_2, and the receive event timestamp $\langle 54, 0 \rangle$.

6   Generating the SMT Formula

Now we illustrate how the monitor will generate a correct formula to send to the SMT solver to detect predicate satisfaction. The basic setting is that for each process P_i, we have three variables: v_i, l_i, and c_i that correspond to a variable value and an HLC timestamp for that variable value. The formula we create will be satisfiable if there is a way to set all $3n$ variables such that the formula is satisfied. The intuition behind a satisfying variable assignment is that they specify a valid snapshot; i.e., a consistent snapshot where the formula is satisfied. We add several constraints to ensure that only consistent snapshots will satisfy the SMT formula, some of which are *static constraints* that do not depend on the actual run. Others are *dynamic constraints* that depend on the actual run.

Clock Synchronization Constraints. We first enforce the clock synchronization requirement of a consistent snapshot. Specifically, all the logical clock values l_i must be at most ϵ apart from each other. We enforce this by adding the following static constraint:

$$\forall i, j \quad 1 \leq i < j \leq n : |l_i - l_j| \leq \epsilon$$

Communication Constraints. We next enforce all communication requirements of a consistent snapshot. Specifically, if process P_i sends a message at time $\langle l_s, c_s \rangle$ to process P_j which receives the message at time $\langle l_r, c_r \rangle$, then if process P_j's timestamp in the consistent snapshot is at least $\langle l_r, c_r \rangle$ which means process P_j has received the message, then P_i's timestamp in the consistent snapshot is greater than $\langle l_s, c_s \rangle$ which means that P_i has sent the timestamp. Thus, for each message reported to the monitor, the monitor adds the following constraint:

$$(\langle l_j, c_j \rangle \geq \langle l_r, c_r \rangle) \Rightarrow (\langle l_i, c_i \rangle > \langle l_s, c_s \rangle)$$

These are dynamic constraints as we need one for every inter-process message. Continuing with the example discussed in Fig. 1(b), when the monitor receives the details of message m from process P_2, it adds the following constraint:

$$(\langle l_2, c_2 \rangle \geq \langle 54, 0 \rangle) \Rightarrow (\langle l_1, c_1 \rangle > \langle 51, 0 \rangle)$$

Variable Event Constraints. We now add constraints to ensure that variable v_i takes on the correct value for consistent snapshot. We ensure this by adding one constraint per variable event message received by the monitor. Specifically, if process P_i sends a variable event message $v_i = val$, $[\langle l_1, c_1 \rangle, \langle l_2, c_2 \rangle)$, then we add the constraint:

$$(\langle l_i, c_i \rangle \geq \langle l_1, c_1 \rangle) \wedge (\langle l_i, c_i \rangle < \langle l_2, c_2 \rangle) \quad \Rightarrow \quad v_i = val$$

Predicate Constraints. Finally, we need to ensure that the predicate being monitored is satisfied at the consistent snapshot. This is a static formula that depends only on the n v_i variables. For example, if the predicate being monitored requires that all values of v_i are true simultaneously, then it would be captured by adding $\bigwedge v_i$. If the goal is to check that the sum of all v_i values is at least 10, then it would be captured by adding $\sum v_i \geq 10$.

6.1 Optimizing by Combining l and c Variables

We now present an optimization where we combine variables l_i and c_i for each process P_i into a new variable nl_i thus eliminating n variables from the formula to speed up the SMT solver. The basic idea is that the maximum c value in a typical run is very small [14]. Mostly, we do not need the c value. It is needed to deal with messages that *appear to be from future* due to clock skew. For e.g., if a process with physical clock 10 receives a message from a process with l value 20, the l value of the receive event is set to 20. To ensure this receive event is later than the send event, the c value of the receive event is set to be one larger than c value of the send event. This c value will increase if more events take place at the current process before its physical clock value reaches l. For small ϵ, this is relatively unlikely to happen. Once l is reset, typically c value will return to 0.

Let c_{max} denote the largest c value encountered during the run. Let $c' = c_{max} + 1$. We can combine l_i and c_i by creating a new variable $nl_i = c'l_i + c_i$.

That is, the monitor still receives HLC timestamps with l_i and c_i values. The monitor combines them into nl_i values before sending them to the SMT solver. Specifically, we modify the constraints as follows. Previous work showed that $c_{max} \leq 3$ for typical parameter values; we typically used $c' = 4$ in our experiments. The clock synchronization constraints change from $\forall i, j \quad 1 \leq i < j \leq n :$ $|l_i - l_j| \leq \epsilon$ into $\forall i, j \quad 1 \leq i < j \leq n : |nl_i - nl_j| \leq c'\epsilon$.

Likewise, the communication constraints change from $(\langle l_j, c_j \rangle \geq \langle l_r, c_r \rangle) \Rightarrow$ $(\langle l_i, c_i \rangle > \langle l_s, c_s \rangle)$ into $(nl_j \geq c'l_r + c_r) \Rightarrow (nl_i > c'l_s + c_s)$. And, the variable event constraints change from $(\langle l_i, c_i \rangle \geq \langle l_1, c_1 \rangle) \wedge (\langle l_i, c_i \rangle < \langle l_2, c_2 \rangle) \quad \Rightarrow \quad v_i = val$ into $(nl_i \geq c'l_1 + c_1) \wedge (nl_i < c'l_2 + c_2) \quad \Rightarrow \quad v_i = val$. Finally, no changes are needed for the predicate constraints since they do not use HLC timestamps.

7 Experimental Results

We now present our experimental results. We use a system of 10 independent processes where their clocks differ by at most ϵ. When a process is running, it sends messages to randomly selected processes at some communication frequency mfr. Each message is received after time δ. In one set of experiments, we use a synthetically generated workload where process variable v_i changes value randomly; we consider v_i as both Boolean and integer variables. In another set of experiments, we use an exclusive access to the shared resource in a shared-resource application that has a timing error that can potentially cause two processes to simultaneously access the shared memory. We run our experiments for one second of actual time where we generate event messages as described in Sect. 5. The monitor generates SMT constraints as described in Sect. 6. We then run Z3 on the SMT formula. In our simulation, SMT is invoked periodically (period chosen to be 1 s). It could also be changed so that it is invoked when a new event is received (or when a given threshold number of events is received).

In our experiments, our default parameters are a clock tick of 0.01 ms, a clock drift $\epsilon = 10$ ms (1000 clock ticks), message delay $\delta = 1$ ms (100 clock ticks), $\beta = 1\%$ (the expected time before the variable becomes true is 1 ms), $interval = 0.1$ ms (10 clock ticks) and an average communication frequency of 1000 messages per second (1% chance of sending a message every clock tick). Among all the experiments performed, the predicate of interest is satisfiable approximately 70% of the time. Since we avoid generating instances where the satisfaction of the predicate of interest is *too easy*, we do not observe a clear pattern that indicates a correlation between the time taken by Z3 and whether the predicate of interest is satisfiable, so we omit discussion of whether the given predicate is satisfiable. However, the raw data from the experiments is available at http://cse.msu.edu/~tekkenva/z3monitoringresults/.

Synthetic workload. In our synthetic workload, the v_i variables are either boolean variables or integer variables. When they are integer variables, we restrict them to $\{0, 1\}$. In both cases, whenever v_i is eligible to change, process i changes v_i's value with probability β. Once v_i changes value, it keeps that value for a minimum length of time $interval$ before becoming eligible to change again.

When v_i is a Boolean variable, we consider three different predicates: the conjunctive predicate $\bigwedge v_i$ that requires all v_i variables to be true simultaneously, the exactly 5 predicate, $|\{v_i = true\}| = 5$, that requires exactly 5 v_i variables to be true simultaneously, and the at least 5 predicate, $|\{v_i = true\}| >= 5$, that requires at least 5 v_i variables to be true simultaneously. When v_i is an integer variable, we consider two predicates $\Sigma v_i = 5$ and $\Sigma v_i \geq 5$ that are equivalent to the exactly 5 and at least 5 Boolean predicates, respectively.

Exclusive access workload. We use a time division multiplexing protocol where each process accesses the shared data in its time slot which has length 100 ms and that the clock drift is at most 10 ms. We assume that each process will access the data at the start of its time slot. To ensure that there is no simultaneous access, each process must stop access 10 ms before the end of its time slot. For example, process 1 should access the data in the interval [0 ms, 90 ms), process 2 should access it in the interval [100 ms, 190 ms), and so on. We introduce a chance of error where each process holds on to its access for an extra 1 ms with a probability of 10% which means process i and process $i + 1$ might simultaneously access the data. For this experiment, v_i is a Boolean variable that marks when process i is accessing the shared data, and the predicate is whether two v_i variables might be simultaneously true.

In the rest of this section, we first describe how we discretize time. Then, we identify how one can interpret the results of our experiments. Finally, we present the effect of communication frequency, communication latency, variable stability, and clock skew on the time for monitoring.

7.1   Effect of Discretization of Time

Although time is continuous, we must discretize time to use hybrid logical clocks and SMT solvers. A natural question is whether the level of discretization has any affect on the accuracy and efficiency of monitoring. We first observe that using a clock tick that is too large can have negative modeling effects. To illustrate this issue, consider the following scenario: clock drift is 10 ms, message delay is 1 ms and the expected number of messages sent by a process in 1 ms is one. If we model such a system using a clock tick of 1 ms, then the discrete clocks of processes differ by at most 10 ticks, each message is received at the next clock tick, and each process would have to send one message at every clock tick. In contrast, if use a clock tick of 0.1 ms, then the discrete clocks of processes could differ by at most 100 ticks, a message would be received after 10 clock ticks, and a process would send a message with probability 0.1 at every clock tick and achieve the desired goal of one expected message sent by a process in 1 ms. This is a better model as it allows a process to possibly send no messages or to send multiple messages within 1 ms. We find that the level of discretization does not have a significant impact on the time required for Z3. Hence, in our analysis, we assume that each clock tick is 0.01 ms. In other words, if $\epsilon = 10$ ms, it would be modeled as $\epsilon = 10/0.01 = 1000$.

7.2 Interpreting the Experimental Results

There are two approaches for implementing run-time monitors; a standalone app-roach where a monitor process is independent of the application process, which is how we have described the monitor process so far, and a combined approach where the monitor runs on the same machines as the application processes and uses a certain fraction of resources from those machines. We now describe how to interpret our Z3 timing results using these two perspectives. Recall that we run the application process for one second in all experiments.

Let us start with the standalone monitor. If the monitoring time is at most one second, a single monitor running on the given environment (Windows 8.1 on 2.19 GHz Intel(R) Core(TM) i5 and 8.00 GB RAM) would suffice with a latency of at most 1 s. If the monitoring time is more than one second, say two seconds, then we need two machines and two instances of Z3. If two monitors are used then it could be achieved by sending events at odd time (first, third, fifth second) being sent to the first monitor and sending events at other times to the second monitor. Some overlap may be necessary to ensure that events that span across boundary are recorded correctly. In general, if the Z3 monitoring time (time required for solving the SMT problem) is c seconds, then we need $\lceil c \rceil$ machines and $\lceil c \rceil$ instances of Z3 to keep pace, and the latency would increase to c seconds. Note that we can reduce the machine requirements and latency by getting a more efficient machine or finding a more efficient SMT solver.

Let us now consider the combined approach. In this case, if monitoring one second of execution time on 10 processors takes c seconds, then each process would need to devote roughly $c \times 10\%$ of its resources to the monitor to ensure that the monitoring process can keep up with the application. We can view this as either needing a $c \times 10\%$ more efficient machine or that $\frac{c \times 10}{100 + c \times 10}$ of its resources are devoted to monitoring meaning that the application itself will slow down due to monitoring. The latency in this case will be ten seconds or, in general, n seconds, where n is the number of processors.

7.3 Effect of Communication Frequency

We first show how inter-process communication frequency affects the time required for monitoring. Figure 2(a) summarizes these results. We use our default parameters except that we vary communication frequency from an average of 100 messages per second (0.1% chance of sending a message every clock tick) to an average of 10,000 messages per second (10% chance of sending a message every clock tick). We see that as the communication frequency decreases, the time for verification also decreases. This holds for all predicates we study. Also, monitor-ing the faulty shared memory access protocol requires less time than monitoring the synthetic workloads.

7.4 Effect of Communication Latency

We now show how inter-process communication latency affects the time required for monitoring. Figure 2(b) summarizes these results. We use our default

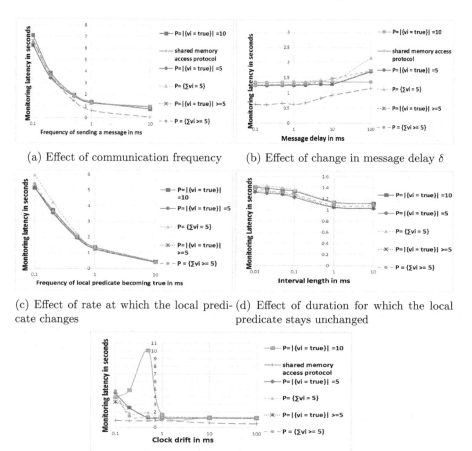

(a) Effect of communication frequency

(b) Effect of change in message delay δ

(c) Effect of rate at which the local predicate changes

(d) Effect of duration for which the local predicate stays unchanged

(e) Effect of change in clock drift ϵ

Fig. 2. Analysis of role of system parameters on monitoring latency

parameters except that we vary communication latency from 0.1 ms to 100 ms. We see that communication latency has a small effect on the time required for monitoring. For all predicates considered, the monitoring time increases with an increase in communication latency, but by at most half a second even when the latency increases from 0.1 ms to 100 ms.

7.5 Effect of Variable Stability

We now show how variable stability affects the time required for monitoring. Note that there are two parameters that affect variable stability in the synthetic workload experiments: β which is the probability of changing the variable value at a given time and *interval* which determines how long the variable value will remain stable after a change. We use our default parameters except we first vary β from 0.1% (the expected time before the variable becomes true is 10 ms) to 10% (the expected time before the variable becomes true is 0.1 ms) in one set of experiments and we vary *interval* from 0.01 ms (1 clock tick) to 10 ms (1000 clock ticks). Figure 2(c) summarizes the results where we vary β and Fig. 2(d) summarizes the results where we vary *interval*. We see that more variable stability leads to faster monitoring. As we decrease the probability of changing variable value or increase the stable interval time, Z3 monitoring time drops.

7.6   Effect of Clock Drift

We now show how clock drift ϵ affects the time required for monitoring. Figure 2(e) summarizes these results. We use our default parameters except that we vary clock drift ϵ from 0.1 ms to 100 ms. We see that unlike other parameters, clock drift does not have a monotonic affect on monitoring time. For some predicates such as conjunctive predicates, the time for monitoring first increases as ϵ increases and then decreases as ϵ increases further. While we do not know the exact reason for this, we suspect the following is true. We are looking for a consistent snapshot where the given predicate is true which in some sense requires examining ϵ-length intervals in the execution. The number of ϵ-length windows is inversely proportional to ϵ. The number of events within an ϵ length window and thus the complexity of the window is proportional to ϵ. Thus, there are competing pressures making the exact complexity a complicated function of ϵ.

8   Related Work

Distributed Predicate Detection with Vector Clocks. The fundamental challenge in distributed predicate detection lies in causality induced by inherent non-determinism [19]. Most existing distributed system monitoring works have focused on asynchronous systems that use vector clocks (VCs) [4–6,12,13,16,26] make minimal assumptions about the underlying system. Unfortunately, asynchronous monitors have several sources of inefficiency that limit their scalability and impede their adoption in real systems. First, general predicate detection with asynchronous monitors is NP-complete [5], although polynomial time algorithms exists for special cases of predicate detection such as linear predicates and conjunctive predicates [5,13]. Second, asynchronous monitors require $\Theta(n)$ space VC timestamps to track all causalities [4] in the system where n is the number of processes. Thus, each message has linear size in the system which limits scalability of asynchronous monitors.

Distributed Predicate Detection with Physical Clock. One way to avoid the overhead of VCs is to use physical time, which has $O(1)$ size timestamps, along with a clock synchronization protocol such as NTP [17], which guarantees that two clocks differ by at most some value ϵ. Stoller [21] has shown that if the inter-event spacing is larger than ϵ, then the number of global states that the system can pass through is $O(kn)$ where k is the maximum number of events in any local process; in contrast, in an asynchronous system, the number of possible states is $\Omega(k^n)$. However, the physical time approach fails to rule out many possible interleavings because it ignores the causality implications of messages. Marzullo [15] described another global state enumeration method that included both logical time and physical time with Hybrid Vector Clocks (HVC). Because of some synchronization, HVC timestamp size may be less than n while preserving properties of VC [24]. In partial synchrony, the trade-off in terms of precision and recall monitoring was discussed in [23]. Namely, Hybrid Logical Clocks (HLC) [14] have been used for efficient predicate detection when imperfect recall is acceptable [25].

Distributed Runtime Monitoring Beyond Predicate Detection. The ultimate goal of runtime monitoring is to monitor expressive properties such as Linear-temporal-logic (LTL) [18,20]. Efficient distributed predicate detection is needed before we can perform efficient distributed LTL monitoring because LTL formula requires predicate detection as a subtask (e.g., consider P leads to Q).

Previous work in distributed monitoring of more expressive properties has focused on developing distributed semantics of the centralized counterpart. Gul [20] considered Past Time Distributed Temporal Logic to express safety properties of distributed message passing systems using vector clocks. Mostafa and Bonakdarpour [18] give a decentralized monitor for LTL specifications in distributed systems; they focus on sound semantics rather than efficiency. In [2,11], the authors designed a decentralized approach for monitoring LTL and regular language specifications using an enhanced automaton assuming that global time is accessible to the local processes. Accessing unambiguous global time requires the use of extremely high precision clocks such as atomic clocks.

Monitoring Distributed Systems in Practice. Intrusive distributed monitoring is a common choice in practice. For example, Facebook TAO [3] designed a distributed database by waiting out the ϵ uncertainty bound during commit-phase so that all events are totally ordered. Google Spanner uses highly synchronized clocks called TrueTime [7,10] which requires transactions to not overlap during the ϵ uncertainty interval. These systems are relatively easy to monitor since blocking execution reduces explosion of number of concurrent states.

9   Conclusion and Future Work

In this paper, we focused on the problem of runtime monitoring partially synchronous distributed systems with the help of SMT solver Z3. We showed how one can map the requirements of runtime monitoring into constraints that need to be satisfied. Based on this analysis, we find that the effort for monitoring reduces with a decrease in communication frequency but increases with communication latency. The time for monitoring also decreases when variables involved in the program change less frequently.

We evaluated our approach for synthetic workload as well as for predicates associated with a program that requires mutual exclusion for shared resource among multiple processes. An interesting observation was that the monitoring time for the synthetic workload was higher. One possible reason is that the constraints created by the synthetic workload does not have any patterns that can be used by the SMT solver. We believe the synthetic workload may represent a hard case and that monitoring may perform better on real protocols. As future work, we plan to test our framework with more predicates and to provide a working tool that can be combined with any application.

References

1. Basin, D., Bhatt, B.N., Traytel, D.: Almost event-rate independent monitoring of metric temporal logic. In: Legay, A., Margaria, T. (eds.) TACAS 2017. LNCS, vol. 10206, pp. 94–112. Springer, Heidelberg (2017). doi:10.1007/978-3-662-54580-5_6
2. Bauer, A., Falcone, Y.: Decentralised LTL monitoring. Form. Methods Syst. Des. **48**(1–2), 46–93 (2016)
3. Bronson, N., Amsden, Z., Cabrera, G., Chakka, P., Dimov, P., Ding, H., Ferris, J., Giardullo, A., Kulkarni, S., Li, H., Marchukov, M., Petrov, D., Puzar, L., Song, Y.J., Venkataramani, V.: Tao: Facebook's distributed data store for the social graph. In: Presented as part of the 2013 USENIX Annual Technical Conference (USENIX ATC 13), San Jose, CA, pp. 49–60. USENIX (2013)
4. Charron-Bost, B.: Concerning the size of logical clocks in distributed systems. Inf. Process. Lett. **39**(1), 11–16 (1991)
5. Chase, C.M., Garg, V.K.: Detection of global predicates: techniques and their limitations. Distrib. Comput. **11**(4), 191–201 (1998)
6. Chauhan, H., Garg, V.K., Natarajan, A., Mittal, N.: A distributed abstraction algorithm for online predicate detection. In: Proceedings of the 2013 IEEE 32nd International Symposium on Reliable Distributed Systems, SRDS 2013, pp. 101–110. IEEE Computer Society, Washington, DC (2013)
7. Corbett, J.C., Dean, J., Epstein, M., Fikes, A., Frost, C., Furman, J.J., Ghemawat, S., Gubarev, A., Heiser, C., Hochschild, P., Hsieh, W., Kanthak, S., Kogan, E., Li, H., Lloyd, A., Melnik, S., Mwaura, D., Nagle, D., Quinlan, S., Rao, R., Rolig, L., Saito, Y., Szymaniak, M., Taylor, C., Wang, R., Woodford, D.: Spanner: Google's globally-distributed database. In: 10th USENIX Symposium on Operating Systems Design and Implementation (OSDI 12), Hollywood, CA, pp. 261–264. USENIX Association (2012)
8. Cristian, F., Fetzer, C.: The timed asynchronous distributed system model. In: Digest of Papers: FTCS-28, The Twenty-Eighth Annual International Symposium on Fault-Tolerant Computing, Munich, Germany, 23–25 June 1998, pp. 140–149 (1998)
9. de Moura, L., Bjørner, N.: Z3: an efficient SMT solver. In: Ramakrishnan, C.R., Rehof, J. (eds.) TACAS 2008. LNCS, vol. 4963, pp. 337–340. Springer, Heidelberg (2008). doi:10.1007/978-3-540-78800-3_24
10. Demirbas, M., Kulkarni, S.: Beyond truetime: using augmentedtime for improving google spanner. In: LADIS 2013: 7th Workshop on Large-Scale Distributed Systems and Middleware (2013)
11. Falcone, Y., Cornebize, T., Fernandez, J.-C.: Efficient and generalized decentralized monitoring of regular languages. In: Ábrahám, E., Palamidessi, C. (eds.) FORTE 2014. LNCS, vol. 8461, pp. 66–83. Springer, Heidelberg (2014). doi:10.1007/978-3-662-43613-4_5

12. Fidge, C.J.: Timestamps in message-passing systems that preserve the partial ordering. In: Proceedings of the 11th Australian Computer Science Conference, vol. 10(1), pp. 56–66 (1988)
13. Garg, V.K., Waldecker, B.: Detection of weak unstable predicates in distributed programs. IEEE Trans. Parallel Distrib. Syst. **5**(3), 299–307 (1994)
14. Kulkarni, S.S., Demirbas, M., Madappa, D., Avva, B., Leone, M.: Logical physical clocks. In: Aguilera, M.K., Querzoni, L., Shapiro, M. (eds.) OPODIS 2014. LNCS, vol. 8878, pp. 17–32. Springer, Cham (2014). doi:10.1007/978-3-319-14472-6_2
15. Marzullo, K., Neiger, G.: Detection of global state predicates. In: Toueg, S., Spirakis, P.G., Kirousis, L. (eds.) WDAG 1991. LNCS, vol. 579, pp. 254–272. Springer, Heidelberg (1992). doi:10.1007/BFb0022452
16. Mattern, F.: Virtual time and global states of distributed systems. In: Parallel and Distributed Algorithms, pp. 215–226. North-Holland (1989)
17. Mills, D.L.: Internet time synchronization: the network time protocol. IEEE Trans. Commun. **39**(10), 1482–1493 (1991)
18. Mostafa, M., Bonakdarpour, B.: Decentralized runtime verification of LTL specifications in distributed systems. In: Proceedings of the 2015 IEEE International Parallel and Distributed Processing Symposium, IPDPS 2015, pp. 494–503. IEEE Computer Society, Washington, DC (2015)
19. Schwarz, R., Mattern, F.: Detecting causal relationships in distributed computations: in search of the holy grail. Distrib. Comput. **7**(3), 149–174 (1994)
20. Sen, K., Vardhan, A., Agha, G., Rosu, G.: Efficient decentralized monitoring of safety in distributed systems. In: Proceedings of the 26th International Conference on Software Engineering, ICSE 2004, pp. 418–427. IEEE Computer Society, Washington, DC (2004)
21. Stoller, S.D.: Detecting global predicates in distributed systems with clocks. Distrib. Comput. **13**(2), 85–98 (2000)
22. Valapil, V.T., Yingchareonthawornchai, S., Kulkarni, S., Torng, E., Demirbas, M.: Monitoring partially synchronous distributed systems using SMT solvers-technical report (2017). http://cse.msu.edu/~tekkenva/z3monitoringresults/TechnicalReport.pdf
23. Yingchareonthawornchai, S., Nguyen, D.N., Valapil, V.T., Kulkarni, S.S., Demirbas, M.: Precision, recall, and sensitivity of monitoring partially synchronous distributed systems. In: Falcone, Y., Sánchez, C. (eds.) RV 2016. LNCS, vol. 10012, pp. 420–435. Springer, Cham (2016). doi:10.1007/978-3-319-46982-9_26. arXiv:1607.03369
24. Yingchareonthawornchai, S., Kulkarni, S.S., Demirbas, M.: Analysis of bounds on hybrid vector clocks. In: OPODIS 2015, Rennes, France, 14–17 December 2015, pp. 34:1–34:17 (2015)
25. Yingchareonthawornchai, S., Valapil, V.T., Kulkarni, S., Torng, E., Demirbas, M.: Efficient algorithms for predicate detection using hybrid logical clocks. In: Proceedings of the 18th International Conference on Distributed Computing and Networking, ICDCN 2017, pp. 10:1–10:10. ACM, New York (2017)
26. Zhu, W., Cao, J., Raynal, M.: Predicate detection in asynchronous distributed systems: a probabilistic approach. IEEE Trans. Comput. **65**(1), 173–186 (2016)

Runtime Detection of Temporal Memory Errors

Kostyantyn Vorobyov$^{(\boxtimes)}$, Nikolai Kosmatov, Julien Signoles,
and Arvid Jakobsson

CEA, LIST, Software Reliability and Security Laboratory,
PC 174, 91191 Gif-sur-Yvette, France
{kostyantyn.vorobyov,nikolai.kosmatov,julien.signoles}@cea.fr
arvid.jakobsson@gmail.com

Abstract. State-of-the-art memory debuggers have become efficient in detecting spatial memory errors – dereference of pointers to unallocated memory. These tools, however, cannot always detect errors arising from the use of stale pointers to valid memory (temporal memory errors). This paper presents an approach to reliable detection of temporal memory errors during a run of a program. This technique tracks allocated memory tagging allocated objects and pointers with tokens that allow to reason about their temporal properties. The technique further checks pointer dereferences and detects temporal (and spatial) memory errors before they occur. The present approach has been implemented in E-ACSL – a runtime verification tool for C programs. Experimentation with E-ACSL using TempLIST benchmark comprising small C programs seeded with temporal errors shows that the suggested technique detects temporal memory errors missed by state-of-the-art memory debuggers. Further experiments with computationally intensive runs of programs from SPEC CPU indicate that the overheads of the proposed approach are within acceptable range to be used during testing or debugging.

Keywords: Runtime analysis · Memory safety · Temporal memory error · Shadow memory · Frama-C/E-ACSL

1 Introduction

Low-level memory access and pointer arithmetic make the C programming language an attractive choice for system-level programming. The same features, on the other hand, make it vulnerable to memory access errors. In C, a programmer is permitted to access and modify memory directly using pointers. It is therefore crucial that each pointer is *valid* at the time of its dereference, as dereferencing an invalid pointer can compromise safety and security of a running program, lead to data corruption or crash the program altogether.

This work has received funding for the S3P project from French DGE and BPIFrance, and for the AnaStaSec project from the French National Research Agency (ANR, grant ANR-14-CE28-0014).

© Springer International Publishing AG 2017
S. Lahiri and G. Reger (Eds.): RV 2017, LNCS 10548, pp. 294–311, 2017.
DOI: 10.1007/978-3-319-67531-2_18

A pointer p is said to be valid if it points to an allocated memory object (also referred to as *memory block*) that p is allowed to dereference with respect to ISO C semantics. For instance, at a given program point p is valid if it has been made point to dynamically-allocated memory or a variable within an active scope. Once that memory has been deallocated all its pointers become invalid.

Motivation. State-of-the-art memory debuggers [3, 7, 20, 22] have become efficient in detecting *spatial* memory errors (accesses to unallocated memory). These tools track memory allocated by a program at runtime and report an error if a program attempts to access a memory location that has not been tracked. Memory debuggers, however, cannot detect uses of invalid pointers in all cases. Consider, for instance, the following code snippet.

```
1 int *p = malloc(sizeof(int));
2 free(p);
3 int *q = malloc(sizeof(int));
4 *p = 1;
```

Execution of the assignment at Line 4 leads to an error. This is because the block initially pointed to by p has been deallocated making p a stale pointer to unallocated memory. In a typical execution, however, the second call to `malloc` at Line 3 can reuse the freed space and place the newly allocated block at the same location as the first one implicitly making p point to the allocated memory. A memory debugger analysing the code observes an access to the allocated memory and does not raise an alarm. Such behaviour, however, is not enforced by ISO C semantics, thus another execution can put the second allocation in a different area. Dereference of a pointer to an allocated memory block that has not been made point to it leads to a *temporal* memory error.

Admittedly, memory debuggers try to avoid temporal errors by using so called quarantine zones, an approach that attempts to allocate new blocks at new addresses and make stale pointers refer to unallocated memory. With this strategy the allocator returns fresh addresses within some allocation buffer. However, once the address space of the buffer is exhausted, the allocator starts to reuse freed memory making occurrence of undetected temporal errors possible.

Most importantly, while the present techniques can catch certain instances of temporal errors on a program's heap, they provide little protection against stack-based temporal issues[1]. Consider the example program in Listing 1.

```
1 int main() {
2     int *p;      // 'p' is invalid
3     {
4         int i = 9;
5         p = &i;  // 'p' made point to 'i'
6     }            // 'p' becomes invalid
7     int j = 8;   // 'j' is allocated at the same address as 'i'
8     *p = 1;      // the assignment changes the value of 'j' through 'p'
9 }                // even though 'p' has never been made point to 'j'
```

Listing 1. Example program containing a temporal error.

---

[1] Recent versions of AddressSanitizer provide experimental support for detecting stack-based temporal errors [18, 27]. However, at the time of developing the proposed approach this feature was not enabled in the mainstream version of the tool.

In the assignment *p = 1 at Line 8 p is likely to be invalid temporally but valid spatially. This is because a typical C compiler (such as GCC) allocates i and j at the same address (since i is released before j is allocated). The assignment at Line 8 therefore results in a temporal error and changes the value of j via p even though p has never been set to point to j.

In a typical execution of the program shown in Listing 1 the temporal error at Line 8 is undetected because allocation and deallocation of program variables is delegated to a compiler. Adopting a different allocating strategy by tampering with automatic allocation is not feasible and has the same problems with detecting temporal errors as the heap-based approach.

Other techniques to detecting temporal memory issues exist. For instance, Safe C [2] detects temporal memory errors by associating memory blocks and pointers with *capabilities* that identify allocations uniquely. A pointer is valid if its capability matches the capability of the memory block it points to. Safe C detects temporal errors, but it also modifies pointer representation that breaks legacy programs. MemSafe [24] detects temporal errors by adding additional assignments that convert temporal issues into spatial. This presents a difficulty during dynamic analysis because pointer addresses can be computed at runtime.

Approach. This paper proposes a solution to reliable detection of temporal errors that does not require compiler modifications or customized allocation strategies. Instead, the proposed technique associates tracked allocations with capability-like identifiers that allow to reason about temporal validity of pointers and detect temporal errors.

The present approach has been implemented in the E-ACSL [4] plug-in within the Frama-C [13] source code analysis platform. To assess error detection capabilities of the proposed technique its authors have created a benchmark called TempLIST comprising 15 small C programs seeded with temporal memory errors. Experimentation with E-ACSL using TempLIST programs has shown that the present approach detects errors missed by such state-of-the-art memory debuggers as AddressSanitizer [20] or MemCheck [22]. Further experimentation with programs from SPEC CPU benchmarks [25] has shown an average runtime overhead of 42% compared to conservative checking for spatial violations only.

Contributions

- An approach to runtime detection of temporal memory errors in C programs.
- An implementation of the proposed approach using E-ACSL.
- A C benchmark called TempLIST for evaluating precision of runtime analysers with respect to detection of temporal memory errors.
- Empirical evaluation of the proposed approach
  using TempLIST and SPEC CPU benchmarks.

2   Temporal Error Detection

The present technique instruments an input program P with statements that monitor its execution and detect temporal errors before they occur. A run of an instrumented program P' tracks every memory block B allocated by P using a metadata storage M that tags B with a unique identifier called an *origin* number and records its bounds. Origin numbers allow to distinguish between different allocations even if these allocations occupy the same address space. Block bounds make it possible to identify whether a given address belongs to an allocated memory block and compute the start address and the origin number associated with that block. M also tracks program pointers. Each pointer variable (that is, a left-value of a pointer type) is mapped to a referent number – an origin number of the memory block the pointer (should) refer to. During its execution the instrumented program P' observes assignments that involve aliasing and updates referent numbers. Temporal errors are detected by checking pointer validity before dereference. For every pointer p to an allocated memory block B the monitor compares the tracked referent number of p to the origin number of B. A temporal error is detected if these numbers do not match.

Example. Consider an execution of the program shown in Listing 1 where i and j are allocated at the same address. The temporal error occurring at Line 8 is detected via the proposed approach as follows. Declarations of variables p, i and j (allocated on a program's stack) assign unique origin numbers to each of these variables. Assume p, i and j are assigned 1, 2 and 3 respectively. Direct pointer assignment p = &i at Line 5 (which makes p point to i) stores the origin number of i as the referent number of p. That is, after the execution of the assignment the referent number of p becomes 2. Finally, the temporal error at Line 8 is detected by comparing the referent number of p with the origin number of the memory block p actually points to. Since p has the referent number of 2 while pointing to j (whose origin number is 3), the analysis concludes that even though p points to an allocated memory block its dereference leads to a temporal error.

The following sections now describe the present technique in greater detail.

2.1 Memory Allocation and Validity

At runtime a C program allocates memory in units called *memory blocks* that typically describe memory allocated automatically for program variables or heap allocations via functions such as `malloc`. A memory block is represented by a contiguous memory region described by its start and end addresses. The start address of a memory block B (denoted $start(B)$) is less than or equal to its end address (denoted $end(B)$). The *length* of B is the difference between the block's end and start addresses increased by one. A memory address a is said to *belong* to a memory block B (and B is said to *contain* a) if a is greater than or equal to the start address of B and less than or equal to its end address.

A pointer p is said to *point* to a memory block B (and B is said to be pointed to by p) if p stores an address belonging to B. To simplify the presentation it is assumed that pointer arithmetics operations use byte offsets. For instance, for pointer p of any type that stores address 0×100, $p + 5$ is 0×105.

Let p be a pointer of type $t*$ storing a memory address a. Let sz denote the number of bytes in the pointed location $*p$ (denoted $sizeof(*p)$). At a given program point p is said to be *spatially* valid if a belongs to an allocated memory block B such that $a + sizeof(*p) - 1 \leq end(B)$. That is, the dereference of p (that reads $sizeof(*p)$ bytes from a) should not exceed the bounds of B. At a given program point p is said to be *temporally* valid if it is valid spatially and B has not been deallocated after p has been made point to B.

The notion of spatial and temporal validity is extended to pointer arithmetic expressions of the form $p + i$, where i is an integer expression and p is a pointer (called the *base* of the pointer expression). The dereference of a pointer expression $p + i$ is *spatially* valid if $p + i$ is spatially valid and addresses given by the base p and the expression itself (i.e., $p + i$) belong to the same allocated memory block, and invalid otherwise. A dereference of a spatially invalid expression $p + i$ leads to a spatial memory error. The dereference of a spatially valid pointer expression $p + i$ is *temporally* valid if p is temporally valid. The dereference of a temporally invalid expression $p + i$ leads to a temporal memory error.

For every allocated memory block B, a unique identifier, called the *origin number* of B and denoted $\alpha(B)$, is associated with B. If a is a memory address belonging to B, then $\alpha(a) = \alpha(B)$. For a pointer variable p (identified by its address $\&p$) that has been made point to block B via address a (e.g. via $p = a$), the *referent number* of p, denoted $\gamma(\&p)$, is defined as the origin number of a, that is, $\gamma(\&p) = \alpha(a)$.

Dynamic metadata storage M that tracks information about memory allocation during a run of an instrumented program is represented by the substructures M_b and M_p. M_b keeps track of every memory block B allocated by the program at runtime recording its bounds and origin number $\alpha(B)$. M_p tracks program pointers such that each pointer p in M_p, identified by its address $\&p$, is mapped to a referent number $\gamma(\&p)$. Relevant implementation details of M are further discussed in Sect. 3.

2.2 Key Instrumentations

Tracking allocated memory, updating referent numbers and checking validity of program pointers before their dereference is delegated to specific functions called from the instrumented program. This section discusses details of these functions and shows relevant examples of their use.

Tracking Memory Blocks. Tracking allocated memory during a run of an instrumented program is enabled via functions *store* and *delete*. *store*(a, s) records a memory block of s bytes in length and a start address of a to the metadata storage M_b. Calls to *store* are added after declarations of variables or calls to memory allocating functions (e.g., `malloc`). *delete*(a) removes a memory block with start address a from M_b. Calls to *delete* are added at the end of scope of variable declarations or before calls to memory-deallocating functions such as `free`. The present approach also takes into account abrupt scope terminations (e.g., via `goto` statements) and emits additional *store* or *delete* statements as required. An example showing the use of *store* and *delete* in an instrumented program is shown in Sect. 2.4.

Updating Referent Numbers. Referent numbers of pointers are updated using functions *mapOrigin* and *mapReferent*. *mapOrigin*$(\&p, a)$ associates a pointer variable p identified by its address $\&p$ with an origin number of address a (i.e., $\gamma(\&p) = \alpha(a)$). For the case when a lies outside of a program's allocation the referent number of a is mapped to an invalid referent number that indicates that dereferencing of p would result in a spatial memory error. *mapReferent*$(\&p, \&q)$ sets the referent number of p to the referent number carried by another pointer variable $\&q$ identified by its address $\&q$ (that is, $\gamma(\&p) = \gamma(\&q)$).

The following snippet shows instrumentation example using *mapOrigin* and *mapReferent* functions. In the original program (shown to the left), pointer p

Original program

```
1 char *p = malloc(sizeof(char));
2 char *q = p;
```

Instrumented program

```
1 char *p = malloc(sizeof(char));
2 mapOrigin(&p, p);      // γ(&p) = α(p)
3 char *q = p;
4 mapReferent(&q, &p);   // γ(&q) = γ(&p)
```

is first assigned an allocated memory block and then q is made point to the same block via p. To update the referent number of p after the first assignment program instrumentation adds function call *mapOrigin*$(\&p, p)$ that updates the referent of p to the origin number of the allocated block. Further, the instrumentation uses *mapReferent*$(\&q, \&p)$ to set the referent number of q to that of p because the aliasing of q is performed indirectly using p. This paper further describes rules by which referent numbers are updated in Sect. 2.3.

Verifying Validity of Pointers. Validity of pointers is established by functions *svalid* and *tvalid* that check spatial and temporal validity of pointer expressions.

Function call *svalid*$(a, base, sz)$ checks spatial validity of pointer expressions and returns a non-zero value if memory addresses a, $a + sz - 1$ and $base$ belong to the same allocated memory block and zero otherwise. Consider an expression $p + i$, where p is a pointer and i is an integer expression. Spatial validity of this expression can then be established using *svalid*$(p + i, p, sizeof(*p))$. That is, *svalid* checks whether $p + i$ belongs to the same allocated block as p (i.e., $\alpha(p + i) = \alpha(p)$) and dereferencing of $p + i$ does not exceed the bounds of the memory block it points to. This approach facilitates detection of overflows into allocated areas, as if p and $p + i$ refer to different blocks, then $p + i$ accesses memory outside of bounds of an allocated object (i.e., memory block pointed to by p). Similarly, if p belongs to unallocated area, then it is invalid and thus using p to access another memory address (even if that address belongs to allocated space) also results in a memory error.

Temporal validity of pointers is determined using function *tvalid*. Function call *tvalid*$(\&p, a)$, where $\&p$ is the address of a pointer variable p and a is an address, checks whether a belongs to a block p should point to. In other words, *tvalid*(p, a) returns a non-zero value if $\alpha(a)$ and $\gamma(\&p)$ have the same value and zero otherwise. *tvalid* expects p to be spatially valid. For instance, for an assignment *(p + 5) = 1, where p is a pointer variable of type char*, the instrumentation adds the following assertions:

```
assert(svalid(p + 5, p, sizeof(*p)));  // Spatial validity error
assert(tvalid(&p, p));                 // Temporal validity error
```

2.3   Rules for Updating Referent Numbers

This section now discusses the key rules for updating pointer referent numbers. Their purpose is to track the origin number of the block that was referred to at the moment *when the reference was initially created*. Assignments considered by the rules $R2$, $R3$ and $R5$ below create a new reference to a block and thus the block's origin number is stored as a referent number. The rules $R1$ and $R4$ copy (and potentially modify) an existing reference, therefore the referent number is copied as well. Rule $R6$ is derived from rules $R1$–$R5$.

($R1$) **Pointer Assignments.** For an assignment of pointers of the form $p = q + i$, where both p and q are pointer variables and i in an integer expression, the referent number of p is set to the referent number of q, i.e., $\gamma(\&p) = \gamma(\&q)$. The referent number of p is set to invalid if either q or $q + i$ points to unallocated memory, or if q and $q + i$ refer to different memory blocks.

($R2$) **Pointer-from-Address Assignments.** Assignments of the form $p = \&lval$, where p is a pointer and $lval$ is a left value expression evaluating to some address a, sets the referent number of p to the origin number of the memory block containing a. That is, $\gamma(\&p) = \alpha(\&lval)$. Assignments involving pointer arithmetic in their left-hand-side parts (e.g., $p = \&lval + i$ or $p = \&lval[i]$, where i is an integer expression) are handled similarly in that $\alpha(\&lval)$ is taken for the referent number of p. For the cases when address $\&lval + i$ evaluates to an address that does not belong to an allocated block or if addresses $\&lval$ and $\&lval + i$ belong to different memory blocks, the referent number of p is set to an invalid value indicating that p is invalid and its dereference will lead to a memory error.

($R3$) **Pointer-from-non-Pointer Assignments by Cast.** If an assignment is of the form $p = rval$, where p is a pointer and $rval$ is a right-value expression of non-pointer type which has been casted to it, then the referent number of p is set to the origin number of $rval$, that is, $\gamma(\&p) = \alpha(rval)$. Notably, such an update is potential source of imprecision as it make it possible to bypass temporal errors. We further discuss this issue in Sect. 3.

($R4$) **Non-Pointer Assignments.** Non-pointer assignments of the form $lval = rval$, where $lval$ and $rval$ are left- and right-value expressions are handled based on the type $lval$ as follows. If $lval$ is of integral or a floating point type, or if $lval$ is of struct or a union type that contains no pointer (sub-)fields then no referent numbers are updated. Otherwise, if the assignment leads to copying pointer (sub-)fields, then all referent information is copied as well. For instance, in the assignment s1 = s2, where s1 and s2 have type struct { int *p; int *q; }, the referent number of s2.p is copied to s1.p and that of s2.q is assigned to s1.q. That is, $\gamma(\&s1.p) = \gamma(\&s2.p)$ and $\gamma(\&s1.q) = \gamma(\&s2.q)$.

($\mathcal{R}5$) **Library Calls.** If an assignment is of the form $p = f(arg)$, where p is a pointer and $f(arg)$ is a call to a library or external function whose source code is not available then the referent number of p is set to the origin number of the memory block returned by $f(arg)$ (i.e., $\gamma(\&p) = \alpha(p)$). This is suitable for many common functions returning a pointer to a newly allocated block (such as malloc) or returning a pointer to a pre-existing block (e.g. strchr) as long as f itself does not create temporally invalid pointer expressions. Approximations required to handle library functions are further discussed in Sect. 3.

($\mathcal{R}6$) **Functions.** Function calls with arguments are treated as implicit assignments where transfer of referent numbers to parameters is performed using the above rules. Return values are treated similarly. Section 3 further discusses related implementation details.

2.4 Instrumentation Example

Listing 2 shows the resulting instrumented program for the program in Listing 1. The statements added by the program instrumentation are shown in italic font.

```
1 int main() {
2       char *p;
3       store(&p, sizeof(char*));      // Record 'p' to M with origin '1'
4       mapOrigin(&p, NULL);           // Set referent of 'p' to be invalid
5       {
6           char i = 9;
7           store(&i, sizeof(char));   // Record 'i' to M with origin '2'
8           p = &i;
9           mapOrigin(&p, &i);         // Set referent of 'p' to origin of 'i'
10          delete(&i);                // Remove 'i' from M */
11      }
12      char j = 8;
13      store(&j, sizeof(char));       // Record 'j' to M with origin '3'
14      /* Spatial: Does 'p' belong to allocated memory? Pass */
15      assert(svalid(p, p, sizeof(*p)));
16      /* Temporal: Are referent of 'p'(2) and origin of 'p'(3) equal? Fail */
17      assert(tvalid(&p, p));
18      *p = 1;
19      delete(&j);                    // Remove 'j' from M
20      delete(&p);                    // Remove 'p' from M
21 }
```

Listing 2. Example of instrumentation for the program from Listing 1.

The instrumentation process proceeds as follows. It first adds calls to *store* and *delete* that track memory blocks allocated by the program. Statements recording allocated memory blocks to dynamic meta-storage M (via definitions of p, i and j) are shown at Lines 3, 7 and 13. Calls to *delete* that remove these variables from tracking are shown via Lines 10, 19 and 20.

Statements that update referent number of p are shown via calls to *mapOrigin* at Lines 4 and 9. The first call to *mapOrigin* at Line 4 sets the referent number of p to invalid (since p has no initializer). Further, once the pointer assignment which aliases p to i at Line 8 is executed, the call to *mapOrigin* at Line 9 updates the referent number of p to the origin number of i.

The final step of the instrumentation process adds assertions that check validity of pointer expressions before their dereferences. In the example shown in Listing 2 the assignment at Line 18 that dereferences p is guarded by two assertions: the assertion at Line 15 verifies the spatial validity of p and the assertion at Line 17 checks whether p is valid temporally before its dereference.

Since at the time of its dereference p is a stale pointer to a valid memory block described by j, its dereference leads to a temporal error. During the execution of the instrumented program shown above this violation is detected via the assertion at Line 17 that fails since the referent number $\gamma(\&p) = 2$ carried by p and the origin number of its actual pointee $\alpha(p) = 3$ differ.

3   Implementation Details

The present approach to detection of temporal errors has been implemented in the E-ACSL [4] plug-in within the Frama-C [13] source code analysis framework. E-ACSL plug-in is a runtime verification tool that accepts a C program P annotated with formal specifications written in the E-ACSL specification language and generates a new program P' that fails at runtime whenever an annotation is violated. A run of P' that satisfies all annotations is functionally equivalent to the run of P. In other words the E-ACSL plug-in instruments a program with inline monitors generated from formal specifications that can either be provided by the end-user or generated automatically by another tool. For instance, the RTE plug-in [8] of Frama-C can automatically generate such annotations for most undefined behaviours (e.g., out-of-bounds errors or arithmetic overflows). Among others, E-ACSL specifications include memory-related annotations such as \valid(p) and \base_addr(p) that respectively denote the validity of a pointer p and the start address of the memory block p belongs to. To support its memory predicates E-ACSL relies on a C runtime memory library (RTL). Memory modifications of the program are recorded by the monitor. Before program instrumentation, static analysis can be performed to safely remove unnecessary instrumentations and improve efficiency of the monitor [9,10].

Metadata Storage. RTL is based on a specialized shadow memory scheme that allows to capture boundaries of allocated blocks [28]. The key feature of this scheme is that given an address it can identify whether that address belongs to allocated memory and if so compute the start address and the length of the block containing that address. For the purpose of this presentation the shadow memory space implementing this scheme is referred to as *spatial* shadow space.

To enable detection of temporal errors RTL has been extended to include an additional *temporal* shadow space that captures origin numbers of memory blocks and pointer referent numbers. Assuming a 64-bit architecture with pointers comprising 8 bytes, the temporal shadow space represents an application memory block B by 8-byte segments. Application blocks are tracked by shadow blocks of the same size such that an application segment is tracked via its shadow counterpart. Origin and referent numbers are represented by 32-bit integers. The first 4 bytes of a shadow block B' tracking application block B are used to capture the origin number of B. The 4 higher bytes of each 8-byte segment of B' store a referent number. Stack blocks whose size is less than 4 bytes are aligned at a boundary of 4. This is to provide enough space to capture an origin number in the shadow. Blocks whose sizes are between 1 and 7 bytes do not require storing referent numbers because they do not provide sufficient space to store a memory address. In 32-bit architectures, where the size of a program pointer is only 4 bytes, the shadow compression ratio increases meaning that 4 bytes of application memory need to be tracked using 8 bytes of shadow memory.

Generating origin numbers is delegated to a counter incremented each time a memory block is recorded to the meta-storage. To store an origin number x associated with a memory block B the approach writes x to a shadow memory location corresponding to the start address of B. Given an address a from block B one can retrieve its origin number by first computing the start address s of B (using capabilities of the spatial shadow space) and then reading an integer stored in a shadow location mapped to s. To map a pointer at address a to a referent number x one computes the shadow address s tracking a, increments it by 4 bytes and writes x at that location. Retrieval of a referent number is similar except one reads a referent number instead of writing it.

Source Code Availability. The present technique operates at a source code level of the C programming language, therefore it should make approximations when handling calls to functions for which the source code is not available. The present implementation assumes that the change to a pointer structure after such a call can only occur through calls to memcpy, memccpy, memmove, and memset functions, while treating the rest of the functions as *safe* in that their execution does not require updates in referent numbers. It handles a call to memcpy(dest, src,n) that copies n bytes from address src to address dest as follows. Since memcpy can duplicate pointers the monitor also updates referent numbers in the shadow memory to reflect this change. Calls to memccpy and memmove are treated in a similar way. memset(s, c, n) that fills the first n bytes of the memory area pointed to by s with the constant byte c effectively destroys all points-to relationships in that area. Once a call to memset is executed the monitor nullifies the portion of shadow space capturing referent numbers.

Function Calls. As indicated in Sect. 2.3 function calls with arguments are treated as implicit assignments. The transfer of referent numbers from arguments to function parameters, however, poses a practical problem due to a change of stack frame. This is because the address of an argument can only be known before the call. The location where the parameter will be stored, however, is not known before the new stack-frame of the called function has been created. Transfer of a referent number requires both addresses. The instrumentation solves this problem by using a global buffer to transfer referent numbers between function calls. This is such that before each call referent numbers of the function arguments are placed to this buffer. Further, once the function is called and the new stack frame is created the instrumentation transfers referent values from the global buffer to function parameters. Referent numbers associated with return values are transferred similarly.

Limitations. One limitation of the present approach stems from imprecision in referent number updates via rule $\mathcal{R}3$, Sect. 2. Consider the following snippet.

```
uintptr_t i = (uintptr_t)q;   // Assume q is temporally invalid
int *p = (int*)i;
```

Let pointer q be temporally invalid. The first assignment stores the address of the q's pointee in the integer i. Then, by Rule $\mathcal{R}3$ p is assigned the origin number of the memory block whose address was given via i. This makes p temporally valid even though it has been assigned from a temporally invalid pointer. Another limitation arises from referent number updates through calls to external functions (rule $\mathcal{R}5$ in Sect. 2). Indeed, an assignment $p = f()$, associates p with the origin number of the memory block address a returned by $f()$ belongs to. The dereference of p is valid as long as the a belongs to allocated space. In practice $f()$ can return an address through a temporally invalid pointer. Such an issue cannot be detected because the source code for f is not available. At a present stage of implementation temporal validity of pointers assigned through integer values and within external functions should be validated by the users of the approach. To draw the users' attention to such issues E-ACSL emits appropriate warnings.

Presently E-ACSL does not support detection of temporal errors in multi-threaded programs. In practice, given that each allocation is identified uniquely (which can be achieved by synchronization), extending the proposed approach to tracking temporal memory errors during runs of multi-threaded programs is straightforward but requires engineering effort.

4   Experimental Results

This section now presents the results of the experimentation with the E-ACSL plug-in. The main objective of this experimentation is to evaluate precision and runtime performance of the present approach with respect to detecting temporal errors in C programs. The objective is addressed using two experiments discussed in the following sections. The platform for all results reported here was 2.30 GHz Intel i7 processor with 16 Gb RAM, running 64-bit Gentoo Linux.

Temporal Error Detection. The first experiment aims to evaluate precision of the present analysis. During this experiment E-ACSL is used to check small programs seeded with temporal errors. The same programs are then analysed using AddressSanitizer [20] (embedded in GCC-5.4.0), Dr. Memory [3] (version 1.11.0) and MemCheck [22] (version 3.10.1) memory debuggers.

The programs used in this experiment belong to a small benchmarking suite called TempLIST. Programs from TempLIST are aimed at evaluating precision of runtime analysers with respect to detection of temporal memory errors. The suite has been created by the authors of this paper for the purpose of assessing temporal error detection capabilities of the present approach. The authors have resorted to creating their own benchmark only because detection of temporal memory errors is not a well-studied area and appropriate code samples either do not exist or are not easy to acquire. The TempLIST benchmark has been made publicly available[2] in hope that the researchers working in related areas may find it useful. Presently TempLIST comprises 15 programs ranging from 20 to 46 lines of code. Each program, containing one or two clearly marked errors explores a scenario leading to a temporal memory safety violation. Code examples derived from TempLIST have been shown in Sect. 1.

During this experiment E-ACSL has been successful in detecting all 23 temporal errors present in the benchmark used. AddressSanitizer, Dr. Memory and MemCheck have been able to detect only 5 errors of 23. Issues discovered by these tools stem from `malloc-free-malloc` sequences (see discussion in Sect. 1) that can be detected using quarantine zones. However, once multiple reallocations that exhaust quarantine areas are involved such issues go unnoticed. An example of such an issue is shown in the following snippet.

```
1 int *p , *q;
2 p = q = (int*)malloc(sizeof(int));
3 ...
4 do {
5   free(q);
6   ...
7   q = malloc(sizeof(int));
8 } while (...);
9 ...
10 *p = 1;
```

Performance Overheads. The second experiment assesses runtime costs of the present temporal analysis. During this experiment E-ACSL was used to monitor programs from SPEC datasets [25] for CPU testing. A series of runs of original and instrumented programs were performed and their runtime measured. A runtime of a program accounts for real time between the program's invocation and its termination. This experimentation calculates performance overhead of executions that check temporal and spatial validity relative to the runtime performance of runs that enable spatial checks only. To account for variance due to external factors, such as test automation process or system I/O, the overhead was calculated using an arithmetic mean over 10 runs of the modified and the original executables. It should be noted that the focus of this experiment is on the cost of temporal analysis rather than of overall E-ACSL performance. Comparative analysis of E-ACSL overhead with respect to the overhead of the state-of-the-art memory debuggers has been recently reported [28].

The programs monitored by E-ACSL were instrumented using the annotations that validate memory safety of pointer or array accesses. The annotations were generated automatically by the RTE plug-in of Frama-C (see Sect. 3). To

---

[2] http://nikolai.kosmatov.free.fr/TempLIST.zip.

take into account all factors contributing to the programs' overhead this experimentation disabled static analysis pass during E-ACSL instrumentations.

This experimentation uses 15 C programs from SPEC CPU 2000 and 2006 datasets ranging from 1,155 to 36,037 lines of code. Remaining C programs were rejected due to current limitations of Frama-C and E-ACSL instrumentation engine independent of the proposed technique. 998.specrand and 999.specrand programs were also excluded from this experiment due to their small size and absence of temporal checks. Runs of SPEC programs were performed using inputs provided by the test input dataset of SPEC.

Figure 1 shows runtime overhead of E-ACSL with temporal analysis enabled relative to the normalized execution time of E-ACSL using only spatial analysis. The results of this experimentation show that introduction of temporal analysis results in an average slowdown factor of 42% with the maximal result of 91% in 197.parser and the minimal result of 17% in 433.milc. One of the main factors contributing to the runtime overhead is the amount of pointer assignments and dereference operations. This is because each pointer assignment results in a transfer of referent numbers, whereas pointer dereferences trigger additional checks. That is, programs, using mostly integer or array operations are likely to result in lower overhead, whereas programs that mostly manipulate pointers are prone to incurring greater overhead.

The overhead of temporal analysis with respect to the runtimes of unobserved programs ranges from approximately 16 times in 470.lbm to approximately 67 times in 433.milc and averages to 35 times. Note that these results have been collected using purely dynamic technique that monitored each potential temporal violation. Using static analysis to remove unnecessary checks typically leads to a better performance. For instance, with static analysis enabled the runtime

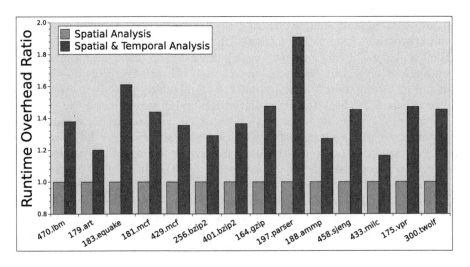

Fig. 1. Runtime overhead of SPEC programs

overhead of 256.bzip of over 40 times drops to only 14.44 times, and 47.31 times overhead of 458.sjeng is reduced to approximately 27 times.

In summary, even though the overhead of temporal analysis is high, it is likely to be within an acceptable range to be used with testing or debugging. In [28] spatial analysis of E-ACSL has been shown to have overhead comparable to such popular tools as Dr. Memory or MemCheck; an average overhead increase of 42% that has an added benefit of temporal error detection should not present an issue in practice.

Threats to Validity. The first issue that may have affected the validity of the presented results is the choice of programs. The experiment evaluating precision of temporal analysis uses programs from a small benchmarking suite developed specifically for evaluating the present approach. While authors have tried to develop representative examples of temporal errors it is possible that they have overlooked certain types of issues that might have affected the results. Further, during the experiment evaluating runtime overhead of the proposed technique programs from SPEC CPU benchmarking suites were used. Even though SPEC are well suited for estimating runtime overhead of memory monitoring tools, different programs or input values may result in different overheads. Additionally, because of technical issues with Frama-C and E-ACSL instrumentation engine several SPEC CPU programs were excluded from the experiment. Using those programs may have also affected the averaged overhead results. The final issue corresponds to the platform used. The experiments were performed on a machine with a 64-bit architecture where a width of a pointer is 8 bytes. This setup allows to use 1:1 compression ratio for tracking referent and origin numbers. 32-bit architectures require twice as much memory to track temporal information. As such, in 32-bit architectures overhead results may differ to the overhead incurred in 64-bit machines.

5 Related Work

One popular way to detect memory errors at runtime is called memory debugging. This approach tracks memory allocated by a program (typically via shadow mappings) and checks that accessed memory locations have been properly allocated and/or initialized. Rational Purify [7] uses compile-time instrumentations to add instructions tracking the memory state of an executing program directly into object files. MemCheck [22], a memory debugger built atop the Valgrind instrumentation platform [16,17], uses dynamic binary instrumentation (DBI) to instrument a program at runtime and track heap memory with bit-level precision. SGCheck [23] is a similar effort targeting stack and global memory. Another notable DBI-based memory debugger is Dr. Memory [3]. AddressSanitizer [20] is a popular memory debugger targeting out-of-bounds accesses and use-after-free violations. AddressSanitizer [20] is known for its low runtime overheads due to a compact shadow state encoding that tracks 8-byte sequences by 3 bits. Address-Sanitizer, initially built on top of a Clang compiler, has now been ported to

GCC replacing mudflap [6]. MemorySanitizer [26] and ThreadSanitizer [21] are similar tools aiming detection of initialization errors and data races.

While effective for detection of spatial violations memory debuggers have a limited capacity for detecting temporal errors. Their detection is based upon custom allocation strategies that try to allocate new memory blocks at new addresses as much as possible making stale pointers refer to unallocated portions. Such an approach, however, is unsound, making stale pointers refer to allocated memory eventually possible. Such an approach is also not suitable for stack allocations typically handled by a compiler. The present approach is different in that it tracks temporal metadata allowing to identify temporal memory errors without the need for a custom allocation strategy or modification to compile or runtime environments.

An orthogonal way of tracking memory is by using *fat pointers*, a technique that extends pointers to carry metadata about their pointees. Safe C [2] detects temporal memory errors by associating memory blocks and pointers with "capabilities" that identify allocations uniquely. A temporal error is detected if a capability of dereferenced pointer is the same as that of the memory block it points to. The use of fat pointers has been explored by various researchers [11,14,15].

Detecting temporal errors using Safe C capabilities is similar to origin and referent numbers used by the present technique. One key difference, however, is the way to track memory. Using fat pointers leads to changes in pointer layout that often break legacy programs. Further, Safe C requires "well-behaved" code in which pointer values are not created from or manipulated as non-pointer values. The present technique has no such limitation.

Another way to detect memory errors is by using backwards compatible techniques [1,5,12,19] that use in-memory databases to associate pointer addresses with bounds metadata of their pointees. Even though these techniques solve issues associated with the use of fat pointers by keeping the pointer layout intact, their primary concern is detection of spatial violations.

A notable effort to ensuring safety of C programs is MemSafe [24] that uses a combination of pointer and object metadata. MemSafe maps each allocated object to a unique identifier and each pointer to an identifier of the object the pointer refers to. Pointer identifiers are used to compute object metadata and check spatial validity of pointers before their dereference. MemSafe detects temporal errors by adding statements that forcibly assign invalid values to stale pointers. Additionally, since each allocated object is unique, a stale pointer can be identified by matching the identifier of its referent against object metadata.

One limitation of MemSafe the use of pointer metadata to determine properties of allocated objects. On the contrary, the present approach computes metadata at an address level. This facilitates detection of overflows into allocated areas (unsupported by MemSafe) and ensures that referent numbers are updated correctly. Another key benefit of the present technique is management of referent numbers using shadow memory. This ensures correct updates of referent numbers even during bulk copy of memory areas, where several objects containing pointers can be copied at once (e.g., via `memcpy`). Since MemSafe utilizes pointer metadata it requires approximations to handle such issues.

6 Conclusion

This paper presented a dynamic technique to detection of temporal memory errors in C programs. This approach consumes a C program P and instruments it with statements that track memory allocated by a program at runtime and assertions that verify validity of pointer dereferences. A run of an instrumented program P' that attempts to dereference an invalid pointer (either spatially or temporally) is aborted and the discovered vulnerability is reported. During its execution P' allocates and associates memory objects with origin numbers that uniquely identify memory allocations. Program pointers in turn are associated with referent numbers – origin numbers of the objects they should point to. Dereferencing a pointer to allocated memory whose referent number mismatches the origin number of the object it points to detects a temporal error.

The present technique has been implemented in E-ACSL, a runtime verification tool built on top of the Frama-C source code analysis platform. Experimentation with E-ACSL using TempLIST benchmarks has shown that the present approach is capable of reliable and systematic detection of temporal memory errors missed by such state-of-the-art memory debuggers as AddressSanitizer, Dr. Memory and MemCheck. Further experimentation with SPEC CPU benchmarks has shown that the presented technique incurred an average runtime overhead of 42% compared to monitoring only spatial memory errors. Such results suggest that the present technique is suitable for use during testing and debugging of real programs where an increased analysis cost is amortized by the value of the analysis capable of detecting a wider class of errors.

References

1. Akritidis, P., Costa, M., Castro, M., Hand, S.: Baggy bounds checking: an efficient and backwards-compatible defense against out-of-bounds errors. In: Proceedings of the USENIX Security Symposium, pp. 51–66. USENIX Association, August 2009
2. Austin, T.M., Breach, S.E., Sohi, G.S.: Efficient detection of all pointer and array access errors. In: Proceedings of the ACM SIGPLAN Conference on Programming Language Design and Implementation, pp. 290–301. ACM, June 1994
3. Bruening, D., Zhao, Q.: Practical memory checking with Dr. Memory. In: Proceedings of the Annual IEEE/ACM International Symposium on Code Generation and Optimization, CGO 2011, pp. 213–223. IEEE Computer Society, Washington, DC (2011)
4. Delahaye, M., Kosmatov, N., Signoles, J.: Common specification language for static and dynamic analysis of C programs. In: Proceedings of the ACM Symposium on Applied Computing, pp. 1230–1235. ACM, March 2013
5. Dhurjati, D., Adve, V.S.: Backwards-compatible array bounds checking for C with very low overhead. In: Proceedings of the International Conference on Software Engineering, pp. 162–171. ACM, May 2006
6. Eigler, F.C.: Mudflap: pointer use checking for C/C++. In: Proceedings of the GCC Developers Summit, pp. 57–70, May 2003
7. Hastings, R., Joyce, B.: Purify: fast detection of memory leaks and access errors. In: Proceedings of the Winter USENIX Conference, pp. 125–136, January 1992

8. Herrmann, P., Signoles, J.: Frama-C's annotation generator plug-in. CEA LIST, Software Safety Laboratory, Saclay, F-91191 (2016). https://frama-c.com/rte.html

9. Jakobsson, A., Kosmatov, N., Signoles, J.: Fast as a shadow, expressive as a tree: optimized memory monitoring for C. Sci. Comput. Program. **132**(Part 2), 226–246 (2016). Special Issue on Software Verification and Testing (SAC-SVT'15)

10. Jakobsson, A., Kosmatov, N., Signoles, J.: Rester statique pour devenir plus rapide, plus précis et plus mince. In: Baelde, D., Alglave, J. (eds.) Journes Francophones des Langages Applicatifs. Le Val d'Ajol, France, January 2015

11. Jim, T., Morrisett, J.G., Grossman, D., Hicks, M.W., Cheney, J., Wang, Y.: Cyclone: a safe dialect of C. In: Proceedings of the General Track: 2002 USENIX Annual Technical Conference, pp. 275–288. USENIX, June 2002

12. Jones, R.W.M., Kelly, P.H.J.: Backwards-compatible bounds checking for arrays and pointers in C programs. In: Proceedings of the International Workshop on Automatic Debugging, pp. 13–26. Linköping University Electronic Press, September 1997

13. Kirchner, F., Kosmatov, N., Prevosto, V., Signoles, J., Yakobowski, B.: Frama-C: a software analysis perspective. Formal Aspects Comput. **27**(3), 573–609 (2015)

14. Kwon, A., Dhawan, U., Smith, J.M., Knight Jr., F.K., DeHon, A.: Low-fat pointers: compact encoding and efficient gate-level implementation of fat pointers for spatial safety and capability-based security. In: Proceedings of the ACM SIGSAC Conference on Computer and Communications Security, pp. 721–732. ACM, November 2013

15. Necula, G.C., Condit, J., Harren, M., McPeak, S., Weimer, W.: CCured: type-safe retrofitting of legacy software. ACM Trans. Program. Lang. Syst. **27**(3), 477–526 (2005)

16. Nethercote, N., Seward, J.: Valgrind: a program supervision framework. Electron. Not. Theor. Comput. Sci. **89**(2), 44–66 (2003)

17. Nethercote, N., Seward, J.: Valgrind: a framework for heavyweight dynamic binary instrumentation. SIGPLAN Not. **42**(6), 89–100 (2007)

18. Potapenko, A.: AddressSanitizerUseAfterReturn (2015). https://github.com/google/sanitizers/wiki/AddressSanitizerUseAfterReturn

19. Ruwase, O., Lam, M.S.: A practical dynamic buffer overflow detector. In: Proceedings of the Network and Distributed System Security Symposium. The Internet Society, December 2004

20. Serebryany, K., Bruening, D., Potapenko, A., Vyukov, D.: AddressSanitizer: a fast address sanity checker. In: Proceedings of the USENIX Annual Technical Conference, pp. 309–319. USENIX Association, June 2012

21. Serebryany, K., Potapenko, A., Iskhodzhanov, T., Vyukov, D.: Dynamic race detection with LLVM compiler — compile-time instrumentation for ThreadSanitizer. In: Khurshid, S., Sen, K. (eds.) RV 2011. LNCS, vol. 7186, pp. 110–114. Springer, Heidelberg (2012). doi:10.1007/978-3-642-29860-8_9

22. Seward, J., Nethercote, N.: Using Valgrind to detect undefined value errors with bit-precision. In: Proceedings of the USENIX Annual Technical Conference, pp. 17–30. USENIX (2005)

23. SGCheck: an experimental stack and global array overrun detector. http://valgrind.org/docs/manual/sg-manual.html

24. Simpson, M.S., Barua, R.: MemSafe: ensuring the spatial and temporal memory safety of C at runtime. Softw. Practice Exp. **43**(1), 93–128 (2013)

25. Standard Performance Evaluation Corporation: SPEC CPU (2006). http://www.spec.org/benchmarks.html

26. Stepanov, E., Serebryany, K.: MemorySanitizer: fast detector of uninitialized memory use in C++. In: Proceedings of the Annual IEEE/ACM International Symposium on Code Generation and Optimization, pp. 46–55. IEEE Computer Society, February 2015
27. Stepanov, E.: AddressSanitizerUseAfterScope (2016). https://github.com/google/sanitizers/wiki/AddressSanitizerUseAfterScope
28. Vorobyov, K., Signoles, J., Kosmatov, N.: Shadow state encoding for efficient monitoring of block-level properties. In: Proceedings of the International Symposium on Memory Management, pp. 47–58. ACM, June 2017

Control Dependencies in Interpretive Systems

Babak Yadegari$^{(\boxtimes)}$ and Saumya Debray

Computer Science Department, University of Arizona, Tucson, USA
{babaky,debray}@cs.arizona.edu

Abstract. Interpreters and just-in-time (JIT) compilers are ubiquitous in modern computer systems, making it important to have good program analyses for reasoning about such systems. Control dependence, which plays a fundamental role in a number of program analyses, is an important contender in this regard. Existing algorithms for (dynamic) control dependence analysis do not take into account some important runtime characteristics of interpretive computations, and as a result produce results that may be imprecise and/or unsound. This paper describes a new notion of control dependence and an analysis algorithm for interpretive systems. This significantly improves dynamic control dependence information, with corresponding improvements in client analyses such as dynamic program slicing and reverse engineering. To the best of our knowledge, this is the first proposal to reason about low-level dynamic control dependencies in interpretive systems in the presence of dynamic code generation and optimization.

1 Introduction

Interpretive systems—interpreters, often accompanied by dynamic code transformation via just-in-time (JIT) compilers, together with input programs—are ubiquitous in modern computer systems. Their ubiquity and complexity make it important to devise algorithms to reason about such systems. An especially important analysis in this context is that of *control dependence*, which specifies whether or not one statement in a program controls the execution of some other statement. Control dependence analysis plays a fundamental role in a number of important program analyses and applications, including code optimization [16], program parallelization [28,31], program slicing [24,33,35], and information flow analysis [14,27].

This paper is concerned with low-level reasoning about control dependencies during an execution of an interpretive system. There are several reasons for considering the system holistically in this manner. The first is that the behavior of such systems is intimately tied to the control flow logic of both the interpreter and the interpreted program as well as the optimization logic of the JIT compiler. Second, in the presence of JIT compilation, a complete and accurate understanding of the execution behavior of such a system necessarily requires a low-level analysis at the level of IR or machine instructions, including instructions that may be

© Springer International Publishing AG 2017
S. Lahiri and G. Reger (Eds.): RV 2017, LNCS 10548, pp. 312–329, 2017.
DOI: 10.1007/978-3-319-67531-2_19

dynamically generated or modified (cf. Balakrishnan's work showing that source-level reasoning may not suffice for understanding low-level program behavior [6], which applies even more strongly to dynamically modified code).

Unfortunately, classical notions of control dependence are not very helpful for such reasoning about the execution behavior of interpretive systems; interactions between the interpreted program, the interpreter, and the JIT compiler; and code generated or modified dynamically. As a result, existing control dependence analyses produce results that can be imprecise when reasoning about the low-level behavior of such systems, including in particular input-specific interactions between the interpreter and JIT compiler (such interactions can give rise to bugs that can be difficult to track down [10,34]). The widespread use of interpreters and interpretive systems makes this a highly problematic situation. This paper takes a step towards addressing this problem by proposing an improved approach to control dependence analysis for interpretive systems.

This paper makes the following technical contributions. First, it identifies an important shortcoming of existing control dependence analyses in the context of modern interpretive systems. Second, it extends the classical notion of control dependence to interpretive systems in a way that handles a wide class of dynamic optimizations cleanly and uniformly. Experiments using a prototype implementation of our ideas, built on top of a Python system equipped with an LLVM-based back-end JIT compiler [36], show that our notion of control dependence significantly improves the results for client analyses such as dynamic program slicing. To the best of our knowledge, this is the first proposal to reason about low-level dynamic control dependencies in interpretive systems in the presence of dynamic code generation and optimization.

The rest of the paper is organized as follows: Sect. 2 discusses some back-grounds and motivating example. Section 3 discusses terminology and notation as well as the traditional notion of the control dependency. Section 4 presents our ideas and algorithms to handle control dependencies in the interpreters. This is followed by implementation details in Sect. 5 with evaluations and experimental results in Sect. 6. Section 7 discusses related work followed by conclusions in Sect. 8.

2   Background and Motivation

2.1   Interpreters

An interpreter implements a virtual machine (VM) in software. Programs are expressed in the instruction set of the VM, and encoded in a manner determined by the interpreter's architecture (e.g., byte-code, direct-threaded). Each operation x in the VM's instruction set is processed within the interpreter using a fragment of code called the handler for x (written $handler(x)$). The interpreter uses a *virtual instruction pointer* (vip) to access successive VM instructions in the input program and a *dispatch* routine to transfer control to appropriate handler code.

An interpreter must accommodate all control flow behaviors possible for all of its input programs despite having a fixed control flow graph itself. This is done by transforming control dependencies to data dependencies through vip and controlling the execution by appropriately updating the vip value for the next VM instruction that should be executed. Control then goes from the handler to the dispatch code, which uses the updated vip to fetch the appropriate next VM instruction. In other words, control flow in the input program is handled via updates to vip within the interpreter depending on the semantics of the executed byte-code. As a result, control dependencies in the input program are transformed into data dependencies through vip in the interpreter's execution. This also means that the handlers are no longer control dependent on each other, but rather are all control dependent on the dispatch code.

2.2 JIT Compilation

Just-in-time (JIT) compilers are widely used in conjunction with interpreters to improve performance by compiling selected portions of the interpreted program into (optimized) code at runtime.

While the specifics vary from one system to another, the general idea is to use runtime profiling to identify frequently-executed fragments of code, then—once one or more such fragments are considered to be "hot enough"—to apply optimization transformations to improve the code. The very first such optimization is to transform the code from an interpreted representation, such as byte code, into native code. Some JIT compilers support multiple levels of runtime optimization, where the dynamically created code can be subjected to additional optimization if this is deemed profitable [30]. We refer to such dynamically-generated native code as "JITted code."

For our purposes, JIT compilation can be seen as a sequence of alternations between two phases: execution, where code from the input program—which may or may not include previously JITted code—is executed; and optimization, where code transformations are applied to hot code to improve its quality. We refer to each such optimization phase as a *round* of JIT compilation.

2.3 Motivating Example

Dynamic slicing is helpful for fault localization in debugging [38]. For simplicity we consider a small interpreter containing an obvious bug; in practice, interpreters are usually much larger and more complex, and even more so when JIT compilation is included.

Consider the backward program slicing problem [2,24] posed for a simple interpreter, shown in Fig. 1(b), executing the input program in Fig. 1(a). Figure 1(c) shows the dynamic dependence graph (DDG) over the execution instances of the interpreter in Fig. 1(b) with the input program in Fig. 1(a) with an input other than 5. The nodes in the DDG graph represent execution instances of the statements in the interpreter program of Fig. 1(b). Each node in the DDG graph contains a pair < first, second > where first corresponds to the statement in the interpreter code and second corresponds to the line number in the input program of Fig. 1(a) that caused the first to be executed in the

```
I1 : vip = 0;
I2 : while (true)
I3 :   op0, op1, dest =
           GetOperands(vip)
I4 :   switch(InputPgm[vip++])
       case ASSIGNMENT:
I5 :     *op1 = op0
         break
       case IF_EQ:
         /*== should be !=*/
I6 :     if (op0 == op1)
I7 :       vip = dest
           break
       case IF_NOT_EQ:
I8 :     if (op0 == op1)
I9 :       vip = dest
           break
       case PRINT:
I10 :    print(op0)
         break
       case INPUT:
I11 :    *op0 = input()
         break
       case HALT:
I12 :    exit()
```

```
1:  n =
      input()
2:  y = 1
3:  x = 1
4:  if n != 5
5:     y = 6
6:  if n == 5
7:     x = 5
8:  print x
9:  halt
```

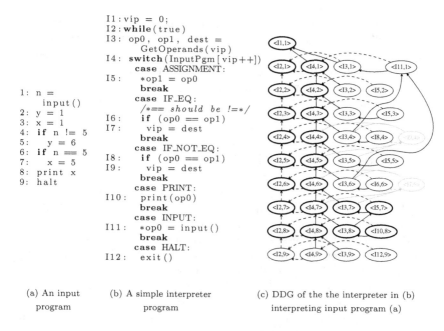

(a) An input
    program

(b) A simple interpreter
    program

(c) DDG of the the interpreter in (b)
    interpreting input program (a)

Fig. 1. A motivating example

interpreter. Dashed edges in the graph show the control dependencies between statements in the code; solid edges show the data dependency and bold nodes represent the program statements that were included in the computed program slice. Gray nodes represent those statements that did not execute in this particular execution. We want to compute a slice with the criterion (8, x) of the input program in Fig. 1.

There is a bug in the interpreter at I6 where the predicate for the conditional operator is wrong. Applying the slicing algorithm on the input program will correctly include lines 7, 6 and 1 in the slice because indeed the value of x at line 8 depends on all those statements. Suppose we want to do the slicing on machine level instructions executed by the interpreter, using the dynamic program slicing algorithm [2] with the slicing criterion (I10, op0). The algorithm starts from the node < I10, 8 > of the DDG that is the interpreter's code implementing the call to the **print** function of the input program. Nodes that are included in the program slice are made bold. According to the input program, node < I6, 6 > should be included because of a control dependency between lines 6 and 7 of the input program. However, this control dependence edge is missing in the DDG of the interpreter because I5 is not control dependent on I6 in the interpreter and so < I6, 6 > is not included in the computed slice.

Relevant slicing [3]—which includes predicates that did not affect the output but could have affected it were they evaluated differently—can improve slicing results where execution omission causes broken dependencies. Using relevant slicing, node < I6, 6 > will be included in the slice because < I7, 6 > could have affected the output. However, for the same reason, node $< 18, 4 >$ will also be included in the slice (the predicate at line 4 of the input program) because of node $< 19, 4 >$. So although relevant slicing helps including the missing statements in the slice computed by dynamic program slicing, it also includes irrelevant statements because of the data dependencies carried over the whole program by vip and this increases the size of the slice significantly for programs with larger sizes.

3   Terminology and Notation

Interpreters on modern computer systems often work in close concert with just-in-time (JIT) compilers to execute input programs.[1] To emphasize this, we refer to the combination of an interpreter and an associated JIT compiler as an *interpretive system*: an interpretive system with interpreter $\mathbf{I}$ and JIT compiler $\mathbf{J}$ is denoted by $\mathcal{I}(\mathbf{I}, \mathbf{J})$; where the interpreter and JIT compiler are clear from the context, or do not need to be referred to explicitly, we sometimes write the interpretive system as $\mathcal{I}$. The set of all possible execution traces of an interpretive system $\mathcal{I}$ on an input program P is denoted by $\mathcal{I}(P)$.

We assume a sequential model of execution. An *execution trace* for a program P is the sequence of (machine-level) instructions encountered when P is executed with some given input. A *dynamic instance* of an instruction x in an execution refers to x together with the runtime values of its operands at some specific point in the execution when x is executed. An instruction x in the static code for P may correspond to many different dynamic instances in an execution trace for P (e.g., if x occurs in a loop); where necessary to avoid confusion, we use positional subscripts such as x_m, to refer to a particular dynamic instance of an instruction x. We use $\prec$ to denote the sequential ordering on the instructions in a trace: thus, $x \prec y$ denotes that x is executed before y.

The idea of control dependence characterizes when one instruction controls whether or not another instruction is executed. This notion is defined formally as follows [16]:

Definition 1. Static Control Dependence: y *is* statically control dependent *on* x *in a given* control flow graph G *(written* $y \xrightarrow{static(G)} x$*) if and only if:*

1. *there is a path π in G from x to y such that for every z on π ($z \neq x, y$), y post-dominates z; and*
2. *y does not post-dominate x in G.*

In addition to static control dependency which reasons about the program statically, Dynamic Control Dependence [37] reasons about control dependencies between program statements over a particular execution of the program.

---

[1] There may be additional software components in the runtime system, e.g., a profiler to identify hot code that should be JIT-compiled, a garbage collector, etc. For the purposes of this paper we focus on the interpreter and the JIT compiler.

Definition 2. Dynamic Control Dependence: y_n *is dynamically control dependent on x_m in a given execution trace and control flow graph G (written as $y_n \xrightarrow{dynamic(G)} x_m$) if and only if: (i) $x_m \prec y_n$; (ii) $y \xrightarrow{static(G)} x$; and (iii) for all z_k such that $x_m \prec z_k \prec y_n$ it is the case that $z \xrightarrow{static(G)} x$.*

The intuition here is that if y is control dependent on x, statically or dynamically, then one control flow successor of x always leads to y while the other may or may not lead to y.

Control dependence is, intuitively, a dynamic property, typically phrased informally as "one statement (or instruction) controlling whether another is executed." The reformulation of this dynamic property in terms of the structure of a static control flow graph, as in the definitions given above, rests on two implicit assumptions. The first, which we refer to as the *realizable paths assumption*, assumes that all "realizable" paths in a program—i.e., all paths subject to the constraint that procedure calls are matched up correctly with returns—are executable; or, equivalently, that either branch of any conditional can always be executed. This assumption, which Barth refers to as "precision up to symbolic execution" [8], is standard in the program analysis literature and is fundamental to sidestepping the undecidability problems arising from Rice's Theorem [20]. The second assumption is that the static control flow graph of the program contains all of the control flow logic of the computation.

The first of these two assumptions is arguably applicable to interpreters and interpretive systems. However, the second assumption does not hold in interpretive systems. There are two reasons for this: first, the logic of the input program necessarily influences the control flow behavior of an interpreter's computation; and second, JIT compilation can introduce new code at runtime whose control flow behavior is not accounted for in such definitions.

4 Control Dependence in Interpretive Systems

4.1 Semantic Control Dependency

To account for these aspects of interpretive computations that are problematic for the traditional notion of control dependency, we adapt the notion of control dependency in two ways. First, instead of considering all possible executions of the interpreter on all possible input programs—which is what we get from the traditional notion of control dependence applied to the control flow graph of the interpreter—we focus on all possible executions of the interpreter for a given input program being interpreted; this is helpful in our context because our goal is to improve the results of dynamic analyses of interpretive systems. Second, instead of tying our notion of control dependence to a fixed static control flow graph—an approach that does not work in the presence of dynamically generated code—we give a semantic definition in terms of execution traces.

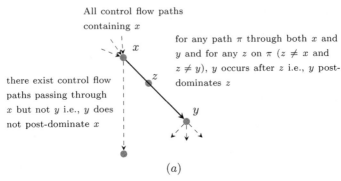

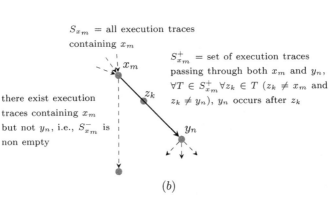

Fig. 2. Parallels between static and semantic control dependence; (a) Static control dependence; (b) Semantic control dependence

Definition 3. Semantic Control Dependence: *Given an interpretive system $\mathcal{I}$ and an input program P, let x_m and y_n be dynamic instances of instructions on some execution of $\mathcal{I}(P)$ such that $x_m \prec y_n$. Let $S_{x_m} \subseteq \mathcal{I}(P)$ be the set of all execution traces in $\mathcal{I}(P)$ that contain the instruction instance x_m. Then y_n is semantically control dependent on x_m (written $y_n \xrightarrow{\ semantic\ } x_m$) if and only if S_{x_m} can be partitioned into two nonempty sets $S_{x_m}^+$ and $S_{x_m}^-$ satisfying the following:*

1. *$y_n \in S_{x_m}^+$ and $y_n \notin S_{x_m}^-$*
2. *$\forall z_k$ such that $x_m \prec z_k \prec y_n$, $z_k \in S_{x_m}^+$ and $z_k \notin S_{x_m}^-$*

This definition parallels the traditional definition of control dependence, as shown in Fig. 2. The notion of static control dependence (Definition 1), shown in Fig. 2(a), uses the structure of the static control flow graph of the program to express the idea that, in the static program code, when we consider the control flow paths that contain x, some execution paths from x lead to y while others do not. Figure 2(b) uses the notion of execution traces—the dynamic analogue of control flow paths—to express the idea, in the dynamic program code, when we consider the set of execution traces that contain x_m, some traces from x_m lead to y_n while others do not; here, $S_{x_m}^+$ denotes the set of execution traces that lead from x_m to y_n while $S_{x_m}^-$ denotes those that do not.

This notion of semantic control dependence differs from the traditional notion of static control dependence in two crucial respects. First, it takes into account both the interpretive system $\mathcal{I}$ and the input program P. Second, it is not tied to a fixed static control flow graph and therefore can be used for situations, such as with JIT compilers, where the code executed changes at runtime.

Definition 3 is not computable as stated and so cannot be embedded directly into an algorithm for computing control dependencies. Instead, we use this definition to reason about the soundness of our approach by showing that, considered in conjunction with the realizable paths assumption, it specifies exactly the set of control dependencies that is computed by our definition.

4.2   Interpretive Control Dependencies

We use a mechanism called instruction origin functions to incorporate control dependence information from the input program into the determination of control dependencies in the (low-level) execution trace. The essential intuition here is as follows. Suppose that, for each instruction Q in the input program, we can determine the set of instructions in the interpreter implementing $handler(Q)$, then the instruction origin function maps x to the input program instruction Q that x "originated from" if one exists; and $\bot$ (denoting "undefined") otherwise. More formally:

Definition 4. *Given an instruction x in the execution of an interpreter, an instruction origin function Γ is defined as:*

$$\Gamma(x) = \begin{cases} Q & \text{if there exists an instruction } Q \text{ in the input program} \\ & \text{such that } x \in handler(Q); \\ \\ \bot & \text{otherwise} \end{cases}$$

Conceptually, Γ can be thought of in terms of labels associated with instructions in the input program that are propagated into the interpreter code, with the handler code in the interpreter getting labeled with the label of the instruction it handles. Γ is a many-to-one mapping of dynamic executed instances of instructions to static instructions in the input program. An instruction Q in the input program may be used in different places in the code, resulting in $handler(Q)$ getting executed multiple times. In this case Γ maps each executed interpreter instruction to the appropriate instruction in the input program. Moreover, if input program instruction Q causes $handler(Q)$ to be executed multiple times (e.g. a loop in the input program), they are all mapped to the same input instruction.

Given an execution trace of an interpretive system $\mathcal{I}$ on an input program P, in order to reason about the control flow influences due to the computational logic of both $\mathcal{I}$ and P, we define a notion of *interpretive control dependence* ("*i-control-dependence*" for short) that combines control dependence information from $\mathcal{I}$ and P and any code that may be dynamically created/modified by the JIT compiler (if any):

Definition 5. *i*-control Dependence: *Given an interpretive system $\mathcal{I}$ and an input program P, let x_m and y_n be dynamic instances of instructions on some execution of $\mathcal{I}(P)$ with k rounds of JIT compilation such that $x_m \prec y_n$ and let $\mathbf{J}_i$ be the JITted code added at round i of JIT compilation. We define $y_n \xrightarrow{interp} x_m$ if either one of the following hold:*

1. *both x_m and y_n are in JITted code, i.e., $\exists i \leq k : x_m, y_n \in \mathbf{J}_i$, and $y_n \xrightarrow{dynamic(\mathbf{J}_i)} x_m$; or*

2. *at least one of x_m and y_n is not in JITted code, and either $y_n \xrightarrow{dynamic(\mathcal{I})} x_m$ or $\Gamma(y_n) \xrightarrow{static(P)} \Gamma(x_m)$.*

The notion of *i*-control-dependency uses the idea of dynamic control dependence to capture the control dependencies between interpreter instructions and JITted code. However, previously defined notions of control dependencies cannot be applied directly to capture the logic of the input program. To capture the control dependencies resulting from the control flow logic of the input program in both the interpreter code and JITted instructions, *i*-control-dependency uses the origin function. The intuition is that for input program instructions Q and R in P where $R \xrightarrow{static(P)} Q$, if there are instructions x and y in the execution trace such that $\Gamma(x_m) = Q$ and $\Gamma(y_n) = R$, then the execution of y_n depends on the execution of x_m and hence they are *semantically* control dependent but this can not be inferred by only looking at the CFG of the interpreter. The reason is that x_m and y_n belong to handlers of the interpreter which are not control dependent according to the interpreter's CFG.

Since JITted code executes natively without any interpretation, in the case where $x_m, y_n \in \mathbf{J}_i$, *i*-control-dependency uses the standard notion of control dependency (through the CFG of $\mathbf{J}_i$) to identify control dependencies between them. This allows *i*-control-dependency to handle situations where the JIT-compiler transformations may not preserve control dependence relationships in the input program (e.g., loop unrolling, loop permutation). However, if one of the instructions belongs to **I** and the other belongs to $\mathbf{J}_i$, it is still required to use Γ to look up control dependencies in the input program.

The reason for using the static control dependence definition for the input program P is that the function Γ maps instructions in the execution trace to static instructions in the input program, not their execution instances. Static control dependencies can be computed from the static CFG of the input program and given an execution trace in $\mathcal{I}(P)$, dynamic control dependencies for interpreter instructions can be computed using the CFG of the interpreter and Definition 2. Likewise for JITted instructions, dynamic control dependencies can be computed by the CFG of the created code at runtime.

The relationship $\xrightarrow{\text{dynamic}(\mathcal{I})}$ contains all the control dependencies in the interpreter code and the runtime generated JITted code that are computed using the standard notion of control dependency, i.e., $y_n \xrightarrow{\text{dynamic}(\mathcal{I})} x_m$ means that for $x_m, y_n \in \mathbf{I}$; or, for $x, y \in \mathbf{J}_i$, y_n is dynamically control dependent on x_m; the former using the CFG of the interpreter and the latter from CFG of the runtime generated code.

We next give a soundness result for the notion of i-control-dependence: namely, that under the realizable-paths assumption in program analysis, the notion of i-control-dependence is identical to that of semantic control dependence.

Lemma 1. *Given an interpretive system $\mathcal{I}$ and an input program P that both satisfy the realizable paths assumption, let x_m and y_n be instructions in an execution trace in $\mathcal{I}(P)$. Then, $y_n \xrightarrow{\text{semantic}} x_m$ implies $y_n \xrightarrow{\text{interp}} x_m$.*

Proof. By induction on the number of rounds $k \geq 0$ of JIT compilation.

Lemma 2. *Given an interpretive system $\mathcal{I}$ and an input program P that both satisfy the realizable paths assumption, let x_m and y_n be dynamic instances of instructions in an execution trace in $\mathcal{I}(P)$. Then, $y_n \xrightarrow{\text{interp}} x_m$ implies $y_n \xrightarrow{\text{semantic}} x_m$.*

Proof. From Definition 5, $y_n \xrightarrow{\text{interp}} x_m$ implies that either (1) $y_n \xrightarrow{\text{dynamic}(\mathcal{I})} x_m$; (2) $y_n \xrightarrow{\text{dynamic}(\mathbf{J})} x_m$; or (3) $\Gamma(y_n) \xrightarrow{\text{static}(\mathbf{P})} \Gamma(x_m)$. In the first two cases, the lemma follows from the definition of dynamic control dependence (Definition 2) applied to the code of the interpreter or the JITted code; In the second case, we use the definition of Γ to apply the definition of static control dependence to the input program.

The following result is now immediate.

Theorem 1. *Given an interpretive system $\mathcal{I}$ and an input program P that both satisfy the realizable paths assumption, let x_m and y_n be instructions in an execution trace in $\mathcal{I}(P)$. Then, $y_n \xrightarrow{\text{interp}} x_m$ if and only if $y_n \xrightarrow{\text{semantic}} x_m$.*

5 Implementation

We have implemented a prototype of our control dependence analysis algorithm in the context of the *Unladen-swallow* implementation of Python [36], an open-source integration of a Python interpreter with a JIT compiler. *Unladen-swallow* uses the LLVM compiler framework [25] to dynamically map frequently executed code to LLVM-IR, which is then optimized and written out as JIT-compiled native code. *Unladen-swallow* was chosen because it is built up on two popular components, Python interpreter and LLVM compiler that are widely used both by researchers and in industry. Furthermore, *Unladen-swallow* provides mechanisms to control the JIT compiler behavior from the input program, e.g. forcing the JIT compilation of a piece of code, that simplifies the evaluation.

To obtain the CFG of the interpreter, we disassemble[2] the interpreter (CPython) and reconstruct its control flow graph, from which we compute (intra-procedural) control dependencies in the interpreter and the JIT compiler. To simplify the implementation effort of our prototype, our current implementation treats the LLVM code generator as an external library that is not included in this control flow graph; this is simply for convenience and there is nothing precluding the inclusion of the LLVM libraries if so desired.

To identify control dependencies among the native code instructions, we use the CFG of the byte-code produced by the CPython compiler and mark the instructions in the execution trace. We instrumented the LLVM back-end JIT compiler to produce CFG of the compiled code that can be used to identify control dependencies among the JITted instructions.

Usually debug information is enough to compute the Γ function to map the executed instructions to the VM byte-codes in the input program. Interpreters, as well as JIT compilers, need to keep some debug information that relates executed instructions to the source program statements to make step-by-step debugging possible. In order to do this, an interpreter needs to keep information about the source program to individual byte-codes, and so for each handler code, the information about the source is accessible through these debug information.

We have instrumented the CPython compiler used in *Unladen-swallow* to produce and emit the control flow graph of the byte-coded input program. Moreover, specific parts in the interpreter handlers that implement control flow transfers in the input program were marked to map conditional jumps in the input program (bytecode) to the machine-level instructions. This helps identifying the actual predicates and control transfer instructions in the execution trace when a basic block in the input program is found control dependent on another one. This was a matter of simplicity and convenience, and is not in any way fundamental to the ideas presented here: other approaches, e.g., reverse engineering the byte code obtained from the front-end compiler, e.g. see [29], would have produced exactly the same results. The modified interpreter inserts markers at the beginning of each basic block where we can map instructions in the execution trace to basic blocks in the input program. This information combined with the mapping information allows us to find the control dependencies in the input program.

For the JIT compiler, on the other hand, we instrumented the LLVM backend to generate the CFG of the dynamically generated native code. We cannot rely on debug information to extract control dependencies in the JITted code because the JIT compiler's transformations may not preserve control dependencies from the original code. The safest option is to have the JIT compiler dump

---

[2] We currently use the `objdump` utility for disassembly, invoking it as 'objdump --disassemble --source'; however, any other disassembler would work. The '--source' option allows us to identify control flow targets for indirect jumps corresponding to `switch` statements.

the CFG of the compiled code and use that to identify control dependencies. We modified the LLVM compiler to dump the CFG for the native code that is produced in the last step. This did not require more than 20 lines of code since the compiler needs to produce the CFG anyway and we just dumped this information.

6   Experimental Results

We evaluated our idea of control dependency presented in this paper using *dynamic program slicing* by applying the i-control-dependency notion discussed in 4.2. Our experiments were performed on a machine with 2×2.60 GHz six-core Intel Xeon processors with 64 GB of RAM running Ubuntu. We used a tracing tool built on top of Pin [26] to collect execution traces. The tracing tool records each instruction with some runtime information such as instruction address.

Two crucial properties of a desired program slice is to include the buggy parts of the code in the slice while keeping the slice size minimal. To evaluate the effects of our notion of control dependency, we apply dynamic program slicing algorithm where the control dependencies are computed using (1) i-control-dependence, and (2) standard control dependence. For the first approach, our dynamic slicing algorithm ignores the data dependencies caused by the vip of the interpreter.

Each experiment was done for two execution modes: *Pure Interpreter* and *Interpreter Plus JIT*. In Pure Interpreter mode, the input program was only interpreted whereas in the Interpreter Plus JIT execution mode, all or some part of the input program was JITted. Our hypothesis is that slices computed using standard notion of control dependencies may be incorrect due to missed control dependencies in the input program while being larger mainly due to spurious data dependencies though the vip. We used a prototype implementation described in Sect. 5 and ran experiments on a collection of Python programs including three samples resembling already known bugs both in the interpreter and the JIT compiler, as well as five Python scripts taken from standard Python libraries that are included in the Python distributed package.

6.1   Buggy Samples

From three buggy samples, two of them are reported in the Python bug tracking system at http://bugs.python.org/[3] and the third one is adapted from a reported bug in C# JIT compiler.[4] All the three samples have a common characteristic where the wrong behavior is because of a bug in the interpreter or the JIT compiler that is only triggered by a particular input program. We constructed examples of the bugs and executed them with the Python interpreter used in *Unladen-swallow*. For the Interpreter Plus JIT experiment, we annotated the code triggering the bug so as to force it to be JITted at runtime. The samples

---

[3] Issues 4296 and 3720 can be found at http://bugs.python.org/issue4296 and http://bugs.python.org/issue3720 respectively.

[4] https://www.infoq.com/news/2015/07/NET46-bug2.

are representative of a class of issues that may arise due to the imprecision of the analysis discussed in this paper and share similar characteristics. The goal of the experiment is to use dynamic program slicing from the point in the program where the wrong behavior is observed and determine whether the buggy code (either in the interpreter or in the JIT compiler) is included in the slice or not.

Table 1 presents the slicing results for the all the three buggy samples. The first two rows show the slicing results for the Pure Interpreter execution mode. As it can be seen from the table, for the two issues we examined, the slicing algorithm based on control dependencies computed with traditional definitions failed to include the sources of the bugs in the program slice because of missing control dependencies in the input program that was necessary to accurately pin down the bug. In the contrary, using i-control-dependency for interpreters, slicing algorithm was able to realize precise dependencies which resulted in the sources of the bug being included in the computed slice.

Table 1. Program slicing results

Exec. mode	Issue No.	Trace size	Std control dependency		i-Control-dependency	
	(bug id.)	(instrs)	Slice size	Bug found	Slice size	Bug found
Pure interpreter	python-3720	11,837	265 (2.23%)	×	192 (1.62%)	✓
	python-4296	6,028	318 (5.27%)	×	222 (3.68%)	✓
Interpreter+JIT	python-3720	248,816	258 (0.10%)	×	22,769 (9.15%)	✓
	python-4296	269,928	21,924 (8.12%)	×	19,861 (7.35%)	✓
	C#-1299	259,802	269 (0.10%)	×	20,608 (7.93%)	✓

The last three rows show the slicing results where the buggy code is JITted during the execution. For the two Python bugs, the actual bug is in the runtime produced (JITted) code because the bug is in the interpreter, but the JITted code make calls to the interpreter. For the third sample, the bug is in the JIT compiler so an accurate slicing algorithm should include the compiler code that produces wrong result. As can be seen from the table, the slicing algorithm using standard notion of control dependency fails to include those parts of the JITted code or the compilation step where the source of the bug is. This is because of missing control dependencies in the runtime generated JIT code. With standard control dependence analysis, the slicing algorithm is only able to identify data dependencies in the JITted code. i-control-dependency helps slicing algorithm to include the bug in the slice.

Table 1 also shows the size of the computed slices for both slicing algorithms. The sizes are given in both raw instruction numbers and normalized to the size of the code observed in the execution trace. Since we are computing dynamic program slice, the size of the static code that was observed in the execution trace was considered as the program size. It can be seen that the slice sizes using i-control-dependence are smaller in the experiments not involving the JIT compiler. This is because the resulting slice is not polluted with spurious dependencies due to the vip, although our slicing algorithm includes additional control dependencies. However, in cases involving JIT-compilation, the traditional slic-ing algorithm does not include any of the JITted code and hence the slice using the proposed algorithm might be larger, which includes JITted code, if any, as well as the compiler code that generated the JITted code.

6.2   Python Library Samples

The second experiment involves five python scripts taken from widely used Python libraries found in their distribution package:

- *binhex*: is a module to encode and decode files in `binhex4` format
- *socket*: provides a low-level networking interface
- *zipfile*: is a module to manipulate files in `ZIP` format
- *StringIO*: provides a file-like class to read/write string buffers
- *HTMLParser*: is a simple `HTML` and `XML` parser library

All the above samples have significantly large and complex logic. We used these samples to show how commonly the slicing results are computed incorrectly when applied to an interpreter code or when JIT-compilation is involved. For each sample we manually inserted slicing criteria on the execution trace of the samples and carried out dynamic slicing.

Table 2. Program slicing results: pure interpreter

Exec. mode	Program	Trace size	Std control dependency		i-Control-dependency
		(instrs)	Slice size	Missed Pred.	Slice size
Pure interpreter	binhex	37,565	4,798 (12.77%)	13	3,561 (09.47%)
	socket	47,929	6,307 (13.15%)	13	5,681 (11.85%)
	zipfile	63,268	9,636 (15.23%)	17	7,837 (12.38%)
	StringIO	20,458	2,458 (12.01%)	10	1,512 (07.39%)
	HTMLParser	104,192	21,027 (20.18%)	14	16,637 (15.96%)
Interpreter+JIT	binhex	303,031	27,348 (9.02%)	36	27,906 (09.20%)
	socket	342,634	34,655 (10.11%)	1	34,130 (09.96%)
	zipfile	337,070	35,215 (10.44%)	68	35,478 (10.52%)
	StringIO	295,877	28,013 (09.46%)	30	28,285 (09.55%)
	HTMLParser	354,758	41,578 (11.72%)	10	40,921 (11.53%)

Table 2 presents the slicing results for the samples from the Python library. Missed predicates column, only given for the dynamic slicing using standard control dependency, shows the number of predicate instructions included in the slice computed using i-control-dependency but not included when standard con-trol dependency was used. The inaccuracy is mainly due to situations similar to what was shown on Fig. 1. For the Pure Interpreter case, missed predicate column indicates missing control dependencies in the input program that are reflected in the interpreter code, while for the Interpreter Plus JIT execution mode it indicates the missing predicates only in the JITted code. The larger the number of missed predicates is, the less accurate the computed slice is, because in addition to missing predicates in the slice, data dependencies to these predicates are also missing which increases the inaccuracy of the slice even more.

Similar to the analysis of buggy samples, the slice sizes are included in Table 2. As it can be seen from the table, the slicing algorithm based on i-control-dependency produces smaller slices even though it includes more control dependencies in the slice, which as mentioned before is mainly due to spurious data dependencies of the interpreter vip. Smaller slice size difference for the Interpreter Plus JIT execution mode is because JIT compilation optimizes away the spurious data dependencies through the vip making the resulting slices smaller.

The running time of the analysis mostly depends on the size of the execution trace. Running time for our three largest traces are 15.12, 37.61 and 201.23 minutes with trace sizes of 423,641,006; 696,851,223 and 1,886,810,614 instructions respectively. The trace sizes for the Interpreter+JIT case are significantly larger than the Interpreter only execution mode.

7   Related Work

There is an extensive body of research on control and data dependence analysis, including: program representations for control and data dependencies [16,21]; frameworks for control dependence analysis [9]; handling control-flow features of modern program structures and reactive systems [4,13]; and efficient algorithms and representations for control dependence analysis [12,37]. None of these definitions consider dynamic code modification due to JIT compiler optimization.

The issue of imprecision of analysis resulting from "overestimation" of control dependencies, which in the interpretive systems arises from the transformation of control dependencies in the original program to data dependencies through vip in the interpreter, has conceptual similarities with problems due to over-tainting that arise when dealing with implicit flows in the context of dynamic information flow analysis. The latter problem is discussed by Bao et al. [7] and Kang et al. [23], who propose algorithms for considering control dependencies selectively, i.e., disregarding dependencies that do not satisfy certain properties of interest. High-level conceptual parallels notwithstanding, the details of the problems are very different from those considered here, as are the proposed solutions.

There is a lot of work on analysis and optimization of interpreters and interpretive systems, but much of this focuses on individual components of interpretive systems—e.g., the input program [11,17], the interpreter [15,18], or the JIT compiler [1,5,19]. Research on partial evaluation has considered the effect of specializing interpreters with respect to their input programs and shown that this is essentially equivalent to compiling the input program [22,32].

8   Conclusion

Interpretive systems—the combination of interpreters and JIT compilers—are ubiquitous in modern software tools and applications. This ubiquity, combined with their complexity, makes it important to develop good algorithms for reasoning about their behavior, in particular with relation to control dependences. Unfortunately, existing algorithms fall short in this regard. This paper introduces a notion of "interpretive control dependence" that can be used to reason about computations of interpretive systems, including code dynamically generated by the JIT compiler. Experimental results show that this notion leads to significantly improved precision in client analyses such as dynamic slicing and CFG recovery.

Acknowledgment. This research was supported in part by the National Science Foundation (NSF) under grants CNS-1115829, CNS-1145913, III-1318343, CNS-1318955, and CNS-1525820.

References

1. Adl-Tabatabai, A.R., Cierniak, M., Lueh, G.Y., Parikh, V.M., Stichnoth, J.M.: Fast, effective code generation in a just-in-time Java compiler. In: Proceedings of the PLDI 1998, pp. 280–290, June 1998
2. Agrawal, H., Horgan, J.R.: Dynamic program slicing. In: Proceedings of the PLDI 1990, pp. 246–256, June 1990
3. Agrawal, H., Horgan, J.R., Krauser, E.W., London, S.: Incremental regression testing. In: ICSM, vol. 93, pp. 348–357. Citeseer (1993)
4. Amtoft, T., Androutsopoulos, K., Clark, D., Harman, M., Li, Z.: An alternative characterization of weak order dependence. Inf. Process. Lett. **110**(21), 939–943 (2010)
5. Arnold, M., Fink, S.J., Grove, D., Hind, M., Sweeney, P.F.: A survey of adaptive optimization in virtual machines. Proc. IEEE **93**(2), 449–466 (2005)
6. Balakrishnan, G.: WYSINWYX: What you see is not what you eXecute. Ph.D. thesis, Computer Science Department, University of Wisconsin, Madison (2007)
7. Bao, T., Zheng, Y., Lin, Z., Zhang, X., Xu, D.: Strict control dependence and its effect on dynamic information flow analyses. In: Proceedings of the 19th ISSTA, pp. 13–24 (2010)
8. Barth, J.M.: A practical interprocedural data flow analysis algorithm. Commun. ACM **21**(9), 724–736 (1978)
9. Bilardi, G., Pingali, K.: A framework for generalized control dependence. ACM SIGPLAN Not. **31**(5), 291–300 (1996)
10. Chen, H., Cutler, C., Kim, T., Mao, Y., Wang, X., Zeldovich, N., Kaashoek, M.F.: Security bugs in embedded interpreters. In: Proceedings of the 4th Asia-Pacific Workshop on Systems, p. 17. ACM (2013)
11. Clausen, L.R.: A java bytecode optimizer using side-effect analysis. Concurrency Pract. Experience **9**(11), 1031–1045 (1997)
12. Cytron, R., Ferrante, J., Sarkar, V.: Compact representations for control dependence. In: Proceedings of the PLDI 1990, pp. 337–351 (1990)
13. Danicic, S., Barraclough, R.W., Harman, M., Howroyd, J.D., Kiss, A., Laurence, M.R.: A unifying theory of control dependence and its application to arbitrary program structures. Theoret. Comput. Sci. **412**(49), 6809–6842 (2011)
14. Denning, D.E.: A lattice model of secure information flow. Commun. ACM **19**(5), 236–243 (1976)

15. Ertl, M.A., Gregg, D.: The structure and performance of efficient interpreters. J. Instr. Level Parallelism **5**, 1–25 (2003)
16. Ferrante, J., Ottenstein, K.J., Warren, J.D.: The program dependence graph and its use in optimization. ACM Trans. Program. Lang. Syst. (TOPLAS) **9**(3), 319–349 (1987)
17. Franz, M.: Adaptive compression of syntax trees and iterative dynamic code optimization: Two basic technologies for mobile object systems. In: Vitek, J., Tschudin, C. (eds.) MOS 1996. LNCS, vol. 1222, pp. 263–276. Springer, Heidelberg (1997). doi:10.1007/3-540-62852-5_19
18. Gagnon, E., Hendren, L.: Effective inline-threaded interpretation of java bytecode using preparation sequences. In: Hedin, G. (ed.) CC 2003. LNCS, vol. 2622, pp. 170–184. Springer, Heidelberg (2003). doi:10.1007/3-540-36579-6_13
19. Gal, A., et al.: Trace-based just-in-time type specialization for dynamic languages. In: Proceedings of the 30th SIGPLAN Conference on Programming Language Design and Implementation, pp. 465–478 (2009)
20. Hopcroft, J.E., Motwani, R., Ullman, J.D.: Introduction to Automata Theory, Languages, and Computation. Addison Wesley, Reading (1979)
21. Horwitz, S., Reps, T., Binkley, D.: Interprocedural slicing using dependence graphs. ACM Trans. Program. Lang. Syst. (TOPLAS) **12**(1), 26–60 (1990)
22. Jones, N.D., Gomard, C.K., Sestoft, P.: Partial Evaluation and Automatic Program Generation. Prentice Hall, Upper Saddle River (1993)
23. Kang, M.G., McCamant, S., Poosankam, P., Song, D.: DTA++: Dynamic taint analysis with targeted control-flow propagation. In: NDSS (2011)
24. Korel, B., Laski, J.: Dynamic program slicing. Inf. Process. Lett. **29**(3), 155–163 (1988)
25. Lattner, C., Adve, V.: LLVM: A compilation framework for lifelong program analysis & transformation. In: International Symposium on Code Generation and Optimization, pp. 75–86 (2004)
26. Luk, C.K., et al.: Pin: Building customized program analysis tools with dynamic instrumentation. In: Proceedings of the ACM Conference on Programming Language Design and Implementation, pp. 190–200, June 2005
27. Masri, W., Podgurski, A., Leon, D.: Detecting and debugging insecure information flows. In: ISSRE 2004, pp. 198–209 (2004)
28. Midkiff, S.P.: Automatic parallelization: an overview of fundamental compiler techniques. Synth. Lect. Comput. Architect. **7**(1), 1–169 (2012)
29. Sharif, M., Lanzi, A., Giffin, J., Lee, W.: Automatic reverse engineering of malware emulators. In: 2009 Proceedings of the IEEE Symposium on Security and Privacy, May 2009
30. Smith, J., Nair, R.: Virtual Machines: Versatile Platforms for Systems and Processes. Elsevier, Amsterdam (2005)
31. Srinivasan, V., Reps, T.: Partial evaluation of machine code. In: ACM SIGPLAN Notices, vol. 50, pp. 860–879. ACM (2015)
32. Thibault, S., Consel, C., Lawall, J.L., Marlet, R., Muller, G.: Static and dynamic program compilation by interpreter specialization. High.-Order Symbolic Comput. **13**(3), 161–178 (2000)
33. Tip, F.: A survey of program slicing techniques. J. Program. Lang. **3**, 121–189 (1995)
34. Wang, X., et al.: Jitk: a trustworthy in-kernel interpreter infrastructure. In: Proceedings of the USENIX conference on Operating Systems Design and Implementation, pp. 33–47 (2014)

35. Weiser, M.: Program slicing. IEEE Trans. Softw. Eng. **10**(4), 352–357 (1984)
36. Wouters, T., Yasskin, J., Winter, C.: unladen-swallow: A faster implementation of python, https://code.google.com/p/unladen-swallow/
37. Xin, B., Zhang, X.: Efficient online detection of dynamic control dependence. In: Proceedings of the 2007 International Symposium on Software Testing and Analysis, pp. 185–195. ACM (2007)
38. Zhang, X., Gupta, N., Gupta, R.: A study of effectiveness of dynamic slicing in locating real faults. Empirical Softw. Eng. **12**(2), 143–160 (2007)

Monitoring Time Intervals

Teng Zhang[1]([⊠]), John Wiegley[2], Insup Lee[1], and Oleg Sokolsky[1]

[1] University of Pennsylvania, Philadelphia, PA, USA
{tengz,lee,sokolsky}@cis.upenn.edu
[2] BAE Systems, Burlington, MA, USA
john.wiegley@baesystems.com

Abstract. Run-time checking of timed properties requires to monitor events occurring within a specified time interval. In a distributed setting, working with intervals is complicated due to uncertainties about network delays and clock synchronization. Determining that an interval can be closed – i.e., that all events occurring within the interval have been observed – cannot be done without a delay. In this paper, we consider how an appropriate delay can be determined based on parameters of a monitoring setup, such as network delay, clock skew and clock rate. We then propose a generic scheme for monitoring time intervals, parameterized by the detection delay, and discuss the use of this monitoring scheme to check different timed specifications, including real-time temporal logics and rate calculations.

Keywords: Runtime verification · Time interval monitoring · Real-time properties

1 Introduction

In this paper, we consider runtime verification of timing properties, such as one event occurring after another event within certain time bound or counting the number of events that occur during an interval of time. In both cases, a monitor needs to not only evaluate the logic of the property but also determine whether events fall within a given time interval. We consider the situation when the system being monitored (referred to as the target system or just system, when the context is clear) and the monitor are deployed in an asynchronous environment. On the one hand, the asynchronous approach makes monitoring more difficult, due to uncertain delays introduced by the network delivering events from the system to the monitor and also due to the differences between the system and monitor clocks. On the other hand, by using the monitor clock that is different from the system clock, we may be able to detect that timing behavior of the target system is incorrect because the system clock is wrong.

This work is supported in part by DARPA BRASS program under contract FA8750-16-C-0007 and by ONR SBIR contract N00014-15-C-0126.

© Springer International Publishing AG 2017
S. Lahiri and G. Reger (Eds.): RV 2017, LNCS 10548, pp. 330–345, 2017.
DOI: 10.1007/978-3-319-67531-2_20

We propose a monitor architecture that clearly separates monitoring of time intervals from the rest of property checking. The property is checked in an event-driven fashion similar to common approaches to runtime verification. To enable checking of the timing in this way, we extend the set of events with a new kind of event that represents the end of a time interval, which we call *interval closure*. Now, we can reduce time checking to *temporal ordering*: if a system event arrives before the closure event, it occurred within the time interval, while if the closure event arrives first, the system event is outside of the interval. In order to produce closure events in the right order, we introduce the *interval handler* module into the monitor.

The second aspect addressed in the paper is the design of the interval handler. We note two particular design considerations for the handler: one is *correctness* and the other is *timeliness*. On the one hand, the handler needs to correctly monitor intervals, in the sense that it should close an interval – that is, raise the closure event – only after any event occurring within the interval has been received. In the presence of uncertainty, correct monitoring is possible only if the handler waits long enough to make sure it has seen all relevant events. On the other hand, closing the interval too late may increase unnecessary resource consumption for monitoring, which should be avoided. Moreover, we should know what the tight one is, in order to be certain that the deadline to be set is larger than the tight one. It is therefore important to set the monitoring *deadline* as small as possible under the premise that correctness of the closure is guaranteed.

To summarize, this paper addresses the following problem: *"Given an asynchronous environment with uncertain communication delay and imperfect clock synchronization between target system and monitor, under what conditions can correctness of monitoring time intervals be ensured and how to achieve it?"*

In this paper, we consider three parameters of monitoring setup, network delay, clock skew and clock rate, and study how they influence monitoring time intervals. We explore the parameter space and present a scheme for setting the deadline of monitoring for each interval. We then introduce an algorithm that the interval handler uses to monitor intervals.

Related Works. In [1], Sammapun considered properties represented with time-bound operators and analyzed several different implementations of checking properties based on timer and heartbeats with bounded or unbounded network delay. However, clock rate and clock skew were not taken into consideration. Moreover, properties using aggregate operators were not studied. In [2], Lee and Davidson proposed algorithms for implementing timed synchronous communication among processes having different clocks such that all processes will decide whether the communication is successfull within their own absolute deadlines and they agree on the same decision. Two communication schemes, multiple senders with one receiver and N-way communication were analyzed. In [3], they further analyzed the performance of two algorithms of timed synchronous communication using probabilistic models. We do not consider synchronous communication in this paper so the method of setting the deadline is different. In [4], Pinisetty et al. proposed a paradigm of runtime enforcement using time retardants on events to ensure that a system satisfies timed properties. While we are not aiming at an enforcement scenario, we will rely on a similar technique in the case when events may be delivered from the system to the monitor out of order. Jahanian et al. studied the runtime monitoring of time constraints specified by Real-Time Logic (RTL) in the distributed real-time system [5]. However, the monitoring procedure of time intervals was not discussed. Finkbeiner et al. presented a query language for asynchronously collecting statistic information and proposed algebraic alternating automata for evaluating the queries in [6]. Colombo et al. presented the tool LarvaStat [7], which supports statistic operations based on the incrementally computable statistics. It also supports the specification of intervals opened and closed by special events. However, the issue of monitoring intervals was not discussed in detail. Basin et al. extended MFOTL (metric first-order temporal logic) with SQL-like aggregate operators over time and corresponding monitoring algorithms [8]. In [9], they further raised the problem of imprecise timestamps of traces influencing the correct verification of the properties specified by MTL formulas. The paper gave the conclusion that certain MTL fragments can be verified by existing monitors for precise traces over traces with imprecise timestamps. In our work, we do not verify properties using a specific logic but rather focus on studying the issue of monitoring intervals. To summarize, little work has been done in monitoring time intervals in a distributed environment based on the analysis of parameters of the monitoring setup.

Paper organization. The paper is organized as follows. Section 2 provides motivation for the work and gives examples of timed property specifications that can be checked in the proposed fashion. Based on this motivation, we introduce the monitor architecture in Sect. 3 and lay out requirements for the interval handler. We then introduce the system model and definitions of parameters considered: network delay, clock skew and clock rate. Based on these, Sect. 4 presents the exploration of the parameter space and addresses the problem of setting deadline for monitoring time intervals. Section 5 proposes a procedure for monitoring intervals. Section 6 gives a further discussion on cases when the correctness of interval monitoring cannot be guaranteed and introduces future work.

2   Motivation

Several kinds of commonly used timed specifications involve reasoning over time intervals. We note that, while the logic of evaluating these properties over a stream of events is different, it invariably involves reasoning about intervals of time given in the specification and whether the timestamp of a given observation falls within an interval or outside of it. As we discuss below, parameters of the monitoring setup, such as clock skew or the latency of delivering observations to the monitor, have an impact on how this reasoning should be performed. We therefore want to separate the logic of property evaluation, which depends only on the semantics of the specification language, and interval management, which depends on properties of the monitoring setup.

To illustrate our approach, we first briefly revisit two of them: LTL with interval operators and interval statistics.

LTL with time-bound operators. In LTL, operator Until(U), Weak-until(W) and R(Release) are used to specify properties in a trace. For instance, property $\phi_1 U \phi_2$ is satisfied in a trace if ϕ_1 is satisfied at each location of the trace until ϕ_2 is satisfied at a certain point. The verdict can not be given to this property until getting the result from the verification of ϕ_2. To restrict the time of getting the result, the time-bound operator is utilized [1]. If we want to express the property that ϕ_2 becomes satisfied within 5 time unit from ϕ_1 becoming true, the formula is written as $\phi_1 U_{[0,5]} \phi_2$.

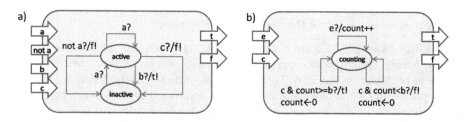

Fig. 1. Evaluation of interval operators

In many runtime verification approaches [10–12], temporal operators are evaluated in an event-driven fashion. Arriving events, which could be observations from the target system or results of sub formula evaluation, trigger changes in the operator evaluation status. We want to extend the same approach to interval operators. Consider, for example, evaluation of the bounded-until $aU_{[0,t_1]}b$, where a and b are target system observations. As Fig. 1(a) shows, evaluation of the operator is a state machine that takes as inputs events a, b, and c. Event *not a* represents the absence of a. We refer to the event c as the *interval closure*, which denotes that t_1 time units have elapsed. Note that t_1 is measured in the sense of perfect clock, which may be different from the clock on the system and the monitor side due to the clock skew. Evaluation is activated by an arrival of a, and while further occurrences of a arrive, the state of the evaluation is unresolved. As soon as *not a* arrives, or if the interval is closed, the operator evaluates to false, denoted by raising an event f. But if b arrives before the interval is closed, the operator evaluates to true and an event t is raised. In this way, evaluation of the operator does not depend on the value of the time bound and does not need direct access to the clock. It is straightforward to extend this scheme to cover intervals of the form $[t_1, t_2]$, as well as cover other commonly used temporal operators. Note that to monitor $aU_{[t_1,t_2]}b$ we consider intervals $[0, t_1)$ and $[t_1, t_2]$. When b arrives, we determine, which of the two interval it falls into, or if it is outside of both. For technical reasons that will be discussed later, we open both intervals when a arrives.

Interval statistics. Some properties needs to collect statistics over a time interval. These properties can be represented in a similar way as SQL queries using aggregate operators [8]. For instance, $Sum_{[0,t_1]}(occur(e)) >= b)$ specifies the property of the number of occurrences of event e over the time interval

$[0,t_1]$ is equal or greater than b. Figure 1(b) shows the evaluation scheme for this operator in a fashion similar to the previous case. Variable *count* increases with arrivals of event e. When *interval closure* event c arrives, the interval is closed. An event t is raised if *count* is greater or equal than b; otherwise an event f is raised.

In contrast to interval operators discussed above, calculation of interval statistics is different in the sense that intervals are *recurrent*. On the system side, once an interval ends, the next one is immediately started and statistics calculation continues for the next interval, effectively partitioning the time line into intervals of the same size, starting from some initial event. We can view recurrent intervals as an extension of the two-interval case above.

Checking example. Figure 2 shows a concrete scenario for monitoring of $aU_{[t_1,t_2]}b$ when system events can be delivered with a delay. Assume first that the clocks in both the system and the monitor are perfect. On the monitor side, we begin processing when the event a arrives at relative time 0. To correctly evaluate this property, the monitor needs to tell whether b falls within $i_1 = [0,t_1)$ or within $i_2 = [t_1,t_2]$. Suppose an event b is raised before t_1 but is delayed more than a was and thus arrives after the time t_1 on the monitor side. Thus, at t_1 the monitor cannot yet conclude that i_1 has expired. From the monitor perspective, i_1 and i_2 *overlap*; that is, an incoming event may belong to either interval. However, once we see the timestamp of b, we can tell whether it belongs to i_1 or i_2. Therefore, we do not need to measure duration of i_1 or i_2 on the monitor side. Now consider the case when b does not arrive within i_2. In order to conclude that b did not arrive in time, the monitor has to wait. Eventually, another event with a large enough timestamp may arrive and the monitor may be able to make the conclusion based on that. But what if it arrives after a very long time or, worse, if the missing b was meant to be the last observation? To proceed in a more timely fashion, the monitor has to use a timer. This timer, essentially, sets the *deadline* for b to arrive. This observation underlies our monitoring approach: we use the timer only to safely close the interval, while all other conclusions – whether the interval has started and whether an event is within the interval – are made based on event timestamps.

Apart from the network delay, the clock rate of the system and the monitor also influence interval monitoring. Using the same example above, assume first that there is no clock skew and delivery delay is ranged from 0 to 1 in the sense of the perfect clock. Suppose the clock rate of the perfect clock r_p is 1, clock rate of the system r_s is 0.5 and clock rate of the monitor r_m is within range $[0.8, 1.5]$. Interval i_1 to be monitored is $[0,6]$ measured by the perfect clock and the monitor begins monitoring it at time 0. To guarantee that all events occurring in i_1 arrive before the monitor finishes monitoring this interval, the deadline of monitoring is set at time 10.5 of the monitor clock, as in the worst case, an event occurs at 3 of system clock (corresponding to time 6 in the sense of the perfect clock as the clock rate is 0.5) arrives at time 10.5 of the monitor clock with the largest delay. If the actual rate of r_m is 1.5, when an event b happens at time 3.1 of the system clock and the network delay is 0.2 then, it arrives at the monitor at

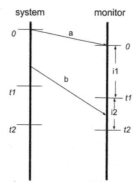

Fig. 2. Monitoring time intervals of $aU_{[t_1,t_2]}b$

time 9.6 (calculated by 3.1*3 + 0.2*1.5). However, since we know the clock rate of the system is 0.5, the time on the perfect clock will be 6.2, which is larger than 6. Therefore, even if b arrives when the monitor is monitoring the interval, the monitor can still determine b does not belong to it. This example suggests that the deadline for monitoring an interval depends only on the duration of the interval and the relationship between the monitoring clock and the perfect clock, but not on the system clock. At the same time, to determine whether an event is within an interval depends on the relationship between the system clock and the perfect clock, but not on the monitor clock. We will make this intuition precise in Sects. 4 and 5.

3   System Architecture and Preliminaries

In this section, we will present the architecture for monitoring time intervals. Then some preliminaries are given, including definitions of some key concepts and parameters of monitoring setup to be explored in the paper.

3.1   Architecture

Figure 3 illustrates the architecture for monitoring time intervals. To separate the logic of time management, a module $IntervalHandler$ is introduced into the monitor between the target system and the property checker. Both the Interval-Handler and checker run under the monitor clock. The checker implements the logic the property to be checked so the implementation detail is out of scope of this paper. It receives two types of events from the IntervalHandler, one is the original events for property evaluation. Another is a special event *interval closure* introduced above, which is used to acknowledge to the checker the end of a time interval.

A checker correctly evaluates the property for a time interval i if all events occurring in i are delivered to the checker when the property is being evaluated.

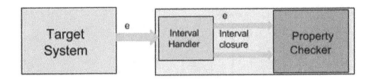

Fig. 3. Architecture for monitoring time intervals

In the ideal situation, when events are delivered from the system to the monitor immediately and there is no timing uncertainty, this can be easily achieved by setting the timer in the IntervalHandler for the duration of i. Any event arriving before the timer expires would be within i, while any event arriving after it expires is outside i. Expiration of the timer immediately raises the closure event. If events can be delayed, however, this approach may clearly result in incorrect checking. The closure event must be delayed to accommodate for late events. In order to close the interval in a timely manner, we need to set a *deadline* for raising the closure event that would, on the one hand, guarantee correct monitoring and, on the other hand, minimize the delay in closing the interval. According to the duration on the time interval and parameters of the monitoring setup, the IntervalHandler can calculate the deadline for each interval when the monitoring process begins. When the current time at the monitor reaches the deadline, the IntervalHandler will send interval closure event to the checker to finish the evaluation of the property for this interval.

The deadline discussed above is useful in another way. If events can arrive out of order, they also should be re-ordered according to their timestamps before being passed on to the checker which, as we discussed above, does not reason about time. In our approach, the IntervalHandler is storing events in a queue in the timestamp order and uses the same deadline to release events from the queue to the checker. We discuss event reordering further in Sect. 5.

3.2   Preliminaries

Time model. There are three time domains assumed: T_m for the monitor clock, T_s for the system clock and T_p for the perfect clock. The monitor takes streams of events as input. Events are observations originated from the system. They are timestamped using the *system clock* in the time domain T_s. The event and monitor clocks can be skewed and run at different rates. In addition, there may be unpredictable delays in delivering events from the target system to the monitor. As a result, event timestamps are not directly comparable with readings of the system clock. Moreover, elements in the time domain T_m and T_s are totally ordered. An event stream E_T is a sequence of timestamped observations $\langle (o_1, t_1), (o_2, t_2), ... \rangle$, where o_i is a value observed at time $t_i \in T_m$. The perfect clock c_p in T_p is used to measure the length of the time interval being monitored.

Time interval is a period of time between two events, the duration of which is measured by the perfect clock. In the remainder of the paper, when we refer the interval on the system, we use "start" and "end" to denote the beginning and ending of the interval. On the monitor side, an interval is "opened" or "closed" by the monitor. A closed interval i that starts at t_1 and ends at t_2 is denoted as $i_{[t_1,t_2]}$. For an event e originated from the system and an interval i, if $t_1 \leq t_e \leq t_2$, then $e \in i_{[t_1,t_2]}$ where t_e is the timestamp of e. Note that if we don't care about events occurring on the bound(s), the interval could also be half-open or open and the denotation will be modified accordingly.

Network delay, denoted as nd, represents the time to send the event from the system to the monitor. The absolute value of the delay is measured in the sense of perfect clock.

Clock rate is the interval of the finest time unit. It is assumed that the clock rate of c_p, denoted as r_p, is 1. The clock rate of the system and the monitor are respectively denoted as r_s and r_m. If r_s (r_m) is greater than 1, then the system (monitor) clock runs ahead of the perfect clock.

Clock skew, denoted as ts, represents the time difference $t_m - t_s$ between the monitor and the system where t_s is the time of the system and t_m is the time of the monitor. In this paper, we assume that time synchronization is periodically conducted between (1) the system clock and the perfect clock and (2) the monitor clock and the perfect clock.

4 Setting the Interval Deadline

In this section, we explore the parameter space of network delay, clock skew and clock rate and identify several cases where correctness of monitoring can be ensured. For each case, we describe how to calculate the deadline for closing the interval. The monitor uses this deadline to set the timer; when the timer expires, we can be certain that no further events belonging to this interval can arrive and the closure event is sent to the checker. Patterns of setting the timer for non-recurrent and recurrent intervals are presented respectively. Case analysis on the three parameters is conducted.

4.1 Patterns of Setting Timer

We rely on timers to determine when an interval can be closed. The timers are set differently based on whether the interval is recurrent or non-recurrent, shown in Fig. 4. Note that the clock rate of the system rs is used to calculate the actual time on the system side.

Non-recurrent intervals. Here we only consider the case involving two consecutive intervals such as the property $aU_{[t_1,t_2]}b$. In $aU_{[t_1,t_2]}b$, two intervals, $[0,t_1)$ and $[t_1,t_2]$, are involved. The monitor begins checking $[0,t_1)$ and $[t_1,t_2]$ when a arrives and two corresponding timers are set to close the intervals.

Recurrent intervals. As the number of intervals to be monitored is unbounded, only the timer for the first interval is set. Then every time an interval is closed, the timer for closing the next interval is set with a proper monitoring deadline. In the following section, we will denote the duration of the recurrent interval as d.

In order to set the deadline as accurate as possible, two steps have to be done. The first step is to estimate the time on the monitor side when e occurs on the system side, denoted as t_0 in Fig. 4. The second step is to calculate deadlines for each monitor based on t_0, which is introduced below.

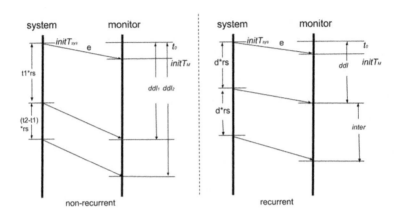

Fig. 4. Scheme of setting deadlines for non-recurrent and recurrent intervals

4.2   Scheme of Setting Deadline

Here we give the case analysis with varying the values of the clock rate, network delay and clock skew with the assumption of bounded network delay. Figure 4 illustrates the scheme of setting deadline for non-recurrent and recurrent intervals. The time when the initial event e occurs on the system side is denoted as $initT_{sys}$, measured by the system clock and $initT_M$ is the time at the monitor when e arrives at the monitor.

The monitor begins the monitoring process at $initT_M$. For the non-recurrent case, ddl_1 and ddl_2 for interval $[0, t_1)$ and $[t_1, t_2]$ need to be calculated. Then, as the timers are set at $initT_M$ with a relative value, deadline for $[0, t_1)$ is set with value $ddl1 - initT_M + t_0$ and deadline for $[t_1, t_2]$ is set with value $ddl2 - initT_M + t_0$. For the recurrent case, the deadline for the first interval can be calculated in a similar way to the non-recurrent case: ddl is calculated according to the duration of interval and the monitoring setup and the deadline for the first interval is $ddl - initT_M + t_0$. From the second interval, timers are set with a period $inter$. The reason the first interval is different from the rest of them is that for the initial event e, we know the exact time when e arrives at the monitor, but for the rest of intervals, we only consider the worst case where the last event for a interval occurs at the boundary and the delay for the delivery is the maximum value of the network delay. In the following case analysis, we will estimate the value of t_0 and calculate ddl_1 and ddl_2 for the non-recurrent case; ddl and $inter$ for the recurrent case.

Case 1: $r_s = 1$, $r_m = 1$, $nd = 0$. In this case, interval durations of the system and monitor are identical and there is no delay, so $t_0 = initT_M$. For the case of non-recurrent intervals, ddl_1 and ddl_2 are respectively t_1 and t_2. For the case of recurrent intervals, ddl and $inter$ have the same value d since there is no network delay.

Case 2: $r_s = 1$, $r_m = 1$, nd is fixed and known. In this case, clock skew ts can be directly calculated by $initT_M - initT_{sys} - nd$ and $t_0 = initT_{sys} + ts$. For the case of non-recurrent intervals, ddl_1 and ddl_2 are respectively $t_1 + nd$ and $t_2 + nd$ since events occurring at the boundary of these two intervals have the delay of nd. For the case of recurrent intervals, ddl is set to $d + nd$, similar to the case of the non-recurrent interval. The value of $inter$ is set to d because the interval is of length d and the network delay has already been taken into consideration when calculating the deadline of the first interval.

Case 3: $r_s = 1$, $r_m = 1$, $nd \in [b1, b2]$, ts is known. As ts is known, $t_0 = initT_{sys} + ts$. We only need to consider the worst case in which network delay has the maximum value, which is when an event e with timestamp t arrives on the monitor side at $t + b2$. The least delay $b1$ is not relevant for computing deadlines. For the case of non-recurrent intervals, ddl_1 and ddl_2 are respectively $t_1 + b2$ and $t_2 + b2$. For the case of recurrent intervals, ddl is $d + b2$ and $inter$ has value d.

Case 4: $r_s = 1$, $r_m = 1$, $nd \in [b1, b2]$, ts is unknown. The analysis is similar to the case 4 but t_0 cannot be determined precisely since ts is unknown and network delay is not fixed. Consequently, we approximate its value using the network delay. The worst case is when the value of t_0 is as late as possible. Therefore, we set $t_0 = initT_M - b1$. The same formulas setting deadlines used in case 3 are also used here.

Case 5: r_s is fixed, $r_m \in [r3, r4]$, $nd \in [b1, b2]$, ts at time $initT_{sys}$ is known. Like in case 3, t_0 is calculated using the formula $t_0 = initT_{sys} + ts$. Because of the clock rate difference between the system and the monitor, clock skew may change. However, since we do not compare time values between the system and the monitor anywhere else, the value of the clock skew does not affect calculations of the deadline value. To cover the worst case of event arrival when calculating the deadline, r_m and nd need to be at their upper bounds. For the case of non-recurrent intervals, ddl_1 and ddl_2 are respectively $(t_1 + b2) * r4$ and $(t_2 + b2) * r4$. For the case recurrent intervals, ddl has value $(d + b2) * r4$ and $inter$ has value $d * r4$.

Case 6: r_s is fixed, $r_m \in [r3, r4]$, $nd \in [b1, b2]$, ts is unknown. Similar with case 4, we need to approximate t_0 using its maximum value: $initT_M - b1 * r3$. The formulas used in case 6 are used in this case.

One can observe that case 5 and 6 are generalization of special cases 1 to 4 and there is no conflicts between them. The summary of case analysis on deadline setting is shown in Table 1. We can prove that given monitoring setup in case 5 and 6, correctness of monitoring intervals can be guaranteed, shown in Lemma 1.

Table 1. Summary of deadline setting scheme

Monitoring setup		Non-recurrent		Recurrent	
	t_0	$ddl1$	$ddl2$	ddl	$inter$
$r_s = 1$, $r_m = 1$, $nd = 0$	$initT_M$	t_1	t_2	d	d
$r_s = 1$, $r_m = 1$, nd is fixed and known, ts is known	$initT_{sys} + ts$	$t_1 + nd$	$t_2 + nd$	$d + nd$	
$r_s = 1$, $r_m = 1$, $nd \in [b1, b2]$, ts is known	$initT_{sys} + ts$	$t_1 + b2$	$t_2 + b2$	$d + b2$	
$r_s = 1$, $r_m = 1$, $nd \in [b1, b2]$, ts is unknown	$initT_M - b1$				
r_s is fixed, $r_m \in [r3, r4]$, $nd \in [b1, b2]$, ts at time $initT_{sys}$ is known	$initT_{sys} + ts$	$(t_1 + b2) * r4$	$(t_2 + b2) * r4$	$(d + b2) * r4$	$d * r4$
r_s is fixed, $r_m \in [r3, r4]$, $nd \in [b1, b2]$, ts is unknown	$initT_M - b1 * r3$				

Lemma 1 (Correctness of Monitoring Interval for Setup in Case 5 and 6). *If r_s is fixed, $r_m \in [r3, r4]$ and $nd \in [b1, b2]$, we can always set a deadline for monitored intervals as illustrated in Table 1, such that all events of the interval will fall within the deadline.*

Proof Sketch. Based on whether ts is known at the beginning of monitoring process, we split into two cases corresponding to case 5 and 6 above. Here we give the sketch for proving the case of monitoring non-recurrent intervals $[0, t_1)$. The proof for interval $[t_1, t_2]$ and recurrent intervals is similar. Recall that t_0 is the estimated time, by the monitor clock, when the initial event occurs on the system side. The deadline is set in two steps, illustrated in Fig. 4, and we argue correctness of these two steps separately. First, we compute the largest possible value for t_0 and this is correct because (1) if ts known, we can calculate the accurate time t_0 of the monitor given the timestamp of $initTsys$ when the initial event occurs on the system side; and (2) if ts is not known, we compute t_0 having the maximum value using the $initT_M$ and the lower bound of nd. Then, we set the deadline relative to t_0 and we do it correctly because we over-estimate the deadline with the upper bound of r_m and nd. We then compare the deadline with t_r, the relative time between $initT_{sys}$ and the latest possible arrival time of the event occurring at t_1 at the monitor. The value of t_r is $t_1 + b2$ in the sense of perfect clock. Translating deadline to the perfect time scale, the value would be $(t_1 + b2) * r4/r_m$, which is greater than or equal to t_r. Since t_0 is equal to or greater than the time when the initial event occurring within the interval, we can always ensure that all events will fall within the deadline.

Lemma 1 can be extended to Theorem 1 describing sufficient condition for correctly monitoring time intervals.

Theorem 1 (Correctness of Monitoring Interval). *If r_s is fixed, r_m is bounded and nd is bounded, we can set a deadline for each monitored interval as illustrated in Table 1 such that all events of the interval will arrive at the monitor within the deadline.*

Proof Sketch. The proof proceeds by case analysis of entries in Table 1. Note that cases 1–4 are special cases of 5 and 6 and need not be considered separately. The union of the monitoring setup conditions in Table 1 is exactly the premise of the theorem. Therefore, correctness of cases 5 and 6, established by Lemma 1, proves the theorem.

5   Monitoring Procedure

This section presents the procedure for monitoring time intervals using the scheme of setting monitoring deadline proposed in the previous section. The procedure describes operation of the IntervalHandler introduced in Sect. 3.1.

The procedure relies of two key functions. First, *calculateDeadline* sets the deadline for each interval according to Sect. 4. Second, procedure *getInterval* is given an event and returns an interval to which this event belongs, as follows. Given an event e with the timestamp t and $initT_{sys}$ which indicates the occurring time of the initial event, we need to get the interval that e belongs to. With the condition that the rate of the system r_s is fixed, the interval can be determined. For the non-recurrent interval, if $t - initT_{sys} < t_1 * rs$, e belongs to the interval $[0, t_1)$; if $t_1 * rs \leq t - initT_{sys} \leq t_2 * rs$, e belongs to the interval $[t_1, t_2]$; otherwise, e falls out of these two intervals. For the recurrent interval, the interval is calculated using the formula $\lfloor (t - initT_{sys})/(d * rs) \rfloor$.

Figure 5 shows the detailed structure of the *IntervalHandler* and how it connects to the *PropertyChecker*. IntervalHandler is responsible for managing intervals and the checker evaluates the logic of the property. Note that the monitoring process is slightly different between the cases of in-order-delivery and out-of-order delivery. *IntervalList* is the data structure representing intervals of interest. In the non-recurrent case, these are the two intervals $[0, t_1)$ and $[t_1, t_2]$. In the recurrent case, if in-order delivery is assumed, we just need to remember the earliest non-closed interval. For out-of-order delivery, *IntervalList* needs to remember all non-closed intervals for which at least one event has been received. We also associate a data structure $eventQueue(i)$ for each interval i in the *IntervalList*: each arrived event is put into corresponding $eventQueue$ ordered by the timestamp. Once the interval i is closed — that is, no more events from this interval can arrive, — the IntervalHandler sends all events in the $eventQueue(i)$ to the checker, followed by the interval closure event.

In the IntervalHandler, *intervalManager* is used to relay events from the system and manage intervals. It first examines whether the received event e is the initial event arriving at the monitor. If so, it computes the deadline and

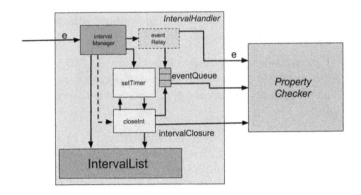

Fig. 5. Structure for the IntervalHandler

sets the timer for the first interval. Note that in the case of properties involving two non-recurrent intervals, two timers with corresponding deadlines need to be set. Then, the interval i that e belongs to is computed. If in-order delivery is assumed, the current interval being evaluated by the checker, denoted as i', is obtained from *IntervalList* by calling the procedure *getLeastOpenedInt*. If i is not equal to i', i' is closed and corresponding closing timer will also be unset. Event e is then sent to the checker. If out-of-order delivery is assumed, it is put into corresponding *eventQueue(i)*.

```
void intervalManager (){
    while(true) {
        Interval i;
        Event e = receiveEvent();
        if (initialEvent (e)){
            initialTS = e.getSystemTimeStamp();
            initialTM = getcurrentTime();
            deadline = calculateDeadline();
            setTimer(deadline,0);
        }
        i = getInterval(e);
        if (out-of-order-delivery){
            addQueue(e,eventQueue(i));
        }else{
            i' = getLeastOpenedInt();
            if(i != i'){
                closeInt(i');
                unsetTimer(i');
            }
            PropertyChecker.handlingEvents(e);
        }
    }
}
```

Procedure $closeInt(i)$ is responsible for closing the interval i, which is called when the corresponding timer is up or an event for the next interval has arrived in the case of in-order delivery. It first calculates the deadline for the next interval $i + 1$ to be evaluated and sets the corresponding timer. For the case of non-recurrent interval, the timer will not be not set. Then the queued events from $eventQueue(i)$ are sent to the checker if out-of-order delivery is assumed. Finally, procedure $intervalClosure(i)$ is called to close interval i and modify $IntervalList$. For the case of recurrent interval, interval i is removed from $IntervalList$ and $i+1$ is set as the earliest non-closed interval if in-order delivery is assumed.

```
void closeInt(integer i){
    ddl = calculateDeadline();
    setTimer(ddl, i+1);
    if (out-of-order-delivery){
        liste = getEventsForQueue(eventQueue(i));
        PropertyChecker.handlingEvents(liste);
    }
    intervalClosure(i);
}
```

6   Discussion and Conclusions

This paper presented an approach to monitoring of time intervals in an event-driven fashion. To do this, we introduced an interval closure event, with the property that all events that fall into the interval occur before the interval closure. The two challenges are (1) correctness of the procedure and (2) timeliness of the event closure. To address these two challenges, we offer a procedure to determine when all events that can fit into the interval have been observed. The answer to this question depends on parameters of monitoring setup, namely network delay, clock skew between the system and the monitor and clock rates of the two. We perform case analysis and show how to close intervals in different cases.

This work has two limitations. First, we can exactly determine when we have seen all the events only if the network delay is bounded. Second, we assumed that we can precisely determine whether a given event is within the bounds of an interval or outside. In general, neither of these two assumptions are true. This means that the monitoring procedure needs to be augmented to accommodate the uncertainty. Below, we offer preliminary remarks on what extensions may be needed.

Unbounded network delay. If the monitoring system is built on a complicated network environment, the network delay can be unbounded. This means we cannot guarantee that the deadline will be sufficiently large to receive all events from the system. We have to accept that, occasionally, an interval will be closed prematurely. A possible approach is to quantify the probability of error.

For example, we consider the delay distribution where events are independent with each other. To simplify the analysis, following assumptions are also made: (1) the system and the monitor has perfect clocks, (2) there is no clock skew, and (3) the event occurrence is distributed uniformly. With these assumptions, we can set a deadline that ensures the probability for one event occurring in the current interval falls out of it is less than $1 - p$. This relation can be represented as the formula below. According to the assumption, $P_1(t)$ is $1/d$ and P_2 is the CDF of delay distribution.

$$\int_0^d P_1(t)P_2(delay \geq d + deadline - t) < 1 - p$$

For a more realistic approach, we can consider more widely used *self-similar* traffic models [13] such as Pareto distribution and Weibull distribution. Different from the memoryless Poisson distribution, self-similar traffic models can perform better in modeling burstiness of traffic in the multiple time scales [14]. Events are not independent with each other and arrivals of events will heavily influence the model.

With this approach we can have a monitoring procedure with probabilistic guarantees of correctness. Moreover, once we discover an event that belongs to an already-closed interval, we know that a monitoring error has occurred. The property checker needs to be notified of the error, which may invalidate some of the checking results. In the case of interval statistics, it may be acceptable to discard the statistics for one of the intervals. In the case of temporal monitoring, we need to determine, which parts of the formula are affected by the error. We will consider a three-valued semantics for the temporal logic, with the "unknown" value corresponding to an error.

Uncertainty in the system clock rate. We need to determine whether an event, timestamped with the system clock, falls within an interval, whose boundaries are determined by the perfect clock. However, if r_s can vary, then an event close enough to an interval boundary cannot be precisely placed. In this case, we can also use a 3-valued semantics, with the third value representing the uncertainty whether the event occurs before or after the interval closure event.

It remains to be seen whether the two three-valued approaches – the one capturing an error and the one capturing the ordering uncertainty – can be combined together in an effective checking procedure. We will explore these questions in future work.

References

1. Sammapun, U.: Monitoring and checking of real-time and probabilistic properties. Ph.D. thesis, University of Pennsylvania (2009)
2. Lee, I., Davidson, S.B.: Adding time to synchronous process communications. IEEE Trans. Comput. **100**(8), 941–948 (1987)

3. Lee, I., Davidson, S.B.: A performance analysis of timed synchronous communication primitives. IEEE Trans. Comput. **39**(9), 1117–1131 (1990)
4. Pinisetty, S., Falcone, Y., Jéron, T., Marchand, H., Rollet, A., Timo, O.N.: Runtime enforcement of timed properties revisited. Formal Methods Syst. Des. **45**(3), 381–422 (2014)
5. Jahanian, F., Rajkumar, R., Raju, S.C.: Runtime monitoring of timing constraints in distributed real-time systems. Real-Time Syst. **7**(3), 247–273 (1994)
6. Finkbeiner, B., Sankaranarayanan, S., Sipma, H.B.: Collecting statistics over runtime executions. Formal Methods Syst. Des. **27**(3), 253–274 (2005)
7. Colombo, C., Gauci, A., Pace, G.J.: LarvaStat: Monitoring of statistical properties. In: Barringer, H., Falcone, Y., Finkbeiner, B., Havelund, K., Lee, I., Pace, G., Roşu, G., Sokolsky, O., Tillmann, N. (eds.) RV 2010. LNCS, vol. 6418, pp. 480–484. Springer, Heidelberg (2010). doi:10.1007/978-3-642-16612-9_38
8. Basin, D., Klaedtke, F., Marinovic, S., Zălinescu, E.: Monitoring of temporal first-order properties with aggregations. In: Legay, A., Bensalem, S. (eds.) RV 2013. LNCS, vol. 8174, pp. 40–58. Springer, Heidelberg (2013). doi:10.1007/978-3-642-40787-1_3
9. Basin, D., Klaedtke, F., Marinovic, S., Zălinescu, E.: On real-time monitoring with imprecise timestamps. In: Bonakdarpour, B., Smolka, S.A. (eds.) RV 2014. LNCS, vol. 8734, pp. 193–198. Springer, Cham (2014). doi:10.1007/978-3-319-11164-3_16
10. Kim, M., Kannan, S., Lee, I., Sokolsky, O., Viswanathan, M.: Java-MaC: a runtime assurance approach for Java programs. Formal Methods Syst. Des. **24**(2), 129–155 (2004)
11. Barringer, H., Rydeheard, D., Havelund, K.: Rule systems for run-time monitoring: from Eagle to RuleR. J. Logic Comput. **20**(3), 675–706 (2010)
12. Roşu, G., Havelund, K.: Rewriting-based techniques for runtime verification. Autom. Softw. Eng. **12**(2), 151–197 (2005)
13. Leland, W.E., Taqqu, M.S., Willinger, W., Wilson, D.V.: On the self-similar nature of ethernet traffic. In: ACM SIGCOMM Computer Communication Review, vol. 23, pp. 183–193. ACM (1993)
14. Becchi, M.: From poisson processes to self-similarity: a survey of network traffic models. Washington University in St. Louis, Technical Report (2008)

Tool Papers

SVAuth – A Single-Sign-On Integration Solution with Runtime Verification

Shuo Chen[1(✉)], Matt McCutchen[2], Phuong Cao[3],
Shaz Qadeer[1], and Ravishankar K. Iyer[3]

[1] Microsoft Research, One Microsoft Way, Redmond, WA 98052, USA
shuochen@microsoft.com
[2] Massachusetts Institute of Technology, Cambridge, MA 02139, USA
[3] University of Illinois at Urbana-Champaign, Urbana, IL 61801, USA

Abstract. SSO (single-sign-on) services, such as those provided by Facebook, Google and Microsoft Azure, are integrated into tens of millions of websites and cloud services, just like lock manufacturers offering locks for every home. Imagine you are a website developer, typically unfamiliar with SSO protocols. Your manager wants you to integrate a particular SSO service into a website written in a particular language (e.g., PHP, ASP.NET or Python). You are likely overwhelmed by the amount of work for finding a suitable SSO library, understanding its programming guide, and writing your code. Moreover, studies have shown that many SSO integrations on real-world websites are incorrect, and thus vulnerable to security attacks! SVAuth is an open-source project that tries to provide integration solutions for all major SSO services in all major web languages. Its correctness is ensured by a technology called self-verifying execution, which performs program verification at runtime. SVAuth is so easy to adopt that a website developer does not need any knowledge about SSO protocols or implementations. This paper describes the architecture of SVAuth and how to use it on real-world websites.

1 Introduction

SSO (single-sign-on) services, such as those provided by Facebook, Google and Microsoft Azure, are integrated into tens of millions of apps, websites and cloud services, just like lock manufacturers offering locks for every home. However, the integration practice is very ad-hoc: on one hand, protocol documentation and usage guides of SSO libraries are written by experts, who are like experienced "locksmiths"; one the other hand, most website programmers are not "locksmiths", and inevitably fall into many pitfalls due to misunderstandings of such informal documentation. Security bugs in SSO integrations are continuously discovered in the field, which leave the front door of the cloud wide-open for attackers. SSO bugs are the primary examples when the Cloud Security Alliance ranked API integration bugs as the No. 4 top security threat [10]. These bugs have become a familiar theme in academic conferences [1, 4, 7, 15, 17, 18, 20] and Black Hat conferences [7, 19].

© Springer International Publishing AG 2017
S. Lahiri and G. Reger (Eds.): RV 2017, LNCS 10548, pp. 349–358, 2017.
DOI: 10.1007/978-3-319-67531-2_21

We are working on an open-source project, called SVAuth, to provide every website with a SSO integration fundamentally immune from the aforementioned bugs. Moreover, we try to make SVAuth a very easy and widely applicable solution for real-world adoption: (1) it is language independent, so it works with web apps in any language, such as PHP, ASP.NET, Python; (2) the default solution only requires installing an executable (or simply copying a folder), without any library integration effort; (3) a programmer can customize the default solutions for his/her special requirement. The customized solutions enjoy the same correctness assurance as the default ones; (4) the SVAuth framework can accommodate all SSO services.

The correctness of every SSO solution in SVAuth is assured using our published technology called self-verifying execution (SVX) [14]. The basic idea of SVX is to perform program verification on a per-execution basis. In this sense, SVX is a type of *runtime verification* approach. We will briefly describe how the SVAuth's object-oriented framework incorporates the SVX verification technology. This ensures that a correctness property defined at the most abstract level is satisfied in every execution of every concrete website implementation.

Besides explaining the basic idea, the paper focuses on the source code architecture of SVAuth, and provides a walk-through on how to use SVAuth in various scenarios. We will also show the integration of SVAuth with MediaWiki and HotCRP as examples.

Secure programming of web-based protocols is a nice problem space to apply runtime verification technologies like SVX. We hope programmers and researchers will join the SVAuth effort by contributing code to the project or by adopting the SSO solutions for their websites.

2   The SVAuth Framework

This section explains the design and underlying technology of SVAuth. Readers who only want to use SVAuth can skip this section and jump to Sect. 3.

SSO is a user authentication mechanism commonly seen on websites. For example, NYTimes.com's login page has a button "Log in with Facebook". When a user clicks the button, through an SSO protocol, Facebook will convince NYTimes.com that the visiting user is a particular user recognized by Facebook. In SSO's terminology, Facebook is called the identity provider; NYTimes.com is called the relying party.

SVAuth provides a solution for relying parties to easily and securely integrate SSO services provided by identity providers. The code of SVAuth is publicly available at https://github.com/cs0317/svAuth. Figure 1 illustrates the class hierarchy of the code, written in C# targeting the .NET Core runtime [1]. It has four levels. The first level defines the most generic concepts, like identity provider (IdP), relying party (RP) and authentication conclusion. More importantly, it defines a correctness property φ to capture the intrinsic meaning of "an RP's conclusion about the client's identity is correct". Defining φ is a non-trivial job, involving fairly deep understandings about the notion of "authentication". We skip the details of φ in this paper. Readers can consider φ as a property that all SSO systems should maintain.

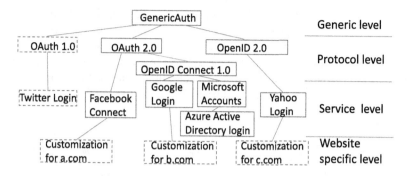

Fig. 1. The class hierarchy of SVAuth

The protocol level consists of classes derived from the generic level. These classes match the protocol specifications, such as those for OAuth 2.0 and OpenID Connect 1.0. Note that the boxes with dashed lines represent namespaces that we have not yet implemented. At the service level, more concrete classes are defined to implement SSO functionalities provided by various companies. There are over 30 major companies in the world providing SSO services. SVAuth has implemented 7 namespaces, each covering one service. We are expanding the coverage, and hope to support most SSO services. At the website specific level, a developer can choose to customize the SSO system by deriving classes from the upper levels in order to fit the specific need of a website.

The verification goal. Having this class hierarchy, the verification goal of the SVAuth framework is: *every concrete implementation in SVAuth should satisfy property φ defined at the generic level.* Next, we briefly explain the self-verifying execution approach to achieve this goal.

2.1 Self-Verifying Execution (SVX)

The basic idea of self-verifying execution (SVX) is to perform code verification at runtime on a per-execution basis. The details are described in our earlier paper [14], which explains the advantages of SVX and how it works. Below, we use a simple example to explain the technology.

Imagine there are three *collaborative* websites, Alice.com, Bob.com and Charlie.com. Each website has an integer constant. They want to run a web-based protocol (i.e., a protocol driven by a browser) to determine which website holds the largest integer. Alice.com has a public method grab() to return Alice's integer value; Bob.com has a method compare(m) to compare its own value against the value in the input message m, and return the larger one; Charlies.com has a method finish(m) to compare its own value against the value in the input message m, and calls a local method conclude(conc). The correctness property φ is that: whenever conclude(conc) is reached, conc.value should be the largest value and conc.who should indicate the website holding the value.

Figure 2 shows two executions when the three websites hold values 10, 40 and 5 respectively. The left execution is expected by the programmer, and it results in the correct conclusion <40, "Bob"> . However, the system is actually vulnerable because a malicious client can trigger an execution on the right, which results in <10, "Alice"> . The traditional goal of program verification is to find such attacks and reject the implementation. However, as we explained in the earlier paper [14], this kind of verification requires the programmer to build a precise model for the client, and the theorem to prove has to be inductive, because the client is basically an infinite loop to interact with the websites.

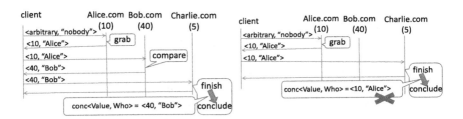

Fig. 2. An expected execution (left) and a successful attack (right).

SVX is much simpler. It does not require the modeling of the client. Instead, it lets a real client trigger an actual execution. During the execution, SVX records the method sequence being executed. In the end of each execution, it only proves that *this method sequence* satisfies property φ, rather than that *every possible execution* will satisfy property φ. Therefore, the theorem to prove is much simpler; it usually requires no induction and can be proven fully automatically.

Figure 3 shows the SVX-enhanced execution. The only addition of SVX is the third message field, which is called SymT (symbolic transaction). In SymT, #grab, #compare and #finish are hash values automatically computed over the code of the corresponding methods using the reflection capability of the language. The hash values represent the unique semantics of these methods. To determine whether a conclusion is correct, we only need to prove that the final SymT logically implies φ. For example, Charlie.com:#finish(Bob.com::#compare(Alice.com::#grab())) implies φ, so <40, "Bob"> is correct and thus accepted. On the other hand, the previous attack sequence

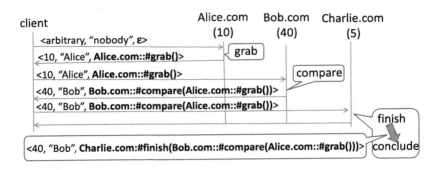

Fig. 3. A concrete execution of SVX.

Charlie.com:#finish(Alice.com::#grab()) does not imply φ, so the conclusion <10, "Alice"> is incorrect, so it is rejected at runtime.

The detailed specification of the SymT is given in Sect. 4. A in reference [6]. A SymT captures the facts whether a message is *signed* or *unsigned*, and whether it is *a server-to-server call* or a *browser-redirection*. These determine whether the output of each method call was authenticated as coming from a known party or should be treated as untrustworthy and nondeterministic in our verification. Due to space constraints, we skip the details here.

The current SVX library uses an off-the-shelf C# verifier, consisting of Bytecode Translator [5] and Corral [12] (see [14] for details).

Runtime overhead of SVX. For every execution, SVX proves a theorem corresponding to the executed code sequence, so the runtime overhead seems too high to be practical. However, since the SymT only represents the code, not any concrete data value, every theorem can be effectively cached (by Charles.com in our example). Therefore, the runtime overhead of SVX is near zero, unless an attacker triggers a new execution sequence or the source code is revised.

2.2 Incorporating SVX into the Class Hierarchy

Recall that the verification goal of SVAuth is to ensure all *concrete* implementations to satisfy the property defined at the *generic* level. A significant advantage of SVX is that the self-verifying capability can be inherited automatically, thus scaled up to all concrete systems. In SVAuth, only the upper two levels, i.e., the generic level and the protocol level, are aware of SVX. Programmers at the lower two levels only need to do normal OO inheritance, and every execution on every concrete implementation will be verified.

It is worth pointing out that this advantage does not exist in static verification techniques. There is a well-known dilemma that a property statically proven for a base class may not hold for a derived class, which is usually discussed in the context of the Liskov Substitution Principle (LSP) [13]. The dilemma of LSP in real-world scenarios is often explained using the "Rectangle-and-Square" example [11].

3   Using SVAuth on Websites

Section 2 explains the SVAuth framework and the underlying verification technology. None of the knowledge is needed for a website programmer to use SVAuth. This section explains how to deploy SVAuth. From the deployment standpoint, SVAuth consists of two components, shown in Fig. 4:

(1) **Agent**: this is the C# code implementing the class hierarchy in Sect. 2, with the SVX capability built in. The agent runs on the .NET Core runtime as an executable, listening on its own port. It bundles a verification toolchain that currently depends on .NET Framework and thus only runs on Windows, but we see no fundamental obstacle to porting the verification toolchain to .NET Core or adding support for the agent to use a remote verification service running on Windows.

(2) **Adaptor**: a language-specific but protocol-agnostic component that is added to the RP website, communicates with the agent and makes the authenticated user identity available to the RP web application framework. For example, we have a PHP adaptor, an ASP.NET adaptor, etc.

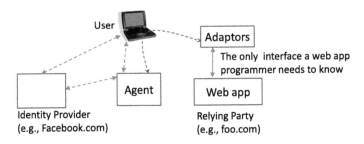

Fig. 4. Agent and adaptors.

The agent handles complex interactions represented by the dashed lines: suppose the identity provider is Facebook.com and the web app is written in PHP, then the agent's job is to authenticate the user through Facebook.com, and call the PHP adaptor to set the authentication conclusion into a set of PHP session variables. However, the web app programmer does not see any of these interactions, but only need to remember the following simple interface:

(1) "http://foo.com/SVAuth/adaptors/php/start.php?provider=Facebook" is the URL to start the Facebook sign-on;
(2) The information about the authenticated user will be in the session variables, such as SVAuth_UserID, SVAuth_Email, SVAuth_FullName, etc.

3.1 Three Scenarios for Deploying the Agent

Figure 4 does not explicitly show where the agent runs. There are three possible scenarios for the agent's placement.

Public agent. In the GitHub repository of SVAuth, we have a release of the adaptors. Using this release is the simplest way to incorporate SSO logins, because it by default uses a public agent running on port 3020 of server https://authjs.westus.clou-dapp.azure.com. The web app programmer's job is extremely simple: just copy the released *adaptors* folder into the website directory http://foo.com/SVAuth.

Local agent. If a programmer does not want to use the public agent, perhaps because he/she wants to derive some customized classes in the agent, then setting up a local agent is an option. A local agent runs on the same server as the web app, i.e., foo.com. The programmer's job is also simple: just do "git clone" the SVAuth repository onto the foo.com server. The "git clone" command will pull the whole SVAuth code, including the agent, the adaptors, as well as the dependencies BCT and Corral. To run the agent, install the .NET Core runtime, and use the command "dotnet run" inside the folder/

SVAuth/SVAuth of the cloned repository. By default, the adaptors know that the agent runs on port 3000 of the local server.

Private agent. A private organization can set up a server to run the agent, which serves all websites inside the organization. For example, the company owning the domain *foo.com* can set up a server *SVAuth.foo.com* to run the agent. The programmer uses "git clone" to get the code onto the *SVAuth.foo.com* server, following the steps described in the "local agent" scenario. Then, the programmer of every website follows the steps described in the "public agent" scenario, except that the configuration file of the adaptors should specify "*SVAuth.foo.com*" as the agent and ".*foo.com*" as the agent's scope.

3.2 Integrating SVAuth with Real-World Web Apps

The interface between the web app and the adaptors is really simple, as described earlier. All the web app programmer needs to do is to read user's identity data from the session variables. This is independent of the SSO service and the language of the web app. To show the ease of the integration, we have integrated SVAuth with MediaWiki and HotCRP. MediaWiki is the software powering Wikipedia.org, and HotCRP is a sophisticated conference management system. The following two URLs are the two systems with SVAuth integrated:

The MediaWiki demo: http://authjs.westus.cloudapp.azure.com

The HotCRP demo: http://authjs.westus.cloudapp.azure.com:8000/

The integrations were very easy. The MediaWiki integration only needs 8 lines of code changes to the MediaWiki user login plugin. The HotCRP integration has only 21 lines of changes. These integrations are documented in the "IntegrationExamples" folder in the code repository.

Inside Microsoft Research, a MediaWiki website has been using SVAuth for nearly a year, which authenticates users through Microsoft Azure Active Directory.

3.3 Currently Supported SSO Services and Web Languages

The SSO services currently supported by SVAuth are: Facebook, Microsoft, Microsoft Azure Active Directory, Google, Yahoo, LinkedIn and Weibo (a major identity provider in China). The demo page for these services is at http://authjs.westus.cloudapp.azure.com/SVAuth/adapters/php/AllInOne.php. The currently supported languages are: PHP, ASP.NET and Python. We are expanding the coverage for SSO services and web languages.

4 SVX and SVAuth in the Context of Runtime Verification

We believe that SVX and SVAuth bring some new perspectives to the research community. In this section, we discuss them in the context of runtime verification.

SVX's relation to other runtime verification techniques. Similar to other runtime verification techniques, SVX performs the actual verification at runtime on a per-execution basis. The SymT string is a representation of an execution trace, and SVX is able to verify *safety* properties about traces. Relations can be drawn between SVX and Monitoring-Oriented Programming (MOP) [9]. MOP is a generic framework for programmers to specify relevant events and safety properties. The MOP framework automatically instruments the code to monitor these events, maintain monitored states and verify the safety properties. It will be valuable to think how SVX can utilize the automatic mechanisms in MOP. Currently, SVX requires the programmer to manually call the SVX library to compute the SymT (analogous to MOP's event monitoring) and to verify a property (analogous to MOP's property checking). In addition to automation, another advantage of MOP is to separate the monitoring logic from the logic of the monitored program.

SSO and other potential domains for runtime verification. SSO is a good domain for runtime verification, because (1) it is a problem faced by many programmers, and its engineering practice is ad-hoc today; (2) it involves multiple organizations: protocol working groups, identity provider companies, SDK solution providers and website programmers, who work collaboratively across different abstraction levels, as shown in Fig. 1; and (3) the desired safety assurances can be defined as trace properties. Thus, SVAuth, which builds SVX into the OO class hierarchy, is a suitable solution.

Besides SSO, *user authorization* can be another problem domain. Mobile apps, social sharing web apps and IoT devices all require proper user authorization. It meets the above conditions (1) and (2). A new challenge is that the authorization objectives are often much more diverse than those for SSO. A research question is: how to precisely define these diverse properties (by individual programmers on a case-by-case basis)?

Also, SVAuth is an instance of "protocol spec as code". This concept has been put in practice in other areas. For example, the TPM (Trusted Platform Module) 2.0 library specification [16] is primarily C code with a substantial amount of English comments (unlike most of today's protocol specs, written in English with pseudo code samples as "comments"). It is valuable for the runtime verification community to identify other areas where industrial specifications can be written as code (e.g., like the abstract classes in SVAuth). The specifications can be for distributed systems, device drivers, online payments, and IoT (e.g., the AllJoyn framework [2]).

5   Summary

Integrating SSO services is often seen as a non-trivial programming job, which demands expertise and time. Moreover, the current practice is too ad-hoc, and SSO vulnerabilities are so pervasive that they have become a trendy topic in security conferences. We want to promote the SVAuth solution – it provides a higher correctness assurance, and is an easy solution for websites to integrate SSO.

The underlying technology is self-verifying execution (SVX), which is a runtime verification mechanism. It is combined with the OO class hierarchy to form the framework for all concrete implementations to be verified with respect to a generic property defined over the base classes. SVAuth is extensible, so we hope researchers working on verification technologies contribute to the core components of the project, or build more SSO solutions within the SVAuth framework.

References

1. .NET Core. https://www.microsoft.com/net/core
2. AllJoyn® Framework. https://allseenalliance.org/framework
3. Bansal, C., Bhargavan, K., Maffeis, S.: Discovering concrete attacks on website authorization by formal analysis. In: 25th IEEE Computer Security Foundations Symposium, CSF (2012)
4. Bai, G., Lei, J., Meng, G., Venkatraman, S.S., Saxena, P., Sun, J., Liu, Y., Dong, J.S.: Authscan: Automatic extraction of web authentication protocols from implementations. In: ISOC Network and Distributed System Security Symposium (2013)
5. Barnett, M., Qadeer, S.: BCT: A translator from MSIL to Boogie. In: Seventh Workshop on Bytecode Semantics, Verification, Analysis and Transformation (2012)
6. Chen, E., Chen, S., Qadeer, S., Wang, R.: Securing multiparty online services via certification of symbolic transactions. In: IEEE Symposium on Security and Privacy (2015)
7. Chen, E., Pei, Y., Tian, Y., Chen, S., Kotcher, R., Tague, P.: 1000 Ways to Die in Mobile OAuth. Blackhat, USA (2016)
8. Chen, F., d'Amorim, M., Rosu, G.: Checking and correcting behaviors of java programs at runtime with java-MOP. In: The Runtime Verification Workshop (2005)
9. Chen, F., Rosu, G.: MOP: An efficient and generic runtime verification framework. In: The ACM SIGPLAN Conference on Systems, Programming, Languages and Applications (OOPSLA) (2007)
10. Cloud Security Alliance. The Notorious Nine – Cloud Computing Top Threats in 2013. https://downloads.cloudsecurityalliance.org/initiatives/top_threats/The_Notorious_Nine_Cloud_Computing_Top_Threats_in_2013.pdf
11. DZone.com. The Liskov Substitution Principle (With Examples). https://dzone.com/articles/the-liskov-substitution-principle-with-examples
12. Lal, A., Qadeer, S., Lahiri, S.: A solver for reachability modulo theories. In: Computer Aided Verification (2012)
13. Liskov, B.H., Wing, J.M.: A behavioral notion of subtyping. ACM Trans. Program. Lang. Syst. **16**(6), 1811–1841 (1994)
14. McCutchen, M., Song, D., Chen, S., Qadeer, S.: Self-verifying execution (Position Paper). In: Proceedings of the IEEE Cybersecurity Development Conference (SecDev) (2016)
15. Sun, S.-T., Beznosov, K.: The devil is in the (implementation) details: an empirical analysis of OAuth SSO systems. In: ACM conference on Computer and Communications Security (2012)
16. Trusted Computing Group. Trusted Platform Module Library Specification 2.0. http://www.trustedcomputinggroup.org/resources/tpm_library_specification
17. Wang, R., Chen, S., Wang, X.F.: Signing me onto your accounts through facebook and google: a traffic-guided security study of commercially deployed single-sign-on web services. In: IEEE Symposium on Security and Privacy (2012)

18. Wang, R., Zhou, Y., Chen, S., Qadeer, S., Evans, D., Gurevich, Y.: Explicating SDKs: Uncovering Assumptions Underlying Secure Authentication and Authorization. USENIX Security (2013)
19. Yang, R., Lau, W.C., Liu, T.: Signing into One Billion Mobile App Accounts Effortlessly with OAuth 2.0. Blackhat, Europe (2016)
20. Zhou, Y., Evans, D.: SSOScan: Automated Testing of Web Applications for Single Sign-On Vulnerabilities. USENIX Security (2014)

Event Stream Processing with Multiple Threads

Sylvain Hallé[(✉)], Raphaël Khoury, and Sébastien Gaboury

Laboratoire d'informatique Formelle,
Université du Québec à Chicoutimi, Saguenay, Canada
shalle@acm.org

Abstract. We present an extension to the BeepBeep 3 event stream engine that allows the use of multiple threads during the evaluation of a query. Compared to the single-threaded version of BeepBeep, the allocation of just a few threads to specific portions of a query provides improvement in terms of throughput.

1 Introduction

Among the many techniques developed to improve the performance of Runtime Verification tools, the leveraging of parallelism in existing computer systems has seldom been studied. Since the validity of an event with respect to a temporal specification may depend on past and future events, the handling of parts of the trace in parallel and independent processes seems to be disqualified at the onset. Case in point, a review of available solutions in Sect. 2 of this paper observes that most existing trace validation tools are based on algorithms that do not take advantage of parallelism.

In Sect. 3, we present an extension of the BeepBeep 3 event stream engine; this extension provides a set of patterns that allow the use of multiple threads in the evaluation of queries on traces of events. The techniques we propose are based on the idea of "wrapping" BeepBeep's basic computing units, called *processors*, into one of a few special, thread-aware containers. This has for effect that any part of an event stream query can be parallelized, without requiring the wrapped processors to be aware of the availability of multiple threads.

Thanks to this architecture, any existing computation can be made to leverage parallelism with very minimal modifications to the original query. To this effect, Sect. 4 shows experimentally the potential impact of these mult-threading patterns. Based on a sample of properties taken from the latest Competition on Runtime Verification (CRV), it reveals that five out of six queries show improved throughput with the use of parallelism, sometimes running as much as 4.4 times faster than their single-thread version.

2 Parallelism in Runtime Verification

A distinction must be made between the runtime verification *of* parallel and concurrent systems [17,21,22,26,28,29] and the use of parallelism *for* runtime verification. This paper is concerned with the latter question.

An extended version of this paper is available as a technical report [14].

© Springer International Publishing AG 2017
S. Lahiri and G. Reger (Eds.): RV 2017, LNCS 10548, pp. 359–369, 2017.
DOI: 10.1007/978-3-319-67531-2_22

A first set of works provide improvements to elements that are peripheral to the evaluation of the property, such as the communication between the monitor and the program, or the use of a separate chip to run the monitor. Pellizzoni et al. [25] utilized dedicated commercial-off-the-shelf (COTS) hardware [8] to facilitate the runtime monitoring of critical embedded systems whose properties were expressed in Past-time Temporal Linear Logic (PTLTL). Ha et al. [12] introduced a buffering design called Cache-friendly Asymmetric Buffering (CAB) to improve the communications between application and runtime monitor by exploiting the shared cache of the multi-core architecture; Berkovich et al. [6] proposed a GPU-based solution that effectively utilizes the available cores of the GPU, so that the monitor designed and implemented with their method can run in parallel with the target program and evaluate LTL properties.

These previous works address issues that are preipheral to the evaluation of a temporal property. A second family of works attempt to split the computation steps of evaluating a query on a trace into blocks that can be executed independently over multiple processes. When trace properties are expressed as Linear Temporal Logic, Kuhtz and Finkbeiner showed that the path checking problem can be efficiently split by evaluating entire blocks of events in parallel [19]. However, a specific type of Boolean circuit requires to be built in advance, which depends on the length of the trace to evaluate. Moreover, the argument consists of a formal proof; deriving a concrete, usable implementation of this technique remains an open question.

In an offline context, the leveraging of a cluster infrastructure was first suggested by Hallé et al. , who introduced an algorithm for the automated verification of Linear Temporal Logic formulæ on event traces, using a cloud computing framework called MapReduce [15]. A different architecture using MapReduce was proposed by Basin et al. [5]. These techniques only apply in a batch (i.e.offline) context. Moreover, both are tailored to one specific query language —in both cases an extension of Linear Temporal Logic. It remains unclear how computing other types of results over an event trace could be done in the same framework.

Much more work on parallelism and distribution was undertaken from the database point of view. The evaluation of SQL queries using multiple cores has spawned a large line of works [4, 10, 11, 18, 20, 24]. Some recent data stream processing systems naturally support processing units to be distributed on multiple machines that exchange data through a network communication. By manually assigning fragments of the query to different machines, distribution of computation can effectively be achieved. Such systems include Aurora, Borealis [1], Cayuga [7], Apache Storm [3], Apache S4 [23] and Apache Samza [2]. This form of parallelism is called "inter-host", as the computation is performed on physically distinct devices.

3   Multi-threading in BeepBeep 3

In this section, we describe how multi-threading capabilities can be added to BeepBeep 3, an open source event stream processing engine that has been developed over the recent years.[1] BeepBeep is organized around *processors*, which are a stateful objects that take zero or more event *traces*, and produce zero or more event *traces* as its output. Any processors with compatible types can be freely composed, with the output of a processor used as the input of another one. Processors produce their output in a *streaming* fashion: they do not wait to read their entire input trace before starting to produce output events.

The main part of BeepBeep is called the *engine*, which provides the basic classes for creating processors, and contains a handful of general-purpose processors for manipulating traces. For example, the `Function` processor applies an arbitrary function to each input event and returns the output. A few other processors can be used to alter the sequence of events received. Hence, the `CountDecimate` processor returns every n-th input event and discards the others. Other processors allow a trace to be filtered, windowed, and sliced in various ways. The reader is referred to a recent tutorial for complete details about the system and its architecture [16].

3.1   Thread Management Model

The first extension added to BeepBeep is a global thread management system. To this end, the instantiation of all threads is controlled by one or more instances of a new `ThreadManager` class. Each thread manager is responsible for the allocation of a pool of threads of bounded size. A processor wishing to obtain a new thread instance asks permission from its designated thread manager. If the maximum number of live threads reserved to this manager is not exceeded, the manager provides a new thread instance to the processor. The processor can then associate any task to this thread and start it.

The distinguishing point of this model resides in the actions taken when the manager refuses to provide a new thread to the caller. Typically, the call for a new thread would become blocking until a thread finally becomes available. In BeepBeep, on the contrary, the call simply returns `null`; this indicates that whatever actions the processor wished to execute in parallel in a new thread should instead be executed sequentially within the *current* thread. Moreover, various parts of a query can be assigned to different thread manager instances with their own thread pool, giving flexible control over how much parallelism is allowed, and to what fragments of the computation. Hence the amount of threading can be easily modulated, or even completely turned off, by changing the value of a single parameter. Since thread instances are requested dynamically and are generally short-lived, this means that changes in the threading strategy can also be made during the processing of an event stream.

3.2   Non-blocking Push/Pull

In BeepBeep, events can either be pushed into a processing chain from upstream, or pulled for the downstream end of the processing chain, using objects implementing the `Pushable` and `Pullable` interfaces, respectively. In a single-thread

---

[1] http://liflab.github.io/beepbeep-3.

computation, a call to any of these objects' methods is *blocking*. For example, calling pull() on one of a processor's Pushable objects involves a call to the processor's input pullables pull() in order to retrieve input events, followed by the computation of the processor's output event. The original call returns only when this chain of operations is finished.

The Pushable and Pullable interfaces have been extended to also provide a non-blocking version of the push and pull operations, respectively called push-Fast() and pullFast(). These methods perform the same task as their blocking counterparts, but *may* return control to the caller before the operation is finished. In order to "catch up" with the end of the operation, the caller must, at a later time, call method waitFor() on the same instance. This time, this method blocks until the push or pull operation that was started is indeed finished. Following the spirit of transparency explained earlier, pushFast() and pullFast() are not required to be non-blocking. As a matter of fact, their default behaviour is to act as a proxy to their blocking equivalents. Thus, for a processor that does not wish to implement non-blocking operations, calling pushFast() followed by waitFor() falls back to standard, blocking processing.

Rather than implementing non-blocking operations separately for each type of processor, an easier way consists of enclosing an existing processor within an instance of the new NonBlockingProcessor class. When push() or pull() is called on this processor, a new thread is asked to its designated thread manager. The actual call to push() (resp. pull()) on the underlying processor is started in that thread and the control is immediately returned to the caller. Using a simple Boolean semaphore, a call to method waitFor() of the NonBlocking-Processor sleep-loops until that thread stops, indicating that the operation is finished.

Non-blocking push/pull can prove useful in situations where one calls push() or pull() on a processor, performs some other task T, and retrieves the result of that push() (resp. pull()) at a later time. If the call is done in a non-blocking manner, the computation of that operation can be done in parallel with the execution of T in the current thread. It turns out that a couple of commonly used processors in BeepBeep operate in this fashion, and can hence benefit from the presence of non blocking push/pull methods. For example, the *sliding window* processor returns the output of a copy of some processor φ on events $e_0 e_1 \ldots e_{n-1}$, followed by the output of a fresh copy of φ on events $e_1 e_2 \ldots e_n$, and so on. The sliding window is implemented by keeping in memory up to $n-1$ copies of φ, such that copy φ_i has been fed the last i events received. Upon processing a new input event, the window pushes this event to each of the φ_i, and retrieves the output of φ_{n-1}. This processor copy is then destroyed, the index of the remaining copies is incremented by 1, and a new copy φ_0 is created.

Figure 1a shows a sequence diagram of these operations when performed in a blocking way. Figure 1b shows the same operations, this time using non-blocking calls. The window processor first calls push() on each copy in rapid-fire succession. Each copy of φ can update its state in a separate thread; the processor

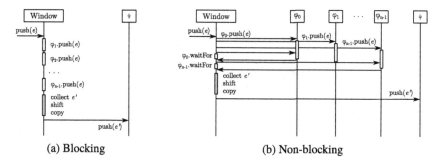

Fig. 1. Sequence diagram for the Window processor: (a) using blocking calls to φ; (b) using non-blocking calls running in separate threads.

then waits for each of these calls to be finished, by calling `waitFor()` on each copy of φ. The remaining operations are then performed identically.

While this pattern works for sliding windows, actually any query that requires an event to be processed by multiple copies of the same processor can benefit from non-blocking push/pull. This includes LTL temporal operators, first-order quantifiers, and the trace slicing processor.

3.3 Pre-emptive Pulling

A second strategy consists of continuously pulling for new outputs on a processor P, and storing these events in a queue. When a downstream processor P' calls $P's$ `pull()` method, the next event is simply popped from that queue, rather than being computed on-the-fly. If P' is running in a different thread from the process that polls P, each can compute a new event at the same time.

Figure 2a shows the processing of an event when done in a sequential manner. A call to `pull()` on ψ results in a pull on φ, which produces some output event e. This event is then processed by ψ, which produces some other output e'. If T_φ and T_ψ correspond to the computation times of φ and ψ, respectively, then the total time to fetch each event from ψ is their sum, $T_\varphi + T_\psi$. On the contrary, Fig. 2b shows the same process, with pre-emptive pulling on φ occurring in a separate thread. One can see that in this case, φ produces a new output event while ψ is busy doing its computation on the previous one. The first output event still takes time $T_\varphi + T_\psi$ to be produced, but later ones can be retrieved in time $\max\{T_\varphi, T_\psi\}$.

In a manner similar to the `NonBlockingProcessor`, pre-emptive pulling is enabled by enclosing a group of processors inside a new object called a `PullGroup`. This processor behaves like a `GroupProcessor`: a set of connected processors can be added to the group, and this group can then be manipulated, piped and copied as if it were a single "black box". The difference is that a call to the `start()` method of a `PullGroup` creates a new thread where the repeated polling of its outputs occurs. To avoid needlessly producing too many events that are not retrieved by downstream calls to `pull()`, the polling stops when

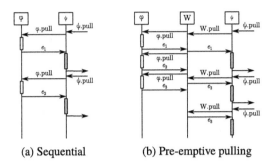

(a) Sequential   (b) Pre-emptive pulling

Fig. 2. Sequence diagram for pre-emptive pulling: (a) no pre-emptive pulling; (b) W performs pre-emptive pulling on φ in a separate thread.

the queue reaches a predefined size; polling resumes when some events of that queue are finally pulled.

3.4 Pipelining

Pipelining is the process of reading n input events $e_1 e_2 \ldots e_n$, creating n copies of a given processor, and launching each of them on one of the input events. A pipeline then waits until the processor assigned to e_1 produces output events; these events are made available at the output of the pipeline as they are collected. Once the e_1 processor has no more output events to produce, it is discarded, the collection resumes on the processor for e_2, and so on. At this point, there is now room for creating a new processor copy and assign it to the next input event, e_{n+1}. This rolling process goes on until no input event is available. In such a scheme, the order of the output events is preserved: in sequential processing, the batch of output of events produced by reading event e_1 comes before any output event resulting from processing e_2 is output (Fig. 3).

Although pipelining borrows features from both pre-emptive pulling and non-blocking pull, it is distinct from these two techniques. As in non-blocking pull, it sends input events in parallel to multiple copies of a processor; however, rather than sending the same event to multiple, independent instances of φ, it sends events that should be processed in sequence by a single processor instance each to a distinct copy of φ and collects their result. In the sequence $e_1 e_2 \ldots$, this means that one copy of φ processes the subtrace e_1, while another one processes (in parallel) the subtrace e_2, and so on.

Obviously, this "trick" does not guarantee the correct result on all processors, as some of them have an output that depends on the complete trace. However, there do exist processors for which pipelining can be applied; this is the case of all FunctionProcessors, which by definition apply a stateless function to each of their input events. While this might seem limiting, it turns out that, in the sample of queries evaluated experimentally later in this paper, a large part of the computing load comes from the application of a few such functions, and that pipelining proves very effective in these situations.

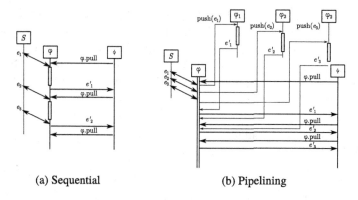

(a) Sequential   (b) Pipelining

Fig. 3. Sequence diagram for pipelining: (a) no pipelining; (b) φ pulls multiple events from S and evaluates each of them on a copy of φ in a separate thread.

4   Implementation and Experiments

In order to showcase the usage of using multiple threads according to our proposed architecture, we setup a set of experiments where our extended version of BeepBeep is run on queries and input traces taken from the Offline track of the 2016 Competition on Runtime Verification [27]. For each property, BeepBeep is run in two configurations: 1. The original query, without any thread-aware processors 2. The same query, modified with thread-aware processors inserted by hand. These modifications were done with the help of intuition and manual trial and error, so they may not represent the absolute best way of using threads. The queries use a single thread manager, whose number of threads is set to be equal to the host machine's number of cores. No other modifications to the query have been made.

The experiment measures two elements. The first is *throughput*, measured in Hz, and corresponds to the average number of input events consumed per second. The second is *CPU load*, measured in percentage, and computed as the average instantaneous load of each CPU core over intervals of one second, as reported. Formally, for a system with n cores, let $f_i(t)$ be a function giving the instantaneous load (between 0 and 1) of core i at time t. If T_S and T_E are the start and end time of the execution of a query, then the load resulting from the execution of that query, noted λ, is defined as:

$$\lambda \triangleq \frac{1}{n(T_E - T_S)} \sum_{i=1}^{n} \int_{T_S}^{T_E} f_i(t)dt$$

In the experiments, instantaneous load is approximated as a 1-second wide rectangle, whose height corresponds to the CPU usage as reported by the SIGAR API[2]. Note that this usage includes that of all applications running on the

---

[2] https://support.hyperic.com/display/SIGAR/Home.

host machine, which can be minimized by running it with a limited number of background services. All experiments and data are available for download[3] as a self-contained instance of the LabPal experimental environment [13]. The results of these experiments are summarized in Table 1. For one of the queries of the CRV (*SQL Injection*), none of the patterns introduced in this paper can be applied, and so no experiment was conducted on it.

Table 1. Throughput and load for each query, for the single-thread and multi-thread versions of BeepBeep.

Query	Threading strategy	Throughput	Load
Auction bidding	Multi-threaded	30,487.8	0.345
	None	28,449.5	0.601
Candidate selection	Multi-threaded	127.9	0.906
	None	28.8	0.315
Endless bashing	Multi-threaded	742.5	0.593
	None	511.8	0.374
Spontaneous Pingu creation	Multi-threaded	782.4	0.467
	None	742.1	0.308
Turn around	Multi-threaded	30.9	0.772
	None	16.6	0.353

As one can see, the use of multi-threading has increased the throughput and load of every remaining problem instance. CPU load has increased on average by a factor of 1.7, and throughput by a factor of 2.0. In some cases, such as the *Candidate Selection* property, the impact of parallelism is notable. This is due to the fact that this property evaluates a first-order logic formula with multiple nested quantifiers, of the form $\forall a \in A : \forall b \in B : \exists c \in C : \varphi$. When the cardinality of sets B and C is large, evaluating $\forall b \in B : \exists c \in C : \varphi$ for each value $a \in A$ can efficiently be done in parallel.

5   Conclusion

In this paper, we have introduced a few simple patterns for the introduction of parallelism in the evaluation of queries over streams of events. These patterns can be applied in systems whose computation is expressed as the composition of small units of processing arranged into a graph-like structure, as is the case in the BeepBeep 3 event stream engine. By surrounding appropriate regions of such a graph with special-purpose thread managers, parts of a query can be evaluated using multiple cores of a CPU, therefore harnessing more of a machine's computing power.

---

[3] https://datahub.io/dataset/beepbeep-mt-lab.

Thanks to the simplicity of these patterns and to BeepBeep's modular design, the introduction of parallelism to an existing query requires very limited changes, which amount to the insertion of two or three lines of code at most. To the best of our knowledge, this makes BeepBeep the first runtime verification tool with such parallelization capabilities. Experiments on a sample of existing properties of have shown promising results. As we have observed, the tested properties benefit from an average speed boost of $2\times$ through the careful application of the patterns presented in this paper.

These encouraging numbers warrant further development of this line of research in multiple directions. First, the scalability of this approach with respect to the number of available cores should be studied experimentally. Second, one could relax the way in which properties are evaluated, and tolerate that finite prefixes of an output trace be different from the exact result. This notion of "eventual consistency" could allow multiple slices of an input to be evaluated without the need for lock-step synchronization. Finally, special care should be given to the way queries are expressed; when several equivalent representations of the same computation exist, one should favor those that lend themselves to parallelization.

In counterpart, the current implementation of multi-threading in BeepBeep requires the user to explicitly define the regions of a query graph that are to be executed using multiple threads. This requires some knowledge of the underlying computations that are being executed in various parts of the query, and some intuition as to which of them could best benefit from the availability of more than one thread. Therefore, the architecture proposed in this paper should be taken as a first step. It breaks new ground by providing a simple way to add multi-threading to the evaluation of an arbitrary query; however, in the medium term, higher-level techniques for selecting the best regions of a query suitable for parallelism should be developed.

References

1. Abadi, D.J., Ahmad, Y., Balazinska, M., Çetintemel, U., Cherniack, M., Hwang, J.-H., Lindner, W., Maskey, A., Rasin, A., Ryvkina, E., Tatbul, N., Xing, Y., Zdonik, S.B.: The design of the Borealis stream processing engine. In: CIDR, pp. 277–289 (2005)
2. Apache Software Foundation. Samza. Accessed 1st December 2016
3. Apache Software Foundation. Storm incubation status. Accessed 1st December 2016
4. Apers, P.M.G., van den Berg, C.A., Flokstra, J., Grefen, P.W.P.J., Kersten, M.L., Wilschut, A.N.: PRISMA/DB: a parallel main memory relational DBMS. IEEE Trans. Knowl. Data Eng. 4(6), 541–554 (1992)
5. Basin, D.A., Caronni, G., Ereth, S., Harvan, M., Klaedtke, F., Mantel, H.: Scalable offline monitoring of temporal specifications. Formal Methods Syst. Des. 49(1–2), 75–108 (2016)
6. Berkovich, S., Bonakdarpour, B., Fischmeister, S.: Runtime verification with minimal intrusion through parallelism. Formal Methods Syst. Des. 46(3), 317–348 (2015)

7. Brenna, L., Demers, A.J., Gehrke, J., Hong, M., Ossher, J., Panda, B., Riedewald, M., Thatte, M., White, W.M.: Cayuga: a high-performance event processing engine. In: Chan, C.Y., Ooi, B.C., Zhou, A. (eds.) Proceedings of the ACM SIGMOD International Conference on Management of Data, Beijing, China, June 12–14, 2007, pp. 1100–1102. ACM (2007)
8. Emerson, E.A.: Temporal and modal logic. In: Handbook of Theoretical Computer Science, Volume B: Formal Models and Sematics (B), vol. 995(1072), p. 5 (1990)
9. Falcone, Y., Sánchez, C. (eds.): RV 2016. LNCS, vol. 10012. Springer, Cham (2016)
10. Ganguly, S., Hasan, W., Krishnamurthy, R.: Query optimization for parallel execution. In: Stonebraker, M. (ed.) Proceedings of the 1992 ACM SIGMOD International Conference on Management of Data, San Diego, California, June 2–5, 1992, pp. 9–18. ACM Press (1992)
11. Graefe, G.: Parallel query execution algorithms. In: Liu, L., Özsu, M.T. (eds.) Encyclopedia of Database Systems, pp. 2030–2035. Springer, New York (2009)
12. Ha, J., Arnold, M., Blackburn, S.M., McKinley, K.S.: A concurrent dynamic analysis framework for multicore hardware. ACM SIGPLAN Not. **44**, 155–174 (2009). ACM
13. Hallé, S.: LabPal: repeatable computer experiments made easy. In: Bultan, T., Sen, K. (eds.) International Symposium on Software Testing and Analysis, ISSTA 2017, Santa Barbara, CA, USA, July 10–14, 2017, pp. 404–407. ACM (2013)
14. Hallé, S., Khoury, R., Gaboury, S.: Event stream processing with multiple threads (extended version). CoRR, abs/1707.02600 (2017)
15. Hallé, S., Soucy-Boivin, M.: MapReduce for parallel trace validation of LTL properties. J. Cloud Comp. **4**, 8 (2015)
16. Hallé, S.: When RV meets CEP. In: Falcone and Sánchez [9], pp. 68–91
17. Harrow, J.J.: Runtime checking of multithreaded applications with visual threads. In: Havelund, K., Penix, J., Visser, W. (eds.) SPIN 2000. LNCS, vol. 1885, pp. 331–342. Springer, Heidelberg (2000). doi:10.1007/10722468_20
18. Krikellas, K., Viglas, S., Cintra, M.: Modeling multithreaded query execution on chip multiprocessors. In: Bordawekar, R., Lang, C.A. (eds.) International Workshop on Accelerating Data Management Systems Using Modern Processor and Storage Architectures - ADMS 2010, Singapore, September 13, 2010, pp. 22–33 (2010)
19. Kuhtz, L., Finkbeiner, B.: Efficient parallel path checking for linear-time temporal logic with past and bounds. Log. Methods Comput. Sci. **8**(4), 1–24 (2012)
20. Li, K., Kavi, M., Naz, A., Sweany, P.H.: Speculative thread execution in a multithreaded dataflow architecture. In: Peterson, G.D. (ed.) Proceedings of the ISCA 19th International Conference on Parallel and Distributed Computing Systems, September 20–11, 2006, San Francisco, California, USA, pp. 102–107. ISCA (2006)
21. Luo, Q., Rosu, G.: EnforceMOP: a runtime property enforcement system for multithreaded programs. In: Pezzè, M., Harman, M. (eds.) International Symposium on Software Testing and Analysis, ISSTA 2013, Lugano, Switzerland, July 15–20, 2013, pp. 156–166. ACM (2013)
22. Nazarpour, H., Falcone, Y., Bensalem, S., Bozga, M., Combaz, J.: Monitoring multi-threaded component-based systems. In: Ábrahám, E., Huisman, M. (eds.) IFM 2016. LNCS, vol. 9681, pp. 141–159. Springer, Cham (2016). doi:10.1007/978-3-319-33693-0_10
23. Neumeyer, L., Robbins, B., Nair, A., Kesari, A.: S4: distributed stream computing platform. In: Fan, W., Hsu, W., Webb, G.I., Liu, B., Zhang, C., Gunopulos, D., Wu, X. (eds.) ICDMW 2010, The 10th IEEE International Conference on Data Mining Workshops, Sydney, Australia, 13 December 2010, pp. 170–177. IEEE Computer Society (2010)

24. Paes, M., Lima, A.A.B., Valduriez, P., Mattoso, M.: High-performance query processing of a real-world OLAP database with ParGRES. In: Palma, J.M.L.M., Amestoy, P.R., Daydé, M., Mattoso, M., Lopes, J.C. (eds.) VECPAR 2008. LNCS, vol. 5336, pp. 188–200. Springer, Heidelberg (2008). doi:10.1007/978-3-540-92859-1_18

25. Pellizzoni, R., Meredith, P., Caccamo, M., Rosu, G.: Hardware runtime monitoring for dependable cots-based real-time embedded systems. In: Real-Time Systems Symposium, pp. 481–491. IEEE (2008)

26. Qadeer, S., Tasiran, S.: Runtime verification of concurrency-specific correctness criteria. STTT **14**(3), 291–305 (2012)

27. Reger, G., Hallé, S., Falcone, Y.: Third international competition on runtime verification - CRV 2016. In: Falcone and Sánchez [9], pp. 21–37

28. Savage, S., Burrows, M., Nelson, G., Sobalvarro, P., Anderson, T.E.: Eraser: a dynamic data race detector for multithreaded programs. ACM Trans. Comput. Syst. **15**(4), 391–411 (1997)

29. Sen, K., Rosu, G., Agha, G.: Runtime safety analysis of multithreaded programs. In: Paakki, J., Inverardi, P. (eds.) Proceedings of the 11th ACM SIGSOFT Symposium on Foundations of Software Engineering 2003 held jointly with 9th European Software Engineering Conference, ESEC/FSE 2003, Helsinki, Finland, September 1–5, 2003, pp. 337–346. ACM (2003)

HySIA: Tool for Simulating and Monitoring Hybrid Automata Based on Interval Analysis

Daisuke Ishii[1]([⊠]) and Alexandre Goldsztejn[2]

[1] University of Fukui, Fukui, Japan
dsksh@acm.org
[2] CNRS/LS2N, Nantes, France
alexandre.goldsztejn@gmail.com

Abstract. We present HySIA: a reliable runtime verification tool for nonlinear hybrid automata (HA) and signal temporal logic (STL) properties. HySIA simulates an HA with interval analysis techniques so that a trajectory is enclosed sharply within a set of intervals. Then, HySIA computes whether the simulated trajectory satisfies a given STL property; the computation is performed again with interval analysis to achieve reliability. Simulation and verification using HySIA are demonstrated through several example HA and STL formulas.

1 Introduction

Runtime verification of hybrid systems is realized with monitoring tools (e.g., [1, 5]) and statistical model checkers (e.g., [4,18,19]) based on numerical simulation. These tools are practical because they can utilize de-facto standard environment (e.g., MATLAB/Simulink) for modeling and simulating industrial systems that are large and nonlinear. However, their underlying numerical computation is unreliable due to numerical errors and can result in incorrect verification results. Conversely, computation of a rigorous overapproximation of a behavior (or a reachable region) suffers a trade-off in the precision of resulting enclosures and computational costs [3,11,15]. A large *wrapping effect* may occur when a model involves nonlinear expressions.

This paper presents the HySIA tool, a reliable simulator and verifier for hybrid systems. HySIA supports nonlinear hybrid automata (HA) whose ODEs, guards, and reset functions are specified with nonlinear expressions. It assumes a deterministic class of HA; a transition to another location happens whenever a guard condition holds. The main functionalities of HySIA are the following:

Simulation. HySIA simulates an HA based on interval analysis; it computes an overapproximation of a bounded trajectory (or a set of trajectories) that is composed of *boxes* (i.e., closed interval vectors) and *parallelotopes* (linear transformed intervals) using our proposed method [12]. The computation can also be regarded as reachability analysis. Intensive use of interval analysis techniques distinguishes HySIA from other reachability analysis tools. First, the simulation

© Springer International Publishing AG 2017
S. Lahiri and G. Reger (Eds.): RV 2017, LNCS 10548, pp. 370–379, 2017.
DOI: 10.1007/978-3-319-67531-2_23

process carefully reduces the wrapping effect that can expand an enclosure interval. As a result, HySIA is able to simulate an HA for a greater number of steps than other overapproximation-based tools; e.g., it can simulate a periodic bouncing ball for more than a thousand steps. Second, HySIA relies on the soundness of interval computation so that the resulting overapproximation is verified to contain a theoretical trajectory. This verification may fail, e.g., when an ODE is *stiff* or when a trajectory and a guard are close to tangent, resulting in an enclosure too large to enable any inference. Due to this *quasi-complete* manner, the simulation process of HySIA performs efficiently whenever a numerically manageable model is given.

Monitoring. HySIA takes a temporal property as an input and monitors whether a simulated trajectory of an HA satisfies the property. Otherwise, HySIA is able to compute a *robustness* signal [7] for the property. The monitoring process [7,16] for *signal temporal logic* (STL) formulas is extended to handle overapproximation of trajectories. The soundness of interval computation is again utilized here to evaluate the logical negation against an overapproximated trajectory [14].

1.1   Related Work

Several tools for simulation and reachability analysis of hybrid systems based on interval analysis have been developed, including Acumen [8], dReach [15], Flow* [3], iSAT-ODE [9], and HySon [2]. They enclose a trajectory with a sequence of numerical processes e.g., for ODE integration, guard detection, and discrete jump computation; therefore, they suffer from the wrapping effect because each process outputs a result as an explicit overapproximation. In contrast, HySIA regards a continuous and a discrete change as a composite function and evaluates it with a single overapproximation process. Comparison results between HySIA and Flow* or dReach are reported in [12] or [13], respectively. With sufficiently small uncertainties, HySIA outperforms other tools. Conversely, Flow* aims at handling models with large uncertainties by enclosing a state with a higher-order representation and outperforms HySIA in this respect.

SReach [18] and ProbReach [17] are statistical model checkers based on interval analysis. SReach cooperates with dReach to exploit its reachability analysis results. ProbReach evaluates the continuous density function with interval analysis computation. RobSim [10] utilizes an interval-based integration method for checking the correctness and robustness of the numerical simulator of Simulink. HySIA can be involved within the frameworks proposed in these tools.

2   Implementation

The brief structure of HySIA is shown in Fig. 1. The front end of HySIA is implemented in OCaml and the back end is implemented in C++. The source repository is available at https://github.com/dsksh/hysia.

The front end contains a parser and a data structure to process hybrid system specifications. Then, a resulting abstract representation is processed by the simulation module. After a simulation, the resulting trajectory is processed by the monitoring module to check whether the attached property is satisfied. Basic interval analysis procedures, e.g., ODE solving, guard evaluation, and jump computation, are imple-

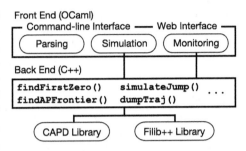

Fig. 1. System structure of HySIA.

mented in the C++ part. Both OCaml simulation and monitoring modules are built using these procedures. HySIA also provides a GUI to users via web browsers (Fig. 2).

Each component is detailed in the following subsections.

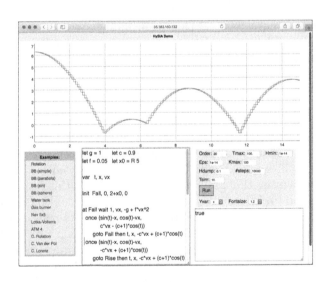

Fig. 2. Web interface available at https://dsksh.github.io/hysia/.

2.1   Specification Language

Figure 3 shows an example HA (referred to as *bb-sin* in the sequel) and an STL property described in HySIA's specification language. This HA models a

```
 1  let g = 1   let c = 0.9   let f = 0.05   let x0 = R 5
 2
 3  var   t, x, vx
 4
 5  init  Fall, 0, 2+x0, 0
 6
 7  at Fall wait 1, vx, -g + f*vx^2
 8      once (sin(t)-x, cos(t)-vx, c*vx - (c+1)*cos(t))
 9                      goto Fall then t, x, -c*vx + (c+1)*cos(t)
10      once (sin(t)-x, cos(t)-vx, -c*vx + (c+1)*cos(t))
11                      goto Rise then t, x, -c*vx + (c+1)*cos(t)
12  end
13  at Rise wait 1, vx, -g - f*vx^2
14      once (vx, true) goto Fall then t, x, vx
15      once (sin(t)-x, cos(t)-vx)
16                      goto Rise then t, x, -c*vx + (c+1)*cos(t)
17  end
18
19  prop  G[0,10] F[0,5] (x-2)
```

Fig. 3. Example of an HA and an STL property.

1D ball that bounces off a table that is moving sinusoidally; a trajectory of the ball is illustrated in Figs. 2 and 4. Line 1 includes the definition of the constants g, c, f, and $x0$; "R 5" represents a value randomly taken from $[0, 5]$ at the execution time. Line 3 presents the state variables t, x, and vx. Line 5 includes the description of the initial location and the initial value for each of the state variables, e.g., $x := 2 + x0$. Lines 7–12 and 13–17 specify the locations Fall and Rise, respectively. After the keyword wait, the derivative of each state variable is specified. Moreover, line 7 is interpreted as follows:

$$\tfrac{d}{dt}t(t) = 1, \tfrac{d}{dt}x(t) = vx(t), \tfrac{d}{dt}vx(t) = -g + f\ vx(t)^2.$$

A sentence starting with once describes a location transition; each of the following expressions is the left-hand side of a guard equation and inequalities; line 8 specifies

$$\sin t - x = 0 \wedge \cos t - vx > 0 \wedge c\ vx - (c+1)\cos t > 0.$$

The expression after then specifies the reset of the state

$$(t, x, vx) := (t, x, -c\ vx + (c+1)\cos t).$$

The STL property $G_{[0,10]}\ F_{[0,5]}\ x - 2 > 0$ is given in line 19 (see Sect. 3.2).

2.2   Interval Analysis Procedures

Every numerical computation in HySIA is performed as a validated interval computation. Instead of a real value $r \in \mathbb{R}$, we handle a closed interval $[l, u]$, where $l, u \in \mathbb{F}$ ($\mathbb{F}$ denotes the set of floating-point numbers), that encloses r (i.e., $l \leq r \leq u$). Instead of a real vector, we handle a *box* $([l_1, u_1], \ldots, [l_n, u_n])$, i.e., an interval vector, or a *parallelotope*, i.e., a linear transformed box. A parallelotope is represented as $\langle A, \boldsymbol{u}, \tilde{x} \rangle$ and interpreted as a region $\{\tilde{x} + Au \mid u \in \boldsymbol{u}\}$, where A is a matrix $\in \mathbb{F}^{n \times n}$, $\boldsymbol{u}$ is a box, and $\tilde{x}$ is a vector $\in \mathbb{F}^n$. The CAPD library[1] and the underlying Filib++ library[2] are used for the ODE integration and interval arithmetic, respectively.

2.3   Simulation Module

The simulation module iteratively computes a set of parallelotopes, each enclosing a state within the trajectory of the input HA; it (i) searches for a state that evolves from the initial state and satisfies the guard of a transition, and (ii) computes the next initial state after a discrete transition. HySIA implements an algorithm that takes into account the wrapping effect that occurs both when integrating an ODE and when computing a discrete transition [12]. More precisely, the algorithm is designed based on a consideration that an evolution of an HA state x for the duration t, *over a discrete jump*, can be represented as a composite function

$$\omega(x, t) := \varphi_2(\delta(\varphi_1(x, \tau(x))), t - \tau(x)),$$

where φ_1 and φ_2 are continuous trajectories in locations before and after the jump, respectively; δ is a jump function; τ is a function that returns the time at which the jump occurs. The algorithm provides a *parallelotope extension* $\langle \omega \rangle$ of the function ω, i.e., for every simulation time t, $\forall x \in \boldsymbol{x}$, $\omega(x, t) \in \langle \omega \rangle(\boldsymbol{x}, t)$ holds, given a parallelotope $\boldsymbol{x}$. By iterating this algorithm, we can simulate k jumps from an initial parallelotope $\boldsymbol{x}_0$ as

$$\boldsymbol{x}_1 := \langle \omega_1 \rangle(\boldsymbol{x}_0, \overline{\tau_1(\boldsymbol{x}_0)}), \quad \ldots, \quad \boldsymbol{x}_k := \langle \omega_k \rangle(\boldsymbol{x}_{k-1}, \overline{\tau_k(\boldsymbol{x}_{k-1})}),$$

where $\overline{\tau_i(\boldsymbol{x}_{i-1})}$ represents the upper bound of the time interval.

Involving interval values within a parallelotope extension is straightforward; therefore, HySIA allows input HA to involve an interval value within the specification. For instance, the initial value of a trajectory of an HA can be parameterized by an interval vector. Using the interval analysis techniques, a value of the parallelotope extension is verified to contain a unique state of the trajectory for each initial value. Overall, the verification process of HySIA proves

$$\forall x_0 \in \boldsymbol{x}_0, \ \forall i \in \{1, \ldots, k\}, \ \exists! x_i \in \langle \omega_i \rangle(\boldsymbol{x}_{i-1}, \overline{\tau_i(\boldsymbol{x}_{i-1})}), \ x_i = \omega_i(x_{i-1}, \overline{\tau_i(\boldsymbol{x}_{i-1})}).$$

2.4   Monitoring Module

The monitoring module evaluates an STL formula based on both boolean-valued [16] and real-valued (i.e., robustness) [7] semantics. The procedure implemented in HySIA is incomplete: it outputs either valid, unsat, or *unknown*. Given

---

[1] http://capd.ii.uj.edu.pl/.
[2] http://www2.math.uni-wuppertal.de/~xsc/software/filib.html.

an HA and an STL property, the output valid implies that every trajectory of the HA satisties the property; the output unsat implies that no trajectory of the HA satisfies the property. The inconclusive result is obtained either when (i) the simulation module fails to verify the unique existence of a solution trajectory or (ii) the result is affected by a precise boundary interval as described below.

For boolean-valued monitoring, (interval enclosures of) zero-crossing points for each atomic proposition p in the STL formula are tracked by the simulation module. As a result, a list of time intervals is obtained, within which p holds. The bounds of the time intervals are represented as intervals, where the satisfiability of p is unknown. Then, the monitoring module processes the lists according to the STL formula in a bottom-up fashion to check whether the STL formula holds at time 0 [14, 16]; the module outputs unknown when a boundary interval intersects time 0.

For real-valued semantics, the monitoring module performs the dedicated algorithm [6], which is extended to handle the interval overapproximation of signals. The current version of the module supports the untimed portion of STL evaluated with bounded-length trajectories. In the monitoring process, the module maintains a list of objects, each of which represents an enclosure of a segment of the resulting signal, where the signal value changes monotonically. Again the list may contain small segments where the monotonicity is unknown because of the overapproximation.

3   Examples

In this section, we show the basic functionalities of HySIA: simulation and monitoring of HA. The reported experiments were run using a 2.7 GHz Intel Core i5 processor with 16 GB RAM. See the documentation[3] for more details.

3.1   Validated Numerical Simulation

Simulation of Nonlinear HA. HySIA correctly simulates nonlinear HA such as the *bb-sin* example in Sect. 2.1. Figure 4 shows simulation results of the two instances of *bb-sin* (Fig. 3) computed with HySIA and MATLAB/Simulink (R2016b; we use the simulator "ODE45" and refine the minimum step size to 10^{-8}). The two results for each instance differ as simulation time proceeds indicating that nonvalidated numerical methods may output a wrong result.

Another example is the *lotka-volterra* system [12] that switches two nonlinear ODEs. We can also consider a 3D *bb-sph* example [12], in which a ball bounces off a sphere based on the universal gravitation between the ball and the sphere. Its ODE and the guard can be modeled as

$$\frac{d^2}{dt^2}x(t) = -\frac{x(t)}{\|x(t)\|_2^3}, \qquad g(x(t)) \equiv \|x(t)\|_2^2 - r^2 = 0 \ \wedge \ \frac{d}{dt}x(t) \cdot \nabla(\|x(t)\|_2^2) > 0,$$

where x represents the position of the ball and ∇ is the gradient operator. A simulation result for this example is shown in Fig. 5.

---

[3] https://dsksh.github.io/hysia/manual.pdf.

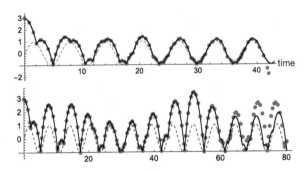

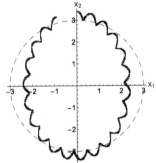

Fig. 4. Trajectories for the variable x of two *bb-sin* instances with the initial value x = 3; the constant c is set as 1 in the experiment below. Solid lines are enclosures computed by HySIA, dots are values computed by MATLAB/Simulink, and dashed lines are the solutions of the guard equations.

Fig. 5. Trajectory of *bb-sph*$_{3.4}$, where the initial value is set as $(0, 0, 3.4, 1, 1, 0)$. Thick and dashed lines represent the computed enclosures and the outline of the sphere, respectively.

Simulation for a Long Duration. HySIA is able to simulate a number of jumps for input HA with its reduction mechanism of the wrapping effect. If the possible number of jumps is unbounded, the enclosure of the trajectory enlarges as the simulation proceeds, and the simulation results in an error due to failure of the verification process. Table 1 illustrates the results of several simulation experiments. In the experiments, HySIA simulates more jumps compared to the naive interval-based method; it outperforms other reachability tools when the interval enclosure of the state is sufficiently tight. The computation time is efficient and most of the timing is taken by the ODE integration process; a *stiff* ODE of larger dimension may require a longer computation time.

Simulation of HA Involving Interval Values. HySIA allows an HA to involve an interval value within the model; in the last experiment reported in Table 1, an interval value is set as the initial height. However, putting an interval in the model easily make the verification process difficult; as a result, the number of simulated jumps decreases in the experiment.

3.2   STL Property Monitoring

Table 2 shows experimental results of boolean-valued monitoring of the STL property against the *bb-sin* example. The property

$$G_{[0,t]} \, F_{[0,5]} \, x - 2 > 0 \quad \equiv \quad \neg(\text{true} \, U_{[0,t]} \, \text{true} \, U_{[0,5]} \, x - 2 > 0),$$

where t is set as either 10 or 100, means that the value of x exceeds 2 within every 5 time units for the initial t time units. In the three experiments, 1000 runs are

Table 1. Simulation results. Each column shows the problem, the dimension of the state variable, the number of jumps HySIA can simulate, the number of jumps a naive box-enclosure method can simulate, and the average CPU time taken for a continuous phase and a jump.

problem	dim	# jumps	box	time
bb-sin	2	1433	24	<0.1 s
navigation	4	24731	51	<0.1 s
lotka-volterra	2	1875	59	<0.1 s
bb-sph$_{3.4}$	6	285	14	0.29 s
bb-sph$_{3.1}$	6	554	17	0.14 s
bb-sph$_{3.1+[-10^{-8},10^{-8}]}$	6	86	9	0.14 s

Table 2. Monitoring results of the STL formula $G_{[0,t]}F_{[0,5]}x-2>0$ against the *bb-sin* example. Each column shows the value t, the width of an interval initial value of x, the numbers of runs for each output value, and the average CPU time taken for a run.

t	width	# valid	# unsat	# unknown	time
10	0	238	762	0	0.2 s
10	0.01	123	10	867	0.2 s
100	0	134	17	849	0.9 s

performed with different settings. HySIA evaluates the property to valid or unsat only when the result is reliable. In the first experiment, the monitoring process successfully checks whether or not the property holds; we count the number of outputs valid and unsat in Table 2 (the result differs from that in [13] because the value of f is different and the verification process is slightly modified). When a monitoring run is badly conditioned, so that the verification process in the monitoring process fails, HySIA will output unknown (or terminate with an error information for some cases). In the second experiment, when an initial value of x is set as an interval of 0.01 width, we obtain the result unknown for 867 times. In the third experiment, we set t as 100 to monitor for 105 time units; then we have the result unknown for 849 times. Even though the unknown results are inconclusive, we consider this verification mechanism is valuable for monitoring a system reliably and efficiently (cf. timings in the last column).

HySIA provides a real-valued monitoring feature for continuous systems, i.e., HA consisting of a location and no transitions. HySIA can compute a robustness signal for unbounded STL properties within a given bounded time horizon. Figure 6 illustrates a computed signal of a property of a simple rotation system.

4   Conclusion and Future Work

The HySIA tool is presented. A web demonstation is available at https://dsksh. github.io/hysia/. We consider that HySIA is a promising testbed for reliable

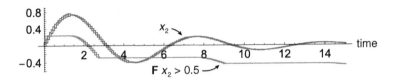

Fig. 6. Interval enclosure of a robustness signal of $Fx_2 > 0.5$.

runtime verification of nonlinear hybrid systems. The whole process of HySIA for simulation and monitoring is implemented using various interval analysis techniques. The tool is able to simulate and monitor various HA and properties for reasonable duration, with a computational efficiency.

As a future work, more detailed analysis and explanation of the inconclusive results will be needed. Extension of HySIA can be planned to incorporate reliable simulation into various runtime verifications such as statistical model checking and conformance testing of hybrid systems.

Acknowledgments. This work was partially funded by JSPS (KAKENHI 25880008, 15K15968, and 26280024).

References

1. Annpureddy, Y., Liu, C., Fainekos, G., Sankaranarayanan, S.: S-TaLiRo: a tool for temporal logic falsification for hybrid systems. In: Abdulla, P.A., Leino, K.R.M. (eds.) TACAS 2011. LNCS, vol. 6605, pp. 254–257. Springer, Heidelberg (2011). doi:10.1007/978-3-642-19835-9_21

2. Bouissou, O., Mimram, S., Chapoutot, A., Paristech, E.: HySon: Set-based simulation of hybrid systems. In: 23rd IEEE International Symposium on Rapid System Prototyping (RSP), pp. 79–85 (2012)

3. Chen, X., Ábrahám, E., Sankaranarayanan, S.: Flow*: an analyzer for non-linear hybrid systems. In: Sharygina, N., Veith, H. (eds.) CAV 2013. LNCS, vol. 8044, pp. 258–263. Springer, Heidelberg (2013). doi:10.1007/978-3-642-39799-8_18

4. David, A., Du, D., Larsen, K.G., Legay, A., Mikučionis, M., Poulsen, D.B., Sedwards, S.: Statistical model checking for stochastic hybrid systems. Electron. Proc. Theor. Comput. Sci. **92**, 122–136 (2012)

5. Donzé, A.: Breach, a toolbox for verification and parameter synthesis of hybrid systems. In: Touili, T., Cook, B., Jackson, P. (eds.) CAV 2010. LNCS, vol. 6174, pp. 167–170. Springer, Heidelberg (2010). doi:10.1007/978-3-642-14295-6_17

6. Donzé, A., Ferrère, T., Maler, O.: Efficient robust monitoring for STL. In: Sharygina, N., Veith, H. (eds.) CAV 2013. LNCS, vol. 8044, pp. 264–279. Springer, Heidelberg (2013). doi:10.1007/978-3-642-39799-8_19

7. Donzé, A., Maler, O.: Robust satisfaction of temporal logic over real-valued signals. In: Chatterjee, K., Henzinger, T.A. (eds.) FORMATS 2010. LNCS, vol. 6246, pp. 92–106. Springer, Heidelberg (2010). doi:10.1007/978-3-642-15297-9_9

8. Duracz, A., Bartha, F.A., Taha, W.: Accurate rigorous simulation should be possible for good designs. In: Workshop on Symbolic and Numerical Methods for Reachability Analysis (SNR), pp. 1–10 (2016)

9. Eggers, A., Ramdani, N., Nedialkov, N., Franzle, M.: Improving the SAT modulo ODE approach to hybrid systems analysis by combining different enclosure methods. Softw. Syst. Model. **14**, 121–148 (2012)

10. Fainekos, G.E., Sankaranarayanan, S., Ivančić, F., Gupta, A.: Robustness of model-based simulations. In: RTSS, pp. 345–354 (2009)

11. Frehse, G., et al.: SpaceEx: scalable verification of hybrid systems. In: Gopalakrishnan, G., Qadeer, S. (eds.) CAV 2011. LNCS, vol. 6806, pp. 379–395. Springer, Heidelberg (2011). doi:10.1007/978-3-642-22110-1_30

12. Goldsztejn, A., Ishii, D.: A parallelotope method for hybrid system simulation. Reliab. Comput. **23**, 163–185 (2016)

13. Ishii, D., Yonezaki, N., Goldsztejn, A.: Monitoring bounded LTL properties using interval analysis. In: Workshop on Numerical Software Verification (NSV), pp. 85–100. ENTCS317 (2015)

14. Ishii, D., Yonezaki, N., Goldsztejn, A.: Monitoring temporal properties using interval analysis. IEICE Trans. Fundam. Electron. Commun. Comput. Sci. **E99–A**, 442–453 (2016)

15. Kong, S., Gao, S., Chen, W., Clarke, E.: dReach: δ-reachability analysis for hybrid systems. In: Baier, C., Tinelli, C. (eds.) TACAS 2015. LNCS, vol. 9035, pp. 200–205. Springer, Heidelberg (2015). doi:10.1007/978-3-662-46681-0_15

16. Maler, O., Nickovic, D.: Monitoring temporal properties of continuous signals. In: Lakhnech, Y., Yovine, S. (eds.) FORMATS/FTRTFT -2004. LNCS, vol. 3253, pp. 152–166. Springer, Heidelberg (2004). doi:10.1007/978-3-540-30206-3_12

17. Shmarov, F., Zuliani, P.: ProbReach : Verified probabilistic delta-reachability for stochastic hybrid systems. In: HSCC, pp. 134–139 (2015)

18. Wang, Q., Zuliani, P., Kong, S., Gao, S., Clarke, E.M.: SReach: A bounded model checker for stochastic hybrid systems. CoRR, abs/1404.7206 (2014)

19. Zuliani, P., Platzer, A., Clarke, E.M.: Bayesian statistical model checking with application to Stateflow/Simulink verification. Formal Methods Syst. Des. **43**(2), 338–367 (2013)

EmbedSanitizer: Runtime Race Detection Tool for 32-bit Embedded ARM

Hassan Salehe Matar[✉], Serdar Tasiran, and Didem Unat

Koç University, Istanbul, Turkey
{hmatar,stasiran,dunat}@ku.edu.tr

Abstract. We propose EmbedSanitizer, a tool for detecting concurrency data races in 32-bit ARM-based multithreaded C/C++ applications. Moreover, we motivate the idea of detecting data races in embedded systems software natively; without virtualization or emulation or use of alternative architecture. Detecting data races in applications on a target hardware provides more precise results and increased throughput and hence enhanced developer productivity. EmbedSanitizer extends ThreadSanitizer, a race detection tool for 64-bit applications, to do race detection for 32-bit ARM applications. We evaluate Embed-Sanitizer using PARSEC benchmarks on an ARMv7 CPU with 4 logical cores and 933 MB of RAM. Our race detection results precisely match with results when the same benchmarks run on 64-bit machine using ThreadSanitizer. Moreover, the performance overhead of EmbedSanitizer is relatively low as compared to running race detection on an emulator, which is a common platform for embedded software development.

1 Introduction

Embedded systems are everywhere: from TVs to robots to smartphones to Internet of Things. Moreover, the computing capability of these systems has tremendously increased in recent years due to multicore support. This has enabled the implementation of complex multithreaded parallel applications. Unfortunately, these applications are prone to concurrency errors such as data races. These bugs are hard to detect in nature and the availability of relevant tools for embedded systems is still limited.

Most of the software development environment for Embedded systems rely on hardware emulations, which tend to be slow. Race detection of embedded system software through emulation can add even more overhead. Nevertheless, running software for race detection on a real hardware not only provides precise race reports but also is faster and hence more productive.

Moreover, many practical race detection tools for C++ applications have not focused on embedded system architectures. Therefore, the alternative is to compile 32-bit embedded C++ applications for other architectures and do race detection there. Unfortunately, some parts of the software that use special features of the target hardware may not be checked due to unavailability of such

© Springer International Publishing AG 2017
S. Lahiri and G. Reger (Eds.): RV 2017, LNCS 10548, pp. 380–389, 2017.
DOI: 10.1007/978-3-319-67531-2_24

features in alternative platforms. Further, it is more appealing to use full features of the software on the target devices for race detection.

We propose a tool named *EmbedSanitizer* [1] for detecting data races for multithreaded 32-bit Embedded ARM software at runtime by running the instrumented application in the target platform. There are two advantages of this approach: (a) parts of software which use unique features, like sensors and actuators, can be analyzed. (b) enhanced developer productivity and throughput attained due to increased performance of race detection compared to hardware emulator. Our tool modifies *ThreadSanitizer* [17] to support race detection for the embedded ARMv7 architecture. Moreover, LLVM/Clang is modified to support *EmbedSanitizer* so that it launches in a similar manner to *ThreadSanitizer*. For simplicity, *EmbedSanitizer* has an automated script which downloads necessary components and builds them together with LLVM/Clang as a cross-compiler. Multithreaded C/C++ programs through this compiler are instrumented and finally run on the target 32-bit ARM hardware for race detection.

The key contributions of this paper are as following:

1. We present a tool for detecting data races in C/C++ multithreaded programs for 32-bit embedded ARM. The tool is easily accessed through Clang compiler chain like *ThreadSanitizer*.
2. We motivate the idea of supporting race detection in native embedded systems hardware and show usability of race detection on such architectures.
3. We evaluate our tool and show its applicability by running PARSEC benchmark applications on a TV with ARMv7 CPU.

2   Motivation

We aim to promote utilization of existing race detection tools by adapting them to different hardware architectures. To show benefits of this approach, consider a theoretical multithreaded example in Fig. 1. It models a TV software component which has two concurrent threads. `ReceiveThread` reads TV signals from an antenna and puts data in a shared queue *queue*. Then `DisplayThread` removes the data from the queue and displays on the TV screen. For the sake of motivation, the implementation of the queue is abstracted away but uses no synchronization to protect concurrent accesses. Since `ReceiveThread` and `DisplayThread` do not use a common a lock (`LK1 & LK2` are used) to protect accesses to *queue*, there is a data race at lines 5(a) and 4(b).

Assume that the developer chooses a method other than the proposed one for race detection. She has two challenges: (1) Modeling the *receipt* as well as the *display* of the video signal data. (2) After that, she can do race detection on an alternative architecture, emulation or virtualization rather than the target architecture. Further overhead is incurred if emulation or virtualization is used. Conversely, the target hardware already has these features and may be faster and thus increasing developer productivity. Moreover, the advantage of instrumenting program and later detecting races on a target hardware is that the developer uses real features for receiving and displaying the signals. This aligns exactly well with our proposed solution.

```
0                          VideoSignalQueue queue;

1 void ReceiveThread() {                 1 void DisplayThread() {
2   while(true) {                        2   while(true) {
3     Signal s = receive(); // from antenna  3     acquire_lock(LK2)
4     acquire_lock(LK1)                  4     Signal s = queue.get();
5     queue.put(s);                      5     release_lock(LK2)
6     release_lock(LK1)                  6     display(s); // to screen
7   }                                    7   }
8 }                                      8 }
                 (a)                                      (b)
```

Fig. 1. A motivating example with two threads concurrently accessing a shared queue. A thread in (a) reads video signals from TV antenna and puts them into the queue, (b) reads from the queue and display to a screen.

3   Related Work

Zeus Virtual Machine® Dynamic Framework [20,21] is a hardware-agnostic platform which contains tools for detecting runtime data races for kernel and user-space multithreaded applications. These tools rely on virtualization and may abstract away real target system interactions with external peripherals like sensors. Moreover, these tools are proprietary and not much relevant information is in the literature. Conversely, *EmbedSanitizer* is open-source and does not rely on virtualization. Differently, from these tools, we motivate the use of the real target hardware for race detection. This improves runtime performance with high precision and developer productivity.

Most of the related solutions for detecting data races do target low end interrupt based, non-multithreaded embedded systems [6,18,19,22]. Therefore, these solutions can not be directly applied to the multithreaded software for ARMv7. Moreover, Keul [11] and Chen [6] use static analysis techniques for race detection in interrupt-driven systems applications. Unfortunately, these techniques do not capture the runtime behavior of the program. Therefore, they fail to infer many of execution patterns which would otherwise result in data races.

Goldilocks [7] is a framework for Java programs which triggers an exception when a race is about to happen. It uses lockset-based and happens-before approaches to improve precision of race detection as well as static analysis to filter out local memory accesses for improved runtime overhead. Differently from our approach, Goldilocks targets Java programs and needs Java virtual machine which may not be ideal for embedded systems.

Finally, *Intel Inspector XE* [10], *Valgrind DRD* [3,13] and *ThreadSanitizer* [17] are race detection tools for C/C++ multithreaded programs. Despite running on native hardware, these tools have limited support for 32-bit ARM architectures. Therefore, they can not directly be used for ARMv7 [4]. *ThreadSanitizer* [17], for example, is developed by default for x86_64 architecture.

4   Background

This section discusses various concepts employed in *EmbedSanitizer*.

ThreadSanitizer. *ThreadSanitizer* [17] is an industrial-level and open-source race detection tool for Go, and C/C++ for 64-bit architectures. This tool is accessible through GCC and LLVM/Clang [12] using compiler flag -fsanitize=thread. It instruments the program under compilation by identifying shared memory and synchronization operations and injecting runtime callbacks. The instrumented executable is then run on a target platform for detecting races.

ThreadSanitizer has been successful mainly for two reasons. First, it uses a hybrid of *happens-before* and *lockset* algorithms to improve its precision. Second, it uses 64-bit architectural capability to store race detection meta-data called *shadow memory* for performance and memory efficiency. The authors of *ThreadSanitizer* claim that extending it for 32-bit applications is *unreliable and problematic* [2]. Therefore, we benefit from its instrumentation part and extend it to support race detection of 32-bit ARM applications.

Data Races. A data race [14,16] occurs when two concurrently executing threads access a shared memory location without proper synchronization and at least one of these accesses is a write. Availability of data races in a program can be a symptom of higher concurrency errors such as atomicity and linearizability violations, and deadlocks. Moreover, data races may result in non-deterministic behavior like memory violations and program crashes.

FastTrack Race Detection Algorithm. FastTrack [8] is an efficient and precise race detection algorithm which improves on purely happens-before vector clock algorithms such as DJIT++ [15]. FastTrack shows that majority of memory access patterns do not require a whole vector clock to detect data races. Instead, an *epoch*, a simple pair of thread identifier and clock suffices. Without sacrificing precision, this significantly improves the performance of race detection of a single memory access from $O(n)$ to $O(1)$ where n is the number of concurrent threads in the program under test. Moreover, its runtime performance is better than most of the race detection algorithms in the literature [23]. Finally, there are further improvements to FastTrack algorithm but tend to sacrifice precision [9].

5   Methodology

EmbedSanitizer improves on *ThreadSanitizer*. It can also be launched through Clang's compiler flag -fsanitize=thread. To achieve this, we modified the LLVM/Clang compiler argument parser to support instrumentation of 32-bit ARM programs when the relevant flag is supplied at compile time. Next, *Embed-Sanitizer* enhances parts of the *ThreadSanitizer* to instrument the target program. Furthermore, it replaces the 64-bit race detection runtime with a custom implementation of the efficient and precise FastTrack race detection algorithm, for 32-bit platforms. In this section, we discuss the important parts of *Embed-Sanitizer* as well as its simplified installation process.

5.1   Architecture and Workflow

Workflow of the *ThreadSanitizer* and the changes done by *EmbedSanitizer* are described in Fig. 2. Figure 2(a) shows default and unmodified relevant components of *ThreadSanitizer* in LLVM/Clang. In Fig. 2(b) these parts are modified to enable instrumentation and detection of races for 32-bit ARM applications.

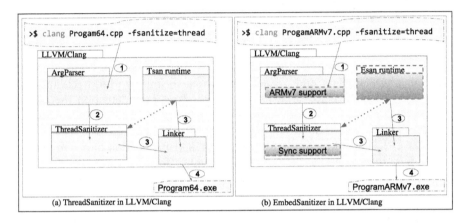

Fig. 2. High level abstraction of *ThreadSanitizer* and *EmbedSanitizer* in LLVM/Clang. In (a) *ThreadSanitizer*: essential LLVM modules for race detection. In (b) *EmbedSanitizer*: same modules modified to instrument and detect races for 32-bit ARM

At ① in Fig. 2(a), the Clang front-end reads the compiler arguments and parses them. If the target architecture is 64-bit, Clang passes the program under compilation through *ThreadSanitizer* compiler pass for instrumentation ②. The pass then identifies all shared memory operations in the program and injects relevant race detection callbacks which are implemented in a race detection runtime library called *tsan*. Furthermore, the instrumented application and the runtime are linked together by the linker ③ to produce an instrumented executable ④. This executable once runs on a target 64-bit platform, it reports race warning in the program. We modify components in the workflow as discussed next.

(a) Enabling Instrumentation of 32-Bit ARM Code in LLVM/Clang: We modify the argument parser of LLVM/Clang to support instrumentation once *EmbedSanitizer* is in place, Fig. 2(b). Therefore, if -fsanitize=thread flag is passed while compiling a program for 32-bit ARM code, the instrumentation takes place. To do this we identified the locations where Clang processes the flag and checks the hardware before skipping the launching of *ThreadSanitizer* instrumentation module because of unsupported architecture.

(b) Modifying the *ThreadSanitizer* Instrumentation Pass: Despite its instrumentation pass, *ThreadSanitizer* has become complex, partly due to its integration into the LLVM's compiler runtime. We extended the available instrumentation pass to identify and instrument synchronization events and inject relevant callbacks and kept instrumentation of memory accesses as it is.

(c) Implementation of Race Detection Runtime: The default race detection runtime in *ThreadSanitizer* uses memory shadow structures which rely on 64-bit architectural support. Due to the complicated structure of ThreadSanitizer, it was not possible to adopt its runtime for 32-bit ARM platform. Therefore, we implemented a race detection runtime by applying the FastTrack race detection algorithm. The library is then compiled for 32-bit ARM and is linked to the final executable of the embedded program at compile time.

5.2 Installation

Figure 3 shows the building process of LLVM compiler infrastructure with *EmbedSanitizer* support. To simplify this process we developed an automated script with five steps. In the first step, it downloads the LLVM source code from the remote repository. Then it replaces files of the LLVM/Clang compiler argument (flags) parser with our modified code to enable *ThreadSanitizer* support for ARMv7. Third, the LLVM code is compiled using GNU tools to produce a cross-compiler which targets 32-bit ARM and supports our tool, *EmbedSanitizer*. Fourth, the race detection runtime which we implemented is compiled separately and integrated into the built cross-compiler binary. Finally, the built cross-compiler is installed which can eventually be used to compile 32-bit ARM applications with race detection support. This whole process is applied once.

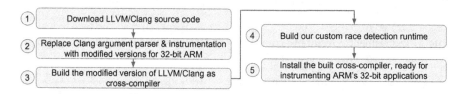

Fig. 3. Showing the automated process for building *ThreadSanitizer* for the first time.

6   Evaluation

We evaluate *EmbedSanitizer* for detecting runtime data races for 32-bit embedded ARM applications, based on two categories. First, we want to see how the precision of race detection in *EmbedSanitizer* deviates from that of *ThreadSanitizer* [17] since *EmbedSanitizer* extends it by using its instrumentation features, and implements a custom FastTrack [8] for detecting races. Second, we want to compare the overhead of *EmbedSanitizer* when running on a target embedded device against when running on an emulator. The key motivation is to show that running race detection on a target device is better than on emulation.

For experimental setup, we built LLVM/Clang, with *EmbedSanitizer* tool, as a cross-compiler in a development machine running Ubuntu 16.04 LTS with Intel i7 (x86_64) CPU and 8 GB of RAM. As our benchmarks, we picked four(4) of the PARSEC benchmark [5] applications. We adopted these applications to Clang compiler and our embedded system architecture. A short summary about the applications we used for evaluation is given below.

- *Blackscholes:* parallelizes the calculation of pricing options of assets using the Black-Scholes differential equation.
- *Fluidanimate:* uses spatial partitioning to parallelize the simulation of fluid flows which are modeled by the Navier-Stokes equations using the renowned Smoothed particle hydrodynamics.
- *Streamcluster:* is a data-mining application which solves the k-means clustering problem.
- *Swaptions:* employs Heath-Jarrow-Morton framework with Monte Carlo simulation to compute the price of a set of swaptions.

6.1   Tool Precision Evaluation

We compare the race reports detected by *EmbedSanitizer* against *ThreadSanitizer*. To do this we run the same benchmark applications with *ThreadSanitizer*, as well as with *EmbedSanitizer*. The instrumented program using *ThreadSanitizer* is run on an x86_64 machine, whereas the binary compiled through *EmbedSanitizer* is executed on ARM Cortex A17 TV. In this setting of four PARSEC benchmark applications, in an application where *ThreadSanitizer* reported races, *EmbedSanitizer* also reported them as shown in Table 1. Therefore *EmbedSanitizer* did not sacrifice any race detection precision.

Table 1. Experimental results to compare race detection in ARMv7 using *EmbedSanitizer* vs in x86_64 with *ThreadSanitizer*.

Benchmark	Input size	Threads	Addresses	Reads	Writes	Locks	*ThreadSanitizer* Races	*EmbedSanitizer* Races
Blackscholes	4 K options	2+1	28686	5324630	409590	0	NO	NO
Fluidanimate	5 K particles	2+1	149711	25832663	8457516	790	YES	YES
Streamcluster	512 points	2+1	11752	21710589	352605	2	YES	YES
Swaptions	400 Simulations	2+1	243945	11000763	3377226	0	NO	NO

6.2   Tool Performance Evaluation

To compare race detection overhead, we ran non-instrumented and instrumented versions of the benchmarks on embedded TV with ARM-Cortex A17 CPUs of 4 logic cores and 933 MB of RAM, and on Qemu-ARM emulator running on a workstation. The slowdown is calculated as a ratio of the execution time of the instrumented program with race detection on and the execution time of the program without race detection. The number of threads was 3 because using the full set of 4 logical cores was crashing the TV. Next, the input sizes were the same in each benchmark setting. Results in Fig. 4 show that detecting races in an emulator incurs between 13× and 371× slowdown whereas the slowdown in the TV is between 12× and 214×. In overall, results in Fig. 4 suggest that detecting races in a target hardware is faster than in an emulator.

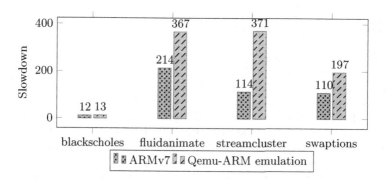

Fig. 4. Slowdown comparison of race detection on ARMv7 vs on Qemu-ARM

7 Conclusion and Future Work

This paper presented *EmbedSanitizer*, a tool for detecting data races for applications targeting 32-bit ARM architecture. *EmbedSanitizer* extends *ThreadSanitizer*, a race detection tool widely accessible through Clang and GCC, by enhancing its instrumentation. Moreover, we implemented our own 32-bit version of race detection runtime to replace *ThreadSanitizer*'s race detection runtime which is incompatible with 32-bit ARM. Our custom race detection library adopts Fast-Track, an efficient and precise happens-before based algorithm.

To evaluate the consistency of *EmbedSanitizer*, we used four PARSEC benchmark applications. First, we evaluated the precision of the tool by comparing the race report behavior with that of *ThreadSanitizer*. Next, we compared its slowdown with running race detection on the Qemu emulator as a representative for testing ARM code in a high-end developer platform.

As a future work, there are four areas to improve. First, improving the efficiency of the custom race detection runtime by hybridizing it with other race detection algorithms. Second, supporting other 32-bit based architectures like the Intel's IA-32. Third, evaluating *EmbedSanitizer* with real-world applications which use special features of the embedded systems such as sensors and actuators, which is the real motivation of our work.

Acknowledgements. This work has been funded under the Affordable Safe & Secure Mobility Evolution (ASSUME) project for smart mobility. We also thank Arçelik A.Ş. for providing the platforms to evaluate our method.

References

1. Embedsanitizer. https://www.github.com/hassansalehe/embedsanitizer
2. Threadsanitizer documentation. https://clang.llvm.org/docs/ThreadSanitizer.html
3. Valgrind drd (2017). http://valgrind.org/docs/manual/drd-manual.html
4. ARM: Arm architecture reference manual armv7-a and armv7-r edition issue c. https://silver.arm.com/download/download.tm?pv=1603196
5. Bienia, C.: Benchmarking modern multiprocessors. Ph.D. thesis, Princeton University, January 2011
6. Chen, R., Guo, X., Duan, Y., Gu, B., Yang, M.: Static data race detection for interrupt-driven embedded software. In: 2011 Fifth International Conference on Secure Software Integration and Reliability Improvement - Companion, pp. 47–52, June 2011
7. Elmas, T., Qadeer, S., Tasiran, S.: Goldilocks: a race and transaction-aware java runtime. In: Proceedings of the 28th ACM SIGPLAN Conference on Programming Language Design and Implementation, PLDI 2007, NY, USA, pp. 245–255 (2007). 10.1145/1250734.1250762
8. Flanagan, C., Freund, S.N.: FastTrack: efficient and precise dynamic race detection. In: Proceedings of the 30th ACM SIGPLAN Conference on Programming Language Design and Implementation, PLDI 2009, NY, USA, pp. 121–133 (2009). 10.1145/1542476.1542490
9. Ha, O.K., Jun, Y.K.: An efficient algorithm for on-the-fly data race detection using an epoch-based technique. Sci. Program. **2015**, 13:13 (2015). doi:10.1155/2015/205827
10. Intel: Intel inspector xe (2017). https://software.intel.com/en-us/intel-inspector-xe
11. Keul, S.: Tuning static data race analysis for automotive control software. In: 2011 IEEE 11th International Working Conference on Source Code Analysis and Manipulation, pp. 45–54, September 2011
12. Lattner, C., Adve, V.: LLVM: a compilation framework for lifelong program analysis & transformation. In: Proceedings of the 2004 International Symposium on Code Generation and Optimization, CGO 2004, Palo Alto, California, March 2004
13. Nethercote, N., Seward, J.: Valgrind: a framework for heavyweight dynamic binary instrumentation. SIGPLAN Not. **42**(6), 89–100 (2004). doi:10.1145/1273442.1250746
14. Netzer, R.H.B., Miller, B.P.: What are race conditions? Some issues and formalizations. ACM Lett. Program. Lang. Syst. **1**(1), 74–88 (2007). doi:10.1145/130616.130623
15. Pozniansky, E., Schuster, A.: Multirace: efficient on-the-fly data race detection in multithreaded C++ programs: research articles. Concurr. Comput. Pract. Exp. **19**(3), 327–340 (2007)
16. Qadeer, S., Tasiran, S.: Runtime verification of concurrency-specific correctness criteria. Int. J. Softw. Tools Technol. Transfer **14**(3), 291–305 (2012). doi:10.1007/s10009-011-0210-1
17. Serebryany, K., Iskhodzhanov, T.: ThreadSanitizer: data race detection in practice. In: Proceedings of the Workshop on Binary Instrumentation and Applications, WBIA 2009, NY, USA, pp. 62–71 (2009). doi:10.1145/1791194.1791203

18. Tchamgoue, G.M., Kim, K.H., Jun, Y.-K.: Dynamic race detection techniques for interrupt-driven programs. In: Kim, T., Lee, Y., Fang, W. (eds.) FGIT 2012. LNCS, vol. 7709, pp. 148–153. Springer, Heidelberg (2012). doi:10.1007/978-3-642-35585-1_20

19. Tchamgoue, G.M., Kim, K.H., Jun, Y.K.: Verification of data races in concurrent interrupt handlers. International Journal of Distributed Sensor Networks **9**(11), Article ID 953593 (2013). doi:10.1155/2013/953593

20. Wire, B.: Parallocity licenses zeus virtual machine dynamic analysis framework to h3c technologies (2012). http://www.businesswire.com/news/home/20121211005482/en/Parallocity-Licenses-Zeus-Virtual-Machine%C2%AE-Dynamic-Analysis

21. Wire, B.: Akamai selects Parallocity's ZVM-U dynamic software analysis framework (2013). http://www.businesswire.com/news/home/20130305005107/en/Akamai-Selects-Parallocity%E2%80%99s-ZVM-U-Dynamic-Software-Analysis

22. Wu, X., Wen, Y., Chen, L., Dong, W., Wang, J.: Data race detection for interrupt-driven programs via bounded model checking. In: 2013 IEEE Seventh International Conference on Software Security and Reliability Companion, pp. 204–210, June 2013

23. Yu, M., Park, S.M., Chun, I., Bae, D.H.: Experimental performance comparison of dynamic data race detection techniques. ETRI J. **39**(1), 124–134 (2017)

A Wingman for Virtual Appliances

Prashanth Nayak[1], Mike Hibler[2], David Johnson[2], and Eric Eide[2(✉)]

[1] NetApp, Research Triangle Park, NC, USA
prashant.u.nayak@gmail.com
[2] University of Utah, Salt Lake City, UT, USA
{hibler,johnsond,eeide}@cs.utah.edu

Abstract. Wingman is a run-time monitoring system that aims to detect and mitigate anomalies, including malware infections, within virtual appliances (VAs). It observes the kernel state of a VA and uses an expert system to determine when that state is anomalous. Wingman does not simply restart a compromised VA; instead, it attempts to repair the VA, thereby minimizing potential downtime and state loss. This paper describes Wingman and summarizes experiments in which it detected and mitigated three types of malware within a web-server VA. For each attack, Wingman was able to defend the VA by bringing it to an acceptable state.

1 Introduction

A *virtual appliance* [15], or VA, is a virtual machine that is deployed to run a specific application or service. For example, a company might use a VA containing a "LAMP stack"—Linux, Apache, MySQL, and PHP—to serve its web site. VAs are commonly assembled from large software components, and even if this software is high quality, bugs and security issues are inevitable. Research suggests that there are 6–16 bugs per thousand lines of code [12,13], leaving VAs vulnerable to run-time failures and attacks.

The simplest way to recover a compromised VA is to completely reinitialize it. This incurs downtime and loss of state, and in many situations, these costs may not be acceptable to users of the VA—especially since, until the attack vector is closed, the VA may need to be restarted continually. This paper explores an alternative recovery strategy: *online repair*. The goal of online repair is to automatically bring a running but compromised appliance to an *acceptable state*, one in which the VA can perform its primary task while also satisfying administrator-specified integrity properties.

Wingman is our prototype tool that performs online VA repair. It uses virtual-machine introspection (VMI) [6] to collect snapshots of a VA's kernel, and it uses an expert system [14] to determine when a snapshot represents an anomaly. Wingman's data-collection and expert-system components run outside the monitored VA, but to carry out repairs, Wingman invokes a kernel module within the VA. This design eases the implementation of complex repair actions. Wingman's data-collection, anomaly-detection, and repair components are reusable across many different VAs. To target Wingman to a new VA, an administrator only needs to encode a set of facts about the VA's application.

© Springer International Publishing AG 2017
S. Lahiri and G. Reger (Eds.): RV 2017, LNCS 10548, pp. 390–399, 2017.
DOI: 10.1007/978-3-319-67531-2_25

This paper describes Wingman's design and implementation, and it summarizes experiments in which we used Wingman to successfully defend a web-server VA from three types of malware. Additional information about Wingman and its evaluation can be found in Nayak's thesis [11]. The Wingman tool is open-source software [7].

2 Design and Implementation

Figure 1 illustrates Wingman's architecture. Its logical components are (1) state gathering, (2) anomaly detection, and (3) recovery (repair). The state-gathering and anomaly-detection components run in a *control VM* and are thus isolated from the VA being protected. The recovery component is spread across the control VM and the VA.

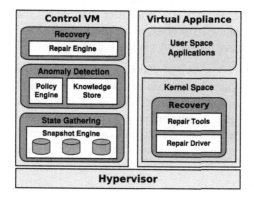

Fig. 1. Wingman's architecture. Logical components are shown as gray rounded rectangles; software components are shown as white rectangles. Adapted from Nayak [11].

The discrete software components of the architecture are shown as white rectangles in Fig. 1. Wingman begins by taking a snapshot of the VA: the *snapshot engine* gathers point-in-time state snapshots of the VA's applications, and it encodes these snapshots as "facts" in the *knowledge store*. Next, the *policy engine* uses those facts and inference rules in the knowledge store to detect anomalies. The *repair engine* uses information in the knowledge store to reason about an appropriate repair strategy and informs the *repair driver*. Finally, the repair driver invokes one or more *repair tools* to carry out the chosen repair. Wingman runs periodically, sampling the state of the VA and detecting and repairing anomalies, and thus works to keep the appliance in an acceptable state.

Wingman is built atop Xen and Linux. The snapshot engine, knowledge store, policy engine, and repair engine execute within the protected Xen dom0 (control VM). The VA's applications, along with the repair driver and tools, execute in a Xen domU running Linux. The snapshot engine gathers state from the VA using the Stackdb [6] VMI libraries. The policy engine is an expert system built using the open-source CLIPS [14] framework. The recovery subsystem is implemented as a combination of a CLIPS-based expert system running in dom0 and Linux kernel modules in domU. The communication channel between the repair engine and the kernel-based repair driver is built with Stackdb.

```
(task-struct
  (comm "mysqld") (pid 663) (tgid 663)   ; process name, ID, thread group ID
  (used_superpriv 1)                     ; has superuser privileges?
  (uid 108) (euid 108) (suid 108)        ; real, effective, and saved user IDs
  (gid 120) (egid 120) (sgid 120)        ; real, effective, and saved group IDs
  (fsuid 108) (fsgid 120)                ; UID, GID for filesystem access
  (parent_pid 1) (parent_name "init"))   ; parent process ID, name
```

Listing 1. Example Base Fact for a `mysqld` Process. Adapted from Nayak [11].

2.1 State Gathering

The snapshot engine is a VMI application that collects the current state of the VA into a "snapshot." It executes periodically in the user space of the control VM, and is thus isolated from possible malware or other problems inside the VA. The engine uses VMI libraries to extract values from the VA's kernel data structures.

Base facts. A snapshot contains data about each process executing in the VA: its credentials, environment variables, scheduling priority, CPU utilization, open files and network sockets, and loaded object files. A snapshot also contains system-wide information, such as CPU load, system-call entry vectors, and loaded kernel modules. All this data is encoded as a collection of records, called *base facts*. Listing 1 shows some of the key fields for an example base fact: a `task-struct` fact representing a `mysqld` process.

2.2 Anomaly Detection

The policy engine and knowledge store run in the control VM. Together, they drive the detection of problems in the VA. The policy engine is an expert system that reasons over collections of facts about the VA—facts that represent the current state of the VA as well as those describing its expected state. As illustrated on the left-hand side of Fig. 2, the policy engine takes as input (1) the *base facts* captured by the snapshot engine, (2) *application-specific facts* representing the expected state of the VA, and (3) *rules* that classify observations as expected or anomalous. From these things, the policy engine generates a set of *anomaly facts* that represent any unexpected state in the VA.

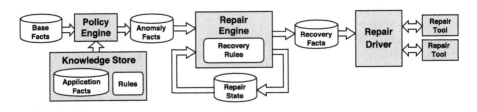

Fig. 2. Anomaly detection and recovery components. Adapted from Nayak [11].

```
;; Declare the allowable processes in the VA.
(known-processes ... "apache2" ...)
;; Declare that Apache *must* be running in the VA.
(mandatory-process (name "apache2") (command /etc/init.d/apache2 start ...))
;; Declare the expected credentials of the Apache process.
(known-process-cred (name "apache2") (parent_name "init" "apache2")
    (uid 33) (euid 33) (suid 33) (fsuid 33) (gid 33) (egid 33) (sgid 33) (fsgid 33))
;; Declare the shared objects of the Apache process.
(known-objects (name "apache2")
    (object-list "apache2" "libnss_files-2.15.so" "libnss_nis-2.15.so"
    "mod_uni_mem.so" "mod_rewrite.so" "mod_alias.so" ...))
```

Listing 2. Example Application Facts for an `apache2` Process

```
(defrule identify-unknown-process
    (task-struct (comm ?name) (pid ?pid) (parent_pid ?ppid))
    (known-processes $?proclist)
    (test (not (member $?name $?proclist)))
=>  (assert (unknown-process (name ?name) (pid ?pid) (ppid ?ppid)))
    (printout t "ANOMALY: Unknown process " ?name " found" crlf))
```

Listing 3. Example Rule for Identifying Unknown Processes. Adapted from Nayak [11].

Application-specific facts. The knowledge store contains Wingman's application-specific knowledge about the VA, provided by the VA's creator or administrator. The application-specific facts represent the expected state of the VA in terms of kernel-visible abstractions such as processes, files, users, sockets, loaded object files (i.e., shared libraries), and kernel modules. Listing 2 shows an example set of facts that capture an administrator's knowledge that an Apache process with the given credentials, possible parent processes, and loaded object files should be executing in the VA.

To protect a particular VA, the administrator or creator of the VA only needs to specify an appropriate set of application-specific facts. He or she can reuse facts created for similar VAs or create an entirely new set of facts. Due to its kernel-centric design, all of the other parts of Wingman are *application-independent* and are reusable for all VAs.

Rules. Inference rules use the application-specific and base facts to validate the state of the VA; they capture an administrator's domain expertise and automate anomaly detection. Listing 3 presents a rule that identifies all unknown processes running in the VA. The clauses above "=>" are the premise, and those following it are the conclusion: if the premise is true, the conclusion is executed. The example rule matches all `task-struct` base facts against the `known-processes` application-specific fact to detect unknown processes. The technique of comparing the VA's dynamic kernel state (base facts) to the properties of acceptable states (application-specific facts) allows Wingman to identify a large and general class of anomalies, including multiple types of malware.

Anomaly facts. Rules produce new facts about observed anomalies. In Listing 3, if any process identified by a `task-struct` is not also present in `known-processes`, the rule creates ("asserts") an `unknown-process` anomaly fact to record the problem.

```
(defrule kill-unknown-process
  ?f <- (unknown-process (name ?name) (pid ?pid))
  (not (exists (unkn-proc-prev-action (prev_action ps_kill | ps_kill_parent)
               (name ?name) (pid ?pid))))
  => (assert (recovery-action (func-name kill_process) (arg_list ?name ?pid)))
     (assert (unkn-proc-prev-action (name ?name) (pid ?pid) (prev_action ps_kill)))
     (retract ?f) (printout t "RECOVERY: Killing the unknown process" ?pid crlf))

(defrule kill-unknown-process_1
  ?f <- (unknown-process (name ?name) (pid ?pid))
  ?of <- (unkn-proc-prev-action (prev_action ps_kill) (name ?name))
  => (assert (recovery-action (func-name kill_parent_proc) (arglist ?pid ?name)))
     (retract ?f) (retract ?of)
     (assert (unkn-proc-prev-action (name ?name) (prev_action ps_kill_parent)))
     (printout t "RECOVERY: Killing the process its parent" crlf))
```

Listing 4. Example "Kill Unknown Process" Recovery Rules. Adapted from Nayak [11].

2.3 Recovery

Once an anomaly has been identified by the policy engine, Wingman's recovery components reason about an appropriate recovery strategy and attempt to restore the VA to an acceptable state. The recovery workflow is shown on the right-hand side of Fig. 2. The repair engine is an expert system that executes in the control VM along with the snapshot engine, policy engine, and knowledge store. It takes as input the *anomaly facts* generated by the policy engine, passes them through a set of *recovery rules*, and generates a set of *recovery facts* that are used to select appropriate repair tools.

Recovery rules. Recovery rules generate recovery facts from anomaly facts, and thus suggest repairs for anomalies, but the mappings are not simply one-to-one. The recovery rules operate over additional *repair state* (facts) kept by the repair engine, such as the history of previous occurrences of the anomaly and recovery actions already taken. This allows the repair engine to better reason about future repair actions.

Listing 4 shows two possible recovery rules that handle unknown processes; they map unknown-process facts to appropriate recovery actions. The kill-unknown-process rule kills newly discovered unknown processes. The premise matches unknown processes for which no recovery action has already been attempted. The conclusion defines the recovery action: asserting a recovery fact that identifies the repair tool to be used (kill_process), asserting a repair-state fact recording that this rule has been tried, and retracting the fact that the process is unknown, since Wingman is about to kill it. It will be rediscovered in the next state-gathering iteration if the kill_process tool fails. The kill-unknown-process_1 rule handles unknown processes that still exist in the VA after Wingman has tried killing them with kill-unknown-process. In this case, the recovery action is to kill both the process and its parent.

Repair tools. Recovery facts identify individual *repair tools*, which are then invoked via the *repair driver*. The repair driver and tools run inside the VA to simplify tool development and make complex repairs feasible. For example, it is straightforward for a tool within the VA's kernel to start a new process or retrieve swapped-out pages, using the kernel's own code. It is practically impossible for an agent entirely outside the VA to perform these tasks through VMI alone. Because the repair engine runs in a different VM than the repair driver and tools (Fig. 1), tool-invocation commands are sent from the repair engine to the driver through an inter-VM communication channel. The result is communicated back to the repair engine through the same channel.

Wingman's most basic tools act on processes and their attributes. The psaction tool terminates a process by traversing the kernel's process list to locate it, and then calling the Linux force_sig function to deliver a SIGKILL. The ps_deescalate tool resets a process's credentials to specified values by modifying the process's cred structure. The kill_socket tool shuts down the open sockets of a process, and the close_file tool closes its opened files. The start_process tool starts a user-space process.

Other tools perform more sophisticated repairs. The system_map_reset tool provides two functions: one to fix corrupt system-call table entries and another to fix overwritten system-call function prologues. The trusted_load and start_process tools work together to start processes in a controlled-boot environment. The trusted_load tool inputs the names of blacklisted objects that are not allowed to be loaded by a process created by start_process. This environment allows only non-blacklisted objects to load during process startup. The tool hooks the open and mmap system calls with versions that return an error when the process tries to load a blacklisted object.

The sled_object tool deals with malicious objects already loaded into process memory by overwriting them. It calls the Linux get_user_pages function to load the pages containing the code segment of an object, and overwrites all non-return instructions with no-ops. Thus, every function in the malicious object is "nullified": calling them does nothing but return. This repair only works on functions with a hook-like API: i.e., that have a void return type and are not required to perform any action.

3   Evaluation

We deployed Wingman to monitor a web-server virtual appliance. We evaluated its effectiveness against three different types of malicious software, including a kernel rootkit, a user-space rootkit, and an application malware.

Experiment context. We ran a web-server VA on a server (64-bit 2.40 GHz quad-core Xeon E5530 CPU, 12 GB RAM) running Xen 4.1.2. Both the control VM and VA ran Ubuntu 12.04 with a Linux 3.8.0 kernel; the VA also ran the Apache 2.2 web server.

The policy in the knowledge store described the VA's acceptable states via 103 CLIPS facts (415 lines of code). It allowed the execution of Apache and PHP processes, MySQL, NTP, and SSH daemons, and standard kernel processes (e.g., kworker).

Wingman's snapshot engine pauses the VA to ensure atomic snapshots, and thus affects VA availability. The average time to capture a complete snapshot is 140.3 ms; during that time, no work is performed by the VA. Wingman does not otherwise affect the VA's availability, since the policy and repair engines run without pausing the VA.

Kernel rootkit. A kernel rootkit is a set of malicious programs that provide continuous, unauthorized root access. The Suterusu [2] rootkit provides features including root-shell access; process, socket, and file hiding, and disabling module loading. Unlike traditional rootkits, Suterusu does not modify the function pointers in the system-call table; instead, it overwrites instructions in the prologues of the functions themselves. This allows Suterusu to evade detection by most rootkit detectors.

Suterusu hides processes by hooking the `proc_root_readdir` function of the /proc filesystem. (Most tools use /proc to list processes.) When run against the infected VA, Wingman found a Suterusu-hidden rogue process because it scans the in-kernel process list; it restored the VA to an acceptable state by killing the process. To detect file-related malicious behaviors, our policy restricted process file access. For instance, if a process violates the policy by opening /etc/shadow, Wingman identifies the access and closes the corresponding file descriptor. Suterusu hooks the `tcp4_seq_show` and `udp4_seq_show` functions (et al.) to hide TCP or UDP sockets. Since the VA's policy allows only specific processes to open sockets, Wingman detects and closes Suterusu-hidden sockets. Because Suterusu hooks normal kernel functions, not system calls, Wingman cannot fully deactivate it—but Wingman *can* suppress its malicious activity.

User-space rootkit. Azazel [1] is a user-space rootkit that infects individual programs at execution time using `LD_PRELOAD` to ensure that its own malicious library functions override standard library functions. This library (named `libselinux.so`) provides functions to spawn root shells, hide processes, and deploy back doors.

When we applied Wingman to our infected web-server VA, it detected the malicious library and recovered over a period of repair iterations. First, Wingman identified the malicious shared object as an anomaly in `sshd`. To recover, the repair engine restarted `sshd`. In the second iteration, Wingman again detected the malicious object in `sshd`'s memory (because Azazel had overwritten the `ld.so.preload` file). This time, `sshd` was restarted in a controlled environment, but failed to run since it was not allowed to load `libselinux.so`. Finally, since previous repair efforts failed, the repair engine chose to nullify ("sled") the object's instructions. In subsequent iterations, if the unknown object were detected in new `sshd` processes, its instructions would be nullified immediately. The `sshd` process became unresponsive to connection requests after the object was "sledded." Its inability to respond is an undetected anomaly—the VA was in an acceptable state by policy, but still had an anomaly. Because the back door was closed and the Apache web server was unaffected, we argue that Wingman successfully recovered the VA.

Azazel can exploit the `su` command to spawn a root shell; if this occurs, Wingman terminates the root shell. Wingman detects such privilege escalations by validating the process lineage in the snapshot against the VA's policy. Azazel also sets up an SSH back door by preloading malicious objects during `sshd` startup. Wingman detects the compromised `sshd` process and restarts it, resulting in the `sshd` session being terminated.

Application malware. Darkleech [9] is an Apache module that injects malicious iframes into legitimate HTTP responses. The iframes redirect clients to malicious sites. Darkleech is loaded at Apache startup via the `LoadModule` configuration file command.

To evaluate Wingman's effectiveness against Darkleech, we created a network consisting of three client hosts and our web-server VA. Each client ran a script that repeatedly made HTTP requests and checked the responses for malicious iframes. As the clients submitted requests, Wingman inspected the web-server VA every five seconds.

In the first iteration, Wingman detected an unknown shared object in the Apache processes, and attempted to restart it. Because Darkleech modified the Apache configuration to load its module at startup, the unknown module was loaded into the restarted process. Thus, in the second iteration, Wingman again detected the unknown module in Apache. Since the previous repair was ineffective, Wingman's repair engine restarted Apache in a controlled-boot environment. As the Apache threads were killed by the repair tool, new threads were spawned by the main Apache process outside Wingman's controlled environment. Thus, in the final iteration, Wingman found the unknown object again. This time, Wingman decided to "sled" the unknown object, replacing its instructions with no-ops. Once this occurred, the responses no longer contained malicious iframes.

Table 1. Malware samples mitigated by Wingman. Adapted from Nayak [11].

Experiment		Mitigated	Acceptable	Outcome
Suterusu	Process hiding	✓	✓	Process detected and terminated
	File access	✓	✓	Detected and stopped
	Network access	✓	✓	Detected and stopped
Azazel	Unauthorized objects	✓	?	Detected, mitigated, but not cleaned
	su exploitation	✓	✓	Detected and privileges restored
	SSH back door	✓	✓	Detected and terminated
Darkleech		✓	✓	Unknown object detected and nullified

Summary. Table 1 summarizes our experiments. Although these malware samples are only a handful of thousands, they are representative of common exploit techniques. Wingman detected all anomalies introduced by these samples. Although it was unable to clear the malicious object loaded by Azazel, it terminated its malicious actions. Wingman successfully mitigated all the actions of the other malware samples. We conclude that Wingman detected the anomalies in the VA and restored it to an acceptable state.

4   Related Work

Several previous research projects, such as Livewire [4], have used VMI to create intrusion-detection systems for virtual-machine guests. Livewire and Wingman both use VMI for anomaly detection, but differ in that Wingman attempts to repair anomalies. IntroVirt [8] uses VMI to detect past intrusions and prevent future exploits of known vulnerabilities. IntroVirt and Wingman provide complementary styles of "stop-gap" protection to VMs: however, IntroVirt does not try to repair existing damage.

Exterior [3] allows processes within a "secure VM" to observe and manipulate the kernel state of a protected "guest VM." Whereas Exterior enables cross-VM execution for repair, Wingman uses a combination of VMI for detection and a kernel module for guest VM repair, and places greater emphasis on *automated* detection and repair.

LKIM [10] combines measures of static data (e.g., code pages) with "contextual inspection" to check the integrity of a kernel's dynamic data. OSck [5] enforces control-flow integrity through means such as write-protecting the kernel's code pages and analyzing the targets of dynamic control-flow transfers. Wingman is similar to these systems in that they all inspect the dynamic data within a VM's kernel and look for integrity violations. Unlike both LKIM and OSck, Wingman attempts to repair violations.

Nayak's thesis [11] presents a more detailed discussion of work related to Wingman.

5 Conclusion

Our Wingman prototype tool demonstrates that automatic, online anomaly detection and repair can help to maintain an acceptable level of integrity within a virtual appliance over time. This is useful when it is important to run a VA continuously, with minimal downtime and state loss. Our evaluation showed that Wingman was able to detect and mitigate three different types of malware within a web-server VA. Although Wingman did not remove the malicious software in our experiments, it substantially and automatically reduced the malware's harmful effects, bringing the VA back to an acceptable state without needing a human to initiate repair.

Acknowledgments. We performed our experiments on machines in the Utah Emulab testbed [16]. This work was supported in part by the Air Force Research Laboratory and DARPA under Contract No. FA8750–10–C–0242. This material is based upon work supported in part by the National Science Foundation under Grant No. 1314945.

References

1. Chokepoint: Azazel userland rootkit, February 2015. https://github.com/chokepoint/azazel
2. Coppola, M.: Suterusu rootkit, September 2014. https://github.com/mncoppola/suterusu
3. Fu, Y., Lin, Z.: Exterior: using a dual-VM based external shell for guest-OS introspection, configuration, and recovery. In: Proceedings VEE, pp. 97–110, March 2013. doi:10.1145/2451512.2451534
4. Garfinkel, T., Rosenblum, M.: A virtual machine introspection based architecture for intrusion detection. In: Proceedings NDSS, pp. 191–206, February 2003. http://www.isoc.org/isoc/conferences/ndss/03/proceedings/papers/13.pdf
5. Hofmann, O.S., Dunn, A.M., Kim, S., Roy, I., Witchel, E.: Ensuring operating system kernel integrity with OSck. In: Proceedings ASPLOS, pp. 279–290, March 2011. doi:10.1145/1950365.1950398
6. Johnson, D., Hibler, M., Eide, E.: Composable multi-level debugging with Stackdb. In: Proceedings VEE, pp. 213–226, March 2014. doi:10.1145/2576195.2576212
7. Johnson, D., Nayak, P., Hibler, M., Burtsev, A., Eide, E.: Wingman and Stackdb software, March 2017. https://gitlab.flux.utah.edu/a3/vmi

8. Joshi, A., King, S.T., Dunlap, G.W., Chen, P.M.: Detecting past and present intrusions through vulnerability-specific predicates. In: Proceedings SOSP, pp. 91–104, October 2005. doi:10.1145/1095810.1095820

9. Landesman, M.: Apache Darkleech compromises, 2 April 2013. http://blogs.cisco.com/security/apache-darkleech-compromises

10. Loscocco, P.A., Wilson, P.W., Pendergrass, J.A., McDonell, C.D.: Linux kernel integrity measurement using contextual inspection. In: Proceedings ACM Workshop on Scalable Trusted Computing (STC), pp. 21–29, November 2007. doi:10.1145/1314354.1314362

11. Nayak, P.: Detecting and mitigating malware in virtual appliances. Master's thesis, University of Utah, December 2014. http://www.flux.utah.edu/paper/pnayak-thesis

12. Ostrand, T.J., Weyuker, E.J.: The distribution of faults in a large industrial software system. In: Proceedings ISSTA, pp. 55–64, July 2002. doi:10.1145/566172.566181

13. Ostrand, T.J., Weyuker, E.J., Bell, R.M.: Where the bugs are. In: Proceedings ISSTA, pp. 86–96, July 2004. doi:10.1145/1007512.1007524

14. Savely, R., Culbert, C., Riley, G., Dantes, B., Ly, B., Ortiz, C., Giarratano, J., Lopez, F.: CLIPS: a tool for building expert systems, May 2015. http://clipsrules.sourceforge.net/

15. Sun, C., He, L., Wang, Q., Willenborg, R.: Simplifying service deployment with virtual appliances. In: Proceedings IEEE International Conference on Services Computing (SCC), pp. 265–272, July 2008. doi:10.1109/SCC.2008.53

16. White, B., Lepreau, J., Stoller, L., Ricci, R., Guruprasad, S., Newbold, M., Hibler, M., Barb, C., Joglekar, A.: An integrated experimental environment for distributed systems and networks. In: Proceedings OSDI, pp. 255–270, December 2002. https://www.usenix.org/legacy/event/osdi02/tech/white.html

Short Papers

Operational Semantics of Process Monitors

Jun Inoue$^{(\boxtimes)}$ and Yoriyuki Yamagata

National Institute of Advanced Industrial Science and Technology (AIST),
1-8-31 Midorigaoka, Ikeda, Osaka 563-8577, Japan
{jun.inoue,yoriyuki.yamagata}@aist.go.jp

Abstract. CSP$_E$ is a specification language for runtime monitors that can directly express concurrency in a bottom-up manner that composes the system from simpler, interacting components. It includes constructs to explicitly flag failures to the monitor, which unlike deadlocks and livelocks in conventional process algebras, propagate globally and aborts the whole system's execution. Although CSP$_E$ has a trace semantics along with an implementation demonstrating acceptable performance, it lacks an operational semantics. An operational semantics is not only more accessible than trace semantics but also indispensable for ensuring the correctness of the implementation. Furthermore, a process algebra like CSP$_E$ admits multiple denotational semantics appropriate for different purposes, and an operational semantics is the basis for justifying such semantics' integrity and relevance. In this paper, we develop an SOS-style operational semantics for CSP$_E$, which properly accounts for explicit failures and will serve as a basis for further study of its properties, its optimization, and its use in runtime verification.

Keywords: Operational semantics · Concurrency · Runtime monitoring · Communicating Sequential Processes

1 Introduction

Specification-based runtime monitoring [7] checks a program's execution trace against a formal specification. Often more rigorous than testing due to the presence of a formal specification, this technique is also computationally much cheaper than formal verification methods like model checking, as it only needs to look at concrete program runs with instrumentation. CSP$_E$ [12] is a language based on Hoare's Communicating Sequential Processes [8] for developing the formal specification. Unlike many other languages in this niche, CSP$_E$ can directly express concurrency. Moreover, it builds up the specification in a bottom-up manner by composing smaller, interacting components, helping to model complex behavior.

CSP$_E$'s main appeal as a specification language, compared to plain CSP, is a *FAIL* construct that signals a global failure, aborting all processes in the model at once. This construct can be used like assert(false) in C or Java, allowing to code invariants that mark some states as (should-be) unreachable. By contrast,

© Springer International Publishing AG 2017
S. Lahiri and G. Reger (Eds.): RV 2017, LNCS 10548, pp. 403–409, 2017.
DOI: 10.1007/978-3-319-67531-2_26

Event	$e \in \Sigma$
Event Variable	$x \in X$
Term	$P, Q \in Terms ::= STOP \mid FAIL \mid ?x : E \to P \mid P \,\square\, Q \mid P \parallel_E Q$
Event Set	$E ::= f(y_1, \ldots, y_n)$ where $f : \Sigma^n \to 2^\Sigma$ is computable
Event Set Param	$y ::= x \mid e$

Fig. 1. Syntax of CSP_E.

deadlocks and livelocks, the conventional notions of failure in CSP, affect only the deadlocked or livelocked process(es). These failures are thus very difficult to propagate into a failure for the entire system, as desired for assertion failures. However, the semantics of how *FAIL* propagates throughout the model requires special treatment. Because the propagation preempts all other activities, normal execution rules must apply only when *FAIL* is not currently propagating. This is a negative constraint, which is generally problematic [6].

While earlier work [12] demonstrated a trace semantics and a reasonably efficient implementation for CSP_E, an operational semantics has been lacking. Developing an operational semantics is highly desirable for several reasons. Firstly, though a trace semantics more naturally defines the set of behaviors (i.e. traces) that comply with a CSP_E specification, an operational semantics more directly defines the implementation. Secondly, process algebras admit multiple denotational semantics capturing different aspects of operationally defined behavior [5]. Investigating the full spectrum of such semantics requires an operational semantics. Finally, an operational semantics provides a more accessible presentation of the semantics than denotational semantics.

1.1   Contributions

In this paper, after reviewing the syntax and trace semantics of CSP_E (Sect. 2), we present the following contributions.

- We define an operational semantics in SOS format [10], which properly captures the propagation of *FAIL* while avoiding the complexities of rules with negative premises (Sect. 3).
- We prove that the operational semantics induces the previously published trace semantics (Sect. 4).

2   Syntax and Trace Semantics of CSP_E

This section reviews the syntax and trace semantics of CSP_E. Figure 1 presents the syntax. A CSP_E term represents a process, which is an entity that successively emits *events* drawn from an alphabet Σ. Terms are built from the following constructs, with the indicated meanings. For a thorougher explanation, see [12].

- The stuck term *STOP* does not emit anything.

- The failing term *FAIL* aborts all processes.
- Prefix $?x : E \rightarrow P$ chooses and emits an event $e \in E$, then executes $[e/x]P$.
- Choice $P \;\square\; Q$ executes P or Q, whichever manages to emit something first.
- Parallel composition $P \;||_E\; Q$ executes P and Q in parallel. Their events are interleaved arbitrarily, except events in E are synchronized.

An event set E can be specified by any computable function parametrized by the x's bound by surrounding prefix operators.

In this short paper, we omit recursion and the terminating action $\checkmark$ in the interest of conciseness. This paper's focus is on analyzing *FAIL*, and $\checkmark$ complicates the presentation substantially without adding anything of conceptual significance. Recursion seems to be similar, though it is still under investigation.

Trace	$s, t \in \Sigma^*$
Trace Set	$T \in \textit{TraceSets} ::= \text{prefix-closed subsets of } \Sigma^*$
Trace Set Operations	

$$eT := \{\varepsilon\} \cup \{et \mid t \in T\}$$

$$T(e) := \{t \mid et \in T\}$$

$$\varnothing \;||_E\; T := T \;||_E\; \varnothing := \varnothing \qquad\qquad (1)$$

$$T_1 \;||_E\; T_2 := \bigcup_{e \in E} e(T_1(e) \;||_E\; T_2(e)) \cup \bigcup_{e \in \Sigma - E} (e(T_1(e) \;||_E\; T_2) \cup e(T_1 \;||_E\; T_2(e))) \qquad (2)$$

Trace Semantics

$$\llbracket STOP \rrbracket := \{\varepsilon\} \qquad\qquad\qquad \llbracket P \;\square\; Q \rrbracket := \llbracket P \rrbracket \cup \llbracket Q \rrbracket$$

$$\llbracket FAIL \rrbracket := \varnothing \qquad\qquad\qquad\quad \llbracket P \;||_E\; Q \rrbracket := \llbracket P \rrbracket \;||_E\; \llbracket Q \rrbracket$$

$$\llbracket ?x : E \rightarrow P \rrbracket := \{\varepsilon\} \cup \bigcup_{e \in E} e \llbracket [e/x]P \rrbracket$$

Fig. 2. Trace semantics of CSP_E. Equation (1) takes precedence over Eq. (2), so the latter applies only if the former does not.

Figure 2 presents the trace semantics. A *trace* is a (possibly empty) sequence of events, and Σ^* is the set of all traces. The concatenation of traces s and t is written st. A *trace set* is any prefix-closed set of traces, which can be empty, unlike in conventional process algebras. The trace semantics of CSP_E assigns to each term P a trace set $\llbracket P \rrbracket$, which is intuitively the set of traces P can emit.

The semantic map uses some operations on trace sets. If T is a trace set, eT prepends e to all members of T and adjoins ε, while $T(e)$ discards all traces in T that do not start with e and drops the leading e from all remaining traces. The $||_E$ operator is defined by Eqs. (1) and (2). Though significantly simplified, these equations are equivalent to the ones found in [12] modulo the absence of $\checkmark$. In [12], this operator was defined "coinductively", which was correct but misleading. Formally, by the Knaster-Tarski Theorem, the defining Eqs. (1) and (2) have a greatest solution in the complete lattice of total binary functions on *TraceSets* ordered by point-wise inclusion, which was taken to be $||_E$. However,

Action	$a ::= e \mid \tau$
Doomed Term	$D \in Doomed ::= FAIL \mid D \square D \mid D \parallel_E P \mid P \parallel_E D$
Viable Term	$\hat{P}, \hat{Q} \in Terms - Doomed$
Operational Semantics	

$$\frac{e \in E}{(?x : E \to P) \overset{e}{\mapsto} [e/x]P} \qquad \frac{P \overset{\tau}{\mapsto} P'}{P \square Q \overset{\tau}{\mapsto} P' \square Q} \qquad \frac{Q \overset{\tau}{\mapsto} Q'}{P \square Q \overset{\tau}{\mapsto} P \square Q'}$$

$$\frac{P \overset{e}{\mapsto} P'}{P \square Q \overset{e}{\mapsto} P'} \qquad \frac{Q \overset{e}{\mapsto} Q'}{P \square Q \overset{e}{\mapsto} Q'} \qquad \frac{P \overset{a}{\mapsto} P' \quad a \notin E}{P \parallel_E \hat{Q} \overset{a}{\mapsto} P' \parallel_E \hat{Q}} \qquad \frac{Q \overset{a}{\mapsto} Q' \quad a \notin E}{\hat{P} \parallel_E Q \overset{a}{\mapsto} \hat{P} \parallel_E Q'}$$

$$\frac{\hat{P} \overset{e}{\mapsto} P' \quad \hat{Q} \overset{e}{\mapsto} Q' \quad e \in E}{\hat{P} \parallel_E \hat{Q} \overset{e}{\mapsto} P' \parallel_E Q'} \qquad \frac{D_1 \overset{\tau}{\mapsto} P_1}{D_1 \parallel_E D_2 \overset{\tau}{\mapsto} P_1 \parallel_E D_2} \qquad \frac{D_2 \overset{\tau}{\mapsto} P_2}{D_1 \parallel_E D_2 \overset{\tau}{\mapsto} D_1 \parallel_E P_2}$$

$$\frac{}{FAIL \square FAIL \overset{\tau}{\mapsto} FAIL} \qquad \frac{}{FAIL \parallel_E P \overset{\tau}{\mapsto} FAIL} \qquad \frac{}{P \parallel_E FAIL \overset{\tau}{\mapsto} FAIL}$$

$$\frac{}{P \overset{\varepsilon}{\Rightarrow} P} \qquad \frac{P \overset{a}{\mapsto} P' \overset{s}{\Rightarrow} P''}{P \overset{as}{\Rightarrow} P''} \qquad \frac{P \overset{\tau}{\mapsto} P' \overset{s}{\Rightarrow} P''}{P \overset{s}{\Rightarrow} P''}$$

Fig. 3. Operational semantics of CSP_E.

if $\parallel_E'$ and $\parallel_E''$ are any two solutions of these equations, then for any T_1 and T_2, every trace in $T_1 \parallel_E' T_2$ is also in $T_1 \parallel_E'' T_2$, by straightforward induction on the trace's length. Thus, the solution is unique, and $\parallel_E$ is this unique solution.

Lemma 1. $\parallel_E$ *is continuous, i.e.* $(\bigcup S_1) \parallel_E (\bigcup S_2) = \bigcup_{T_1 \in S_1, T_2 \in S_2} T_1 \parallel_E T_2$.

Proof. The defining Eqs. (1) and (2) preserve continuity, so in fact the Knaster-Tarski construction can be carried out in the space of continuous binary operators, which is also a complete lattice under point-wise inclusion.

3   Operational Semantics

This section explains the operational semantics, summarized in Fig. 3. *Internal transitions* $P \overset{a}{\mapsto} Q$ emit an event a or the silent action τ. A *visible transition* $P \overset{s}{\Rightarrow} Q$ happens when P internally transitions to Q in zero or more steps, and the non-τ actions it emits along the way form s. The rules are mostly identical to standard CSP, save for the presence of *FAIL* and viability annotations $\hat{P}$.

The purpose of viability annotations is to ensure timely propagation of *FAIL*. For example, in $P \parallel_\varnothing FAIL$, the P must not be allowed to keep emitting events, for then P could do so indefinitely, withholding the propagation of *FAIL*. Instead, *FAIL* should kill all processes including P, transitioning the whole term to *FAIL*. To achieve this effect, the usual rule that allows the left operand to transition must apply only when the right operand is not failing. This constraint is tricky to capture because it is a negative constraint.

The viability annotation syntactically restricts the range of the metavariable $\hat{P}$ to exclude *doomed* terms, i.e. terms for which transitioning to *FAIL* has become inevitable and are now propagating *FAIL* within themselves. These annotations are placed so that when a term is doomed, rules that propagate *FAIL* become the only applicable ones, thus forcing the propagation to take place.

Proposition 2. *A doomed process always transitions to FAIL while emitting nothing but τ.*

Proof. $D \overset{a}{\mapsto} P$ implies $a = \tau \wedge P \in Doomed \wedge |D| > |P|$, where $|P|$ denotes term size, by induction on D. Thus, a doomed term can only τ-transition, and only finitely many times, while staying doomed. Another induction shows $\forall D \neq FAIL. \exists D'. D \overset{\tau}{\mapsto} D'$, so a doomed term keeps transitioning until it reaches *FAIL*.

4   Correspondence Between the Semantics

This section establishes a correspondence between the two semantics: a process' denotation is precisely the set of traces it can emit, up to but not including any transitions that doom the process. This means that the monitor comparing a system to P can declare a failure as soon as the system's trace strays out of $[\![P]\!]$.

Theorem 3. $[\![P]\!] = \{s \mid \exists M. P \overset{s}{\Mapsto} M \notin Doomed\}$.

A special case of this theorem is particularly illuminating: the doomed set is precisely the set of terms with empty trace sets, corresponding to the fact that doomed terms silently transition to *FAIL*.

Proposition 4. $P \in Doomed \Longleftrightarrow [\![P]\!] = \varnothing$.

Proof. Induction on P.

Furthermore, trace sets faithfully follow non-silent transitions, in that the traces which follow an event e in $[\![P]\!]$ are precisely the traces of terms Q that follow P after a sequence of transitions that emit e.

Lemma 5. $[\![P]\!](e) = \bigcup_{P \overset{e}{\Mapsto} Q}[\![Q]\!]$.

Proof. Induction on the size of P, where event sets do not count toward size, e.g. $|?x : E \to P'| := |P'|+1$. This way, $|[e/x]P'| = |P'|$, so when $P = (?x : E \to P')$, the inductive hypothesis applies to $[e/x]P'$, despite it not being a subterm. Several lemmas are needed along the way, two of which are of particular note. Take for example $P = P_1 \|_E P_2$ with $[\![P_1]\!], [\![P_2]\!] \neq \varnothing$ and $e \in E$. Inductive hypotheses give $[\![P]\!](e) = (\bigcup_{P_1 \overset{e}{\Mapsto} Q_1}[\![Q_1]\!]) \|_E (\bigcup_{P_2 \overset{e}{\Mapsto} Q_2}[\![Q_2]\!])$. Then, continuity (Lemma 1) lets us commute the $\bigcup$ and $\|_E$, equating this to $\bigcup_{P_1 \overset{e}{\Mapsto} Q_1, P_2 \overset{e}{\Mapsto} Q_2}([\![Q_1]\!] \|_E [\![Q_2]\!])$. Then, a lemma characterizing those Q with $P \overset{e}{\Mapsto} Q$ equates this to $\bigcup_{P \overset{e}{\Mapsto} Q}[\![Q]\!]$.

Theorem 3 is a straightforward consequence of these facts.

Proof (of Theorem 3). We show $s \in [\![P]\!] \iff \exists Q.\ P \stackrel{s}{\Rightarrow} Q \notin Doomed$ by induction on s. For the base case, $\varepsilon \in [\![P]\!] \iff P \notin Doomed$ by Proposition 4. If $P \notin Doomed$, then $P \stackrel{\varepsilon}{\Rightarrow} P \notin Doomed$, and if $P \in Doomed$, then P can only transition inside $Doomed$ as noted in the proof of Proposition 2. For the inductive step, s breaks down as $s = es'$, and $s \in [\![P]\!] \iff s' \in [\![P]\!](e)$. By Lemma 5, this is equivalent to having $s' \in [\![P']\!]$ and $P \stackrel{e}{\Rightarrow} P'$ for some P', which by inductive hypothesis is equivalent to $\exists P', Q.\ P \stackrel{e}{\Rightarrow} P' \stackrel{s'}{\Rightarrow} Q \notin Doomed$.

5 Related Works

The main issue in CSP_E semantics is the propagation of *FAIL*, which entails the negative constraint that normal computation rules apply only if *FAIL*-propagation rules do not. Negative premises of the form $P \stackrel{g}{\nRightarrow}$ are a natural means for codifying such constraints, but they are generally quite problematic. A transition relation satisfying negative rules may be non-existent, or non-unique, with no obvious guiding principle (such as minimality) in choosing the "right" one. Some formats do guarantee well-definedness, such as GSOS with the witnessing constraint [3] and *ntyft/ntyxt* [6]. But even then, negative rules tend to betray desirable properties such as compositionality of some forms of bisimulation [2].

CSP_E's approach avoids negative premises altogether, essentially turning the system into a positive one, by restricting the range of metavariables in transition rules. The same approach is seen in textbook reduction rules for the call-by-value λ calculus [9], where the argument in a function application should be evaluated only if the function expression cannot be evaluated any further.

Attard and Francalanza translate temporal logic formulas to monitor specifications in a process calculus with *verdicts* [1] which, like *FAIL*, globally communicate success or failure. However, verdicts do not guarantee timely propagation: translated to our setting, the P in $P \parallel_E FAIL$ can transition indefinitely. While this non-determinacy does not hamper the translated monitor's correctness, determinate monitors may still be more desirable for ensuring consistent detection [4]. It remains to be seen if our approach makes such a guarantee, however.

We identify *FAIL*-induced failures by transitions into *FAIL*, but an alternative approach would be to have *FAIL* emit a special event F, just as termination is signalled by $\checkmark$. Though we have not pursued this idea in detail, the central concern there will be to give F higher priority than all other events. Prioritized transition also involves a negative constraint but is known to be well-behaved, being translatable to plain CSP [11]. At the moment, it is not clear if *FAIL* propagation can be translated to the prioritized-transition primitive in [11].

6   Conclusion

We gave an operational semantics for CSP_E that adequately captures the behavior of *FAIL*, the global failure operator, with positive operational rules. This semantics induces the previously defined trace semantics. As noted in the introduction, this development enables studies of other types of denotational semantics, while informing the implementation. A possible direction for future work is to see if CSP_E guarantees consistent detection in the sense of [4]. It would also be interesting to see if *FAIL* can be specified by priorities, and if that approach yields better-behaved semantics.

Acknowledgment. The authors would like to thank Yoshinao Isobe and Adrian Francalanza for comments on an earlier draft of this paper and stimulating discussions.

References

1. Attard, D.P., Francalanza, A.: A monitoring tool for a branching-time logic. In: Falcone, Y., Sánchez, C. (eds.) RV 2016. LNCS, vol. 10012, pp. 473–481. Springer, Cham (2016). doi:10.1007/978-3-319-46982-9_31
2. Bloom, B.: Structural operational semantics for weak bisimulations. Theoret. Comput. Sci. **146**(1), 25–68 (1995)
3. Bloom, B., Istrail, S., Meyer, A.R.: Bisimulation can't be traced. J. ACM **42**(1), 232–268 (1995)
4. Francalanza, A.: Consistently-detecting monitors. In: 28th International Conference on Concurrency Theory (CONCUR 2017) (2017, to appear)
5. van Glabbeek, R.J.: The linear time - branching time spectrum I. In: The Semantics of Concrete, Sequential Processes, Chap. 1, pp. 3–100. Elsevier (2001)
6. Groote, J.F.: Transition system specifications with negative premises. Theoret. Comput. Sci. **118**(2), 263–299 (1993)
7. Havelund, K., Reger, G.: Specification of parametric monitors. In: Drechsler, R., Kühne, U. (eds.) Formal Modeling and Verification of Cyber-Physical Systems, pp. 151–189. Springer, Wiesbaden (2015). doi:10.1007/978-3-658-09994-7_6
8. Hoare, C.A.R.: Communicating Sequential Processes. Prentice-Hall Inc., Upper Saddle River (1985)
9. Mitchell, J.C.: Foundations for Programming Languages. MIT Press, New York (1996)
10. Plotkin, G.D.: A structural approach to operational semantics. J. Logic Algebraic Program. **60**, 17–139 (2004)
11. Roscoe, A.: The expressiveness of CSP with priority. Electron. Notes Theor. Comput. Sci. **319**, 387–401 (2015)
12. Yamagata, Y., Artho, C., Hagiya, M., Inoue, J., Ma, L., Tanabe, Y., Yamamoto, M.: Runtime monitoring for concurrent systems. In: Falcone, Y., Sánchez, C. (eds.) RV 2016. LNCS, vol. 10012, pp. 386–403. Springer, Cham (2016). doi:10.1007/978-3-319-46982-9_24

Runtime Verification of User Interface Guidelines in Mobile Devices

Chafik Meniar[1], Florence Opalvens[1,2], and Sylvain Hallé[1(✉)]

[1] Laboratoire d'informatique formelle, Université du Québec à Chicoutimi,
Chicoutimi, Canada
shalle@acm.org
[2] Université de Strasbourg, Strasbourg, France

Abstract. The design of the user interface of a modern application needs to follow a set of guidelines, codified in a document published by the maintainers of a particular operating system. These guidelines are intended to ensure a minimum level of quality and consistency across applications. Unfortunately, checking compliance with respect to these guidelines is left to the application developer, and is generally done by manual testing. In this paper, we present a methodology, based on runtime verification, for the automated testing of user interface guidelines of Android applications.

1 Introduction

Many application ecosystems have defined sets of constraints on the possible use of user interface widgets, such as buttons, sliders, and lists. Unfortunately, a large number of applications do not follow these guidelines, resulting in a user interaction of lesser quality, and in inconsistencies in the behaviour of components across applications of the same operating system. The problem is exacerbated by the current lack of tools to test applications for conformance to layout constraints, and in particular the short supply of formally defined languages for expressing the desirable properties of an application's content and display.

In this paper, we focus on the user interface constraints of Android applications. In Sect. 2, we show examples from the wide palette of restrictions and suggestions codified in the Android Human Interface Guidelines [2]. In Sect. 3, we describe a methodology for instrumenting an Android application in a generic way. We then show how a monitor can automatically detect violations of UI guidelines whenever the state of the user interface changes; to this end, guidelines are codified in a high level specification language based on first-order Linear Temporal Logic.

These concepts have been implemented in a runtime verification tool called *Cornidroid*. A template Android app, already instrumented for use with Cornidroid, is freely available under an open source license.[1] In time, it is hoped that the use of such a runtime verification tool will help improve the quality of mobile applications by helping developers comply with existing UI guidelines.

---

[1] https://github.com/liflab/cornipickle-android-probe.

© Springer International Publishing AG 2017
S. Lahiri and G. Reger (Eds.): RV 2017, LNCS 10548, pp. 410–415, 2017.
DOI: 10.1007/978-3-319-67531-2_27

2   The Android Human Interface Guidelines

Virtually every OS ecosystem has published a set of constraints that apply on the contents of user interfaces designed by third-party developers. One can mention documents codifying UI guidelines for Apple iOS [3], GNOME [9], Windows [8], and Android products [2]. These documents are motivated by at least two factors. First, third-party applications need to meet high expectations for quality and functionality; enforcing UI guidelines ensures a minimum level of usability, aesthetics and consistency. Second, the ease of use of an application is often increased by the fact that the placement and behaviour of controls is identical across applications for a same system.

We now focus on the particular case of the Android human interface guidelines [2]. This document is divided into sections, each of which provides a set of rules for the design, placement, expected behaviour and use of user interface elements. In the following, we give a few examples of constraints on the use of UI elements. The reader shall keep in mind that UI guidelines specify hundreds of constraints of this kind, written in plain English and scattered across the whole document.

Raised Buttons. "Flat" buttons are text-only buttons, while "Raised" buttons have a rectangular shape. One guideline suggests that, when there are many elements on the interface, raised buttons should preferably be used (instead of flat buttons) to make them more visible. Figure 1 shows the difference between the two.

Fig. 1. An example of raised (left) vs. flat (right) buttons. Notice the appearance of the *Share* and *Explore* buttons.

Bottom Navigation. The bottom navigation bar should expose three to five level destinations inside an app. If there are fewer than three or more than five, developers are asked to consider using tabs instead of a navigation bar.

Text Field Size. In text boxes with a limited amount of characters, a simple red line should be displayed with a character counter showing when the user exceeds the character restriction. Otherwise, the line should be blue to show that there is no overflow (or no constraint at all on the number of characters that can be typed).

Target Touch Size. To ensure balanced density and ease of use, touch targets should have a size of at least 48×48 display pixels (dp). In most cases, there should be 8 dp or more space between them to prevent fingers from sticking too much between them. Moreover, the elements should have a physical size of about 9 mm, regardless of the size of the screen.

ListView Usage. Alphabetical sorting makes information easier to find; therefore, list widgets should not display elements in random order.

Floating Button. As its name implies, a floating button must not be fixed. For example, if clicking on the floating button makes a bottom bar appear, it must be able to rise vertically at the same time as the bar to avoid being hidden and therefore no longer be usable.

3 Runtime Verification of UI Guidelines

In the current state of things, respecting the user interface guidelines described in the previous section is left to the application developer. Android Core Quality Guideline UX-B1 does require an application to be tested for UI compliance [1]; however, the Android ecosystem provides no automated tool for checking that the suggested constraints are actually being followed by applications developed by third parties and released online in the Google Play Store.

To solve this problem, we developed Cornidroid, a runtime verification system designed specifically for the verification of interface-based constraints in Android applications. Cornidroid is a modified and extended version of an earlier tool called Cornipickle, which has been used for the testing of web applications [6].[2]

3.1 Specification Language and Interpreter

Cornidroid is organized along a client-server architecture. Server-side code takes care of gathering and evaluating specifications. To this end, users can write constraints on the contents of an Android user interface using a declarative language based on an first-order extension of Linear Temporal Logic called LTL-FO^+ [7]. The language's grammar is designed to use many plain English words

---

[2] A video of Cornidroid in action is available online: https://youtu.be/YNxxV8hIIzY.

and constructs, resulting in a relatively readable set of constraints. For example, the following block of code stipulates that all buttons in the current window must be raised buttons:

```
We say that $x is a raised button When (
    ((($x's width / the device's device-density) is greater than 47)
    And
    (($x's height / the device's device-density) is greater than 47))
      And (Not ($x's bgcolor matches"RGB\(0,0,0\)"))
).
```

```
"""
    @name Using raised buttons
    @description It is better to use raised buttons instead of
                 flat buttons when there are many details
    @link https://material.io/guidelines/components/buttons.html
    @severity Warning
"""
For each $z in $(Button) ($z is a raised button).
```

As one can see, the properties can be accompanied by Javadoc-like metadata; these elements can be used to display useful information to the developer when the corresponding property is violated. In a typical use case, a developer first starts the Cornidroid interpreter, and feeds it with a set of declarative statements representing the UI constraints to be tested for. This set of statements is stored in memory and is given a unique ID.

3.2   Application Probe

In the application under test, a special Java object, called the *probe*, also needs to be inserted. The probe is the single object taking care of the instrumentation inside the application to be monitored. It is designed to send to the server a snapshot of the relevant UI elements upon every user-triggered event. Moreover, it is tailored to the special way in which user interface elements are created and handled in the Android operating system.

The elements content of the Android user interface can be described either with Java code or in a separate XML document. In XML, we can't collect the dynamically created elements during runtime. Furthermore, the connections between the different activities windows is defined just in the Java code, so to have all information's about UI elements at runtime, it is important to analyze the whole source code.

Visually, a *window activity* is composed of a hierarchy of *views*. Each such view inherits from the View and ViewGroup classes. A ViewGroup is simply a container that can contain other ViewGroups or View. View is the ancestor class of every Android widget; for example, Button is a descendant of View.

When a UI event is detected in the application, the Probe recursively browses all parent and child nodes of the top View object, searches for required nodes with a certain type, and returns them with their attributes in a JSON document, as is illustrated in Fig. 2. The probe fetches only the information required for the evaluation of the specifications provided by the user. Hence the probe is given instructions on what widgets of the application are of interest and attributes are needed on these elements.

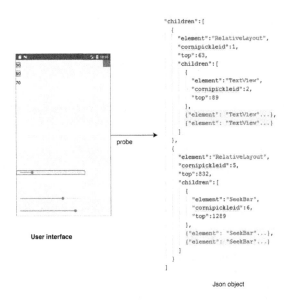

Fig. 2. The properties of the user interface elements are serialized by the Probe object into a JSON document that is sent to the interpreter.

The server receives these events and updates in real time the verdict of each monitored property. Information on the current status of the properties is relayed back to the probe, which interacts with the application's UI to provide visual feedback to the user.

3.3   Related Work

Cornidroid can be distinguished from other recent tools aimed at the monitoring of Android applications. For example, RV-Android [5] generates monitor-enabled versions of existing applications, using AspectJ to instrument the code. The properties that are monitored are mostly related to security issues, and are expressed at the method-call level. Another approach suggests the use of a monitor within an Android application, in order to enforce device usage policies, such as the number of text messages sent per day, or the total time spend playing games [4]. To the best of our knowledge, Cornidroid is the first monitoring solution that focuses on GUI elements.

4   Conclusion and Future Work

In this article, we have presented Cornidroid, an automated approach that automatically detects and reports violations of Android user interface guidelines. Cornidroid has allowed us to automatically catch many common problems encountered in real Android applications. A particularly useful application of the tool is regression testing: when a property of the Android guideline is not respected and has therefore been found, developers can write a rule and use it to ensure this property that is not respected never reappears in future modifications made to the application. Among the additional features not included in this paper, we mention an automated counter-example generation procedure that can be used to pinpoint specific elements of a document responsible for the violation and highlight them in real time.

We have obtained promising preliminary results, which should be confirmed by considering additional case studies. Obviously, a larger number of constraints should be codified in Cornipickle's language, and these constraints should also be classified according to a level of severity. As a future step, we also plan to find a suitable approach by which suggestions to correct the interface will be given to the developer.

References

1. Android: Core app quality (2017). https://developer.android.com/develop/quality-guidelines/core-app-quality.html. Accessed 5 May 2017
2. Android: User interface guidelines (2017). https://developer.android.com/guide/practices/ui_guidelines/index.html. Accessed 7 May 2017
3. Apple: Apple iOS human interface guidelines (2017). https://developer.apple.com/ios/human-interface-guidelines/. Accessed 7 May 2017
4. Chircop, L., Colombo, C., Pace, G.J.: Device-centric monitoring for mobile device management. In: Kofron, J., Tumova, J., Buhnova, B. (eds.) Proceedings of the 13th International Workshop on Formal Engineering Approaches to Software Components and Architectures, FESCA@ETAPS 2016. EPTCS, Eindhoven, The Netherlands, 3rd April 2016, vol. 205, pp. 31–44 (2016)
5. Daian, P., Falcone, Y., Meredith, P., Şerbănuţă, T.F., Shiriashi, S., Iwai, A., Rosu, G.: RV-android: efficient parametric android runtime verification, a brief tutorial. In: Bartocci, E., Majumdar, R. (eds.) RV 2015. LNCS, vol. 9333, pp. 342–357. Springer, Cham (2015). doi:10.1007/978-3-319-23820-3_24
6. Hallé, S., Bergeron, N., Guérin, F., Le Breton, G., Beroual, O.: Declarative layout constraints for testing web applications. J. Log. Algebr. Meth. Program. **85**(5), 737–758 (2016)
7. Hallé, S., Villemaire, R.: Runtime enforcement of web service message contracts with data. IEEE Trans. Serv. Comput. **5**(2), 192–206 (2012)
8. Microsoft Corporation: The Windows Interface: An Application Design Guide. Microsoft Press, Redmond (1992)
9. The GNOME Project: GNOME human interface guidelines (2017). https://developer.gnome.org/hig/stable/. Accessed 7 May 2017

Trusted Mission Operation - Concept and Implementation

Aaron Paulos[1(✉)], Partha Pal[1], Shane S. Clark[1], Kyle Usbeck[1],
and Patrick Hurley[2]

[1] Raytheon BBN Technologies, Cambridge, MA 02138, USA
aaron.paulos@raytheon.com
[2] Air Force Research Laboratory, Rome, NY 13441, USA
patrick.hurley.4@us.af.mil

Abstract. Small unmanned vehicles support many mission critical tasks. However, the provenance of these systems is usually not known, devices may be deployed in contested environments, and operators are often not computer system experts. Yet, the benefits of these systems outweigh the risks, and critical tasks and data are delegated to these systems without a sound basis for assessing trust. This paper describes an approach that can determine an operator's trust in a mission system and applies continuous monitoring to indicate if the performance is within a trusted operating region. In an early prototype we (a) define a multi-dimensional trusted operating region for a given mission, (b) monitor the system in-mission, and (c) detect when anomalous effects put the mission at risk.

1 Introduction

We are developing a framework for continuous monitoring of trust in small commercially available unmanned aerial systems (sUAS). The sUAS autopilot is functionally rich, and is increasingly used in missions that demand a strong *operator-device bond*. However, in many cases, mission operators will not have a deep understanding of sUAS. As a result, they are likely to trust the autopilot with mission tasks and data *implicitly* and perhaps more importantly, *unduly*.

To establish the belief that an autopilot is dependable, we take a compositional approach where observables across system layers and mission aspects are checked against a combined multi-dimensional *trusted operating region*. While our long term vision is to include proofs of system properties and reputation in defining a trusted operating region, this work is primarily focused on runtime verification of measurable aspects from telemetry (I/O) and computation states. Through modeling, analyzing training data, and accommodating for environmental factors, this work discerns patterns or conditions that are indicative of mission success, i.e., behavioral patterns that must be satisfied or conditions for undesirable states that may lead to failure. We refer to our approach as CMT, or Composable and Measurable view of Trust.

© Springer International Publishing AG 2017
S. Lahiri and G. Reger (Eds.): RV 2017, LNCS 10548, pp. 416–423, 2017.
DOI: 10.1007/978-3-319-67531-2_28

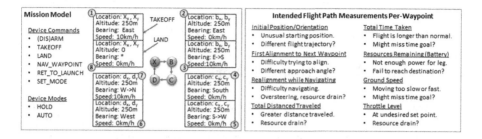

Fig. 1. CMT mission model and example flight constraints

With CMT, a trusted operation region is defined as a collection of *trust criteria*, or a specification of desired outcomes against a *mission model*. Our current mission model is developed against the ArduPilot/Pixhawk sUAS [28,31], and depicted on the left hand of Fig. 1. CMT models both the functional aspects of mission plan and a subset of runtime states for an autopilot software during mission. A companion *device model*, described later in this paper, identifies state and behaviors of the autopilot's execution that can be associated with the mission model, thus capturing runtime software invariants as part of a trust criteria. CMT's two model design allows operators to express mission intent (i.e., outcomes) as human understandable conditions or constraints over the functional aspects of a mission. As an example of intent, we specify eight desired navigation attributes for flight on the right side of Fig. 1, where each property is considered during each leg of the mission plan (e.g., leave 3 and arrive at 4). An operator can also annotate each constraint with what could occur on a failed check (i.e., assertion) and what the implication for the mission might be.

After operator intent is defined, CMT analyzes training runs and simulation to collect expected ranges for telemetry variables and in-memory variables specified in the device model. We are currently focusing on the MAVLink protocol [27] for I/O and the ArduPilot firmware. After a statistically significant amount of data is collected and curated, patterns and ranges of acceptable values begin to emerge for a devices I/O and runtime states. Collectively those derived values will define the system's trusted operating region for the mission. At runtime, CMT adds instrumentation and checks to the autopilot firmware and its I/O channels to detect anomalies that would decrease trust.

A benefit of this work is an early detection and warning capability for errant mission executions. For sUAS, support for multi-layer anomaly detection is currently not a priority. Low-latency and low-bandwidth anomaly detection would enable operators to respond to errant conditions by adjusting mission plans or device configurations. As contributions, this work introduces a framework that reduces the amount of risk that human users must assume in mission. Second, we show that for a given mission, it is possible to determine a trusted operating region based on readily available observables. Finally, we show that it is possible to efficiently detect when an anomalous event puts a mission at risk.

For this paper, Sect. 2 describes related works, Sect. 3 describes the monitoring framework, and Sect. 4 provides a conclusion and next steps.

2   Background and Related Work

Modern systems include security, Quality of Service controls, and runtime monitors that enable resiliency, however, continued operation by itself does not imply trusted operation. Parts of a system are often assumed to be trusted computing bases without proper verification, specifications are often incomplete and imprecise [17], systems components are not adequately tested [18], and the provenance of commodity components is often uncertain [19]. Furthermore, as designed, sophisticated resilience mechanisms actually adapt the system in hard to predict ways [21,22]. Consequently, a large part of the system is assumed to do the right thing without a reasonable basis for that assumption.

This work leverages human factors work [1] on trust and suspicion in automation and technology, that indicates interpersonal trust is believed to be driven by dispositional forces (propensity to trust) and indicators of trustworthiness (ability, integrity, and benevolence) [2–4]. Trust also plays a role in both interpersonal relationships and automation, i.e., human user interactions with computing systems [5–7]. Other foundational research has also revealed that human perceptions of trust predicted the use of automated aids in supervisory control scenarios beyond the true reliability of the system [8,9].

sUAS devices represent similar challenges: a blind sphere of trust and an irrational bias towards trusting the system. At the same time cyber-attacks proliferate and components of questionable origin are now unavoidable [20,23, 24]. As such, an irrational bias for trust becomes not only questionable but irresponsible and risky, and also motivates technologies that enable trust in sUAS.

3   Continuous Monitoring for ArduPilot Missions

This section describes a runtime verification capability for ArduPilot/Pixhawk devices, and a device model based upon the MAVLink protocol, the ArduPilot/Pixhawk firmware, and the Nuttx OS [29]. We first introduce key components of CMT's runtime, and then describe the initial states that we are examining using select sensors. We then show early results that examine the efficiency and overhead of the continuous monitoring runtime.

The left side of Fig. 2 illustrates the components and data flows of CMT's runtime environment. The runtime is composed of software modules enabling trust assessments, and a collection of control probes that extract the I/O and CPU states from a mission system. All boxes with an asterisk are part of a mission system; this includes a ground control station (GCS), simulators, and a device (e.g., ground rover). At the bottom of the figure, we label operations of the CMT runtime: control runtime sensors, estimate the state of a mission system,

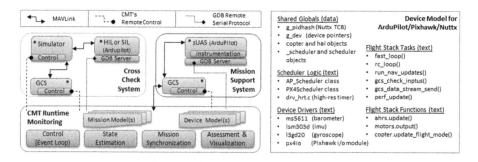

Fig. 2. Continuous monitoring runtime and Pixhawk device model

synchronize a cross-checking framework to an estimated state, and execute trust assessments and visualize results. We now summarize CMT's sensors and control.

ArduPilot Instrumentation: to add a low-overhead, high-fidelity and on-device assessments, we developed an OS task and instrumentation points throughout the Nuttx, PX4 and ArduPilot code. When scheduled, the task examines the Nuttx task control block and pre-specified memory of the flight-stack to examine its integrity. Such instrumentation executes on a live-device with minimal impact at runtime. Results of inspection are periodically exported in a custom-built MAVLink telemetry message to a trusted ground station.

GCS and Simulator Control: to enable programmatic control and comparison with the mission support system, we added interfaces and extensions to the MAVProxy GCS [36] and ArduPilot simulator. These interfaces are used to synchronize mission support system states to values from a live system. Examples of updated states include: device position, orientation, speed, throttle, and resources. This level of control enables CMT to support in-mission cross-checking of intermediate variables returned by our instrumented firmware.

Applying JTAG [30] to Inspect Pixhawk: to enhance the trustworthiness and non-bypassability of our approach, we selectively apply on-chip hardware debugging to verify the integrity of code and data on the Pixhawk (e.g., our embedded instrumentation). To support live in-mission debugging, we mounted a Raspberry Pi and a JTAG debugger onto a ground rover. With this combination, CMT has a higher degree of assurance in its firmware instrumentation, and can also verify the lowest layers of the Pixhawk firmware.

To complement the mission model in Sect. 1, we identified and grouped critical variables that support flight-level operations into five categories as a device model. Those groupings and variables are listed on the right hand of Fig. 3. This was a manual process, but aided by simulation and hardware debugging. While the nuances of the full model are very complex, we aimed to identify the tasks and data that is responsible for collecting data from onboard sensors and producing the outputs for autonomous flight. For the purposes of our work, this model adds transparency to lower-level operations, but more importantly allows CMT to associate runtime states with the operators intent.

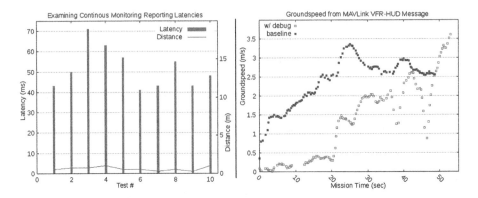

Fig. 3. Latency for anomaly detection (left) and on-chip debugger overhead (right).

To characterize the efficiency and overhead when applying runtime checking against mission constraints we conduct two experiments. First, in simulation, we measure the end-to-end reporting latency for trust violations, and then capture the distance that the vehicle travels after a violation is detected. Then, in a field experiment with a ground rover, we conduct a stress test to measure the effects of on-chip debugging as a trust assessment capability. We plot results from the two experiments side-by-side in Fig. 3.

First, we run 10 simulations of a four waypoint surveillance mission described in earlier work [15]. At a pre-specified time, we inject a synthetic bug that changes the throttle output levels. This change violates the throttle-level flight constraints defined in Sect. 1, Fig. 1. To measure the detection latency we synchronize the time sources of the ground rovers Pixhawk with the continuous monitor constraint checker on a laptop. We also we instrument the fault injector and the constraint checkers notification handler. Taking the difference of the two measurements captures the end-to-end latency, which is graphed in bars, on the primary y-axis of left-hand chart in Fig. 3. We also examine GPS telemetry to estimate the distance the vehicle travels from the time the event occurs until the trust violation is reported. Distance traveled is a function of the reporting latency and the set point for ground speed (here 5 m/s). On average, we observed a latency of 51.4 ms and distance traveled of 2.4 m, which would enable realistic corrective actions from operators (e.g., stop mission or correct throttle).

In field experiments, right hand of Fig. 3, we applied a stress test to estimate the effects of high-rate monitoring of a Pixhawk from a co-resident Raspberry Pi3 and a JTAG debugger. Using a three waypoint mission, we measured runtimes via telemetry with and without on-chip debugging. In the debugging case, we added a single hardware breakpoint to the function symbol that generates HEARTBEAT telemetry (generates 20 messages-per-second). On each message, we extracted a stack trace and read the variable state of the x-axis IMU at the driver-level of the Pixhawk. We assumed this test would produce undesirable outcomes for mission execution (e.g., excessive overhead or real-time panics).

When inspecting the driving paths of the two vehicles using GPS data we found that the debugged vehicle hovered much closer to the linear paths between the three waypoints. However, the rover also wobbled back-and-forth across the mission path during navigation (i.e., the expected effect of the stress test on the nav controller). This finding is interesting when considering the standard navigation metric *Cross Track Error*, which is a continuous measurement of how closely a sUAS aligns itself to a planned trajectory to a waypoint. Since cross track error is reported in MAVLink, an operator might wrongly assume that the debugged mission performed better than the standard run. I.e., the operator would need to examine two or more telemetry states to determine that the system is functioning as expected. We believe this motivates CMT's objective of composing trust across multiple measurements of a mission system.

Examining the ground speed of the two vehicles shows a different story (left hand Fig. 3), where the overhead of stopping the Pixhawks 20 times/sec, extracting state, and performing trust calculations greatly reduces its efficiency, and thus usability. While the rover was able to complete the mission, it incurred a 8.5% timing overhead and maintained a much lower average speed (77%). Moving forward, we believe these overheads can be minimized, especially if we selectively apply JTAG for low-rate and randomized verification of CMT's firmware instrumentation.

4   Conclusion and Next Steps

This work describes a framework for defining operator trust in a sUAS and a continuous monitoring approach for assessing trust throughout a mission. This approach can be used to detect anomalous behaviors and emergent outcomes, in-mission, that may degrade operator trust. In our initial results, we define a trusted operating region for a given mission, and monitor both live and simulated missions to measure overhead of our runtime verification software.

Next steps include (i) testing with software attacks and (ii) extending CMT's models to take into account emergent states introduced by dynamic updates to sUAS and cyber resilience capabilities. The latter will entail model enhancements that provide a stronger association between mission intent and the potential range of a devices embedded computation. A longer term goal is to incorporate proofs of software and operation as part of a composed trust framework, including formal methods that reduce the requirements on continuous monitoring.

Acknowledgements. The work presented in this paper is supported by the US Air Force Research Laboratory (AFRL), under contract number FA8750-15-C-0057. The content of the paper does not reflect the official position or policy of the US Air Force or the US Government.

DISTRIBUTION A. Approved for public release: distribution unlimited. 88ABW-2017-2014 on April 27, 2017.

References

1. Lyons, J.B., Stokes, C.K., Eschleman, K.J., Alarcon, G.M., Barelka, A.: Trust-worthiness and IT suspicion: an evaluation of the nomological network. J. Hum. Factors **53**(3), 219–229 (2011)
2. Colquitt, J.A., Scott, B.A., LePine, J.A.: Trust, trustworthiness, and trust propensity a meta-analytic test of their unique relationships with risk taking and job performance. J. Appl. Psychol. **92**(4), 909–927 (2007)
3. Mayer, R.C., Davis, J.H., Schoorman, F.D.: An integrative model of organizational trust. Acad. Manag. Rev. **20**(3), 709–734 (1995)
4. Mayer, R.C., Davis, J.H.: The effects of the performance appraisal system on trust for management: a field quasi-experiment. J. Appl. Psychol. **84**(1), 123–136 (1999)
5. Lee, J.D., See, K.A.: Trust in automation: designing for appropriate reliance. Hum. Factors **46**(1), 50–80 (2004)
6. Madhavan, P., Wiegmann, D.A.: Similarities and differences between human-human and human-automation trust: an integrated review. Theoret. Issues Ergon. Sci. **8**, 277–301 (2007)
7. Parasuraman, R., Riley, V.: Humans and automation: use, misuse, disuse, and abuse. Hum. Factors **39**, 230–253 (1997)
8. Lee, J.D., Moray, N.: Trust, self-confidence, and operators adaptation to automation. Int. J. Hum Comput Stud. **46**, 17–30 (1994)
9. Muir, B.M., Moray, N.: Trust in automation: part II. Experimental studies of trust and human intervention in a process control simulation. Ergonomics **39**, 429–460 (1996)
10. Jian, J., Bisantz, A.M., Drury, C.G.: Foundations for an empirically determined scale of trust in automated systems. Int. J. Cogn. Ergon. **4**, 53–71 (2000)
11. Sheridan, T.B.: Trustworthiness of command and control systems. In: Proceedings of the IFAC/IFIP/IEA/IFORS Conference on Man Machine Systems, Pergamon, Elmsford (1988)
12. Lewicki, R.J., McAllister, D.J., Bies, R.J.: Trust and distrust: new relationships and realities. Acad. Manag. Rev. **23**, 438–458 (1998)
13. Levine, T.R., McCornack, S.A.: The dark side of trust: conceptualizing and measuring types of communicative suspicion. Commun. Q. **39**, 325–340 (1991)
14. Aven, T.: Quantitative Risk Assessment: The Scientific Platform. Cambridge University Press, Cambridge (2011)
15. Highnam, K., Angstadt, K., Leach, K., Weimer, W., Paulos, A., Hurley, P.: An uncrewed aerial vehicle attack scenario and trustworthy repair architecture. In: Proceedings of the 46th International Conference on Dependable Systems and Networks Workshop (DSN-W), pp. 222–225 (2016)
16. Harrison McKnight, D., Chervany, N.L.: Trust and distrust definitions: one bite at a time. In: Falcone, R., Singh, M., Tan, Y.-H. (eds.) Trust in Cyber-societies. LNCS, vol. 2246, pp. 27–54. Springer, Heidelberg (2001). doi:10.1007/3-540-45547-7_3
17. Menghi, C.: Verifying incomplete and evolving specifications. In: Proceedings of the 36th International Conference on Software Engineering (ICSE), pp. 670–673 (2014)
18. Ahmed, I., Gopinath, R., Brindescu, C., Groce, A., Jensen, C.: Can testedness be effectively measured? In: Proceedings of the 24th International Symposium on Foundations of Software Engineering (FSE), pp. 547–558 (2016)
19. Paar, C.: Hardware trojans and other threats against embedded systems. In: Asia Conference on Computer and Communications Security (Asia CCS) (2017)

20. Costello, P.: Identifying and exploiting vulnerabilities in civilian unmanned aerial vehicle systems and evaluating and countering potential threats against the United States Airspace. In: ACM SIGCSE Technical Symposium on Computer Science Education, pp. 761–762 (2017)
21. Salehie, M., Tahvildari, L.: Self-adaptive software: landscape and research challenges. ACM Trans. Auton. Adapt. Syst. (TAAS) **4**, 14 (2009)
22. Multari, N., Singhal, A., Manz, D., Cowles, R., Cuellar, J., Oehmen, C., Shannon, G.: Testing, evaluation for active, resilient cyber systems panel verification of active, resilient systems: practical or utopian? In: Workshop on Automated Decision Making for Active Cyber Defense (SafeConfig) (2016)
23. Kamkar, S.: SkyJack: Autonomous Drone Hacking. http://samy.pl/skyjack/. Accessed 18 Jan 2017
24. MalDrone - First Ever Backdoor for Drones. http://thehackernews.com/2015/01/MalDrone-backdoor-drone-malware.html. Accessed 18 Jan 2017
25. Language-theoretic Security. http://langsec.org/. Accessed 18 Jan 2017
26. Waypoint Protocol - QgroundControl GCS. http://www.qgroundcontrol.org/mavlink/waypointprotocol. Accessed 18 Jan 2017
27. GitHub - mavlink/mavlink: MAVLink micro air vehicle marshalling/communication library. https://github.com/mavlink/mavlink/. Accessed 18 Jan 2017
28. GitHub - ArduPilot/ardupilot: ArduPlane, ArduCopter, ArduRover source. https://github.com/ArduPilot/ardupilot/. Accessed 18 Jan 2017
29. Nuttx Real-Time Operating System. http://nuttx.org. Accessed 18 Jan 2017
30. Home - blacksphere/blackmagic Wiki - GitHub. https://github.com/blacksphere/blackmagic/wiki. Accessed 18 Jan 2017
31. Pixhawk Flight Controller Hardware Project. https://pixhawk.org. Accessed 18 Jan 2017
32. Organizational Information Bylaws of the Academy of Model Aeronautics, Incorporated. www.modelaircraft.org/files/001bylaws.pdf. Accessed 18 Jan 2017
33. Unmanned Aircraft Systems (UAS) Regulations and Policies. https://www.faa.gov/uas/resources/uas_regulations_policy/. Accessed 18 Jan 2017
34. RCGroups.com: The ABCs of Radio Control - Aircraft, Boats, and Cars! https://www.rcgroups.com/forums/index.php. Accessed 18 Jan 2017
35. Flite Test — RC Planes, Quadcopters, Videos, Articles & More. www.flitetest.com. Accessed 18 Jan 2017
36. GitHub - ArduPilot/MAVProxy. https://github.com/ArduPilot/MAVProxy. Accessed 18 Jan 2017

Verifying the Output of a Distributed Algorithm Using Certification

Kim Völlinger$^{(\boxtimes)}$

Humboldt University of Berlin, Berlin, Germany
voellinger@hu-berlin.de

Abstract. A *certifying algorithm* verifies the correctness of its output at runtime by producing a *witness* in addition to an input-output pair. If a *witness predicate* holds for the triple, the input-output pair is correct. A *checker* algorithm decides the witness predicate. While certifying *sequential* algorithms are well-established, we consider *distributed* algorithms. In this paper, we investigate certifying distributed algorithms that verify their distributed output. While the witness predicate states a property in the network, for distributed checking, additional predicates are decided for each component. We illustrate the applicability by examples.

Keywords: Runtime verification · Certifying algorithm · Distributed algorithm

1 Introduction

A major problem is assuring the quality of software; formal verification is often too costly and testing is not complete. Another method is runtime verification: for instance, using a certifying algorithm to verify an input-output pair at runtime. A *certifying algorithm* produces a *witness* in addition to each input-output pair. If a *witness predicate* holds for the triple, the input-output pair is correct. A *checker* algorithm decides the witness predicate. Usually in runtime verification, a monitor gets events from an instrumented system and indicates whether a property holds [1]. Now, the monitor is the checker, and the instrumented system the certifying algorithm. While certifying *sequential* algorithms are well-established, we consider *distributed* algorithms which behave differently.

2 Preliminaries

We recap certifying sequential algorithms [4] and distributed algorithms [3,6].

2.1 Certifying Sequential Algorithms

Let X, Y, W be sets of potential inputs, outputs and witnesses, and the precondition $\phi \subseteq X$ and postcondition $\psi \subseteq X \times Y$ a specification. A *witness predicate* for the specification is a predicate $\Gamma \subseteq X \times Y \times W$ with the *witness property*:

$$\forall x \in X, y \in Y, w \in W : (\phi(x) \wedge \Gamma(x,y,w)) \longrightarrow \psi(x,y) \tag{1}$$

© Springer International Publishing AG 2017
S. Lahiri and G. Reger (Eds.): RV 2017, LNCS 10548, pp. 424–430, 2017.
DOI: 10.1007/978-3-319-67531-2_29

A *certifying algorithm* produces a *witness* w in addition to an input-output pair (x, y) such that the witness predicate holds. A *checker* algorithm decides the witness predicate. If the precondition holds and the checker accepts on (x, y, w), then (x, y) satisfies the specification (even if the certifying algorithm is buggy). As an example, consider the decision if a graph is bipartite (i.e. its vertices can be divided in two partitions so that each edge has a vertex in both partitions). For a bipartite graph, a bipartition is a witness by definition. For a non-bipartite graph, an odd cycle in the graph is a witness since it is not bipartite itself. Figure 1 sums up the concept of a certifying algorithm. The user has to trust the checker. The rationale is that checking is easier than construction.

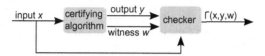

Fig. 1. A certifying algorithm accompanied by its checker.

2.2   Distributed Algorithms

We consider *networks* where components communicate over channels. A *distributed algorithm* describes for each component a reactive algorithm such that all components together solve one problem (e.g. leader election, mutual exclusion or coloring). We call the algorithm running on a component a *local algorithm*, and distinguish the *global input* of the network from the *local input* of a component. We consider terminating algorithms and use the same terminology for an output. We focus on networks that are *asynchronous* (i.e. no global clock), *static* (i.e. unchanged topology) and *id-based* (i.e. unique identifiers).

3   Distributed Algorithms Certifying Their Global Output

We investigate terminating distributed algorithms certifying their global output. A witness is computed in a distributed manner. While the witness predicate states a property in the network, for distributed checking, additional predicates are decided for each component.

We fix the following: The network is presented by a connected undirected graph $N = (V, E)$ with $|V| = n$ where a vertex is a component and an edge a channel. Let X, Y, W be sets of local inputs, outputs and witnesses, and X^n, Y^n, W^n sets of global inputs, outputs, witnesses. To ease the formalization, we assume only global inputs fulfilling a precondition. Hence, the correctness of an input-output pair is specified by a postcondition $\psi \subseteq X^n \times Y^n$. We call a predicate stating a property over the network a *global predicate*, and a predicate stating a property over a component a *local predicate*.

In analogy to certifying sequential algorithms, we define a witness predicate.

Definition 1 (witness predicate). *A global predicate $\Gamma \subseteq X^n \times Y^n \times W^n$ with*

$$\forall \boldsymbol{x} \in X^n, \boldsymbol{y} \in Y^n, \boldsymbol{w} \in W^n : \Gamma(\boldsymbol{x}, \boldsymbol{y}, \boldsymbol{w}) \longrightarrow \psi(\boldsymbol{x}, \boldsymbol{y}) \tag{2}$$

is a witness predicate *for ψ.*

The property (2) is the *witness property*: if the witness predicate holds, the global input-output pair is correct. For a triple $(\mathbf{x}, \mathbf{y}, \mathbf{w}) \in \Gamma$, we call $\mathbf{w}$ a *global witness*, and w_i a *local witness* of component i. By letting each component compute a local witness, we have a distributed algorithm that computes a global witness.

For distributed checking, we define local predicates to be decided for each component. A global predicate may hold in a network if a property holds *for all* components:

Definition 2 (universal distributable). *A global predicate $\Gamma \subseteq X^n \times Y^n \times W^n$ is* universal distributable *if there exists a local predicate $\gamma \subseteq X \times Y \times W$ such that*

$$\forall \boldsymbol{x} \in X^n, \boldsymbol{y} \in Y^n, \boldsymbol{w} \in W^n : (\forall i \in V : \gamma(x_i, y_i, w_i)) \longrightarrow \Gamma(\boldsymbol{x}, \boldsymbol{y}, \boldsymbol{w}) \tag{3}$$

Example 1 (Network is Bipartite). For a bipartite network, a bipartition of the components is a global witness. The according witness predicate is universal distributable with a local predicate that holds if a component has only neighbors with the other color. If each component has a bipartition in its neighborhood, then by overlapping neighborhoods it follows that there is a bipartition of the components in the network.

There is always a witness predicate that is universal distributable, for instance, with each component having its computation and message history as a local witness. For proving the witness property, we have to establish the correctness of the algorithm. Hence, this certifying variant is not interesting in general.

Moreover, not every global predicate is universal distributable. A global predicate may hold in a network if a property holds *for at least one* component:

Definition 3 (existential distributable). *A global predicate $\Gamma \subseteq X^n \times Y^n \times W^n$ is* existential distributable *if there exists a local predicate $\gamma \subseteq X \times Y \times W$ such that*

$$\forall \boldsymbol{x} \in X^n, \boldsymbol{y} \in Y^n, \boldsymbol{w} \in W^n : (\exists i \in V : \gamma(x_i, y_i, w_i)) \longrightarrow \Gamma(\boldsymbol{x}, \boldsymbol{y}, \boldsymbol{w}) \tag{4}$$

Example 2 (Not a Bipartition of the Network). A pair of same colored neighbors are witnessing that a 2-coloring is not a bipartition. The according witness predicate is existential distributable with a local predicate that holds if a component has a neighbor with the same color. Note that same colored neighbors do not verify that a network is non-bipartite but only that a particular coloring is not a bipartition.

Not every global predicate is universal or existential distributable in a network. A global predicate in a network may hold if some properties hold for all components while others hold for at least one:

Definition 4 (distributable). *A global predicate $\Gamma \subseteq X^n \times Y^n \times W^n$ is distributable if one of the following holds:*

1. *Γ is universal distributable.*
2. *Γ is existential distributable.*
3. *There exists a distributable global predicate Γ_1 such that*

$$\forall x \in X^n, y \in Y^n, w \in W^n : (\neg \Gamma_1(x, y, w)) \longrightarrow \Gamma(x, y, w).$$

4. *There exist distributable global predicates Γ_1, Γ_2 such that*

$$\forall x \in X^n, y \in Y^n, w \in W^n : (\Gamma_1(x, y, w) \wedge \Gamma_2(x, y, w)) \longrightarrow \Gamma(x, y, w).$$

5. *There exist distributable global predicates Γ_1, Γ_2 such that*

$$\forall x \in X^n, y \in Y^n, w \in W^n : (\Gamma_1(x, y, w) \vee \Gamma_2(x, y, w)) \longrightarrow \Gamma(x, y, w).$$

The global predicates used in 3, 4 and 5 separate properties in universal distributable and existential distributable ones. We call such predicates the *subpredicates* of Γ. Not every global predicate is distributable due to the chosen restrictions on combining logical quantifiers. However, the chosen restrictions are useful for distributed checking of the witness predicate.

Example 3 (Network is Non-Bipartite). An odd cycle is a global witness for a network not being bipartite. The according witness predicate Γ is distributable. We give subpredicates Γ_1, Γ_2, and Γ_3 such that $\Gamma_1 \wedge \Gamma_2 \wedge \Gamma_3 \longrightarrow \Gamma$.

To this end, we assume a rooted spanning tree with a bipartition. If a component has a neighbor with the same color, the components are connected by a channel not belonging to the tree – a *non-tree channel*. Such a non-tree channel implies that the network contains an odd cycle. Let i and j be two same colored components connected by a non-tree channel. Since i and j are connected by a spanning tree, they either have a common ancestor k different from i and j, or one is the ancestor of the other. Figure 2 illustrates the two cases. If i and j have a common ancestor k, then the path in the spanning tree between i and k, and j and k have either both odd or even length. With the additional non-tree channel (i, j), there is an odd cycle. Otherwise we assume i is an ancestor of j w.l.o.g. Since i and j have the same color, the path in the tree between i and j has even length. With the non-tree channel (i, j), there is an odd cycle.

We use this property to give subpredicates for Γ. We have to verify the spanning tree, its bipartition and the same colored neighbors: Γ_1 holds if the network contains a spanning tree, Γ_2 if the spanning tree has a bipartition, and Γ_3 if two neighbors have the same color. Thus, it holds:

$$\forall \mathbf{x} \in X^n, \mathbf{y} \in Y^n, \mathbf{w} \in W^n : \Gamma_1(\mathbf{x}, \mathbf{y}, \mathbf{w}) \wedge \Gamma_2(\mathbf{x}, \mathbf{y}, \mathbf{w}) \wedge \Gamma_3(\mathbf{x}, \mathbf{y}, \mathbf{w}) \longrightarrow \Gamma(\mathbf{x}, \mathbf{y}, \mathbf{w}).$$

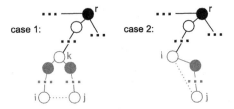

Fig. 2. r is root of the spanning tree. i and j are connected by a non-tree channel (dotted line). Case 1: k is a common ancestor in the tree. Case 2: i is j's ancestor in the tree. In both cases, the odd cycle is highlighted in red. (Color figure online)

The subpredicate Γ_1 ("spanning tree") is universal distributable by using a characterization of a spanning tree given by the parent and the distance function. For details see [7] where a spanning tree is certified in the context of certifying leader election. As previously discussed, subpredicate Γ_2 ("bipartition") is universal distributable, and Γ_3 existential distributable.

We define a certifying variant of a terminating distributed algorithm that solves a problem specified by ψ:

Definition 5 (Certifying Terminating Distributed Algorithm). *Let $\Gamma \subseteq X^n \times Y^n \times W^n$ be a distributable witness predicate for ψ. Let $\Gamma_1, \Gamma_2, .., \Gamma_k$ be subpredicates of Γ. Let each Γ_j with $j = 1, .., k$ be universal/existential distributable with a local predicate $\gamma_j \subseteq X \times Y \times W$. A certifying distributed algorithm computes for each global input $\mathbf{x} \in X^n$ a global output $\mathbf{y} \in Y^n$ and a global witness $\mathbf{w} \in W^n$ in the way that it holds, for each component i, there are $\gamma_j(x_i, y_i, w_i)$ with $j = 1, .., k$ such that $(\mathbf{x}, \mathbf{y}, \mathbf{x}) \in \Gamma$.*

Example 4 (Certifying Distributed Bipartite Testing). For distributed bipartite testing, the components decide whether the network[1] itself is bipartite: the components construct a spanning tree and color its levels alternately. If the coloring is a bipartition in the network, the network is bipartite, otherwise not. For a certifying variant, the components additionally compute a global witness – either a bipartition or an odd cycle. For a bipartition, the local witness of a component is its own color and the colors of its neighbors. For an odd cycle, the local witness of a component, is its parent (root is its own parent), its distance from the root, its parent's distance from the root, its color, its neighbors' colors and the identifier of root. Since distributed bipartite testing uses a rooted spanning tree with a bipartition, the information can be collected during construction.

For distributed checking, each component i has a *local checker* that gets its local input, output and witness, and after termination, decides γ_j with $j = 1, .., k$ on (x_i, y_i, w_i) as illustrated in Fig. 3. We distinguish communication from the input and output since the postcondition specifies correctness for the global input-output pair. As often done in distributed algorithms, we abstract from

---

[1] For distributed algorithms, the global input is often the network itself.

distributing the input, and assume an initialization. Moreover, since local witnesses build the global witness, it is crucial that local witnesses are *consistent* with each other, i.e. information about the same fact contained in two local witnesses are the same. Consistency can be checked by local checkers communicating with neighboring local checkers. We evaluate the subpredicates $\Gamma_1, \Gamma_2, .., \Gamma_k$ by using a spanning tree to combine the k-tuples of the checkers. Each position of a k-tuple has to be either combined by a logic conjunction or disjunction since it is either universal or existential quantified. Finally, the root evaluates the witness predicate Γ, and if it holds, the global input-output pair is verified.

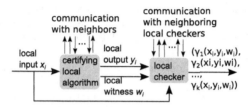

Fig. 3. Component i with its local checker.

4 Related Work

A theory of certifying algorithms and further reading is given in [4]. This work was done for *sequential* algorithms. In previous work, we give a certifying variant of distributed Bellman-Ford algorithm [8] and leader election [7]. To our knowledge, there is no other research on certifying *distributed* algorithms. However, there are similarities to proof labeling schemes [2] where a universal distributable global predicate is decided, and to decentralized runtime verification [5].

5 Conclusion

We applied the concept of certification to distributed terminating algorithms. While the witness predicate states a property in the network, for distributed checking, we considered local predicates for each component. We distinguished three ways of distributing a witness predicate over the network and illustrated each by an example.

Future work is to develop further certifying distributed algorithms. One direction is to consider non-termination. To this end, certification of data structures, decentralized runtime verification and self-stabilizing algorithms are fields of interest. Another direction is to consider certifying distributed algorithms that verify local outputs instead of the global output.

References

1. Hallé, S.: When RV meets CEP. In: Falcone, Y., Sánchez, C. (eds.) RV 2016. LNCS, vol. 10012, pp. 68–91. Springer, Cham (2016). doi:10.1007/978-3-319-46982-9_6
2. Korman, A., Kutten, S., Peleg, D.: Proof labeling schemes. Distrib. Comput. **22**(4), 215–233 (2010). doi:10.1007/s00446-010-0095-3
3. Lynch, N.A.: Distributed Algorithms. Morgan Kaufmann Publishers Inc., San Francisco (1996)
4. McConnell, R.M., Mehlhorn, K., Näher, S., Schweitzer, P.: Certifying algorithms. Comput. Sci. Rev. **5**, 119–161 (2011)
5. Mostafa, M., Bonakdarpour, B.: Decentralized runtime verification of ltl specifications in distributed systems. In: Proceedings of the 2015 IEEE International Parallel and Distributed Processing Symposium, IPDPS 2015, pp. 494–503. IEEE Computer Society, Washington, DC (2015)
6. Raynal, M.: Distributed Algorithms for Message-Passing Systems. Springer, Heidelberg (2013)
7. Völlinger, K., Akili, S.: Verifying a class of certifying distributed programs. In: Barrett, C., Davies, M., Kahsai, T. (eds.) NFM 2017. LNCS, vol. 10227, pp. 373–388. Springer, Cham (2017). doi:10.1007/978-3-319-57288-8_27
8. Völlinger, K., Reisig, W.: Certification of distributed algorithms solving problems with optimal substructure. In: Calinescu, R., Rumpe, B. (eds.) SEFM 2015. LNCS, vol. 9276, pp. 190–195. Springer, Cham (2015). doi:10.1007/978-3-319-22969-0_14

Author Index

Printed in the United States
By Bookmasters